Gente Rutheni, Natione Poloni:
The Ruthenians of Polish Nationality
in Habsburg Galicia

The Peter Jacyk Centre
for
Ukrainian Historical Research

Monograph Series
Number nine

Adam Świątek

Gente Rutheni, Natione Poloni:
The Ruthenians of Polish Nationality in Habsburg Galicia

Translated from the Polish
by Guy Russell Torr

Preface
by Frank E. Sysyn

Canadian Institute of Ukrainian Studies Press
in cooperation with Księgarnia Akademicka
Edmonton, Toronto   2019   Cracow

Canadian Institute of Ukrainian Studies Press

University of Alberta
Edmonton, Alberta
CANADA T6G 2H8
<www.ciuspress.com>

University of Toronto
Toronto, Ontario
CANADA M5T 1W5

Ksiegarnia Akademicka
ul. św. Anny 6
31-008 Kraków, Poland
<www.akademicka.pl>

ISBN 978-1-894865-55-5 (paperback)

Library and Archives Canada Cataloguing in Publication

Title: *Gente Rutheni, Natione Poloni*: the Ruthenians of Polish Nationality in Habsburg Gal-
icia / Adam Swiatek.
Other titles: Gente Rutheni, Natione Poloni. English
Names: Świątek, Adam. author.
Series: Monograph series (Peter Jacyk Centre for Ukrainian Historical Research); no. 9.
Description: Series statement: The Peter Jacyk Centre for Ukrainian historical research
monograph series; number nine | Translation of: *Gente Rutheni, Natione Poloni: z dzie-
jów Rusinów narodowości polskiej w Galicji* (Cracow, 2014). | Includes bibliographical
references and index.
Identifiers: Canadiana 20190136634 | ISBN 978-1-894865-55-5.

Subjects: LCSH: Ruthenians—Galicia (Poland and Ukraine)—History. | LCSH: Poloniza-
tion—Galicia (Poland and Ukraine)—History. | LCSH: Group identity—Galicia (Po-
land and Ukraine)—History. | LCSH: Galicia (Poland and Ukraine)—Ethnic relations.
Classification: LCC DK4600.G345 S9513 2019 | DDC 943.8/6—dc23

Cover design: Paweł Sepielak

Publication financed under the program of the Minister of Science and Higher Education
under the name "National Development Program of Humanities" in 2016–2019 (agreement no. 0242/NPRH4/H3a/83/2016)

NATIONAL PROGRAMME
FOR THE DEVELOPMENT OF HUMANITIES

A generous grant toward this publication has been provided by the Cosbild Investment
Club Endowment Fund at the Canadian Institute of Ukrainian Studies, University of
Alberta.

Printed in Canada

To my family

Table of Contents

Preface

Gente Ruthenus, Natione Polonus

When I undertook my research on a biography of Adam Kysil [Adam Kisiel, 1600–53] many decades ago, I assumed he was the classic case of a *gente Ruthenus, natione Polonus*, an appellation for an ethnic Ruthenian who belonged to the Polish political nation—a phenomenon common to the early modern Polish-Lithuanian Commonwealth.[1] Although I was struck by not finding the exact term in his own voluminous writings, I did find many ways in which he juxtaposed his Ruthenian and Polish identities, and I remarked that while I could not find an instance in which he referred to the Poles as his *gens*, I could find cases in which the Ruthenians were his *natio*. I stated that I had avoided the cliché *gente Ruthenus, natione Polonus* because I found it clouded the issue of early modern nationhood more than it clarified it. But I accepted the received opinion that it had been first used by the sixteenth-century figure Stanisław Orzechowski [Stanislav Orikhovsky] and that *gens* meant tribe or ethnic group, while *natio* designated a higher identity of a national or state community. My own interests focused on how Kysil and his generation expressed Ruthenian identity, and here, following the research of Mykhailo Hrushevsky and Viacheslav Lypynsky [Wacław Lipiński], I found a maturing conceptualization of the Ruthenians as a people with its own history and language in the late sixteenth and early seventeenth centuries. Through examining Kysil's writings, I perceived how the Ukrainian territories annexed by the Kingdom of Poland from the Grand Duchy of Lithuania in 1569 were conceived of as a regional Rus' entity embodied with rights and privileges. My interests were centered on the relation of these phenomena to the rise of Cossack Ukraine.

Only after reading David Althoen's dissertation[2] many years later did I come to see the phrase—which became current in the literature on the early modern period—that assumed a subordination of a *gens* to a *natio* not only did not occur in the works of Orzechowski, to whom it was ascribed, but that it was essentially a creation of the nineteenth century and the age of nationalism. While the early modern period had

---

[1] See my monograph *Between Poland and the Ukraine: The Dilemma of Adam Kysil (1600–1653)* (Cambridge, Mass., 1985).
[2] D. Althoen, "That Noble Quest: From True Nobility to Enlightened Society in the Polish-Lithuanian Commonwealth, 1550–1830," PhD diss. (University of Michigan, 2001).

a complex web of identities and Ruthenian nobles such as Kysil had come to see the Commonwealth as their *ojczyzna* (fatherland), the phrase *gente Ruthenus, natione Polonus* had obfuscated the study of early modern concepts of nation and diverted scholars' attention from the centrality of *ojczyzna* in explaining the Ruthenian nobles' relation to Crown Poland (Korona Polska) and the Commonwealth (Rzeczpospolita). Polish scholars, concentrating their attention on the Ukrainian lands that remained in the Commonwealth after the Khmelnytsky revolution, tended to focus on the processes of acculturation and assimilation of the Ruthenians into the Commonwealth and Poland. Ukrainian scholars were more likely to focus on the lands where the revolt succeeded and on the emergence of Cossack polities and the culture of the Hetmanate. More recent research has pointed to how "Ukraine on both banks of the Dnipro" emerged as a fatherland (Ukrainian: *otchyzna)* in the late seventeenth century and how its culture and political traditions served as a crucial building block for Ukrainian nation-building, including for the Ukrainian lands that remained in the Commonwealth down to the end of the eighteenth century.[3]

Whatever the impact and use of the phrase on the study of the seventeenth century, *gente Ruthenus, natione Polonus* came to play a major role in identity discussions in nineteenth- and early twentieth-century Galicia. The phrase came, above all, to describe those in the Austrian crownland of Galicia who identified themselves as in some sense "Ruthenian" and sought to integrate themselves into projects to restore the Polish-Lithuanian Commonwealth or find a place for Ruthenians in Polish state- and nation-building projects. Ultimately the *gente Ruthenus, natione Polonus* option proved unviable because its adherents could not create a stable Ruthenian identity within a Polish nation and because the majority of Galicia's Ruthenians chose other identity projects, conceiving themselves as a nation separate from the Poles and increasingly as part of a Ukrainian nation. In essence they took on the seventeenth-century choice of those who had rebelled against the Commonwealth. In so doing they affirmed a Cossack historical tradition that was antithetical to the Commonwealth, and they adopted a modern vernacular literary language that they shared with the Ruthenians/Ukrainians of the Russian Empire. Indeed one of the problems of the "Ruthenian of Polish nationality" project that sought to resurrect the Polish-Lithuanian Commonwealth in its borders of 1772 was that it cut off the territories of Left-Bank and Sloboda Ukraine, whose large num-

---

[3] For a summary of this research, see Frank E. Sysyn, "Ukrainian Nation-building in the Early Modern Period: New Research Finds," in *Theatrum humanae vitae: Studia in honorem Natala Jakovenko / Studii na poshanu Natali Iakovenko* (Kyiv, 2012), pp. 358–70.

ber of Ukrainian speakers many viewed as the same people as the Ruthenians west of the Dnipro. Hence, for those who saw nationhood as associated with the people's or folk language, the political goals of the "Ruthenians of Polish nationality" would have divided the Ukrainian speakers. Already in 1881 Mykhailo Drahomanov, who had tremendous influence on the formation of a populist and ultimately Ukrainian movement in Galicia, had condemned Polish restorationist goals and insurrections because they were aimed at dividing the Ukrainian people (whatever nomenclature one used for them) along the Dnipro.[4]

Adam Świątek sees this process of affirmation of an ethnos as a nation that sought to establish a state as the usual path of "nationalism." Many scholars would see the Ukrainian case as more complex than just the affirmation of an ethno-linguistic group as a nation, in that it derived in great part from the political culture of the Cossack Hetmanate, including the conceptualization of Cossack Ukraine as a fatherland. Certainly the Achilles heel of various Polish projects to encompass the Ruthenians of Galicia or of the Right Bank in nation- and state-building came from the social and cultural movements deriving from the Hetmanate, the lands that withdrew from the Commonwealth. In the same way, the Polish projects to unite Poles and Galician Ruthenians on the basis of belonging to the Catholic Church faced problems over attempts to diminish distinctions between the Latin and Greek rites or to overestimate those between the Uniates and the Orthodox majority of Ukrainian speakers. In the same way, plans to emphasize the differences between Ruthenians and Orthodox Russians—plans that in many ways worked in favour of the Ruthenians identifying themselves as a nation separate from the Russians—encountered problems because they would also have cut off the Orthodox "Little Russians" beyond the Dnipro, not to speak of those Ruthenians of the Right Bank who had affirmed the abolition of the Union of Berestia/Brest.

Dr. Świątek has undertaken a massive recovery project to restore the voices of those Ruthenians who adopted Polish "nationality," and of those Poles who aimed to gain Ruthenians' loyalty for Polish projects. In many ways his research fits recent trends examining multiple and hierarchical identities. It also contributes to research on national indifferentism. Dr. Świątek has decided to take up the course of an amorphous and ultimately losing trend that does not fit well into either the Polish or the Ukrainian national narrative. At least for the Polish

---

[4] For a discussion of Drahomanov's views, see Serhiy Bilenky, "Preface to Drahomanov, 'Jews and Poles in the Southwestern Region'," in *Fashioning Modern Ukraine: Selected Writings of Mykola Kostomarov, Volodymyr Antonovych, and Mykhailo Drahomanov*, ed. Serhiy Bilenky (Edmonton–Toronto, 2013), pp. 307–9.

narrative, the cliché and the purported phenomenon occupied a significant place in historical and political writing and in family genealogies. For those who wish to see *gente Rutheni, natione Poloni* as a positive phenomenon and a chance that was missed, Dr. Świątek's book offers many challenges. The phenomenon occupies a much more negative role in the Ukrainian popular imagination, where it is associated with the periods of national decline and individual opportunism. Above all, it is associated with those who wanted to hold back Ruthenian/Ukrainian development as a nation or culture. The upholders of *gente Rutheni, natione Poloni* identity can so easily be seen as Uncle Toms or, to use the phrase that at least from the 1880s was coined for those who sold their votes, *khruni* (swine), which in Western Ukraine became a synonym for traitors. Here, too, Dr. Świątek's work will challenge stereotypes and present individuals who wholeheartedly backed a Polish alternative, yet often furthered the development of Ruthenian identity. The great strength of his book is that it examines the advocates and carriers of a series of ideas, identities, and cultural formations associated with *gente Rutheni, natione Poloni* over Galicia's long nineteenth century, in fact from the late eighteenth to the early twentieth century.

Written for a Polish reading public often well versed in the realia of Polish political and cultural affairs in Galicia, the volume has been adapted for the English-language reader. Still, we recognize that the reader may have to consult a wide array of books on Polish and Ukrainian history to follow all of the narrative and fill in the groups that are not examined. Fortunately recent decades have seen a great increase in such literature available in English. Translating Dr. Świątek's book has not been an easy task, which even the title makes clear. If, from the time of the writings of scholars such as Stanisław Kot, the phrase *gente Rutheni, natione Poloni* for the early modern period would have been automatically translated as "of Ruthenian tribe/stock/ethnicity and the Polish nation," David Althoen has given us credible evidence that these translations of *gens* and *natio* do not correspond to early modern usage and that *natio* was frequently used to describe an ethno-linguistic community rather than a political one. Fortunately Kot's vision, though codified only in the 1930s, does coincide with the way *gente Ruthenus, natione Polonus* was employed at least from the 1860s. The groups Dr. Świątek has placed under this rubric have been called "of Ruthenian provenance and Polish nationality." Just what provenance and nationality meant in various periods and situations is the centre of his study.

The English reader should also be aware of how the terms "patriots" and "nationalists" have been used in the Polish lexicon. "Patriots" was used in the nineteenth century, and many contemporary authors continue using it thus, to describe groups who wished to restore a Polish state, usually on the territory the Commonwealth held until 1772. "Nationalists" is often reserved for those dedicated to Polish ethnicity as the criteria for Polish nationhood (or assimilation to this ethnicity) and who conceived of an independent Poland as this nation's state. The distinction was not always seen in similar terms by those who rejected Polish identity, and Ukrainian activists of the late nineteenth century used the term "*patrioty*" as a synonym for Polish chauvinists. Similar translation problems occur in the Ukrainian case for groups usually called "*narodovtsi*," who are often called populists or Ukrainophiles. The *narodovtsi* adopted a belief that the simple folk had retained their nationality and vernacular language, and that this peasantry would be the basis of the Ruthenian nation, which by the late nineteenth century came to be called Ukrainian. The term "populists" has acquired a very negative connotation today rather than being remembered as the defining name of the nineteenth-century movement for universal male suffrage and economic and political rights for the peasant majority.

The most confusing term for English readers may be the language called "Ruthenian," though this somewhat reflects the nineteenth-century situation and its carry over in the present volume. The Ruthenians of Galicia spoke Ukrainian dialects, which most observers have seen as related to the Ukrainian dialects in the Russian Empire. The literary language is a very different matter. Throughout the nineteenth century, literary forms based on an earlier book form of Ruthenian (an early modern literary language based on Ukrainian and Belarusian with Polish accretions) greatly influenced by Church Slavonic were used and called Ruthenian. At times these literary forms were heavily influenced by Russian (especially advocated by Russophiles). At other times they were closer to the vernacular and influenced by the Ukrainian literary language emerging in the Russian Empire. Battles over language and what alphabet and orthography the Ruthenians were to use played a major role in influencing identity among these Ukrainian speakers of Galicia. They were resolved in the main only at the end of Habsburg rule in favour of a codified Ukrainian language and identity. The reader should keep these differing uses of the phrase "in Ruthenian" in mind while reading Dr. Świątek's book.

The CIUS Press and the Peter Jacyk Centre for Ukrainian Historical Research at the Canadian Institute of Ukrainian Studies have undertaken the publication of this volume because it is such an important contribution to the study of Polish-Ukrainian relations and of Galicia. As many readers know, those relations were a minefield throughout most of the twentieth century, and scholarship was not the least of the battlefields. Even the term "Ruthenians" (*rusyny*) was involved in this controversy, not least because of the reluctance of some Poles to accept the change of nomenclature to "Ukrainians" and because of the interwar Polish authorities' attempts to divide those who called themselves Ukrainians and Ruthenians. While many Western scholars have used the term "Ukrainians" (e.g. Ivan L. Rudnytsky), we have retained Dr. Świątek's references to the historical Ruthenians for Galicia and even for territories in the Russian Empire. This may disturb some readers of Ukrainian descent, but probably not as much as finding many of their surnames in Polish. Dr. Świątek has requested that for those Ruthenians who advocated a two-tier identity of Ruthenian provenance and Polish nationality, the Polish form of their name be the primary one used. We have ensured that such names' Ukrainian forms also appear upon first use. The process of decision-making is obviously a difficult one since identities changed, and in this text one will find that one member of the famous Ruthenian Triad [*Ruska triitsia*], Ivan Vahylevych, later decided he was Jan Wagilewicz. But, rather than struggling over nomenclature, we have sought to convey the opinions of a scholar who has devoted such intense research to providing a multifaceted approach to examining those who were "*gente Rutheni, natione Poloni.*" As far as place names go, they appear in this book according to current geographic borders, though we know that for some nineteenth-century figures mentioned the city would have been Lwów, not Lviv, or Peremyshl, not Przemyśl. Out of such compromises come joint projects such as this translation, which was undertaken with Księgarnia Akademicka of Cracow, Poland. The result is that, in the new lingua franca, readers and scholars will have the opportunity to enter the complex world of Habsburg Galicia and Ukrainian-Polish relations.

Frank E. Sysyn
Director, Peter Jacyk Centre for Ukrainian Historical Research
Canadian Institute of Ukrainian Studies, University of Alberta

Abbreviations
of Frequently Cited Sources

BJ: Biblioteka Jagiellońska

LNNBU: Lvivs´ka natsional'na naukova biblioteka Ukraïny imeni Vasylia Stefanyka

MNK, DJM: Muzeum Narodowe w Krakowie. Oddział Dom Jana Matejki

PSB: *Polski słownik biograficzny*

TsDIAU: Tsentral´nyi derzhavnyi istorychnyi arkhiv Ukraïny u L'vovi

ZNiO: Zakład Narodowy im. Ossolińskich we Wrocławiu

Introduction

In the 1890s, the teenager Mieczysław Opałek, who would go on to become a renowned Lviv [Lwów] bibliophile, left the city to visit his Ruthenian relatives, the Dykoński [Dykonsky] family. The recollections of this meeting returned to him years later when he was preparing a typed manuscript expounding his youth spent in Lviv:

Besides the mythologically themed pictures hanging on the wall, there were other lithographs displayed at the Dykoński residence; images not lacking in mustached figures clothed in traditional felt coats—*burkas*—and four-cornered caps. In recalling these prints, I feel a former sensation of pleasant amazement awakening inside me. Uncle Dykoński was a Ruthenian, an official at the Greek Catholic consistory, and he lived in lodgings that were part and parcel of the Uniate Church next to the Cathedral of St. George. Both of his daughters had been married off to Ruthenians, one of whom was a Uniate priest. At that time none of this seemed to be at odds whatsoever with the Polish subject matter of the pictures held in such esteem in [...] Ruthenian households. At times, there could be found in these same houses [...] a lithographic representation by [Edward] Stolz of Prince Lev [Danylovych], and occasionally even a portrait of Taras Shevchenko. The times had not yet arrived for a likeness of Bohdan Khmelnytsky. The curious collection of pictures that graced the flats of some Ruthenians was like an iconological documentation of the slogan contained in the Polish-Ruthenian poet Platon Kostecki's tetrastich:

> In the name of the Father, and the Son
> It is our prayer,
> That the Trinity be one,
> One of Poland, Rus' and Lithuania

I also came across pictures imbued with a Polish theme in the flat of my teacher, Michał Janusz [Mykhailo Ianush] of the folk school. He was also a Ruthenian. A dozen or so years later, all was to be changed beyond recognition. The walls of Ruthenian homes were to be thoroughly cleansed of all "Polish" images, even eradicating at times the very image of Our Lady of Częstochowa.[1]

The author, a Pole, spoke of these times as if they were long-lost and never destined to return. They were characterized by a harmony,

---

[1] Mieczysław Opałek, "Książka o Lwowie i mojej młodości. Kartki z pamiętnika 1881–1901" (Frysztak, 1958), pp. 15–16, Zakład Narodowy im. Ossolińskich in Wrocław (subsequently: ZNiO), sygn. 13535/II (MF 3269).

a brotherhood, a coexistence of Poles and Ruthenians joined not merely by their physical proximity in the same land but by bonds of blood, and, at times, even a shared community of values and ideas. Opałek's observations, albeit written down years after the events in question, bear witness to an array of similar recollections from this period, and to the author's perception of those most radical of changes within Ruthenian-Polish relations that were about to occur. During this period, territories under Austrian rule witnessed the rise of a modern Ukrainian nation, a nation with its own aspirations at odds with Polish interests. These were not reconcilable with Polish retrospections of the past nor with their dreams of a joint future realized on a common territory. Furthermore, for the majority of the Polish Galician-based elite, the notion of Ruthenians becoming a nation of equal standing was not only for a long time something wholly unacceptable, but quite simply unimaginable.

It is common practice of late, within the relevant subject literature, to write about the period of partitions as if Polish-Ruthenian relations had been characterized for decades by a rivalry that intensified from the beginning of the twentieth century. If this had been the case, then it would have meant that Poles and Ruthenians had, up until that moment, lived not with each other but simply beside each other, as two separate communities. At the same time, there existed a group of Ruthenians who constituted a somewhat different example of Polish-Ruthenian relations in Galicia. And here we shall add that already at the level of the very designation itself, "Polish-Ruthenian," a certain phraseological inadequacy is detectable in relation to the question examined in this study. For the notion implies, if not a complete opposition of the two elements, then at least their distinction—as if they had been two subjects independent of each other. Yet can one divide something that was in many instances joint and common or—to put things differently—in between? Zbigniew Pucek has noted that traditionally when statistics were given for the percentage of Poles, Ruthenians, and Jews amongst the inhabitants of Galicia, there was no exploration whatsoever regarding the nature of the internal relations that existed within the territory under Austrian rule. For these people functioned in an ambivalent world, their existence subject to two sometimes contrary principles of social life: the territorial (family-neighbour orientated) and national (ideologically based). They created a truly "intercultural" community, not simply through living in a single place but through mixed genealogy as a result of inter-confessional marriages. Simultaneously, the ideological principle contravened territorial integrity as it assumed the creation of a national entity, implying the separation of something that without the use of force and family and community upheaval could not be separated.[2]

Today our view of the Ruthenian past as played out on those lands once under Austrian rule is often conditioned by the epilogue to this period—the Polish-Ukrainian War for Eastern Galicia, or the bloody events of the Second World War. Yet this development of a "national" option was in the Ruthenian case not the only route available, although it was the one that would prove victorious. Often in our search for the roots of the modern Ukrainian and Polish nations we are oblivious to all the branches, those that at first glance do not appear to fit onto the "trunk" of either nation. Such thinking is in line with the spirit of historical determinism. Yet these branches also had significance; although from the perspective of history they were to turn out to be secondary, they were by no means unimportant. To this end the view of the British historian Hugh Trevor-Roper is particularly pertinent: "History is not merely what happened; it is what happened in the context of what might have happened. Therefore it must incorporate, as a necessary element, the alternatives, the might-have-beens."[3]

Ivan Lysiak-Rudnytsky, in developing Trevor-Roper's thinking, showed that the historian's obligation is to "accord full hearing to all alternatives which at a given time contended for supremacy, but he is also under an obligation to account adequately for the reasons of the success of the one that ultimately prevailed."[4] In the case of the Ruthenian population, there are several historical alternatives that never came to pass. Instead of becoming Ukrainians, Ruthenians could have as easily become—in the political sense—Russians, Austrians, or Poles.[5] The final alternative—occasionally awkwardly worded within Polonophile literature—was to create a people that with time were to be referred to as *gente Rutheni, natione Poloni,* or "Ruthenians of Polish nationality." The key to understanding who these people were lies in the tetrastich cited by Opałek and composed by a representative of this very group, Platon Kostecki (Kostetsky). This extract from his best--known poem "Our Prayer" ["Nasza mołytwa"], written in 1861, was

---

[2] Cf. Zbigniew Pucek, "Galicyjskie doświadczenie wielokulturowości a problem więzi społecznej," in *Społeczeństwo i gospodarka*, eds. Jerzy Chłopecki and Helena Madurowicz--Urbańska (Rzeszów, 1995), pp. 12 ff.

[3] Hugh Trevor-Roper, "History and imagination," *Times Literary Supplement* no. 835 (25 Jul. 1980), quoted after: Ivan L. Rudnytsky, "Carpatho-Ukraine: A People in Search of Their Identity," in Ivan L. Rudnytsky, *Essays in Modern Ukrainian History* (Edmonton, 1987), pp. 358–59.

[4] Ibid., p. 359.

[5] Cf. Andrew Wilson, *The Ukrainians: Unexpected Nation* (New Haven–London, 2015), pp. 114–21, 120.

quick to appear in the press and in a poetry collection.[6] Throughout the decades of the nineteenth century as well as for a part of the twentieth century these words—of Poland, Rus' and Lithuania being like a "Trinity" and as "one"—were sufficient to convey the feelings and beliefs of those inhabitants of the Austrian partition who came from Ruthenian (or mixed) families, spoke in Ruthenian (though equally in Polish) and belonged to the Greek Catholic "Uniate" Church, but who felt themselves to be not merely Ruthenians but also Poles and who dreamed of an independent Poland (or rather a commonwealth of three nations: Poles, Lithuanians, and Ruthenians). This was a dual-level identity, one comprising two components, where the Ruthenian ethnicity was closely subject to the chosen Polish nationality.

Who were *gente Rutheni, natione Poloni*, what characterized their dual-level identity, what is the genesis of their formation, what conditioned their national choice, and finally, what role were they to play in the social, political, and cultural history of Galicia? These are all questions that the present book will attempt to answer.

The Chronological and Geographical Scope of the Study

The book does not fall between neat chronological bookends, and this for two reasons. First, the very term "Galicia" means that we are dealing with history post-1772 when, as a result of the First Partition of Poland, the Habsburg monarchy had the lands of southern Poland incorporated into their empire: from the southern part of the Cracow voivodeship (province) without the city of Cracow itself right up to the Zbruch River in the east. As a result of the Third Partition of 1795, Austria was to annex subsequent lands: the northern part of the Cracow province along with the city of Cracow, the Lublin lands, and parts of Podlachia and Mazovia. The situation in these areas—with the exception of Cracow and environs—was certainly not my focus due to the short time period this region was actually held by Austria (1795–1809). Nonetheless, the above-mentioned territories, also inhabited by Ruthenians of the Uniate rite, will occasionally appear in the book as a background

---

[6] Platon Kostecki, *Poezyi* (Lviv, 1862), p. 1. The piece was printed in *Dziennik Literacki* no. 39 (1861), p. 312. The manuscript in a later copy by the author can be found in: Platon Kostecki, "Nasza mołytwa" (Lviv, 1891), Lvivs'ka natsional'na naukova Biblioteka Ukraïny imeni Vasylia Stefanyka (subsequently: LNNBU), fond 5: Zbirka rukopysiv, avtohrafiv, hramot i dyplomiv biblioteky Natsional'noho zakladu im. Ossolins'kykh u m. Lvovi, op. 2: Avtohrafy, spr. 5146/II.

for key deliberations, for they did constitute a neighbouring territory to that of Galicia itself. Following the annulment of the Union of Brest on the occupied territories, the Uniate Church in the Congress Kingdom of Poland was headed primarily by Catholic priests of the Greek rite from Galicia; there, the gradual process of Polonizing the Uniate population also occurred—proof of which lies in the attitudes of the Uniates as evidenced by the eve of the January Uprising (1863) and immediately after the breakout of this national revolt. Finally, when in the 1870s the Uniate Church was eradicated in the Lublin region and Podlachia, those oppressed and persecuted received support from the inhabitants of the Austrian partition, where they fled and where they were warmly received. I also do not cover the area of Bukovyna, even though it belonged to Galicia—on admittedly different legal principles—for the period from 1786 to 1849. This is because this area was a borderland region of a Romanian-Ruthenian rather than Polish-Ruthenian character, despite growing Polish settlement during the Austrian period which saw an increase in the region's Polish element. The book will, however, include Cracow and in principle the lands of the Cracow Commonwealth, incorporated into the Austrian state as the Grand Duchy of Cracow, and joined with the Kingdom of Galicia and Lodomeria into a single province in 1846. Cracow, even though located in the western, ethnically Polish, part of the region, was to play an important role in the history of Galicia as a whole, as well as in the individual lives of Ruthenians of Polish nationality, hence the frequent references I shall make to this former capital of Poland. Galicia was to exist within these borders until 1918, and following the Polish-Ukrainian War over Eastern Galicia and the victory against the Bolsheviks, it was to survive as Little Poland [Małopolska] right up until the Second World War.

The second and possibly most important reason as to why there are no bracketed dates demarcating the research period is contained in the question: can one insist on fixing temporal limits of historical processes that naturally result from earlier events and have consequences for the future, thereby creating a chronological chain of interdependence? I am of the view that this does not need to be done. As a result, this study will also make references to modern times when the gentry *gente Rutheni, natione Poloni* existed in a form different from that of the nineteenth century. In the post-partition period when no Polish state existed, to answer the question "Who are you?" was to make a dramatic and necessary choice.

Although principally focused on the period of the partitions, the present study has no grand dividing line as such, despite the fact that Poland subsequently gained independence. This is simply because many Ruthenians of Polish nationality who were born in the nineteenth century were still alive after 1918. Then, the *gente Rutheni, natione Poloni* were to find state support, since even a new concept of "Greek Catholic Poles" was created, which would separate the concept of religious rite from that of nationality (hitherto Greek Catholics had often been equated with Ukrainians, while Roman Catholics were considered Poles). The ethnic element (*gente Rutheni*) was abolished from the designation *gente Rutheni, natione Poloni*; for in the face of shaping both nationalities, Polish and Ukrainian, ethnic matters took on a secondary importance. In such an understanding, rite was no longer seen as a designation of nationality.

A certain symbolic boundary does, however, exist, and limit the research I have undertaken, one which corresponds not so much with an end to the very notion of *gente Rutheni, natione Poloni*, but rather to the conditions that would have allowed for its continuation. This is the era of growing nationalisms, which naturally excluded any further functioning of a two-layer model for identity within a territory that found itself the object of heightened attention on the part of two opposing national ideologies (conjecturing the construction of a state based on this very territory). Several culminating points and stages in the development of these nationalisms may be noted, beginning with the final years of the nineteenth century when the ideas of National Democracy [*Narodowa Demokracja*] were formulated in the Polish lands and analogically nationalist ideas amongst Ruthenians of the national camp, through to the Polish-Ukrainian War for Eastern Galicia and ending in the 1940s. At that time, as a result of the massacres witnessed in Volhynia and Eastern Galicia, the border changes, the deportations during the war and afterwards of Poles from the area of Eastern Galicia, and the deportation of Ukrainians by the Polish communist authorities during the Operation "Vistula," the demography of the Polish-Ukrainian borderland, which had existed in the eastern part of Galicia and which had been forged over centuries, was almost completely destroyed.

Terminology and Onomastics

The problem of the spelling of ethnonyms is a crucial one facing all who research the inter-ethnic relations of Galicia. These include notions such as "Rus'," "Ukraine," as well as the terms "Ruthenian" and "Ukrainian." These problems arise from the fact that Ukraine as a state came into existence only in the twentieth century, though the name has been in existence for a considerably longer period and had been used to designate the lands lying along the Dnipro River. Similarly, during the period I am covering, this name did not apply to those lands which today constitute Western Ukraine. Consequently, in the present study I use the term "Ukraine" in its former geographical and not political sense, employing it when referring to those lands (Kyiv, Podilia and Volhynia provinces) situated under the political control of tsarist Russia. Polish politicians (among them *gente Rutheni, natione Poloni*) rarely understood the term "Ukraine" in its contemporary borders. Not only was Eastern Galicia excluded from this term, but also Left-Bank Ukraine. While the term "Rus'" is one with an even longer history, I employ it in a most general sense as a land once under the rule of the Kyivan princes, which went on to exist with this same designation following the inclusion of these lands within the Polish state. This term covers the eastern Galician lands and consequently those of Red Rus'. Often the formulation "Rus'" appears in the book as a notion less confined by closely defined borders, whether geographical or ethnic, and more in the form of a headword intended to emphasize that former and future Poland included or was to include some Ruthenian territories. Hence the term "Rus'" does not always take on those same dimensions as understood by the authors quoted in the source works.

I have intentionally used in large parts of the book the ethnonym "Ruthenian" to define a representative of the Ruthenian ethnic group,[7] regardless of whether this referred to the nationally conscious elite or the Ruthenian peasantry. Ethnic Ruthenians also included representatives of *gente Rutheni, natione Poloni* as well as those who chose a Russophile orientation. In order to indicate to the reader to the type of viewpoint held by a given individual, I often specify whether we are dealing with Ruthenians with a national populist outlook, Russophiles, or Ruthenians of Polish nationality. Many historians, especially during the period of the Polish People's Republic, consciously employed an anachronistic designation by assigning to all Galician Ruthenians the ethnonym "Ukrainian" for the time period when they themselves did not use such a designation. There would be nothing wrong with this per se, if it had not resulted in a muddying of the identificational ambiguity that characterized the representatives of the Ruthenian group in nineteenth-century Galicia. Ruthenians of Polish nationality are often referred to in these works as Polonophile Ukrainians, and yet this constitutes a significant difference, distorting their identity as they often considered themselves to be nationally Polish and not Ukrainians.

The term "Ukrainian" was used within Galicia to underline the union of two parts of a nation divided as a result of the Austro-Hun-

---

[7] The term "Rusyns" ("Ruthenians") was introduced in Austria in 1843 at the request of Metropolitan Mykhailo Levytsky, rejecting other designations. This term did not cover the Ukrainian population of the Russian Empire, where the state apparatus referred to them as "Little Russians." Cf. Jan Kozik, *The Ukrainian National Movement in Galicia 1815–1849*, ed. and introd. Lawrence D. Orton, trans. Andrew Gorski and Lawrence D. Orton (Edmonton, 1986), pp. 162–63.

garian-Russian border along the Zbruch; this term already had a definite national character and not an ethnic one.[8] It started to be adopted within Galician society at the turn of the twentieth century, although as early as the 1860s we note the first use of the term in the magazine *Sioło* [Village] (edited by Paulin Święcicki [Pavlyn Svientsitsky]) in relation to the region's Ruthenian inhabitants. I also employ both terms, "Ruthenian" and "Ukrainian," interchangeably in those parts of the book dealing with the turn of the century or a later period, which more or less covers the beginning of the adoption by Galician Ruthenians of this new name for their nationality.

A certain problem linked to the above considerations on the correct rendering of geographical, ethnic, and national names occurs in relation to the spelling of first names and surnames. Very often the protagonists of the present study used their first names and surnames in two language variants: Polish and Ruthenian. For example, when publishing in Ruthenian the *gente Ruthenus, natione Polonus* Platon Kostecki used a Ruthenian-sounding version of his surname. Likewise, many Ruthenians who did not feel Polish appear in Polish sources and literature under Polish variants of their surnames. I have therefore decided to intentionally apply a spelling to surnames that in my opinion best reflects how the given individual felt about their identity. And if someone was to change their affiliation during the course of their life—as in the case of Ivan Vahylevych, later Jan Wagilewicz—then I have used both spellings of his name depending on the period in question. Despite a degree of artificiality in the spelling of certain surnames, I am of the view that this allows the reader to instantly recognize whether the individuals in question felt themselves to be Ruthenian or Polish. In instances where I have not been able to establish the identity of the person under consideration, I have used the spelling of the name most commonly employed by the individual and which is best known within the literature on the subject. At the request of the publisher, to the first entry of a Ruthenian of Polish nationality's name was added the Ukrainian spelling variant in brackets next to the Polish.

In the case of place names, the modern version of the name was given as the basic version for towns and villages in Ukraine and Poland. For some towns now in Ukraine, the Polish name was also given in brackets, and for some places in contemporary Poland inhabited (or formerly inhabited) by the Ukrainian population—the Ukrainian variant.

---

[8] On the role played by the ethnonym "Ukrainian" in the shaping of national consciousness and awareness see, among others: Mirosława Papierzyńska-Turek, *Od tożsamości do niepodległości. Studia i szkice z dziejów kształtowania się ukraińskiej świadomości narodowej* (Toruń, 2012), pp. 54–57, 119–25.

Structure of the Book

The book attempts to deal with the vast and somewhat enigmatic problem that is *gente Rutheni, natione Poloni*. The very fact that we are talking here about an amorphous phenomenon, one more concerned rather with the nature of the soul than of the body, with thoughts rather than deeds, means that the problem is difficult to present in a coherent and ordered way. Readers may even be under the impression that the book is asymmetrical, unbalanced, and what is more, unchronological. They will also note that important political problems from the epoch are mixed with trivial (from the present-day perspective) events, influential propaganda works with literary and poetical ones, great processes in social change with the personal routes taken by the book's heroes. At times Ruthenians of Polish nationality speak from the rostrum of the Galician Diet (*Sejm Krajowy/Kraiovyi soim*), at times they compose a poem or write a newspaper article in the quiet of their homes; they ride to raucous commemorations of the Union of Lublin, while at other times they give a speech at the funeral of a friend of a similar dual identity. Yet, all these facets combine to present a holistic picture of the group *gente Rutheni, natione Poloni*, a fact that has influenced the decision to construct the current analysis around problem areas rather than chronology. Consequently, some events, or the biographies of certain individuals, will seem to randomly pop up in various parts of the book; yet, it is the author's hope that the reader will understand the principle of such a presentation.

The book begins with the chapter "*Gente Rutheni, Natione Poloni*: The Characteristics of the Formation." The aim of this chapter is to gradually introduce the reader to the general problem of defining the term *gente Rutheni, natione Poloni*. Here I try to refer to concepts such as "ethnicity," "nation," and "identity." Although there is not sufficient room here to examine the huge academic debate around these terms, it does seem imperative to note that the question under consideration in this study is framed by the national changes occurring during the nineteenth century. The next part of this chapter attempts to show the structure of the two-tier (dual) identity of Ruthenians of Polish nationality, taking into consideration as broadly as possible the spectrum of issues arising within the lives of individuals as well as those factors which impacted the development of their national consciousness. In it, I try to characterize the formation of *gente Rutheni, natione Poloni* in order to place the phenomenon within time and geographical expanse and to show how it manifested itself across various social strata. I also introduce the reader to the main characters of the book, dealing subsequently with those elements of daily life that often decided whether Ruthenians chose the Polish nationality option. Here mention is made of family, the Uniate

Church, school, language, conflict situations with Ruthenians of other political persuasions, and finally a fascination with Polish culture.

Chapter Two, "Rus' in the Historical Consciousness of Poles," attempts to illustrate the Polish cultural input in the shaping of the world outlook of many Galician Ruthenians. I consider nineteenth-century literature, art, and historiography to be fundamental in the creation of people's historical consciousness, and with it their identity. For Polish cultural heritage, they not only recalled the former might of a state now lost, but also built up the myth of the unbroken bonds linking Poland, Lithuania, and Rus'. With time, certain members of *gente Rutheni, natione Poloni* started to adopt and develop this, as was the case with the "icon" of this formation, Platon Kostecki.

Chapters One and Two are not chronological in nature, attempting to illustrate the cultural foundations of *gente Rutheni, natione Poloni* as a form of identity. The third chapter, "From Enlightened Centralism to the Romantic Brotherhood of Peoples," is effectively an introduction to Chapter Four. It presents the genesis of the political demands made by Ruthenians of Polish nationality in 1848. This part of the book returns to the Age of Enlightenment in order to illuminate the significance of the centralist views on "the state" and "the nation." These views, fused together with the Romantic slogans on matters of social change and a brotherhood of peoples, were to cause the creation of a certain stock of demands upon which the plotters of the Galician conspiracies of the 1830s and 1840s drew. This chapter attempts to shed light on those Ruthenians of Polish nationality who came to prominence at the time through their political and social activities, often risking their lives and liberty, with many receiving severe punishments of long-term imprisonment. Their life stories are important not only because of the views they expressed, but also because of the aura of conspiratorial legend that motivated them to act and excel during the Revolutions of 1848.

Chapter four, "*Gente Rutheni, Natione Poloni* during the Revolutions of 1848," shows how Ruthenians of Polish nationality emerged as political players in the revolutionary events that came to a head in 1848. The Ruthenian Council, the only political organization in history assembling Ruthenians of Polish nationality, and the journal *Dnewnyk Ruskij* [The Ruthenian Daily] published by them, were at the time entities sufficiently strong to constitute competition to the Supreme Ruthenian Council, the political organ of the Ruthenians who espoused a national orientation. In this chapter I attempt to draw attention not only to political events, but also to those contemporary dilemmas in Ruthenian circles that were to result in the lack of group consolidation later on, and consequently matters of acknowledging or refuting the existence of Ruthenian nationality. The defeat of the Galician Poles during the Revolutions of 1848 at the same time saw the failure of Ruthenians of Polish nationality. Nonetheless, those who made themselves heard were to continue propagating their principles on the public stage and implementing them through the social and political posts they held in Galicia.

Chapter Five, entitled "Ruthenians and the Return of Absolutism," depicts the situation within the Austrian partition at the time of renewed Habsburg absolutism after 1849 as it relates to the activities of Ruthenians of Polish nationality. Discussion centers on the still unresolved questions of equal status for both languages in Galicia, schooling, and finally the matter of an alphabet for the Ruthenian language. The appointment of a Pole—Count Agenor Gołuchowski—to the office of governor for Galicia during this difficult time enabled the implementation of initiatives beneficial to the interests of Ruthenians of Polish nationality. This was chiefly due to the huge role played by Euzebiusz Czerkawski [Ievzevii Cherkavsky] in aiding this immensely rich count, who was a key figure in the Galician school system of that time, and subsequently during the period of autonomy.

Chapter Six deals with the January Uprising (1863), which was the only Polish national revolt where the standards bore not only the Polish Eagle and Lithuanian Vytis coat-of-arms but also the Ruthenian Archangel Michael. The Uprising's defeat in 1864 ended any hope for independence within a state as dreamed of by *gente Rutheni, natione Poloni*. These dreams were not to fade immediately, but only with the passing of the subsequent years and the failure of the democratic camp in Galicia to achieve Galician sovereignty after the reconstruction of the Habsburg monarchy following its defeat in the 1866 war with Prussia and the defeat of France—the Poles' only ally in the world—to the same foe in 1871. These three defeats erased any romantic hopes for a swift liberation. The political activists of the day, including Ruthenians of Polish nationality, had to undertake, in the language of the positivists, "organic work."

The next two chapters, "*Gente Rutheni, Natione Poloni* in Power" and "Manifestation of Ideas," require almost parallel reading. They illustrate the efforts made by many Ruthenians of Polish nationality within political and social life to ensure decent relations between the Galician Polish and Ruthenian communities. Many important posts were held by Ruthenians of Polish nationality, particularly in the 1860s, 1870s and 1890s. This allowed them to not only display denominational outlooks (particularly on the so-called "Ruthenian question"), but also to implement many important solutions within public life (including in the education system). At the same time, from the 1880s onwards, *gente Rutheni, natione Poloni* gradually disappeared from the political life of Galicia, while the programs of the Polish political parties of the time failed to take into consideration the demands of this group. There is a brief presentation in the chapter of how Galician groupings of conservatives, socialists, 'populars' (peasant movement, *ludowcy*), and national democrats (*narodowcy, endecy*) reacted to the Ruthenian question.

Equally significant was the highlighting of Ruthenian involvement during important jubilee celebrations commemorating Polish historical anniversaries, which took the form of political demonstrations. In this way the notion of Rus' as being bound for centuries to Poland was constantly referenced and talked about everywhere from grand ceremonies to private gatherings and even funeral services. The final political position on the part Ruthenians of Polish nationality was to be Teofil Merunowicz's peace treaty project for the Versailles Congress.

Source Base

The most difficult problem encountered during the research stage for this book was the absence of a set of sources that cover in their entirety the construct *gente Rutheni, natione Poloni*; no single archive has a collection of documents devoted exclusively to this grouping. Moreover, it is not sufficient when researching the subject simply to choose a set type of source material. For we are not able to grasp the essence of such an enigmatic formation simply through letters, memorabilia, literature, or mere press accounts. Material on Ruthenians of Polish nationality can be found in the entire historical heritage of Galicia for the period of the partitions and following Poland's recovery of independence. *Gente Rutheni, natione Poloni* and their related problems appeared in the press, propaganda publications, poetry, literary works, paintings, funerary objects, statistical materials, church and state documents, police and court protocols, parliamentary and council minutes and records, and a host of other sources. Ruthenians of Polish nationality—as a group existing through almost the entirety of the partitions—were to leave behind innumerable traces within diverse sources. The current study was able to employ only a mere fraction of the immense nineteenth-century Galician source materials. My selection of materials was chosen so as to sufficiently sketch the phenomenon of *gente Rutheni, natione Poloni* on the various planes in which it manifested itself during the period of the partition.

The archival research was conducted in Lviv, Wrocław, and Cracow. At the Central Ukrainian State Historical Archive in Lviv I made use of several collections including the diaries and memoirs of Florian Ziemiałkowski (fond 93), collections of documents on the January Uprising including the police lists of those arrested for aiding the insurgents (fond 102), documents pertaining to Metropolitan Andrei Sheptytsky (fond 358), and viceroy acts (fond 146). Of special significance in my research was fond 474, a sizeable collection of various documents about the November Uprising (1830–31) and particularly the period 1848–49 in Galicia. There I found numerous printed leaflets, appeals, and proc-lamations, which helped me especially in work on the third and key fourth chapter of the book.

Even more documents, brochures, and first and foremost rare sets of all the editions of *Dnewnyk Ruskij* — the only journal in the history of the *gente Rutheni, natione Poloni* formation—were found in the Rare Books Department of the Vasyl Stefanyk National Scientific Library in Lviv. Some of the materials relating to the 1848 Revolutions—chiefly letters and pamphlet proclamations—were found in the manuscripts department of the same library in the Pawlikowski family manuscripts and archive (fond 76). Here I also made use of other fonds created out of various former Lviv library collections. The fundamental collection here is fond 5, which is a pre-war collection of manuscripts from the Ossoliński National Institute in Lviv. I also used materials on the Revo-lutions of 1848, a reproduction of Henryk Bogdański's hand-written diary, the original of Józef Fedkowicz's *History of the Polish-Ruthenian--Lithuanian Commonwealth* [*Historyia Rzeczypospolitej Polsko-Rusko-Litew-skiej*], and finally the letters and works of Julian Horoszkiewicz and Pla-ton Kostecki. The latter's poems may also be found in the collection of Polish autographs (fond 215). Additionally, I made use of individual items found in other fonds: the Baworowski collections (fond 4), private acquisitions (fond 9), as well as the archive of the Dzieduszycki family (fond 45).

At the Ossoliński National Institute in Wrocław, besides utilizing the rich stock of nineteenth-century journals, I also made use of indi-vidual items from a range of collections. These included the diary of Maurycy Dzieduszycki and the typed memoirs of Mieczysław Opałek, as well as manuscripts (partly preserved on microfilm) on the period of the Revolutions of 1848.

I used materials on the January Uprising in the collection of the Na-tional Archive in Cracow, as well as the notes of Bronisław Łoziński from Euzebiusz Czerkawski's diary, preserved in the Manuscript De-partment of the Jagiellonian Library in Cracow. I also conducted in this library the main part of my research based on old journals, prints, lite-rary and historiographical works, diaries and memoirs, the records and minutes of the Galician Diet, as well as scholarly works.

All the assembled sources appear throughout the various chapters, their fragments showing the specific nature of the group of *gente Ru-theni, natione Poloni* within the context of daily life and the problems of identity based chiefly on diary, biographical, and correspondence sources. Several Ruthenians of Polish nationality wrote memoirs. Be-sides Eugeniusz Czerkawski, memoirs were written by Julian Horoszkiewicz [Iuliian Horoshkevych], Zygmunt Sawczyński [Syhizmund Savchynsky] (during his school days), Platon Kostecki [Kostetsky] (manuscript 3063/II at the Stefanyk Library, entitled *On the Ruthenian Question* [W sprawie ruskiej], contains autobiographical information), Mikołaj Zyblikiewicz [Mykola Zyblykevych] (a short autobiographical sketch of life in the pages of *Czas* [The Time]), Antoni Dąbczański [Antin Dombchansky] (his diary and the reminiscences about him by his daughter—Helena Dąbczańska), Józef Doboszyński [Iosyf Doboshynsky] (a diary reflecting the perspective of an ordinary civil servant), Józef Matkowski [Iosyf Matkovsky] (recollections from the period of the Napoleonic Wars), and Klemens Mochnacki [Klyment Mokhnatsky] (memories from the period of the Galician conspiracies). Information on Ruthenians of Polish nationality may be found in other diaries, ones kept by those who knew the heroes of the present study (a detailed list is given in the bibliography).

The second chapter of the book, devoted to ideas and consequently literature, painting, and historiography, obviously draws on poetic and prose works, pictures, and historiographical works from the epoch.

In Chapters Three to Eight, where the subject matter concerns the political and social activity of the group *gente Rutheni, natione Poloni*, and subsequently its gradual disappearance, I have referenced publications and works of a political character, newspaper articles, the aforementioned archival sources, stenographic minutes and reports of the Galician Diet, and finally numerous books from the period of interest.

The sources selected, despite any negative consequences deriving from the selection process itself, are as a whole sufficient to present the basic problems associated with the functioning of the group of Ruthenians of Polish nationality in nineteenth-century Galician society. For there emerges from the varied spectrum of sources not only the individual perspective of particular Ruthenians of Polish nationality themselves, but also the views of external observers. It is important to not merely establish the biographical facts about Ruthenians of Polish nationality, but also to grasp an understanding—in as far as this is possible—of their own reflections upon their identity and the life choices they made.

Gente Rutheni, Natione Poloni in the Subject Literature

Interest in *gente Rutheni, natione Poloni* can be seen in the literature of the interwar period in Poland, undoubtedly a result of the recent Polish-Ukrainian war over Eastern Galicia and the dispute regarding the area's subsequent sovereignty. Firstly, the annexation of the said territory, now known as Eastern Little Poland, required substantiation that the lands of Red Rus' should be joined to Poland as a result of their historical associations. Secondly, the identity of *gente Rutheni, natione Poloni*, which in the nineteenth century had been a natural phenomenon resulting from the fluidity of national formulae and the mixing of cultures, was now to become a slogan in a political state striving to assimilate minorities. The colonization of the Ruthenian minority was to occur in various aspects of daily life, taking on the most varied of forms and affecting an array of aspects of social life from the army,[9] through journalism, and ending with religion. It is obviously a usual state of affairs that a country aims for an integration of its citizens. Fears over potential separatist acts on the part of the national minorities inhabiting interwar Poland resulted in many preventative actions, particularly in the face of the various acts of resistance and terror often employed by Ukrainian nationalists. On the one hand this resembled the multi-ethnic Poland of yore, while on the other it represented a struggle against difference.

It is worth mentioning here the recollections of Marian Tyrowicz, the well-known historian and researcher of Lviv. He wrote thus about the former capital of Galicia:

A manoeuvring between periods of calm and peace and sudden outbursts and explosions was to constitute a permanent feature of life in the city, although the take on matters presented in the newspapers was somewhat different. The government attempted to neutralize nationalism with Ukrainian economic concessions, school and educational sweeteners, while on the other hand carrying out a search for the so-called minor gentry, i.e., families once Ruthenian of the genus *gente*

---

[9] For more on this subject see: Maciej Krotofil, "Ukraińcy w Wojsku Polskim w okresie międzywojennym," in *Mniejszości narodowe i wyznaniowe w siłach zbrojnych Drugiej Rzeczypospolitej 1918–1939. Zbiór studiów*, eds. Zbigniew Karpus and Waldemar Rezmer (Toruń, 2001), pp. 123–52; Tadeusz Antoni Kowalski, *Mniejszości narodowe w siłach zbrojnych Drugiej Rzeczypospolitej Polskiej (1918–1939)* (Toruń, 1997); Piotr Siwicki, "Duszpasterstwo greckokatolickie w Wojsku Polskim 1918–2003," in *Historia duszpasterstwa wojskowego na ziemiach polskich*, eds. Jan Ziółek et al. (Lublin, 2004), pp. 383–408; Piotr Stawecki, "Kilka uwag o roli wojska w procesach integracyjnych i dezintegracyjnych II Rzeczpospolitej," in *Drogi integracji społeczeństwa w Polsce XIX i XX w.*, ed. Henryk Zieliński (Wrocław, 1976), pp. 193–215; Piotr Stawecki, "Polityka narodowościowa w wojsku Drugiej Rzeczypospolitej," in *Mniejszości narodowe i wyznaniowe*, pp. 11–36. The Polish military authorities attempted to integrate the army and assimilate minorities doing military service through an educational program, and also by sending Greek Catholic soldiers to the western territories of the Polish Republic. It was expected that the recruits would be impressed by the higher civilizational level of life when compared to the less developed east of the country (Stawecki, "Polityka narodowościowa," p. 19). An important instrument in the process of instilling a sense of loyalty towards the Polish state was the presence of Greek Catholic priests in the Polish army. The military authorities expected these clergymen to educate the Greek Catholic soldiers through talks, choosing appropriate topics for sermons, and giving relevant speeches to mark various anniversaries and celebrations (Siwicki, "Duszpasterstwo greckokatolickie," p. 391).

Rutheni, natione Poloni. Archivists, teachers and young unemployed historians (oh, and how many there were!) hastily rummaged through parish and local authority ledgers, searching for documents of royal issue bestowed on those distinguished in battle to cement Polishness east of the San River. Stories of such ilk intertwined on the pages of the Lviv press with others, ones more harrowing, discussing the pacification of villages in Eastern Little Poland.[10]

The Second Polish Republic created favourable conditions for those Ruthenians who wished to be neither Ukrainians nor Russians but Poles. Within the social sphere, these conditions were reflected by the existence of relevant organizations and journals. We shall mention the Friends of the Union Association in Cracow and the Poles and Greek Catholics Union in Lviv, as well as journals such as *Unia* [Union] and *Greko-Katolik* [Greek Catholic]; the latter would change its name twice. On the one hand, organizations and journals of this type gave their members and readers a sense of security and tolerance for their ethnicity; on the other, they constituted an instrument of inciting rivalry between Ukrainians and Russians.

Let us consider the organ of Polish Greek Catholics, *Greko-Katolik.* The journal was established in 1933 in Cracow, with the editorial board situated at 14 Szewska Street. The editor-in-chief was one Teofil Stupnicki [Stupnytsky], a former Polish legionnaire, with the editorial committee comprised of Prof. Mikołaj Mazanowski [Mykola Mazanovsky], Mikołaj Ilnicki [Mykola Ilnytsky], Włodzimierz Sawulak [Volodymyr Savulak], and Michał Pasławski [Mykhailo Paslavsky].[11] The first edition of 1934 (carrying the subtitle of *A Monthly for Greek Catholic Poles*) proclaimed in the introduction the magazine's whole ethos, something worth quoting at length:

> *Greko-Katolik* aims at defending Polish tradition, the Polish national and state course amongst those Greek Catholic citizens in Poland who considered themselves Poles and who went under the designation: "Gente Ruthenus—natione Polonus" ("Ruthenian by birth—Pole by nation"). It desires to renew, strengthen, and maintain a Polish spirit amongst the younger generation, their children. Our journal has finally set itself the goal of familiarizing Polish society with the Greek Catholic and Ruthenian ethnicity issue, to bring both sides closer to each other: the Greek Catholic to Polishness and Polishness to Greek Catholicism; for

---

[10] Marian Tyrowicz, *Wspomnienia o życiu kulturalnym i obyczajowym Lwowa 1918–1939* (Wrocław–Warsaw–Cracow–Gdańsk–Łódź, 1991), p. 69.
[11] Tadeusz Jagmin, *Polacy grekokatolicy na ziemi czerwieńskiej* (Lviv, 1939), p. 21. Cf. also: Bogumił Grott, "Nacjonalizm ukraiński w cerkwi greckokatolickiej i jego praktyka dyskryminacji Polaków i polskości w latach II Rzeczypospolitej," in *Różne oblicza nacjonalizmów. Polityka, religia, etos*, ed. Bogumił Grott (Cracow, 2010), p. 274.

in days of yore the Polish nation was composed of two equal parts, though two differing in rite: Roman and Greek Catholics. We aspire for the great ideal of our forefathers to rule once again in the resurrected Poland, within our ranks that have been weakened in this respect by the occupiers.[12]

The journal contained articles about the threat posed for Poland and its populace by Ukrainians. Various examples of disgraceful acts on the part of the Ukrainian side were given to create the atmosphere of a "besieged fortress." Recalled were honoured figures for the whole *gente Rutheni, natione Poloni* movement, whether from the period of the Galician conspiracies, the Revolutions of 1848, or the war over Eastern Galicia,[13] but also lesser known individuals and events. The goal was to cultivate the long tradition of loyalty amongst Ruthenians, especially Uniates, in relation to Poland. That the phenomenon of *gente Rutheni, natione Poloni* still existed was demonstrated by, for example, the giving of the number of "Greek-Poles" in tertiary education.[14] The journal also tried to prove to its readership the validity of the nineteenth-century assertion that there was but a single Polish nation, and a single Polish language, differentiated merely by dialects.[15] From 1935 the journal began to include the posthumous recollections of select Ruthenians of Polish nationality, from which we are able to learn the names of more or less well-known individuals from this group for the period under discussion.[16] The journal's editorial board also spoke out on political matters. For example, when elections to the Polish lower house [*Sejm*] were taking place in 1935, it called on its readership to vote not for Ukrainians but for Poles. At the same time it expressed regret that no *gente Ruthenus, natione Polonus* was standing for office.[17]

---

[12] "Od Wydawnictwa," *Greko-Katolik* 2, no. 1 (Mar. 1934), p. 1.

[13] Cf. the articles: "Zwycięstwo wiary nad ukraińską polityką," *Greko-Katolik* 2, no. 2 (Apr. 1934), pp. 1–2; "Rocznica obrony Lwowa," *Greko-Katolik* 2, no. 5 (Nov. 1934), p. 1–2; "Udział Unitów w obronie Lwowa," *Greko-Katolik* 2, no. 5 (Nov. 1934), p. 4.

[14] In one of the editions it was stated that in 1931 at the Jan Kazimierz University in Lviv 81 such persons studied there, while only 30 studied at the Jagiellonian University in Cracow. It was joyfully proclaimed that "This is a symptom of the Greek Catholic return to Polishness". See "Greko-Polacy w szkołach," *Greko-Katolik* 2, no. 4 (Oct. 1934), p. 4.

[15] "Jedna Polska—jeden naród," *Greko-Katolik* 3, no. 1 (Jan. 1935), p. 1.

[16] The paper recalled: Jarosław Korczyński [Iaroslav Korchynsky] the builder ["Z żałobnej karty," *Greko-Katolik* 3, no. 1 (Jan. 1935), p. 8], the editor of the journal *Ruski selanyn* [Ruthenian Villager] Witold Demiańczuk [Vytovt Demianchuk] ["Zgon niezłomnego rycerza," *Greko-Katolik* 3, no. 3 (Mar. 1935), p. 6.], the editor of *Kurier Krakowski* [The Cracow Courier] and also an association member of the Friends of the Konstanty Srokowski Union [Kostiantyn Srokovsky] ["Zgon wielkiego Polaka greckiego obrządku," *Greko-Katolik* 3, no. 6–7 (Jun.–Jul. 1935), p. 6] and also Father Henryk Polański ["Z żałobnej karty," *Greko-Katolik* 3, no. 10 (Oct. 1935), p. 5].

[17] "Wybory do Sejmu a Greko-Polacy," *Greko-Katolik* 3, no. 8–9 (Aug.–Sep. 1935), p. 1.

In 1936 the journal proposed a new term to designate Poles of the Ruthenian rite, "Greek Pole," with the journal adopting the same name. At the same time the journal started to become increasingly bold in stating its case, speaking of the persecution of the Polish language in the Greek Catholic Church and consequent attacks on the entirety of Polish Uniate society.[18] It went on to again change its title, this time to *Polak Greko-Katolik* [The Greek Catholic Pole], with the magazine becoming a sociocultural publication abandoning its strict religious-political origins. Its mandate was to inform its readers about all aspects of life in the Second Republic, not merely on matters concerning the persecution of Uniate Poles by Ukrainians. The full title of the journal now read: *Polak Greko-Katolik. Czasopismo miesięczne dla grekokatolików polskiej narodowości (religione Ruthenus—natione Polonus)* [The Greek Catholic Pole. A Monthly Magazine for Greek Catholics of Polish Nationality (*Religione Ruthenus—Natione Polonus*)]. From 1 September 1938 it was published every two weeks, continuing its observation and analysis of events important for Greek Catholic Poles.[19] It built up the tradition of the entire movement, recalling the history of Uniate Poles in a series of non-specialist articles[20] as well as appealing for the construction of memorials or the unveiling of plaques to commemorate the Greek Catholic conspirators of the 1830s and 1840s.[21] The grassroots activities of Teofil Stupnicki were aimed at countering the growing Ukrainization of Galician Uniates, and were also an attempt to regain the "stolen souls" of the Ruthenian minor gentry. Additionally, proposals were advanced for the creation of a Polish Greek Catholic clergy. This was to be aided by the establishment of halls of residence for Uniate Poles and support for the creation of Polish sections at Greek Catholic seminaries, with the ultimate aim of establishing separate Polish Greek Catholic seminaries.[22]

Besides surfacing in the press, *gente Rutheni, natione Poloni* started to become a topic of discussion in academic literature. Here the foremost mention should be made of the eminent historian Stanisław Zakrzewski, president of the Lviv Section of the Polish Historical Association and publisher of the journal *Ziemia Czerwieńska* [The Cherven

---

[18] "Zamiast 'Greko-Katolik'—'Greko-Polak,'" *Greko-Polak* 4, no. 1 (Jan. 1936), p. 1.

[19] With great joy it was announced that on 17 July 1938 the Greek Catholic military parish in Lviv would have a new parish priest—Father Stefan Hrab. At the time the Mass was celebrated in Polish, with a sermon given in Polish and Ukrainian, Polish hymns (including "Boże, coś Polskę" ["God save Poland"]) and the national anthem played at the end. See "Nowy lwowski proboszcz greckokatolicki," *Polak Greko-Katolik* 5, no. 13–14 (ed. B) (Jul. 1938), p. 4. With similar pomp it was announced that on 21 May Jerzy Kuryłowicz had been victorious in the elections to the Lviv Municipal Council. See: "Zwycięstwo polskich grekokatolików," *Polak Greko-Katolik* 6, no. 10 (30 May / 1 Jun. 1939), p. 9.

[20] Cf. for example, about Kasper Cięglewicz: "Grekokatolicy związani z polską kulturą," *Polak Greko-Katolik* 6, no. 12 (1 Jul. 1939), p. 8.

[21] "O uczczenie gr. kat. księży i kleryków," *Polak Greko-Katolik* 6, no. 12 (1 Jun. 1939), p. 4.

[22] Cf. Grott, "Nacjonalizm ukraiński," pp. 276, 281.

Land] (concerned with the eastern Galician past[23]). His work frequently formulated theses and opinions arguing for the Jagiellonian idea as historically justified, something that was to be of significance in the course of Poland's struggle for independence and the subsequent delineation of its borders, as these drew upon varied conceptions of the territorial shape of the revived state and the eastern lands which had once comprised part of Poland-Lithuania. While still a student at the Jagiellonian University in the 1890s, he had opposed the views of the Ukrainian writer and historian of literature Ivan Franko, advocating instead for the harmonious coexistence of Poles and Ruthenians.[24] Later, as a lecturer in the auxiliary historical sciences at Lviv University, he concentrated his research on the Poland of the Piast dynasty, as well as the question of Poland's genesis. He equated nationality with national sentiment, which enabled him to think about the notion of nation in political categories and not ethnic ones. Paradoxically, during the first decade of the twentieth century he was to be associated with the camp of the Polish nationalist leader Roman Dmowski, which centred on the concept of ethnic nationality. Zakrzewski was of the view that a Pole — in the understanding of state nationality — could be a Lithuanian or Ruthenian. As Zakrzewski's biographer Krystyna Śreniowska notes, in 1902 the historian wrote a highly criticized article about the Ruthenian origins of St. Stanislaus. Later, he pointed out the non-Polish roots of the Renaissance humanist and writer Stanisław Orzechowski [Stanislav Orikhovsky]. In the book *The West and the East in Polish History* [*Zachód i Wschód w historji Polski*] he traced the links between Poland and Rus' from the depths of the Middle Ages onwards, accentuating the impact of Ruthenian elements on Polish culture and finally concluding that in the former Poland, Poles and Ruthenians were so close to each other that they created not a dual but a single coherent society. He believed that if it had not been for a difference in rite, Poles and Ruthenians would not differ from each other at all.[25] Here he noted the free will that had accompanied Poland's union with Rus', the religious tolerance within the joint state, and the benefits brought by the Polish expansion of Latin culture into Ruthenian territory.[26]

---

[23] On the *Ziemia Czerwieńska* and its community see: Helena Madurowicz-Urbańska, "Karta z dziejów lwowskiej nauki. 'Ziemia Czerwieńska' — Rocznik Oddziału Polskiego Towarzystwa Historycznego we Lwowie (1935–1938)," in *Poprzez stulecia. Księga pamiątkowa ofiarowana Profesorowi Antoniemu Podrazie w 80. rocznicę Jego urodzin*, ed. Danuta Czerska (Cracow, 2000), pp. 299–307.

[24] Krystyna Śreniowska, *Stanisław Zakrzewski. Przyczynek do charakterystyki prądów ideologicznych w historiografii polskiej 1893–1936* (Łódź, 1956), pp. 23–24.

[25] Stanisław Zakrzewski, "Zachód i Wschód w historji Polski," in Stanisław Zakrzewski, *Zagadnienia historyczne*, vol. 2 (Lviv, 1936), pp. 1–50; Cf. Śreniowska, *Stanisław Zakrzewski*, pp. 64–71.

[26] Ibid., p. 104.

Zakrzewski expanded upon these notions a dozen or so years later in the work *Poles and Ruthenians in the Cherven Land of the Past* [*Polacy i Rusini na Ziemi Czerwieńskiej w przeszłości*], in which the author presented the core of his reflections on the Ruthenian question within the Polish historical context.[27] In this study Zakrzewski attempts to prove that from as early as the tenth century, even though an ethnographic division between Poles and Ruthenians existed, one cannot talk about a resistance to the flow of cultural influences. He emphasizes that since the Middle Ages Poles had been the indigenous people inhabiting the area between the Bug and San rivers and the Dnister River. His entire argument is that Poles and Ruthenians enjoyed a cordial and friendly coexistence for centuries. Zakrzewski in no way negates the impact of either Polish culture or colonization on the inhabitants of the Ruthenian lands, seeing Rus' as a net beneficiary of this process. Here he cites many examples of individuals from the *gente Rutheni, natione Poloni* formation who had naturally sworn allegiance to the Polish state, though in doing so were fully conscious of their Ruthenian origins. Several individuals he identifies are Stanisław Orzechowski, as the son of a Pole and a Ruthenian woman; Father Józef Wereszczyński [Iosyf Vereshchynsky] of the Chełm [Kholm] lands and subsequently bishop of Kyiv; and finally, Jan Andrzej Próchnicki, the archbishop of Lviv. Zakrzewski does not refute that these individuals were, in fact, the product of Polonization, but he also does not see anything negative in this fact: "the process of Latinization and Polonization conducted within the very core of Ruthenian families was done in a way that was wholly domestic, family-driven against a background that was purely sociocultural in its coloration."[28] According to him, it was the Union of Brest that had acted as the dominant factor in bringing the adherents of Orthodoxy from the eastern part of the Polish-Lithuanian state to Polishness. This was to endow the Polish nation with Ruthenians such as the magnate and Grand Hetman of Lithuania Kostiantyn Ostrozky [Konstanty Ostrogski]—who was, according to Zakrzewski, "the true deputy king and deputy patriarch of the Ruthenian Church"—Ipatii Potii [Hipacy Pociej], Iosyf Veliamyn Rutsky [Józef Welamin Rucki], and first and foremost Adam Kysil [Kisiel], the voivode of Kyiv who "during the most difficult periods of the Cossack wars represented the

---

[27] Stanisław Zakrzewski, "Polacy i Rusini na Ziemi Czerwieńskiej w przeszłości," in Eugeniusz Romer, Stanisław Zakrzewski, Stanisław Pawłowski, *W obronie Galicyi Wschodniej* (Lviv, 1919), pp. 15–57. Another in-depth study into the historiographic views of Zakrzewski on Polish history besides the mentioned text *Zachód i Wschód w historji Polski* may be found in the article "Ze studiów nad dziejami unji polsko-litewskiej," in Zakrzewski, *Zagadnienia historyczne*, vol. 2, pp. 177–229.

[28] Zakrzewski, "Polacy i Rusini," p. 43.

notion of loyalty to the Commonwealth across the entirety of Rus'."[29]
Evidence of Rus' loyalty to the state as a whole was seen by Zakrzewski in the approach adopted by cities such as Lviv or Zamość, which
defended themselves staunchly against the Cossacks. He explains the
acts of plunder and murder carried out at this time by Ruthenian peasants as "acts of disorder socially motivated not derived from national issues."[30] He saw the vitality of *gente Rutheni, natione Poloni* in the
Ruthenian support for Polish independence, starting from 1794. The
Ruthenian dislike of Poles that he witnessed was explained in relation
to the impact of Austrian Habsburg administration. Zakrzewski's study
was published in 1919, during the Polish-Ukrainian War for Eastern
Galicia. He crowns it with the hope that "in the future the Ruthenian
people would want to belong to Poland as they had in centuries past."[31]

Zakrzewski placed great score on the Union of Lublin, and even
more on the Treaty of Hadiach. He was critical of the Polish conservative historian and politician Michał Bobrzyński, who negatively evaluated both of these political acts, suggesting that a better solution would
have been the absorption of these eastern neighbours into a centralized
state because, otherwise, conditions for the outbreak of anarchy had
been created. As a supporter of the Jagiellonian idea, Zakrzewski noted
in a review of Bobrzyński's *History of Poland: An Outline* [Dzieje Polski
w zarysie] that it was precisely the suppression of Rus' that resulted in
Cossack revolts.[32] For Zakrzewski, the Treaty of Hadiach of 1659 was
simply an unrealized symbol of the Jagiellonian idea.

Under communism, Zakrzewski was accused of "a nationalistic
haughtiness combined [in Zakrzewski's works—A.Ś.], with a clear
program of subordinating other nations."[33] Zakrzewski's writing and

---

[29] Ibid., p. 45.

[30] Ibid., p. 46.

[31] Ibid., p. 57.

[32] Stanisław Zakrzewski, "Z powodu czwartego wydania 'Dziejów Polski w zarysie'
Michała Bobrzyńskiego," in Zakrzewski, *Zagadnienia historyczne*, vol. 1, pp. 237–41.

[33] Śreniowska, *Stanisław Zakrzewski*, p. 71. As proof, Krystyna Śreniowska gave the example of the letter used by Oswald Balzer to Zakrzewski with the intention of increasing
the remuneration of the town hall caretaker, Michał Majba, as a result of his conversion
from the Uniate to the Roman Catholic faith. (See ibid., p. 71, footnote 83). This example
speaks more of Balzer's mindset than that of Zakrzewski's. In addition, Śreniowska herself quotes the content of Zakrzewski's lecture of 1921 (*The Impact of the Ruthenian Question on the Polish State in the Fourteenth Century* [Wpływ sprawy ruskiej na państwo polskie
w XIV w.]), in which the historian states that "In the Ruthenian people, the state obtained
a committed working class used extensively in the fields of feudal service, and which
later also played a creative role in the area of our culture" (ibid., p. 71). In her book she
also gives the contents of a letter of Zakrzewski's to Father Jan Fijałek of 1922, in which
the historian proposes that Ruthenian-Polish sources or their regesta be published on the
model of the publication: *Monumenta Poloniae Historica* (ibid., p. 129). This is by far the
clearest proof that Zakrzewski was especially sensitive in his approach toward Rus'.

activities were never meant to argue for the superiority of Poles over Ruthenians or the subordination of the latter to Poland. Quite the contrary; everywhere the author emphasizes the symbiotic advantages for each culture that resulted from their mutual relations. Such benefits in no way required the introduction of administratively endorsed Polonization. In the article "Germany, Russia, and the Polish Question" [Niemcy, Rosja i kwestia polska...] he underlines that there could never have been talk "about Poles having to make Poles out of Ruthenians." Further on, he notes: "a strengthening in the development of the Ruthenian nation, with the only reservation that this does not affect Poles detrimentally, has to be incorporated in the program of every Polish activist."[34] It is also worth recalling that in 1920 and during the peace negotiations with the Bolsheviks, Zakrzewski, sharing the views of the Polish head of state Józef Piłsudski, spoke out in favour of adopting the pre-partition borders and subsequently creating the buffer states of Ukraine and Belarus.[35] Zakrzewski, dreaming at this time of the development of relations between Poland and a federated Ukraine, constructed the myth—one drawn from many centuries of tradition—of a federal commonwealth that had once existed in the form of the Polish-Lithuanian Commonwealth. Even though such a vision was never to be a reality, thanks to Zakrzewski and many other like-minded historians it became strongly embedded within Polish historical consciousness. Zakrzewski was undoubtedly the first historian to devote more space in his research to Ruthenians of Polish nationality.

Another work that is key to the whole discussion about *gente Rutheni, natione Poloni* is the article by Stanisław Kot on national consciousness in modern Poland, published in *Kwartalnik Historyczny* [Historical Quarterly] in 1938.[36] Kot was the first to attempt to define what the phenomenon of *gente Rutheni, natione Poloni* actually was. His notions, such as "respective *gentes* merged into a single *nation*,"[37] have entered into the canon of the literature on the subject and have been referred to not so much by researchers into the history of the partitions, but by those historians examining the internal state of affairs in the Commonwealth of Two Nations (Poland-Lithuania). From here onwards the notion was used to describe the Ruthenian gentry in pre-partition Poland.[38]

---

[34] [Stanisław Zakrzewski] Z., "Niemcy, Rosja i kwestia polska. Z powodu książki Dmowskiego pod tymże tytułem," *Ateneum Polskie* 4 (1908), p. 74. Cf. also: Śreniowska, *Stanisław Zakrzewski*, p. 99.

[35] Śreniowska, *Stanisław Zakrzewski*, pp. 89, 101.

[36] Stanisław Kot, "Świadomość narodowa w Polsce w. XV–XVII," *Kwartalnik Historyczny* 52, no. 1 (1938), pp. 15–33.

[37] Ibid., p. 26.

[38] See, for example: Teresa Chynczewska-Hennel, *Świadomość narodowa szlachty ukraińskiej i kozaczyzny od schyłku XVI do połowy XVII w.* (Warsaw, 1985), pp. 133–46; Teresa

It is also worth recalling another text of a less academic nature, which had the fortune to be published just before the Second World War broke out. Numbering a mere thirty pages, this piece by Tadeusz Jagmin[39] was an attempt to show the situation of Poles of the Greek Catholic rite and their relations to the Uniate hierarchy. The author clearly states his aims in the very first sentences:

> The fate of Greek Catholic Poles constitutes one of the darker sides of our Polish reality as played out across those ancient lands of the Piasts and Jagiellonians.
>
> But this booklet was not written to bemoan and enumerate grievances but to show the routes to concentrate forces and to unharness them in the rhythm of a victory for progressive Polish labour on this Earth.[40]

In his publication, the author explored the issues of the size of the Greek Catholic community; of how the Greek Catholic Church's attitude towards Poland and Poles changed over the centuries; and of the underprivileged and disadvantaged status of the Polish Greek Catholics. The final chapter contained seven demands made by this community. They demanded the creation of Polish Greek Catholic parishes in localities inhabited mainly by Polish Greek Catholics. Where they constituted a minority, they appealed for a Mass to be celebrated in the Polish language. They also made demands for confession, prayers, and hymns as well as religious studies to be in Polish, and called for the recruitment of Poles to Greek Catholic seminaries and the creation there of separate classes for them. Other demands were to end the practice of politicized sermons in church, and to include Greek Catholic clergy of Polish nationality in parish affairs. These petitions were obviously never to be satisfied, for they hit hard and fundamentally at the exclusively Ukrainian nature of the Uniate Church.

However, the problem was to be brutally resolved by the Second World War. The ethnic cleansing, the moving of borders, and the mass deportation of peoples resulted in the annihilation of the multicultural border region that had been former Eastern Galicia, now mainly annexed by and incorporated into the USSR. Likewise, within its new borders communist Poland was to become an almost exclusively monoethnic state, one in which ethnicity neatly overlapped with nationality. As the Polish historian Andrzej Walicki wrote:

Chynczewska-Hennel, "Gente Ruthenus—Natione Polonus," *Warszawskie Zeszyty Ukrainoznawcze* 6–7: *Spotkania polsko-ukraińskie. Studia Ucrainica* (1998), ed. Stefan Kozak, pp. 35–44.

[39] Jagmin, *Polacy grekokatolicy.*

[40] Ibid., p. 3.

(...) a Polish nation created exclusively on the basis of a Polish-
-language-speaking ethnic group is not what was desired and what was
planned by the Polish intelligentsia of the era of uprisings and its numerous ideological heirs. (...) In no way negating the massive significance of nationalist ideologies, one must admit that ethnicity was to be
a hard fact of life, one resistant to the ideological constructs trying to
lessen its role.[41]

In this way, the long generational chain of ethnoses living side by
side was severed, and the Polish nation lost the ethnic input of non-
Polish elements, such as that of the Ruthenians of Polish nationality as
they had been in the nineteenth century. The phenomenon of *gente Rutheni, natione Poloni* ceased to function as a political issue. This is not to
say, however, that Poles of the Greek Catholic rite no longer existed, for
we can find a series of examples of Greek Catholics publicly appearing
in Polish political life during the second half of the twentieth century.
Under such conditions, the subject of *gente Rutheni, natione Poloni* remained merely an academic problem and one that even then was increasingly marginalized.

Researchers of Galicia from both the Polish People's Republic and
the USSR were obviously aware of this group's previous existence.
Nonetheless, they mention it only on the margins of broader studies,
particularly those referring to Polish-Ukrainian relations in Galicia. The
matter is most commonly raised in political contexts, and more precisely when describing the revolutions of 1848 or the work of the Galician
Diet. The *gente Rutheni, natione Poloni* were rarely examined in a more
thorough way, and thus most attention was given to the political dimension of this phenomenon instead of its cultural, social, and finally,
ideological ones. That said, numerous studies into the most important
political events in nineteenth-century Galicia, the biographies of well-
known individuals, and source publications such as memoirs have
resulted in a greater number of researchers discovering many border
figures, their activities and works, and the processes in which the *gente
Rutheni, natione Poloni* were involved. Taking this into consideration, it
is therefore very important to consider the following question from the
outset: has the subject of *gente Rutheni, natione Poloni* appeared within
Polish historiography during the study of other events or phenomena?

The topic surfaces mainly during discussions of the history and society of the Polish-Lithuanian Commonwealth. Teresa Chynczewska-
-Hennel, in particular, has examined the attitudes of the Polonized

---

[41] Andrzej Walicki, "Koncepcje tożsamości narodowej i terytorium narodowego w myśli
polskiej czasów porozbiorowych," *Archiwum Historii Filozofii i Myśli Społecznej* 38 (1993),
p. 231.

Ruthenian gentry during the period of the Cossack wars, devoting an entire chapter in her book and a whole article to the matter.[42] In turn, Henryk Litwin has drawn attention to aspects of the Ruthenian gentry's political choices and the ambiguities of these choices. One of his texts analyzes various attitudes exhibited by the nobles in Rus': from the time of the Union of Lublin to the Khmelnytsky Uprising; from pro-Polish sentiments through conciliatory relations between Poles and Ruthenians and the attempts to broaden the Polish-Lithuanian state to include a third, Ruthenian, royal land; and finally, cooperation with the Cossacks.[43] No less important are the works of Janusz Tazbir, which analyze the changes taking place within the national consciousness of the Polish gentry where the adoption of Polish nationality on the part of Ruthenian boyars was widespread.[44] Perhaps the most prominent Ukrainian historian to research the matter at hand is Natalia Yakovenko, who has written on the identity of the Ruthenian gentry.[45] The American researcher David Althoen and the Ukrainian-American Serhii Plokhy[46] have also worked on the formula *gente Rutheni, natione Poloni* within the context of the "noble nation" of former Poland.[47] Yet none of this research has gone much beyond the early modern epoch.

In the second half of the twentieth century, many studies appeared on the subject of Galicia. Given the socioethnic nature of the subject, these studies were unable to avoid mentioning the presence of Ruthenians of Polish nationality within the sociopolitical life of this territory under Austrian rule. It will suffice to mention the numerous studies published in Poland on the Galician conspiracies, the Revolutions of 1848, the January Uprising, or the political and national life in the Habsburg Monarchy; works by Zbigniew Fras,[48] Sławomir Kalembka,[49]

---

[42] Chynczewska-Hennel, *Świadomość narodowa*, pp. 133–46; Chynczewska-Hennel, "Gente Ruthenus," pp. 35–44.

[43] Henryk Litwin, "Katolicyzacja szlachty ruskiej a procesy asymilacyjne na Ukrainie w latach 1569–1648," in *Tryumfy i porażki. Studia z dziejów kultury polskiej XVI–XVIII w.*, ed. Maria Bogucka (Warsaw, 1989), pp. 47–73.

[44] Cf., for example: Janusz Tazbir, "Procesy polonizacyjne w szlacheckiej Rzeczypospolitej," in *Tryumfy i porażki*, pp. 9–45; Janusz Tazbir, "Tradycje wieloetnicznej Rzeczypospolitej," in *Inni wśród swoich*, ed. Wiesław Władyka (Warsaw, 1994), pp. 12–23.

[45] Teresa Chynczewska-Hennel and Natalia Jakowenko, "Społeczeństwo, religia, kultura," in *Między sobą. Szkice historyczne polsko-ukraińskie*, eds. Teresa Chynczewska-Hennel and Natalia Jakowenko (Lublin, 2000), pp. 111–51.

[46] David Althoen, "*Natione Polonus* and the *Naród szlachecki*: Two myths of national identity and noble solidarity," *Zeitschrift für Ostmitteleuropa-Forschung* 52 (2003), pp. 475–508.

[47] Serhii Plokhii, *The Origins of the Slavic Nations: Premodern Identities in Russia, Ukraine, and Belarus* (Cambridge, 2006), pp. 169–73.

[48] Zbigniew Fras, *Demokraci w życiu politycznym Galicji w latach 1848–1873* (Wrocław, 1997); Zbigniew Fras, *Galicja* (Wrocław, 2000).

[49] Sławomir Kalembka, *Wiosna Ludów w Europie* (Warsaw, 1991), p. 188.

Stefan Kieniewicz,[50] Jan Kozik,[51] Bolesław Łopuszański,[52] Piotr Łossowski,[53] Marian Stolarczyk,[54] and Henryk Wereszycki.[55] Of special note is the article by Anna Wróbel on the subject of the portrayal of the Polish intelligentsia by foreign representatives and minorities, including Ruthenians. The problem of *gente Rutheni, natione Poloni* is also dealt with in her work.[56]

A more detailed and direct handling of the problem, framed within the context of the period of partitions, was only to appear in 1995 when Andrzej A. Zięba published his then fundamental article on the topic in *Studies of the Eastern European Commission* at the Polish Academy of Learning.[57] To this day it remains the fundamental Polish-language study on the subject. In his extensive article he draws attention to the changes in the national consciousness of the Galician landed gentry and intelligentsia, providing numerous examples of individuals and families for whom the question of national identification was a straightforward one. For several years after its publication the matter was left largely unexplored; possible exceptions were Antonina Kłoskowska's book which examined the difficulties cultural formations pose for any

---

[50] Stanisław Kieniewicz, *Czyn Polski w dobie Wiosny Ludów* (Warsaw, 1948); Stanisław Kieniewicz, *Konspiracje galicyjskie (1831–1845)* (Warsaw, 1950); Stanisław Kieniewicz, "'Rusyn na praznyku' i dalsze jego losy," in *Problemy wiedzy o kulturze. Prace dedykowane Stefanowi Żółkiewskiemu*, eds. Alina Brodzka, Maryla Hopfinger and Janusz Lalewicz (Wrocław–Warsaw–Cracow–Gdańsk–Łódź, 1986), pp. 327–41; Stanisław Kieniewicz, *Adam Sapieha 1828–1903* (Warsaw, 1993).

[51] Jan Kozik, *Ukraiński ruch narodowy w Galicji w latach 1830–1848* (Cracow, 1973); Jan Kozik, *Między reakcją a rewolucją. Studia z dziejów ukraińskiego ruchu narodowego w Galicji w latach 1848–1849* (Warsaw–Cracow, 1975); Jan Kozik, "Stosunki ukraińsko-polskie w Galicji w okresie rewolucji 1848–1849. Próba charakterystyki," *Prace Historyczne* 54: *Z dziejów współpracy Polaków, Ukraińców i Rosjan* (1975), pp. 29–53. In English: Kozik, *The Ukrainian National Movement*.

[52] Bolesław Łopuszański, "'Wskazówka dla nauczycieli ludu ruskiego' Kaspra Cięglewicza (z literatury chłopomańskiej pierwszej połowy XIX w.)," *Rocznik Muzeum Etnograficznego w Krakowie* 5 (1974), pp. 239–56; Bolesław Łopuszański, *Stowarzyszenie Ludu Polskiego (1835–1841). Geneza i dzieje* (Cracow, 1975).

[53] Piotr Łossowski and Zygmunt Młynarski, *Rosjanie, Białorusini i Ukraińcy w powstaniu styczniowym* (Wrocław, 1959).

[54] Marian Stolarczyk, *Działalność Lwowskiej Centralnej Rady Narodowej. W świetle źródeł polskich* (Rzeszów, 1994).

[55] Henryk Wereszycki, *Pod berłem Habsburgów. Zagadnienia narodowościowe* (Cracow, 1986), pp. 143–44.

[56] Anna Wróbel, "Od 'Galileuszy' do Polaków. Wejście do polskiej inteligencji przedstawicieli ludności napływowej i mniejszości w Galicji w XIX w.," in *Inteligencja polska XIX i XX wieku. Studia 5*, ed. Ryszarda Czepulis-Rastenis (Warsaw, 1987), pp. 173–90 (particularly pp. 185–87).

[57] Andrzej A. Zięba, "Gente Rutheni, natione Poloni," in *Prace Komisji Wschodnioeuropejskiej PAU*, vol. 2, eds. Ryszard Łużny and Andrzej A. Zięba (Cracow, 1995), pp. 61–77.

researcher of national cultures,[58] and also the sociological study by Łucja Kapralska, who looked into the phenomenon of cultural and ethnic pluralism during the period of the Second Polish Republic, simultaneously bringing to the fore the notion of assimilation (citing the example of *gente Rutheni, natione Poloni*).[59] Andrzej A. Zięba returned to the issue a dozen or so years later with the publication of an extensive two-part article on the ethnic identity of Rusyns (Lemkos) from the Lemko region, in which examples of individuals from the group of interest to us are given.[60] The same author also wrote about Ruthenians sympathizing with Poland during the January Uprising, placing them amongst similar ethnic examples, in an article that constituted a part of the publication *On the Year 1863. The Jagiellonian University and the January Uprising* [*Rzecz o roku 1863. Uniwersytet Jagielloński wobec powstania styczniowego*].[61]

Jarosław Moklak has also dealt with the political activity of Ruthenians of Polish nationality in his research into the language issues settled during the session of the Galician Diet.[62] Renata Dutkowa has touched on those representatives of *gente Rutheni, natione Poloni* who were active in the ratification of the language act (1866/1867), and subsequently the creation of the framework for the Galicia's Provincial School Board [*Rada Szkolna Krajowa/Kraiova Shkil'na Rada*]. Her study of *gente Rutheni, natione Poloni* does not go into much detail, as this was not its aim.[63] In turn, the presence of Ruthenian deputies of Polish

---

[58] Antonina Kłoskowska, *National Cultures at the Grass-root Level* (Budapest, 2001), p. 51, 128.

[59] Łucja Kapralska, *Pluralizm kulturowy i etniczny a odrębność regionalna Kresów południowo-wschodnich w latach 1918–1939* (Cracow, 2000), pp. 143–64.

[60] Andrzej A. Zięba, "Tożsamość etniczna jako obiekt manipulacji politycznej. Przypadek Rusinów łemkowskich XVIII–XX w. (część pierwsza)," *Rocznik Ruskiej Bursy* (2007), pp. 59–94; Andrzej A. Zięba, "Tożsamość etniczna jako obiekt manipulacji politycznej. Przypadek Rusinów łemkowskich XVIII–XX w. (część druga)," *Rocznik Ruskiej Bursy* (2008), pp. 59–71.

[61] Andrzej A. Zięba, "Inne 'Tamte światy'," in *Rzecz o roku 1863. Uniwersytet Jagielloński wobec powstania styczniowego*, ed. Andrzej A. Zięba (Cracow, 2013), pp. 83–87.

[62] Jarosław Moklak, "Stanowisko posłów polskich gente Ruthenus i ruskich (ukraińskich) w Sejmie Krajowym galicyjskim wobec projektu ustawy o języku wykładowym w szkołach ludowych i średnich w 1866 r.," *Biuletyn Ukrainoznawczy* 8 (2002), pp. 28–41; Jarosław Moklak, "Spór polsko–ukraiński o język obrad sejmu galicyjskiego (1865–1866). Wnioski Antona Petruszewycza i Aleksandra Borkowskiego. Przyczynek do kształtowania się nacjonalizmów w Galicji Wschodniej," *Biuletyn Ukrainoznawczy* 9 (2003), pp. 40–51; Jarosław Moklak, *W walce o tożsamość Ukraińców. Zagadnienie języka wykładowego w szkołach ludowych i średnich w pracach galicyjskiego Sejmu Krajowego 1866–1892* (Cracow, 2004).

[63] Renata Dutkowa, "Polityka szkolna w Galicji 1866–1890," in *Nauka i oświata*, eds. Andrzej Meissner and Jerzy Wyrozumski (Rzeszów, 1995), pp. 137–49; Renata Dutkowa, *Polityka szkolna w Galicji. Między autonomią a centralizmem (1861–1875)* (Cracow, 1995).

leanings—including Ruthenians of Polish nationality—at the Imperial Council (*Reichsrat*) in Vienna in the 1860s and 1870s has been mentioned by Stanisław Pijaj.[64] It is also relevant to mention Włodzimierz Osadczy, a researcher of Russophilism in Galicia, in whose works the subject of *gente Rutheni, natione Poloni* as a competitive formation also appears.[65] This historian has also written an article devoted to the myth of the Polish-Lithuanian-Ruthenian union, one especially cultivated by Galician Ruthenians of Polish nationality.[66] The *gente Rutheni, natione Poloni* attitudes prevalent amongst the minor gentry of the Sambir district have been dealt with by Magdalena Kwiecińska,[67] while Czesław Partacz, in writing about Polish-Ukrainian relations on the eve of the heyday of nationalism, has concentrated on rural Greek Catholic Poles at the close of the epoch studied here.[68] It is also worth mentioning three recently published books on the question of the shaping of Ruthenian/Ukrainian identity, in which the matter of *gente Rutheni, natione Poloni* is also examined. Here we are speaking about Bernadetta Wójtowicz-Huber's book on the role of Uniate priests in the process of creating national awareness amongst Ruthenians,[69] the book *Another Galicia* [*Inna Galicja*] by Danuta Sosnowska, in which the author in an original, though contestable, way shows the various national dilemmas that appeared within nineteenth-century Galician society,[70] and Magdalena Nowak's book which deals with the problem of shaping Andrei Sheptytsky's national identity.[71] Marceli Handelsman has undertaken an examination

---

[64] Stanisław Pijaj, *Między polskim patriotyzmem a habsburskim lojalizmem. Polacy wobec przemian ustrojowych monarchii habsburskiej (1866–1871)* (Cracow, 2003); Stanisław Pijaj, "Posłowie ruscy w parlamencie wiedeńskim w latach 1848–1879," in *Ukraińskie tradycje parlamentarne. XIX–XXI wiek*, ed. Jarosław Moklak (Cracow, 2006), pp. 95–126; Stanisław Pijaj, *Opozycja w wiedeńskiej Radzie Państwa w latach siedemdziesiątych XIX w. (skład, organizacja, funkcjonowanie)* (Cracow, 2011).

[65] Włodzimierz Osadczy, *Święta Ruś. Rozwój i oddziaływanie idei prawosławia w Galicji* (Lublin, 2007), p. 85.

[66] Włodzimierz Osadczy, "Galicyjski mit unii polsko-litewsko-ruskiej," in *Unia lubelska. Unia Europejska*, ed. Iwona Hofman (Lublin, 2010), pp. 169–75.

[67] Magdalena Kwiecińska, "Poczucie tożsamości stanowej i narodowej rodu Kulczyckich z Kulczyc koło Sambora, na Ukrainie Zachodniej," *Literatura Ludowa* no. 4–5 (2004), pp. 105–24; Magdalena Kwiecińska, "Drobna szlachta w Galicji—między polskim a ukraińskim ruchem narodowym," *Sprawy Narodowościowe. Seria Nowa* 34 (2009), pp. 83–97.

[68] Czesław Partacz, "Stosunki religijne w Galicji Wschodniej. Rusini łacinnicy i Polacy grekokatolicy," *Rocznik Przemyski* 28 (1991–92), pp. 140–46; Czesław Partacz, *Od Badeniego do Potockiego. Stosunki polsko-ukraińskie w Galicji w latach 1888–1908* (Toruń, 1997), pp. 180–84.

[69] Bernadetta Wójtowicz-Huber, *'Ojcowie narodu'. Duchowieństwo greckokatolickie w ruchu narodowym Rusinów galicyjskich (1867–1918)* (Warsaw, 2008).

[70] Danuta Sosnowska, *Inna Galicja* (Warsaw, 2008).

[71] Magdalena Nowak, *Dwa światy. Zagadnienie identyfikacji narodowej Andrzeja Szeptyckiego w latach 1865–1914* (Gdańsk, 2018).

of the matter of *gente Rutheni, natione Poloni* in Galicia from an émigré perspective, building upon Joanna Nowak's article in which she writes about the reflections of the Great Emigration on the subject of Ruthenians.[72] Stanisław Grodziski deals with the disappearance of the *gente Rutheni, natione Poloni* phenomenon in his popular book on Galicia, enumerating examples of Ruthenians who felt themselves to be Poles as well as reverse examples of Poles who proclaimed affiliation to Ukrainian nationality.[73]

The question of *gente Rutheni, natione Poloni* also arises in descriptions of the more frequent phenomenon of multiculturalism. Many studies in this field, often based on the example of Galician small towns, have been conducted by Jadwiga Hoff.[74] It is also important to make special mention of Tomasz Pudłocki's book on the Przemyśl intelligentsia. Here he mentions the phenomenon of *gente Rutheni, natione Poloni* in his region of interest within the context of a "hybridization of culture."[75]

The subject of Ruthenians of Polish nationality has also generated interest and research beyond Poland's eastern border. In Soviet, Russian, and Ukrainian historiography one must mention the studies of well-known historians such as Vladimir Boris,[76] Hryhorii Herbilsky,[77] Grigory Marakhov,[78] and Feodosi Stebly.[79] The essay by the émigré

---

[72] Marceli Handelsman, *Ukraińska polityka ks. Adama Czartoryskiego przed wojną krymską* (Warsaw, 1937); Joanna Nowak, "*Gente Ruthenus, natione Polonus*. Rusini w refleksji Wielkiej Emigracji," *Sprawy Narodowościowe. Seria Nowa* 23 (2003), pp. 43–62.

[73] Stanisław Grodziski, *Wzdłuż Wisły, Dniestru i Zbrucza Wędrówki po Galicji dyliżansem, koleją, samochodem* (Cracow, 2006), pp. 323–24.

[74] Jadwiga Hoff, "Żydzi, Polacy i Rusini w małych miastach Galicji Wschodniej w drugiej połowie XIX w. Sąsiedzi, obcy, wrogowie?," in *Społeczeństwo w dobie przemian. Wiek XIX i XX. Księga jubileuszowa profesor Anny Żarnowskiej*, eds. Maria Nietyksza, Andrzej Szwarc and Krystyna Sierakowska (Warsaw, 2003), pp. 337–44; Jadwiga Hoff, *Mieszkańcy małych miast Galicji Wschodniej w okresie autonomicznym* (Rzeszów, 2005); Jadwiga Hoff, "Inteligencja galicyjska—niepokorna czy lojalna?," *Rocznik Przemyski* 46, no. 4: *Historia* (2010), pp. 51–58.

[75] Tomasz Pudłocki, *Iskra światła czy kopcąca pochodnia? Inteligencja w Przemyślu w latach 1867–1939* (Cracow, 2009), pp. 418–19.

[76] Włodzimierz Borys, "W kręgu rewolucyjnym Szymona Konarskiego, Piotra Kotkiewicza i Ignacego Kulczyńskiego," *Przegląd Historyczny* 66, no. 3 (1975), pp. 461–72; Włodzimierz Borys, "Wyprawa J. Zaliwskiego i polskie organizacje spiskowe w Galicji w latach 1832–1835," in *Społeczeństwo polskie i próby wznowienia walki zbrojnej w 1833 roku*, eds. Władimir Djakow, Stanisław Kieniewicz, Wiktoria Śliwowska and Feodosij Steblij (Wrocław–Warsaw–Cracow–Gdańsk–Łódź, 1984), pp. 83–105; Włodzimierz Borys, "Z dziejów walk o wyzwolenie narodowe i społeczne w Galicji w pierwszej połowie XIX w.," *Przemyskie Zapiski Historyczne* 4–5 (1987), pp. 223–30.

[77] Hryhorii Herbil's'kyi, *Peredova suspil'na dumka v Halychyni (30-i – seredyna 40-kh rokiv XIX stolittia)* (Lviv, 1959); Hryhorii Herbil's'kyi, *Rozvytok prohresyvnykh idei v Halychyni u pershii polovyni XIX st. (do 1848 r.)* (Lviv, 1964).

[78] Grigorij Marachow, "Polsko-ukraińskie związki rewolucyjne (50.–70. lata XIX wieku)," *Prace Historyczne* 54: *Z dziejów współpracy Polaków, Ukraińców i Rosjan* (1975), pp. 55–70.

[79] Feodosij Steblij, "Polskie spiski lat trzydziestych XIX w. a społeczeństwo ukraińskie w Galicji," in *Społeczeństwo polskie*, pp. 106–18; Feodosii Steblii, "Ukraïntsi i poliaky

Ukrainian historian Ivan Lysiak-Rudnytsky entitled *The Ukrainians in Galicia under Austrian Rule* is particularly valuable. In this study, the author treats the phenomenon of *gente Rutheni, natione Poloni* as an example of cultural mixing.[80] Yaroslav Hrytsak[81] has also made several mentions of the phenomenon of Polonized Ruthenians in his groundbreaking study of Ivan Franko. He again mentioned the phenomenon of *gente Rutheni, natione Poloni* in various contexts in a book of interviews, which presents a broad spectrum of the historian's ideas.[82]

The leading specialist on the *gente Rutheni, natione Poloni* is, however, undoubtedly the Lviv historian Marian Mudry. He has published a range of articles devoted to the political aspects of this phenomenon. In these he examines, among other things, Ruthenians in the Central National Council [*Centralna Rada Narodowa*],[83] the organization of the Ruthenian Sobor [*Sobór Ruski/Rus'kyi Sobor*] and its members,[84] the ideological questions of this political organization,[85] its relations with the Supreme Ruthenian Council [*Holovna Rus'ka Rada*],[86] and the documents generated therein.[87] He has also explored the views of Ruthenians of Polish nationality during the pre-autonomous period, looking at the delegations that derived from this formation in the Galician Diet during the 1860s right up to the celebrations held to mark the 300th anniversary of the Union of Lublin,[88] as well as the general attempts that were made

---

Halychyny v 30–40-kh rr. XIX st. Poshuky politychnoho partnerstva," in *Polska – Ukraina. Historia, polityka, kultura. Materiały międzynarodowej konferencji naukowej*, ed. Stefan Zabrowarny (Szczecin–Warsaw, 2003), pp. 44–61.

[80] Ivan L. Rudnytsky, "Ukrainians in Galicia under Austrian Rule," in Rudnytsky, *Essays in Modern Ukrainian History*, p. 326.

[81] Yaroslav Hrytsak, *Ivan Franko and His Community*, trans. Marta Olynyk (Edmonton–Toronto, 2018).

[82] Jarosław Hrycak, *Ukraina. Przewodnik krytyki politycznej. Z Jarosławem Hrycakiem rozmawia Iza Chruślińska*, preface by A. Michnik (Gdańsk–Warsaw, 2009).

[83] Marian Mudryi, "*Gente Rutheni* v Pol's'kii Tsentral'nii Radi Narodovii 1848 roku," *Zapysky Naukovoho Tovarystva imeni Shevchenka* 256: *Pratsi filosofs'koï sektsiï*, ed. O. Kupchyns'kyi (2008), pp. 244–81.

[84] Marian Mudryi, "Rus'kyi sobor 1848 roku. Orhanizatsiia ta chleny," *Ukraïna. Kul'turna spadshchyna, natsional'na svidomist', derzhavnist'* 16: *Iubileinyi zbirnyk na poshanu Ivana Patera* (2008), pp. 107–26.

[85] Marian Mudryi, "Ideolohiia chy svitohliad? Do pytannia pro teoretychni zasady Rus'koho Soboru 1848 roku," *Visnyk L'vivs'koho universytetu. Seriia istorychna* 44 (2009), pp. 75–106.

[86] Marian Mudryi, "'Jesteśmy rozdwojonymi członkami jednego ciała': Do pytannia pro vidnosyny mizh Holovnoiu Rus'koiu Radoiu i Rus'kym Soborom 1848 roku," *Zapysky naukovoho tovarystva imeni Shevchenka* 265: *Pratsi Istorychno-filosofs'koï sektsiï* (2013), pp. 54–80.

[87] Marian Mudryi, "Rus'kyi sobor 1848 roku. Istoriohrafichnyi ta dzhereloznavchyi ohliad," *Visnyk L'vivs'koho universytetu. Seriia knyhoznavstvo, bibliotekoznavstvo ta informatsiini tekhnolohiï* 8 (2014), pp. 193–206.

[88] Marian Mudryi, "Ideia pol's'ko-ukraïns'koi uniï ta 'Rusyny pol's'koï natsiï' v etnopolitychnomu dyskursi Halychyny 1859–1869 rokiv," *Visnyk L'vivs'koho universytetu. Seriia*

in Galicia to reach agreement and reconciliation between Poles and Ruthenians.[89] He also has drawn attention to *gente Rutheni, natione Poloni* within the context of the January Uprising. Here he shows the phenomenon as not merely a cultural choice on the part of Ruthenians, but also as a certain ideological mindset, an idea coinciding with the political program of the leadership of the January Uprising.[90] Besides the aforementioned currents of research, Marian Mudry has analysed the formation of *gente Rutheni, natione Poloni* more broadly—e.g., within the context of the notion of fatherland as understood by representatives of this group, or as a case of discovering one's own identity.[91] At present he is completing a monograph on the Ruthenian Sobor, which will undoubtedly shed further light on this research area.

Olena Arkusha has also dealt with the notion of *gente Rutheni, natione Poloni* in her research into the political life of Galicia. The group appears in several of her articles, particularly in relation to the direction taken in the development of Ruthenian national consciousness under Austrian rule. She has also looked at a certain dependency within the political thought of various political camps in Galicia, particularly those of a conservative leaning.[92] Together with Marian Mudry she has written an article on the attitude of Polish landowners to the development

---

istorychna 39–40 (2005), pp. 83–148; Marjan Mudryj, "Dylematy narodowościowe w Sejmie Krajowym galicyjskim (na przykładzie posłów formacji gente Rutheni natione Poloni)," in *Ukraińskie tradycje parlamentarne*, pp. 59–94.

[89] Marian Mudryi, "Sproby ukraïns'ko-pol's'koho porozuminnia v Halychyni (60–70-i roky XIX st.)," *Ukraïna. Kul'turna spadshchyna, natsional'na svidomist', derzhavnist'* 3–4: *Zbirnyk naukovykh prats'* (1997), pp. 58–117.

[90] Marian Mudryi, "Sichneve povstannia ta seredovyshche 'rusyniv pol's'koi natsiï' (*gente Rutheni, natione Poloni*) v Halychyni," in *Galicja a powstanie styczniowe*, eds. Mariola Hoszowska, Agnieszka Kawalec and Leonid Zaszkilniak (Warsaw–Rzeszów, 2013), pp. 135–46; Marian Mudryj, "Powstanie styczniowe a środowisko *gente Rutheni, natione Poloni* w Galicji," in *Powstanie styczniowe. Odniesienia, interpretacje, pamięć*, ed. Tomasz Kargol (Cracow, 2013), pp. 67–78.

[91] Marian Mudryi, "Rusyny pol's'koï natsiï (*gente Rutheni, natione Poloni*) v Halychyni XIX st. i poniattia vitchyzny," *Ukraïna. Kul'turna spadshchyna, natsional'na svidomist', derzhavnist'* 15: *Confraternitas. Iuvileinyi zbirnyk na poshanu Iaroslava Isaievycha* (2006–7), pp. 461–74; Marian Mudryj, "Formacja *gente Rutheni, natione Poloni* w XIX-wiecznej Galicji a pojęcie ojczyzny," in *Formuły patriotyzmu w Europie Wschodniej i Środkowej od nowożytności do współczesności*, eds. Andrzej Nowak and Andrzej A. Zięba (Cracow, 2009), pp. 285–98; Marian Mudryj, "Poszukiwania tożsamości narodowej i pojęcie ojczyzny w dziewiętnastowiecznej Galicji (na przykładzie *gente Rutheni, natione Poloni*)," in *'Duża i mała ojczyzna' w świadomości historycznej, źródłach i edukacji*, eds. Bogumiła Burda and Małgorzata Szymczak (Zielona Góra, 2010), pp. 29–42.

[92] Ołena Arkusza, "Ukraińskie przedstawicielstwo w sejmie galicyjskim," in *Ukraińskie tradycje parlamentarne*, pp. 13–57; Olena Arkusha, "Krakivs'kyi konservatyzm ta problema ukraïns'ko-pol's'kykh vzaiemyn u Halychyni na pochatku XX stolittia," *Zapysky naukovoho tovarystva imeni Shevchenka* 256: *Pratsi filosofs'koï sektsiï*, ed. O. Kupchyns'kyi (2008), pp. 282–316; Ołena Arkusza, "Polacy i Ukraińcy w Galicji wobec 'dużych i małych

of Ruthenian national aspirations where the problem area of *gente Rutheni, natione Poloni* also manifested itself.[93]

Western researchers involved in the awakening and subsequent multi-directional development of Ukrainian nationalism in Galicia have also had contact with the subject of our research. Two notable examples are the English-Canadian historian Peter Brock[94] and the Canadian researcher John-Paul Himka who, in examining the trajectories of Ruthenians in Galicia, pay special attention to those of *gente Rutheni, natione Poloni* orientation.[95]

It finally follows to devote some space to the numerous biographers of Ruthenians of Polish nationality. Mikołaj Zyblikiewicz is the sole *gente Ruthenus, natione Polonus* whose biography was published in Polish. Irena Homola's broader studies also deal with the figure of Zyblikiewicz.[96] Aleksander Skórski started a biography of another Ruthenian of Polish nationality, Euzebiusz Czerkawski, but failed to finish it; the section devoted to the first half of his life was published in fragments in the journal *Muzeum* [Museum].[97] The subject was taken up again in the 1920s by Zygmunt Zborucki, who published a book concerning Czerkawski's book on the educational school act of 1867.[98] In addition, a dozen years or so ago, Wiesława Duszkiewicz wrote an article on Czerkawski's educational views.[99] This same collection includes Elżbieta Głaz's text on the subject of another

---

ojczyzn.' Ewolucja pojęcia ojczyzny jako wynik modernizacji świadomości narodowej na przełomie XIX i XX stulecia," in *Duża i mała ojczyzna*, pp. 43–58.

[93] Ołena Arkusza, Marian Mudryj, "XIX-wieczna arystokracja polska w Galicji Wschodniej wobec ruskich (ukraińskich) aspiracji narodowych," *Krakowskie Pismo Kresowe* 4: *Galicja jako pogranicze kultur* (2012), pp. 145–71.

[94] Peter Brock, "Ivan Vahylevych (1811–1866) and the Ukrainian National Identity," *Canadian Slavonic Papers* 14, no. 2 (1972), pp. 153–90; Peter Brock, *Nationalism and Populism in Partitioned Poland: Selected essays* (London, 1973); Peter Brock, "The Polish Identity," in *The Tradition of Polish Ideals: Essays in History and Literature*, ed. Władysław Józef Stankiewicz (London, 1981), pp. 23–51.

[95] John-Paul Himka, "The Construction of Nationality in Galician Rus': Icarian Flights in almost All Directions," in *Intellectuals and the Articulation of the Nation*, eds. Ronald Grigor Suny and Michael D. Kennedy (Ann Arbor, 2001), pp. 109–64. Cf. also the older article: John-Paul Himka, "The Greek Catholic Church and nation-building in Galicia, 1772–1918," *Harvard Ukrainian Studies* 8, no. 3–4 (1984), pp. 426–52.

[96] Irena Homola-Dzikowska, *Mikołaj Zyblikiewicz (1823–1887)* (Wrocław–Warsaw–Cracow, 1964); Irena Homola-Dzikowska, *Kraków za prezydentury Mikołaja Zyblikiewicza (1874–1881)* (Cracow, 1976).

[97] Alexander Skórski, "Euzebiusz Czerkawski," *Muzeum* 12 (1896), pp. 685–99, 751–61, 815–31; 13 (1897), pp. 12–26, 87–93, 166–71, 238–44, 342–49, 503–19; 14 (1898), pp. 99–131, 169–82, 225–37, 297–318, 583–95, 698–705.

[98] Zygmunt Zborucki, *Euzebiusz Czerkawski i galicyjska ustawa szkolna z 1867 r.* (Lviv, 1927).

[99] Wiesława Duszkiewicz, "Euzebiusz Czerkawski i jego poglądy na szkolnictwo średnie," in *Biografie pedagogiczne. Szkice do portretu galicyjskiej pedagogii*, eds. Czesław Majorek and Jerzy Potoczny (Rzeszów, 1997), pp. 25–40.

eminent teacher, Zygmunt Sawczyński, also a Ruthenian of Polish nationality.[100] Andrzej A. Zięba published an extensive biography in article format of Emilian Czyrniański [Emilian Chyrniansky], a professor of the Jagiellonian University and a Lemko by provenance,[101] while Janusz Łosowski wrote about the career of another Cracow-based scholar, Anatol Lewicki [Anatol Levytsky].[102] Aside from the aforementioned examples, a certain amount of attention has been paid to the central ideas running through the poetry of Platon Kostecki.[103] Another eminent literary figure, Jan Zachariasiewicz, was also the subject of research interest, particularly by Czesław Kłak, who devoted a series of academic papers to him. It is worth adding that many of these studies not only focused on the life and fate of Jan Zachariasiewicz, but also placed him and his novels within the context of Polish-Ruthenian relations in nineteenth-century Galicia.[104] From the Ukrainian side the

---

[100] Elżbieta Głaz, "Zygmunt Sawczyński – pedagog, polityk i działacz oświatowy," in *Biografie pedagogiczne*, pp. 41–58.

[101] Andrzej A. Zięba, "Profesor Emilian Czyrniański," in *Łemkowie i łemkoznawstwo w Polsce*, ed. Andrzej A. Zięba (Cracow, 1997), pp. 15–27.

[102] Janusz Łosowski, *Anatol Lewicki* (Przemyśl, 1981); Janusz Łosowski, "Anatol Lewicki jako historyk," in Anatol Lewicki, *Obrazki najdawniejszych dziejów Przemyśla* (Przemyśl, 1994), pp. vii–xxxviii.

[103] Not counting the headwords for *Polski słownik biograficzny* [The Polish Biographical Dictionary] together with the less extensive biographical notes therein, until recently only a single article about Kostecki existed within academic circles, in conjunction with an article about Calderon's text that he himself had translated. See Jarosław Komorowski, "Platona Kosteckiego Hołd Calderonowi," *Pamiętnik Teatralny* 48, no. 3–4 (1999), pp. 96– 108. Recently several new texts about Kostecki have appeared: Ihor Chornovol, "Ostannii *gente Rutheni, natione Poloni*. Platon Kostets'kyi," *Lviv's'ka hazeta* no. 119 (13 Jul. 2007); Adam Świątek, "Wizja Rzeczypospolitej w twórczości literackiej Platona Kosteckiego," in *Piłsudski i jego czasy*, eds. Marek Hańderek and Adam Świątek (Cracow, 2007), pp. 203–10; Adam Świątek, "'Serdeczny Mistrzu, Tyś dziejów nie mierzył. Łokciem dziesiątków lat, Ty w Ruś uwierzył.' Platon Kostecki a Jan Matejko – historia niezwykłej znajomości," in *Per aspera ad astra. Materiały z XVI Ogólnopolskiego Zjazdu Historyków Studentów*, ed. Adam Świątek (Cracow, 2008), pp. 169–77; Adam Świątek, "Platon Kostecki – zapomniany propagator unii polsko-rusko-litewskiej," in *Shevchenkivs'ka vesna. Materialy mizhnarodnoï naukovo-praktychnoï konferentsiï molodykh uchenykh*, vol. 6, part 2: *Pratsi aspirantiv ta studentiv*, vol. 2, ed. V. Kolesnyk (Kyiv, 2008), pp. 241–44; Adam Świątek, "Kostecki Platon," in *Przemyski słownik biograficzny*, vol. 1 (Przemyśl, 2009), pp. 39–44; Adam Świątek, "Platon Kostecki – swój czy obcy w polsko-ukraińskim społeczeństwie Galicji Wschodniej drugiej połowy XIX wieku," in *'Swój' i 'obcy'. Materiały z I Międzynarodowej Sesji Humanistycznej, Toruń 17–19 V 2009*, eds. Anna Zglińska et al. (Toruń–Warsaw [2009]), pp. 175–84; Adam Świątek, "W sprawie ruskiej Platona Kosteckiego," *Galicja. Studia i materiały* 3 (2017), pp. 350–413.

[104] Maria Janion, "Powieść o chłopskim buntowniku," in Jan Zacharyasiewicz, *Jarema. Studium z wewnętrznych dziejów Galicji*, ed. Maria Janion (Warsaw, 1957), pp. 5–17; Czesław Kłak, "Literacka młodość Jana Zachariasiewicza," in *Z tradycji kulturalnych Rzeszowa i Rzeszowszczyzny. Księga pamiątkowa dla uczczenia X-lecia rzeszowskiego oddziału Towarzystwa Literackiego im. Adama Mickiewicza*, eds. Stanisław Frycie and Stefan

most interest has understandably been directed towards Jan Wagile-wicz, the co-creator of the Ruthenian Triad, known more commonly as Ivan Vahylevych.[105] The aforementioned researcher Peter Brock, in writing about Vahylevych, added as an aside that the Ruthenian Sobor was not so much an expression on the part of Ruthenians of pro-Polish tendencies as proof of their support for the evolution of a constitutional process within the state, while at the same time constituting opposition to the loyalist activities of the Supreme Ruthenian Council.[106] Brock de-velops the character of Wagilewicz further, contextualizing him within the heterogeneous group of Ruthenians of Polish nationality (some-thing he clearly emphasized) as well as within the general Ukrainian national consciousness in the nineteenth century.[107] Several members of *gente Rutheni, natione Poloni* were to see their own bibliographical entries in the *Polish Biographical Dictionary* [*Polski słownik biograficzny*]; these publications are cited in the bibliography of this book.

Lastly, it is worth mentioning that the subject of *gente Rutheni, na-tione Poloni*, although marginalized for many years by researchers, was nevertheless still present in a series of studies and compilations. The Canadian researcher Paul Robert Magocsi cited the group as an example of Polonophile tendencies amongst Galician Ruthenians.[108]

Reczek (Rzeszów, 1966), pp. 141–82; Maria Grzędzielska, "Drogi Jana Zachariasiewicza," in *Z dziejów kultury i literatury ziemi przemyskiej. Zbiór szkiców, opracowań i utworów lite-rackich*, ed. Stefania Kostrzewska-Kratochwilowa (Przemyśl, 1969), pp. 107–24; Czesław Kłak, "Powieści biograficzne Jana Zachariasiewicza," in *Z dziejów kultury i literatury*, pp. 125–72; Czesław Kłak, "Powieści historyczne Jana Zachariasiewicza zwierciadłem sporów politycznych między demokratami i konserwatystami galicyjskimi," *Prace Huma-nistyczne. Rzeszowskie Towarzystwo Przyjaciół Nauk. Wydział Nauk Humanistycznych. Komi-sja Historycznoliteracka* 1, series 1, no. 1 (1970), pp. 153–92; Czesław Kłak, "Glosa do Czer-wonej czapki Jana Zachariasiewicza," in Czesław Kłak, *Pisarze galicyjscy. Szkice literackie* (Rzeszów, 1994), pp. 57–76; Roman Koropeckyj, "Wizerunek narodowego ruchu ruskiego w powieści Jana Zachariasiewicza 'Święty Jur,'" *Krakowskie Zeszyty Ukrainoznawcze* 3–4 (1994–1995), pp. 305–23.

[105] A more extensive subject literature is given by the publisher of one of Wagilewicz's works: Rotysław Radyszewśkyj, "Przedmowa," in Jan Dalibor Wagilewicz, *Pisarze pol-scy Rusini wraz z dodatkiem Pisarze łacińscy Rusini*, ed. Rotysław Radyszewśkyj (Przemyśl, 1996), pp. 5–22. See also: Ihor Chornovol, "Ieretyk. Ivan Vahylevych," *Lvivs'ka hazeta* 156 (2 Sep. 2005); Leonid Zashkil'niak, "Ivan Vahylevych na tli svoho chasu ta istoriohrafii," in *Bahatokul'turne istorychne seredovyshche L'vova v XIX i XX stolittiakh / Wielokulturowe środowisko historyczne Lwowa w XIX i XX wieku* 4, eds. Leonid Zashkil'niak and Iezhy Maternits'ki (Lviv–Rzeszow, 2006), pp. 146–53; Leonid Zaszkilniak, "Iwan Wahyłewicz (1811–1866)," in *Złota księga historiografii lwowskiej XIX i XX wieku*, eds. Jerzy Maternicki and Leonid Zaszkilniak (Rzeszów, 2007), pp. 63–80.

[106] Brock, *Ivan Vahylevych*, p. 179.

[107] Ibid., p. 180. The same article was published later in the edition of the author's col-lected works—see Brock, *Nationalism and Populism*, pp. 102–41.

[108] Paul Robert Magocsi, *A History of Ukraine: The Land and its People* (Toronto–Buffalo–London, 2010), p. 468.

Mention was also given by Andrzej Chwalba in his academic textbook on the Polish history of the nineteenth century, in which he devoted several lines to Platon Kostecki as the most clearly recognizable representative of the demographic.[109] Kostecki is also cited in a Ukrainian--language compilation of Polish history, published by a team of Polish academics.[110] Besides this, *gente Rutheni, natione Poloni* has appeared (not always by name) in various works where recourse has been made to the participation of Kasper Cięglewicz [Kasper Tsenglevych] in the conspiracies of the 1830s, and first and foremost in relation to the period of the 1848 Revolutions when the Ruthenian Sobor came into being, acting as a forum for the assembly of Ruthenians of Polish nationality.[111]

Although several studies have indeed appeared about *gente Rutheni, natione Poloni*, especially beyond Poland's eastern border, the matter has yet to be examined with appropriate depth. In addition, aside from the texts of Andrzej A. Zięba and Marian Mudry, it still remains on the margins of academic interest. Historians have been far more eager to pursue subject matter concerning the national histories of Poles and Ukrainians or studies of the conflicts between the two nations than to research phenomena that seemed to unite Poles and Ruthenians. By creating a multifaceted narrative of *gente Rutheni, natione Poloni* in Galicia, the present book aims to draw attention to the problem of fluidity within nineteenth-century national identities. Many other important Ruthenians of Polish nationality stand in the shadows of history, as does a range of different problems affecting this community. Hopefully this book will encourage readers to search for similar examples and biographies of individuals who seemed to bring together what from the present-day perspective appears impossible to combine.

*** *

This translation is based on the Polish original published in 2014 under the title *Gente Rutheni, natione Poloni. Z dziejów Rusinów narodowości polskiej w Galicji* by Księgarnia Akademicka in Cracow. Certain sections have been shortened, while others have been modified. However, in

---

[109] Andrzej Chwalba, *Historia Polski 1795–1918* (Cracow, 2005), p. 478.

[110] Matsei Ianovs'kyi, "Syroty Rechi Pospolytoï. Vid stanovoho suspil'stva do suchasnykh natsiï 1795–1918," in *Pol'shcha. Narys Istoriï*, eds. Vlodzimiezh Mendzhets'kyi and Iezhy Bratsysevich, trans. Ivan Svarnyk (Warsaw, 2015), pp. 209–10.

[111] Cf. among others Marian Zgórniak, *Polska w czasach walk o niepodległość (1815–1864)* (Cracow, 2001), pp. 187, 225; Władysław A. Serczyk, *Historia Ukrainy* (Wrocław, 2001), p. 188; Wilson, *The Ukrainians*, p. 116; Karol Grünberg, Bolesław Sprengel, *Trudne sąsiedztwo. Stosunki polsko-ukraińskie w X–XX wieku* (Warsaw, 2005), pp. 154, 161, 164.

terms of thesis and argumentation the present study repeats the views expressed in the Polish original.

This book would not have come into being without the involvement and help of a number of people. First and foremost, words of gratitude go to my wife Wiktoria Kudela-Świątek for believing in me and motivating me to work. To my sons—Antoni and Ignacy—for their understanding.

I would also like to express a big thank you to all those involved in either the Polish original or this edition. Thanks go to Michał Baczkowski, Tomasz Gąsowski, Jadwiga Hoff, Marian Mudry, Kszysztof Popek, Andrew Sorokowski, and Frank E. Sysyn. Lastly, I extend a word of recognition to the translator, Guy Russell Torr, and the co-publisher of the present monograph, the Canadian Institute of Ukrainian Studies in Toronto (in particular Marko R. Stech) as well as Księgarnia Akademicka in Cracow (especially Adam Lejczak, and editors: Diana Osmęda and Małgorzata Manterys-Rachwał).

The generous help extended by all the above named in no way frees me from the responsibility for the content of the present book. For any potential oversights and inadequacies I remain solely responsible.

Chapter I
Gente Rutheni, Natione Poloni
The Characteristics of Formation

Definitions

A study of the subject literature brings to the fore various definitions of the notion *gente Rutheni, natione Poloni*. Włodzimierz Wilczyński has claimed that this term constitutes:

> The self-designation for the period from the sixteenth to the seventeenth century on the part of representatives of the Ukrainian nobility as equally the Ukrainian intelligentsia in Eastern Galicia in the nineteenth–twentieth century who had adopted a pro-Polish orientation and as a consequence had undergone a process of Polonization.[1]

This rather vague definition has been expanded upon by the authors of a lexicon devoted to borderland (marches) culture. They also credited Stanisław Orzechowski with coining the term:

> *Gente Ruthenus, natione Polonus* (Latin 'a Ruthenian by provenance of Polish nationality'). A formula utilized by Stanisław Orzechowski. Expressed within it is an attempt to define (ca. the mid-sixteenth century) the national and ethnic [dimensions] within the Ruthenian nobility of Red Rus' provenance. Orzechowski, being a Ruthenian (his mother being of the Orthodox faith), emphasized his Ruthenian origins while simultaneously strongly accentuating his affiliation to the political nation that was the Polish nobility. This belonging to *natio Polona* (the Polish nation) was also a manifestation of an attachment to Western culture — that of Latin civilization.[2]

However basing the definition on the sole and singular example of Stanisław Orzechowski and accrediting him with having first coined the formula of *gente Rutheni, natione Poloni*, is, as David Althoen argues, not entirely valid.[3]

---

[1] Włodzimierz Wilczyński, "Gente Ruthenus, natione Polonus," in Włodzimierz Wilczyński, *Ukraina. Leksykon. Historia, gospodarka, kultura* (Warsaw, 2010), p. 75.

[2] J[akub] N[iedźwiedź], "Gente Ruthenus natione Polonus," in *Kultura pogranicza wschodniego. Zarys encyklopedyczny*, eds. Tadeusz Budrewicz, Tadeusz Bujnicki and Jerzy Stefan Ossowski (Warsaw, 2011), p. 136.

[3] David Althoen claims that Orzechowski comprehends the meanings of the words *gens* and *natio* in a completely different way than they have been interpreted since the nineteenth century. Furthermore, while the formulation *gente Rutheni, natione Poloni* has been

This understanding of *gente Rutheni, natione Poloni* undoubtedly came into existence during the nineteenth century, enjoying more widespread usage from the 1860s onwards.[4] Yet the roots of this phenomenon may actually stretch back to the Old Polish period, particularly to the reign of King Casimir III the Great, when Red Rus' was permanently incorporated into the Kingdom of Poland. This event initiated extensive cultural exchange that lasted for the entirety of the existence of the Polish state, and subsequently that of Poland-Lithuania. This exchange further developed following the 1569 Union of Lublin. The Ruthenian lands incorporated in the fourteenth and sixteenth centuries adopted Polish law and culture, while the boyars often also adopted Catholicism. In the Ruthenian lands, Catholicism was held in higher esteem than the faith of the Orthodox Church, which was seen as being backward compared to the Latin Church and existing on the periphery of the Greek Orthodox world. This conversion of Orthodox Ruthenians to Catholicism had occurred from the very inception of the Roman Catholic metropolitanate in Halych. The Union of Brest in 1596 constituted an additional factor ensuring the integration of Rus' with the Polish Kingdom. This Union also joined the Orthodox faith, in the form of the Uniate Church, to Catholicism. The Ruthenian nobility, in accepting the Crown's cultural achievements, gradually underwent a process of assimilation and integration within the framework of a single state. However, this phenomenon chiefly affected the privileged (upper) social strata, since it was primarily connected with the responsibilities, duties, and privileges derived from estate affiliation, and therefore with a participation in governance and the consequent responsibility for the state. Such responsibilities were expressed by, for example, levy en masse, participation at diets, or the holding of state functions and offices. The Cracow historian Stanisław Kot presented this state of affairs in terms that suggested the initiation of *gente Rutheni, natione Poloni* as a phenomenon in Polish history:

> Coexistence within a single state organism quickly created a common tradition of its employment at diets, assemblies, tribunals, posts and offices, its defences during military expeditions, material and bloody

---

ascribed to Orzechowski, it has yet to be discovered in his work. The closest to the designation we can find in two of his religious treatises is that of *gente Roxolanus, natione vero Polonus*, but as Althoen claims this does not appear within a context of Orzechowski explaining his national identity, nor is it reconcilable with our current understanding of the formulation *gente Rutheni, natione Poloni*. Cf. David Althoen, "Natione Polonus and the Naród szlachecki: Two Myths of National Identity and Noble Solidarity," *Zeitschrift für Ostmitteleuropa-Forschung* 52 (2003), pp. 475–508.

[4] I write more extensively on the matter in: Adam Świątek, "Przypadek gente Rutheni, natione Poloni w Galicji," *Prace Historyczne* 144, no. 2: *Kształty galicyjskich tożsamości*, ed. Adam Świątek (2017), pp. 303–22.

sacrifices. The participants in this collective life were initially brought together by language, slowly by custom, and primarily by faith, and what was the most important — the attachment to common devices considered to be their own, attachment to freedoms so advanced that it protected even those who had stood apart and removed themselves from certain forms of coexistence (for example in matters of religion).

And thus all of a sudden the respective *gentes* merged into a single *natio*, which no longer constituted citizens of a single state, albeit of various provenance and language, but now citizens united within a common community of language, institutions, and what was the most important — within a single Polish national consciousness.[5]

Close attention should be given to Stanisław Kot's terminology — *gens* and *natio*. He goes on in his article to explain the meaning of these terms:

> The tradition of the Middle Ages understood *gens* in a narrower sense as generation, kith, a tribe joined by common origin, while *natio* was community, one also based on ancestral bonds, but at a higher level, connected by a common consciousness (…) *Natio* could incorporate the inhabitants of a single state, linked through common tradition and common aspirations although of different descent and language (…).[6]

In taking this route, we should understand the formulation *gente Rutheni, natione Poloni* as literally: "of Ruthenian kith, of Polish nationality," which suggests that the said "Ruthenian kith" was contained within the broader collectivism of Polish nationality. Some find Kot's understanding of this phenomenon to be problematic. He has been increasingly reproached by scholars for his instrumental use of Orzechowski to prove the concept of a multi-ethnic Polish "political nation."[7] Despite this, as Teresa Chynczewska-Hennel demonstrates, Kot's concept "served many historians as a brief explanation of the Ruthenian nobility's national affiliation."[8] This was understood in the following manner: the Ruthenian nobility (Orthodox and subsequently Catholic of the Greek rite, from Ruthenian families and originating from Ruthenian lands) was of Polish nationality because its state was Poland. If one is to understand nationality in a political sense, then Polish was the only

---

[5] Stanisław Kot, "Świadomość narodowa w Polsce w. XV-XVII," *Kwartalnik Historyczny* 52, no. 1 (1938), pp. 26–27.

[6] Ibid., p. 20.

[7] Cf. among others: Althoen, "Natione Polonus," pp. 475–76, footnote 3; Wioletta Pawlikowska-Butterwick, "A 'Foreign' Elite?: The Territorial Origins of the Canons and Prelates of the Cathedral Chapter of Vilna in the Second Half of the Sixteenth Century," *Slavonic and East European Review* 92, no. 1 (2014), p. 51, footnote 26.

[8] Teresa Chynczewska-Hennel, *Świadomość narodowa szlachty ukraińskiej i kozaczyzny od schyłku XVI do połowy XVII w.* (Warsaw, 1985), p. 133.

nationality that the Ruthenian boyars could have had, for if they had had their own sense of nationality then they would have pushed for the creation of an independent Ruthenian state of their own. The Cossack uprisings were undoubtedly such an attempt at nation creation. For, at a certain moment, they were to take on a state-creating—and subsequently nation-creating—character. The Cossacks however were not supported by the majority of the Ruthenian nobility, who elected to stay loyal to the king. In the political sense, this nobility was Polish. But does this enable us to view them as *gente Rutheni, natione Poloni,* that is, of Polish nationality?

Tomasz Kizwalter has criticized the modern tendency to refer to the concept of a political nation when discussing the nobility. He has emphasized the community of the noble estate cannot be viewed as synonymous with the modern definition of "nation," as "a mere estate structuring of society and a linguistically fluid higher culture are not elements that permit us to talk of the existence of a nation." A community can only be deemed a nation, he argues, when it demonstrates social democratization and an awareness of ethnic affiliation. With such an understanding of nationhood, it would be impossible to locate the beginnings of the Polish nation any earlier than the nineteenth century.[9] A different view of the creation and shaping of nationhood is advanced by Antonina Kłoskowska. Instead of regarding the creation of the nation as a nineteenth century phenomenon, she prefers to emphasize the historical changeability of nations, albeit through the maintaining of certain traits which justify "using a single concept for the separation of a whole subject to historical modifications."[10]

Juliusz Bardach in turn has also proposed a chronological framework for the development of nations in Europe, dividing the process into three stages.[11] He identifies the first stage as the tribal state or union of tribes, characterized by an origin from a common forefather or set of ancestors and a common language, territory, cult, and set of customs. This type of nation extended to the "early medieval nations formed upon an ethnic basis,"[12] from which feudal political nations—the second stage of development—were created. However, this "nation" only encompassed the gentry and nobility, while lower social groupings were excluded (if only through the loss of an awareness of belonging to a nation as such). At this stage the notion of membership was decided by a political bond and not merely by the ethnic. Indeed,

---

[9] Tomasz Kizwalter, *O nowoczesności narodu. Przypadek Polski* (Warszawa, 1999), p. 84–85.
[10] Antonina Kłoskowska, *National Cultures at the Grass-root Level* (Budapest, 2001), p. 60.
[11] Juliusz Bardach, "Od narodu politycznego do narodu etnicznego w Europie Środkowo-Wschodniej," *Kultura i Społeczeństwo* 37, no. 4 (1993), pp. 3–5.
[12] Ibid., p. 3.

political nations were multi-ethnic in composition, with the strongest factors impacting the weaker, as demonstrated in the Polonization and conversion to Catholicism of the Lithuanian-Ruthenian nobility. Henryk Litwin provides an excellent illustration of the phenomenon of multi-levelled self-identification. He outlines this using a fictitious case of an Orthodox nobleman of the Pinsk (in present-day Belarus) region, who was a deputy to the Diet [*Sejm*]:

> If he were to be asked who he was, then the answer would probably depend on the location and who was doing the asking. Asked outside an Orthodox Church then the reply would most probably be "a Ruthenian." Quizzed at the Diet the retort would be "a Lithuanian." If waylaid somewhere in Germany by a foreigner the probable reply would be – *eques polonus sum*.[13]

In the same fashion, Stanisław Orzechowski used both designations—"Ruthenian" and "Pole"—situationally. He would sign his works with pseudonyms such as *Roxolanus* and *Rutenus*, therein emphasizing his origins in Rus'. For example, in a letter written to Giovanni Francesco Commendone he wrote: "My fatherland of Rus' is situated on the River Tyr, which the local inhabitants call the Dnister."[14] On the other hand, he devoted his own writings to the affairs of Poland, his state fatherland, which he called "the sweetest homeland." As David Althoen has shown, Orzechowski the Pole also underwent a metamorphosis while abroad or when he wished to emphasize his gentry social affiliations, yet he was far more likely to appear as a Ruthenian, accentuating his territorial provenance and identity.[15] Althoen draws attention at the same time to the fact that *gens* (that is what other see as the lower in the two-component hierarchy of identity ranking) was no less important to Orzechowski than *natio*.[16]

So how did the relationship between *gens* and *natio* look at a later stage – in the modern epoch? The disappearance of Poland as a state from the map of Europe resulted in a situation whereby the question of nationality ceased to be an obvious one. National affiliation was subsequently devoid of any direct reference to a state as such, and would have to be defined on the basis of one's ethnic roots or motivated by a conscious ideological choice (or based on both). Juliusz Bardach places the third stage in the periodization of nation development within the industrial era. For it was then, after the French Revolution, that

---

[13] Henryk Litwin, "Narody pierwszej Rzeczypospolitej," in *Tradycje polityczne dawnej Polski*, eds. Anna Sucheni-Grabowska and Alicja Dybowska (Warsaw, 1993), p. 199.

[14] Stanisław Orzechowski, *Wybór pism* (Wrocław, 1972), pp. xiii, 620. In the original: "Roxolania patria est mihi, ad flumen Tyram, Dnestrum vocant accolae (…)."

[15] Althoen, "Natione Polonus," pp. 494–99.

[16] Ibid., pp. 488 ff.

social divisions into estates stopped fulfilling their previous roles and lost most of their importance. The so-called "historic" nations—those with their own statehood or at least the memory of the existence of such—shaped themselves on the basis of the notion of a state or the desire to fight for its independence. Usually due to recourse to tradition and culture, "non-historic" nations (i.e., those that were stateless) had to create their own identity and national culture anew, often mythologizing their own past. Józef Chlebowczyk expresses these two developmental routes in the following manner:

a) state community — linguistic community — national community (state-nation)
b) linguistic community (cultural-civilizational) — national community — state community (state-national).[17]

The first model (a) corresponds more to the processes shaping the Polish nation, while the second (b) correlates to the history of the Ukrainian nation in the nineteenth and twentieth centuries. The Ukrainian nation had to pass through more than two phases: phase I (the linguistic-cultural), which involved the standardization of the language leading to a linguistic self-designation and as a consequence the creation of nationality, and subsequently phase II (the political), which involved the struggle for the right to political self-designation.[18]

Here we are dealing with the clear identity and juxtaposition of both groups. Consequently, where was the place for Ruthenians of Polish nationality? At first glance, this group appears to be ideally located between the two variants. It would follow to view the creation of the *gente Rutheni, natione Poloni* alongside the process of assimilation: each dominating nation (historically, in terms of statehood possession) is to a degree a manifestation of ethnocentricism and a striving towards an integration of ethnically alien factors. This process likewise took place within the territory of revolutionary France, Hungary, and in an analogical fashion across the expanse of former Poland, employing the same mechanism albeit with certain specific variations. Assimilation enforced two tendencies employed by every Enlightenment state in Europe: centralisation and uniformity (the erasing of differences). In the French case, a French citizen was to become a Parisian, a Breton, a Burgundian, and a Lorrainian. In Hungary two concepts were created: Magyar and Hungarian, the latter being possibly both an ethnic Hungarian (Magyar), a Slovak, a Romanian, a Croat, a Serb, or a Ruthe-

---

[17] Józef Chlebowczyk, *O prawie do bytu małych i młodych narodów. Kwestia narodowa i procesy narodotwórcze we wschodniej Europie Środkowej w dobie kapitalizmu (od schyłku XVIII do początków XX w.)* (Warsaw–Cracow, 1983), p. 23.
[18] Ibid., pp. 38–56.

nian. Analogically, the Polish state and later its post-partition elites created the concept of Poland as comprising an array of lands. By means of the instruments available and therefore by language, religion, material position, cultural achievements, and the strength of the apparatus of authority, the dominating group (the majority) impacted the minority group, also the weaker, that found itself at a disadvantaged level of development. The process of assimilation, according to Józef Chlebowczyk, occurred according to the following pattern:

> Initially they [individuals or entire collectives] relaxed the links with the hitherto primary linguo-national community, and increasingly the given individuals or entire collectives became alienated as a result of the influence of the values and models of behaviour of the former community, finally marking out a route to an increasingly fuller identification with the new, in fact hitherto alien cultural-civilizational circle (…) with the perspective of total assimilation (…) under conditions of the development of a modern social consciousness.[19]

Chlebowczyk cites the phenomenon of semi-assimilation (cultural hybridization) as a side effect of the long term process of assimilation.[20] The Ruthenians of Polish nationality in Galicia were such a group, caught halfway between acculturation and total assimilation. To put it another way, their ethnic roots were Ruthenian while their national choice (the idea) was Polish. Therefore, we should understand that beneath the concept of *gente Rutheni, natione Poloni* lay individuals of Ruthenian ethnic provenance who identified with the Polish nation in terms of their political, social, and creative activity and a manifestation or declaration of their national identity, though simultaneously maintaining many characteristics of the Ruthenian ethnic group, such as rite, language, culture and custom, and family and communal contacts. They recognized a separate historical tradition based on a private notion of homeland—that of Rus'—while at the same time strongly proclaiming their connection to their ideological homeland of Poland.'[21] However, it is important to clarify this definition from the outset. Galicians of *gente Rutheni, natione Poloni* did not constitute an integrated group with externally recognized characteristics that distinguished them from others. Consequently, we should not use the notion of *gente Rutheni, natione Poloni* to designate a closed community that can be researched within a concrete time and across a designated territory, and we should em-

---

[19] Ibid., p. 62.
[20] Ibid., pp. 37–38, 62.
[21] Cf.: Adam Świątek, "Z rozważań nad problematyką tożsamości narodowo-etnicznej *Gente Rutheni, natione Poloni* w XIX-wiecznej Galicji," in *Odmiany tożsamości*, eds. Robert Szwed, Leon Dyczewski and Justyna Szulich-Kałuża (Lublin, 2010), p. 98.

ploy this "label" most cautiously and only when we are describing individuals who themselves employed the designation in relation to themselves or in relation to those whose life choices and attitudes clearly labelled them as such.

Discussions on Ethnicity, Nation, and National Identity

The definition given above contains two designations, "ethnic group" and "nation." For the historian familiar with the source matter this distinction is intuitively understandable, yet the understanding of these terms varies depending on the academic discipline. Additionally, the discussion that has developed over decades has created such a rich panoply of definitions and theories, including those that are often mutually exclusive, that it is difficult to find an adequate model which could be consistently used in relation to a grouping such as *gente Rutheni, natione Poloni*. This does not mean, however, that Ruthenians of Polish nationality were a unique cultural phenomenon in the European context.[22] Nonetheless their complex, two-tiered identity is burdened with a series of problems that make it difficult to pigeonhole them as either Ruthenians or Poles through the direct application of existing terminology.

To start, we need to consider the first component of our formula *gente Rutheni, natione Poloni*, i.e. *gens*. Stanisław Kot has translated this term as "clan" or "tribe." Such words can be related to ethnicity, which can be academically defined in an array of ways. Helpful here is the definition proposed by Anthony D. Smith, who has differentiated the following elements as typical for an ethnic community (which he terms an "ethnie"): a common provenance, joint history and recollections, separate and distinct culture and traditions, a connection to a given territory,

---

[22] Analogical phenomena have occurred in other European countries (e.g., the Germanization of the Czech nobility, Croatian Hungarians, Lithuanian *krajowcy* [Polish intellectuals who opposed the division of the Polish-Lithuanian Commonwealth into "nation" states – G.T.]) and among representatives of other ethnicities across the former Polish lands. Polish national identity was possessed or adopted in Galicia by Jews, Armenians, Czechs, and Austrian Germans. On the latter see: Isabel Röskau-Rydel, *Niemiecko--austriackie rodziny urzędnicze w Galicji 1772–1918. Kariery zawodowe, środowisko, akulturacja i asymilacja* (Cracow, 2011), pp. 159–338. See also: Ivan L. Rudnytsky, "Ukrainians in Galicia under Austrian Rule," in Ivan L. Rudnytsky, *Essays in Modern Ukrainian History*, ed. Peter L. Rudnytsky (Edmonton, 1987), p. 348–49, footnote 32; Anna Wróbel, "Od 'Galileuszy' do Polaków. Wejście do polskiej inteligencji przedstawicieli ludności napływowej i mniejszości w Galicji w XIX w.," in *Inteligencja polska XIX i XX wieku. Studia 5*, ed. Ryszarda Czepulis-Rastenis (Warsaw, 1987), pp. 173–90.

and a sense of solidarity and identity.[23] But how might one define the ethnicity of the "Ruthenianism" of Ruthenians of Polish nationality? To use Smith's framework, they would be characterized by their origin within the territory of old Rus', the eastern rite (initially Orthodox, later Greek Catholic), Ruthenian as a language, common mores, a sense of connectivity with other Ruthenians, and finally, an affiliation to their place of birth. Recollections of their (Ruthenian) kith's past would also be important for some. *Gens* based on a territorial, ethnic, or neighbourhood sense of community was often much stronger than *natio*, and was for a long time understood as belonging to a privileged class or stratum. The nineteenth century, which witnessed a fundamental reconstruction of the social order—and the consequent change in the organization of political life enabling the participation of the increasingly conscious masses—differs from the previous epoch in that a greater role than that of ethnicity was being played by ideological factors along with the need for self-identification. It is incredibly important to pay attention to self-designation, as it allows the researcher to grasp the moment of reflection on the part of the individual on their own identity and conscious choice of nationality. This choice, determined by internal and external factors, does not necessarily result from ethnic provenance.

Here we shall tackle the other part of our designation—*natio*. The term "nation" has for a long time generated heated debate within academia, firstly because of the array of definitions; secondly, as this multitude of definitions renders it nearly impossible to establish objective and universal criteria which would allow one to define a given community as a "nation"; and thirdly, as a result of the various viewpoints regarding the chronological determination of the beginnings of given nationalities. There is not enough room here to enumerate the various debates over the definition of "nation." An awareness of the differences (and simultaneously faults) in the approaches to the question of nationhood makes it impossible to unconditionally adopt a single approach, particularly in the case of research that touches on two or more academic disciplines; this is indeed the case of research into the nationality question of borderland and marches regions in the past. Therefore, it is worth shifting the focus of the discussion to the question of "national identity," that is, to the question of who the individual is within the world that surrounds them. Only then should one attempt to deliberate the national identity of the collective, bearing in mind that this collectivity is made up of the identity of individuals.

---

[23] Anthony D. Smith, *The Cultural Foundations of Nations: Hierarchy, Covenant, and Republic* (Malden, MA–Oxford–Carlton, 2008), pp. 30–31. Cf. also: Barbara Szacka, *Wprowadzenie do socjologii* (Warsaw, 2008), pp. 247–48.

The key determinant allowing one to differentiate a nation from an ethnic grouping is politicization, and consequently the participation of a given community in power (self-determination) or the desire for self-determination (a striving for sovereignty, possible autonomy). Though the political aspect plays an important role when the matter concerns the whole of society, much can be gleaned from looking at its effect on the individual. For the individual to be able to feel like a member of a nation, he has to participate within a certain universe, relate to it, and accept that it alone will determine his life choices. Here it is worth recalling the so-called "culturalist" approach coined by the Polish sociologist Antonina Kłoskowska. She places particular emphasis on the role of culturalization in determining national identification, highlighting "the initiation and entrance into the universe of symbolic culture in general, including national culture."[24] The assimilation of culture by the individual, known as "cultural assimilation" or one's attitude to culture, occurs in three dimensions: through knowledge about the cultural community, through emotional-affectionate bonds, and finally, through undertaking certain actions and a way of being/behaving. A cultural community that has arisen from the transformations of ethnic communities is a nation.[25] National culture is "the broad and complex system (syndrome) of means of action, values, symbols, beliefs, and symbolic works which are considered by a certain social collective to be its/theirs (…)."[26] This approach places great store on individual identity in the context of drawing models of action, symbols, and knowledge from national culture.

I am an adherent of adopting a subjective approach which draws attention to the individual's will to decide on their identity regardless of ethnic provenance, assuming there is no dismissal of any of those attributes that shape national identity (language, religion, history, territory), or attachment to a state, and even more so to a culture. In order to understand the principles of this approach, it is worth recalling the words of Grzegorz Babiński, who has written on the question of the Polish-Ukrainian marches. He argues that attachment to a nation is determined by the consciousness of the individual and a desire to belong to a national community "regardless of the family into which they were born and which language is used on a daily basis."[27] So let us consider what triggered the desire among a part of the Ruthenian ethnic group to affiliate themselves with Polishness.

---

[24] Kłoskowska, *National Cultures*, p. 98.
[25] Paweł Ścigaj, *Tożsamość narodowa. Zarys problematyki* (Cracow, 2012), pp. 305–13.
[26] Ibid., p. 315.
[27] Grzegorz Babiński, *Pogranicze polsko-ukraińskie. Etniczność – tożsamość narodowa – zróżnicowanie religijne* (Cracow, 1997), pp. 24–25.

National Self-Determination

The possibility of national self-determination for the inhabitants of Galicia gave rise to numerous situations in which there occurred attempts to fight for independence or manifest Polishness. Here the matter concerns problematic moments in their entirety, including wars, armed uprisings, conspiratorial acts and associations, as well as creative and social works aimed at strengthening and giving heart to the people, and political activities as demonstrated in the Galician Diet or the Imperial Council in Vienna.[28] This phenomenon needs to be examined not merely at the level of the social elite. Sometimes problematic situations, those which forced self-reflection over one's own identity, spilled out onto the streets, into work, and into the family or living space. In fact, it was exactly those situations and incidents that are most telling about the phenomenon of how certain representatives of *gente Rutheni* became *natione Poloni*. But one need also be aware that Ruthenian participation in conspiracies or uprisings did not always represent a defence of Polish national identity; slogans backing social change also provoked national uprisings. Furthermore, these people, namely the developing intelligentsia, had quite simply no other alternative than Poland, for over the course of the first decades of the nineteenth century it was rather difficult to talk of a modern Ruthenian nation as such. Only a small number were conscious of their national differentiation from Poles. These were the representatives of the newly established Ruthenian intellectual elite in Galicia, comprised mainly, but not exclusively, of members of the Greek Catholic clergy. These clergymen also sometimes felt themselves to be Poles and engaged in Polish conspiratorial acts. During this time, the Ruthenian noble elites often underwent Polonization and Latinization.[29] It was only after the 1830s, as a result of the Ruthenian Triad affair, that an awakening of Ruthenian national movement was to occur. Up until this point, the *gente Rutheni, natione Poloni* did not recognize Ruthenian nationality as a valid option. John-Paul Himka has referred to this state as "the larvae state,"[30] while Danuta Sosnowska, following

---

[28] Marian Mudry, in analyzing the *gente Rutheni, natione Poloni* deputies in the Galician Diet, wrote: "It is difficult to say to what degree the Galician Diet created and to what extent it influenced the consciousness of *gente Rutheni natione Poloni*. What is certain is that Diet discussions were conducive to bringing to the fore such a consciousness and the displaying of attitudes hitherto hidden." See Marjan Mudryj, "Dylematy narodowo-ściowe w Sejmie Krajowym galicyjskim (na przykładzie posłów formacji gente Rutheni natione Poloni)," in *Ukraińskie tradycje parlamentarne. XIX-XXI wiek*, ed. Jarosław Moklak (Cracow, 2006), p. 63.

[29] Mieczysław Adamczyk, *Edukacja a awans społeczny plebejuszy 1764–1848* (Wrocław, 1990), pp. 108–9.

[30] John-Paul Himka, "The Construction of Nationality in Galician Rus': Icarian Flights in Almost all Directions," in *Intellectuals and the Articulation of the Nation*, eds. Ronald Grigor Suny and Michael D. Kennedy (Ann Arbor, 2001), p. 111.

the terminology of Miroslav Hroch, defines this stage of development as "phase A" of the creation of the Ukrainian nation, prior to its political shaping.[31]

The situation would only drastically change with the onset of the Revolutions of 1848, when political demands were advanced by Ruthenians for the first time. At this time, there emerged an alternative to choosing between strictly Polish or Ruthenian nationalities. Many researchers point to the fact that the year 1848 gave rise to several extremely realistic scenarios within the development of Ruthenian nationality. Danuta Sosnowska enumerates five cultural models existing in parallel among this same ethnic group, though in point of fact this affected only its elite: Polonization, Ukrainization, Russification, Rusynification, and Ruthenification.[32] The victory of Ukrainization (also called Ukrainophilism, pro-Ukrainianism) over the many options and routes that could have been taken by this very same people has been explained by Yaroslav Hrytsak, who points out that the reason lay in the greater degree of radicalization and modernization that Ukrainization entailed. Neither the conservative nor the conciliatory, but rather the radical movements turned out to be the most effective in Europe at that time. In the Ukrainian case nationalism was to play a most important role, one far more significant than demonstrated in the Polish case. In addition, it was radically-charged nationalist ideologies that found the largest number of adherents amongst the young, perhaps because these ideologies proved the most inspiring.[33] The Ukrainian option, built on an oppositional spectrum (nationalist in relation to Poles and Russians; social in relation to the landowners; religious in terms of the dominant Roman Catholic Church in Galicia), proved more attractive than gradual assimilation or the stagnation of national development. Galician Ruthenian activists (Ukrainians) drew their model from none other than their Polish neighbours. What is more, this "new" Ruthenian (Ukrainian) nationality was also inspired by Polish politicians, particularly by the Cracow conservatives. Conscious of the threat emanating from Russian panslavism, they preferred to support the Ruthenian national movement as a means of opposing the expansion of the Orthodox Church and the idea of a Great Russia.

The political possibilities which later would enable Galician autonomy allowed the shaping of the political thinking of the Ruthenian elite and its consequent articulation, a process that would embolden the elite

---

[31] Danuta Sosnowska, *Inna Galicja* (Warsaw, 2008), pp. 22–23. Cf. Mirosław Hroch, „National Self-Determination from a Historical Perspective", *Canadian Slavonic Papers* 37, no. 3–4 (1995), pp. 284, 288.

[32] Sosnowska, *Inna Galicja*, p. 25.

[33] Cf. [Jarosław Hrycak], *Ukraina. Przewodnik krytyki politycznej. Z Jarosławem Hrycakiem rozmawia Iza Chruślińska*, prefaced by Adam Michnik (Gdańsk–Warsaw, 2009), pp. 130–31.

to fight for their own goals.[34] With that being said, until the end of the nineteenth century it remained worthwhile for many Ruthenians to continue to function within Polish elitist circles, which lay at the pinnacle of the Galician social hierarchy. This was the result of the development level and attractiveness of Polish culture, but also chiefly because of its long-time domination over the Ruthenian culture, which was principally identified with the peasantry and the Uniate clergy. The majority of cultural centres were Polish, as was a significant proportion of publications, the administrative elite, and the University of Lviv, which was gradually Polonized in the 1870s. As Jarosław Moklak writes:

> Polish culture absorbed many intellectuals and politicians of Galician Ruthenian origin. They operated in public institutions, involved themselves in science and education, and as deputies sat in the Lviv [Galician] Diet, together deciding on the country's legislation. [35]

The ability to be split between a sense of Ruthenianness and Polishness was possible in Galicia only until such a time that the conflict between Poles and Ukrainians had become clearly demarcated. Conflict should be understood as the "final violent confrontation between nations or ethnic groups, in which cultural and ethnic identities of the sides represent a more significant factor than possessions, authority, or information."[36] Particular displays of strength during this conflict, such as the non-conformist rule of politicians from both nations, an increasingly vehement press smear campaign (the aim of which ceased to be the presentation of the views of a few individuals but the entirety of a neighbouring culture), the symbolic murder of the governor of Galicia Andrzej Potocki in 1908, and most importantly, the Polish-Ukrainian war over Eastern Galicia itself. These events forced the inhabitants of Galicia to ally with one of the sides. The result of this forced allegiance was varied, at times even dividing families. In the face of conflict national affiliation changed, with the final decision to choose one option or another driven by a fear of exclusion. On the whole, such a process of identification resulted in the complete severing of one's ethnic roots and subsequent total assimilation to the chosen group, understood as the identification of the individual with their social surroundings (in this case Polish) to such a degree that they stop being viewed as alien.[37]

---

[34] Mudryj, *Dylematy narodowościowe*, p. 63.

[35] Jarosław Moklak, *W walce o tożsamość Ukraińców. Zagadnienie języka wykładowego w szkołach ludowych i średnich w pracach galicyjskiego Sejmu Krajowego 1866–1892* (Cracow, 2004), p. 7.

[36] Krzysztof Kwaśniewski, "Konflikt etniczny," *Sprawy Narodowościowe. Seria nowa* 3, (1994), p. 52.

[37] Hieronim Kubiak, "Asymilacja," in *Encyklopedia socjologii. Suplement*, comp. Zbigniew Bokszański et al., eds. Hieronim Kubiak et al. (Warsaw, 2005), p. 29.

Michel Morineau wrote about "sweet nectare of belonging," which "answer the primary desire to belong, to belong to a group, to be accepted by someone else, to be taken in, to be the confirmed recipient of support, allies (...)."[38] This notion is expounded by Zygmunt Bauman:

> The "we" made of inclusion, acceptance, and confirmation is the realm of gratifying safety cut out (though never securely enough) from the frightening wilderness of the *outside* populated by "them." The safety would not be felt unless the "we" were trusted to possess the binding power of acceptance and the strenght to protect those already accepted.[39]

In the same manner as other inhabitants of Galicia who deliberated over their own identity, *Gente Rutheni, natione Poloni*, initially adopted Polish culture with the aim of securing their material status and consequently advancing socially through belonging to an elite, or simply through self-realisation. Later, however, they sought protection through their allegiance in the face of conflict. The "terrifying alienness of the external world" for Ruthenians who had chosen Polish nationality was realized in the Ukrainian national movement. In not wanting to be seen as "them," they declared their Polishness, depriving themselves of elements of Ruthenian ethnicity. Acculturation in the face of the ground-breaking political events at the turn of the twentieth century and beyond changed into an instantly realized assimilation. Hence the more intense the conflict fuelled by nationalist elements became, the rarer was talk of the *gente Rutheni, natione Poloni* model. Instead, discourse favoured a severing of roots and total assimilation. The reverse process also occurred, though this was less common, whereby certain individuals in an identification dilemma adopted Ukrainian nationality and cut themselves off from their Polishness. Gradually, belief in the possibility of an amicable and brotherly solution to Ukrainian-Polish relations forged within a single state faded. Yet many found themselves in a very difficult situation as a result of the crystallization of these separate nationalities, the Polish and the Ukrainian. Hence their national conversions were often unexpected and surprising, but first and foremost difficult. It is also untrue that only those who were not yet nationally classified were able to choose between nations. Identity was still fluid in the nineteenth century, and the opportunity for choice remained.

---

[38] Michel Morineau, "La douceur d'être inclus," in *Sociabilité, pouvoirs et société. Actes du Coloque de Rouen, 24/26 Novembre 1983*, coll. by Françoise Thelamon (Rouen, 1987), p. 19, quoted after: Zygmunt Bauman, "Soil, Blood and Identity," *The Sociological Review* 40, no. 4 (1992), p. 679.

[39] Ibid.

The Social Structure and Identity Type of *Gente Rutheni, Natione Poloni*

In the face of the changes occurring in Central-Eastern Europe in the nineteenth century, all social strata started to consciously participate in matters of nation, including those who, during the period of the Polish--Lithuanian Commonwealth, had actually been excluded from power. This was a time when all social groups could proclaim their inclusion within the Polish nation. These processes were to take place in various social strata in different ways and at different times. The situation was the same in the formation of *gente Rutheni, natione Poloni*, which, although manifesting itself within higher social levels, did nevertheless draw recruits from the lower classes. Andrzej A. Zięba wrote:

> And so the formation of *gente Rutheni, natione Poloni* broadened its social base to include non-gentry circles and ceased to be a phenomenon taken from gentry ideology for it became one of the categories of enlightened national consciousness.[40]

To glean a holistic picture of the phenomenon, it is essential to examine what this awareness looked like within the various social layers of the Ruthenian population of Galicia.

The Landed Gentry

In the Ruthenian lands, any identification with Poland up until the moment of the partitions came from the landed gentry. Its representatives had fulfilled an array of political and administrative functions in the Polish state, and had taken up the mission of defending it. Despite their Ruthenian origins, they had for centuries been connected with Polish culture and had undergone a process of Polonization and its accompanying Latinization. The process of assimilation of the knighthood that had taken place from the fourteenth century until the end of the Polish-Lithuanian state's existence had almost come to an end. This was characterized by not only the adoption of Polish as a language, but by the rate of conversion to the Roman Catholic Church. As Włodzimierz Osadczy writes, already in the eighteenth century there was no longer a splendid Rus' knighthood that would stand by the Eastern Church. He claims that:

---

[40] Andrzej A. Zięba, "Gente Rutheni, natione Poloni," in *Prace Komisji Wschodnioeuropejskiej*, vol. 2, eds. Ryszard Łużny and Andrzej A. Zięba (Cracow, 1995), p. 66.

The designation of the time *ritus ruthenus – ritus rusticus* conveyed the true state of the Uniate rite in its social aspect. The Union, one based chiefly on the peasantry, had neither intellectual elites nor believers fully conscious in their affiliation to their rite.[41]

While assimilation in the Polish-Lithuanian epoch had chiefly resulted from political factors, with the cultural dimension being somewhat less prevalent, in post-partition Poland it was the latter that was to encourage a continued commitment to Polishness. According to earlier researchers, this constituted the best proof of the Poles' civilizational superiority over Ruthenians,[42] but a more accurate explanation would be the lack of an attractive alternative political tradition to which one could have turned within the territory of Eastern Galicia at the moment of Poland's loss of statehood. The times of the Principality of Galicia--Volhynia were distant memories and seen exclusively as an antiquated Ruthenian past, while the tradition of the Cossack hetmanship was of no interest to the heirs of those Ruthenian boyar dynasties which for hundreds of years had found themselves within the Polish cultural orbit. Consequently many representatives of the richer gentry class, even if they had not renounced their eastern rite by participating in the "political nation" itself, were by the very nature of things eager first to save Poland and then to win its independence.

An excellent example of such a family is the Matkivsky [Matkowski] family. Although originally from the Podilia region, later generations were to obtain and hold sizeable tracts of land in the Eastern Carpathians. Stefan Swieżawski describes the family thus:

> (...) The Matkowski family are typical representatives of the said *gente Rutheni et natione Poloni*. Within the family, Ruthenian traditions (as yet still not deemed as Ukrainian) were harmonized with Polish ones, while patriotism was expressed by hard work for the country and by a love for the federative and unitary ideals of the former Commonwealth.[43]

It is worth noting how the representatives of this Ruthenian family, even when entering into the period of the partitions, would still remain loyal to their former state.

Father Bazyli Matkowski [Vasyl Matkivsky], in addition to being the Greek Catholic parish priest in Bar, was an abbot and prelate who was

---

[41] Włodzimierz Osadczy, *Kościół i Cerkiew na wspólnej drodze. Concordia 1863. Z dziejów porozumienia między obrządkiem greckokatolickim a łacińskim w Galicji Wschodniej* (Lublin, 1999), p. 87.

[42] Stanisław Pawłowski, *Ludność rzymsko-katolicka w polsko-ruskiej części Galicji z dwoma mapami* (Lviv, 1919), p. 10.

[43] Stefan Swieżawski, *Wielki przełom 1907–1945*, ed. Mirosław Daniluk, preface by Tadeusz Fedorowicz (Lublin, 1989), p. 17.

made a protonotary by the pope in 1768. He died during a Russian attack on the town during the course of the confederation in 1768. His son, Józef [Iosyf], having moved to Eastern Galicia, became a lawyer and also purchased vast lands in the Eastern Carpathians. His estates included Veldizh [present-day Shevchenkove], Patsykiv, Senechiv, and Vyshkiv. During the Kościuszko Insurrection of 1794 he was a member of the Centralization of Lviv, becoming a member of the Duchy of Warsaw's Council of Ministers in 1809. He married Teresa Au (from a Polonized German family) and had two children with her: a daughter, Ludwika, who went on to marry Erazm Hoszowski [Erazm Hoshovsky]—also from a family of the inclination *gente Rutheni, natione Poloni*—and a son, Józef [Iosyf].[44]

Józef excelled as a captain in the engineering corps of the Duchy of Warsaw's army. Despite his Ruthenian origins he considered himself unequivocally Polish. In his memoirs, he cites his conversation with the French commander General Dominique Vandamme, who:

> (…) avidly asked what lineage I was and when I told him a Pole from Austrian Poland [colloquial name of Galicia – A. Ś.] he scowled and asked how could I dare serve against my own monarch, for war was to be declared. I answered him though that I only wish to serve those who will return our lost homeland to us and consequently I serve the Emperor Napoleon. He then started to slap me heartedly on the shoulder and praise the way I thought. (…)[45]

Józef Matkowski would demonstrate his patriotism on the battlefield. He fought in Prince Józef Poniatowski's corps at Smolensk, Mozhaisk, and Chirikovo, and helped take Moscow, subsequently seeing action at the Biarezina River. After his wounds had healed he took part in the defence of Dresden, where he was captured by the Austrians but freed as a result of his Galician origins. For a dozen or so years he managed the family estates within the Austrian area of partition. He eventually joined his compatriots again during the November Uprising of 1830, although he participated not by fighting but by hiding insurgents at his manor house.[46]

We know of other eminent gentry families who produced well-known Ruthenians of Polish nationality. The best example is Father Onufry Krynicki [Onufrii Krynytsky], a professor at Lviv University,

---

[44] Ibid., 16–17. We know in detail the biography of Józef (the son) Matkowski, including the course of his military career thanks to the memoirs he wrote. See Józef Matkowski, "Zbiór niektórych szczegółów życia mego," preface by Ryszard Grabowski, in *Pamiętniki z lat 1792–1849*, comp. Ryszard Grabowski (Wrocław, 1961), pp. 95–176.

[45] Matkowski, "Zbiór," p. 143.

[46] Bolesław Łopuszański, "Matkowski Józef," in *Polski słownik biograficzny* (subsequently: *PSB*), vol. 20 (Wrocław–Warsaw–Gdańsk–Cracow,1975), p. 203.

who even held the office of rector at the academy three times. He came from the Krynicki-Eliasz [Krynytsky-Illiash] noble family of the Korab coat-of-arms.[47]

The representatives of the landed gentry were drawn to one another as a result of their social standing and not because of ethnicity or religious rite. This does not mean that despite Polonization and Latinization—the changing of rite to that of the Roman Catholic—they instantly severed all contact with their roots. Sometimes they cultivated past customs and often

1. Onufry Krynicki

used Ruthenian as a language and, consequently, did not treat the Ruthenian peasant as someone alien, at least not in the ethnic sense.[48] In addition, as Andrzej A. Zięba pointed out in his article, in the first half of the nineteenth century many of these eminent families started to return to their Ruthenian roots. This was the result of genealogical research and the cultivating of family traditions. Zięba gives the example of the Fedorovych [Fedorowicz] family, which, on discovering "its Ruthenianness," returned to the Uniate rite abandoned by their ancestors and began to communicate in Ruthenian.[49] However, these were usually passing whims, and in general after these momentary discoveries of their roots families would return to Polish culture. Zięba writes:

> Similar twists and turns were experienced by the Dzieduszycki, Szeptycki, Gużkowski, Komarnicki, Jelski, Jasiński, and even, though to a lesser degree, by the Sapieha family. With the exception of the Szeptycki Family, where there was a return to the most strongly felt family traditions including religious motifs and a few other similar cases, these families did not on the whole decide to adopt a Ukrainian national consciousness.[50]

The Sheptytsky/Szeptycki family example requires special consideration. Usually when the surname is mentioned recourse is made to the conversion of Roman Szeptycki [Roman Sheptytsky], who, fol-

[47] Marian Tyrowicz, "Krynicki Onufry," in *PSB*, vol. 15 (Wrocław–Warsaw–Cracow, 1970), p. 463.
[48] Mieczysław Adamczyk, "Społeczno-gospodarcze położenie ludności unickiej diecezji przemyskiej w latach 1772–1848," *Przemyskie Zapiski Historyczne* 4–5 (1986–87), p. 113.
[49] Zięba, "Gente Rutheni," pp. 71–72.
[50] Ibid., p. 72.

lowing his nomination as Uniate metropolitan in Lviv Andrei, was to become the leader and foremost national authority for Galician Ukrainians. His sense of identity represented a return to his former roots. Jan Kazimierz Szeptycki, in researching the reasons behind Roman Szeptycki's decision to enter the Order of the Basilian Monks, unequivocally points to the family's origins as a cause. The trajectory of his ancestors was typical for a *gente Rutheni, natione Poloni* landed gentry family. In pre-partition Poland, the Sheptytskys were an Orthodox family that converted to the Union following the Synod of Brest of 1596. Many representatives of this family were involved in the church, with some members becoming bishops and even metropolitans (for example, Atanasii Sheptytsky [Atanazy Andrzej Szeptycki], bishop of Przemyśl, who went on to become Uniate metropolitan). Roman's great great grandfather, Vasyl Sheptytsky [Bazyli Szeptycki] (1735–1800), was probably the very last direct Uniate ancestor of the future metropolitan. Following the change in rite to Roman Catholicism, the family continued to preserve the memory of their Ruthenian past despite the ongoing ubiquitous Polonization of their social circles. The Szeptycki family, who had assembled Ruthenian artefacts for generations, passed on family traditions and maintained a cordial relationship with the Greek Catholic Church, participating in Uniate liturgies as well as inviting the Ruthenian clergy to partake in family celebrations and joint holiday celebrations. Taking into account the fact that Prylbychi, the Szeptycki family estate, was on the whole inhabited by Ruthenians, and that Roman himself also spoke fluent Ruthenian, the conversion is easily understandable and was in fact simply a return to the bosom of the Greek Catholic Church.[51] This occurred despite the completely different national views of Roman's parents or those held by his younger brother, Stanisław, an officer in the Austrian army who had commanded the Third Polish Legion Brigade during the First World War and had overseen the north-eastern front during Polish--Soviet War 1919–21.

There were also other cases of total assimilation within the burgeoning Ukrainian movement. A prominent example is Wacław Lipiński of Polish gentry stock who was to become Viacheslav Lypynsky, the

---

[51] Jan Kazimierz Szeptycki, "Gdy w rodzinie ważyły się losy syna... (Rzecz o Romanie Marii Aleksandrze Szeptyckim – późniejszym metropolicie Andrzeju – w świetle dokumentów rodzinnych)," in *Polska–Ukraina. 1000 lat sąsiedztwa*, vol. 1: *Studia z dziejów chrześcijaństwa na pograniczu etnicznym*, ed. Stanisław Stępień (Przemyśl, 1990), pp. 183–84. Cf. also Andrzej A. Zięba, "W sprawie genezy decyzji Romana Szeptyckiego o zmianie obrządku," in *Metropolita Andrzej Szeptycki. Studia i materiały*, ed. Andrzej A. Zięba (Cracow, 1991), pp. 43–64 as well as Piotr Mikietyński, *Generał Stanisław hr. Szeptycki. Między Habsburgami a Rzeczpospolitą (okres 1867–1918)* (Cracow, 1999), pp. 15–16.

historian and conservative Ukrainian politician.[52] In the case of the Galician aristocracy it is also important to emphasize that there was a large
number of people who employed the notion of "Ruthenian" in matters of self-identification, though they did so chiefly for political reasons. Many landowner deputies declared themselves to be Ruthenian
with the intent of legitimizing either their possessional rank or various political or administrative functions entrusted to them in a "Ruthenian" land. Such was the case with the Golejewski, Puzyna, Dunin-
Borkowski, or Jabłonowski families. The majority of wealthy Galician
landowners were, as a rule, already completely Polonized, making it
difficult to see their representatives as individuals with a dual identity. For they had found themselves immersed in Polish culture, while
their connection with Rus' as such was at that time almost exclusively
a territorial matter. A somewhat rare example of dual identity within
the group is the Sapieha family, which was a dynastic line Polonized
over many generations, yet with a good degree of understanding for
Ruthenian aspirations. On the cusp of the constitutional epoch, Adam
Sapieha, the son of Leon Sapieha—who had been ready to make concessions to Ruthenians during the Revolutions of 1848 and was later
the Galician Diet marshal—argued that representatives of Polish magnate families of Ruthenian provenance should adopt the Greek Catholic
rite, and subsequently should take over the leadership of Eastern Galicia as the Ruthenian upper stratum, which would allow them to control the burgeoning Ruthenian national movement.[53] In a letter to his
uncle Prince Adam Czartoryski, Adam Sapieha expounds on the need
for a least a dozen magnates to convert with Rome's blessing to the
Greek Catholic rite, with this allowing the "Ruthenian dreamers" and
the whole Ruthenian nation to come to an accord with Poland. He emphasized that if even nine willing men could be found then he himself
would change his denomination, to which Czartoryski, who himself
was broadly inclined towards the idea of gaining the cooperation of the
inhabitants of the Ruthenian-Ukrainian lands, responded advising his
relative against changing his religious denomination for merely political aims. As an alternative, Czartoryski suggested supporting the conservative element amongst the Ruthenians and taking care of the Uniate
Church, something that Sapieha attempted to do in subsequent years.

---

[52] Bogdan Gancarz, *My, szlachta ukraińska. Zarys życia i działalności Wacława Lipińskiego 1882–1914* (Cracow, 2006).

[53] Stefan Kieniewicz addressed this theme in researching Sapieha's correspondence with Adam Czartoryski, housed at the Czartoryski Library in Cracow. See Stefan Kieniewicz, *Adam Sapieha 1828–1903* (Warsaw, 1993), pp. 353–55; Cf. also: Jan Kozik, *The Ukrainian National Movement in Galicia 1815-1849*, ed. and introd. Lawrence D. Orton, trans. Andrew Gorski and Lawrence D. Orton (Edmonton, 1986), p. 129.

One might say that the plans of Czartoryski and Sapieha were at a later stage of realization, although they were not to bring about the expected result. For the Cracow conservatives did indeed support the Ruthenian movement, while the Greek Catholic metropolitan of Lviv was to be selected from one of the most eminent noble families, the Szeptyckis, yet the Ruthenians were in no way about to turn back from their now chosen route which would lead to a separation from Polishness.

The Gentry

In addition to the powerful landowning dynasties, it is necessary to examine the impoverished descendants of the old gentry class, particularly in relation to the political, administrative, and economic changes that occurred at the beginning of the period of partitions. There is no need to enumerate the various reasons that resulted in the declassing of huge numbers amongst the gentry in Galicia, but it is worth pointing out the requirement to prove their nobility before the heraldist. An inability to demonstrate lineage resulted, particularly in the case of the impoverished gentry, in exclusion from this estate. Magdalena Kwiecińska noted in her research the significance of the problem of identity for Ruthenians of Polish nationality recruited from this very social stratum.[54] The reorganization of the gentry estate conducted by the Austrian authorities as well as the political demands articulated by Ruthenians at that time, which undermined the notion of the old Poland as represented by the Polish elite and the landed nobles, led to ideological dilemmas. In earlier times, the gentry had expressed their political allegiance to the Polish nation as a result of their inherited class responsibilities, and subsequently in the adherence to this very tradition which was handed down from generation to generation. After 1848 the matter of estate and class became secondary in importance to the self-designation which had to be expressed in the face of Polish--Ruthenian political rivalry. Kwiecińska writes in the context of *gente Rutheni, natione Poloni*:

> (…) it was the *natione Poloni*, constituting allegiance to a political-administrative community, that proved to be inadequate to a situation of nations arising and awakening in consciousness.[55]

Those representatives of the gentry of Ruthenian provenance had three options. Firstly, as an answer to their own career aspirations

---

[54] Cf. Magdalena Kwiecińska, "Drobna szlachta w Galicji – między polskim a ukraińskim ruchem narodowym," *Sprawy Narodowościowe. Seria Nowa* 34 (2009), pp. 83–97.
[55] Ibid., p. 92.

they could join the ranks of the newly formed social group, the intelligentsia, which was for the most part Polish. Within its ranks national awareness blossomed, and members were able to gain entrance into the Polish current of political and cultural life. The second possibility was to maintain an ambivalent stance. The third solution was the process of becoming Ruthenian, undertaken with ease for those living in the countryside among a predominantly Ruthenian peasant population. While education favoured the first option, the other two options were likewise bolstered by provincial abodes and a physical distancing from Polish cultural institutions, including the Roman Catholic Church. It is worth adding that according to certain researchers the petty gentry of Galicia in no way needed to undergo a process of Ruthenization, for they already were in their ethnic character Ruthenian, and therein exhibited no signs of Polishness. The Ukrainian historian Liubov Slyvka, in her debate with some Polish scholars, argued that the affiliation of the Ruthenian petty gentry majority to the Greek Catholic Church and the fact that they spoke Ruthenian at home allowed them to be included within the Ukrainian nation.[56] She also demonstrated that the influence of the Greek Catholic Church was in no way strong enough that it could decisively bring about the Ruthenization of this social class over the course of a single century, consequently suggesting that they must have been Ruthenian even earlier. According to such an interpretation the Ruthenian gentry in Eastern Galicia was never *natione Poloni*. For this reason alone the thesis is at the very least disputable, for it was from this very stratum that numerous members of the Polish intelligentsia came. Furthermore, one cannot underestimate the impact of the Greek Catholic Church on their parishioners, peasants and petty gentry alike. The priest fulfilled not merely a spiritual role but also often involved himself in political and national matters. Therefore, in those places of gentry residence where there was no Roman Catholic church or where it was at a significant distance away, it was easy for not only the Greek Catholic gentry to adopt a Ruthenian national consciousness, but also for the Roman Catholics to abandon their rite and gradually undergo a process of de-Polonization.

Magdalena Kwiecińska gives an example of the Kulczycki [Kulchytsky] family which had moved to the Sambir district from Western Galicia. Contact with the local Ruthenians resulted in their rejection of the

---

[56] Liubov Slyvka, *Halyts′ka dribna shliakhta v Avstro-Uhorshchyni (1772–1914 rr.)* (Ivano-Frankivsk, 2009), pp. 127–31. She has, however, also emphasized that this gentry group also spoke Polish, though this usage was reserved for certain situations requiring a more prestigious language, chiefly in urban settings. Also they peppered their Ruthenian with many Polonized forms and Latinisms in order to emphasize their higher social status in their rural dealings with the non-gentry populace (cf. ibid., p. 130).

Roman Catholic Church, aided by the fact that in Kulchytsi there was no Roman Catholic church but there were four Greek Catholic temples. This, in turn, led to a gradual process of de-Polonization.[57] Yaroslav Hrytsak has also written about the Kulchytsky/Kulczycki family, although not necessarily about the same members, and has analyzed the fate of the descendants of Ivan Franko on the distaff side. He has managed to establish that a part of this declassed family assimilated with their Ruthenian surroundings, while the rest identified with the tradition of the former Poland to such a degree that they took part in Polish national uprisings, the best evidence of which is the death of Ivan Franko's uncle, who died fighting in the January Uprising of 1863. In turn another relative of Franko, a certain Aunt Koshytska [Koszycka], was an example of ambivalence; she attended services of both rites, sang Polish and Ruthenian songs, but when she argued with her husband she chose Polish as the language of dispute.[58]

We can see the various routes taken by the petty gentry in Eastern Galicia. A large number renounced their Polishness within the new social reality and forgot about their bonds with Poland as such, yet there were those who remained true to their former homeland or at least shunned the Ruthenian national movement.

The question of the petty gentry and their relationship with identity was fundamental, and one that continued to arouse interest in the interwar period. Władysław Pulnarowicz wrote about the gentry of the Turka district in 1929:

> For here the so-called "clog gentry" live in sizeable numbers, impoverished, living predominantly in a close knit mass. Although admittedly being of the Greek Catholic rite and speaking Ruthenian, as a result of the Polish family traditions and their flaunting of their noble descent to which they made constant reference, they were not considered Ruthenians.[59]

The author estimated their number to be one hundred thousand. He wrote that they lived in the administrative divisions of Turka, Staryi Sambir, Sambir, Sokal, Stryi, Dolyna, and Zhydachiv, among others.

> The gentry were simply the collators in their local village parishes with the clergy in many respects being dependent on them; hence the fre-

---

[57] Magdalena Kwiecińska, "Poczucie tożsamości stanowej i narodowej rodu Kulczyckich z Kulczyc koło Sambora, na Ukrainie Zachodniej," *Literatura Ludowa* no. 4–5 (2004): pp. 109–10.

[58] Yaroslav Hrytsak, *Iwan Franko and His Community*, trans. Marta Olynyk (Edmonton–Toronto, 2018), p. 33.

[59] Władysław Pulnarowicz, *U źródeł Sanu, Stryja i Dniestru. Historia powiatu turczańskiego* (Turka, 1929), p. 133.

quent wrangles, feuds, and disagreement with the priests, as the gentry threatened under any pretext to convert to Roman Catholicism. Although they were devout observers of the Greek Catholic rite, there were always many converters to the Latin Church in their families. They held Roman Catholicism in fond regard and in no way felt out of place in a [Roman] Catholic church; quite the opposite, they willingly took part in Roman Catholic ceremonies.[60]

In reality many representatives of this group did not have their concept of national affiliation firmly worked out. On the one hand they belonged to the gentry and preserved this tradition, while on the other, they differed little from the Ruthenian peasantry among which they lived. They spoke the same language (Ruthenian), they met up at the local Greek Catholic church, and they shared the same daily problems. They even lived in houses more closely resembling country cottages than noble residences.[61] Consequently, their social and economic situation meant that they very easily could adopt Ukrainian nationality, and many of them did.

Magdalena Kwiecińska describes the example of the Association of the Ruthenian Gentry in Galicia which, set up a branch in Sambir at the beginning of the twentieth century. The aim was to attract those of Ruthenian provenance and of the Greek Catholic rite. The mission of this association was to organize of social life in the form of meetings, presentations, and concerts; provide grants for students of gentry origin; and provide support and further education for the peasantry. They wanted to maintain their position as a privileged group, while simultaneously looked to certain Ukrainian politicians as their defenders. The Polish nationalist press even feared that the association wanted to Ukrainianize fifty thousand members of *gente Rutheni.*[62] An internal rivalry operating within the Ruthenian camp between the Rusophiles and the Ukrainian national activists should be noted at this point. Andriy Zayarnyuk, in his monograph on the peasant class in Galicia, has shown that the latter were successful in their "nationalizing" of the Ruthenian gentry in the Sambir region. A telling example could be the fact that in the elections to Galician Diet of 1912 only a single nobleman in the Sambir electoral district voted for a Polish candidate. The Ukrainian project, which in the place of class divisions proposed a new identity formula—one not dependent on social strata but on the question of nationality— would become far more attractive for this group, to such a degree that the gentry would not lose its affiliation to Ukrainianness

---

[60] Ibid., 134.
[61] Slyvka, *Halyts'ka dribna shliakhta,* pp. 84–85.
[62] Kwiecińska, "Drobna szlachta," pp. 94–95.

even during the period of the Second Polish Republic.[63] Here Zayarnyuk advances an hypothesis that suggests several factors which might have resulted in the defeat of the Polish option among this social group: the impact of the Greek Catholic clergy who were Ruthenian patriots; the frailty of Polish organizations in the region; and the significance of the Ruthenian petty gentry for the Ukrainian national narrative, which was of far more significance than it was in the Polish case.[64]

The example of the Sambir Ruthenian gentry undoubtedly shows the broader tendency of Ruthenianzation taking place in Eastern Galicia among representatives of the declassed Ruthenian gentry. In the nineteenth century it became Ruthenianized in spite of its gentry heritage in a similar way as the Polish peasantry became assimilated, largely a result of the numerical domination of the Ruthenian peasant majority. This was an atypical situation given the previous state of affairs where the gentry as a rule identified themselves as being Polish, while the peasants identified themselves as Ruthenian. A policy of re-Polonization was therefore undertaken in the interwar period—not without opposition on the Ukrainian side—among the Ruthenized petty gentry of Eastern Galicia (through The Union of the Farming Gentry [*Związek Szlachty Zagrodowej*]).[65] The journal *Greko-Katolik* raised the alarm in 1935 that "our petty gentry of the Greek Catholic rite has been completely persuaded to Polonize, to praise the Polish coat-of-arms and to be faithful to everything Polish.'[66] The means of achieving this Polonization was by conversion to Roman Catholicism.[67] However, the broad range of undertakings launched on the part of the Polish authorities did not bring about the desired effects.[68]

---

[63] Andriy Zayarnyuk, *Framing the Ukrainian Peasantry in Habsburg Galicia, 1846–1914* (Edmonton–Toronto, 2013), pp. 372–73.

[64] Andriy Zayarnyuk, "The Greek Catholic Rustic Gentry and the Ukrainian National Movement in Habsburg-Ruled Galicia," *Journal of Ukrainian Studies* 35–36 (2010–11), p. 102.

[65] Jan Piotr Jarosz, "Akcja repolonizacyjna na terytoriach południowo-wschodnich Rzeczypospolitej w latach 1935–1939," in *Polacy i Ukraińcy dawniej i dziś*, ed. Bogumił Grott (Cracow, 2002), pp. 61–66.

[66] "Polska szlachta chodaczkowa," *Greko-Katolik* 3, no. 4 (Apr. 1935), p. 7.

[67] The Latinization was encouraged, among others, by the dissemination of the journal *Pobudka*. Anna Krochmal, "Stosunki międzywyznaniowe i międzyobrządkowe w parafiach greckokatolickiej diecezji przemyskiej w latach 1918–1939," in *Polska–Ukraina*, vol. 3: *Studia z dziejów greckokatolickiej diecezji przemyskiej*, ed. Stanisław Stępień (Przemyśl, 1996), p. 223.

[68] Maciej Krotofil, "Ukraińcy w Wojsku Polskim w okresie międzywojennym," in *Mniejszości narodowe i wyznaniowe w siłach zbrojnych Drugiej Rzeczypospolitej 1918–1939. Zbiór studiów*, eds. Zbigniew Karpus and Waldemar Rezmer (Toruń, 2001), p. 141.

The Intelligentsia

We shall move to examine the individuals who were set on gaining an education and finding their place among the elite circles of the day—namely, the intelligentsia. This social estate included civil servants, administrators and clerks (state and private), teachers, lawyers, doctors, architects, academics, artists, literary figures, as well as the clergy, with their ranks later being expanded by bankers and industrialists.[69] This was a class that *de facto* only came into being during the mid-nineteenth century. It is worth remembering that this new socio-professional circle was fuelled first and foremost by people with petty gentry or bourgeois roots, and only later by an input from the peasantry.

According to estimations made by Mieczysław Adamczyk, at the end of the eighteenth century those members of the intelligentsia of gentry provenance still noticeably dominated when compared to those of plebeian origins. With time these proportions were to change, but over the territory of Eastern Galicia (with the exception of the district of Lviv) the intelligentsia would continue to be recruited from among the propertied classes.[70] The gentry intelligentsia had a hereditary affiliation to Polishness within the framework of the gentry class, but with time this was also to become a choice made on the basis of national considerations. In the case of the plebeian intelligentsia we are dealing exclusively with an independent choice of nationality, at times inspired by external factors.

The events in Galicia of the 1830s and 1840s ushered in a period where the intelligentsia could accept responsibilities of a political nature. Even if it did not hold power, education allowed its members to enter into the world of ideas and their creative development. Earlier members of this social stratum had had significant trouble relating to patriotic or nationalistic ideology, a problem which persisted, although later it diminished in scale. Andrzej A. Zięba writes:

> The *gente Rutheni* intelligentsia, as a social grouping in the process of its formation, was devoid of its own traditions (…). Lacking any solid historical foundations which could have imposed the group's past upon national history, it would oscillate far over to the Polish side, then to the Russian, declaring, often alternating in its affiliation to these nations and their historical traditions.[71]

---

[69] Jadwiga Hoff, "Inteligencja galicyjska – niepokorna czy lojalna?," *Rocznik Przemyski* 46, no. 4: *Historia* (2010), pp. 51–52.

[70] Adamczyk, *Edukacja a awans*, p. 109.

[71] Zięba, "Gente Rutheni," p. 73.

Here one must examine Platon Kostecki's reflections which he voiced in an unpublished essay entitled "On the Ruthenian Question" [W sprawie ruskiej]. The text was probably written in the summer of 1863 and is an interesting analysis of the state of awareness among the Ruthenian population in Galicia with differentiation by the various social divisions. The author is of the view that the Ruthenian intelligentsia comprises five groups: the clergy, seminarians at the Greek Catholic seminaries in Przemyśl and Lviv, professors/teachers, students and secondary school pupils, and "several secular individuals living by their own means." According to Kostecki:

> All of these branches of the intelligentsia are a) for Poland, b) for Slavdom, or c) indifferent. However, all have one thing in common: they do not dream, at least in the near future, about *Rus' as an independent self-sufficient entity*. All of them, with very few exceptions, are similar in that they do not hold decisive convictions and do not have self-sacrificial attitudes. They are directed by whoever has in his hands the authority over their fate and the fate of their families.[72]

Jadwiga Hoff gives an interesting example reflecting the problem of self-identification. She cites the figure of a lawyer from Drohobych, [Czubaty], who "to the end of his life was not able to solve the question as to whether he was a Pole or a Ruthenian for the term Ukrainian had as yet not reached him. 'It seems that I am first a Drohobychan [resident of Drohobych – A. Ś.]', he would often repeat."[73]

It was the storm of ensuing political events that would force individuals from this stratum to deliberate over their national identity. The widespread emergence of national slogans did not only influence how the individuals decided to view their nationality, regardless of their ethnic origins, but also inspired them to act in accordance with their choice. Kostecki wrote that almost all those representing liberal professions supported Poland, this being also the case for clerks and civil servants, while in turn the clergy were already more inclined towards the Russophile option, although in their majority, they displayed indifference.[74]

Let us examine some well-known names among the Galician intelligentsia who, despite their Ruthenian origins, finally aligned themselves with the Polish side. These are chiefly representatives of liberal profes-

---

[72] Platon Kostecki, "W sprawie ruskiej," [Lviv, 1863], LNNBU, fond 5: *Zbirka rukopysiv, avtohrafiv, hramot i dyplomiv biblioteky Natsional'noho zakladu im. Ossolins'kykh u m. Lvovi*, op. 1: Rukopysy, spr. 3063/II, p. 1–1v; Adam Świątek, "*W sprawie ruskiej* Platona Kosteckiego," *Galicja. Studia i materiały* 3 (2017), p. 368.

[73] Hoff, "Inteligencja galicyjska," p. 58.

[74] LNNBU, fond 5, op. 1, spr. 3063/II, p. 1–2; Świątek, "*W sprawie ruskiej*," pp. 368–70.

sions. Besides Platon Kostecki, a journalist, publicist as well as poet, one
should mention another literary figure
of Ruthenian-Armenian background:
Jan Zachariasiewicz [Ivan Zakhar-
iasevych], the author of numerous immensely popular novellas which often
revealed the specifics of Ruthenian-
Polish relations in Galicia. Also worthy
of mention is Volodymyr Stebelsky, originally a Ruthenian poet who in the end
became a thoroughly Polish literary
figure, signing his poems and novellas

2. *Emil Hołowkiewicz*

"Włodzimierz Stebelski";[75] the deputies to the Galician Diet: the Marshal
of the Diet [National Speaker] and mayor of Cracow, Mikołaj Zyblikiewicz, the teachers Euzebiusz Czerkawski and Zygmunt Sawczyński,
and the lawyer Antoni Dąbczański, who was particularly active during the period of the 1848 Revolutions.[76] The route to Polishness often
meandered thorough a personal involvement in political events linked
to conscious decisions and choices, an example of which can be found
in the figures of Samuel Leligdowicz [Samiilo Leligdovych]—a provincial translator who fought in the November Uprising of 1830 and was
later actively involved in the events of the Revolutions of 1848[77]— and
the economic activist and journalist Teofil Merunowicz [Merunovych],
who had been an insurgent in the January Uprising of 1863. It was not
necessary to take up arms to demonstrate one's affinity for Polishness,
however. Many notable individuals who modestly operated in ordinary day-to-day life chose a Polish identity. Here one might mention
Emil Hołowkiewicz [Holovkevych], a forester, who as a secondary
school pupil in Sambir was involved in open confrontation with teachers who implemented the policy of Germanization.[78] Father Tomasz
Barewicz [Toma Barevych], who years later would take up the position
of principal in this very same school, was a former Galician Diet deputy, an adherent of cooperation between Ruthenians and Poles, and an
opponent of the so-called Old Ruthenians or representatives of "the

---

[75] Cf. Hrytsak, *Ivan Franko*, pp. 99–100. For Stebelsky's biography, see Małgorzata Kamela, Andrzej A. Zięba, "Stebelski Włodzimierz," in *PSB*, vol. 43 (Warsaw–Cracow, 2004–5),
pp. 40–45.
[76] Aleksander Czołowski, "Dąbczański Antoni," in *PSB*, vol. 4 (Cracow, 1938), pp. 466–67.
[77] Zbigniew Fras, *Demokraci w życiu politycznym Galicji w latach 1848–1873* (Wrocław,
1997), p. 68.
[78] Józef Broda, "Hołowkiewicz Emil," in *PSB*, vol. 9 (Wrocław–Cracow–Warsaw, 1960–
61), pp. 599–600.

Saint George party" [the party of Saint George Cathedral in Lviv – A. Ś.].[79] The decision to choose Polishness did not always have an ideological background, but was often a subconscious choice. A classic example is the case of the administrator Józef Doboszyński [Iosyf Doboshynsky], whose memoirs speak volumes about society in Galicia during this time.[80]

For considerable periods of the nineteenth century, Ruthenians did not have at their disposal anything of sufficient cultural interest that could attract the intelligentsia of Ruthenian provenance. Paramount was the development of the Ruthenian language itself. The Ruthe-

3. *Emilian Czyrniański*

nian language, lexically inferior to Polish and even more so to German at this stage in its development, acted as a barrier to involvement in an array of academic disciplines. This largely explains why Ruthenians who wanted to pursue an academic career were forced to become a part of Polish academic life, and therefore often underwent the process of Polonization. Prominent Ruthenians who entered the world of Polish science and scholarship included Michał Borysiekiewicz [Mykhailo Borysykevych] of Bilobozhnytsia, a renowned ophthalmologist and professor at Graz;[81] Józef Czerlunczakiewicz [Iosyf Cherlunchakevych], a lecturer in theology and church law at Lviv University and the Jagiellonian University;[82] and Emilian Czyrniański, a former member of the Ruthenian Sobor and a professor in chemistry at the Jagiellonian University, a doctor *honoris causa* and rector of the same university, and member of the Polish Academy of Learning in Cracow. Czyrniański educated the renowned chemists Karol Krzyżanowski and Karol Olszewski.[83] He was well known for his fierce resistance against the continuous Germanization of the Jagiellonian University, for which he almost

---

[79] For more on this subject see: Władysław Cichocki, *Sambor przed pół wiekiem. Ku upamiętnieniu 40-ej rocznicy matury zdawanej w samborskiem gimnazjum w czerwcu 1884 roku* (Cracow, 1925), pp. 24–26.

[80] Józef Doboszyński, "Pamiętnik," in *Pamiętniki urzędników galicyjskich*, eds. Irena Homola and Bolesław Łopuszański (Cracow, 1978).

[81] Adam Bednarski, "Borysiekiewicz Michał," in *PSB*, vol. 2 (Cracow, 1936), p. 357.

[82] Karol Lewicki, "Czerlunczakiewicz Józef," in *PSB*, vol. 4, p. 336.

[83] Olszewski was the first in the world to liquefy oxygen, nitrogen, and carbon dioxide from the atmosphere in a stable state.

lost his job.[84] A pupil of Czyrniański's who was also *gente Ruthenus, natione Polonus*, Walery Jaworski [Valerii Iavorsky], the son of a Greek Catholic priest, made a career as a gastroenterologist. Referred to as the father of Polish gastroenterology, he was renowned for being the first to employ X-rays in internal medical clinical practice, and for being the founder of the Museum of Medicine in Cracow.[85] Finally, one should also mention Anatol Lewicki [Anatol Levytsky], a teacher and historian who lectured at the Jagiellonian University.[86]

4. *Walery Jaworski*

Besides the influx of lecturers, the boom in Galician education owed a great deal to the teaching institutions in which *gente Rutheni, natione Poloni* were particularly active. The aforementioned Euzebiusz Czerkawski and Zygmunt Sawczyński, activists at the National School Council, played a significant role in the development of the Galician school system at the time of Poland's autonomy. It must be noted that this system, though guaranteeing the right to instruction in Ruthenian at the primary level, resulted in the fact that the number of Ruthenian secondary schools was noticeably lower than that of Polish secondary schools. In universities the language of instruction was an even more vital issue, as the universities in Lviv and Cracow were Polonized (though limited instruction in Ruthenian was offered in Lviv). Not only was this a cause of conflict between Ruthenian and Polish deputies at the Galician Diet, but it was also the reason why Ruthenian youth, upon commencing university education, were obliged, at least in theory, to gravitate towards an increasingly Polish intellectual world. An important role in influencing students was played by their teachers and school principals. It is easy to find within the teaching institutions examples of those who held an outlook representative of *gente Rutheni, natione Poloni*. Such individuals include Julian Dolnicki [Iuliian Dolnytsky],

---

[84] Karol Estreicher, "Czyrniański Emilian," in *PSB*, vol. 4, pp. 378–79; Helena Duć-Fajfer, "Udział Łemków w życiu religijnym, umysłowym, kulturalno-społecznym Galicji w 2. połowie XIX i na początku XX wieku," in *Poprzez stulecia. Księga pamiątkowa ofiarowana Profesorowi Antoniemu Podrazie w 80. rocznicę Jego urodzin*, ed. Danuta Czerska (Cracow, 2000), p. 206.

[85] Mieczysław Skulimowski, "Jaworski Walery," in *PSB*, vol. 11 (Wrocław–Warsaw–Cracow, 1964–65), pp. 113–15; Duć-Fajfer, "Udział Łemków," p. 207.

[86] Józef Mitkowski, "Lewicki Anatol," in *PSB*, vol. 17 (Wrocław–Warsaw–Cracow–Gdańsk, 1972), pp. 224–25.

a secondary school teacher in Zolochiv and Lviv, and principal at the gymnasium in Stryi, who co-founded the journal *Muzeum*;[87] Piotr Hrabyk [Petro Hrabyk], a doctor of philosophy and a historian, who taught at schools in Bibrka, Lviv, Cracow, and Przemyśl, founded a girls' secondary school in Przemyśl and joined the Przemyśl Friends of Science Society;[88] Mikołaj Zyblikiewicz, a teacher at the Tarnów secondary school; and Zygmunt Sawczyński, a teacher at schools in Cracow and Lviv. There are, however, individuals who entered the annals of Galician education through their dedicated work for the cause of interethnic reconciliation and equality. These were teachers at local village and secondary schools who on a daily basis worked for Ruthenian-Polish conciliation and their stories still need to be told by historians. Their funerals would often turn into demonstrations of harmonious relations within what were heavily ethnically mixed environments, and were reported on by the press of the day.[89]

The Greek Catholic Clergy

At the turn of the nineteenth century, a process of Polonization similar to that of the gentry occurred within the Uniate clergy in terms of language and other aspects. The Ukrainian researcher Nadiia Stokolos wrote that "up until the mid-nineteenth century a significant part of the Greek Catholic clergy in Galicia, brought up within Polish cultural norms and on the basis of Polish political ideas, considered no national difference to exist between Poles and Ukrainians"; additionally, the process of Polonization was supported by the upper echelons of the Church hierarchy.[90] This was a result of the fact that the higher levels of the Uniate Church came from the gentry, which had already been Polonized. Polonized Uniate clergy held key positions in the Church right up until the end of the nineteenth century, an example of which was the election in 1899 of Julian Kuiłowski [Iuliian Kuilovsky-Sas],

---

[87] Antoni Knot, "Dolnicki Julian," in *PSB*, vol. 4, p. 288.

[88] Stefan Uhma, "Hrabyk Piotr," in *PSB*, vol. 10 (Wrocław–Warsaw–Cracow, 1962–64), p. 50.

[89] Adam Świątek, "Problem patriotycznego wychowania ludu na łamach lwowskiej „Szkoły" w czasach autonomii galicyjskiej," in *Czasopiśmiennictwo XIX i początków XX wieku jako źródło do historii edukacji*, eds. Iwonna Michalska and Grzegorz Michalski (Łódź, 2010), pp. 180–81 as well as Adam Świątek, "'Poległ wśród boju nauczycielskiego'. Wspomnienia pośmiertne na łamach czasopisma 'Szkoła' jako źródło do historii nauczycielstwa galicyjskiego," in *Addenda do dziejów oświaty. Z badań nad prasą XIX i początków XX wieku*, eds. Iwonna Michalska and Grzegorz Michalski (Łódź, 2013), pp. 122–23.

[90] Nadiia Stokolos, *Konfesiino-etnichni transformatsii v Ukraïni (XIX – persha polovyna XX st.)* (Rivne, 2003), p. 104.

a participant in the Revolutions of 1848 and then an émigré connected with the Hôtel Lambert camp in Paris, for the position of Lviv Greek Catholic metropolitan.[91] One can find many Ruthenian clergymen involved in Polish matters across the entirety of Galicia during the times of the partitions. Worthy of mention is the Basilian Leon Demkowicz [Demkovych] of Volhynia, who was an engaged activist in the National Education Commission and collaborated with Tadeusz Czacki. During the Napoleonic Wars he moved to Cracow, where he took over the local Greek Catholic par-

5. Metropolitan Julian Kuiłowski

ish.[92] The Catholic Church of St. Norbert was for a long time a point of assembly for clergy of a pro-Polish disposition as well as sometimes Ruthenians of Polish nationality.[93] For the years 1834–1854 the parish priest was Father Leon Laurysiewicz [Lavrysevych] from the Lublin area, who was highly unlikely to support the Ruthenian national movement, later becoming a professor at the Jagiellonian University, a dean of the Theology Faculty, and eventually rector. At the time of the January Uprising of 1863, Leon's brother, Father Stefan Laurysiewicz [Lavrysevych], was the parish priest there and he become well-known for his organization of boisterous celebrations in 1861 to commemorate the Union of Horodło in Congress Poland.[94] In the period from 1867 to 1883 the position of parish priest was held there by another *gente Ruthenus, natione Polonus* Father Józef Czerlunczakiewicz.

Many Greek Catholic priests actively involved themselves in Polish social and political undertakings even during the uprisings. Here, first and foremost, attention should be paid to the conspirators of the 1830s and 1840s. Notable among the many seminary graduates in Lviv and Przemyśl was Romuald Krzyżanowski [Kryzhanivsky], who actively supported the insurgent unit of Józef Zaliwski, and later the Association of the Polish People [*Stowarzyszenie Ludu*

---

[91] Adamczyk, *Edukacja a awans*, pp. 108–9.

[92] Jozafat Skruteń, "Demkowicz Leon," in *PSB*, vol. 4, pp. 105–6.

[93] Adam Świątek, "Rusini, Ukraińcy czy Polacy? Przyczynek do badań nad problematyką narodowości studentów obrządku greckokatolickiego studiujących na Uniwersytecie Jagiellońskim w latach 1850/1851–1917/1918," in *Amico, socio et viro docto. Księga ku czci profesora Andrzeja Kazimierza Banacha*, eds. Tomasz Pudłocki and Krzysztof Stopka (Cracow, 2015), pp. 353–54.

[94] Kazimierz Gregorowicz, *Zarys główniejszych wypadków w województwie lubelskim w r. 1861*, comp. Wiesław Śladkowski (Lublin, 1984), pp. 97–98.

Polskiego] and Young Sarmatia [*Młoda Sarmacja*]. Following his arrest and deportation to Spilberk Castle—a prison for Austrian "state prisoners"—the Greek Catholic Church hierarchy revoked his right to practice as a priest. In 1848 he joined the revolutionary upheaval as a member of the Ruthenian Sobor.[95] Father Onufry Krynicki, possibly the most politically active Uniate priest of Polish nationality, was to act in a similar fashion. Hailing from the Lemko region, he was a prefect at the Lviv seminary, later the rector of Lviv University, and during the Revolutions of 1848 one of the most engaged activists on the Ruthenian Sobor. This in no way stopped him from twice more becoming rector of his Lviv *alma mater* and thrice becoming a deputy to the imperial court.[96]

With time the number of Uniate clergymen of Polish nationality fell. From the mid-nineteenth century onwards the clergy estate drew its candidature from the Ruthenian intelligentsia, from both those with a national populist as well as a Russophile orientation. Consequently, in the second half of the nineteenth century Greek Catholic clergymen from Eastern Galicia who considered themselves to be Polish were becoming increasingly rare. Kostecki had already written in 1863 that "Priests who are genuinely for Poland are a very small part, in my view barely a twentieth; the rest dream of pan-Slavism, or like the overall majority are simply indifferent."[97] The latter were, according to Kostecki, loyalists to the Habsburg monarchy for purely pragmatic reasons. Also of significance was the age of a priest and the time period in which he was ordained. Kostecki noted:

> There are more priests of an older age who support Poland than is the case with the young, that is those ordained after 1848 and in particular after 1860. For there is at least a greater sense of political awareness among them, less indifference so that propaganda would be slower to permeate than before.[98]

Nonetheless the old priests were still alive; those of the "old school"—as they are usually referred to in Polish sources —who were raised within Polish culture and were not well orientated in the new national trends that were becoming popular among the younger clergy. In order to illustrate this phenomenon, we shall quote an interesting account by Franciszk Rawita-Gawroński on the subject of Father Kobłosz [Koblosh], the parish priest in Tarnawa, where the Polish writer had a residence:

---

[95] Bolesław Łopuszański, "Krzyżanowski Romuald," in *PSB*, vol. 15, pp. 615–16.
[96] Tyrowicz, "Krynicki Onufry," p. 463; Duć-Fajfer, "Udział Łemków," p. 205.
[97] LNNBU, fond 5, op. 1, spr. 3063/II, p. 1v; Świątek, „*W sprawie ruskiej*," p. 369.
[98] Ibid.

Kobłosz, the priest, was an old and decent fellow. Already at the time [1896 – A.Ś.] he had turned eighty. He was a Uniate priest of the old school. At home he spoke Polish, he prayed in Polish, but under pressure from the younger clergy of the surrounding area he had subscribed to the magazine *Halychanyn* [Galician], not really knowing what was Ukrainian and what was pro-Muscovite. Ukrainianism had only just been born. He was a man of coarse habits who led an extremely modest life, and was good and gentle as a man. And so these old men lived out their days in village backwaters, dividing their time between the farmstead and the church, but in accord and harmony with Poles.[99]

Until the end of the nineteenth century there existed a fraternal union between the Latin and Greek Churches despite the clear and increasingly open Polish-Ukrainian political conflict, which was slowly manifesting itself within the Church as well. The Przemyśl bishop Ivan Stupnytsky [Jan Stupnicki], a zealous Polonophile actively engaged in combating the influence of Orthodoxy on the Greek Catholic Church, was not liked by the Ruthenians. The situation was similar for Julian Kuiłowski, who became the Greek Catholic metropolitan of Lviv from 1899–1900. Already on his first day in office a conflict emerged between him and the Ruthenians as the metropolitan had given a sermon in Polish during his installation.[100] The next metropolitan, Andrei Sheptytsky, was held in great esteem as a leader of the Galician Ruthenians. Interestingly, he also reached out to the Poles of the Greek Catholic rite. In 1904 he wrote a pastoral letter to Poles of the Uniate denomination.[101] In the introduction to the letter the metropolitan explained:

---

[99] Franciszek Rawita-Gawroński, *Ludzie i czasy mego wieku. Wspomnienia, wypadki, zapiski (1892–1914)*, comp. Eugeniusz Koko (Gdańsk, 2012), pp. 67–68.

[100] Ibid., p. 219.

[101] „List pasterski metropolity halickiego, arcybiskupa lwowskiego Andrzeja Szeptyckiego do Polaków-grekokatolików," 16 May 1904, Tsentral'nyi derzhavnyi istorychnyi arkhiv Ukraïny u Lvovi (subsequently: TsDIAU), fond 358: Sheptyts'kyi Andrei, op. 2, spr. 5: Pastyrs'ki poslannia Sheptyts'koho do dukhovenstva i narodu, pp. 37–44. The letter itself was published in: Andrzej Szeptycki, *Pisma wybrane*, comp. Maria H. Szeptycka, Marek Skórka (Cracow, 2000), pp. 92–107. Analyses have been undertaken several times in the relevant subject literature. Cf. Felicja Wysocka, "List pasterski arcybiskupa Andrzeja Szeptyckiego do Polaków obrządku greckokatolickiego z roku 1904," in *Unia brzeska – geneza, dzieje i konsekwencje w kulturze narodów słowiańskich*, eds. Ryszard Łużny, Franciszek Ziejka and Andrzej Kępiński (Cracow, 1994), pp. 139–50; Włodzimierz Osadczy, "Dialog arcybiskupów. Andrzej Szeptycki i Józef Teodorowicz o stosunkach międzyobrzędowych w Galicji Wschodniej na przełomie XIX i XX wieku," *Chrześcijanin w Świecie* no. 2 (1995), pp. 95–103; Piotr Siwicki, "Miejsce nie-Ukraińców w Ukraińskim Kościele Greckokatolickim w świetle nauczania Metropolity Andrzeja Szeptyckiego (Konferencja naukowa z okazji 10-lecia ustanowienia Diecezji Wrocławsko-Gdańskiej, Wrocław [September 29, 2006])," *Kościół Unicki na Hrubieszowszczyźnie*, accessed 1 Sep. 2019, https://unici.forumoteka.pl/temat,16,metr-a-szeptycki-o-grekokatolikach-nie-ukraincach-w-ukgk.html as well as Andrzej A. Zięba, "National majority – religious minority: Polish Greek-Catholics

For a long time now, oh, our most beloved Lord Jesus Christ in his grace, I have so yearned to address you in a separate letter written in the Polish language, for in that way I can bestow on you proof of the tenderness and devotion to your salvation.[102]

In this letter he explained that no beliefs of a national character can be imposed on the faithful (in the sense of a Greek Catholic being a Ukrainian), but that he as metropolitan did not wish to be perceived as an opponent to anyone in matter of politics or nationality. He also wrote that he left Polish Greek Catholics with the "freedom to be Poles." He distanced himself from the imposition of Ruthenian patriotism and elaborated that his sole concern was that every life be a Christian life. At the same time he reminded his addressees that it was permitted for the sacraments be taken in the temples of both denominations.[103] Sheptytsky's correspondence was viewed, however, with mistrust. The Armenian archbishop of Lviv, Józef Teodorowicz, saw an agenda in the metropolitan's actions, by which it would be possible for the Uniate clergy to absorb the remaining Uniate Poles into the Ukrainian national fold.[104] This conviction came from the fact that Polish society at this time had already stopped believing in the existence of a Uniate clergy of Polish nationality that the metropolitan had written about in his letter. Teodorowicz did not believe that Sheptytsky was acting out of the good of his heart when addressing this handful of three thousand Lviv Poles of the Uniate rite who were effectively "lost in the millions."[105]

The Peasants

The final social stratum in which we can also find examples of Ruthenians of Polish nationality is the peasantry. For almost the entire period in question their identity was to be primarily ethnic and not national.[106]

As Włodzimierz Osadczy wrote, the peasantry did not distinguish national differences between Ruthenians and Poles.[107] For most of the nineteenth century it was language and chiefly faith that identified

---

in the 20th century (Toronto Seminar in Ukrainian Studies, March 9, 1989)", *Historycy.org*, accessed 1 Sep. 2019, http://www.historycy.org/historia/index.php/t6310-50.html.

[102] TsDIAU, fond 358, op. 2, spr. 5, p. 45.

[103] Cf. ibid.

[104] Osadczy, *Kościół i Cerkiew*, pp. 224–25.

[105] Osadczy, "Dialog arcybiskupów", pp. 161–63.

[106] Ryszard Radzik writes that the Polish and Ruthenian peasants possessed up until 1848 "a consciousness of ethnic difference," but not of state/national differentiation. Ryszard Radzik, "Społeczne uwarunkowania formowania się ukraińskiej świadomości narodowej w Galicji wschodniej w latach 1830–1863," *Kultura i Społeczeństwo* 25, no. 1–2 (1981), p. 299.

[107] Osadczy, *Kościół i Cerkiew*, p. 74.

them. Only a handful of those living in the countryside were conscious of distinct nationalities. The social structure of the village made for an elite comprised of only two social groupings: the gentry and the Uniate priest. In as far as the former organised the economic life of the village, so the latter fulfilled a more important role that transcended religious duties and affected every aspect of village life, for he was quite possibly the only member of the intelligentsia in the parish. It was chiefly he who acted as the moral and spiritual authority that shaped the world outlook of the Ruthenian peasant. At the same time the landowner, as a representative of another linguistic and social world, often of a different rite, was placed in a disadvantageous position the very moment any conflict emerged. The nature of social relations in the provinces has been skilfully captured by Władysław Zawadzki, who was travelling across Galicia in the mid-nineteenth century:

> (...) The influence of the priest in general and his position within his flock is most significant. The flock, although capable of engaging in dispute with the priest on many matters, still sees in him the only person of trust; and it is to him they turn for advice on all matters and disputes, whether with the manor or amongst themselves. The priest's word, although not always liked, always finds a receptive audience in such cases. The priest is the indisputable authority in the village and no important matter happens without his knowledge. This is the result of his daily contact with each and every parishioner, his knowledge of their temperament and relations, his closeness to life and custom itself. For this the local peasant considers the Ruthenian priest as someone close, as a member of his lineage and ancestry. The opposite is true in regards to the gentry: even though the gentleman was born on the same piece of land, fed with Ruthenian buckwheat, a Ruthenian through and through, he nevertheless dresses differently and appears to the peasant to be seemingly aloof and alien.[108]

The role of the Greek Catholic clergy in the shaping of not only attitudes but also the national identity of the peasants was immense. From 1848 onwards, when the Uniate clergy started to exhibit their differences in relation to the Polish stance on political matters in the capital and other large towns of Galicia, an awareness of a Ruthenian political programme gradually started to seep into the provinces, although not yet on a mass scale. Influence on the Ruthenian peasantry was first and foremost exerted by the Greek Catholic clergy and only then—and here the ground needed to be prepared—by the burgeoning secular Ruthenian (national populist) intelligentsia through the various organizations and associations of a cultural-educational nature, such as Ruska Besida Society. This gives a sense of the answer to the question of why the

---

[108] Władysław Zawadzki, *Obrazy Rusi Czerwonej* (Poznań, 1869), pp. 19–20.

gente Rutheni, natione Poloni intelligentsia did not play a significant role in the shaping of the national identity of the Ruthenian peasantry. The only representatives of this circle were the Galician conspirators of the 1830s and 1840s, such as Julian Horoszkiewicz and Kasper Cięglewicz. They directed their leaflets towards the peasants, using the peasants' own Ruthenian language to attack the old social order, which they believed was responsible for the collapse of Poland and the failure of the November Uprising of 1830. They attacked the feudal system, in which they believed the Roman Catholic Church and Greek Catholic Church were complicit. In Galicia in 1848 hundreds of leaflets addressed to Polish and Ruthenian peasants were written and printed. The last attempts were made to convince the idea of Polish-Ruthenian fraternity. Despite the political ignorance of the peasantry in the first half of the nineteenth century, any attack on the very individuals who enjoyed authority and status within local communities—the priests—was unlikely to draw many supporters to the *gente Rutheni, natione Poloni* intelligentsia from among the peasantry itself. This is not to say, however, that exceptions did not occur.

One such example is that of Jan Gudziak [Ivan Hudziak], a revolutionary peasant who was infected with the notion of Polish-Ruthenian fraternity by the conspirators of the 1830s to such a degree that he joined the Association of the Polish People.[109] Another interesting example, albeit from a later period, is of a certain "nanny," a Lemko woman, of Bogusław Longchamps de Bérier. The Polish officer was to recall her years later: "Oh nanny, you illiterate woman, oh nanny, you peasant, oh nanny, you Ruthenian, how close in childhood you were to my heart and mind and how close you remain a whole half century later!"[110] This nanny not only had a rich and patriotic past but was also an individual consciously moulded by her ideological and political surroundings. The author of the recollections states that his nanny "was an ardent opponent of Austria and especially of Austrian bureaucracy"; furthermore, he notes that she felt similarly towards the Mazurians or the Polish peasantry. What is even more interesting is that her abhorrence of those of the same social stratum had its groundings in some tragic recollections from the peasant revolt of 1846, when she recalled that "The Madzury [!] sawed the masters in half."[111] Yet these constitute the only few known examples, as the vast majority of the Ruthenian peasantry remained indifferent to political affairs. If interest was

---

[109] Marian Tyrowicz, "Gudziak Jan," in *PSB*, vol. 9, pp. 137–38.

[110] Bogusław Longchamps de Bérier, *Ochrzczony na szablach powstańczych... Wspomnienia (1884–1918)*, eds. Włodzimierz Suleja and Wojciech Wrzesiński (Wrocław–Warsaw–Cracow–Gdańsk–Łódź, 1983), p. 35.

[111] Ibid., p. 34.

shown, then they preferred to listen to the Ruthenian "fathers of the nation"—the priests.

From these observations, the question arises as to whether the phenomenon of *gente Rutheni, natione Poloni* could have enveloped the peasant class. Speaking of the 1860s, Kostecki wrote that the peasants were first and foremost highly conservative in outlook, resistant consequently to political agitation and only loyal in relation to the Austrian administration.[112] Therefore the mechanisms that had worked on the intelligentsia would have made no inroads here. An important factor in the intelligentsia's choice of Polishness had been their inclusion within cultural, literary, and social Polish circles. In the countryside, contact with these was possible in only three places: at church, in school, and possibly at some cultural-educational association gatherings. As Czesław Partacz has stated, there were far fewer Polish schools and Polish reading rooms in Eastern Galicia than the demographic statistics would suggest.[113]

But it was not only contact with the institutionalized life of the nation that was significant; the environment one lived in also exerted considerable influence. Individuals tended to adapt to the majority's traditions and customs. In as far as the majority of the Galician elite were Poles, the relations in the countryside were the complete opposite. In Eastern Galicia the Polish peasant minority, also known as Mazurians, adopted the Ruthenian language and thereby integrated themselves within the framework of a single stratum along with the Ruthenian peasants in opposition to the masters. Anna Wróbel wrote:

> Language, liturgy, and the acts of the clergy stimulated both religious and national experiences. Such support did not emanate from the Latin faith and consequently rarer were cases of a transition to the Polish side by this rural and uneducated populace.[114]

Far more often peasants of the Latin rite learned and used the Ruthenian language. Because of this, a fairly sizeable group of so-called *latynnyky* [*łacinnicy*] came into being. This is merely proof that Ruthenian folklore was far more appealing to the Polish peasantry than the incomprehensible culture of the Galician Polish elite, whether the gentry or the urban intelligentsia. This state of affairs was aptly characterized by the Polish historian of peasant movements, Franciszek Bujak, over one hundred years ago:

---

[112] LNNBU, fond 5, op. 1, spr. 3063/II, p. 1; Świątek, *W sprawie ruskiej*, p. 367.
[113] Czesław Partacz, *Od Badeniego do Potockiego. Stosunki polsko-ukraińskie w Galicji w latach 1888–1908* (Toruń, 1997), pp. 174–75. The author gives several examples. E.g., in Skalat Poles constituted 43% of the population, yet only 8% of the reading rooms were Polish.
[114] Wróbel, "Od 'Galileuszy,'" p. 186.

The Polish peasant most eagerly learnt to sing wistful *dumkas*, decorate their clothes and tools in rich Ruthenian ornamental motifs, work less, and observe the world and life in the way the surrounding and far more numerous Ruthenian people did, and [thus, he] lost his national identity.[115]

A link subsequently developed between the social and the national question. A peasant identified with the designation "Ruthenian," placed in opposition to the master who was identified as a Pole.[116] It is important to ask the question whether the affiliation to the Latin rite allows one to equate a peasant *latynnyk* with a Ruthenized Pole. The Ukrainian researcher Oleh Pavlyshyn presented the former group not as Polish peasants who had undergone Ruthenization after centuries spent on the lands of Red Rus', but as an indigenous Ruthenian peasantry—and even a part of the petty gentry and the bourgeoisie—which had changed its denomination in the past to the Latin rite.[117] In such a case, one could not speak of a national conversion, as this phenomenon was interpreted one hundred years ago.

Regardless of whether the *latynnyky* were Latinized Ruthenians or Ruthenized Poles, the fact remains that this group struggled with the question of its identity. Czesław Partacz illustrates that the adoption of Ruthenian nationality on the part of the *latynnyky* was far from straightforward. He examines how de-Polonization and simultaneous Ruthenization did not immediately represent an approval of the Ukrainian national idea, as the *latynnyky* were to remain indifferent in the question of identity.[118] The ambivalent attitude to national identity held by these circles was also highlighted by Pavlyshyn. He states that the case of such a grouping—actually one of many such types in Europe—is also proof that one cannot treat religious rite and language as the only categories determining national affiliation.[119]

The real battle for peasant identity was to begin in the last two decades of the nineteenth century, and particularly in the first decade of the twentieth. Significant to this period was the activity of Lviv (and later Cracow) Roman Catholic Bishop Jan Puzyna and the Lviv Roman Catholic archbishop Józef Bilczewski, the latter of whom instigated the growth in the network of chapels and parishes in Eastern Galicia. The

---

[115] Franciszek Bujak, *Galicya*, vol. 1: *Kraj, ludność, społeczeństwo, rolnictwo* (Lviv–Warsaw, 1908), p. 83.

[116] Ibid., p. 84.

[117] Oleh Pavlyshyn, "Dylema identychnosty, abo istoriia pro te, iak 'latynnyky' (ne) staly ukraïntsiamy/poliakamy (Halychyna, seredyna XIX–XX st)," *Ukraïna moderna* 21: *Natsionalism na skhodi Evropy. Chyslo na poshanu Romana Shporliuka* (2014), pp. 188 ff.

[118] Partacz, *Od Badeniego*, pp. 172–73.

[119] Pavlyshyn, "Dylema identychnosty," pp. 192.

agricultural strikes of 1902 and 1903, in which chiefly Ruthenian peasants took part, and the agitation on the part of Ukrainian national activists created conditions in which the *latynnyky* in Eastern Galician villages could become more aware of their distinctiveness from Ruthenians.
Polish national democrats and the Eastern Galician conservatives, the
Podolians (*Podolacy*),[120] were extremely active in their efforts to bring
this group to the Polish side. Those who did indeed cross over could
also be classified as *gente Rutheni, natione Poloni* on the basis of their
return to Polish identity, but we are not able to speak of the motives
for their choice of nationality. Worthy of similar consideration are the
choices of nationality made by the peasants belonging to the group of
Greek Catholic Poles in the Eastern Galician countryside. As Czesław
Partacz noted, they adopted Greek Catholicism as a result of the so-
called "soul stealing" that took place in the Eastern Galician countryside because of a lack of parishes, churches, and Roman Catholic clergy
before the Concord of 1863. Yet, can they be included within the group
of *gente Rutheni, natione Poloni*, when the only thing linking them to the
Ruthenian ethnos was membership in the same Church?

The real difficulty in researching the peasant consciousness, identity
changes, and national conversions lies in the limited amount of sources
available. Searching for examples of Ruthenian peasants of Polish nationality is complicated when we have at our disposal a narrow pool
of narrative sources (correspondence, memoirs, etc.) from a class that
was to remain largely illiterate until the development of rural schools
in Galicia. An enlightened Ruthenian of Polish nationality left behind
books, letters, press articles, correspondence, poetry—in broad terms,
some form of an intellectual legacy. Peasants as a rule left nothing of
that kind, except in rare cases when an ethnologist had visited a rural
area and noted down their choices and attitudes. To what extent these
sources constitute an actual description of the state of peasant consciousness and to what extent they are the creations of the authors
themselves remains an open and debatable question.

The only truly dependable sources were created by those individuals
of peasant origin who "broke out" and made a career for themselves,
particularly those who studied at the universities of Lviv and Cracow.[121]
An analysis of the nationality declaration given by Cracow students of

---

[120] Partacz, *Od Badeniego*, pp. 177–80. Cf. also Artur Górski, *Podolacy. Obóz polityczny i jego liderzy* (Warsaw, 2013), pp. 28–29.

[121] The presence of peasants at the Jagiellonian University was the subject of a monograph by Andrzej Banach. See Andrzej Kazimierz Banach, *Młodzież chłopska na Uniwersytecie Jagiellońskim w latach 1860/61–1917/18* (Cracow, 1997), pp. 125 ff. He showed that during the period of Galician autonomy as many as 142 peasants of the Greek Catholic rite
studied at the Jagiellonian University, which represented 4.2% of the entire student body.

the Greek Catholic rite for the period 1850/1851–1917/1918 shows that a full 14% of them declared their nationality to be Polish. What is more, a number of Greek Catholics actually changed their nationality declaration, sometimes several times, which illustrates a search for identity on the part of the young people in question. Almost 30% of the undecided were to finally decide on Polishness, even if they had previously marked themselves as Ruthenians. Summarizing these results, we end up with a figure of 132 Greek Catholic students who either felt Polish or were ultimately to arrive at this choice, a number which represented almost 14% of Greek Catholic youth at the Jagiellonian University. Among these Greek Catholic students the majority came from the lower social classes. These figures prove that in the process of being educated many (albeit not all) peasants' sons adopted Polish culture, regardless of provenance, and when asked about nationality stated that they were Poles. These statistics beg the question, however, as to whether we are still speaking about peasants belonging to *gente Rutheni, natione Poloni*, or if the demographic instead represents the intelligentsia.[122]

The Geographical Scope of the Phenomenon and Numbers

Gente Rutheni, natione Poloni inhabited the entirety of the eastern Polish marches region, an area where the Polish and Ruthenian ethnic groups intermingled. It covered Eastern Galicia and the Lemko region area stretching along the Beskyd [Beskid] Mountains range and driving a wedge into Western Galicia. We can chiefly find examples of those functioning within and identifying themselves with both ethno-national groups in the towns and villages of the region. The reason for this is twofold. It was predominantly a rural population who belonged to the Greek Catholic Church in the territory under discussion; the population, as a rule, nationally unconscious, although the intelligentsia, townspeople, and the Church hierarchy also constituted a demographic within this geographic area. The Latin rite was chiefly maintained by the gentry, often of Ruthenian origin, but who had assimilated long ago and undergone conversion to Roman Catholicism, and in addition by those Polish peasants, known as Mazurians, who had settled the area over the course of many centuries, as well as the majority of the townspeople.

The role of the towns in instilling a national consciousness in their inhabitants cannot be overestimated. This was chiefly the result of the ease of access to Polish literature, art, learning, and the Polish

---

[122] Świątek, "Rusini, Ukraińcy czy Polacy?", pp. 352–53.

press, which was to have a huge influence on the world view of urban societies. The countryside at that time, long denied access to the urban world of ideas, was to remain unchangingly Ruthenian. Time passed slower in the countryside and new currents, ideas, or slogans—if they were to appear at all—were viewed with suspicion. These areas lacked the intellectual activity of the towns, as well as involvement, even a passive one, in politics. In the countryside, a Ruthenian was a peasant and a Pole was a master. As was mentioned in the previous section, the rural Polish populace would sometimes willingly become Ruthenian, feeling a greater affinity with their Ruthenian neighbours than with the gentry in the manor house. The opposite process was taking place in the towns, where the Uniate townspeople and intelligentsia underwent Polonization.[123] Consequently it was largely representatives of the urban intelligentsia that strengthened the group *gente Rutheni, natione Poloni*, which explains why the Ruthenians of Polish nationality were mainly found in the towns.

It is also important to draw attention to the geographical aspect of the national awareness process during the nineteenth century. The earliest national self-designations of Ruthenians were to occur in the large towns of Eastern Galicia, particularly in Przemyśl and Lviv. In Western Galicia, where the Polish element dominated, the use of Polish on the part of the Ruthenians living there was a natural occurrence. The renowned Sembratovychs/Sembratowiczs of the Lemko region were a family that serves as an example of *gente Rutheni, natione Poloni* during the 1860s. We shall cite Kazimierz Chłędowski's interesting note about that family:

> My private tutor was the older pupil Sembratowicz, the brother of the Lviv cardinal and metropolitan-to-be. The Sembratowicz family were Ruthenians from the mountains, but at that time in Sącz we still did not differentiate the Polish nationality from the Ruthenian one. In the eastern part of Western Galicia, where there were few Ruthenians, there simply was no difference between us. Sembratowicz spoke Polish as correctly as all the rest of us, and he lived in the same close relations with us as any other school friend. And even though these Sembratowiczs—and there were three priests among them as I remember—were later to become fairly radical Ruthenians and cut off close ties with the Poles, they were not as obstinate in relation to the Poles as those Ruthenians who had been brought up under different influences, like the Lytvynovych, Pavlykiv, Pelesh, and other families.[124]

In Eastern Galicia the situation was different. Inhabited by two national elements, often in conflict with each other, a sizeable part of the

---

[123] Cf. Osadczy, *Kościół i Cerkiew*, pp. 120–24.
[124] Kazimierz Chłędowski, *Pamiętniki*, vol. 1: *Galicja (1843–1880)*, ed. Antoni Knot (Cracow, 1957), p. 63.

population was forced to choose a self-designation. What is more, analysis of the biographies of well-known Ruthenians of Polish nationality shows that they were educated individuals who, as a minimum, had completed their secondary school education. It can be argued, therefore, that the adoption of a Polish identity lay chiefly in the education that could be acquired in the larger urban centres which had secondary schools and institutions of higher education, for example in Lviv. As a result of its political system (shaped by the influence of the autonomous political institutions, a well-developed press, manifestations and demonstrations of a social and national character) as well as its academic institutions (Lviv University, the Ossolineum, museums, libraries, and secondary schools), the capital of Galicia was naturally a place which inspired one to develop one's own well-defined identity. An individual who participated in salons, associations, and organizations and who held public posts was not able to remain a person of undefined identity, at least not for long. But it is not only Lviv that abounded in examples of *gente Rutheni, natione Poloni*. Other towns also experienced the same processes, and particularly those in the Polish-Ruthenian ethnic border area: in the western parts of Eastern Galicia and in Podilia. This did not mean, however, that the countryside was totally passive in matters of nationality for the entire period under consideration. It must be noted that the rural areas functioned in a constant connection with the towns. From the countryside people migrated to the towns and, having acquired education, they would often return to the country. Indeed, the majority of the *gente Rutheni, natione Poloni* known to us came from rural areas. Towards the end of the nineteenth century, and particularly at the beginning of the twentieth, various cultural-educational associations in the countryside became increasingly active. Similarly important was the development of the network of Roman Catholic parishes in Eastern Galicia, something that must have had an effect on identity changes for the rural population. Among this demographic we find not only peasants but also numerous de-classed gentry living like peasants. Andrzej Chwalba attributed the high number of Polish-speaking Uniates in Galicia (in 1910 around 20% of the Uniates in the Lviv administrative district spoke Polish, while in 1914 3% of the entire population of Galicia were Polish-speaking Greek Catholics) to two causes: firstly, the region was inhabited by many Poles; and secondly, the area had undergone a high degree of Polonization at the beginning of the twentieth century under the influence of the Roman Catholic clergy with the support of the local gentry.[125] Here we are dealing not only with Lviv and

---

[125] Andrzej Chwalba, "Krajobrazy etniczne Galicji Wschodniej," in *Poprzez stulecia*, pp. 177–78.

the south-east borderland of Galicia but also Przemyśl, Sanok, Stryi, and first and foremost, Sambir. The Sambir area was a region subject to several phases of Polish colonization during the second half of the eighteenth century.[126] This was also a region with a particularly high proportion of gentry: Hipolit Stupnicki in 1849 numbered the gentry in Galicia at 32,200, over a quarter of whom resided in the lands around Sambir.[127] For this reason, Sambir and its environs were to become the most profusely populated region for *gente Rutheni, natione Poloni*. Aleksander Kuczera, the author of a two-volume monograph on the region, spoke of the identity choices made in the nineteenth century by inhabitants of these lands:

> (…) the most influential and the wealthiest part of the Polish gentry of the Greek rite willingly, without any coercion, adopted the Roman Catholic rite. It was clear that this was not done for material gain or with a view to the future but rather brought about by state patriotism and a desire to document their national affiliation, which might be questioned by someone as a result of them holding the Greek Catholic faith.
>
> Yet, the petty gentry, regardless of any change in denomination or language, has remained in its political conviction Polish gentry, linking their prosperity and happiness to the joint, homogenous state organization that is Poland. Which is why one sees at every step through the Sambir area that strange type of citizen, one rarely meets these days, deemed *gente Ruthenus, natione Polonus*, shedding blood for a common homeland, "for your and our freedom."[128]

Later in his book Kuczera recalls that the process also occurred the other way around, when members of the Polish gentry would adopt Ruthenian ways, language, and finally even convert to the Greek rite itself.

The changes in identity occurring among the inhabitants of this Galician town can be illustrated in three stages. During the first phase, until 1848, there was a unity amongst Poles and Ruthenians as a result of the absence of a national identity within the Ruthenian community. This state of affairs started to change in the light of the Revolutions of 1848, from the moment the first political demands were made by the Ruthenian elite in Lviv, demands which initiated the second stage. This is very aptly portrayed in Józef Doboszyński's account of his native Sambir:

---

[126] Tomasz Gąsowski, „Struktura narodowościowa ludności miejskiej w autonomicznej Galicji", *Prace Historyczne* 125, ed. Krzysztof Baczkowski (1998), p. 107, footnote 33.

[127] Hippolit Stupnicki, *Galicya pod względem geograficzno-topograficzno-historycznym* (Lviv, 1849): table p. 3. J. Kozik drew attention to this estimate in: *The Ukrainian National Movement*, pp. 18 and 376, footnote 6.

[128] Aleksander Kuczera, *Samborszczyzna. Ilustrowana monografja miasta Sambora i ekonomii samborskiej*, vol. 1 (Sambor, 1935), p. 418.

Sambir was, and has remained, a purely Polish town with no known division, at that time, into Poles and Ruthenians, regardless of denomination. Up until 1848 all those with a superior intellect considered themselves Poles—any identification of nationality with a religious rite simply did not exist. The sons of the impoverished petty gentry freely settled in the environs of Sambir, people who had generally left home speaking Ruthenian, yet who after a short stay in the town spoke Polish, in spite of the presence of German schools, and boasted of their Polish nobility, while the sons of the Ruthenian clergy brought from home a knowledge of the Polish language and the Ruthenian priests of superior intellect used this language at home.[129]

Despite the conflict in 1848, the second stage—the period leading up to the end of the nineteenth century—would not result in any particular interethnic animosity in small towns; instead, there existed a relative harmony amongst the Polish and Ruthenian communities.[130] The third stage—from the turn of the twentieth century to the period of infusing the daily life with nationalism—was when the matter of dual-culturalism (and also interculturalism) had to give way to the dynamically developing nationalist movements.

Establishing the scale of the *gente Rutheni, natione Poloni* phenomenon in nineteenth-century Galicia presents its own set of problems. It is impossible to estimate the number of Ruthenians of Polish nationality, particularly in the first half of the century, for a myriad of reasons: Firstly, the majority of society—that is, the rural population—was indifferent to the question of nationality; secondly, a full crystallization of the Ruthenian national identity had yet to take place; and thirdly, we do not have at our disposal the relevant research materials in the form of statistical sources, as a population census was only to be implemented within the Habsburg lands in 1857.

Stanisław Pawłowski, the author of the 1919 work *The Roman Catholic Population in the Polish-Ruthenian Part of Galicia* [*Ludność rzymsko--katolicka w polsko-ruskiej części Galicji*], working off the 1825 findings of Stanisław Plater,[131] has shown that in the first decades of the nineteenth century there were around 200,000 Greek Catholics who considered

---

[129] Doboszyński, "Pamiętnik," pp. 364–65.

[130] Cf. Jadwiga Hoff, *Mieszkańcy małych miast Galicji Wschodniej w okresie autonomicznym* (Rzeszów, 2005), p. 42.

[131] [Stanisław Plater] S.H.P., *Jeografia wschodniey części Europy czyli opis krajów przez wielorakie narody słowiańskie zamieszkanych obejmujący Prusy, Xięztwo Poznańskie, Szlązk Pruski, Gallicyą, Rzeczpospolitę Krakowską, Królestwo Polskie i Litwę* (Wrocław, 1825), p. 83. This author, unfortunately without providing the source of this information, writes that in Galicia with the population of "4,000,000 heads," there lived 1.7 million Poles (i.e., Polish-speaking) and 1.8 million Ruthenians (Ruthenian-speaking), wherein 1.48 million were Roman Catholic and 2 million Greek Catholic.

Polish to be their first language, which at least gives us a group frame-work within which we may start to look for the *gente Rutheni, natione Poloni*. Unfortunately Pawłowski fails to develop his research, conclud-ing only that as a result of the development of a Ruthenian national con-sciousness the percentage of Uniate Poles was to gradually fall over the subsequent decades until a point was reached, at the beginning of the twentieth century, where there were more people declaring Ruthenian as their first language than there were Greek Catholics themselves.[132]

The second half of the nineteenth century would allow for more detailed findings, with the Austrian census being conducted every ten years. Nonetheless the questions the census asked concerned denomin-ation and so-called "social" language (this box was added in 1880),[133] but not nationality. As Tomasz Gąsowski wrote:

> There officially existed in the Habsburg monarchy only "peoples" as groups of an ethnic character. For the notion of "nationality" contains, and this was correctly picked up on, a political element which initial-ly potentially and later quite realistically threatens the cohesion of the state.[134]

While our interest lies in how many of those who indicated the Greek Catholic rite actually felt an affiliation to the concept of Polish nationality, the census questionnaire did not ask about nationality. However, contemporary researchers, in analyzing the census results, made various statements which have proven helpful. The closest thing to a statement of nationality was commonly interpreted as being a dec-laration of Polish as the "social" language.[135] Within certain circles, par-ticularly those of the intelligentsia (for example in Lviv), such a declara-tion could indeed reflect a sense of national affiliation; however, for the overwhelming majority of Galician society, the declared language was usually whatever the individual had been brought up speaking and continued to use on a daily basis.

Usually researchers wishing to establish the number of Greek Cath-olic Poles at the end of the Galician period compare the language and denominational censuses, intending to calculate how many of those indicating Greek Catholic as their rite simultaneously marked "Polish" in response to these other questions. Edward Prus used this method to

---

[132] Pawłowski, *Ludność rzymsko-katolicka*, p. 11–12.
[133] Lidia A. Zyblikiewicz, "Powszechne spisy ludności w monarchii Habsburgów," in *Celem nauki jest człowiek… Studia z historii społecznej i gospodarczej ofiarowane Helenie Madu-rowicz-Urbańskiej*, ed. Piotr Franaszek (Cracow, 2000), p. 398.
[134] Gąsowski, "Struktura narodowościowa", p. 91.
[135] See, for example: Stanisław Kasznica and Marcin Nadobnik, *Najważniejsze wyniki spisu ludności i spisu zwierząt domowych według stanu z d. 31 grudnia 1910 r.* (Lviv, 1911), pp. xxxviii–xlii as well as tab. IV, pp. 17–27.

conduct his research, going on to assert in his book that "in 1900 there resided in Lviv 29,327 Greek Catholics but only 15,159 Ruthenians. This means that 14,168 were Greek Catholic Poles."[136] Prus's sum is purely the result of mathematical subtraction, a process far too simplistic to account for the actual number of *gente Rutheni, natione Poloni* in Galicia. As far back as the start of the twentieth century, Józef Buzek provided insight into the difficulties involved in such a calculation. Wanting to enumerate the Greek Catholic population declaring their Polishness by determining how many Greek Catholics used Polish as a language of social discourse, he quickly realized the fundamental difficulty presented by this type of calculation:

> With the state statistics in this combination not differentiating the Roman Catholic from the Greek Catholic, we consequently have no exact figure for those of the Roman Catholic faith who have stated their use of Ruthenian, or those numbers of Greek Catholics that stated their use of Polish.[137]

These problems aside, Buzek tried to tackle the problem not by simply subtracting the number of Greek Catholics who declared their language of social communication to be Ruthenian, but also by attempting to exclude those of other denominations who declared themselves as speakers of Polish or Ruthenian. Buzek arrived at a figure of 71,061 Uniates out of a number of 3,982,033 Polish speakers. He considered, however, this estimate to be too low a figure. There was also a parallel process to *gente Rutheni, natione Poloni*, namely the Ruthenization of Roman Catholics. Buzek calculated 36,000 to be the number of those who spoke Ruthenian and who belonged to the Roman Catholic Church, and this enabled him to raise the number of Polish-language Ruthenians to around 107,000.[138] At the beginning of the twentieth century these figures were to be confirmed by the Ruthenian publicist, professional statistician, and socio-political activist Volodymyr Okhrymovych.[139]

In subsequent years estimates for the number of Poles of the Greek Catholic rite were to increase, a result of the inflamed situation between Poles and Ukrainians developing in Galicia. According to the 1910 estimates of Stanisław Pawłowski, as many as 235,328 Greek Catholics stated Polish as their language of choice, with 42,822 Roman

---

[136] Edward Prus, *Hulajpole. Burzliwe dzieje Kresów Ukrainnych (od słowiańskiego świtu do Cudu nad Wisłą)* (Wrocław, 2003), p. 311.
[137] Józef Buzek, *Rozsiedlenie ludności Galicyi według wyznania i języka* (Lviv, 1909), p. 155.
[138] Ibid., p. 156.
[139] According to Dariusz Maciak, Okhrymovych "calculated the 'census' losses of Ruthenians in 1900 to be at least 100,000." Dariusz Maciak, *Próba porozumienia polsko-ukraińskiego w Galicji w latach 1888–1895* (Warsaw, 2006), p. 50, footnote 100.

Catholics declaring Ruthenian.[140] If that was indeed the case it would have meant that in the course of ten years the number of Uniates who spoke in Polish had doubled. Pawłowski's research was cited during the Polish-Ukrainian War for Eastern Galicia. Published at the time was a collection of texts entitled *In Defence of Eastern Galicia* [*W obronie Galicyi Wschodniej*], in which Pawłowski quoted his estimates of over 200,000 Polish-speaking Greek Catholics.[141] He concluded that "Polish" Greek Catholics would increase the number of Poles in Eastern Galicia, depending on the administrative district, by 1 to 13%. The greatest number of Greek Catholics to use Polish were found in the administrative districts (counties) of: Łańcut (34%), Lviv and in the region's capital (24%), Brzozów (over 20%), Jarosław (below 20%), and Przemyśl, Sanok, and Ternopil [Tarnopol] (10%). In other counties (with the exception of the nine not mentioned by Pawłowski) this percentage was less than 10%. Pawłowski additionally forecasted that the proportion of Greek Catholics within the Polish nation would gradually increase.[142] He concluded that on the territory of Galicia, "it is impossible to establish any ethnographic boundary whatsoever across such a mixed area."[143] It must be understood that Pawłowski was not advocating the division of the province, but its total inclusion within the Polish state that would soon come into existence.

Stanisław Zakrzewski, about whom more will be said later, agreed with Pawłowski's estimates. In his text he emphasized one more problem: how is one to understand nationality? He saw it in terms of consciousness or self-awareness, not something based on language or religion, and thus he re-examined Pawłowski's calculations. In his sketch *Poles and Ruthenians in the Cherven Lands in the Past* [*Polacy i Rusini na Ziemi Czerwieńskiej w przeszłości*] we read that:

> Affiliation on the basis of provenance and blood ties to a given ethnic group does not determine national affiliation. A half ethnic consciousness cannot be compared to a full sense of national awareness. (…) a belonging to a particular nation is neither decided by one's origin, nor religion, but by the conscious wish of the individual to belong to one and not another national mass.[144]

According to Zakrzewski's calculations, 2,219,561 individuals qualified for inclusion into Polish society across the territories of the for-

---

[140] Pawłowski, *Ludność rzymsko-katolicka*, p. 12.
[141] Stanisław Pawłowski, "Stosunki narodowościowe w Galicyi Wschodniej," in Eugeniusz Romer, Stanisław Zakrzewski and Stanisław Pawłowski, *W obronie Galicyi Wschodniej* (Lviv, 1919), p. 63.
[142] Ibid., 72–73.
[143] Ibid., 81.
[144] Stanisław Zakrzewski, "Polacy i Rusini na Ziemi Czerwieńskiej w przeszłości," in Romer, Zakrzewski, Pawłowski, *W obronie*, pp. 17–18.

mer Red Rus'. His composition breakdown read as follows: 1.3 million Roman Catholics and 235,000 Uniates in Eastern Galicia, with also 456,900 *latynnyky* and 119,000 Orthodox believers in the Chełm region, over 77,000 adherents to Judaism, and 20,000 others, including Protestants and Armenian Catholics. The total number of Poles in these areas was almost the same as the number of Ruthenians — 2,423,525. Zakrzewski calculated the Ruthenian population to be 2.26 million Greek Catholics from Eastern Galicia and 46,500 *latynnyky*, as well as 119,000 Orthodox believers in the Chełm region.[145]

Of course, it must be emphasized that a Uniate individual designating their language as Polish in no way meant that they felt themselves to be Polish. In fact, many had an indifferent relationship to nationality, while some Ruthenians simply did not know the Ruthenian language or chose not to use it. In order to ascertain the number of *gente Rutheni, natione Poloni*, one would need the results of research into the degree of national consciousness among the inhabitants of Galicia, and such research was never conducted. In summary, any analysis of the number of Greek Catholics who considered themselves to be Poles is simply impossible because of the absence of the category of "nationality" in the Austrian censuses. Keeping with the defining premises adopted at the beginning of this study, it is not possible to include someone within a given nationality exclusively on the basis of language or rite. One could define a given individual or group as "potentially" Polish or Ukrainian, but not necessarily as definitive members of these nationalities. Hence, in dealing with an individual who declares their use of Polish and their membership of the Uniate Church, we should not draw the conclusion that the said individual is a Ruthenian of Polish nationality. One needs to be extremely careful when analyzing the numbers from the censuses taken during the period of the partition.

It was only in the censuses of the Second Polish Republic that the category of "nationality" was to appear. In light of the new information provided by these censuses, it seems that the ambitious aforementioned estimate made by Edward Prus as to the number of Greek Catholic Poles in Lviv was at least twice the actual figure. In the journal *Greko-Katolik* — which should be regarded with caution in respect to objectivity — it was written that in 1921 there were 27,269 Greek Catholics in Lviv, of whom nine thousand were Poles, while Prus set the number at fourteen thousand in the year 1900. The journal also states that in the Lviv administrative district, out of a total of 67,000 Greek Catholics as many as 25% were Poles.[146] The situation in Przemyśl is evaluated even

---

[145] Ibid.
[146] "Wzrost greko-katolików we Lwowie," *Greko-Katolik* 3, no. 6–7 (Jun.–Jul., 1935), p. 4.

more favourably, for out of a figure of 8,278 Greek Catholics 3,271 were Poles, making up 40% of the town's Uniate population.[147] As far as the whole of Galicia was concerned, the journal in question wrote proudly in 1935 that: "There exists a huge number of Ruthenians, numbering half a million, who consider themselves to be Poles."[148] This data was most clearly based on state censuses, the objectivity of which raised serious doubts and still continues to do so within contemporary academic research. Nonetheless, as there is no possibility of comparing and contrasting them with other statistical sources we must humbly concede that we will never know the actual numbers from this period. It is, therefore, important to remember that all subsequent research has been based upon these very figures that, most probably, did not accurately reflect reality.

In 1939 Tadeusz Jagmin published a booklet in which he undertook a detailed population analysis of Galicia in relation to the number of Polish Uniates. On the basis of the 1931 census he established that Greek Catholic Poles at the time represented 13% of the Uniate Church faithful for Eastern Galicia, and therefore they numbered 430,000 (6.9% of the population for the entire territory), of which 74,400 were urban and 355,900 rural residents.[149]

Table 1. The number of Greek Catholic Poles in Eastern Galicia (figures as of 1931) according to Tadeusz Jagmin

Province	In total		Urban		Rural	
	in 1000s	%	in 1000s	%	in 1000s	%
Lviv	229.1	7.3	42.4	5.4	186.7	7.9
Stanyslaviv	59.2	3.9	11.6	4.0	47.6	4.0
Ternopil	141.9	8.9	20.4	7.4	121.6	9.2
Total	430.2	6.9	74.4	5.5	355.9	7.3

Source: T. Jagmin, *Polacy grekokatolicy na ziemi czerwieńskiej*, Lviv 1939, p. 7.

---

[147] "Większość greko-katolików w Przemyślu jest polską!," *Greko-Katolik* 3, no. 8–9 (Aug.–Sep., 1935), p. 2.
[148] "Polska winna poprzeć greko Polaków," *Greko-Katolik* 3, no. 3 (Mar., 1935), p. 2.
[149] Tadeusz Jagmin, *Polacy grekokatolicy na ziemi czerwieńskiej* (Lviv, 1939), p. 7. Cf. also: Prus, *Hulajpole*, p. 311.

Table 2. The number of Greek Catholic Poles in selected towns of Eastern Galicia (figures as of 1931) according to Tadeusz Jagmin

Town	Number of Greek Catholic Poles	% of population
Lviv	14 600	4.6
Stanyslaviv	1780	3.0
Ternopil	3950	11.1
Przemyśl	3270	6.4
Boryslav	1750	4.2
Drohobych	2800	8.9
Jarosław	2450	11.1
Sambir	840	3.9
Stryi	1029	3.3
Kolomyia	2470	7.3

Source: T. Jagmin, *op. cit.*, p. 7.

Jagmin's data as well as that of later researchers who referenced him is, however, based uncritically on the results of the census. Was it possible that in the course of three decades the number of Uniate Poles could rise from 107,000 (Buzek's estimate) to 430,000 (Jagmin's estimate)? In regards to inhabitants of towns, it is possible that the urban intelligentsia during the time of the Second Polish Republic might acquire a sufficiently developed Polish national consciousness, so that it could, in spite of its Uniate affiliations, identify itself as Polish and increasingly voice this identity. However, when we look at the third of a million Uniate Poles in rural areas, we need to ask the question as to whether a Greek Catholic, filling out the census in 1931, selected "Polish" because they actually felt they belonged to that nationality or whether they were not entirely conscious of the meaning of the nationality question, and quite simply marked the adjective "Polish" thinking it referred to citizenship or their inclusion within a political state. One also cannot exclude deliberate falsification of the results or pressure exerted by officials to mark that option, something that the Ukrainian side often accused the Poles of doing.[150] Grzegorz Hryciuk, a researcher in this field, has also underlined yet another factor influencing the problem of national self-designation: the widespread phenomenon of bilingualism.[151]

---

[150] For more on the census of 1931 see: Grzegorz Hryciuk, *Przemiany narodowościowe i ludnościowe w Galicji Wschodniej i na Wołyniu w latach 1931–1948* (Toruń, 2005), pp. 62–101.
[151] Ibid., p. 104.

Enumerating the *gente Rutheni, natione Poloni* is complicated not only by research difficulties, but also by the political factors at work during the first half of the twentieth century. Simply put, Ruthenians of Polish nationality would, from the Polish perspective, bolster the argument that Poland should rightfully hold Eastern Galicia. Given that we have population estimates of between 107,000 and 430,000 for the first decades of the twentieth century, I am tempted to adhere to the lower figure, with the provision that we are only talking about potential Ruthenians of Polish nationality, for this data refers only to Polish-speaking Uniates. In his monograph on national population changes in the 1930s and 1940s, Hryciuk quotes researchers who have reduced the number even more radically to a figure of only 26,000. He also points out, following the logic of Włodzimierz Mędrzecki, that the group of Greek Catholic Poles had anyway only a temporary character.[152] Keep in mind that the number of Ruthenians of Polish nationality did not necessarily increase with demographic progress. With the emerging Polish-Ukrainian conflict, the *gente Rutheni, natione Poloni* were to completely Polonize themselves, discarding even at times those religious beliefs that had become the only difference dividing them from Poles, but which had begun to cause unease due to the increasingly Ukrainian character of the Galician Greek Catholic Church.

Yet, another question can be examined as an offshoot of the aforementioned statistical findings. The representatives of the *gente Rutheni, natione Poloni* formation were often chiefly recruited from mixed Polish-Ruthenian families, with such marriages representing a sizeable percentage of all marital unions within Galician society. Zdzisław Budzyński, conducting research into inter-faith relations in the South-Eastern marches and chiefly within Eastern Galicia, wrote that in the second half of the eighteenth century an event occurred that brought both Catholic communities together: the increase in the number of mixed marriages. The average number of such unions for the whole territory was 3–5%, while in particular regions it is estimated the number could have reached even 20% of the marriage total, particularly in urban parishes. These nuptials were chiefly held in Roman Catholic churches, not in Greek Catholic ones; in large parishes in particular, it was the Roman Catholic communities who took care of mixed families.[153] Of course, this did not necessarily indicate the gradual Polonization of the whole family. The holding of interfaith weddings in Roman Catholic churches frequently resulted in conflicts between the clergy of both rites. The unions and rifts created by interfaith marriages indicate

---

[152] Ibid., pp. 105–06.
[153] Zdzisław Budzyński, *Kresy południowo-wschodnie w drugiej połowie XVIII wieku*, vol. 3: *Studia z dziejów społecznych* (Przemyśl–Rzeszów, 2008), pp. 172–78, 322.

a social contract that could, on the one hand, create a bicultural environment, and on the other hand unite those who grew up in these families as *gente Rutheni, natione Poloni*.

A complex identity derived from such interfaith family conditions, can explain the unwillingness to separate both cultures in the consciousness of such individuals. It was difficult to divide the Ruthenian elements of identity from the Polish when the entire upbringing at home had been based on a bicultural family model, even if traditionally the son was to inherit the faith and, with it, the nationality of the father, while the daughter was to follow in her mother's footsteps. No estimates exist as to the scale of mixed marriages in the first half of the nineteenth century. This type of marriage was very common and was considered natural and normal at the time, as a sharp conflict between the ethnic groups did not yet exist. The number of mixed marriages inevitably fell over time, but as Franciszek Bujak noted, as many as 20% of marriages were mixed as late as 1908. He also highlighted that many Ruthenians had Polish roots as a result of the intense Polish colonization of the territories of Red Rus', Podilia, and Ukraine in a past.[154] Such multiculturalism within the framework of the family itself brought about a practical, and not ideological, link between Ruthenians and Poles.

The Family and the Choice of Identity

The multicultural nature of Galicia was established not merely by bonds between neighbours within individual communities, but primarily through familial ties. Multicultural families provided the conditions needed for an orientation like *gente Rutheni, natione Poloni* to freely exist. The combination of Polish and Ruthenian identity markers was not viewed as contradictory within mixed families. This is best conveyed in the reflections of Mieczysław Opałek, which show the permeation of family life with religious customs:

> It was a custom to go with Mother to my aunt and uncle's on the Ruthenian holidays of Christmas and Easter. The first of these, not being a moveable feast day, always fell in January and tied in with our Epiphany, and was called in the Ruthenian calendar *Rozhdestvo Khrysta* [Christmas]; the second, *Voskreseniie Hospoda* [Resurrection Sunday] was observed in April or May (…).
> (…) at Aunt Katarzyna's [Dykońska; Kateryna Dykonska] the air was heavy with [!] dried fruits and honey, and brioche, strudels, *mazurka*

---

[154] Bujak, *Galicya*, pp. 80–81.

short crust cakes and layer cakes, traditional *kutia* and sparkling currant wine—all homemade (...) all representing temptation itself. (...)

After the hospitality had run its course, Uncle with his grey moustache on his pensive Cossack face would start to sing carols. The first song to which he set his already rusty vocal cords was the Ruthenian carol "Boh predvichnyj nam narodyv sia" ["Eternal God Born Tonight". Then uncle [Dykoński] would sing most heartily the Polish carols "A wczora z wieczora z niebieskiego dwora" ["On the Yersterday's Eve"], "Z narodzenia Pana dziś dzień wesoły" ["'Tis Joyful Morning"], and also "Pan z nieba i łona Ojca przychodzi" ["The Lord Comes from Heaven and Father's Womb"].[155]

They would meet with both sides often, if only out of a desire to maintain family ties. An excellent opportunity for such gatherings were religious holidays (*praznyky* in Ruthenian).

Another interesting account was provided by the Lviv architect Wawrzyniec Dayczak, whose parents took him as a boy to his Ruthenian family in Horodyshche for a Ruthenian *praznyk*. He recalled that first they attended the church service, and then they went to their relatives for the celebratory meal:

On that occasion a relation, a powerfully built but pleasant bloke named Petro, gave me a moral talking to about being decent with people and defending the family honour and not bringing shame to the [family] name. In general the atmosphere at this celebratory meal was pleasant, relaxed, and sincere, in quite the same way it was at home when our Ruthenian relatives would visit us for Christmas or on other occasions. One of my old Ruthenian aunts would always bring up some complicated religious question or other which would be pounced upon and discussed at length, though without any firm outcome (...) This was my father's oldest sister, he being the son of a Pole and a Ruthenian mother. The common life lived by both nationalities was in every respect totally harmonious, with mutual respect shown to religious ceremonies and customs. Mutual relations were friendly and even sincere. And so it was in the times when Poles and Ruthenians lived in harmony. Unfortunately this was not to last for long.[156]

Concrete nineteenth-century evidence for the existence of biculturalism across the Austrian partition can also be found in the sepulchral legacy of the region—cemeteries, tombs, and memorial plaques. Walking around necropolises, as well as rural cemeteries, one comes across a host of graves and tombs with inscriptions that, on the one hand, be-

[155] Mieczysław Opałek, „Książka o Lwowie i mojej młodości. Kartki z pamiętnika 1881–1901" (Frysztak, 1958), ZNiO, sygn. 13535/II (MF 3269), pp. 16–17.
[156] Maria Dayczak-Domanasiewicz, „Z dni wielkich przemian. Wspomnienia architekta Wawrzyńca Dayczaka (1882–1968)," *Rocznik Biblioteki Naukowej PAU i PAN w Krakowie* 53 (2008), pp. 420–21.

tray the biculturalism of individual families while, on the other, nationalist dilemmas.

Let us examine first the cemetery in Buchach, a small town in Eastern Galicia within the Stanyslaviv [Stanisławów, present-day Ivano--Frankivsk] district. There the necropolis is a fantastic example of a cultural border region. Not only do we find the graves of Poles and Ruthenians right next to one another, but this biculturalism may be observed on a single grave. In the case of the Kryzhanivsky [Krzyżanowski] grave of Hryhorii and his wife Agnieszka (née Ufryjewicz), the inscription for the former is in Cyrillic, while that of the latter is written in Polish.[157] An even more interesting example is the grave of Władysław Niedźwiński [Volodyslav Nedvinsky], an eighth-grade secondary-school pupil and the son of a court counsellor. At the base of the gravestone is a stone plaque on which is engraved the self same information about the deceased but in two different languages: Polish on the left hand side and Ruthenian on the right.[158]

An analogical case is that of Father Tomasz Polański [Toma Poliansky], a deputy at the Galician Diet and Imperial Council and a beloved teacher and principal at secondary schools in Sambir and Przemyśl. On the gravestone funded—as one can read from the inscription—by "grateful pupils," there exist two versions of the text devoted to him: the Ruthenian in Cyrillic and the Polish in Latin script.

Another interesting example, the gravestone of the Kulczycki/ Kulchytsky family in Międzybrodzie near Sanok [Sianik], has been documented by Joachim Śliwa. At the local Greek Catholic cemetery, close to the Greek Catholic church funded by Dr. Aleksander Wajcowicz, there lies a grave in the shape of a pyramid in which rest Maria Ludwika (née Michałowska) Kulczycka [Kulchytska], Prof. Volodymyr Kulchystky, and their son Prof. Jerzy Kulczycki [Iurii Kulchytsky]. The latter, an archaeologist, was fascinated by the Orient and Egypt in particular, which explains the unusual form of the tomb. Above the entrance to the pyramid's interior is engraved in Ruthenian language: "ГРІБ КУЛЬЧИЦЬКИХ і ДОБРЯНСЬКИХ," [the grave of Kulchytsky and Dobriansky families]; carved on the entrance door are the family coat-of-arms and inscriptions to each of the three people buried there, with the inscriptions for Maria Ludwika née Michałowski and Jerzy Kulczycki in Polish, while that of the Volodymyr is in Ruthenian ("Володымир Кульчыцькый").[159] This member of the gentry, born

[157] Anna Sylwia Czyż and Bartłomiej Gutowski, *Cmentarz Miejski w Buczaczu* (Warsaw, 2009), p. 69.

[158] Ibid., p. 93.

[159] Joachim Śliwa, "Egipskie piramidy w polskim krajobrazie. Grobowiec rodziny Kulczyckich w Międzybrodziu koło Sanoka," *Rocznik Biblioteki Naukowej PAU i PAN w Krakowie* 52 (2007), pp. 499–503, also the photographs therein.

in Przemyśl in 1862, finished his secondary school in Kolomyia and studied the natural sciences in Vienna, finishing with a successful PhD defence at the University of Lviv. He worked in the field of zoology and was an enthusiastic collector of oriental fabrics, publishing a series of articles on the subject. He also organized exhibitions held during the days of the Second Polish Republic. Most interestingly, despite his Greek Catholic rite and Ruthenian origins (and indeed, the Cyrillic inscription on the gravestone), his biographer notes that "he considered himself to be Polish."[160].

Several tombstones leave no doubt of the deceased's two-tiered identity. On the now non-existent grave of Konstanty Łękawski [Konstantyn Lenkavsky], a member of the Ruthenian Sobor and a participant in the Hungarian Uprising of 1848–49, the following inscription was etched:

A band of brothers of sword and thought
These words to a wanderer's memory did wrought:
Here lies gente Ruthenus natione Polonus
By birth a Ruthenian, by nation a Pole.[161]

Such an explicit sentiment is not found on the graves of all those functioning within bicultural families. At the Lychakiv cemetery in Lviv lies the grave of the Merunowicz/Merunovych family, not of the line of the politician Teofil Merunowicz, but that of his brother Józef [Iosyf], the renowned doctor.[162] The surnames of his wife and children as well as of other unidentified relatives are written in Latin script. A similar Polish inscription can be found on the Lychakiv obelisk of another well-known Ruthenian of Polish nationality, Dymitr Koczyndyk [Dmytro Kochyndyk]. The use of Polish for gravestone inscriptions was common for Ruthenians of Polish nationality who were buried outside of their birthplaces. The Polish inscription on the grave of Mikołaj Zyblikiewicz at the Rakowice cemetery in Cracow comes as no surprise, nor does the plaque commemorating Father Emilian Sieniewicz [Senevych], an insurgent in the January Uprising of 1863 who, fearing the eradication of the Uniate Church in the Kingdom of Poland, moved to Cracow where he was to live out his days.[163] His services to the nation were posthumously commemorated by the people of Cracow, who buried him at

---

[160] Zdzisław Kosiek, "Kulczycki Włodzimierz Sas," in *PSB*, vol. 16 (Wrocław–Warsaw–Cracow–Gdańsk, 1971), p. 137.
[161] *Co mnie dzisiaj, jutro tobie. Polskie wiersze nagrobne* comp. Jacek Kolbuszewski (Wrocław, 1996), p. 247.
[162] Jerzy Lisiewicz and Anna Pituch, "Merunowicz Józef," in *PSB*, vol. 20, pp. 454–55.
[163] "Krakowskie echa. Kraków 10 grudnia," *Przegląd Lwowski* 10, no. 24 (15 Dec., 1880), p. 656.

the Rakowice cemetery in the tomb to the insurgents of the November and January Uprisings.[164]

The family served as the environment within which an individual's identity was shaped from their earliest years. If the family was bicultural, the question of "who am I?" became more complicated. Children who were products of mixed marriages were able to become acquainted with two cultures, learn two languages, and then have the option to choose one for themselves. It was certainly not the case that the son took up the father's nationality, or the daughter adopted that of her mother. It was from these very families that a well-known part of *gente Rutheni, natione Poloni* came, with the father usually being a Ruthenian, and often a Greek Catholic priest. For some time, the process of Polonization was favoured as a result of a better home education and the higher ambitions of such children. Indeed, the priest was often the only representative of the intelligentsia in the provinces. A priest's children naturally started off with higher aspirations than their peers. Several notable sons of priests were: Euzebiusz Czerkawski,[165] Józef Czerlunczakiewicz,[166] the Lviv and Warsaw veterinary surgeon Konstanty Łopatyński [Konstantyn Lopatynsky],[167] the optician Michał Borysiekiewicz,[168] Platon Kostecki,[169] Onufry Krynicki,[170] the renowned photographer Melecjusz Dutkiewicz [Meletii Dutkevych],[171] Walery Jaworski,[172] the famous historian Anatol Lewicki,[173] the German scholar Witold Barewicz [Vitold Barevych],[174] the forester and writer Emil Hołowkiewicz,[175] and finally Ivan Vahylevych [Jan Wagilewicz], who was to become a priest himself, subsequently converting from Catholicism to Lutheranism.[176] In analyzing the origin of *gente Rutheni, natione Poloni*, we also come across the sons of state civil servants and private clerks along with the

---

[164] Adam Świątek, "Grobowiec weteranów z 1831 i 1863 roku na cmentarzu Rakowickim w Krakowie. Materiały z projektu inwentaryzacyjnego," *Sowiniec* no. 43 (2013), p. 47.

[165] Antoni Knot, "Czerkawski Euzebiusz," in *PSB*, vol. 4, p. 333.

[166] Lewicki, "Czerlunczakiewicz Józef," p. 336.

[167] Krzysztof Wojciechowski, "Łopatyński Konstanty," in *PSB*, vol. 18 (Wrocław–Warsaw–Cracow–Gdańsk, 1973), p. 409.

[168] Bednarski, "Borysiekiewicz Michał," p. 357.

[169] Marian Tyrowicz, "Kostecki Platon," in *PSB*, vol. 14 (Wrocław–Warsaw–Cracow, 1968–1969), p. 340.

[170] Tyrowicz, "Krynicki Onufry," p. 463.

[171] Aleksander Maciesza, "Dutkiewicz Melecjusz," in *PSB*, vol. 6 (Cracow, 1948), p. 15.

[172] Skulimowski, "Jaworski Walery," p. 113.

[173] Mitkowski, "Lewicki Anatol," p. 224.

[174] Zdzisław Żygulski, "Barewicz Witołd," in *PSB*, vol. 1 (Cracow, 1935), p. 304.

[175] Broda, "Hołowkiewicz Emil," p. 599.

[176] Rotysław Radyszewśkyj, "Przedmowa," in Jan Dalibor Wagilewicz, *Pisarze polscy Rusini wraz z dodatkiem Pisarze łacińscy Rusini*, ed. Rotysław Radyszewśkyj (Przemyśl, 1996), p. 6.

representatives of liberal professions. Julian Horoszkiewicz and Zygmunt Sawczyński were the sons of court officials,[177] Antoni Dąbczański's father was a notary public,[178] Romuald Krzyżanowski's father was a legal advisor at the National Court,[179] and Henryk Rewakowicz's [Revakovych's] father was a rural primary school teacher.[180] Those known examples of Ruthenians of Polish nationality in Galicia prove that this formation was shaped chiefly within the intelligentsia.

How long could an identity such as that of the *gente Rutheni, natione Poloni* be maintained among enlightened social strata? To answer such a question, one needs to focus on the identity of individuals of various generations within the same family. Zygmunt Sawczyński and his family present an interesting case study. Sawczyński's affiliation to Polishness was not a break with familial tradition; as Kazimierz Chłędowski recalled, he belonged to "a Polish-feeling family."[181] Sawczyński married Jadwiga Ekielska, a highly educated and well-read woman from Cracow, and resided in Lviv.[182] As a couple they were exceptionally hospitable. Chłędowski wrote that "without any great preparation and announcement, a group of the most interesting people would gather there almost daily over a modest cup of tea, while the upper echelon of Cracow would not dream of passing through Lviv without paying a call on the Sawczyńskis."[183] The Sawczyński children, Leonia Paszkowska and Jan Henryk Sawczyński, underwent complete Polonization. Jan Henryk, who gained the degree of doctor of law at Lviv University, was to pursue the tedious career of an administrative clerk while an employee of the National Department of the Galician Diet in Lviv, while at the same time serving as a lecturer in History and Polish Literature at the Agricultural Academy in Dubliany. One of his sons, Henryk (1896–1919), died from wounds sustained during skirmishes with Ukrainians in the battle for Lviv,[184] while the other, Adam Tymoteusz, fought in the Polish-Soviet War of 1919–1920 and commanded the artillery of the 41st Polish Infantry Division during World War II.[185]

---

[177] Henryk Wereszycki, "Horoszkiewicz Julian," in *PSB*, vol. 10, p. 10; Zbigniew Fras, "Sawczyński Zygmunt," in *PSB*, vol. 35 (Warsaw–Cracow, 1994), p. 290.

[178] Czołowski, "Dąbczański Antoni," p. 467.

[179] Łopuszański, "Krzyżanowski Romuald," p. 615.

[180] Krzysztof Dunin-Wąsowicz, "Rewakowicz Henryk Karol" in *PSB*, vol. 31 (Wrocław–Warsaw–Cracow–Gdańsk–Łódź, 1988–89), p. 169.

[181] Chłędowski, *Pamiętniki*, p. 75.

[182] An interesting aside is that their flat was in a building belonging to a certain Mr. Dymat, who traded in church requisites for the Greek Catholic Church.

[183] Ibid., p. 222.

[184] Alina Szklarska-Lohmannowa, "Sawczyński Jan Henryk," in *PSB*, vol. 35, pp. 289–90.

[185] Henryk Bułhak, "Sawczyński Adam Tymoteusz," in *PSB*, vol. 35, pp. 287–89.

The descendants of those who actively defined their identity as *gente Rutheni, natione Poloni* rarely ever felt themselves to be Ruthenians. As a rule, they were people who had already severed their ties with Ruthenianism (or who avoided it altogether), and who were fully Polish in their consciousness. An example of this mentality is the well-known Lviv bibliophile Helena Dąbczańska, the daughter of the Ruthenian lawyer Antoni Dąbczański, one of the most active members of the Ruthenian Sobor and whose house at 4 Citadel Street was an important centre for the Polish patriotic movement. She felt that she was completely Polish, with her life and activities in no way characterized by anything at all reminiscent of matters Ruthenian.[186] This negligence of her Ruthenian roots is best illustrated by her diary, in which she mentions her father but never discusses his adherence to the Greek Catholic rite or his Ruthenian provenance.[187] Similarly, the son of Antoni Dąbczański, Leszek, had no doubt about his ethnic affiliations. He fought in the January Uprising of 1863, holding the rank of major. His biographer wrote: "He grew up in a patriotic atmosphere, at his father's home, the known Lviv activist."[188]

Another interesting case is that of Józef Daniluk [Iosyf Danyliuk] and his son Leon. The former fought in the January Uprising and then joined and became active in the socialist movement, which became dissociated from nationalistic issues. Daniluk himself did not renounce any element of his nationality. The question of identity manifested itself differently in the case of his son. Leon wrote in 1904 the booklet *"Wiz i perewiz" or the True Face of Galician Ukraine* [*"Wiz i perewiz" czyli Ukraina galicyjska w prawdziwym oświetleniu*] and published it using the pseudonym "Ukrainiec" ["The Ukrainian"].[189] This designation does not mean, however, that he felt himself to be Ukrainian in the way those representatives of the Ukrainian national movement did at the time. He intentionally did not call himself Ruthenian in an attempt to return to the former ethnonym of "Ukrainian," a name less burdened with political baggage. His booklet includes a criticism of Ruthenian national populist activists, with Ivan Franko at the head. Leon Daniluk wrote that the poet was "undoubtedly the most talented contemporary Ruthenian writer, but as great as he may be a literary figure, he is as weak as

---

[186] Irena Gruchała, "Pasja bibliofilska Heleny Dąbczańskiej," in *Kraków – Lwów. Książki, czasopisma, biblioteki XIX i XX wieku*, vol. 9, part 1, eds. Halina Kosętka, Barbara Góra and Ewa Wójcik (Cracow, 2009), pp. 265–76.

[187] Helena Dąbczańska-Budzynowska, "Pamiętnik," ed. Józef Fijałek, *Rocznik Biblioteki Polskiej Akademii Nauk w Krakowie* 9 (1963), pp. 313–14.

[188] Justyn Sokulski, "Dąbczański Leszek," in *PSB*, vol. 4, p. 467.

[189] [Leon Daniluk] Ukrainiec, *"Wiz i perewiz" czyli Ukraina galicyjska w prawdziwem oświetleniu* (Lviv, 1904).

a man.'[190] He then goes on to expose an array of Ukrainian politicians and social organizations, pointing out their vices. At the end of his work he underlines that the pamphlet had not been patronized or commissioned by Poles. If this is indeed true, then his opinions must derive from his identity as a *gente Ruthenus, natione Polonus*.

Andrzej A. Zięba has provided several other interesting examples of the total Polonization of Ruthenians of Polish nationality, this time from the Lemko region. Such figures include Jan Jaworski [Ivan Iavorsky], the Greek Catholic priest in the village of Florynka and the father of Prof. Walery Jaworski, and the priest's daughter, Maria, who married Piotr Olbrycht, a veterinary surgeon from Sanok and whose children were brought up as Poles. Of Maria and Piotr's sons, Jan Olbrycht lectured in Court Medicine at the Jagiellonian University in Cracow, Tadeusz Olbrycht became a zoo technician and geneticist at the Academy of Veterinary Medicine in Lviv, and Bruno Olbrycht served as a general in the Polish Army.

In turn, Teofil Feliks Wisłocki, the son of Bazyli Wisłocki [Vasyl Vyslotsky], a rural primary school teacher in Tymbark, and then a teacher at the secondary school in Przemyśl, was a professor in Medicine at Warsaw University, and edited the journal *Świt* [Dawn] in Lviv. Teofil's son, also a doctor, fought during the January Uprising of 1863, as did the descendants of Prof. Emilian Czyrniański.[191] While studying at the Jagiellonian University during the years 1877–1883, the youngest of the professor's sons, Julian Tadeusz Czyrniański, declared himself to be a Pole every term on the student questionnaires. This self-designation serves as an example of identification with the Polish nation.[192]

While the conclusion to be drawn from these examples is unequivocal, it must be remembered that the conscious sense of belonging to the formation *gente Rutheni, natione Poloni* was, in the nineteenth century, the self-designation for representatives of the assimilated generation who for the first time had to define their own national identity, yet did not want to immediately sever their ties with their families' Ruthenian past. However, national change did not always take the form of Polonization; sometimes the opposite process occurred. Andrzej A. Zięba cites the figures of the Lemko priest Father Mikołaj Baczyński [Mykola Bachynsky] and his wife, who considered themselves *gente Rutheni, natione Poloni* and were widely read in Mickiewicz and Słowacki. Their

---

[190] Ibid., p. 8.

[191] Andrzej A. Zięba, "Tożsamość etniczna jako obiekt manipulacji politycznej. Przypadek Rusinów łemkowskich XVIII-XX w. (część pierwsza)," *Rocznik Ruskiej Bursy* (2007), p. 81.

[192] *Corpus studiosorum Universitatis Iagellonicae 1850–1918*, [vol.] 1: *A-D*, ed. Jerzy Michalewicz (Cracow, 1999), p. 697.

son and daughter, however, considered themselves to be Ukrainian. What is more, they held their parents personally responsible for the wretched state of Ukraine.[193]

The Problem of the Choice of Identity

If Ruthenians did not assume a sense of Polish national consciousness from their home, then they most commonly acquired it from their education (most often unofficial) and from their school peers. Many of the best-known Ruthenians of Polish nationality were the children of Uniate priests, and therefore individuals who had a much higher level of education than the Ruthenian population on average. An upbringing in an ecclesiastical family was not merely a good climate for moral development, but also provided incentive for children to mirror the example of their parents. Knowing the importance and value of education, priests sent their children to secondary school and then to seminaries and universities. Education created a new social stratum, that of the intelligentsia, enabling them to make a career and to forge contacts with social elites who were on the whole Polish. Often *gente Rutheni* became *natione Poloni* not only because they wanted to become Poles, but also because after entering into higher social spheres they no longer wanted to be Ruthenian, which frequently had connotations of being plebeian. An important reason for abandoning Ruthenian roots was also conflict with their own community.

We will turn to the case study of Euzebiusz Czerkawski, born in 1822 in the village of Tuchapy. He was the son of Tymotei Cherkavsky, a parish priest of the Greek Catholic rite, and Maria, the Ruthenian daughter of Father Teodor Kyverovych, the deacon at Oleszyce[194] Euzebiusz Czerkawski finished school in Przemyśl, then studied philosophy at Lviv University. He became a teacher in Tarnów, vying unsuccessfully for a post at the Department of Contemporary History and the Austrian State at Lviv University. Czerkawski's biographist Aleksander Skórski writes:

(…) it would not have been possible at the time to say whether Czerkawski was *gente Ruthenus – natione Polonus*. For he would clearly state [Czerkawski – A.Ś.] that "in terms of nationality he is a Ruthenian," and would place such emphasis on his talent for speaking Ruthenian that

---

[193] Zięba, "Tożsamość etniczna (część pierwsza)", p. 80; Andrzej Zięba, "Inne 'Tamte światy'," in *Rzecz o roku 1863. Uniwersytet Jagielloński wobec powstania styczniowego*, ed. Andrzej A. Zięba (Cracow, 2013), p. 87.
[194] Aleksander Skórski, "Euzebiusz Czerkawski," *Muzeum* 12 (1896), p. 686.

it would seem as if the department was reserved exclusively for candidates who lectured in Ruthenian.'[195]

Even when Czerkawski became a secondary school inspector in 1850, he behaved more like a loyal enforcer of educational policy for the Habsburg Empire than a Pole. Only through work in the field of education, first in Western Galicia then later in Eastern Galicia, was Czerkawski's character to be shaped. Through dealing with language problems and opposing the expectations of the Ruthenians who often had Russophile leanings, Czerkawski started to develop his stance as a defender of the rights of Polish as a language in opposition to Ruthenian demands. Yet, his Polish identity was ultimately cemented by Ruthenian opposition to several of his major plans, including his proposal for the introduction of the Latin script, the cleansing of the Polish language from Ruthenianisms, and a change in calendar from the Julian to the Gregorian.[196] He was, however, to remain first and foremost a loyalist, though not one detrimental to Polish patriotism, as demonstrated by his behaviour on 29 November 1860. On this day, a Mass was being conducted for Adam Mickiewicz at the St. Ann Church in Cracow at the same time when Czerkawski was inspecting a city secondary school. Czerkawski extended the duration of the inspection by an hour, but did not forbid the youth from attending the Mass; consequently, many pupils were able to leave the school without being penalized for their actions. Despite this, Czerkawski's inspection itself was interpreted by the pupils as an attack on the youth's sense of patriotism, and he was attacked that very same day, insulted, pelted with stones, and then beaten with sticks. The abused inspector, following a court case, ultimately forgave the culprits.[197] Czerkawski found himself out of favour with both the Ruthenian as well as the Polish side. At this time, he left to work in Graz, returning home only in 1866. Upon his return he ran in the elections for the Galician Diet as a candidate for the Chortkiv constituency.[198] A key moment in his life was when he publically presented his draft act on the language of instruction for primary and secondary schools at a plenary session of the Galician Diet (31 December 1866), which was completely boycotted by the Ruthenian deputies but passed on the strength of Polish votes.[199] From this point onwards, Czerkawski abandoned any Ruthenian sympathies and fully embraced Polishness.

---

[195] Ibid., p. 751.

[196] Ibid., pp. 819–20.

[197] Ibid., pp. 828–29. Kazimierz Chłędowski has given a different reason for the "beating of Czerkawski"—the alleged aversion to Polish lectures at the Jagiellonian University. Cf. Chłędowski, *Pamiętniki*, pp. 84–85.

[198] Skórski, "Euzebiusz Czerkawski," *Muzeum* 13 (1897), pp. 19–21.

[199] Ibid., pp. 87–88.

Two years later, in 1868, as Aleksander Skórski noted, Czerkawski "was already recognized in the Diet as an ardent spokesman for Polish national aspirations."[200]

It is worth mentioning another figure important to Ukrainians, Ivan Vahylevych, a Ruthenian folklorist, writer, and researcher of folk language. While studying in Lviv in the 1830s he was associated with those young Ruthenian intellectuals referred to as the "Ruthenian Triad" who worked to develop the literature and culture of Galician Ruthenians. Together with his colleagues Yakiv Holovatsky and Markiian Shashkevych, in 1836 he published the first Ruthenian periodical *Rusalka Dnistrovaia*, which was confiscated by the Austrian authorities. Nonetheless, this publication shaped Vahylevych's reputation as the "awakener of Ruthenian nationality." Several years later he also published a grammar of the Ruthenian language.[201] Following his marriage to Amalia Piekarska, he was ordained a priest, despite initial complications. He tried to obtain work at the universities in Lviv, Warsaw, and Poznań, and even contemplated moving to Russia.[202] Danuta Sosnowska wrote that a variant of Ruthenization, similar to that of Holovatsky—that is, joining the Russophile camp—was extremely likely to have happened to Vahylevych.[203] It was political events that finally forced Vahylevych to define his identity. Having fallen into conflict with the Greek Catholic Church, he arrived in Lviv and was swiftly drawn into the Ruthenian Sobor by his university friends August Bielowski and Korecki, and "was there welcomed with open arms and hearts by his friends and was, as a priest and Uniate, the most splendid pillar and support for the cause represented by the Sobor."[204] He was soon offered the editorship of *Dnewnyk Ruskij*. Therefore, he was not associated with the Supreme Ruthenian Council, but with the pro-Polish Ruthenian Sobor, the organization assembling Polish landowners of Ruthenian background as well as Ruthenians of Polish nationality like himself. After he chose this political orientation, there was no place for him among the Ruthenian intelligentsia. He did not become a lecturer in Ruthenian at the university (the post went to Yakiv Holovatsky), nor did he take up the post of editor at the Ruthenian journal *Zoria Halytska* [Galician Dawn]. Finally, following his conflict with the Greek Catholic Church, he converted to Lutheranism. Finding himself with no means to live, he gladly took up a position at the National Ossoliński Institute, subsequently supporting

---

[200] Ibid., p. 167.

[201] Jan Wagilewicz, *Grammatyka języka małoruskiego w Galicii* (Lviv, 1845).

[202] Radyszewśkyj, "Przedmowa," pp. 6–9.

[203] Sosnowska, *Inna Galicja*, pp. 174–75.

[204] Julian Horoszkiewicz, *Notatki z życia*, ed. Henryk Wereszycki (Wrocław–Cracow, 1957), pp. 290–91.

academics connected with this institution through his research work.[205] He also worked as a translator, compiling shorthand minutes during the Galician Diet sessions. In Wagilewicz, Poles had gained a valuable scholar, writer, and specialist on the Ruthenian question.

The Polonization of Józef Barewicz [Iosyf Barevych] also occurred in the face of national confrontation. He was the son of Father Tomasz Barewicz, the principal of the state secondary school in Sambir. A former pupil, Władysław Cichocki, wrote that Father Barewicz was "the only brave soul in the whole of Sambir," who had the "nerve" to read the newspaper *Czas*.[206] Other Greek Catholic priests allegedly accused him of "prostrating himself to Poles," for which reason one of his pupils—the son of another Greek Catholic priest, the parish priest of Listowate near Ustrzyki Dolne, Sas-Lyskovatsky—struck Barevych in the face. This insubordinate pupil was

6. Father Tomasz Barewicz

expelled from school while his school colleague, the victim's son Józef Barewicz, "took such offence against all Ruthenians over the affront to his father that he 'joined' the Poles (…) accepted Polish nationality even though he was of the Greek Catholic rite, and officially referred to himself as *gente Ruthenus, natione Polonus*."[207] Subsequently, Witold Barewicz, the second son of Father Tomasz Barewicz, turned away from his Ruthenian origins, even in time rejecting the Greek Catholic faith.[208] For Ruthenian patriots, Tomasz Barewicz was an example of a traitor. After his death, the newspaper *Halychanyn* published a comprehensive obituary, in which he was accused of "hatred of Ruthenian youth" and that his "Polish chauvinist patriotism opened him a way to the Diet in Lviv and the Imperial Council in Vienna"[209]. But the newspaper also reported that with the passing of time even the Poles had pushed him into the background because he did not fit his views into the reality of the so-called "a New Era" in Polish-Ruthenian relationships in Galicia (following a settlement, concluded between Kazimierz Badeni and Yuliian Romanchuk in 1890)[210].

The nationalist ideas and notions, which in the Polish case took the form of the program of National Democrats, were also to exclude

[205] Radyszewśkyj, "Przedmowa," pp. 9–11.
[206] Cichocki, *Sambor*, p. 15.
[207] AV, "Lwów oczami Ukraińców," *Kultura* no. 9 (107) (1956), p. 138.
[208] Żygulski, "Barewicz Witołd," p. 304.
[209] *Halychanyn* no. 141 (1894), p. 3.
[210] Ibid.

a bicultural model for Galician society. Nationality was to be clearly defined and proclaimed; those with dual identities (even given its two-tiered nature) were to be assimilated, while those ambivalent to their nationality were to be won over to the Polish idea.

The Srokowski [Srokovsky] family constitutes another example of a family whose choices were conditioned by politics. The trajectories of two cousins, Konstanty [Konstantyn] and Stanisław [Stanyslav], are worthy of analysis. The former went to the Ruthenian academic gymnasium in Lviv, published in *Literaturno-Naukovy Vistnyk* [Literary and Scholarly Herald], and even authored a volume of short stories in Ruthenian in 1899. Later, however, he was to enter into Lviv Polish literary circles. He worked for the newspapers *Słowo Polskie* [Polish Word], *Nowe Słowo Polskie* [New Polish Word], then left for Warsaw to take up a position at *Kurier Polski* [Polish Courier] and *Słowo* [Word]. He subsequently travelled to Russia where he was associated with the Polish journal *Kraj* [Country], published in St. Petersburg. In Russia he worked as the correspondent for the Cracow newspaper *Nowa Reforma* [New Reform], with which he was to collaborate even more closely on his return to Cracow in 1906. It was at this time that he commenced his political activities within the Polish Democratic Party. His particular interests were Ruthenian and Jewish matters.[211] An insight into his thinking is offered by his article published in *Krytyka* [Criticism], entitled "The Polish Raison d'Être on Ruthenian Issues" ["Polska racya stanu w sprawie ruskiej"], where he chiefly distanced himself from "pseudo-ethnic clichés of 'brotherly harmony,' 'mutual understanding' or 'neighbourly kindness'" long-dead in society but still lingering in the Diet.[212] He soberly evaluated the relations between the two nations, accusing the Ruthenians of not wanting to retract their mandate of driving the Poles west of the San River, and criticizing Polish political formations for foolishly believing that Poles would be able to permanently guarantee the rights of the Polish minority in Eastern Galicia.[213] In analyzing the "Polish raison d'être," he showed that

7. *Konstanty Srokowski*

---

[211] Zięba, "Srokowski Konstanty," in *PSB*, vol. 41 (Warsaw–Cracow, 2002) pp. 231–32.

[212] Konstanty Srokowski, "Polska racya stanu w sprawie ruskiej," *Krytyka* 9, vol. 1 (1907), p. 320.

[213] Ibid., p. 454.

their initial concern was securing and gradually broadening existing achievements. This twofold mission meant that Poles divided themselves into those involved in the former and those who implemented the latter; there was no balanced approach for the realization of both goals. As an example, Konstanty cited the Eastern Galician landed gentry, the Podolians, as well as the conservative elite of Cracow. The gentry wanted to maintain their properties and possessions, while the elite were of the view that Eastern Galician matters should be left alone. Srokowski criticized the Podolians for not being the "source of worldly strengths for the Commonwealth," for in Eastern Galicia "there have emerged the most anarchic and wildest magnate tendencies of the Commonwealth." Such a situation contributed to the propagation of the stereotypical notion of Polish-Ruthenian relations as one of conflict between the Polish landowner and the Ruthenian agricultural labourer. Further he pointed out that Poles themselves contributed to Ruthenian nationalism because "we oppose the democratic and most progressive nationalist politics of the Ruthenians with a reactionary, aristocratic nationalist-Polish policy." He was also critical of the view that Polish "aristocratic nationalism" could effectively handle Ruthenian "democratic nationalism." He had but a single recipe for this situation: the fundamental democratization of Polish policy towards the Ruthenians and reaching a conclusion as to whether the national development of Ruthenians was favourable for Polish interests or not. He personally considered such a development to be positive for the simple reason that sooner or later Ruthenians would develop as a nation. Consequently there was absolutely no point in fighting them, but it made sense to work with them to achieve a form of cultural-political autonomy for the whole of Galicia, rejecting any nationalist territorial projects, including the Ruthenian demands for a division of Galicia itself.[214] After many years the presence of Ruthenians of Polish nationality in the socio-political life of Galicia, it was only Srokowski who was able to soberly evaluate Polish-Ruthenian relations, proposing guidelines for their improvement while advocating the loyalty of Galicia to the Polish state. Here he fought against the delusions which had been disseminated in earlier decades by those who were *gente Rutheni, natione Poloni.* However, despite his seemingly temperate views on Polish-Ukrainian relations, he was unable to avoid criticism, particularly in regards to his two-tier identity. Such disparagement was to occur during the elections to the Galician Diet in 1913. The highly critical *Głos Narodu* [The Voice of Nation], in addition to asking questions regarding Jewish issues, criticized Srokowski for being a Ruthenian:

---

[214] *Krytyka* 9, vol. 2 (1907), pp. 63–74.

Mr. Srokowski is also, as is well known, a better Ruthenian than the Ruthenians themselves, for not all Ruthenians demand the founding of a Ruthenian university [!] in Lviv, while Mr. Srokowski in the Warsaw *Świat* pointed to Lviv as the only fitting location for a Ruthenian university. This should not be surprising, for it is difficult to forget the "ideals" Mr. Srokowski so zealously expounded during his youth.[215]

This line was further developed by an article published on 8 July in *Gazeta Narodowa* [National Gazette]. It argued that Srokowski, who was the son of a Ruthenian and maternal grandson of a Greek Catholic priest, remained a Ruthenian regardless of the fact that he himself was married in a Roman Catholic church. It also recalled his involvement in Ruthenian cultural life since he wrote articles and short stories in Ruthenian.[216] A reply soon appeared in *Nowa Reforma*, which considered the arguments on Srokowski's non-Polishness to be bizarre as *Gazeta Narodowa* was a newspaper that Jan Dobrzański, Platon Kostecki, Teofil Merunowicz, and Henryk Rewakowicz had worked on for many years, and all of them were Uniates exactly like Srokowski.[217] Srokowski himself also published a text in which he defended his Polishness and that of his family.[218] A dozen or so days later *Dziennik Polski* [Polish Daily] came to Srokowski's defence and provided an extensive list of Polonized individuals, both those already mentioned in *Nowa Reforma* as well as other ones from among the townspeople of German origin.

In his memoirs, the nationalist Franciszek Rawita-Gawroński called Srokowski the "Temporal Bone" (a play on his name in Polish) and was of the view that his currently declared nationality was the result of his present interests. He was outraged that years earlier when he had met Srokowski in the editorial offices of *Słowo Polskie*, Srokowski had been indignant about Gawroński's criticism of the *haidamaka* movement when speaking of the Ruthenian question. Srokowski allegedly said: "I am a Ruthenian and you, sir, are insulting my nationality."[219] For this reason, Gawroński's perception of Srokowski was largely negative:

Srokowski first of all said: I am more a Ruthenian than I am a Pole. We cannot deny our own words; either they come from the depth of our soul and then are worth something or they conceal—heaven knows what (…).

Further on he writes:

---

[215] "Pan Srokowski i żydzi," *Głos Narodu* no. 149 (2 Jul., 1913), p. 2.

[216] *Gazeta Narodowa* no. 156 (8 Jul., 1913), p. 3.

[217] *Nowa Reforma* no. 312 (9 Jul., 1913), p. 2.

[218] Konstanty Srokowski, "Pro domo mea," *Nowa Reforma* no. 322 (15 Jul., 1913), p. 2.

[219] Rawita-Gawroński, *Ludzie i czasy*, p. 215.

The fault does not lie in the fact that he adheres to Polishness while being a Ruthenian, but that this admittance is hypocritical and too late. When was he a Pole? Was it when he talked to me in the offices of *Słowo Polskie*, or when he worked in *Kraj*, or was it in Cracow that he suddenly felt himself Polish?[220]

Gawroński was acting in accordance with the adage he would later cite: "a bird defends its nest and a nation has to defend itself too.'[221] It seems as if these words best convey the attitudes of that part of Polish society at the beginning of the twentieth century that had absorbed nationalist ideas in relation to those of a *gente Rutheni, natione Poloni* identity. What is particularly interesting is that *Gazeta Narodowa* also started to employ such rhetoric, althought their former editor-in-chief, Platon Kostecki, had to his credit a sizeable Ruthenian-language output. The conclusion to be drawn from the smear campaign against Srokowski is unequivocal: there was no place for those of a two-tiered identity in the Galician society at the beginning of the twentieth century during the period of the development of nationalism, at least not within the public sphere.

At the beginning of the twentieth century an unambiguous identity choice had to be made if one did not wish to attract criticism from either side. Hence many Ruthenians with a Polish affiliation wished to radically sever their ties with their Ruthenian past. Stanisław Srokowski, the cousin of the aforementioned Konstanty, was one such individual. Although he came from a Ruthenian family, his grandmother had brought him up within the spirit of Polish patriotic traditions. He studied at Polish schools, and then went on to attend the Jagiellonian University in Cracow; later he worked at Lviv University. He was also to become a teacher of the Polish language, first in Rzeszów and then in Ternopil, where he was president of the the Association of People's Schools [*Towarzystwo Szkoły Ludowej*]. It was here that his rivalry with the Ruthenians took shape. He tried to prevent those inhabiting the regions around Ternopil, Terebovlia, Skalat and Zbarazh from being influenced by the Prosvita society.[222] Significantly, he spoke out against the Ruthenians more strongly than many pure-blooded Poles. While running for election to the Galician Diet in Ternopil in 1906, Stanisław Srokowski urged his compatriots, the peasants, not to vote for the Ruthenian candidates:

We are addressing first and foremost the Polish peasantry, for the Ruthenians can do what they like. Let them listen to the array of ringleaders promising them mountains of gold. Anyone can make promises;

---

[220] Ibid., p. 224.
[221] Ibid., p. 225.
[222] Andrzej A. Zięba, "Srokowski Stanisław Józef," in *PSB*, vol. 41, pp. 238–39.

actually doing something is the realm of the few. Wait a few years and then you'll see how far the Ruthenians' agitation has got them, which even the emperor himself reprimanded a few days ago when the Ruthenian delegation travelled to Vienna. Not for the first time, the Ruthenians have initiated fights and unrest, and their history repeats itself every hundred years or so. First they talk, then they start to boil over, the Orthodox priests bless the knives and finally they revolt, and everything ends in a great disaster for their nation [all highlighting as in the original – A.Ś.]. And because they listen to these incitements, thousands of them die, while the common people find themselves poorer still after every revolt. Hundreds of children cry for their fathers, wives for their husbands, parents for their children. Poles have no fear of the *haidamaka* knife whatsoever, especially these days.[223]

Srokowski painted a very bleak picture of what would occur if the peasants were not to vote for Polish candidates. Yet, the programme he and his colleague, also national-democratic politician, Jan Zamorski, proposed was in actuality disheartening for the peasants themselves because it opposed equal electoral rights. Srokowski and Zamorski feared that the landowners, chiefly Poles, would disappear amidst the Ruthenians, who numerically dominated in Eastern Galicia. Therefore they believed that only curial voting would ensure the election of Poles as deputies:

Although Eastern Galicia is an eternal Polish land, even though we are the legitimate lords here and although we have put into this land so much labour, expense, and blood, this land could so easily fall from our grasp into the hands of the poorly enlightened Ruthenians who hold sway over this, our Polish land; they could push us westward beyond the San River or slowly turn us into Ruthenians, taking away our churches, schools (…).[224]

It therefore comes as no surprise to learn that the Ruthenians reprinted Srokowski's and Zamorski's appeal as an "anti-example." They simply added a commentary in Polish so that the Polish peasantry could see that both politicians were more interested in supporting the old feudal system than defending the peasantry. They appealed to their readers:

Read this letter, brothers, and get to know the soul of this lackey to the lords, get to know the man to whom you wish to hand over your fate and that of your children.[225]

---

[223] Stanisław Srokowski and Jan Zamorski, *Do Braci Włościan* (Ternopil, 1906), LNNBU, fond 9: Okremi nadkhodzhennia, spr. 2295: Zbirka vidozv, oholoshen', statutiv tovarystv, vypysky z hazet ta in., p. 9.
[224] Ibid.
[225] Ibid.

Four years later Stanisław Srokowski became involved in a dispute with the newspaper *Gwiazda* [Star] for libelling its members, including January Uprising insurgents, who had not wanted to join in the political war he was waging against the Ruthenians. Srokowski was later to explain on the pages of *Głos Polski* [Voice of Poland] that he had never called the members of *Gwiazda* street thugs, but his words nevertheless caused an outcry. A certain Adolf Gawalewicz even wrote a public notice in which he enumerated Srokowski's faults as a Polonized ex-Ruthenian nationalist. He characterized his struggles with his own identity in the following way:

> Having gotten rid of his original nationality and Ruthenian beliefs, not accepted by the Roman Catholic church, rejected by the Armenian rite, he would surely have joined now, together with his Siamese brother: the Great Prophet and deputy [Rudolf] Gall, the sect being created *ad hoc* that will create assimilated Polish-Jewish or Jewish-Polish nationalities.[226]

He went on to criticize his activities:

> Himself being a traitor to his faith and nationality, this renegade has the nerve to refuse to acknowledge patriotism in those old men who were born and brought up as Poles and who worked for the good of the fatherland through the entirety of their laborious lives right up until their grey-haired days, living the memories of the lofty moments of the year 1863. He denies them reverence due to a true Pole through his exclusion of them from the Association of Primary Education because they are different from him and his terrorised satellites — those political Lilliputians — because they understand the responsibilities of a Pole. A democrat would never extend a hand to the "National Democracy terror groups" who see salvation for the Fatherland in an exterminating war with their brother Ruthenians and in their constant affront to their most holy national feelings, which would ultimately result in a fratricidal battle of knives and inevitable doom for both Poland and Rus', and with it the total triumph of our mutual enemies.[227]

The example of the Srokowski cousins deftly illustrates the problem of Poles of Ruthenian provenance at the beginning of the twentieth century. Konstanty, in quietly maintaining his Ruthenian roots yet acting for the advancement of the Polish cause, was vehemently attacked by nationalists for not breaking with the past. In turn, his cousin Stanisław completely rejected his origins and operated within the nationalist political current of the day. This represented complete Polonization and a total resignation from all things Ruthenian. The symbolic act in this

---

[226] Adolf Gawalewicz, *List otwarty (w imię kłamstwa)* (Ternopil, 1910), LNNBU, fond 9, spr. 2295, p. 11.
[227] Ibid.

rejection was his leaving the Greek Catholic rite following the murder of the governor Andrzej Potocki in 1908.[228] However, he was not alone in deciding to sever his ties with his Ruthenian roots in this way.

It must be remembered, however, that the direction of change was not always towards Polonization. There are known cases of individuals who could have become *gente Rutheni, natione Poloni*, but in the decisive situations rejected this route and remained within the Ruthenian camp. Such a figure was Iosyp Lozynsky [Józef Łoziński], who in 1835 had written a well-known text for the Lviv *Rozmaitości* [Varieties] on the subject of employing the Latin alphabet for the needs of the Ruthenian language. Following the Revolutions of 1848 he changed his outlook and became a Ruthenian patriot. He also distanced himself from his proposal to introduce the "Polish alphabet" into Ruthenian spelling. He officially opposed his earlier proposition at a special language commission called by Agenor Gołuchowski in 1859.[229]

An unexpected return to his roots—albeit in a new, national Ukrainian form—was undertaken by Damian Savchak [Damian Sawczak]. The son of a Lemko psalmist and primary school teacher from Nowa Wieś [Nove Selo], Savchak was married to a Polish woman, Ewelina Dąbrowska. He worked initially as the secretary to Władysław Zamoyski at Kórnik near Poznań, and then obtained his PhD at Lviv University. He became a deputy of the Galician Diet, where he helped to win over Ukrainian national populists for the agreement of 1890. He was highly involved in Polish social life and belonged to the committee formed to bring the remains of Adam Mickiewicz to the Wawel Castle in Cracow for burial. In the face of the tense Polish-Ukrainian relations at the turn of the twentieth century, he underwent a political evolution that set him firmly in the Ukrainian camp. Despite this, one of his three sons, Jarosław Sawczak [Iaroslav Savchak], a doctor practicing in Zakopane, continued to remain on "the Polish side."[230] Often the choice of identity was not decided according to geographical borders but as a result of internal family relations. The inner divisions within families was to become the greatest problem for multicultural Galician society when the hour of trial came. Before the conflict between Poles and Ukrainians assumed clearly defined outlines, events could have taken a different course. Apart from familial and domestic conditions there were other influences that impacted the biculturalism of Galicia's inhabitants, particularly the use of Polish in Greek

---

[228] Zięba, "Srokowski Stanisław Józef," p. 239.
[229] Czesław Lechicki, "Łoziński Józef," in *PSB*, vol. 18, pp. 455–56.
[230] Zięba, "Tożsamość etniczna (część pierwsza)," pp. 93–94 as well as footnote 100. For Savchak's biography, see Zbigniew Fras, "Sawczak Damian," in *PSB*, vol. 35, pp. 284–85.

Catholic churches and within the school system, as well as the effect exerted by literature.

Polish in the Greek Catholic Church

In pre-partition Poland, especially during the last years of its existence, the features that had distinguished Ruthenians from other citizens of the Commonwealth were the Uniate rite and their Ruthenian ethnicity. Language was secondary, as both nobles and urban commoners had adapted to the Polish linguistic culture out of the necessity for social advancement.[231] The Greek Catholic rite had long been of enormous importance to the Ruthenian people as an element of identity, for it gave them a sense of separateness that distinguished them from the Orthodox Russians and the Roman Catholic Poles. Nonetheless, even the Greek Catholic Church would gradually undergo Polonization. In the first half of the nineteenth century not only did priests receive pastoral instruction in Polish or Latin, but they themselves would deliver sermons in Polish, including those given at the St. George Cathedral.[232] Furthermore, all official Church correspondence was in Polish and many Uniate clergymen simply did not know the Ruthenian language.[233] Aleksander Morgenbesser recalls that:

> (…) they were only Ruthenians when in church, outside of church both Uniates and Roman Catholics were good Poles; the government did not allow for any (…) divisions and nominated twice as many [Roman] Catholics as catechism teachers and twice as many [Roman Catholic] priests in the army simply because of the difference in rite. Polish was considered by Ruthenians to be their literary language. Sermons were delivered in church in Polish, policies were joint, Ruthenians and Poles fought for the same things and ended up groaning together in prisons.[234]

Language differences did not influence the decision as to which church services to attend: in a Greek Catholic church or in a Roman Catholic one. It was invariably a physical distance to the church that decided the matter. The faithful would transfer from one rite to another even though this was in fact forbidden by canon law. Tellingly, during the first half of the nineteenth century there was nothing strange in ordaining Uniates as Roman Catholic priests and vice

---

[231] Radzik, "Społeczne uwarunkowania," pp. 307–8.
[232] Osadczy, *Kościół i Cerkiew*, p. 57.
[233] Kozik, *The Ukrainian National Movement*, p. 26.
[234] Aleksander Morgenbesser, *Wspomnienia z lwowskiego więzienia*, ed. Rafał Leszczyński (Warsaw, 1993), p. 19.

versa.[235] Erasing the difference in ecclesiastical practices and rituals between the two Churches was seen as paramount. Włodzimierz Osadczy enumerates the following examples of this phenomenon: the celebration of the Holy Mass in Eastern Catholic churches; the removal of elements of the liturgy characteristic of the Eastern Church; the changing of the rite by families of Greek Catholic clergy to Roman Catholicism; the choosing of a life of celibacy by the sons of Greek Catholic priests after completing seminary in the manner of Roman Catholic priests; Uniates entering Latin seminaries; the celebration in Greek Catholic churches of masses and prayers to saints from the Roman Catholic Church; blessing people after the Holy Mass; genuflection rather than bowing upon raising the Host; the introduction of pews and altar bells; the changing of the look of liturgical garments to make them similar to those of the Latin rite, etc.[236] The erasure of ritual differences created a cordial atmosphere of coexistence and brought these ethnically different peoples together. It was easier for Ruthenians raised in such an environment to adopt Polish culture, as Polish customs and the Roman Catholic Church were not alien to them.

The situation was to change only with the advent of the Revolutions of 1848. At this time a decisive Ruthenization of the Greek Catholic Church occurred, shocking those Greek Catholics who saw themselves more as Poles than representatives of the awakening Ruthenian nation. Józef Doboszyński recalls this change, seen in the example of students of both denominations:

> Up until 1848 the catechists were usually Roman Catholic priests. For the daily service students of both rites would attend the Latin Church, formerly a Jesuit temple and the closest church to school; only for communion would the Uniates go to the Greek Catholic church, where the sermon was given in Polish for all assembled and not simply for the students. The faithful, regardless of denomination, would attend services—sometimes here and sometimes there, wherever was closest. But now all this has changed, for the Uniate students are taken to the Greek Catholic Church and sermons are now delivered in Ruthenian.[237]

The Revolutions of 1848 struck the final blow in a situation that had been gradually breaking down for decades. The only significant difference between Poles and Ruthenians was that of religious rite. From the very moment the Greek Catholic Church started to fulfil the leading

---

[235] Jan Niemirowski, *Pojednanie braci duchownych i świeckich rzymsko- z grecko-katolickiemi w drodze zlania obódwóch obrządków w jedno ciało, czyli Wieniec Haliczanki Skromnej i Nadobnej ułożone i kobietom zacnym ofiarowane* (Lviv, 1848), p. 12.

[236] Osadczy, *Kościół i Cerkiew*, pp. 90, 115.

[237] Doboszyński, "Pamiętnik," p. 373.

role for the Ruthenian nation, those on the Polish side simultaneously started to find their defence in the Roman Catholic Church. From 1848 there occurred a process of politicization of the clergy—initially the Greek Catholic and later the Roman Catholic—which manifested itself in the violent "cleansing" of each denomination of those foreign influences taken from the neighbouring culture.[238]

Changes of these sort helped make Ruthenian people nationally conscious, but also resulted in deteriorating relations between the clergy and those adherents of Greek Catholicism who in no way wished to sever their links with Polishness. As Ruthenian nationality came to be identified with the Greek Catholic Church, choices between nationality and faith became more frequent, which often began as an initial rejection of religious practice and culminated with a rejection of the denomination as a whole. Doboszyński recalled that after the Revolutions of 1848 his father, a Uniate, simply stopped going to the Greek Catholic Church but did not go as far as to change his faith.[239]

The Problem of Greek Catholic Church Affiliation in the Life of *Gente Rutheni, Natione Poloni*

The Galician elite was for the most part an exclusively Polish stratum almost until the end of the nineteenth century, basing itself on Polish culture and drawing from the gentry mores of pre-partition Poland. Any Ruthenian element of those *gente Rutheni, natione Poloni* who had joined this elite grouping was to become burdensome to the individual. Entering the elite came with the price of accepting the culture and habits of the upper echelons, in this case Polish. Polish was the language of speaking, writing, and correspondence; the people they interacted with, worked with, and married were Poles. In such a situation the Ruthenian element of one's identity—which usually meant the affiliation with the Greek Catholic Church—became shameful and onerous to Ruthenians of Polish nationality. This is exemplified by Michał Tustanowski [Mykhailo Tustanovsky], a PhD, lawyer and friend of the Fredro family. He, a Ruthenian of Polish nationality, fulfilled the classic trajectory of marrying into the Polish gentry and entering the circle of Lviv's Polish elite. Despite all this, he maintained his denomination and would regularly attend masses at Greek Catholic churches. However, his presence at the Cathedral of St. George became a cause of embar-

---

[238] Osadczy, *Kościół i Cerkiew*, pp. 91–92, 102.
[239] Doboszyński, "Pamiętnik," p. 373.

rassment to him. Zofia Szeptycka, née Fredro, the mother of the future metropolitan Andrei, wrote of him:

> They no longer said to his face that he did not like to admit to being of the Ruthenian rite, to which, however, he was tied to with all his heart. They say, that Tustan [i.e. Tustanowski] would stealthily creep along the fencing to the Cathedral of St. George to attend a mass on the Ruthenian holidays; and during the blessing his hand would hold the collar of his coat so as not to betray the white tie. Perhaps he simply feared being the subject of some joke or other which might ridicule that most precious treasure from his childhood orphaned years, which he brought to the world together with his plain child's ragged shirt.[240]

It was not only Tustanowski who was ashamed of his faith. For Zofia Szeptycka, the fact that her son Roman would join the Basilian order and would later become Metropolitan Andrei Sheptytsky, proved to be a real drama. She quotes her son's words in her recollections and recalls her feelings:

> (...) his [Roman's – A.Ś.] words struck me like lightning: "So, mother I've decided to join the Basilian [order] and to become a novice."
>
> And did I say anything in reply, did I pray during mass? I simply can't say. Everything is blurred in my mind as is the case of someone losing consciousness after a heavy blow... There were only moments in which some consciousness would return and from these I remember what concerned me. But on hearing those words (those blessed words, as today my heart forces me to write), all of Bratkówka, the whole family, guests, everything drowned, as if in the roar of a hurricane, in that constant thunderous thought: "[Roman] is of a different rite than I!" At that time this meant to me of "another faith."[241]

These sentiments were rooted in the tendency of the Roman-Catholic landowners to treat their neighbouring denomination as something inferior. Thus Szeptycka adopted this view, even though her husband Jan's ancestors had been Greek Catholic metropolitans and bishops themselves before the entire family converted to the Latin rite. In her memoirs, she writes:

> I heard from my earliest years how the Ruthenian clergy was held in the contempt it deserved because of its utter ignorance, greed, and its customs. I knew nothing of the rite itself, having seen only its repre-

---

[240] Zofia Szeptycka, *Wspomnienia z lat ubiegłych*, introd. Bogdan Zakrzewski (Wrocław–Warsaw–Cracow, 1967), p. 78.
[241] Zofia Szeptycka, *Młodość i powołanie ojca Romana Andrzeja Szeptyckiego zakonu św. Bazylego Wielkiego opowiedziane przez Matkę jego 1865–1892*, ed. Bogdan Zakrzewski (Wrocław, 1993), p. 48.

sentatives among the lowest, most despicable layer of society. And in this social layer, which was terrifying and generated pure revulsion, even those who weren't ignorant and depraved had for a dozen or so years been acting as the enemy of the Latin Church and of the Polish nation. [242]

There is no room here to cite the extensive passages from Szeptycka's recollections, in which she over the course of several diary pages describes her regret mixed with outrage and depression, revealing all of the prejudices of the Polish landed gentry against the Ruthenian people and the Uniate rite as well as the repetitious stereotypes on the subject. One such stereotype was the perception of the Ruthenian rite as something devised for rural types and thus inferior to the Roman Catholic faith. Szeptycka quotes herself in conversation with Father Henryk Jackowski: "Father, he will become a total yokel by living among them!"[243]

The father, Jan Szeptycki, had even more difficulty to accept his son's decision. For a long time he refused to accept it. He even sent his son off to the army for a year—which ended when Roman Szeptycki came down with a serious illness. But his father's actions in no way stopped Roman from carrying out his conversion. The Szeptycki family, itself of Ruthenian provenance, was critical of the Uniate Church even though for many centuries its ancestors had taken part in services conducted in the eastern rite. Advancement, development, and career choices drew them unequivocally toward the Polish elites, one aspect of which was the Roman Catholic Church. Any diversion from this "natural" process was extremely painful. It was easier for someone from the upper echelons to wholly Polonize than it was to diverge from this route[244].

A number of Ruthenians willingly abandoned the Greek Catholic rite for the Roman Catholic one, and vice versa. Yakiv Holovatsky wrote:

> A person in Galicia usually calls himself a Ruthenian only if he professes Greek Catholicism; as soon as he changes his faith to the Latin rite, which often happens now, he ceases to be a Ruthenian and is called a Pole.[245]

---

[242] Ibid., p. 50.

[243] Ibid., p. 51.

[244] The dilemma of Roman Szeptycki/Andrei Sheptytsky's identity and its tear between two cultures has been devoted to extensive study by Magdalena Nowak. This very new and well-documented case study is an important voice in the discussion on the problem of the identity of the population of the cultural borderland, which was Galicia in the 19th century. See: Magdalena Nowak, *Dwa światy. Zagadnienie identyfikacji narodowej Andrzeja Szeptyckiego w latach 1865–1914* (Gdańsk, 2018).

[245] Quoted from: Kozik, *The Ukrainian National Movement*, p. 17.

The best known example is that of Jan Wagilewicz, who converted to Protestantism. It was not, however, simply the Polonization he was subjected to that forced him into such a choice; he was also motivated by his financial situation and his relations with superiors within the Greek Catholic Church.[246] Another example is that of Marcjan Łapczyński [Martselii Lapchynsky], the son of a Greek Catholic parish priest. As a twenty-two-year-old man in the 1830s he had been involved in Polish conspiratorial activities. Initially he had participated in the work of the Association of the Polish People, then he jointly founded the organization Free Galicians [Wolni Haliczanie] and subsequently conspired within the ranks of the Sons of the Fatherland [*Synowie Ojczyzny*]. He was arrested for his conspiratorial activities and then sentenced to death, the sentence being reprieved by the emperor. After this, Łapczyński avoided any political activity. He worked as a teacher, and in 1851 changed his religious denomination to Roman Catholicism and joined the Bernardine Order in Lviv, where he spent the next twenty years of his life.[247]

In 1858, Platon Kostecki also wished to join the Basilian religious order, as he expressed in his correspondence with Mieczysław Romanowski. Ultimately he decided not to go through with it,[248] and began his journalistic and literary career.

Another interesting example is Father Stanisław Stojałowski, the well-known peasant activist and defiant Roman Catholic priest. Though to include him in the category *gente Rutheni, natione Poloni* would be an exaggeration (he was already firmly within the Polish sphere), this designation could be applied with much justice to his ancestors. He was the grandson of Bazyli Stojałowski [Vasyl Stoialovsky], the Greek Catholic parish priest at the village of Hlivchany in the Zhovkva administrative district. However, Stanisław was to become a Jesuit novice in 1863 in Stara Wieś and a Roman Catholic priest. His younger sister, Wanda, also chose to serve within the Roman Catholic Church, entering the order of the Felician Sisters in 1872, while the elder brother was known as a Polish patriot, fighting in the January Uprising of 1863 and the Battle of Radyvyliv [Radziwiłłów].[249] Only the fourth of the children, Jan Stojałowski [Ivan Stoialovsky], was to become a Greek Catholic

---

[246] Radyszewśkyj, "Przedmowa," p. 10.
[247] Bolesław Łopuszański, "Łapczyński Marcjan," in *PSB*, vol. 18, p. 209.
[248] *W promieniu Lwowa, Żukowa i Medyki. Listy Mieczysława Romanowskiego 1853-1863*, eds. Bolesław Gawin and Zbigniew Sudolski (Warsaw, 1972), pp. 295–96; Platon Kostecki, „11 listów i wiersze, listy do Mieczysława Romanowskiego" (Lviv, Shehyni, 1854–83), LNNBU, fond 76: Kolektsiia Pavlikovs'kykh, op. 2: Arkhiv Pavlikovs'kykh, spr. 214, p. 27, 29v.
[249] Tomasz Latos, "Stojałowski Stanisław," in *PSB*, vol. 44 (Warsaw–Cracow, 2006–7), pp. 11–17.

priest. When Tadeusz Jagmin wrote about Jan Stojałowski in 1939, he was already an eighty-two-year-old priest in the village of Iavora in the Turka administrative district, but he was unable to fulfil his vocation because of an "assigned Ukrainian guardian," who "does not allow him to perform any church acts yet takes all the incomes."[250] Jan Stojałowski and his family eventually approached the president of Poland Ignacy Mościcki for help.

The Ruthenian Language in the School System

Up until the mid-nineteenth century and in some cases even later, Polish was not only the language of the elites and the Greek Catholic Church in Galicia, but also the language of educated Ruthenian people. The use of Polish at the middle and higher tiers of learning instead of, or with a reduction in the role of Ruthenian, became the subject of long and rowdy Galician Diet debates over the course of the 1860s. These debates were chiefly conducted by *gente Rutheni, natione Poloni* teachers. There is no doubt that at this time Polish was a lexically richer language than Ruthenian, which until the mid-nineteenth century had been used chiefly by peasants and the lower-ranking Greek Catholic clergy.[251] Andrzej A. Zięba correctly notes that under the umbrella of "Ruthenian" there existed many local dialects, individual literary notions, and eventually an administratively standardized variant of the language prepared for use within education.[252] The Ukrainian literary language was yet to be fully formed, and consequently it was often inadequate for academic discourse, which used terms that lacked equivalents in the poorer lexical tongue. Besides the advantage of Polish in literary output over Ruthenian, no less important was the zealous participation of Poles in the somewhat clandestine movement of popularizing Polish literature in the face of progressive Germanization, and later during the period of autonomy a fierce involvement in the Polonization of the Galician school system.

As Marceli Handelsman writes:

> Though on the basis of the royal decree of 1786 the peasant language of the Galician Ruthenians had admittedly been recognized as a "national

---

[250] Jagmin, *Polacy grekokatolicy*, p. 20. Cf. also: Partacz, "Stosunki religijne w Galicji Wschodniej. Rusini łacinnicy i Polacy grekokatolicy." *Rocznik Przemyski* 28 (1991–92), pp. 141–42; Partacz, *Od Badeniego*, p. 181.

[251] Roman Pelczar, *Szkoły parafialne na pograniczu polsko-ruskim (ukraińskim) w Galicji w latach 1772–1869* (Lublin, 2009), pp. 17–18.

[252] Andrzej A. Zięba, "Tożsamość etniczna jako obiekt manipulacji politycznej: Przypadek Rusinów łemkowskich XVIII–XX w. (część druga)," *Rocznik Ruskiej Bursy* (2008), p. 59.

language," in which school instruction and the training of the priesthood were to be conducted, there has now (…) occurred a violent process of Polonization never before seen during the times of the former
independent Poland.[253]

Before this occurred, the Galician school system had been moulded
under conditions of an official policy of Germanization. The lands
under the Austrian area of partition did not initially see many parish schools in operation, either Roman Catholic or Greek Catholic,
and those that existed were chiefly single-class schools. The children
of both denominations could learn their basic skills including reading
and oration in their own language (in Roman Catholic schools in Polish, in Greek Catholic in Ruthenian). Based on the assessment of parish
schools alone, the state of schooling was, however, most inadequate. It
should also be remembered that the provinces (then without Cracow)
missed the reforms enacted by the Commision for National Education
in the still existing, though truncated, Poland.

At this time the Austrian authorities, wishing to create an alternative
option to parish schools, decided to create a network of primary schools.
The school system in Galicia was organized on the basis of the educational model formulated by the Austrian educational reformer, the Aug-
ustinian Johann Ignaz Felbiger. This new model was to be introduced
in all the key countries of the Habsburg Monarchy from 1774 (in Galicia
from 1777). Education was implemented in three types of schools: trivium schools (functioning in small towns and villages), major schools (in
towns), and normal schools, also known as model schools (designated
for an entire province). This system of primary education was to function alongside the parish school system and to gradually supersede it.
The network of state schools was developed very slowly, the level of
teachers' qualifications was terrible, and the furnishing and equipment
of the schools themselves was so limited that many parents decided
not to send their children to school at all. The situation was not even
helped by various types of restrictions and additional legislation aimed
at enhancing the implementation of the compulsory schooling and the
funding of new schools. Given these failures, Emperor Francis I issued
a decree in 1805 for German-language primary schools. This decree envisaged a primary school for every parish. In the same year a patent
was issued which entrusted school care to the clergy. Two years later
the clergy were obliged to submit a report on the state of the school
system, while in 1815, as a result of the edict of the Lviv province, it was
decided that schools were to be under the supervision of consistories

---

[253] Marceli Handelsman, *Ukraińska polityka ks. Adama Czartoryskiego przed wojną krymską*
(Warsaw, 1937), p. 60.

of the relevant denomination. Such a state of affairs was to plague the school system right up until 1848, and, after certain modifications, in principle right up until the period of so-called Galician autonomy.[254]

Education in the light of the new act was to be conducted within three types of school, known as public schools: trivium schools, major schools, and real schools (*Realschulen*). The principle behind the establishment of the system of state schools was for the purpose of training civil servants loyal to the Habsburg monarchy. Only one method of teaching was tolerated—memory exercises through the repetition of texts from German textbooks. Corporeal punishment was rife. As Antoni Knot writes, "life's derelicts" and "a completely chance element" worked in these schools. The aim of state school education was "to gain proficiency in German, master German grammar and spelling as well as the main functions of arithmetic."[255] Such schools were blatantly directed towards Germanization. In trivium schools German was taught, as well as Polish and Ruthenian, while in major schools the language of instruction was to be only German, though during the first years of education Polish was also taught. The Ruthenian language was not taught in the major schools.[256] As Czesław Majorek writes, the teaching of national languages was purely auxiliary in character, used only to facilitate the process of teaching children German.[257] Only religion could be taught in the national languages, but often a bilingual catechism was employed in which one part was in German while the second in a local language translation.

The Galician intelligentsia were to recall their school years as a time of particular misfortune. Zygmunt Sawczyński, *gente Ruthenus, natione Polonus*, wrote in his memoirs that when he cast his mind back to his primary school days he shuddered and thanked the Lord that he was experiencing only memories and not reality all over again. The Germanized school of his memory did not teach pupils to think about or comprehend the materials taught. Teaching merely entailed the recitation out loud of textbooks, and was accompanied by exceptionally severe punishments:

> (…) the teachers "beat" students, but this word is too soft and vague to convey the nature of the action; for they did not beat but, and here

[254] For more on the subject of Galician education for the period in question see: Teofil Fiutowski, *Szkolnictwo ludowe w Galicyi* (Lviv, 1913); Antoni Knot, "Wstęp," in *Galicyjskie wspomnienia szkolne*, ed. Antoni Knot (Cracow, 1955); Florentyna Rzemieniuk, *Unickie szkoły początkowe w Królestwie Polskim i w Galicji 1772–1914* (Lublin, 1991); Roman Pelczar, *Rzymskokatolickie szkoły trywialne w Galicji w latach 1774–1875* (Lublin, 2014).

[255] Knot, "Wstęp," p. xix–xxi.

[256] Rzemieniuk, *Unickie szkoły*, pp. 126–27.

[257] Czesław Majorek, *Historia utylitarna i erudycyjna. Szkolna edukacja historyczna w Galicji (1772–1918)* (Warsaw, 1990), p. 19.

often in a most refined fashion, mutilated a lad if he made a mistake, or stopped while reciting a lesson, or simply did not know where the recitation or the reading of the boy before him had finished.[258]

Many families were spared from Germanization by being educated at home or through boycotting the educational system altogether. Attempts were made to increase the number of lessons given in Polish and Ruthenian. In the case of Ruthenian, efforts were made in 1815 to take advantage of the changeover in school supervision by consistories from the relevant denomination. It was established at the time that religion in schools under the supervision of the Greek Catholic Church would be conducted in Ruthenian, in schools under the supervision of the Roman Catholic Church in Polish, and in schools with an ethnic mix also in Polish but with a guarantee that Ruthenians could be taught religion in their own language. In those settlements where an ethnic mix existed such schools could be set up, but if the area already contained schools under the supervision of the Latin Church then as a rule the building of new schools was forbidden by the authorities.[259] In 1816 the Greek Catholic metropolitan Mykhailo Levytsky approached the Galician provincial office with the request to introduce the teaching of Ruthenian into schools. The provincial office refused, basing its decision on the fact that "the Ruthenian language is, at this moment, merely an uneducated dialect of Polish and consequently constitutes no benefit to the country whatsoever."[260] After an appeal to the emperor, a special school commission was established with the involvement of the archbishops Mykhailo Levytsky and Andrzej Ankwicz, but it was unable to forge a breakthrough. In the commission's statement it was decided that, as Włodzimierz Osadczy notes, "the introduction of Ruthenian classes to primary schools in Galicia is illogical, for Polish is the educated local language while Ruthenian as merely one of its dialects does not lend itself to educational ends and goals."[261] There was even the suggestion that the Greek Catholic catechism be translated into Polish.

Ruthenian was similarly discriminated against in the secondary schools or gymnasiums, which had also suffered because of the policy of Germanization. In 1784, as numerous monasteries were being closed, the majority of existing Galician secondary schools were disbanded (chiefly Jesuit, Piarist, Theatine, and Basilian colleges).[262] Suddenly

---

[258] Zygmunt Sawczyński, "Galicyjska szkoła elementarna przed 1848 r.," in *Galicyjskie wspomnienia,* p. 156.

[259] Rzemieniuk, *Unickie szkoły,* p. 129; Pelczar, *Szkoły parafialne,* p. 27.

[260] Włodzimierz Osadczy, *Święta Ruś. Rozwój i oddziaływanie idei prawosławia w Galicji* (Lublin, 2007), p. 81.

[261] Ibid., p. 82.

[262] Knot, "Wstęp," p. xxiv.

there were only six of them left: in Lviv (that is the famous academic gymnasium where in the future classes were to be conducted in Ruthenian/Ukrainian), Przemyśl, Stanyslaviv, and Tarnów, as well as private schools in Rzeszów and Zamość which still belonged at the time to Austria. Teaching was mainly in Latin. In 1811 reforms were carried out to the Galician educational system, which resulted in the introduction of German-language secondary schools where all classes were conducted in German with the exception of mathematics and Latin. Secondary education was subject to another set of changes in 1819, though these made no improvements. In his study on Galician secondary schools, Stefan Ignacy Możdżeń wrote: "Gymnasiums destroyed the native first language of the youth through the means of the so-called *signum linguae*, and it blacklisted Polish literature."[263] These changes did not mean, however, that pupils brought up in Polish patriotic homes agreed and accepted this imposition of a new "Galician" identity[264]; similarly Ruthenians continued to read Polish poets. Józef Doboszyński, a Galician civil servant, wrote in his diary that with the end of the 1830s "no one even dreamt about Ruthenian, it being considered a local dialect only. In an educated class everyone considered themselves a Pole regardless of religion and rite."[265]

Ruthenians generally found themselves under the overwhelming influence of the Polish language, deemed the only attractive alternative to the officially imposed and largely abhorred German. So marginalized was Ruthenian that in 1848, when classes in German were momentarily withdrawn and religious education was to be taught in the relevant national language that Ruthenian pupils preferred the instruction to be in Polish for they simply did not know any Ruthenian. Such was the situation in the school in Sambir which Józef Doboszyński attended and in which Jan Wagilewicz taught.[266] Not only did the pupils want to be taught in Polish, but there was also an absence of textbooks and of teachers who were able to conduct classes in Ruthenian (in the major schools only Polish grammar was taught).[267] Sometimes even religion was taught to Greek Catholics by Poles if they knew Ruthenian, which was at odds with the principle that religion was supposed to be taught by a teacher of the same denomination as the pupil.

---

[263] Stefan Ignacy Możdżeń, *Historia wychowania 1795–1918* (Sandomierz, 2006), p. 181.

[264] On the failure of the project to make the people (especially Poles) of Galicia the 'Habsburg' or even 'Galician' nation—in other words 'the state nation'—treats the text of Andrzej A. Zięba, "Polacy galicyjscy, czy Polacy w Galicji – refleksje na temat przeobrażeń tożsamości polskiej w zaborze austriackim," *Prace Historyczne* 144, no. 2: *Kształty galicyjskich tożsamości*, ed. Adam Świątek (2017), pp. 215–32.

[265] Doboszyński, "Pamiętnik," p. 362.

[266] Ibid., p. 372.

[267] Pelczar, *Szkoły parafialne*, p. 211.

Following the thaw in interethnic relations in the immediate after-math of the Revolutions of 1848, the Germanization of educational institutions was resumed. At this time the Ruthenian language was introduced as a compulsory subject for all schools in Eastern Galicia, regardless of the pupils' nationality. All other subjects were taught in German. Similarly, in Western Galicia Polish could be taught. Despite the character of a Germanized school system, there was no lack of indi-viduals who worked within it that were wholly committed to the Polish cause and were able, regardless of the language of instruction, to exert a strong influence on the shaping of pupils' identities. At the St. Ann Gymnasium in Cracow during the 1850s Stanisław Tarnowski and Józef Szujski regarded their teacher of history and the Polish language with reverence—a Ruthenian of Polish nationality, Zygmunt Sawczyński. Tarnowski wrote: "to get a bad mark in German or mathematics was just a matter of the mark but to do badly in Mr. Sawczyński's class was shameful and most humiliating."[268] Later on in his recollections Tarn-owski states that

> (...) he awakened [in pupils – A.Ś.] an interest in history and literature, a reverence for what was beautiful in one and the other, but above all [he fostered] the ability to think, which he placed great score on and de-manded of us, and which he would praise when perceived. We under-stood each other exceptionally well in matters of feelings, particularly patriotic ones, and here without saying a word—we trusted him im-plicitly. There was no way to talk about convictions in children, but he infected us with his ideas, and perfectly matched our own instincts. During every history lesson one could effortlessly sense who was good and who was bad (...). Since he came from the Austrian school [sys-tem], being educated chiefly on the basis of German textbooks, and as a historian was obliged to know [these textbooks], it was really strange how very little of all that had an impact on him, particularly given his young age. [269]

Kazimierz Chłędowski writes about Sawczyński in similarly glow-ing terms:

> The greatest teachers that I had at secondary school were Zygmunt Sawczyński and Teodor Stahlberger. The former was a Ruthenian but from a Polish-orientated family (...). A certain Ukrainian lethargy and carelessness had subdued in him all impulses of partaking in a more energetic activity; he read a lot, absorbed what he read, and taught superbly, yet he didn't manage to muster the energy to produce a de-cent academic work or a literary text. He taught us Polish literature in

---

[268] Stanisław Tarnowski, "Dwa lata na ławie szkolnej z Józefem Szujskim," in *Galicyjskie wspomnienia,* p. 201.
[269] Ibid., p. 207.

an easy, warm, and accessible way, he was interested in the minds of the young people, and with genuine engagement we listened to him whenever he stepped up to the lectern.[270]

Another *gente Ruthenus, natione Polonus*, Mikołaj Zyblikiewicz, was given a job at the secondary school in Tarnów in November 1848, but lost his position within a year. He was dismissed because he used a Polish textbook when teaching the theory of pronunciation instead of the requisite Latin textbooks, even though the school in this period used Polish as the language of instruction![271] Years later he confided:

> I worked too much on fostering the Polish language, how could I have stayed in such a position given the reaction that was to occur in Austria in 1849.[272]

The examples cited thus far concern teaching in Western Galicia, but how did the situation look in the eastern part of the region? There we can find cases of Ruthenian teachers who, despite making different choices later on in life, supported the notion of a Polish educational upbringing. In Bolesław Adam Baranowski's memoirs he mentions Father Michał Polański [Mykhailo Poliansky]:

> [He was] of the Greek Catholic rite but—like many at the time —thought and felt Polish. If he was angry with one pupil or another he would place him in the centre of the classroom, give him a good shake and holler "You Muscovite!" He taught natural history, encouraged the collecting of beetles, and treated the pupils of both top classes, as they say, in a friendly manner. He taught the Polish language as an optional subject.[273]

In the Stanyslaviv gymnasium where Polański worked, Ruthenian as a language was a compulsory subject, with only those who had come from Galicia being able to learn Polish though even they had to attend a course of Ruthenian. Only later, when he became a teacher at the First Academic Gymnasium in Lviv, did Father Polański "completely renounce Polishness."[274]

The descriptions of these Ruthenian teachers demonstrate that teaching in a Germanized school did not necessarily preclude an education

---

[270] Kazimierz Chłędowski, "Karta szkolna z pamiętnika literata i ministra 1853–1861," in *Galicyjskie wspomnienia*, pp. 266–67.

[271] Irena Homola-Dzikowska, *Mikołaj Zyblikiewicz (1823–1887)* (Wrocław–Warsaw–Cracow, 1964), p. 10.

[272] [Mikołaj Zyblikiewicz], "Autobiografia Mikołaja Zyblikiewicza," *Czas* no. 116 (22 May, 1887), p. 1.

[273] Bolesław Adam Baranowski, "Kołomyjska *Kreis-Hauptschule* i gimnazjum w Stanisławowie," in *Galicyjskie wspomnienia*, pp. 242–43.

[274] Ibid., p. 243.

that was patriotic and Polish, and that also it often was these Ruthenian teachers that kindled a Polish spirit in the young.

From 1860 onwards, at a time of political change within the monarchy, German was removed from schools as the language of instruction. A rivalry between Polish and Ruthenian began as to which should be used at all levels of the school educational system. Interestingly, there were cases of Ruthenians themselves protesting the introduction of Ruthenian as a language. The situation that unfolded in Khyriv in 1863 is worthy of note, when a group of inhabitants protested against the decision taken by another group in the name of the whole community to hand the school over to the control of a Greek Catholic consistory.[275] Twenty-eight people signed the letter, including fourteen Greek Catholics. We know this because the denominational aspect was added to the signatures,[276] presumably to show that even Uniates were against giving the school over to a consistory of their own rite. Antoni Golejewski reported a similar situation during a discussion on the language act of 1866, though for demonstrational purposes only. He responded to the critical views expressed by Ruthenian deputies about the act by citing the example of the village of Liadske, where the inhabitants had produced a petition in which the Ruthenian population themselves asked the Galician Diet for a Latin consistory to be appointed as they were being made to learn in Ruthenian, a language they did not understand.[277]

Now we shall turn our attention to higher education in nineteenth-century Galicia. In 1784 Emperor Joseph II founded a state university in Lviv in place of the Jesuit academic school, although this university would be reduced in status to a secondary school in 1805. At the university Ruthenian clergy were taught in Latin and not in their own language. Similarly, in the Lviv Studium Ruthenum founded in 1787, the classes in philosophy and theology were more often given in Polish than in Ruthenian, usually at the request of the students themselves.

---

[275] „List mieszczan chyrowskich do Jaśnie Wielmożnego Najprzewielebniejszego Konsystorza obrządku łacińskiego w Przemyślu", 12 Apr. 1863, TsDIAU, fond 146: Halytske namisnytsvo m. Lviv, op. 66, vol. 2, spr. 1708: Materialy pro borot'bu ukraïns'koho nasellennia proty latynizatsii i polonizatsii ukraïns'koi shkil'noi molodi v m. Khyrovi (donesennia, lystuvannia i inshi), pp. 56–57.

[276] We can discern the signatures of the following Uniates on the document: Jan Lepecki (the initiator of the action), Jan Smyk, Michał Mazurski, Michał Kurykowski, Grzegorz Macuski, Father Jan Podkut, Father Jan Kaliczak, Father Jan Jaremkiewicz, Jan Kaliczak (unknown whether the same or another priest than mentioned above), Michał Czukwiński (?), Father Józef Kamnański, Father Jan Pukacz, Michał Sabara, Jan Jabłoński. Ibid., p. 17.

[277] *Sprawozdanie stenograficzne z 4 sesyi Sejmu Krajowego Królestwa Galicyi i Lodomeryi, wraz z Wielkiem Księstwem Krakowskiem w roku 1866*, p. 528.

The professors were not interested in lecturing in Ruthenian, for Polish was the language they used at home.[278] Polish was used by individuals such as Father Michał Harasiewicz [Mykhailo Harasevych], later known for his Polish patriotic activities, as well as the Greek Catholic metropolitan of Lviv, Father Antin Anhelovych.[279] The same situation existed at Lviv University, re-established in 1817, where the Faculty of Theology was almost entirely Greek Catholic in composition.[280] These included individuals who, in the face of national confrontation in 1848, stood on the Polish side or simply wished to maintain the former *status quo*. An exception was Father Onufry Krynicki, the honorary canon of the Greek Catholic Cathedral in Przemyśl, dean ten times and rector of the university in 1834, who during the Revolutions of 1848 joined in the activities of the Ruthenian Sobor.[281] The problem of the language of instruction at institutions of higher education lasted in some form until World War I. This struggle was exemplified by the Uniate priest Father Józef Czerlunczakiewicz, who from the 1858–59 academic year taught at Lviv University. He gave classes in Latin to clergy of both denominations, which led to conflict with the Ruthenian students. During his lectures, Czerlunczakiewicz criticized the notion of priests having children (even though he was the son of a Greek Catholic priest) and called for the introduction of celibacy as it functioned in the Roman Catholic Church. The culminating point in the conflict with the Uniate students occurred on 13 May 1864, when Czerlunczakiewicz was refused entrance to the lecture hall by Ruthenian clergymen, and then attacked with eggs. The scandal ended with the expulsion of thirty-seven priests, who were subsequently accepted by the Jagiellonian University.[282] In the end, Czerlunczakiewicz himself moved to Cracow where he was given a post at the Jagiellonian University in addition to taking over the Greek Catholic parish on Wiślna Street.[283]

Polish was to be the language of instruction at other faculties of Lviv University. Aleksander Morgenbesser, who in 1835 transferred from the Faculty of Theology to the Faculty of Law, met a professor of criminal law, the Ruthenian Mikołaj Napadziewicz [Mykola Napadzevych], who after delivering lectures in German would talk to the students in Polish.[284] The dominance of Polish was not merely restricted to the

---

[278] Zięba, "Gente Rutheni," p. 68.

[279] Osadczy, *Kościół i Cerkiew*, p. 56. See also John-Paul Himka, "The Greek Catholic Church and Nation-building in Galicia, 1772–1918," *Harvard Ukrainian Studies* 8, no. 3–4 (1984), p. 436.

[280] Osadczy, *Kościół i Cerkiew*, p. 61.

[281] Tyrowicz, "Krynicki Onufry," p. 463.

[282] Świątek, "Rusini, Ukraińcy czy Polacy?".

[283] Lewicki, "Czerlunczakiewicz Józef," p. 336.

[284] Morgenbesser, *Wspomnienia*, p. 32.

heavily Polonized city of Lviv, but was widespread in other towns. For example, almost all documents submitted to the Przemyśl Institute of Psalmists and School Teachers, founded in 1816 by Mykhailo Levytsky, by candidates wanting to study there (chiefly the sons of Greek Catholic parish priests) were written in Polish, never in German or Ruthenian.[285]

To recapitulate, the question of language had not always been associated with national identity. Yaroslav Hrytsak recalls an excerpt from the memoirs of Kornylo Ustyianovych, the son of Mykola Ustyianovych, a well-known Ruthenian activist of the 1830s. In it, he asked his father: "Tell me, Dad. What are we really? We think in German, we speak Polish, but how do we write?—in Russian!"[286] Only following the Revolutions of 1848 did the Ruthenian language become a political point that reflected the needs and aspirations of the Ruthenian nation. From the mid-nineteenth century onwards the language question started to genuinely trouble the representatives of the Ruthenian intelligentsia within the context of national identity.

The significance of language for the creation of Ruthenian nationality was paramount. Language as the instrument of communication among the members of a given group determines the ethnic bonding between them. However, this on its own was not enough for the ethnic group of Ruthenians to become a Ruthenian nation. According to nineteenth-century intellectuals, every nation should have its own literary language in which it is able to articulate thought, create works of literature, conduct science, etc. The absence of such in the case of Galician Ruthenians inspired a small group of Ruthenian writers and national activists, including the renowned Ruthenian Triad, to work on creating such a language; but it also allowed for Ruthenian to be treated as a dialect of Polish. Social problems also influenced the language divisions. Polish was universally viewed as belonging to the world of the "masters," while the peasants, regardless of whether Ruthenian or sometimes even Polish (such as the Mazurians in Eastern Galicia), preferred to use Ruthenian.[287] This is not to say, however, that Ruthenians who were not peasants did not know Ruthenian. It was simply easier for them in day-to-day life to speak Polish, as it was the language of urban communication. Furthermore, by living in the towns they remained under the influence of Polish cultural circles, and in particular the culture of written Polish, which most strongly shaped national consciousness. John-Paul Himka has employed a mathematical equation to illustrate the phenomenon: a Ruthenian + higher education =

---

[285] Rzemieniuk, *Unickie szkoły*, pp. 143, 151; Pelczar, *Szkoły parafialne*, p. 211.

[286] Hrytsak, *Ivan Franko*, p. 15.

[287] Osadczy, *Kościół i Cerkiew*, p. 184.

a Pole.[288] This boiled-down conclusion contains much truth. As Antoni Dąbczański wrote:

> I have never heard an educated Ruthenian speak in his own language; even the servants [in Polish homes] have appropriated this Polish language. In Ruthenian seminaries the Ruthenian language is not taught at all, and to this day there still remains only a tiny number of Ruthenian clergy who know the language enough to read the Church alphabet [Cyrillic script – A.Ś.]. The Stauropegion Institute, founded with the purpose of furthering the propagation of the Ruthenian language, has been unable to employ its printers for anything but Roman Catholic books and works in Polish. Even the most nationally zealous Ruthenians produce their works in Polish. And finally in the local Metropolitan church I have heard nothing but Polish sermons.[289]

The influence of Polish was so strong that even those Ruthenians conscious of their nationality were unable to stop speaking it. Rendering the situation more difficult, Ruthenians from Galicia in contact with Ukrainians from beyond the Austrian-Russian border who belonged to the same conceived "nation," were not always able to understand each other in this mutual yet varied language. Kazimierz Chłędowski recalled that in his youth he met with a Biernatsky from Ukraine who dreamed of a free "Little Rus'." He had a colleague, a Ruthenian from Galicia, but "between themselves however they did not speak Ruthenian but conversed in Polish, for both of them were the sons from the homes of civil servants in Rus'."[290]

The Impact of Polish Literature on Polish-Ruthenian Society in Galicia

Language facilitates self-identification but does not determine it. It constitutes an instrument in the conveyance of specified content, but it is the content itself that shapes a world outlook, and which finally helps to form national identity. As a result of the Germanization of the school system in the first half of the nineteenth century, the only hope of being brought up in the Polish spirit was to undertake it oneself. This realization spurred the formation of an array of interest circles, libraries, and inspired interest in the works of Polish literature, which were passed on and copied, often secretly, out of fear of the Austrian police. Antoni Knot wrote: "Self-reflection and literary rebirth in the national

---

[288] Himka, "The Construction of Nationality," p. 114.

[289] Antoni Dąbczański, *Wyjaśnienie sprawy ruskiej* (Lviv, 1848), p. 20.

[290] Chłędowski, *Pamiętniki*, pp. 107–08.

spirit constitutes the only programme open to the present-day youth of Galicia."[291] This applied to both Poles and Ruthenians. Ruthenians, deprived of the literary heritage available to Poles, were unable to fully participate in the process of self-improvement set into motion by the Poles. The situation was to change in the second half of the nineteenth century, when Ruthenians began to develop more cultural and educational activities.

The literary work of the Polish romantics and those who proceeded them played an important role in acquainting the youth with the history, geography, and culture of a country that had been erased from the map of Europe. It helped to develop their patriotic sentiment and raised awareness of the differences existing within the territory of former Poland, differences not yet comprehended as national factors, but viewed instead as ethnic or regional variants. Those fostering a Polish social consciousness learned about the existence of a unique Ruthenian history, folklore, and language through the pages of novels. It is therefore no surprise that the future rousers of Galician Ruthenian nationality took cues from Polish poets and writers. Before it could have any impact, however, literature in Galicia as a whole had to be reborn from this period of Germanization and collapse.

A significant problem for the development of literature among the young generation in Galicia during the first decades of the nineteenth century was the scant stock of local Polish literature, as well as limited access to what had been produced outside the borders of the Austrian partition. As Władysław Zawadzki wrote: "what existed in Galicia before 1820 cannot be called literature."[292] German literature exerted a huge influence, in particular the writers of the Enlightenment and the Romantic poets, particularly Friedrich Schiller and Johann Wolfgang von Goethe. According to the research of Antoni Knot, the interest in literature that developed into a university movement among the youth had its roots in Polish translations of German literature. A breakthrough moment was the influx into Galicia of Adam Mickiewicz's works—their import, copying, and dissemination—beginning in the 1820s, as well as the growth in interest in the historical prose of Julian Ursyn Niemcewicz and Adam Naruszewicz, who dealt with the affairs of the no longer existent Polish state.[293] These writers found wide readership and inspired Galician authors to write similar works. This interest in Polish literature was a feature of both schools and Lviv University, attested

---

[291] Knot, "Wstęp," pp. xxv.

[292] Władysław Zawadzki, *Literatura w Galicji (1772–1848). Ustęp z pamiętników* (Lviv, 1878), p. 27.

[293] Antoni Knot, *Dążenia oświatowe młodzieży galicyjskiej w latach 1815–1830* (Wrocław, 1959), pp. 13–18.

in the unpublished diary of Ryszard Herman. The original diary perished during a fire at Herman's library, but this diary was copied by another memoirist, Henryk Bogdański. His manuscript ended up at the Ossolineum Institute, and is currently part of the holdings of its successor, the Vasyl Stefanyk Lviv Academic Library of Ukraine. Ryszard Herman, born into a Polish-Czech family, attended one of the schools in Lviv before the November Uprising of 1830. In his memoirs (rewritten by Bogdański) Herman described the passionate literary interests of the young people of the day, from among whom many well-known Polish patriots would later be recruited:

> Attending the colleges, I got to know some of those who loved Polish literature. We agreed among ourselves to set up a literary association. There were several of us from different backgrounds: Ludwik Nabielak, Ignacy Kikiewicz, August Bielowski and his youngest brother Franciszek, Stanisław Jaszowski, [Zygmunt] August Kretowicz, Kasper Cięglewicz, and a few others whose names I can't remember. We chose a chairman and a secretary for our circle. We would meet once a week and then each of us would be obliged to bring and read something of their own work or a translation of something. As far as original poetic works, the most successful were those of Nabielak and [Kikiewicz, while the translated poetry of Bielowski held sway; Jaszowski wrote prose, Kretowicz poetry and prose, I also wrote verse, and Cięglewicz wrote poetry which was pompous and unintelligible. Besides writing, we were obliged to read important poetic works. I don't know how, but Nabielak managed to find Mickiewicz's and Odyniec's latest poetry, and as soon as they would write them our lot would recite them. It is difficult to describe the level of enthusiasm with which we listened [to their poetry] and how it broke our hearts to know we would never come anywhere close to equalling them. We would meet in one of the school rooms which, given that our gatherings took place on Sundays, was empty. This lasted for several months, but the police, upon learning of our illicit meetings, called in Jaszowski and Kretowicz and Jaszowski [!] betrayed us. We excluded them from our circle and continued with further gatherings but now in our own flats. (…) Such literary meetings lasted until probably 1828.[294]

Reading could only take place outside of official education. Works of literature were secretly bought, borrowed, copied, and read because, from the perspective of the absolutist monarchy, the possession of this literature was deemed as revolutionary and tied to dangerous nationalist aspirations. Nonetheless, Romantic literature had an enormous influence on the "Polish spirit," particularly among the youth. Bolesław

---

[294] Henryk Bogdański, „Notaty do pamiętnika Ryszarda Hermana" (Lviv, 1868), LNNBU, fond. 5, op. 1, spr. 3535/III, p. 4.

Adam Baranowski wrote that it was the "external side of education." He recounts in his memories that:

> (…) whoever obtained Czajkowski's novel *Vernyhora*, would keep it under lock and key in his chest, and on free days would sneak off to the loft above the stables, sink into the hay or straw and read the prophetic Ukrainian bard secretly, fearing capture for being in possession of such reprehensible literature.[295]

The first literary journals appeared at that time and attracted admirers of Polish literature through their publication of Romantic literary works. An important role was also played by the Department of Polish Literature and Language which was opened at the Emperor Francis I University (later Lviv University) in 1825.[296]

At the same time various philomath societies were being formed among pupils and university students, which later developed into conspiratorial organisations. The *Gente Ruthenus, natione Polonus* Klemens Mochnacki wrote about his studies in Lviv:

> Here I came into contact with young people from Berezhany, Stanyslaviv, and Buchach, who knew more about Polish literature than those from the Przemyśl or Sambir districts. This proves that teachers exist who can give the youth more than can be found in school books (…) It was the first time I heard of [Adam] Mickiewicz, [Józef Bohdan] Zaleski, [Kazimierz] Brodziński and others. (…) With all the passion of youth I threw myself into reading our poets. The poetry of Mickiewicz, published in Paris, Brodziński, [Antoni Edward] Odyniec, [Franciszek] Karpiński, [Stanisław] Trembecki, the almanac *Melitele noworocznik* [published by Odyniec in Warsaw in 1829], [Aleksander] Fredro's comedies—youth influencing youth. The movement was even stronger in Lviv when [Walenty] Chłędowski published *Haliczanin* [almanac published in two volumines in Lviv in 1830] and young writers appeared for the first time with their works: writers like Leszek and Józef Borkowski, A[ugust] Bielowski, [Ignacy] Kikiewicz, [Ludwik] Nabielak, and L[udwik] Jabłonowski. *Haliczanin* struck the bell and awoke intellect from stupor, but it did not incite political thought. Eugeniusz Brodzki changed things; it was to be 29 November [1830—A.Ś.] that eventually opened everyone's eyes.[297]

Besides works of literature, students often read texts on Polish history. Klemens Mochnacki remembered reading the works of Adam Naruszewicz, Julian Ursyn Niemcewicz, and Franciszek Siarczyński.

---

[295] Baranowski, "Kołomyjska *Kreis-Hauptschule*", p. 251.

[296] Osadczy, *Święta Ruś*, p. 29.

[297] Klemens Mochnacki, *Pamiętnik spiskowca i nauczyciela 1811–1848*, ed. Antoni Knot (Cracow, 1950), pp. 6–7.

As he himself notes, this did not so much affect political views, but rather influenced the "Polish spirit." He wrote: "Only the November Uprising was to revive the spirit of Polish patriotism."[298]

However, before the youth of Galicia were to mobilize and fight, there had to be a reason for revolt. Other factors influenced the general call to arms besides the patriotic-nationalist rapture; the everyday effects of living within the partition, such as the process of Germanization in schools, convinced Polish and Ruthenian youth alike of the need to struggle. Patriotic literature, laden with calls for freedom and the matching slogans, found receptive readers in Galicia among people of both provenances. Because of the lack of a Ruthenian literature, Polish literature was adopted as "one's own" for all of the inhabitants of this Austrian area of partition. The strong influence of Polish is mentioned in the pre-November Uprising poetry by the Lviv poet Ludwik Pietrusiński, later a doctor of law:

> How honest is this Polish child, that Ruthenian right there,
> With a slitless open cape and visibly uncut hair,
> Beaten by a German switch or staff of green
> Next to Polish syllables wrote the German ones,
> Trying to replicate the German catechism.[299]

The force of Polish Romanticism was unusually strong. Ruthenian pupils were reading exactly the same materials as their Polish school colleagues, the interest of both heightened by the fact that these were outlawed works. Ivan Holovatsky, the brother of Yakiv, confided in his brother that as a seventeen-year-old he had absorbed "French-Polish propaganda" including Mickiewicz's *Books of the Polish People and Pilgrimage* [*Księgi narodu i pielgrzymstwa polskiego*].[300] In any case it was not only Ivan but also Yakiv Holovatsky who avidly read the Polish Romantics, something that he later refrained from admitting. It was Danuta Sosnowska who noticed this, drawing attention to Holovatsky's library slips from the time he studied at the seminary.[301] As Handelsman wrote, it was indeed from Polish democracy that:

> The young Ruthenian intelligentsia in Galicia took its revolutionary attitude, social concepts and the impetus to direct action among its own people. It also received a strong push in the direction of patriotism: admittedly it was Polish patriotism, but a change of situation, mood, and influences would be enough for Poland to be replaced in their souls by

---

[298] Ibid., p. 7.
[299] Knot, *Dążenia oświatowe*, p. 39.
[300] Handelsman, *Ukraińska polityka*, p. 65.
[301] Sosnowska, *Inna Galicja*, pp. 165–67.

some other hazily defined fatherland, Rus', all the elements for which had been previously given to them through the preparation of Polish conspiracies.[302]

In summary, the influx of new revolutionary intellectual currents and their promotion by the post-November Uprising Polish emigration found a receptive audience among both Poles and Ruthenians in Galicia. The youth were fascinated by Mickiewicz's messianic visions as well as by the demands for equality advanced by émigré democrats wishing to reform social relations in backward Galicia. Romantic literature did not only initiate the revolutionary activity of insurgents and conspirators; for many years it constituted a canon of Polish literature which evoked universal feeling. The writings of Polish authors from the first half of the nineteenth century filled the shelves of the so-called "good" homes, those of the gentry and bourgeoisie. This explains to a certain degree the access to Polish culture enjoyed by the many Ruthenians who would become *natione Poloni*. Władysław Cichocki, in recalling the popularity of Adam Mickiewicz, Aleksander Chodźko, Wincenty Pol, and Lucjan Siemieński, wrote:

> We have many writers who were shaped on these models alone and reached great heights. I shall mention as an example only Z[ygmunt] Sawczyński, whose works we have often come across in older "excerpts" and whose historical portrait *Kubek sierotka* [The Orphan Mug] is in my opinion an artistic gem in its own right. In this work he showed that he writes magnificently.[303]

Sawczyński was not alone in taking up pen and paper in the manner of the Polish poets. Platon Kostecki, a pupil of the secondary school in Sambir, also wanted to model himself on Mickiewicz. His teachers "would furtively slip (…) books, give advice on the first steps to a literary career," and a certain teacher named Romankiewicz [Romankevych] "secretly acquainted him with Polish literature and poetry."[304]

Literature was a medium that incited one to action and fulfilled a patriotic function. It also resulted in increased social awareness, shaped the world outlook of readers, articulated the bonds between the peoples inhabiting the lands of what had been Poland, and finally drew people's attention to the history of these lands. Rus' was to occupy a special place within this "archive of visions," one that was dependent on Poland itself.

---

[302] Handelsman, *Ukraińska polityka,* p. 66.
[303] Cichocki, *Sambor,* p. 44.
[304] S.P., "Gente Ruthenus, natione Polonus," *Dziennik Polski* no. 18 (18 Jan., 1888), p. 2.

Chapter II
Rus' in the Historical Consciousness of Poles

The Perception of Fatherland

Polish scholarly literature dealing with the notion of the fatherland has been forced to consider the nature of the term not only through a geographical, but also a political lens. The understanding of fatherland, its definition, and finally the strong attachment to the term demonstrated by the inhabitants of Galicia all constitute important aspects in the matter of self-identification. For Ruthenians of Polish nationality, the question of what fatherland meant to them was especially difficult. Although they were descended from Rus' and Ruthenian families, they articulated at the same time a broadly understood attachment to Polishness. They yearned to reconstruct the Poland of old, all the while principally identifying themselves with their most immediate surroundings—the territory of former Red Rus'.

In order to appreciate the significance of this problem in one's individual consciousness, it is worth here to examine Stanisław Ossowski's concept of "private" and "ideological" fatherlands. This sociologist described the relation of man to an ideological fatherland:

> The relation to an ideological fatherland (…) is based (…) on certain convictions: on the conviction of the individual as to his participation in a given collectivity and on the conviction that this is a territorial collectivity connected with this very area.[1]

Elsewhere Ossowski emphasized:

> A fatherland constitutes a rich set of values that plays a significant role in national culture, while a certain specific attitude in relation to a territorial fatherland is indeed an element of this culture. Imperative in this sense is the fact that there would be no basis to call a culture devoid of such an element a national culture, and to refer to such type of collectivity as a nation. The dependence between the fatherland and the nation is therein bilateral.[2]

---

[1] Stanisław Ossowski, "Analiza socjologiczna pojęcia Ojczyzna," in Stanisław Ossowski, *O ojczyźnie i narodzie* (Warsaw, 1984), p. 26.

[2] Stanisław Ossowski, "Ziemia i naród," in Ossowski, *O ojczyźnie*, p. 54.

The ideological fatherland for *gente Rutheni, natione Poloni* was—particularly in the nineteenth century—Poland, while the private, individual fatherland remained Rus' (and in principle its Galician part), which constituted their natural existential environment.

Attention should also be drawn to one more question: who formed the image of an ideological fatherland among the inhabitants of Galicia? The memory of a lost fatherland was passed on within the circles of the more patriotic noble families; however, the entire society that inhabited the lands of former Poland required a developed and cohesive conception, one conveyed by literature—the information transfer of the day—and subsequently the printing press. It was therefore essential in the nineteenth century, given the absence of a Polish state, to nurture the notion of a fatherland as an idea conceivable for the entire nation, as much for those who already felt themselves to be Polish as for those who were only beginning to develop such a notion.[3] Such a concept of territory that would serve as the basis for the construction of the future state had not only to be presented to interested recipients, but had to be first and foremost defined. Yaroslav Hrytsak pointed out that the "creation of a fatherland" in the nineteenth century was a joint venture between politicians, geographers, historians, statisticians, the military, and finally, particularly in the Polish case—literary figures. Hrytsak claims that writers "transformed all their readers into a 'nation of dreamers'."[4] Yet the concept of "creating a fatherland" appears to be somewhat exaggerated; although the matter concerns lands that once belonged to Poland, learned and cultured people "imagined" a fatherland of their own making for their recipients. These were subjective descriptors and representations containing more misrepresentations and omissions than objective facts. The most fundamental aspect, however, was the conveying of love for the fatherland.

What image of the Polish fatherland was shaped in the nineteenth century? Above all, the fatherland was to mirror the territory of the former Poland within the pre-partition borders, with the inclusion of Ruthenian and Lithuanian lands. There was an understanding of the historic and cultural differences of the Ruthenian and Lithuanian lands, but it was nevertheless assumed that the inhabitants of these lands would still want to build a multi-ethnic Polish state in the future. Such a myth was professed and consolidated by generations of Polish politicians, writers, and artists. This notion existed right up to the moment

---

[3] It is worth noting that it was not conceived for a moment that Ruthenians and Lithuanians might actually want their own states.

[4] Cf. Yaroslav Hrytsak, *Ivan Franko and His Community*, trans. Marta Olynyk (Edmonton–Toronto, 2018), p. 78.

territorial demands were articulated by hitherto "fraternal" peoples,[5] which did not mean that the Polish elites wanted to agree to the demand for a reduction in the territorial size of the future state. The antagonism between Poles and Ruthenians over joint settlement of the territory was imaginary in character until the end of the World War I, but it nevertheless did force Ruthenians of Polish nationality to make a concrete choice. As a result of their chosen nationality, *Gente Rutheni, natione Poloni* dreamed of an independent Poland, yet adamantly emphasized that a fundamental element ought to be its federal character. From the 1860s poetry of Platon Kostecki through the political demands of Teofil Merunowicz in 1919, Poland was presented as a comprehensible political commonwealth of ethnic Poland, Lithuania, and Rus'.

It was natural that the increasingly nationally-conscious Ruthenians would not agree to such a vision, but they were not the only group opposed to the idea. The project of constructing a commonwealth of nations from these regions, equal in rights, had also been questioned by a contingent of the Polish Galician political scene, namely the populists and nationalists. According to their political programs, the Polish fatherland was to encompass lands inhabited by a Polish ethnos. However, the nationalists would often recall the most distant border in the east, placing their hopes on a policy of assimilation. At this time, terminology arose that simultaneously encompassed the geographical areas of Poland, i.e., "historic Poland" (also referred to as "Jagiellonian") based on the Commonwealth of Poland and Lithuania, as well as the notion of "ethnic Poland" (Piast), whose eastern borders were not viewed as lying beyond Galicia but rather within it, centred on the rivers Wisłok, San, and Tanew.[6]

The tradition of "historic Poland" was brought to the fore through literature, art, and historiography. Polish cultural works had for generations raised the spirits of the inhabitants of these former Polish lands, especially the inhabitants of Galicia, peoples bound in a spirit of attachment to the former borders stretching up to the Dnipro and Dnister rivers. This love for the land did not necessarily translate into a willingness to acknowledge the non-Polish inhabitants of these expanses. In this way, from the end of the nineteenth century to the first decades of the twentieth century, the relationship of Poles to the non-Polish inhabitants of these areas was defined by sometimes conflicting desires to rebuild historic Poland and to create a society that was strictly

---

[5] Cf. Piotr Eberhardt, *Polska i jej granice. Z historii polskiej geografii politycznej* (Lublin, 2004), p. 38.
[6] Ibid., pp. 63–64.

homogeneous — if not Polish then at least Polonized. Thus from the end of the nineteenth century onwards, both forms of perception entered into the Polish Eastern Marches, ones differing only in terms of the potential border and relations to their non-Polish (in the ethnic sense) inhabitants. For this reason, almost all of nineteenth-century Polish literature and art that referred to the eastern lands of the Poland of old was to place an emphasis increasingly on the territory in the sense of the land rather than on the ethno-national differences existing there, with the latter eventually being subjected to the idea of a common state.

Literature in the First Half of the Nineteenth Century

In the article "The Polish Procession" ["Polski korowód"], Maria Janion aptly presented the essence of the ideas current in nineteenth-century Polish society, and their impact on society during the epoch of the partition. She argues:

> In examining the history of Polish consciousness in the modern epoch, one can easily notice in the nineteenth century the importance of the role played by the intense ideological activity of both artists and politicians as well as that of so-called ordinary people, particularly those drawn into activities creating history itself. What occurred in the sphere of historical events from the collapse of Poland's independence was to find its personal equivalent in imaginary life. It is necessary to emphasize that imagined projects were to affect reality most strongly. We are therefore dealing in this period with an exceptionally clear interaction between reality and imagination.[7]

Citing Norman Davies, Janion claims that it is impossible to research the history of Poland under the partitions without recourse to the so-called "archives of imagination." The scholar must question how romantic visions of the fatherland, dreams about state reconstruction, national myths, and finally the literary and artistic legacy of the inhabitants of the lands of the former Polish state influenced the consciousness of Poles and Ruthenians in Galicia. The strongest influence on the worldview of an educated man in the first half of the nineteenth century was that of Romantic literature. The force of the written word was immense, for a literary work carried a definite vision of the world (in this case of Polish culture, history, people), but also shaped and formed specific attitudes and modes of behaviour. Furthermore, those who

---

[7] Maria Janion, "Polski korowód," in *Mity i stereotypy w dziejach Polski,* ed. Janusz Tazbir (Warsaw, 1991), p. 186.

shaped literature were well aware of its strength; after all, nineteenth-
-century writers were "architects of the imagination." The output of
Polish writing, particularly from the times of Romanticism, was sufficiently powerful across the territorial entirety of the old Poland that it
often served as proof of the Polishness of these particular lands. It was
the literary legacy, not the achievements of technology or industrial development, that was considered for the largest part of the period under
study to be of the greatest cultural value. Consequently, when dozens
of excellent literary works were created in Poland, Rus', or Lithuania,
they formed a belief in the actual existence and development of Polish
culture within these very borders, and therefore for the entire nation.
Wincenty Pol, the most important of the nineteenth-century "architects
of the imagination," wrote about language and literature in the following way:

> The literary language is, as it were, a national transaction of Poland,
> Lithuania, and Rus'; somehow it was only following the joining of
> Lithuania and Rus' with Poland that the written language developed at
> an incomprehensible speed across matters colloquial as well as within
> public life and here across the entirety of the Polish historical expanse.
> (...)
>   No doubt an active element was brought to the language by the
> Lechite tribe, whose language had earlier grown stronger, more power-
> ful and resonant; yet the common heritage of all older Polabians meant
> that as much as some brought to the language others took, and as much
> as they took they themselves gave.
>   The Polish written language was to become in this way the result of
> a historical fact—the unification of the indigenous Polabians into a na-
> tion and the merging of dialects into a common organ of conscious com-
> prehension within the field of spiritual life.
>   This national chemistry joined the dialects together in such a way
> that today, only skill is able to partly illuminate against the field of
> linguistic research what contribution each of the component dialects
> brought to the creation of the written, literary Polish language.[8]

In a later part of his work Pol acknowledges:

> (...) we shall here state that the "expanse of Polish literature" totally
> matches the "area of the Polish language" and that across this expanse
> there could not have been maintained permanently, either through the
> course of the ages or today, any literary language that could have been
> raised to the significance of a literary language of the magnitude and
> literary worth that we can observe in the Polish language and in Polish
> literature.[9]

---

[8] Wincenty Pol, *Historyczny obszar Polski* (Cracow, 1869), pp. 10–11.
[9] Ibid., p. 13.

Understanding literacy as a crucial element of the cultural affiliation of these said lands, Pol came to the conclusion that the languages
used in particular areas were at most dialects, while Polish was the language of high literature; hence, Rus' and other lands were, in actuality,
Polish.[10]

The Polish literature of the nineteenth century frequently dealt with
the subject of Rus', Ukraine, and the Ruthenian people. This was the
result of the new literary current of Romanticism which directed itself
towards the hitherto overlooked element of folk culture, initially Lithuanian and then by analogy, Ruthenian.

Adam Mickiewicz was to take various episodes from Lithuanian
history and combine them with folk tales to spin out stories inspiring
one to patriotic sacrifices. Other writers and poets followed his example
both within Poland and abroad, for it was not simply the famous invocation from *Sir Thaddeus* [Pan Tadeusz]—"Oh Lithuania, my fatherland"—that spoke of the bard's attachment to his own homeland, in
this case Lithuania. He laid out the entire ideology of Polish Romanticism, including the question of the two historical nations, in his *Books
of the Polish Nation and Polish Pilgrimage* written in 1832,[11] when Mickiewicz was an émigré, and translated into English a year later. Here we
can read a description of the unity of Poles and Lithuanians, forged in
a biblical style:

> And God rewarded them for it; for a great country, Lithuania, united
> with Poland, like a betrothed bride with a bridegroom, two souls in one
> body. And there never before had existed such a union of nations—yet,
> hereafter, such a union shall exist.
>   For this union and wedding tie of Lithuania with Poland is but an
> image of a universal union of Christian nations, which is to be effected
> in the name of Faith and Freedom.[12]

In turn, in the 12th Book of Polish Pilgrimage the bard explained to
the Lithuanians and the Mazurians that there were no differences between them, for they were but a part of the same nation: "The Lithuanian and the Mazurian are brothers, and do brothers quarrel, because
the one is named Wladislaw, and the other Witowt [Vytautas – A.Ś.]?
Their common name is the same—that of Poles."[13]

The Lithuanian-Polish bond, deriving from the times of union, was
forcefully emphasized in the literature of Romanticism and firmly en-

---

[10] Cf. Eberhardt, *Polska,* p. 42.
[11] Adam Mickiewicz, *Księgi narodu polskiego i pielgrzymstwa polskiego* (Paris, 1832).
[12] Adam Mickiewicz, *The Books and the Pilgrimage of the Polish Nation* (London, 1833), p. 16.
[13] Ibid., p. 55.

grained in the social consciousness of the partition period. It suffices to examine the universal and frequently accentuated heraldic symbolism. For centuries, Lithuanians had managed to weave themselves into Polish culture, though this was a process involving chiefly the privileged social estates. The peasants, as in the case of the Ruthenians, were to remain indifferent to the national question right up until the turn of the twentieth century. Yet the framing of the union of Poles and Lithuanians not as a fraternity but as a marriage was to remain a key element in Polish historical consciousness throughout the nineteenth century, something obvious but especially articulated in Romantic literature from Mickiewicz's time onwards. An analogical process occurred in the Ruthenian lands. Polish writers coming from Ruthenian territories naturally concentrated on those geographical expanses closest to them, demanding a place for them in Polish literature. Here mention must be made of those figures belonging to the so-called Ukrainian Romantic School: Seweryn Goszczyński, Antoni Malczewski, Bohdan Zaleski, Wincenty Pol, and finally Juliusz Słowacki. Agaton Giller wrote:

> Polish poetry is therefore a tonal union—it is the singular aesthetic output of Poles, Lithuanians and Ruthenians. Without the said Ukrainian school of poets, in which Zaleski occupies one of the leading places, Polish poetry would not be what it is, and this is to its eternal glory: a complement to the beauty of the union of the three nations.[14]

Józef Bohdan Zaleski, the actual founder of the Ukrainian Romantic school, who debuted in 1819 with the poem "Lament for Wacław" ["Duma o Wacławie"], introduced the fascinating world of Ukraine to Polish literature.[15] In researching the Ukrainian *dumka*, Zaleski came to the conclusion that they contained Polish words and were of a Polish character. He modelled his own songs on them. He even considered himself to be the heir of the legendary Rus' bard Boyan. This presumably lay behind his creation of numerous works set in a Ukrainian reality through which was woven the motif of a Polish-Ruthenian brotherhood-in-arms facing the threat posed by Turks and Tatars. Rus' is also a constant element in his works. Leafing through the pages of Zaleski's poetry published in Lviv in 1838, one is transported to the world of a Cossack Ukraine. Heroic, not rebellious, figures feature prominently in his works. It is worth recalling "The Dumka of Hetman Kosinsky" ["Dumka hetmana Kosińskiego"] or "Chaikas: Song of

---

[14] Agaton Giller, *Bohdan Zaleski* (Poznań, 1882), p. 2.
[15] Hugo Zathey, *Młodość Bohdana Zaleskiego (1802–1830)* (Cracow, 1886), p. 7.

the Zaporozhian Cossacks on their Return from a Sea Expedition under Konashevych" ["Czajki. Śpiew Zaporożców w powrocie z wyprawy morskiej Konaszewicza"].[16] Zaleski presented a fatherland composed of three lands, Poland, Lithuania, and Rus', and considered himself a son of the latter. As a devout believer he had no qualms about inciting God, the Holy Virgin, and finally the saints, St. Stanislaus, St. Casimir, and St. Josaphat (as the respective patrons of the Crown, Lithuania, and Rus'), for help in this broadly understood fatherland. We shall recall two stanzas from a very important Zaleski poem, an anthem of sorts, entitled "A Prayer for Poland" ["Modlitwa za Polską"]:

Oh Mary, Mary, Queen on high,
Your grace famed in three lands,
Your three lands – Lithuania – Rus' – the Crown
Stretch before you under your holy feet!
Lithuania – Rus' – Poland
– a three-leafed brotherhood,
O Virgin pure protect your bloom!
The Chosen States oppressed in state
There on high our protectors lord
To the common mother – to Poland – oh to her
Do turn your gaze! Saint Stanislaus,
Saint Casimir, Saint Josaphat
To her – to the Mother in the bloody cloak.[17]

In turn, Wincenty Pol wrote about the expansive borders of Poland and Lithuania extending beyond their ethnic dimensions, and in doing so escorted his readers around the various corners of this broadly understood fatherland, one that also incorporated Rus'. "The Songs of Janusz" ["Pieśni Janusza"] contain the following lines:

I was in Lithuania and in the Crown,
I was on that side and on this,
I was here and I was there;

From the Beskyd Mountains to Pomerania,
From Lithuania to Zaporizhia,
I know Poland the whole.
I know the whole honest tribe,
The Polish seas, the Polish land,
And that Polish salt;

---

[16] Józef Bohdan Zaleski, *Poezye* (Lviv, 1838), pp. 45–54. A *chaika* is a type of Cossack wooden boat – G.T.
[17] [Józef] Bohdan Zaleski, *Poezija* (Paris, 1841), p. 103.

And I dream about all, I fantasize,
And all as if mine,
As if I were the Polish king[18].

This exceptionally telling fragment from "The Songs of Janusz" could serve as an answer to the question from where and in what way the notion of the borders of the then politically nonexistent Poland was derived. Those who read these words would recognize that Rus' was also Poland.

These three poets, Mickiewicz, Zaleski, and Pol, played an important role in the shaping of social consciousness during the period of partition. They not only recalled the history of old, but also emotively explained by means of their poetry such complex terms as "nation" and "fatherland." Their conception of "nation" comprised several ethnic groups, while "fatherland" encompassed various geographical lands, including Rus', within its borders. As Seweryna Duchińska stated:

> Mickiewicz exhilarated our society with recollections of Lithuania, Bohdan Zaleski took us with him across the broad steppes of Ukraine; Wincenty Pol led us through all the districts of our land, and with this miracle of song the reborn Poland grew into a single, inseparable national whole.[19]

Duchińska aptly defined one of the functions of Polish poetry as the "consolidation of the spirit." Poles, Ruthenians, and Lithuanians were to merge into a single nation, regardless of their differences. But for this to happen, over the course of centuries those inhabiting the areas comprising old Poland had to absorb literature that promoted the concept of Rus' as its own land. This mindset was influenced by other poets: Antoni Malczewski in *Maria*,[20] a work emphasizing the value of knighthood in the borderlands; Seweryn Goszczyński in *Kaniv Castle* [*Zamek Kaniowski*],[21] a work presenting Ukraine as a place of mystery, exceptional in its folklore, customs, and superstitions; and finally Michał Czajkowski in *Vernyhora* [*Wernyhora*],[22] Lucjan Siemieński in *The Three Bards* [*Trzy wieszczby*],[23] Juliusz Słowacki in *Wacław*,[24] *Beniowski*[25]

---

[18] Wincenty Pol, *Pieśni Janusza*, vol. 1 (Paris, 1833), pp. 8–9.

[19] Seweryna Duchińska, *Bohdan Zaleski* (Poznań, 1892), p. 3.

[20] Antoni Malczewski, *Marja. Powieść ukraińska* (Warsaw, 1825).

[21] Seweryn Goszczyński, *Zamek kaniowski. Powieść* (Warsaw, 1828).

[22] Michał Czajkowski, *Wernyhora. Wieszcz ukraiński. Powieść historyczna z roku 1768*, vol. 1–2 (Paris, 1838).

[23] Lucjan Siemieński, *Trzy wieszczby* (Paris, 1841).

[24] Juliusz Słowacki, *Wacław* (Lviv, 1879).

[25] Juliusz Słowacki, *Beniowski. Poema. Pięć pierwszych pieśni* (Paris, 1841).

and *Salomea's Silver Dream* [*Sen srebrny Salomei*],[26] and at a later date also Franciszek Rawita-Gawroński in the poem "The Death of Vernyhora" ["Śmierć Wernyhory"].[27] All these poets recall the figure of the Ukrainian prophet Mosii Vernyhora, the bard loyal to Poland at the time of the Koliivshchyna rebellion, the Ruthenian rebellion intent on suppressing the Bar Confederation (1768–72), which was considered to be the first Polish independence uprising against Russia and its influences in Poland. The myth of this Cossack holding the *haidamakas* back from attacking Poles and his prophecy of Poland's restoration has, as a result of literary and artistic works, occupied a coveted place in the canon of Polish culture.[28] This myth was sufficiently strong that works based on him were written in Ruthenian. The November Uprising insurgent Antoni Szaszkiewicz [Antonii Shashkevych], hailing from the Podilia-Volhynia border region, composed the song "Vernyhora" [*Wernyhora*], which was later sung during the January Uprising in 1863.[29] The song, written in Ruthenian but in Latin script, called for taking up arms against the enemy:

> Come on out boys out of the hut
> Pay homage to Vernyhora
> For all of our Honcharykha[30]
> Will see good after the bad,
>
> In the teeth, in the hand, whatever one has;
> Let the iron [weapons] be pulled
> And if something is missing
> Then God will somehow save the day
> Call forth the Poles
> Who is unwilling will get the whip
> Who is not with us, is certainly against us
> To the Moscovite! All in God's time.

---

[26] Juliusz Słowacki, *Sen srebrny Salomei. Romans dramatyczny w pięciu aktach* (Paris, 1844).

[27] Franciszek Rawita-Gawroński, "Śmierć Wernyhory. Baśń ukraińska," *Tygodnik Illustrowany* no. 25 (6 [18] Jun., 1893), pp. 489–510.

[28] On Vernyhora in Polish culture see: Jan Mirosław Kasjan, "Wernyhora," in *Życiorysy historyczne, literackie i legendarne*, eds. Zofia Stefanowska and Janusz Tazbir, vol. 2 (Warsaw, 1989), pp. 155–80; Władysław Stabryła, *Wernyhora w literaturze polskiej* (Cracow, 1996).

[29] On Antoni Szaszkiewicz see: Stefan Buszczyński, "Historyczne wspomnienie o Antonim Szaszkiewiczu. Przyczynek do dziejów naszej walki o wyzwolenie," in [Antoni Szaszkiewicz], *Pieśni Antoniego Szaszkiewicza wraz z jego życiorysem*, published by Stefan Buszczyński (Cracow, 1890), pp. 3–31. Szaszkiewicz was also recalled by: Stabryła, *Wernyhora*, pp. 18, 122–23.

[30] Honcharykha is the name of a ravine near Starokostiantyniv in Ukraine where, according to a prophecy by Vernyhora, the Russians were to experience a future defeat.

Take a farewell oh black browed [Cossacks, young soldiers]!
And be proud that we are there,
That all are ready to die
Our mark we shall make on the enemies.

Let us make accord with the Poles,
Don't let us count their sins,
A single idea, a single cause
For Warsaw is our capital.[31]

Szaszkiewicz, writing to Ruthenians in their own language and rallying a brotherhood-in-arms in the fight against a common enemy, was by no means isolated in his activities. Another such individual propagating Polish-Ruthenian unity came from beyond the Zbruch River—Tomasz Padura, better known as Tymko Padurra. This poet, born into a Polonized gentry family from the area of Carpathian Rus', modelled himself on Julian Ursyn Niemcewicz, the author of *Historical Songs* [*Śpiewy historyczne*], a cycle of songs presenting a vision of Poland's past. Padura decided to write a similar history of Ukraine, but in laments. He chose figures from Cossack history with a friendly disposition towards Poland as his heroes. For an important moment in 1825, Tomasz Padura's life intersected with that of "Emir" Wacław Rzewuski, who prepared a Cossack unit that later undertook action to revive the Zaporozhian Sich in union with Poland. Padura, travelling through Ukraine dressed as a bard and inciting an armed uprising, advocated just this kind of conflict. Following the collapse of the November Uprising, which cancelled Rzewuski's farreaching plans, Padura settled down on his family estate and his works started to take on a life of their own. They were published in Polish journals in Galicia and the other areas of partition. He was eventually able to publish a collection of his Ruthenian poetry written in Latin script in 1844.[32] Padura's biographer Mieczysław Inglot noted the stylization of his poetry "fitted within (…) the main current of the literary fashion of the day, that of Ukrainomania."[33]

Following the example of Padura, who enjoyed popularity in Galicia, other poets and lovers of folklore began collecting Ruthenian poetry or publishing it in the original. A similar process to that taking place in Ukraine occurred in Galicia, where a sizeable group of "researchers" of Ruthenians and their cultural heritage could be found. The first mention should be made of Wacław of Olesko, that is Wacław Zaleski,

---

[31] [Szaszkiewicz], *Pieśni*, pp. 59–60. Cf. Stabryła, *Wernyhora*, pp. 18–19.

[32] Tymko Padurra, *Ukrainky z nutoju* (Warsaw, 1844).

[33] Mieczysław Inglot, "Padurra Tomasz," in *PSB*, vol. 25 (Wrocław–Warsaw–Cracow–Gdańsk, 1980), p. 14.

who would go on to become the governor of Galicia. He was the first to introduce wide-scale ethnographic research into the Eastern Galician countryside, personally collecting folk songs. Marceli Handelsman wrote that Wacław of Olesko was responsible for discovering country-side songs in which a genuinely Slavic spirit was revealed.[34] In 1833 Zaleski managed to publish almost one and a half thousand works of this type,[35] through which he was able to acquaint the Galician elite with the common people of these lands. This was of some significance, especially given the developing interest in this subject area among later poets and researchers. The next work of a similar type appeared in 1839–40: *The Songs of the Ruthenian Folk of Galicia* [*Pieśni ludu ruskiego w Galicyi*], collected by Żegota Pauli. Like his predecessor, he published the Ruthenian songs in Ruthenian but used the Latin alphabet.[36]

This work continued into the next generation with Lew (Leon) Eugeniusz Węgliński, about whom Józef Białynia Chołodecki wrote that "he collected Little Russian songs, laments, dumkas, choral pieces, dances, ballads, etc., and had them printed with Latin letters desiring in this way to contribute to fraternity between the Polish and Ruthenian nations."[37] From the end of the 1850s right up until the 1880s, Węgliński published numerous collections of Ruthenian poetry and songs, transcribing them into Latin script as his predecessors had done. A portion of these works were ethnographic in character and dealt with Galician Rus'.[38]

These "collectors" of Ruthenian songs had a significant influence on acquainting Galician society with the culture of the Ruthenian country-side, and they incorporated this output into the Polish literary heritage. As Aleksander Zyga wrote: "the folk poetry of a fraternal Slavic tribe was treated as if belonging to national Polish poetry."[39] At the same

---

[34] Marceli Handelsman, *Ukraińska polityka ks. Adama Czartoryskiego przed wojną krymską* (Warsaw, 1937), p. 61.

[35] [Wacław Zaleski], *Pieśni polskie i ruskie ludu galicyjskiego z muzyką instrumentowaną przez Karola Lipińskiego*, coll. and publ. by Wacław z Oleska (Lviv, 1833).

[36] Żegota Pauli, *Pieśni ludu ruskiego w Galicyi*, vol. 1–2 (Lviv, 1839–40).

[37] Józef Białynia Chołodecki, *Do dziejów powstania styczniowego. Obrazki z przeszłości Galicyi* (Lviv, 1912), p. 18.

[38] Leon Euzebiusz Węgliński, *Nowyi poezyi małoruski t.j. piśny, dumy, dumki, chory, tańci, ballady etc. w czystom jazyci Czerwono-Rusyniw wedla żytia, zwyczaiw ich i obyczaiw narodnych*, vol. 1–3 (Lwihorod–Peremyszl, 1858). Later he also published: [Leon Euzebiusz Węgliński], *Zwuki ôd našych seł i nyv. Pińja Lirnyka Nad-Nistrańskoho*, vol. 1–2 (Cracow, 1885); [Leon Euzebiusz Węgliński] L. Kost' Prawdolubec z Jezupola, *Hôrkij śmich. Skazki i obrazki z żytia w Hałyczyni* (Cracow, 1885).

[39] Aleksander Zyga, "Ludowa pieśń ukraińska w polskiej krytyce lat 1820–1845," *Rocznik Przemyski* 28 (1991–92), p. 45.

time the decision to publish in Latin letters confirmed the trend, later supported by *gente Rutheni, natione Poloni*, of using this alphabet for the Ruthenian language instead of Cyrillic. Subsequent generations of enthusiasts of Ruthenian folk culture were raised within this current. These works simultaneously inspired the publication of numerous works of travel literature that showed Rus' as a land linked for centuries with Poland. It is sufficient to mention *Images of Red Rus'* [*Obrazy Rusi Czerwonej*] by Władysław Zawadzki, published as a book but also produced in installments on the pages of *Tygodnik Illustrowany* [The Ilustrated Weekly].[40] In this work Zawadzki described the indigenous inhabitants of Eastern Galicia. Ruthenian aspirations are, quite obviously, completely absent from his works. We have on the other hand a beautiful literary description of customs, songs, daily life, and similar activities as observed in the Ruthenian countryside.

Platon Kostecki

Many poets and writers drew inspiration from the Ruthenian folklore of Galicia. One of these was Platon Kostecki, a man who became an iconic figure in the entire *gente Rutheni, natione Poloni* formation largely for his poetic output, which enjoyed immense popularity in the area under Austrian partition. It is worth remembering, however, that his path could have taken a completely different "national" direction during the course of the revolutions of 1848. As he himself recalled, he was still too young to get actively involved in the whirl of the events at the time:

> In the years 1848 and 1849 I was too young (17 and 18) and without the slightest political knowledge, (…) this was a result of other factors beyond my control, far removed as I was from the heart of the movement in Lviv. I knew few Polish journals; the Ruthenian *Zoria* I had read only sporadically; regarding the strife at the time between Ruthenians and Poles, I either did not know of it or simply did not as yet understand it.[41]

Kostecki, the son of a Polish woman and a Uniate parish priest, went to the German secondary school in Sambir. From 1852 to 1854 he studied law at Lviv University, a degree program he was not to complete.

---

[40] Władysław Zawadzki, "Obrazy Rusi Czerwonej," *Tygodnik Illustrowany* 9, no. 223–32 (1864).

[41] Platon Kostecki, „W sprawie ruskiej" [Lviv, 1863], LNNBU, fond 5: Zbirka rukopysiv, avtohrafiv, hramot i dyplomiv biblioteky Natsional'noho zakladu im. Ossolins'kykh u m. Lvovi, op. 1: Rukopysy, spr. 3063/II, p. 23; Adam Świątek, "*W sprawie ruskiej* Platona Kosteckiego," *Galicja. Studia i materiały* 3 (2017), p. 391.

As a result of a lack of money as well
as a conflict that had evolved with one
of the German professors, he ultimately
left the university and took up journalism. At first, he published Ruthenian
and Polish poems for *Nowiny* [News]
and *Przyjaciel Domowy* [Home Friend],
but in 1854–1855 he served on the editorial team of the Ruthenian newspaper
Zoria Halytska, to which he restored its
national Ruthenian character since theis
newspaper had developed a Russophile orientation under the earlier editorship of Bohdan Didytsky. Here Kostecki published many Lemko stories
and other texts under his own name

8. Platon Kostecki

and his pseudonym "Vasyl Susky from Khotsenka" ("Сускій Васил зъ
подъ Хоценки") as well as under the initials of this pseudonym.[42] Due
to a conflict with the Ruthenian clergy, Kostecki resigned from editing
the newspaper.[43] He sought his place for a long time. First, he worked
as an assistant editor of the publishing series titled *Biblioteka Pisarzy Polskich* [Polish Writers' Library] in Sanok and Przemyśl; later, he moved
to Medyka, where he came into contact with the Polish literary milieu
centered around Mieczysław Pawlikowski. Kostecki even became the
secretary of the poet Kornel Ujejski. Because of financial problems (and
seeking stabilization in life), he wanted to join the Basilian monastery,
but after his father's death he had—as the oldest in the family—to take
care of the younger sisters (his mother had died many years earlier).
To earn money, he began to cooperate with Polish newspapers in Lviv,
such as *Dziennik Literacki* [Literary Daily], *Dzwonek* [Bell], *Czytelnia
dla Młodzieży* [Reading Room for the Youth] and *Przegląd Powszechny*
[The Common Review]. He carried out a number of proofreading and

---

[42] Kostecki's works were published in *Zoria Halytska* in 1854–55. Cf. also: Ivan Em[eryk]
Levitskii, *Galitsko-russkaia bibliografiia XIX. stolětiia s" uvzgliadnen'em" russkikh izdanii, poiavivshikhsia v" Ugorshchině i Bukovině (1801–1886)*, vol. 1: *Khronologicheskii spisok" publikatsii
(1801–1860)* (Lviv, 1888), pp. 88, 143; Ivan Franko, "Stara Rus"," in Ivan Franko, *Zibrannia
tvoriv*, vol. 37: *Literaturno-krytychni pratsi (1906–1908)*, ed. Ihor Dzeverin, comment. Mykola Hryciuta (Kyiv, 1982), pp. 100–1; Andrzej A. Zięba, "Tożsamość etniczna jako obiekt
manipulacji politycznej. Przypadek Rusinów łemkowskich XVIII–XX w. (część druga),"
Rocznik Ruskiej Bursy (2008), p. 59.
[43] Platon Kostecki, „11 listów i wiersze, listy do Mieczysława Romanowskiego," (Lviv–
Shehyni, 1854–83), LNNBU, fond 76: Kolektsiia Pavlikovs'kykh, op. 2: Arkhiv Pavlikovs'kykh, spr. 214, p. 4v-5.

editorial projects in these journals, and published poems and publicistic articles. He bore a deep-seated grudge against the "Germanizers" of Lviv University, which became clear when he published a critical article in *Przegląd Powszechny* about the German character of this institution.[44] This article resulted in a court case, which ended with his being sentenced to two months' imprisonment. The political trial and his jail sentence instilled in him patriotic opinions. Kostecki did not waste time during his incarceration: he worked on a slim volume of Ruthenian poetry which he went on to publish shortly after his release. The volume entitled *Poezyi* [Poems], written in Ruthenian in the Latin script, earned him a permanent place among Polish poets. This status was cemented by the poem "Our Prayer"[45]. It starts by emphasizing the indivisibility of Poland, Lithuania, and Rus' through a comparison to the Holy Trinity:

In the name of the Father and the Son
It is our prayer
That the Trinity be one
A single Poland, Rus' and Lithuania

According to Kostecki the union of Poland, Lithuania, and Rus' did not result solely from political conditions but from the fact that these lands found themselves under the care of Our Lady:

United in Our Lady
Pray for us
From Częstochowa, Pochaiv
And from above Ostra Brama.

He also stressed the glory of old Poland's three capitals, Warsaw, Kyiv, and Vilnius [Wilno], which were ruled by three families who also came from the three lands: the Piasts (Poland), the Jagiellonians (Lithuania), and the Korybut family (Rus'):

And yet we live in hope,
Joint glory to us

[44] [Platon Kostecki], "Uniwersytet Lwowski," *Przegląd Powszechny* no. 2 (3 Jan., 1861), p. 2.
[45] Platon Kostecki, *Poezyi* (Lviv, 1862), pp. 1–2. The poem was earlier published in the popular daily *Dziennik Literacki* no. 39 (17 May, 1861), p. 312. In the poem of Platon Kostecki, the relation between Poland and Rus' as a reflection of the relationship between God the Father and the Son of God comes to the fore. Lithuania in this triad is not accidentaly in third place. An interesting interpretation of this poem was recently written by Sergei Temchin, pointing to Kostecki's inspiration by medieval religious apocrypha. See: Sergei Temchin, "Rech' Pospolitaia (Pol'sha, Rus' i Litva) kak Sviataia Troytsa. Srednevekovaiapredystoriia poeticheskogo obraza Platona Kostetskogo (1861)," *Slavistica Vilnensis* 62 (2017), pp. 265–75.

All are equally touched by
Kyiv, Vilnius and Warsaw

Hey, the Cracow bells are ringing
– the sound resounds across the whole world
From the graves there cry out the Jagiellonians
The Piasts, and the Korybuts.

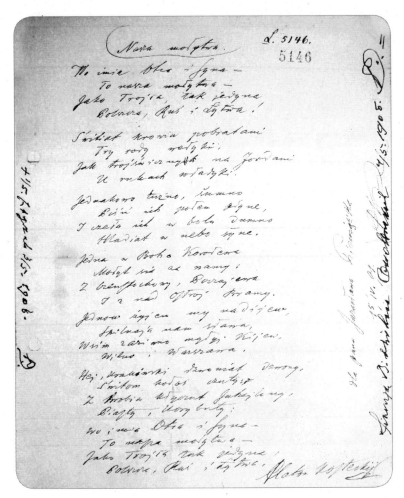

9. The manuscript of Platon Kostecki's poem "Our Prayer"

This poem contains all the elements that characterized its author
and the entire group of *gente Rutheni, natione Poloni*. Aside from "Our
Prayer", other poems from this collection also convey to the reader the
gente Rutheni, natione Poloni worldview. For example, in the poem "The

Order of Peter the Great" ["Prykaz Petra Wełykoho"][46] Kostecki warned
against the designs of the Russian Empire which desired to turn Ruthenians into "Little Russians."

    The success of Platon Kostecki's first volume resulted in the publica-
tion soon afterwards of another collection of poetry, entitled *The Saturn
Years* [*Saturninowe gody*]. This volume was released in 1863 during the
January Uprising.[47] Kostecki did not personally take part in the uprising, but he tried to use his poems to inspire young people to fight. In
the work "The Lonely Ones" ["Samotni"][48] he refers to the bitter memory of defeat in the November Uprising. He claims that the cause of
defeat was a misunderstanding of the slogan "For our and your freedom." The poet considered the union of Poland, Rus', and Lithuania
to be inseparable still, despite the defeat. He demonstrates this in the
poem "Choir" ["Chór"],[49] emphasizing at the same time that Poland
will be resurrected. He saw the cooperation of Poles, Ruthenians, and
Lithuanians to be key to the attainment of independence. This preoccupation with independence runs through the poem "The Reveille"
["Pobudka"],[50] which is bursting with belief in the positive outcome of
the armed struggle:

> The twenty-second [Jan. 1863 – A.Ś.] its promise left unfulfilled
> In shackles Rus', Lithuania and the Crown
> Servants to the tyrant we still remain
> And our faith dulled!
> To arms, to arms!
>
> To arms, brothers, to arms
> Brothers of the Eagle, the Archangel, the Chasing Knight!
> Let us finish what has been set a-rolling,
> For the goals and means are set atoning!
> Jagiełło is watching and Bathory has blessed us
> To arms, to arms!

    It is worth noting that Kostecki, while believing in the achievement
of independence, was in no way blind to the growing antagonism ob-
structing the realization of this noble goal:

> This day here the Vistula, the Warta, and the Dnister's
> Waters have come and merged,

---

[46] Kostecki, *Poezyi*, pp. 103–4.
[47] Platon Kostecki, *Saturninowe gody* (Lviv, 1863).
[48] Ibid., p. 4.
[49] Ibid., pp. 5–6.
[50] Ibid., pp. 12–14.

> While the Dnipro, the Bug and Neman
> Still stagnate under the ice!

Platon Kostecki often refers in his work to historical figures who symbolized the unity of the three countries. In "The Reveille" he refers to Vernyhora's prophecy, which foresaw the restoration of Poland. The poet also predicts how it will appear:

> And on our common lands
> One day it will be good
> I will then stride free
> Making the rounds Heigh-ho from Cracow to Warsaw, Poznań and Lviv
> And from Cieszyn to Vilnius, from Gdańsk
> To Kyiv!

These two small volumes of verse were not the end of Platon Kostecki's poetic output. He continued to write, though now chiefly occasional poetry. Many of these poems, regardless of their purpose, emphasized the ideas expounded earlier by the poet. Even in the verse penned for his godson, Zdzisław Marceli Opolski, to mark his taking of the first sacrament, he wrote:

> O, new knight bearing the martyr's crest
> I greet thee in the cradle, o, new Pole!
> Though today your tiny hands do naught but flutter at your mother's bosom,
> I still regard them with a reverence and awe:
> They one day may
> Be the hands to receive from the Lord the banner holy
> Which, when planted in Warsaw clay
> Will liberate Lithuania, Ruthenia and the Crown![51]

For the goal of gaining independence within the old borders of the fatherland, Kostecki placed his hope in the youth; hence his subsequent involvement with the Sokół [Falcon] Gymnastic Society organization and its activities. His belief in the young generation is expressed in his poem "Three Hopes" ["Trzy nadzieje"]:[52]

> So, 'tis you the Crown… Do you know what Poland is?
> It is a strong back and shoulders of steel!
> And you are Lithuania… Do you know what that is?

---

[51] Platon Kostecki, "Zdzisławowi M. Opolskiemu, mojemu chrześniakowi (Nowy rycerzu męczeńskiego znaku…)," LNNBU, fond 215: Zbirka pol's'kykh aftohrafiv, ZA 427 folio 5: "Kostets'kii, P., Virshi," pp. 5–6.
[52] Platon Kostecki, "Trzy nadzieje," *Gazeta Narodowa*, no. 15 (19 Jan., 1888), p. 3.

A brave heart, and earnest prayer!
And you, oh Rus' of mine... Oh, Ruthenia one and all,
Galicia, Podilia, Volhynia, Ukraine,
In whose entrails the enemy warms his feet,
With suffering as immense as the expanse of the steppe
And poetry as accommodating as an angel's embrace
– 'Tis here Europe's fate they will allot...

For Kostecki, each of the three countries and the three nationalities inhabiting the territory of pre-partition Poland held equal hope for the attainment of independence:

Here you are — the three young hopes,
Each of you worthy at tournaments
With dragons and infidels to clash
Legions of knights and nations whole,
Before any whisk you afar to matrimonial courtship
But the great Mother, our one and only Fatherland,
The one united Ruthenian, Lithuanian and Polish,
Beautiful and grand like you three together.

The poet expresses his belief that independence for the fatherland was within reach in the final appeal:

I here now bless your golden locks,
And beseech you to remember what I tell you:
That Polish leaves, only Polish
Which are simultaneously Lithuanian, Ruthenian, and Polish! –
What splinters and separates, left at the bottom of a Polish hell
Die and vanish, weighed down by an unforgivable sin!

And let us change the slogan's words "She is not yet dead!"
Let you, Poland, be led by a new song!
Pitiful and small is but the temporary enemy's work
Freedom is coming! Oh be of good voice and sing, Polish youth.

This vision of a tripartite state was to undergo a certain transformation over the course of the poet's life. For example, with time the Silesians[53] and Czechs[54] joined the Poles, Lithuanians, and Ruthenians in

---

[53] We can see this in the poem "A Greeting to our Brother from the West": "God so orders!... Hey, Pole, / Silesians, Lithuanians, / All shoulder to shoulder, / Ruthenians together with us! / Like they have marked with us for ages, / So we are together with them, / Whether free or not free – / But equals standing with equals!" Platon Kostecki, *Braci naszej od Zachodu na powitanie* (Lviv, 1871).

[54] In the poem "For the Alliance of Poles and Czechs!" we read: "And for us, Czechs and Poles, / Two victims, or joint work! / The fatherland calls us alive! / Let us pass over what

the struggle for independence. Nonetheless, Kostecki was recognized within (and outside of) the Austrian area of partition as being the bard of the former fatherland not in a single or dual but in a tri-member composition. Kostecki's work is full of hope for the restoration of the state within those borders inhabited by Poles, Ruthenians, and Lithuanians, a state defined by harmony, freedom, and equality. His works, chiefly the manifesto poem "Our Prayer", were widely known in Galicia, and not just among the usual elite circles. An example of this may be seen in the words of Kyrylo Tryliovsky, a Ruthenian pupil at the Kolomyia secondary school, who in 1884 went to Ivan Franko to complain that his history teacher "is distorting history; for entire hours he weaves the topic of 'Ruś, Polszcza i Litwa to odna mołytwa,' ['Ruś, Poland and Lithuania are one prayer,' a line from a poem by Platon Kostecki], makes fun of peasants, etc., without end."[55]

"Our Prayer," in its concise characterization of the essence of the *gente Rutheni, natione Poloni* formula, was cited on numerous occasions. Recourse was made to the work during the 300th anniversary of the Union of Lublin. Józef Łokietek was also inspired by these famous lines when in 1891 he wrote his *Ruthenian Cause* [*Sprawa ruska*]. The sentiment conveyed by Kostecki—"Like the Trinity, so a single Poland, Rus' and Lithuania"— became particularly hallowed in the rhetoric of the leadership of the January Uprising, as demonstrated by Łokietek. Although the collapse of this uprising proved the failure of this very idea, publicists called for the continuation of policy in the same spirit. Łokietek wrote: "It follows to evaluate the situation according to this slogan, to measure the programs of Ruthenian parties by this slogan, to act and fight under this slogan.'[56]

"Our Prayer" was not forgotten over the course of the subsequent decades, even after its author's death. When celebrations took place in 1938 in Warsaw to honour St. Andrzej Bobola (a missionary tortured and killed by Cossacks), a pilgrimage from Galicia entered the city to view the saint's coffin. The pilgrims comprised 550 people, Poles and Ruthenians alike, which aroused significant interest among the inhabitants of Warsaw. During the service Father Iłków, the Łódź army corps chaplain, spoke to the assembled congregation and called for the har-

---

has been taken from us, / But what was given us in dowry / God's hand, once generous!... / The holy bound in alliance, / We shall take all from the enemy's jaws – / Our Elbe, Our Oder!" Platon Kostecki, "Na sojusz Polaków z Czechami!," LNNBU, fond 215, ZA 427, folio 5, pp. 1–4.

[55] Quoted after: Hrytsak, *Ivan Franko*, p. 438, footnote 63.

[56] [Józef Łokietek] Jił, *Sprawa ruska. Wspomnienia, spostrzeżenia, uwagi, wnioski* (Cracow, 1891), p. 15.

monious cohabitation of Greek and Roman Catholics. At the end he cited a "poetic prayer" —as Kostecki's verse was called— after which there followed an ovation and the singing of the Polish national anthem.[57]

Popular Literature in the Second Half of the Nineteenth Century

Besides Kostecki, there were a number of other poets and writers who propagated *gente Rutheni, natione Poloni*-based views, positioning them as the desired direction for the development of Ruthenian nationality. The famous first line of the poem "Our prayer" was quoted by Józef Laskownicki, a folk writer who came from an impoverished gentry family from the district of Sanok, as the motto of his work.[58] Under the pseudonym of "A. Maryan," Laskownicki wrote the historical novel *The Ruthenians* [*Rusini*], published in 1869. It was revised and republished ten years later, which is a good indication of its popularity.[59] The action of the novel takes place just after 1848 in Mohylky, inhabited by a Polish and Ruthenian population who had hitherto lived in harmony. An emissary from Russia named Nikolai Skatutin arrives in the settlement, set on inciting the inhabitants against Poles and Catholicism. One of the protagonists is the old Greek Catholic parish priest and widower, Michał Iwankowski [Mykhailo Ivankovsky], who is an example of the *gente Rutheni, natione Poloni* type of clergyman. His entire family had been brought

10. *The first page of Józef Laskownicki novel* The Ruthenians *(Lviv, 1869) with the first stanza of Platon Kostecki's* "Our Prayer" *as an epigraph*

---

[57] "Polacy i Rusini u trumny św. Andrzeja Boboli," *Polak Greko-Katolik* 5, no. 13–14 (Jul. 1938), p. 7.

[58] Czesław Lechicki, "Laskownicki Józef Albin," in *PSB*, vol. 16 (Wrocław–Warsaw–Cracow–Gdańsk, 1971), pp. 525–26.

[59] [Józef Laskownicki] A. Maryan, *Rusini* (Lviv, 1869; 2. edit. 1878). Discussed in: *Przegląd Polski* 4 (1869), p. 489.

up in this spirit. The son Włodzimierz [Volodymyr] writes Ruthenian *dumkas*, while at the same time being socially active as a Polish man of letters. The priest tells his grandson historical accounts of hetmans and other heroes from Polish history. The second of the priest's sons, Petro [Piotr], supports the Ruthenian option. Despite this, life follows the "old model." During a holiday feast, one of the clergy even raises a toast to Poland, Rus', and Lithuania, patriotic speeches are made, both Polish and Ruthenian songs are sung, and the polonaise, mazurka, and krakowiak are danced. In a word, the presbytery of the Greek Catholic parish priest Iwankowski is presented as an example of the home of a real Ruthenian of Polish nationality. The antagonist, Skatutin, initially wins over first Petro then other Ruthenians, seeking to spread Orthodoxy and combat Polishness in Mohylky. However, this propaganda does not prove successful, and in the end Polish-Ruthenian brotherhood triumphs in the village. The plot of the novel reflects the Galician reality of the mid-nineteenth century: the continuation of the phenomenon of *gente Rutheni, natione Poloni,* which wins out in the novel, as well as the expansion of Orthodoxy resulting in Russophile tendencies among the Ruthenian clergy of the younger generation.

In 1869 Henryk Hugon Wróblewski wrote the poem *The Union* [*Unja*] to mark the 300th anniversary of the Union of Lublin, with an accompanying illustration by Leon Piccard depicting three women

11. The Leon Piccard's illustration in Henryk Hugon Wróblewski's book
The Union (*Cracow, 1869*)

holding hands in an act of fraternity. One has placed her free hand on a shield with a Lithuanian Vytis; behind the second woman there flutters a standard with the Archangel Michael; the third, above whom is a radiant star and behind whose head are the rays of a rising sun, is Poland. Wróblewski's poem begins with an appeal "to brothers from the Vistula, the Neman, Dnipro and Warta." He reminds the reader that the nation has not died yet and assures him that Poland will not share the fate of Carthage. All that is necessary is for the Ruthenians and the Lithuanians to unanimously stand up to awaken the joint fatherland. In a later part of the poem he recalls the country's suffering, the policy of the partitioning powers, and the mood of the people, all in an oscillating melancholic and bombastic stylization. The author's main idea was for a nationwide awakening to occur, defined by the participation of the three peoples, which would resurrect the state:

> Look you, on the corpses life still shines,
> On the ruby lips a prayer just sleeps,
> "O my fatherland, Rus', Poland and Lithuania,
> After union a common cradle of three peoples."[60]

It is worth mentioning at this point writer Julian Jakubowski, largely forgotten to history, who in 1874 wrote the historical poem *Reconciliation* [*Zgoda*], targeted at the Ruthenian population of Galicia.[61] It was in effect a poetic version of Michał Czajkowski's short story entitled *Trakhtemyriv* [*Trechtymirow*], published in Leipzig in 1865 as part of a broader collection.[62] Czajkowski's story tells of Rus' in the twelfth century, a time when Kyiv was under the yoke of Andrei Bogoliubsky. The prince of Vladimir-Suzdal's repressive and bloody governance and his ruthlessness in relation to subordinate Rus' princes engendered resistance. The heroes of the short story are the representatives of two Rus' clans, the Dashkovych and Tymyr families, who feuded with each other as a result of the conflict that had engulfed the Rus' sovereign principalities from the Olhovych and Monomakhovych dynasties. In the name of a common front against the incursion and a desire to unite Rus', the rival families set off with the true ruler of Kyiv, the Galician Prince Iziaslav, to fight against Andrei Bogoliubsky's vassal Meshcherak. The combined forces enable victory over the common enemy, the destruction of his castle, and the construction in its place of a new citadel:

---

[60] Henryk Hugon Wróblewski, *Unja. Poemat* (Cracow, 1869), p. 21.
[61] Julian Jakubowski, *Zgoda. Poemat historyczny. Ruskiej braci poświęca Julian Jakubowski* (Lviv, 1874).
[62] Michał Czajkowski, "Trech-tymirow," in *Pisma Michała Czajkowskiego*, vol. 7: *Koszowata i Ukrainki* (Leipzig, 1865), pp. 215–33.

Trakhtemyriv. The prince gives his blessing to the children from both families, who then marry. The rather limited plot of the story shows that united Ruthenians are able to oppose a common enemy, in this case the Suzdalians, who plunder their lands and are the personification of Tsarist Russia. Michał Czajkowski reveals this in the verse concluding his work:

> To Rus' again evil has come,
> Suzdal shall ride, and with it captivity.
> Oh! Ruthenians, do not lose heart,
> For the taker shall come but then depart.[63]

Czajkowski's piece was entirely directed against Russia occupying Ukraine during the times in which he lived, when the poet was an emissary in the framework of the Hôtel Lambert political camp.

The Galician poet Jakubowski was to bestow a completely different meaning onto the story. A quote from the poem "The Pole and the Ruthenian are Two Bodies," ["Polak i Rusin – to dwa tiła"] by the *gente Rutheni, natione Poloni* poet Dymitr Koczyndyk [Dmytro Kochyndyk], placed on the title page of "Reconciliation," tells us the direction the author intends to follow on the subsequent pages. While the tale is pulled from Czajkowski's work, Jakubowski adds his own introduction and conclusion.

At the very beginning he explains to his Ruthenian reader—for from the subtitle it is clear that the work is addressed to Ruthenians—the essence of Polish-Ruthenian brotherhood while simultaneously appealing to it:

> Ruthenian brothers you will raise your hand,
> To fraternal accord in miserable adversity!
> – A single homeland is our mother
> And the single yoke of long adversity ...
> Together we praise a single God
> – Joint is the history of our line
> And bloody the memory of our knights![64]

By contrast with Czajkowski, the fatherland in Jakubowski's poem refers not only to Rus'-Ukraine, but to a multi-ethnic Poland:

> O poor fatherland! Today alive in the grave
> You must groan in the fetters of captivity;

---

[63] Ibid., p. 233.
[64] Jakubowski, *Zgoda*, p. 3.

The Pole and Lithuanian are lamenting your demise
While the Ruthenian betrays his brother in adversity!...

The above lines suggest the author's intention behind *Reconciliation*: he wished to point out to the Ruthenians of the day the risk of taking their own route, one far from Polish expectations. In recalling the story of the Tymyrs and the Dashkovych, Jakubowski wanted to show the ancient past of Rus' in the context of the history of Poland, a common fatherland for Poles, Lithuanians, and Ruthenians. Admittedly, Poles appear only once in the story, engaged in war with the Teutonic Knights, an aside that explains their absence in the struggle with the forces from Suzdal.

Czajkowski ends his narrative by encouraging the Ruthenians not to lose heart, for they are capable of overcoming Russia. However, Jakubowski reminds the fraternal nation that if it does not observe the "holy reconciliation" and fails to love the "fatherland," then it will perish. The author predicts that Rus' will again be free when it has regained this virtue. The work seeks to define the essence of the Polish-Ruthenian brotherhood that had once somehow survived, and to argue that if it were to exist again it would outlive "all the tsars."[65]

Although Jakubowski's introduction and conclusion seem at odds with the actual content of the story, they show us the author's desire to force home ideas of a Polish-Ruthenian brotherhood. So important was this notion that he notes in the title that the work is devoted to "the Ruthenian brotherhood." We have no indication what reception it generated, but a copy was nevertheless found on the shelves of Ivan Franko's private book collection.[66]

Another literary figure worth mentioning is that of Jan Zachariasiewicz, also of the *gente Rutheni, natione Poloni.* Jan Zachariasiewicz was born in 1825 in Radymno, the son of Aleksander, the town's mayor. He was christened a Greek Catholic, as was his whole family. He subsequently completed

12. *Jan Zachariasiewicz*

[65] Ibid., pp. 47–48.
[66] Halyna Vurlaka et al., *Biblioteka Ivana Franka. Naukovyi opys u chotyr'okh tomakh*, vol. 1, foreword Mykola Zhulyns'kyi (Kyiv, 2010), p. 504.

secondary school in Przemyśl where he belonged to the secret organization "The Sons of the Fatherland," and for that he was arrested and sentenced to a two-year period of incarceration at the fortress in Spielberg. In 1844 he returned to Galicia and settled in Lviv. He knew Ivan Vahylevych quite well. As a *gente Ruthenus, natione Polonus*, he entered the Ruthenian Sobor during the period of the revolutions of 1848. He worked editing various newspapers or wrote articles for them (*Gazeta Lwowska* [Lviv Gazette], *Dziennik Mód Paryskich* [Parisian Fashions Daily], *Postęp* [Progress], *Gazeta Powszechna* [General Gazette], *Tygodnik Polski* [Polish Weekly], *Dziennik Literacki*), and later started to produce his own works, chiefly on historical subjects.[67] He was given a two-year prison sentence (1852–54) in the fortress of Theresienstadt for his poem *The Maccabees* [*Machabeusze*], in which he criticized the partitioning authorities. Many of his works drew upon actual conditions in the Galicia of his day. He was especially critical in his writings of the views held by the Cracow historical school, which saw Poland's defeat as self-inflicted. This did not mean, however, that he did not criticize the attitudes of the Polish gentry responsible—in his view—for "the political destruction of the nation."[68] Zachariasiewicz was an exceptionally popular writer during the period of the partitions, and it is therefore crucial to examine his literary works.

Let us begin with one of Zachariasiewicz's novels dealing directly with Ruthenian affairs—*Saint George* [*Święty Jur*]. In the preface to the second edition of a collection of his works including this novel as well as *Iarema* [*Jarema*], Zachariasiewicz emphasized that the stories depicted the actual state of national relations, which had not changed since 1862 despite "a visible attempt at improvement."[69] It is worth providing a brief summary of the plot of *Saint George*, following the analy-

---

[67] On Jan Zachariasiewicz's youth see: Franciszek Henryk Lewestam, "Jan Zacharyasiewicz: Szkic biograficzno-literacki," *Tygodnik Illustrowany* no. 230 (20 Febr. 1864), pp. 65–66; Anna Wróbel, "Od 'Galileuszy' do Polaków. Wejście do polskiej inteligencji przedstawicieli ludności napływowej i mniejszości w Galicji w XIX w.," in *Inteligencja polska XIX i XX wieku. Studia 5*, ed. Ryszarda Czepulis-Rastenis (Warsaw, 1987), pp. 186–87; Czesław Kłak, "Literacka młodość Jana Zachariasiewicza," in *Z tradycji kulturalnych Rzeszowa i Rzeszowszczyzny. Księga pamiątkowa dla uczczenia X-lecia rzeszowskiego oddziału Towarzystwa Literackiego im. Adama Mickiewicza*, eds. Stanisław Frycie and Stefan Reczek (Rzeszów, 1966), pp. 144–45; Czesław Kłak, "Glosa do *Czerwonej czapki* Jana Zachariasiewicza," in Czesław Kłak, *Pisarze galicyjscy. Szkice literackie*, (Rzeszów, 1994), pp. 63–65; Roman Koropeckyj, "Wizerunek narodowego ruchu ruskiego w powieści Jana Zachariasiewicza 'Święty Jur'," *Krakowskie Zeszyty Ukrainoznawcze* 3–4 (1994–95), pp. 306–07.

[68] Kłak, „Glosa", p. 70.

[69] Jan Zachariasiewicz, *Święty Jur. Jarema. Dwie powieści współczesne*, vol. 1–2 (Leipzig, 1873), p. 1. Other editions: Jan Zachariasiewicz, *Św. Jur. Powieść w trzech częściach* (Lviv, 1862); Jan Zachariasiewicz, *Święty Jur. Powieść współczesna*, vol. 1–3 (Warsaw, 1886) and the newest: Jan Zachariasiewicz, *Święty Jur* (Warsaw, 2018).

ses by Maria Grzędzielska and Roman Koropeckyj. The heroes of the novel are two descendants of the Szetycki [Shetytsky] family (not to be confused with the Szeptycki/Sheptytsky family) in Eastern Galicia: Karol Grocki, a Roman Catholic, and Porfiry [Porfyrii], a Uniate. Both men were orphaned in childhood but raised by the Greek Catholic priest Father Onufry [Onufrii], whose daughter Eudoksja [Yevdoksiia] has in turn been brought up in the Polish spirit through the reading of patriotic works of Romantic literature. Grocki had in the past been active in the Polish national cause, but we become acquainted with him when he is already a man broken by the suffering he had experienced as a consequence of this involvement. In turn, Porfiry, although

13. *The cover of the first edition of Jan Zachariasiewicz's novel* Saint George *(Lviv, 1862)*

he had cooperated with the Poles in 1848 and even gone to prison for his activities, later became a Ruthenian patriot. Both protagonists are therefore positioned as if on opposite sides. At a certain moment in the book, the heroes learn of the death of an uncle. He has left in his will three villages to whoever in the family demonstrates loyalty to the faith of his ancestors. Both potential heirs have to consequently show that they uphold the requirements of the will. In their acts, Grocki is supported by a certain Korybut, and Porfiry by his uncle, a Greek Catholic priest at St. George's Cathedral in Lviv. The aims driving the patrons of the two main heroes are particularly signficant. Korybut sees his support for Grocki as advantageous for Poland, while the Greek Catholic priest believes helping Porfiry will benefit the Ruthenian national movement. Finally, both Grocki and Porfiry get rid of their advisers. Furthermore, Porfiry becomes convinced of the deceptiveness of the Ruthenian program, particularly when at a certain moment he is attacked, as a member of the gentry, by Ruthenian peasants. When patriotic demonstrations break out in Warsaw in 1862, Porfiry and Grocki leave for Ukraine to organize their Ruthenian units to fight against Russia. They finally meet up in Warsaw during a demonstration on 8 April 1862[70]. It is then that a crowd of more than one

---

[70] From 1860, after the funeral of Katarzyna Sowińska (widow of General Józef Sowiński—a hero during the November Uprising of 1830–31), which turned into a national manifestation, the Russian authorities introduced martial law throughout the Congress

hundred thousand gathered on the streets of Warsaw are attacked by the Russian military. One of the priests in the crowd is carrying a cross. As they are killing the priest, this symbol of Christ's torment is taken up by another. After this man is also shot, the crucifix is held up by... a Jew! At this moment Grocki points out to Porfiry the might of the Polish nation. Finally, it falls to them to carry the cross, and having been shot, they fall to the ground; their blood—as proof of the brotherhood of Poles and Ruthenians—runs together. Following this exceptionally solemn scene, both men recover and return to Galicia, where they jointly receive the inheritance mentioned in the will. They subsequently marry, with Porfiry taking the Polonized Eudoksja as his bride. The work ends with the announcement that new owners have opened a folk school, where the Polish and Ruthenian languages are equal in status. The whole novel not only shows the immensity of tensions between Poles and Ruthenians in the Galicia of the 1860s, but also gives hope that if Poles and Ruthenians were to live in reconciliation and were to work for Poland, then all would end well.[71]

Zachariasiewicz valued those who advocated Polish-Ruthenian friendship, as demonstrated in his presentation of various characters in the novel. Koropeckyj has drawn attention to the fact that the task of the Polish heroes in *Saint George* is to raise awareness in the wayward Ruthenians and to render them productive members of Polish society. In his novel, Zachariasiewicz highlights the road that Ruthenians should take, this being the route that he himself had taken as a *gente Ruthenus, natione Polonus*. The existence of the oppositional national Ruthenian movement is linked by Zachariasiewicz to the external forces that are the cause of the internal Galician conflicts. This is especially noticeable in another of his novels, *Iarema*, in which he appears to accuse the Austrian administration of deliberately inciting the Ruthenian peasantry to conflict with the Polish gentry. As Czesław Kłak wrote: "Sympathizing tendencies dictated that he refer to the myth of the symbiosis of Ruthenians and Poles, which had momentarily been seized by the perfidious intrigue of the partitioning powers."[72] Zachariasiewicz in this way presented his interpretation of the Polish-Ruthenian conflict in Galicia. He

---

Kingdom. Nevertheless, national demonstrations aimed against the repressions of the Russian authorities continued to be bloodily suppressed. The events described by the author refer to the tense political atmosphere in Warsaw in the spring of 1862 (a time when the author was writing the first edition of the book), which after a few months will lead to the outbreak of the January Uprising of 1863.

[71] Maria Grzędzielska, "Drogi Jana Zachariasiewicza," in *Z dziejów kultury i literatury ziemi przemyskiej. Zbiór szkiców, opracowań i utworów literackich*, ed. Stefania Kostrzewska--Kratochwilowa (Przemyśl, 1969), pp. 114–16; Koropeckyj, "Wizerunek," pp. 313–16.

[72] Czesław Kłak, „Powieści historyczne Jana Zachariasiewicza zwierciadłem sporów politycznych między demokratami i konserwatystami galicyjskimi." *Prace Humanistyczne*.

places blame solely on the partitioning power, while suggesting that Ruthenians should cooperate with Poles in patriotic work.

The question of national consciousness and its changes also found its way into comic novels. One particularly noteworthy example is the uproarious novel by the renowned Galician writer Jan Lam entitled *Miss Emilia or the Grand World of Capowice* [*Panna Emilia czyli wielki świat Capowic*].[73] The novel's heroes are inhabitants of the fictitious town of Capowice. The main protagonist, Wacław Precliczek, is an Austrian civil servant of Czech descent, while his wife hails from a German family, although it is she who calls him a kraut. They have a daughter Emilia who, having been brought up on the literature of Lviv, is a Polish patriot and speaks French well. As a husband for her, her father is grooming a certain Johann von Sarafanovych, whose family

> (…) right up until 1848 was Polish gentry of the Uniate rite, though in recent times has adopted Austrian nationality, while the -vych instead of -wicz [in the surname] comes from the fact that the uncle of the young lecturer, Father Nabukhovych, was a well-known philologist, the *ringleader* of the nation and its *representative* in Lviv and Vienna; hence Mr. Schmerling's favours fell on the entire family.[74]

This figure becomes, as a result of the changes in nationality, the focus of the author's ridicule. Von Sarafanovych does not know the Ruthenian language well and has to seek assistance from a Roman Catholic curate (!) to help him write. A knowledge of the Cyrillic script is for him, as the author writes, "doubly necessary as the only secular representative of Father Nabukhovych's nationality in the Capowice district."[75] The humour in Sarafanovych's character develops when the proclaimed Ruthenian of Polish nationality, though at present an Austrian, allows himself to be persuaded by the priest that his first language was in fact Polish. However, the Capowice gendarmerie soon starts to follow the said clergyman as if he were a dangerous agitator, while Sarafanovych himself, dreaming of a career as a ministerial counsellor, labours in a search of insurgents from 1863.[76]

Rzeszowskie Towarzystwo Przyjaciół Nauk. Wydział Nauk Humanistycznych. Komisja Historycznoliteracka 1, series 1, no. 1 (1970), p. 160.

[73] Jan Lam, *Wielki świat Capowic* (Cracow, 1869; last edition 2002). Discussed in: "Kronika bibliograficzna," *Przegląd Polski* 1, no. 3 (13) (1869), p. 524. The author of the note was most taken with the book, writing that "it will remain for a long time valuable material for the history of the development of Polish nationality in Galicia." About Lam's novel in English literature see: Agnieszka B. Nance, *Literary and Cultural Images of a Nation without a State: The Case of Nineteenth-Century Poland* (New York, 2008) pp. 85–98.

[74] Lam, *Wielki świat*, p. 43.

[75] Ibid.

[76] Ibid., pp. 43–44.

The problem of the development of Ruthenian nationality is even more interestingly sketched by Lam. Sarafanovych has six brothers, all Greek Catholic parish priests. At one point in the novel he is at Father Nabukhovych's for a feast day (*praznyk*), during which conversations develop on political topics. Not only does Sarafanovych slip in Polish words during the course of this emotive conversation, but "after six o'clock: all are already speaking Polish as a result of 'there not being a Pole in the room'."[77]

The book follows Precliczek's attempts to force his daughter to marry Sarafanovych and the strenuous attempts on the part of the potential son-in-law to win over Emilia, who is far from enthusiastic at the prospect as she considers him to be a Muscovite and an anti-Polish Ruthenian nationalist. The father considers his daughter's resistance to be rooted in the Polish books she has read, which he confiscates and takes to his study.[78] Emilia, however, placed in front of the altar, cleverly manages to avoid marriage by announcing that she has already taken vows to marry a Pole, a January Uprising insurgent named Karol Schreyer. This explanation results in further rows and sparks the intent to take the former conspirator to court. The problem eventually resolves itself when it is revealed that in 1866 the position of governor of Galicia was taken, in place of an Austrian, by the governor of Galicia Agenor Gołuchowski. Within this political constellation Precliczek quickly becomes a Pole, proud of the collection of Polish books he now has in his study. When it turns out that there is no place for him in the local administration, he moves to Lviv and becomes a Czech once again. Karol and Emilia live a long and happy life while Sarafanovych finds himself a Ruthenian woman with whom he settles down.

Apart from its entertainment value, Lam's comedy is one that examines the interesting question of national identity, which was for the ordinary people at this time not a matter for which they were willing to die. The writer showed that it was the economic situation that brought about a change in mentality. Even though Lam sketches in a caricatural way the relations at work within a Galician village, he has also presented the historical reality of the epoch at least in as far as the choice of nationality is concerned, as well as highlighting the nuances connected with the yet unconsolidated Ruthenian nationality and its contemporary evaluations.

---

[77] Ibid., p. 49.
[78] Ibid., p. 99.

Sienkiewicz and Matejko

Besides these popular literary works that attempted to depict Galician social reality (including Polish-Ruthenian relations), no less important in the shaping of the national identity of the inhabitants of this province were literary and artistic works dealing with historical themes. Historical consciousness, understood as knowledge about the past as well as its conceptualization, was to play a significant role in the formation of national self awareness. What is more, as Jerzy Topolski writes, historical consciousness is a "factor determining human actions, to which society bestows cultural meaning and sense."[79] This notion is expanded on and developed by Józef Chlebowczyk, who perceived the role of historical documentation as a factor justifying the right of a host to a given territory, one contested by various national groups. Thus understood, national consciousness is not merely a passive element in a man's identity, for it might result in concrete undertakings. Chlebowczyk, in drawing attention to the importance of historical documentation, ascribed in the Polish case a special role not so much to politicians as to cultural activists, from among whom he listed Henryk Sienkiewicz and Jan Matejko, men of exceptional social influence.[80]

We shall first examine Sienkiewicz's famous work *With Fire and Sword* [*Ogniem i mieczem*], which reached the inhabitants of Galicia not only in book form but also through its serialization in the press. This work is so important due to the author taking a stance in the book on the Cossack question, which in the second half of the nineteenth century had started to slowly take on the status of a Ruthenian national myth[81]. Those who were considered rebels by the Poles were to become heroes in Ruthenian eyes. This explains why within Polish literary and artistic works those motifs that are the building blocks of Ukrainian national

---

[79] Jerzy Szacki, "Świadomość historyczna a wizja przyszłości," *Studia Filozoficzne* no. 8 (1975), p. 41.

[80] Józef Chlebowczyk, "Świadomość historyczna jako element procesów narodotwórczych we wschodniej Europie Środkowej," in *Polska, czeska i słowacka świadomość historyczna XIX wieku. Materiały sympozjum Polsko-Czechosłowackiej Komisji Historycznej 15–16 XI 1977*, ed. Roman Heck (Wrocław–Warsaw–Cracow–Gdańsk, 1979), pp. 23–24. For more on the importance of Jan Matejko's work for the development of the historical consciousness of Poles in the context of their relations to the Ruthenian populace see: Adam Świątek, '*Lach serdeczny*'. *Jan Matejko a Rusini* (Cracow, 2013), pp. 141–42.

[81] On the adaptation of the Cossack myth by the Galician Ruthenians see more: Ostap Sereda, "Formuvannia natsional'noï tradytsiï. Ukraïns'ke kozakofil'stvo u Halychyni v 60-x rokakh XIX stolittia," in *Istoriia, mental'nist', identychnist'*, vol. 4: *Istorychna pam'iat' ukraïntsiv i poliakiv u period formuvannia natsional'noï svidomosti v XIX–pershii polovyni XX stolittia*, eds. Leonid Zashkil'niak, Joanna Pisulińska and Paweł Sierżęga (Lviv, 2011), pp. 395–403.

identity are marginalized or shown in another light. This phenomenon is certainly present in Sienkiewicz; the Cossacks in *With Fire and Sword* are depicted as rebels. However, they are opposed by those Ruthenians of the ilk of Prince Jeremi Wiśniowiecki [Iarema Vyshnevetsky]. The stance of the Ruthenian prince, one who was subject to king and state, was especially close to the reader. Consequently, in Sienkiewicz's work the prince became a symbol of the old Poland a multi-ethnic state. Stanisław Zakrzewski, an authority on this idea and a historian who has impressively interpreted Sienkiewicz and undertaken an article on the subject of Sienkiewicz's *Trilogy* [*Trylogia*] (of which *With Fire and Sword* was the first part), writes:

> Did the Cossacks turn against ethnic Poland, one hundred percent Polish in blood and bone, and also against the Roman Catholic faith? We consider this not to be so. The matter was not one of ethnic Poland; of importance here was Jagiellonian Poland, and more precisely the political ideal of Jagiellonian Poland. The core content of this ideal is well-known; for this is political solidarity in the first order, that of Poland and Lithuania, with the second order being that of Poles, Lithuanians, and Ruthenians, and the third degree within the borders of obviously contemporary conceptions the cooperation of the Roman Catholic world with other denominations, other Churches, and consequently also with the Orthodox.[82]

Jeremi Wiśniowiecki was an ideal symbol for this vision, an alternative to the Cossack identity variant. We shall quote again Zakrzewski, who concluded:

> The Sanguszko [Sanhushko] family, the Ostrogski [Ostrozky] family, the Wiśniowiecki [Vyshnevetsky] family, all Ruthenians not from great grandfathers, but from ancestors, some of Lithuanian blood, others from Ruthenian princely lines, whether of authentic or dubious genealogy, none of this matters for the question under consideration.
> From the position of the history of the Jagiellonian state and that of the house of Vasa they all served Polish political thought, all of them are Poles in the understanding of the state, even the greatest defenders of Lithuanian independence, even the staunchest Ruthenians, the most devout believer in Orthodoxy.
> And to these belonged Jarema Wiśniowiecki (…).[83]

After all, it is not merely Wiśniowiecki who in *Trilogy* is an example of a Ruthenian loyal to Poland. We find in Sienkiewicz a range of fig-

---

[82] Stanisław Zakrzewski, "'Ogniem i mieczem' Sienkiewicza w świetle krytyki historycznej," in Stanisław Zakrzewski, *Zagadnienia historyczne*, vol. 1 (Lviv, 1936), p. 84.
[83] Ibid., p. 85.

ures that totally fulfil all the conditions required to bear such a designation. There is the gentry man Zaćwilichowski, a former officer, a soldier
in the Crown army, a Ruthenian by birth.[84] Literature also discussed
whether the main character of the novel, Jan Skrzetuski, has Ruthenian
roots.[85] Finally, there appears throughout the book the figure of Adam
Kisiel, the Kyiv voivode, loyal to the King of Poland. All these heroes
constituted model figures for society.

At the same time, the history of the Ruthenian lands started to appear
on the canvases of Polish painters. As illustrations of historical scenes
are by their very nature not actual representations of a given event,
such art will always reflect the artist's historiosophical position. We
can observe among Polish painters a frequent reference to Ruthenian/
Ukrainian themes. The heroes of these canvases are often the inhabitants of Rus', common people dressed in colourful attire, though with
an unusual decorousness; the Cossacks, romantic icons of free people
yet full of life's passions, romance, and emotion; and finally, the Ruthenian land itself, with its exceptionally varied landscape, fauna, and
flora. As Nikodem Bończa-Tomaszewski wrote, thanks to the artistic
flair and fascinations of Polish artists, Ukraine was in the second half of
the nineteenth century to become "the fatherland territory of Poles."[86]
In this way, Ukraine was presented on canvases painted by such eminent artists as Aleksander Orłowski, Juliusz Kossak, Piotr Michałowski,
Józef Chełmoński, Józef Brandt, Jan Stanisławski, Wacław Pawliszak,
Kazimierz Pochwalski, Antoni Piotrowski, and ultimately Jan Matejko.[87]

This is an analogous phenomenon to the one we have already seen
in literature; in art there also occurred a depiction of the Ruthenian
lands as idylls. In nineteenth-century paintings no blood flows between
Poles, Ruthenians, or Cossacks.

The best examples of this are the works of Jan Matejko, the painter
who exerted the strongest impact on the historical consciousness of
Poles in the nineteenth century. In all of his paintings he emphasized
the multi-ethnic nature of the former state, making frequent reference
to Ruthenians. It was from his canvases that an inhabitant of the partitioned Polish lands could learn that the bond between Poles and Ruthenians had existed almost since early Slavic times (*Saints Cyril and*

---

[84] Ibid., p. 77.
[85] Ibid., pp. 91–98.
[86] Nikodem Bończa-Tomaszewski, *Źródła narodowości. Powstanie i rozwój polskiej świadomości narodowej w II połowie XIX i na początku XX wieku* (Wrocław, 2006), p. 355.
[87] Cf.: Adam Sviontek, "Mystetstvo na sluzhbi narodu. Rol' maliarstva u formuvanni
uiavlen' poliakiv pro rus'ki zemli v period podiliv," *Istorychni ta kul'turolohichni studii* 6–7
(2014–15), pp. 62–80.

Methodius [*Święci Cyryl i Metody*], 1885), and be informed of events such as the expansion of Poland's civilization into Rus' from the beginning of the reign of Bolesław the Brave (*The Coronation of the First King 1001* [*Koronacja pierwszego króla r.p. 1001*], 1889; *Bolesław the Brave and Svia-topolk at Kyiv's Golden Gate* [*Bolesław Chrobry ze Świątopełkiem przy Złotej Bramie w Kijowie*], 1884); the peaceful incorporation of Red Rus' into the Polish state by Casimir the Great (*The Retaking of Rus': Riches and Education 1366* [*Powtórne zajęcie Rusi – Bogactwo i oświata r.p. 1366*], 1888); the participation of Ruthenian-Lithuanian forces under the command of Grand Duke Vytautas at the Battle of Grunwald (*The Battle of Grunwald* [*Bitwa pod Grunwaldem*], 1878), the political and religious union of Poles and Ruthenians (*The Union of Lublin* [*Unia lubelska*], 1869; the figure of Ipatii Potii in the picture *Skarga's Sermon* [*Kazanie Skargi*], 1864, and in the sketch *The Golden Age of Literature in the Sixteenth Century: The Reformation; The Advance of Catholicism* [*Złoty wiek literatury w wieku XVI – Reformacja – Przewaga katolicyzmu*], 1888); the Cossacks who fought in defence of Poland against foreign invasion (*Ostafii Dashkevych* [*Eustachy Daszkiewicz*], 1874; the figure of Przecław Lanckoroński [*Predslav Liantskoronsky*] in the picture *The Prussian Homage* [*Hołd Pruski*], 1882), here particularly the Cossacks fighting against Russia (the figure of the Cossack hetman Ivan Oryshovsky in the picture *Stefan Batory at Pskov* [*Stefan Batory pod Pskowem*], 1872); St. Josaphat Kuntsevych, the first martyr of the Uniate church (*The Queen of the Polish Crown* [*Królowa Korony Polskiej*], 1887–88), the life of St. Jan of Dukla, only deemed blessed in Matejko's day (*Bohdan Khmelnytsky and Tughay Bey at Lviv* [*Bohdan Chmielnicki z Tuhaj-Bejem pod Lwowem*], 1885); and finally the Cossack Vernyhora preventing the *haidamakas* from staging a bloodbath (*Vernyhora* [*Wernyhora*] 1884).[88]

Jan Matejko was the first Polish artist to propagate the vision of Polish-Ruthenian brotherhood and the solidarity of Roman Catholics and Uniates on such a large scale. He was almost a devotee of the traditions of the Union of Lublin, although not without reservations and criticisms on matters of detail. It is not a surprise that he was to find a common language with the most well-known representative of the *gente Rutheni, natione Poloni* formation, Platon Kostecki.[89] Without doubt the artist's output, as was the case with many other Polish cultural activists of this period, would for many years shape the vision of history held by the inhabitants of Galicia that saw the past of Rus' inextricably connected to the Polish state.

---

[88] For more on the pictures by Matejko devoted to Rus' and the artist's own views on the Ruthenian question see: Świątek, '*Lach serdeczny*', pp. 75–137.
[89] Ibid., pp. 56–59.

Polish Historiography

The vision of the connections between Rus' and Poland illustrated through the canvases of Matejko and the prose of Sienkiewicz would have had no great resonance whatsoever had it not been for the huge output of Polish historical literature during the period of the partitions. Through the course of the nineteenth century it was historiography, alongside literature and art, that constituted one of the most important factors shaping the consciousness of the literate population. This results from the understanding that the writing of history directly influences the formation of the historical consciousness of those who receive it, and consequently there arises an effective medium for the transfer of ideologies of various kinds, the conveyance of views, and finally the actual shaping of people's attitudes. Martyna Deszczyńska wrote that in the first decades of the nineteenth century there occurred "an appropriation of the collective mentality by history, and in particular by historiography, harnessed in the service of the notion of nation-building," though "the bond of history was perceived as only one of the components of nationality."[90] Moreover, the Ukrainian historian Leonid Zashkilniak emphasized that Poland's past, viewed as a great civilizational achievement, represented "an organic element in the consciousness of a modern nation," one moulded simultaneously by Polish literature.[91] During this period, history ceased to be an academic discipline or simply knowledge about the past and became instead an important element in social communication, a narrative shaping the recipient's identity. In the nineteenth century the history of Poland not only filled academic publications and literature but also found a forum for discourse on the pages of magazines, in the creation of museums, in the organization of ceremonies commemorating historical events, etc. Thanks to the omnipresence of historical narratives about the Poland of old, there developed a definite relationship on the part of people to their past, one that was treated as a "reserve of values lost." Of particular importance was Poland's former multi-ethnic nature and the entirety of its historical achievements, along with the long timeline of events influencing the "fraternizing" of the peoples inhabiting its territories, including the Polish and Ruthenian populations.

---

[90] Martyna Deszczyńska, "W sprawie świadomości historycznej polskich elit intelektualnych początku XIX w.," in *Społeczeństwo w dobie przemian. Wiek XIX i XX. Księga jubileuszowa profesor Anny Żarnowskiej*, eds. Maria Nietykisza, Andrzej Szwarc and Krystyna Sierakowska (Warsaw, 2003), p. 422.

[91] Leonid Zaszkilniak, "Polsko-ukraiński spór o Galicję na początku XX wieku. Między świadomością historyczną a realiami," in *Narody i historia*, ed. Arkady Rzegocki (Cracow, 2000), p. 157.

Enlightenment and subsequently Romantic historiography, particularly that which came from the writings of Adam Naruszewicz, Julian Ursyn Niemcewicz, Jerzy Samuel Bandtkie, and Joachim Lelewel, found an audience in the houses of the intelligentsia and gentry, regardless of where they were located in the three areas of partition. This happened even though such narratives were prohibited from officially functioning within a Germanized school system. For a long time, as Andrzej Stępnik wrote, schools were unable to teach the history of the "Polish and Ruthenian national elements," not that the students were uninterested in the topic.

What was the image of Rus' that appeared in these historical works? Above all, the historiography at the end of the eighteenth century treated Red Rus' and Right-Bank Ukraine as an integral part of the Polish state. Stępnik has written that "this was not accompanied by any deeper academic reflection."[92] The writings produced at the end of the eighteenth century expressed the fashionable principles of the day, extolling state integration, which involved the eradication of all forms of regional differences. It was only in the 1830s that the distinctiveness of Rus' was to be perceived, yet never to the extent that this area was conceived as being separate from Poland. Joachim Lelewel, the publisher and—one could say—second author of *The History of Polish Kings and Princes* [*Historia książąt i królów polskich*], written by Teodor Waga, differentiated the Ukrainian lands as those inhabited by a Uniate people and Ruthenian-speaking, from the lands of Red Rus' which, as he argued, were shown to be different by a different attitude of its population toward the figure of Hetman Bohdan Khmelnytsky whom this population treated as an alien figure.[93] In his exceptionally popular *A History of Poland Colloquially Told* [*Dzieje Polski potocznym sposobem*], Lelewel, in turn, said that the incorporation of this territory into Poland by Casimir the Great was "greeted willingly by the majority of the inhabitants of Rus' and took place without warfare."[94] This was an interpretation far from historical reality. Even in his monarchical and Polonocentrist multi-volume work, Adam Naruszewicz was not afraid to speak of the siege of Lviv by the Poles, the starvation of its inhabitants or the pillaging of the princely treasury, but he avoided mentioning the bloodshed in the city.[95]

---

[92] Ibid., p. 31.
[93] Cf. Teodor Waga, *Historya Xiążąt i Królów Polskich krótko zebrana* (Vilnius, 1816), pp. 179, 255. Cf. Andrzej Stępnik, *Ukraina i stosunki polsko-ukraińskie w syntezach i podręcznikach dziejów ojczystych okresu porozbiorowego 1795–1918* (Lublin, 1998).
[94] Joachim Lelewel, *Dzieje Polski potocznym sposobem* (Warsaw, 1829), p. 133.
[95] Adam Naruszewicz, *Historya narodu polskiego od początku chrześcijaństwa. Panowanie Piastów*, vol. 6 (Warsaw, 1785), pp. 97–98.

However, it was not Naruszewicz's but Lelewel's history of the incorporation of Rus' that would dominate Polish history writing and the historical consciousness of Poles for many years to come. In the realities of nineteenth-century Galicia, to speak of the subjection of Rus' to Polish hegemony was to present a counter-argument against the Ruthenian political aspiration to divide the country into two parts, an ambition that lasted from 1848 right up to 1918.

In reality, the incorporation of Rus' was in no way as innocent as Lelewel and his imitators portrayed it to be, as it only came about with the burning down of Lviv and two Polish military expeditions into the territory of Red Rus'. Consequently, the depiction by Ruthenian historians such as Denys Zubrytsky of the beginnings of the Polish-Ruthenian union as being not as harmonious as Poles would like to believe is totally justified. In Polish publications of this period there is an absence of the motifs touched on in 1840 by Zubrytsky in his *Outline of the History of the Ruthenian Nation in Galicia* [*Rys historyi Narodu ruskiego w Galicyi*], such as the sections on the slaughtering of people who took shelter in St. George's Church, the burning of the church, and the pillaging of the starved town and the looting of all "princely, ecclesiastical and private treasures."[96]

The nineteenth century also witnessed the rise of the popular thesis expounding former Slavic unity, the joint ancestors of which were Poles and Ruthenians, in opposition to the Russians, who had succumbed to Asiatic influences. Jerzy Samuel Bandtkie unequivocally separated Ruthenians from Russians.[97] Many later researchers and writers emphasized this differentiation in order to counter nineteenth-century Russian historiography, which proclaimed that Ruthenians were actually "Little Russians," a part of the great Russian nation.[98] Such a historiographical vision nurtured by the Russophile aspirations of many Galician Ruthenians constituted a serious threat to the national development of Ruthenians, and also threatened Poles (and Austrians) with the possibility that in the future Russia might take this corner of the ancient lands of Rus' lying in Eastern Galicia. Here *gente Rutheni, natione Poloni* represented the polar opposite of the Pan-Slavic and Russophile tendencies popular among the Galician Ruthenian population. According to their interpretation of history (seen, for example, in the historical views of

---

[96] Dyonizy Zubrzycki, „Rys Historyi Narodu ruskiego w Galicyi przez Dyonizego Zubrzyckiego. Zeszyt drugi od roku 1340 do roku 1596," LNNBU, fond 4: Biblioteka Bavorovs'kykh, op. 1: Rukopysy, spr. BAW. 1630/III, pp. 4–5.

[97] Jerzy Samuel Bandtkie, *Dzieje Królestwa Polskiego*, vol. 1 (Wrocław, 1820), pp. 24–27.

[98] Stępnik, *Ukraina*, pp. 81–84.

Teofil Merunowicz), Rus' was to become part of an independent Poland, which was to be a federation of equal subjects.

One more important thesis prominent in the nineteenth-century Polish historiography was the notion that Poland's occupation of Rus' was a mission to bring civilization to the East. This was reconciled with the belief in the existence of a superior Western Latin civilization in ˙opposition to the barbarian East. This historical interpretation viewed Red Rus' as deriving benefits from the achievements of Poland's superior medieval culture. This concept was formulated between the November and January Uprisings, with its main initiators being Julian Klaczko and Karol Szajnocha, though Joachim Lelewel was also instrumental.[99] Such an interpretation lived on for a long time in Polish historiography, explaining the legitimacy of the incorporation of Rus' into Poland as motivated by the superiority of Polish culture in relation to the culture of its Ruthenian neighbours. The natural consequence of this outlook was the Polonization of many Ruthenian families. Polish history writers did not critically evaluate the native cultural dominance, but rather considered the Polonization and Latinization of Ruthenians to be simply a consequence of cultural superiority and an inevitable task to be carried out. This is how Karol Szajnocha, the author of the text "How Rus' Became Polonized" ["Jak Ruś polszczała"], perceived this issue:

> The conversion of many Ruthenian families to the Latin rite was a marvellous act in the Polonization of Rus' — but can we observe in the whole undertaking any trace of pressure exerted by the Polish side? The rite introduced by the Poles reconciled enlightened minds, but in relation to Polish rights and freedoms a Ruthenian in the sixteenth century was the equal of a Pole.[100]

Besides the question of the incorporation of Red Rus' into the Polish Crown, of particular interest is one event from the history of Poland—the Union of Lublin, concluded in 1569. This event, like those of the year 1340, was given an array of interpretations, though under Romanticism this political union was evaluated quite positively. Joachim Lelewel even took it upon himself to write *A History of Lithuania and Rus'* [*Dzieje Litwy i Rusi*], in which he made the Union of Lublin the culminating and simultaneously crowning moment. According to Lelewel, it was thanks to this Union that there arose "a single, joint commonwealth, which from two states and nations a single people arose

---

[99] Cf. Ibid., pp. 86–88.
[100] Karol Szajnocha, "Jak Ruś polszczała," in Karol Szajnocha, *Szkice historyczne*, vol. 4 (Lviv, 1869), p. 188.

and bonded."[101] Although Lelewel's work was written in 1839 and was intended as a popular non-specialist book, it nevertheless laid the foundations for his successors who also believed that the Union of Lublin had brought Poles and Lithuanians (as well as Ruthenians) together for centuries as a single nation. Andrzej Wierzbicki emphasized that underlying Lelewel's historiography was the conviction that the republican form of authority was essential to the historical process of development. He characterized Lelewel's work as optimistic, maintained in the spirit of concern for the indigenous population while treating the national problem in a supra-state manner.[102] Lelewel's approach would be adopted for many years in a more or less conscious way by subsequent Polish historians.[103]

Lelewel's thought was further developed in Lviv by Karol Szajnocha and Henryk Schmitt. The former, examining the genesis of the Union of Lublin and therefore the times of Władysław Jagiełło, wrote in his key work *Jadwiga and Jagiełło* [*Jadwiga i Jagiełło*] that in 1401, the Polish lords and Lithuanian boyars swore mutual loyalty. He evaluated this event most positively, writing:

> This was the only example in history of an unenforced union of peoples hostile to each other for centuries, for whom history was to provide a closer bond still. The fortunate interaction of various motives changed this outstanding union of nations into a close union of families and people.[104]

In discussing the Union of Horodło, Karol Szajnocha galloped far ahead to 1569, writing that "the later joining of Poland with Lithuania and Ruthenia supplemented this work of equality."[105] Jerzy Maternicki argues that it was Szajnocha himself who initiated this idyllic perception of the Polish-Lithuanian union, and sees here a significant element in the process of establishing the so-called "Jagiellonian myth" in Polish historiography, which was, among other things, a reply to Ruthenian separatist aspirations for the division of Galicia from 1848 onwards. The Jagiellonian myth was also an argument confirming the legitimacy of the gentry estate landholdings in Red Rus'. In this case the union

---

[101] Joachim Lelewel, *Dzieje Litwy i Rusi aż do unji z Polską w Lublinie 1569 zawartej* (Poznań, 1844), p. 196.

[102] Andrzej Wierzbicki, *Historiografia polska doby romantyzmu* (Wrocław, 1999), pp. 307–8.

[103] Lelewel's historiosophical thought has been analyzed more broadly by Henryk Słoczyński in: Henryk Marek Słoczyński, *Światło w dziejarskiej ciemnicy. Koncepcja dziejów i interpretacja przeszłości Polski Joachima Lelewela* (Cracow, 2010).

[104] Karol Szajnocha, *Jadwiga i Jagiełło 1374–1413. Opowiadanie historyczne*, vol. 4 (Lviv, 1861), p. 318.

[105] Ibid., p. 323.

was a commendable example of the Polish civilizational mission in the East.[106]

Henryk Schmitt was to go even further in his judgements. To mark the occasion of the anniversary of the Union of Lublin in 1869, he published a book devoted to this historical event. In it, he briefly described the history of the Polish-Lithuanian union, not overlooking Jadwiga's incorporation of Rus' and the freeing of this land from the "Hungarian yoke." He drew attention to the phenomenon of the Union of Lublin, which, uniquely, had been achieved without the need for military force. At this time the merging of various "nationalities" into a single nation occurred. Interestingly Schmitt, as *gente Germanus, natione Polonus*, added his own nationality to the three peoples of Poland:

> (…) there merged with each other two Slavic (Poles and Ruthenians) and two foreign (German and Lithuanian) nationalities into a single joint Commonwealth with the complete right to maintain their individuality and national separateness. With time these differences started to blur, from which there formed without coercion or force, without the imposition of hegemony, a national uniformity; the Polish element, being the most politically, socially, and intellectually developed, gained the advantage. This assimilative action was the natural result of the relationship developing amongst the factions comprising the Commonwealth, and this was to occur without injury or oppression of even the best. Polishness as the principle of freedom and equality was adopted in all the provinces of the joint Commonwealth, while (…) the consequence of such an adoption was the Polonization of these provinces, yet no one's rights and freedoms were in the slightest violated, whether this referred to individuals, towns, or provinces.[107]

In another work synthesizing Poland's history, Schmitt emphasized that the Union was a "skillful reconciliation of autonomy and provincial separateness with the principle of the collective unity of the Commonwealth." According to him, "without the use of violence and coercion and without (…) centralism (…) all differences were subsequently slowly blurred and [the nationalities] merged finally into a one-nation Commonwealth." Schmitt praised the Union, stating that "nowhere else has such an undertaking been managed."[108]

---

[106] Cf. Jerzy Maternicki, "Początki mitu jagiellońskiego w historiografii polskiej XIX wieku: Karol Szajnocha i Julian Klaczko," *Przegląd Humanistyczny* 32, no. 11/12 (1988), pp. 35, 38–40.

[107] Henryk Schmitt, *Unja Litwy z Koroną dokonana na sejmie lubelskim 1568–1569. Szkic dziejowy* (Lviv, 1869), pp. 48–49.

[108] Henryk Schmitt, *Dzieje Narodu Polskiego od najdawniejszych do najnowszych czasów, krótko i zwięźle opowiedziane*, vol. 1 (Lviv, 1861), p. 484.

To summarize, the concept of a union of Poles and Ruthenians owes its long life to the developing historical consciousness of the inhabitants of Galicia. Polish historiography placed particular stress on the people inhabiting both lands and on those events that had politically, religiously, or culturally tied Rus' with the Crown. The appearance of a series of authors praising the magnitude of the Union of Lublin allowed Ruthenians leaning towards Polishness to find consistent historical argumentation to justify their identity choices. However, it must be remembered that historical books were initially addressed only to the intelligentsia and the privileged strata, whose members were literate and interested in the study of the past. Eventually initiatives appeared that were directed towards an even broader transmission of this interpretation of history above others. An excellent opportunity for this to occur was presented from the 1860s onwards through the creation of an autonomous Galician school system.

For a period of nine decades the school system in Galicia had been Germanized. As a result, there were no books or textbooks in the school system that could introduce young people to the history of the country through the idea of the former Polish-Ruthenian brotherhood. Indeed, no textbooks on Polish history were even allowed in the school system, since no such subject was taught in schools in the Austrian area of partition.[109] An opportunity for Polish historiography to reach the youth was afforded only after gaining autonomy. And the idea was to produce a textbook that would remind Polish and Ruthenian pupils that their duty, derived from their historical legacy, was to remain together.

Such ideas floated in the minds of many historians, which is why the subject of union with Lithuania and the willing inclusion of Rus' in Poland was present on the pages of most Polish historiographic works, syntheses, textbooks, and articles. One such attempt at showing the centuries-old "marriage" of Poland, Rus', and Lithuania was *A History of the Lithuanian-Ruthenian-Polish Commonwealth for the Young* [*Historya Rzeczypospolitej litewsko-rusko-polskiej dla młodzieży*] by Józef Sielcz Fedkowicz. This book, completed in 1878, was never published. We know the content of this text from a manuscript preserved in the collections of the Ossolineum, currently held by the Lviv National Vasyl Stefanyk Scientific Library of Ukraine. The manuscript of the book numbering 878 pages, was a synthesis of the history of the multi-ethnic state, yet presented differently from those previously produced. We read on one of the pages, "The Polish Commonwealth was here composed of three

---

[109] An independent school system was in operation solely in Cracow, and only when it was a free city.

peoples constituting the Polish nation, the Polish, the Lithuanian, and the Ruthenian peoples."[110] The author attempts to devote equal attention to the three peoples. He ultimately fails to realize this intention, the work being largely a history of the Polish state and not an account of three peoples creating a commonwealth; it did, however, represent an attempt to give uniform coverage of the three nationalities united by the Union of Lublin—"never, absolutely never severed," as he himself notes. The legacy of King Sigismund II Augustus of 1569 is considered by Fedkowicz to be an absolutely decisive event; it merged "the spirit of our hearts into a single sensual flame which in the most distant time of posterity will always (...) foster the spirit of fraternal love in our souls."[111] The entire narrative of the book proceeds in such a tone. The young reader, regardless of his ethnic origins, was thus acquainted with the history of his fatherland, learning that the three, once separate, states—the Polish, Ruthenian, and Lithuanian—were forever linked by the course of historical events. Fedkowicz's work would not, however, see a print.

During the initial years of Galician autonomy, Henryk Schmitt's aforementioned popular book was in general use in schools,[112] recommended by the National School Council in 1872. This was a concise history of Poland, in which the history of Rus' was subordinated to the history of the Crown. A new textbook, approved by the National School Council in 1884, paid more attention to the key role of the Ruthenian lands in the history of old Poland.[113] This textbook for secondary school pupils in Galicia, entitled *A Historical Outline of Poland and the Ruthenian Lands that Are Linked to Poland* [*Zarys historyi Polski i krajów ruskich z nią połączonych*], was written by Anatol Lewicki and reissued a dozen or so times: during the partitions, under the Second Polish Republic, in the emigration, and even for the very last time as a reprint in 1999.[114] The

---

[110] Józef Sielcz Fedkowicz, "Historya Rzeczypospolitej litewsko-rusko-polskiej dla młodzieży" (1878), LNNBU, fond 5, op. 1, spr. 4545/I, p. 23.

[111] Ibid., p. 370.

[112] Henryk Schmitt, *Zdarzenia najważniejsze z przeszłości narodu polskiego zestawił w potocznym opowiadaniu* (Lviv, 1869).

[113] Czesław Majorek, *Historia utylitarna i erudycyjna. Szkolna edukacja historyczna w Galicji (1772–1918)* (Warsaw, 1990), pp. 328–33.

[114] The first publication of the textbook: Antoni Lewicki, *Zarys historyi Polski i krajów ruskich z nią połączonych* (Cracow, 1884). The final edition is *de facto* a reprint from 1947, in which Jan Friedberg increased the chronological scope to 1922. See Antoni Lewicki and Jan Friedberg, *Zarys historii Polski od zarania do roku 1922* (Warsaw–Komorów, 1999). Janusz Łosowski was one of the historians who analyzed this textbook in his "Anatol Lewicki jako historyk," in Anatol Lewicki, *Obrazki najdawniejszych dziejów Przemyśla* (Przemyśl, 1994), pp. xxx–xxxi. For more on Lewicki's treatment of Polish-Ruthenian relations

very title points to the author's relationship to the history of Poland and Rus',
which is all the more interesting given
that he was an authentic *gente Ruthenus,
natione Polonus*. The textbook begins
with a "geographical look at the lands
of the Poland of old." The author lists
the expanses between the Carpathians
and the Baltic, and to the east, the lands
along the Dnipro. He includes within
old Poland not only the Little Poland region, Cuiavia, the Great Poland region,
Mazovia, Pomerania, Prussia, Silesia,
and Podlachia, but also those territories
stretching from the Rus' lands to Livo-

14. Anatol Lewicki

nia. The history of Poland is divided into twelve periods, from Slavic
times right up to the Third Partition; several pages are devoted to the
era from Maria Theresa up to Franz Joseph I.[115] In addition, the textbook
is equipped with geneaological trees of particular rulers, not merely
the Piast or Jagiellonian dynasties but also the Kyivan prince Iaroslav
the Wise and the Sobieski family, whose Ruthenian roots were often
emphasized in the nineteenth century. The table of contents reveals
the author's intent to show the free-willed union of Poland, Lithuania,
and Rus' in history. The best example is the title given to the "second
epoch" in the textbook: *The Lithuanian-Ruthenian-Polish State under the
Jagiellonians: 1386–1572*. According to Lewicki's chapter headings, Red
Rus' under Jadwiga was "The Second Retaking of Red Rus'," and the
"Joining of Galician-Volhynian Rus' to Poland" took place under Casimir the Great. The author explicitly explores the driving concept of his
work by devoting a part of the textbook to the "Joining of Lithuania,
Rus', and Poland," which took place under the governance of King
Władysław Jagiełło. Most unusual for a textbook on Polish history is
the large amount of material on the history of Rus'. The author obviously wanted to convey to the young Polish and Ruthenian inhabitants of
Galicia knowledge about their former, and most importantly, "joint"
state. The inclusion of many interesting episodes from the history of

---

and the image of Ukraine, see: Dorota Malczewska-Pawelec, "Obraz Ukrainy i stosunków polsko-ukraińskich w podręczniku Anatola Lewickiego *Zarys historii Polski i krajów
ruskich z nią połączonych*," in *Stosunki polsko-ukraińskie w szkolnej edukacji historycznej od
XIX do XXI wieku. Materiały konferencji naukowej 21–22 października 2004 r., Cedzyna k. Kielc*,
ed. Hanna Wójcik-Łagan (Kielce, 2005), pp. 145–61.
[115] In subsequent editions the chronological scope was expanded.

Rus' meant that the textbook was not Polonocentric, but rather represented an interpretation of history on which both the Polish and Ruthenian inhabitants of the Austrian partition could be brought up.

It is not simply the textbook under discussion that reveals the historical interests of this Pole of Ruthenian origin. Anatol Lewicki also devoted a series of works to the medieval history of Poland, including the Polish-Lithuanian unions. In his writings the Union is an event without historical parallel.[116] He presented the Union of these states in a similar way in his book on the Švitrigaila Uprising, which was awarded a prize by the Historical-Literary Society in Paris.[117] Lewicki also wrote popular historical works designed for a broader and less specialized readership, a famous example of which is *Images from the Oldest History of Przemyśl*

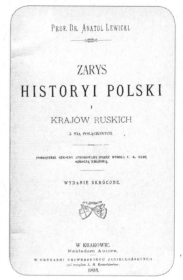

15. The cover of Anatol Lewicki's textbook A Historical Outline of Poland and the Ruthenian Lands that Are Linked to Poland (Cracow, 1893)

[Obrazki z najdawniejszych dziejów Przemyśla]. The whole work shows the medieval history of this important Red Rus' town, which—as the author states—even in "the most distant historical times was a Polish holding."[118]

Lewicki's writings show his historical outlook, but also that of the entire group of *gente Rutheni, natione Poloni* from which he came. By accentuating the benefits derived from the Union of Rus' with Poland, this group hoped to portray a genuine program for Galician Ruthenians: not Russian, not Ukrainian national populist, but one dependent on the

---

[116] Cf. Oksana Ruda, "Otsinka Liublins'koï uniï 1569 r. u pol's'kii istoriohrafiï kintsia XIX – pochatku XX st.," in *Bahatokul'turne istorychne seredovyshche L'vova v XIX i XX stolittiakh / Wielokulturowe środowisko historyczne Lwowa w XIX i XX wieku*, vol. 4, eds. Leonid Zashkil'niak and Jerzy Maternicki (Lviv–Rzeszów, 2006), p. 321.

[117] Anatol Lewicki, *Powstanie Świdrygiełły. Ustęp unii Litwy z Koroną* (Cracow, 1892). The newest edition with and introduction commenting historical view of Lewicki was published in 2015. See: Jarosław Nikodem, „Anatol Lewicki i jego 'Powstanie Świdrygiełły'," in Anatol Lewicki, *Powstanie Świdrygiełły. Ustęp z dziejów unii Litwy z Koroną* (Oświęcim, 2015), pp. 9–19.

[118] Anatol Lewicki, *Obrazki z najdawniejszych dziejów Przemyśla*, ed. Stanisław Stępień (Przemyśl, 1994)

union with Poland, directed not to the east but to the west. Lewicki's
books may today appear to be *gente Rutheni, natione Poloni* propaganda.
However, I would caution against such an evaluation. Without a doubt
these were frank opinions of an author who was searching for a new narrative to relate the history of his "local homeland." Such a presentation
of the past was to naturally incite resistance on the part of Ruthenian
national populists, but Lewicki never feared engaging in debate with
them. In the work *A Word on the Union of Lithuania with the Polish Crown*
[*Nieco o unii Litwy z Koroną*], he refuted the criticism in *Dilo* [The Work]
of one of his books (*The Švitrigaila Uprising* [*Powstanie Świdrygiełły*]),
claiming that the adoption of this viewpoint by the editor was a result
of the contemporary Ruthenian position. Lewicki did not emphasize in
his writings the national oppression of the Ruthenian people by Poles,
which the contemporary Ruthenian critics of his work wished to see. He
defended himself by stating that in the period he studied there could
be no talk of national pressure, for there was no sense of such a thing as
nationality. He pointed out the use of the Ruthenian language by members of the Jagiellonian dynasty, the attempts to strike a union between
the Roman Catholic and Greek Catholic churches, the incorporation of
Ruthenian gentry into Polish families, the equality in laws, etc. Yet this
did not in any way mean that Lewicki neglected the negative aspects
of Polish-Ruthenian unions, reminding his readers that the Catholic
Church did not initially treat schismatics as being equal to Roman Catholics; however, he also emphasized that this should not be treated as an
example of oppression against Ruthenians.[119]

Lewicki never concealed the fact that he was a Ruthenian author.
He valued the history of his homeland and knew the injustices and difficulties which his homeland had endured in the past. Nevertheless, he
emphasized the importance of the attempts undertaken hundreds of
years earlier to unify Ruthenia with Lithuania and Poland.

It was not only Lewicki who wrote about the joining of Rus' to Poland. This subject was undertaken by other authors, ones not always
sensitive to nationality questions. The Romantic current in historiography, together with its apologetic interpretation of the events that
comprised the joining of Lithuania and Ruthenia to Poland, maintained
its hold for a long time. In evaluating not only state history but also that
of the common people, "the people," these currents moved the subsequent evolution of Polish historiography in the direction of nationalist writing. Such tendencies existed already in the Galicia of the 1870s.
Marian Gorzkowski, a nobleman from Ukraine who settled in Galicia,

---

[119] Anatol Lewicki, *Nieco o unii Litwy z Koroną* (Cracow, 1893), pp. 4–7.

was so fascinated with his own personal homeland that he undertook his own historical research, though unfortunately without any academic preparation. Before he became secretary at the Fine Arts School in Cracow, he had released *An Overview of Debatable Questions on Rus'* [*Przegląd kwestyj spornych o Rusi*], in which he had argued—basing his conclusions on a questionable understanding of Nestor the Chronicler[120]— that the Kyivan lands had always been Polish. He presumably considered that the tribe Polanians [Eastern Polans] in Kyiv was identical with the Polanes [Western Polans] from the territory of the Great Poland region, while the Rus' were merely Scandinavian invaders, a thesis often repeated in the Polish historiography of the time. Elsewhere he emphasized that the Ruthenian language was but a dialect of Polish, supporting his statement that Ruthenians were basically Poles.[121] Gorzkowski's writing is an example not only of the denial of the Ruthenians' right to nationhood, but their right to rule over the territory of Rus' and Ukraine, which, in his view, was the exclusive domain of the Poles.

Gorzkowski would not become the chief authority writing from this historical position; this title would belong to Franciszek Rawita-Gawroński, the son-in-law of Zygmunt Miłkowski, known more widely by his pseudonym of Teodor Tomasz Jeż—a leader of Polish emigrants in Switzerland, a chief of Polish Union [*Liga Polska*]. Both authors, descended from Polish gentry families in Ukraine, where they had come into contact with Ukrainians in their childhood, considered themselves to be highly qualified to speak on the subject of the Ruthenian lands and their inhabitants. What is more, they also spoke of themselves as *gente Rutheni, natione Poloni*, although they understood *gente* to designate territorial origin rather than ethnic. Miłkowski in one of his works clearly stated:

> I am—and loudly proclaim the fact—*gente Ruthenus, natione Polonus*. I was born in Rus', I was raised in Rus'; the first sounds to echo in my ears were those of the Ruthenian tongue (…).

---

[120] "(…) Nestor (…) clearly wrote that the lands around Kyiv were Polish before the ninth century; it is not surprising that these lands as if linked by historical lot with Poland should be joined to them as they earlier had been merged before the incursion of the Rus', by blood, provenance, language." Marian Gorzkowski, *Przegląd kwestyj spornych o Rusi* (Cracow, 1875), p. 30.

[121] He wrote: "True Lithuania, Ukraine, Volhynia, Podilia, and Eastern Galicia are inhabited by people that we today refer to as villagers, peasants, and though they speak a separate dialect, it is still an irrefutable fact that they have to be included in the Polish nation, Polish blood, origin and tribe; while their folk language as provincial dialects of the Polish tongue constitutes one and the self same Polish language!" Marian Gorzkowski, *O rusińskiej i rosyjskiej szlachcie* (Cracow, 1876), pp. 199–200.

I became accustomed to the Ruthenian people and loved this folk, I loved it with all my soul, all my heart, and later, when upon this emotional base rational concepts were formed, I came to the understanding that clans develop into nations which, by their nature, possess the right to live and the freedom to develop.[122]

So Miłkowski considered that Ruthenians composed the greater nation of Poles, seeing himself in the very same way. Coming from Ukraine, he had to find and define his place within the Polish nation.[123] As a result, he tended to overly accentuate the federal political model enforced in Poland. He was already writing in 1879 that:

Bondage, foreign rule, the quartering of the country, the parcelling off of land, administrative, legislative and political means, all ways in which Poland has for over a hundred years been abused, did not deprive Poland of the properties that constitute her essence—a core that is first and foremost federal, a union, erected as such at those very times when the Polish state was formed and legally pronounced at the moment when Poland in its state form stood at the culminating point of becoming established. *De facto* and *de iure* the core of Poland is a federation and such must it be as a result of its very genetic make-up and nature. (...)[124]

On subsequent pages he underscores the separateness of Rus' from Poland, while simultaneously adding that "Rus' entered the state complex of Poland not enslaved but liberated," and that "Ruthenianism did not experience any harm" through Polonization.[125]

In the thought of Miłkowski, as Poland had formerly been a federation, Ruthenians remained—in the national sense—Poles. Miłkowski's son-in-law thought in a similar way. Franciszek Rawita-Gawroński, as Zofia Kozarynowa writes, "called himself a Ukrainian in the regional understanding of the day (...), fostering his tribal traditions despite the affiliation to a nation and state which considered him a member and citizen."[126] In a similar way to his father-in-law he also declared

---

[122] Zygmunt Miłkowski, *Sprawa ruska w stosunku do sprawy polskiej* (Lviv, 1902), p. 3.

[123] Adam S'v'iontek, "'Vid kolysky na vse zhyttia' – shchodennyk pol's'koho politychnoho diiacha ta pis'mennyka Zygmunta Milkovs'koho (Teodor Tomash Iezh) iak kraieznavche dzherelo do vyvchennia istorii Podillia," in *Kraieznavstvo v systemi rozvytku dukhovnosti i kul'tury rehionu. Materialy Mizhnarodnoï naukovo-praktychnoï konferentsiï 21–23 zhovtnia 2008 r.*, eds. M. Spytsia et al. (Vinnytsia, 2008), p. 25.

[124] Zygmunt Miłkowski, *Sprawa ruska. Prowodyrowie Rusi spółcześni* (Poznań, 1879), pp. 2–3.

[125] Ibid., pp. 5–6.

[126] Zofia Kozarynowa, *Sto lat. Gawęda o kulturze środowiska* (Wrocław–Warsaw–Cracow, 1992), p. 35.

himself to be *gente Ruthenus, natione Polonus*,[127] as his ancestors, in set-
tling in Podilia in the sixteenth century, had only changed their rite
from the Greek to the Latin at the end of the eighteenth century.[128] Like
Gorzkowski, Franciszek Rawita-Gawroński considered the name Rus'
to be Germanic (Scandinavian), while he denied the Ruthenians the
right to be called a nation. Here he fundamentally opposed Mykhailo
Hrushevsky, the author of the central synthesis of the history of Rus'-
Ukraine and the propagator of a view that the Ukrainian nation was
a composite of the inhabitants of Ukraine and Galician Ruthenians.[129]
Hrushevsky had presented these views much earlier, having written
various academic and journalistic works. Eugeniusz Koko, a researcher
of Gawroński's historical writings, noted that a fundamental difference
lay between the two historians in their understanding of the concept of
a nation. As Koko thinks, Gawroński cultivated the already anachronistic tradition of Gentry Poland, according to which the spirit of Poland was to soar over Ukraine.[130] Hence Gawroński's conviction, noted
in his history of the Cossack movement written after Poland gained
independence in 1918, that "neither in Volhynia, nor in Red Rus' was
there ever a 'Ukraine' or a 'Ukrainian nation.'"[131] Consequently, he
also favourably evaluated the act of the Union of Hadiach of 1658, but
argued that Cossacks raised in Western culture following the experi-

---

[127] Eugeniusz Koko writes about this, *Franciszek Rawita-Gawroński (1846–1930) wobec
Ukrainy i jej przeszłości. Studium archaizmu* (Gdańsk, 2006), p. 125.
[128] Eugeniusz Koko, "Przedmowa," in Franciszek Rawita-Gawroński, *Ludzie i czasy mego
wieku. Wspomnienia, wypadki, zapiski (1892–1914)*, ed. and footnotes Eugeniusz Koko
(Gdańsk, 2012), p. 7.
[129] Mykhailo Hrushevs'kii, *Istoriia Ukraïny-Rusy*, vol. 1–9 (Lviv, 1898–1928). Rawita-Gawroński in his memoirs wrote: "Ruthenians were not yet fashionable in Austria but they
were already loudly shouting about their millions and about the fantastic Ukraine-Rus'
constructed for their history by Hrushevsky, a professor of Lviv University, which they
presented to Austria as an independent state with Habsburg backing or an autonomous
province of a future Greater Austria. The hallucinations of a few Ruthenian ideologists
fed on Polish bread were taken by some as serious, and the noisy clichés of a few pathetic
rags calling themselves the Ruthenian press—as the expression of the opinion of a people
who not only did not know about any Ukraine-Rus', but even had not established names
for themselves, did not know what they were called, and besides the bounds of class and
social envy did not possess any other aspirations whatsoever." Rawita-Gawroński, *Ludzie
i czasy*, pp. 96–97.
[130] Eugeniusz Koko, "Rusini czy Ukraińcy? Kształtowanie się nowoczesnego narodu
ukraińskiego w poglądach Franciszka Rawity-Gawrońskiego," in *Polacy i sąsiedzi – dystanse i przenikanie kultur. Zbiór studiów*, part 1, ed. Roman Wapiński (Ostaszewo Gdańskie, 2000), pp. 33–34.
[131] Franciszek Rawita Gawroński, *Kozaczyzna ukrainna w Rzeczypospolitej Polskiej do końca XVIII wieku. Zarys polityczno-historyczny* (Warsaw–Cracow–Lublin–Łódź–Poznań–Vilnius–Zakopane, 1922), p. 12.

ence of the Pereiaslav Treaty with Moscow noticed the cultural differences between the Cossack lands and Russia and yearned to return to
the "joint fatherland" of Poland. For Gawroński, the Union of Hadiach
was the first treaty in history that guaranteed the rights of Ruthenians,
for whom he could not see a political place outside of Poland.[132]

It was the Cracow historical school that initiated the polemical voice
in the evaluation of Poland's past. Its position was in accordance with
the views of the Stańczyks political faction on the Ruthenian question.
Cracow historians were of the mindset that the Union of Lublin had
squandered the chance for a strong, western-rooted state. The "marriage" of the Lithuanian-Ruthenian lands to Poland, so lauded by Romantics and Eastern Galician circles, was subject to criticism as the very
reason for latter-day anarchy within the state. Although in 1862 Józef
Szujski still emphasized the memorable significance of the Union, he
acknowledged the difficulties in its conclusion and the aversion to it
on the part of many Lithuanians.[133] Eighteen years later, when he published *Twelve Books Concisely Conveying the History of Poland* [*Historii
polskiej treściwie opowiedzianej ksiąg dwanaście*], the Union of Lublin, as
a result of the implementation of a federal model, appeared to him to
be a squandered chance for a strong Poland, which he understood as
a centralized state.[134] Józef Gierowski sums up Szujski's views thus:

> The Union pulled Poland into an undertaking that was to become its mis-
> sion: the bestowing of Western civilization on the territories of Lithuania
> and Rus'. The forces involved here, rather than being concentrated on
> the ethnic area of Poland, resulted in their dissipation and consequently
> in the collapse of the state.[135]

Szujski's views were further developed by his student Michał
Bobrzyński, the future governor of Galicia. In his groundbreaking work
National History, with Particular Consideration of the History of Galicia
[*Dzieje ojczyste ze szczególnym uwzględnieniem historyi Galicyi*], he wrote
that the Union had been the time-consuming "subject of the moral
labourings of several generations," but that it had had "one important

---

[132] Konrad Bobiatyński, "Polska historiografia wobec unii hadziackiej," in *350-lecie unii
hadziackiej (1658–2008)*, eds. Teresa Chynczewska-Hennel, Piotr Kroll and Mirosław Nagielski (Warsaw, 2008), pp. 664–66.
[133] Józef Szujski, *Dzieje Polski podług ostatnich badań spisane*, vol. 2: *Jagielloni* (Lviv, 1862),
pp. 318–24.
[134] Józef Szujski, *Historyi polskiej treściwie opowiedzianej ksiąg dwanaście* (Warsaw, 1880),
p. 196. Por. Stępnik, *Ukraina*, pp. 175–76; Ruda, "Otsinka," pp. 318–19.
[135] Józef A. Gierowski, "Józef Szujski jako historyk czasów nowożytnych," in *Spór o historyczną szkołę krakowską. W stulecie Katedry Historii Polski UJ 1869–1969*, eds. Celina Bobińska and Jerzy Wyrozumski (Cracow, 1972), p. 91.

and fundamental flaw." As an adherent of strong monarchical authority, he criticized the federal solutions implemented in the state (the offices of chancellors, marshals, hetmans, etc.). He wrote that "the sanctifying of a duality of government within a single state became the seed for the lasting and unavoidable dilemma that beset the united countries."[136] Although his criticism would soften with time, with subsequent editions of his work conceding that the expansion of Poland under Casimir the Great incorporated Red Rus', he maintained his general critical appraisal of the Union. Bobrzyński considered the colonization of the Lithuanian and Ruthenian lands to be the dilution of Polish forces in the East, not the work of Poland's historical civilizing mission.[137] Both he and his predecessors writing in the current of the Cracow historical school strongly disputed the "chief historian of Romanticism," Lelewel.[138] Bobrzyński believed that Lelewel's praise of republicanism, the most wondrous historical example of which was purportedly the state union of Poland and Lithuania (and with it of Rus'), had been mistaken. Following Szujski, who believed in the truth of the sentence *historia magistra vitae est*, Bobrzyński searched history for those factors which influenced civilization or state progress.[139] Meanwhile, in observing the cultivation of a completely romanticized conception of union and political alliance (as can be seen alone on the basis of the celebrations, in 1869, of the 300th anniversary of the Union of Lublin), he saw a fundamental contradiction. This observation naturally influenced Bobrzyński's political views. He therefore did not deny the existence of Ruthenian nationality and did not set out to prove to Ruthenains their affiliation to the Polish nation. He based his politics regarding the Ruthenian question on the method of compromise, with the aim of strengthening the Galician authorities within the framework of the Habsburg monarchy.

From where did such a drastically divergent evaluation of Polish-Ruthenian unions come? The representatives of the Cracow school saw a huge involvement of Polish forces in the East, which they did not consider to be beneficial in the least for Poland.[140] From the demo-

---

[136] Michał Bobrzyński, *Dzieje ojczyste ze szczególnem uwzględnieniem historyi Galicyi* (Cracow, 1879), pp. 190–91.

[137] Jerzy Maternicki, "Michał Bobrzyński wobec tzw. idei jagiellońskiej. Ewolucja poglądów i jej uwarunkowania," *Przegląd Humanistyczny* 21, no. 12 (1977), pp. 136–40.

[138] Wojciech M. Bartel, "Michał Bobrzyński (1849–1935)," in *Spór o historyczną szkołę krakowską*, pp. 156, 166–67.

[139] Cf. Gierowski, "Józef Szujski," p. 86; Bartel, "Michał Bobrzyński," pp. 164–65.

[140] Janusz Tazbir, "Procesy polonizacyjne w szlacheckiej Rzeczypospolitej," in *Tryumfy i porażki. Studia z dziejów kultury polskiej XVI–XVIII w.*, ed. Maria Bogucka (Warsaw, 1989), pp. 24–25.

graphic point of view, Poland gained several tens of thousands Polonized gentry (the said *gente Lithuani* and *gente Rutheni*), while it lost
several million Polish colonists, peasants who underwent Lithuaniza-
tion and Ruthenization.[141] Eugeniusz Starczewski explicitly stated that
the "union of Poland with Lithuania perhaps presents a splendid and
brilliant monument of glory," but "future generations have been left in
their legacy to tackle very difficult and extremely important questions
fraught with consequences: the Ruthenian question and the Lithuanian
question."[142] So the Romantic interpretation of the union of Poland with
its eastern neighbours was confronted with the hard facts, including the
aforementioned demographic changes. The loss of millions of potential
Poles for the gain of a small stratum of *gente Rutheni* and *gente Lithuani*
for the *natione Poloni* could hardly be considered praiseworthy.

Romantic historiographical output, so vital in maintaining belief in
the inseparability of nations and in the special mission of subsequent
Polish-Lithuanian unions, was the subject of significant criticism,
echoed in the field of literary studies. Józef Buszko wrote: "If we attempt to compare the historical scholarship with the historical-literary
writing at that time, we can see a common fundamental feature in both
of these disciplines: the evaluation of historical figures and phenomena
in the fields of political and social history, as well as in literature, from
a civic patriotic and moralizing position based on strong conservative
Catholic tendencies (…)."[143] This trend was exemplified by the literary
historian, professor, and rector of the Jagiellonian University, Stanisław
Tarnowski, and the booklet published by him in 1891: *On Rus' and the
Ruthenians* [*O Rusi i Rusinach*]. In this work, the author emphasized that
although the Poles and the Ruthenians came from the same tribe, spoke
similar languages, belonged to the same Church (although of different rites), and finally inhabited the same territory, "we [Poles] are not,
however, the exact same as the Ruthenians, and they are not the same
as we are."[144] Although Tarnowski advocated cooperation between the
two nations, the very admission that Ruthenians are different from
the Polish nation was extremely significant. Such a view could not have
been expressed in the mainsteam Polish historiography of that time or
in the Polish Romantic literature, both of which propagated the idea
of the Poles' special mission in Rus' and Lithuania, a mission plagued

---

[141] Eugeniusz Starczewski, *Sprawa polska* (Cracow, 1912), p. 58.
[142] Ibid., p. 60.
[143] Józef Buszko, "Historycy 'szkoły krakowskiej' w życiu politycznym Galicji," in *Spór
o historyczną szkołę krakowską*, p. 194.
[144] Stanisław Tarnowski, *O Rusi i Rusinach* (Cracow, 1891), p. 3.

by multiple defeats in the era of conspiracies and national uprisings. But it was not only Bobrzyński who criticized the Romantics, laying the blame squarely on their shoulders for driving "ceaselessly towards damaging outbursts and demonstrations."[145] It should be emphasized at the same time that these Cracow intellectuals did not believe their past offered an optimistic vision, witnesssing on a daily basis a reality that was the direct effect of the activities of an ascending group. Living in Galicia, they did not observe much zeal on the part of Ruthenians for the Polish dreams of a fight for independence to resurrect the tripartite state, the Commonwealth of Poland, Lithuania, and Rus'. They did see Ruthenians who presented endless Russophile sympathies or separatist demands. Even if one were to suspect this body of the Cracow historians and politicians of everyday pragmatism in the face of this reality, following the collapse of the January Uprising there was little to no chance of bringing the federal idea back to life. The position taken by the Cracow historical school was born of a sober appraisal of reality, while the historiosophical views of the Stańczyks conservative group were intent on concrete political solutions. Through their historiographical and literary studies, works, and ultimately political activities, the Cracow conservatives opened up a new chapter in the development of the Poles' conceptions of their neighbours in Eastern Galicia. One may even laconically state that the Cracow elite excused themselves from the fruitless attempts to prove to Ruthenians that they were Poles or to convince them that they should collectively rebuild the state together. Instead, this group merely involved themselves in the arrangement of relations aimed at consolidating the autonomous authority secured within the framework of the monarchy and to oppose—which in their minds was a far more serious threat—the development of Russophilism and an interest in Pan-Slavism. It was understood that Russia could one day turn its attention to what was left of the former Rus', which it had yet to exert control over—the lands of Red Rus' which formed part of Galicia.

Despite criticism, the writings of the historians of the Cracow historical school enjoyed long-lasting popularity and gathered an increasing number of adherents. Retrospectively, we can see the correlation between the achievements of the Stańczyks group over the course of several decades and their continued power as a political circle. However, as it turned out, the theses advanced by those researchers representing the Cracow historical school were not able to destroy the notion of the special significance of Polish-Lithuanian unions cultivated for decades within Polish national historiography.

---

[145] Bobrzyński, *Dzieje ojczyste*, p. 325.

Chapter III
From Enlightenment Centralism to the Romantic Fraternity of Peoples

Ruthenians in the Conceptions of the Polish Enlightenment

The previous chapters presented the formulation of *gente Rutheni, natione Poloni*—one universally present within Polish literature, art, and historiography—as a form of identity, an attitude or world outlook, and ultimately as a prescribed model for the ethnically non-Polish inhabitants of the lands of the former Commonwealth. This chapter and those that follow aim to answer the following questions: what events, views, and ideas led *gente Rutheni, natione Poloni* circles to articulate a political program? What guided the formulation by Ruthenians of Polish nationality of specific political demands, demands pursued—both legally and illegally—as far as possible? Finally, how were Ruthenians involved in Polish political life focused on independence for the Polish state or other forms of self-government? In other words, what was the route taken by the Polish political tradition before it was understood that the Ukrainian nation was separate from the Polish? What happened within Polish political thinking that resulted in *gente Rutheni, natione Poloni* becoming the most anticipated direction for the development of an identity of the Ruthenian population of Galicia?

The roots of the problem under discussion should be looked for in the period when the Polish-Lithuanian Commonwealth was still in existence. In 1772, as a result of the first partition of Poland, the southern part of the state found itself located within the borders of the Austrian Empire. This territory was called Old Galicia. For over twenty years it was separated from its main cultural centre, that is, the still functioning Polish-Lithuanian state. In the end, the very fact of partition resulted in the inability of the Polish state apparatus to influence Galicia.[1] Nonetheless, there were still bonds between the Galician elite and the elites of Poland, links based on family, social, and professional relations. The

---

[1] Ryszard Radzik, "Społeczne uwarunkowania formowania się ukraińskiej świadomości narodowej w Galicji wschodniej w latach 1830–1863," *Kultura i Społeczeństwo* 25, no. 1–2 (1981), p. 300.

Galician elite watched what was happening in Warsaw. The ideas of the Polish Enlightenment reached Galicia, although in limited measure, and these carried notions such as state and nation in completely new categories. Even if at the time these concepts had no chance of any practical implementation in Galicia, Polish political activists brought up on Enlightenment rhetoric were still to believe, even after the partitions, in the possibility of turning ideas into political action.

The ideas of the Enlightenment understood the nation as a political community expressing itself in the form of a state. Historical nations were to have the right to their own statehood. Therefore, those who had managed to exist in history, or for whom there existed a state tradition, had such a right. Consequently, even following the partitions, the conviction could still be preserved that the Poles were a nation—admittedly a stateless one—but one convinced that in the future they would obtain their state once again. As Andrzej Walicki wrote: "despite the destruction of state organization there still remained an 'invisible commonwealth,' to which civic service was to be directed." The emphasis had therefore shifted "from joint statehood to a joint political history and non-obsolete civil rights."[2] An excellent example of this phenomenon from Galicia would be the approach taken by the municipal councillors of the city of Lviv in 1772. At the moment of the installation of Austrian authority in the newly acquired province, they were to have said in a memorandum that: "the city of Lviv is unable to swear allegiance to a new ruler given that it has already sworn the said to the most glorious King of Poland."[3]

Another important matter concerned the character of the nation-state in the understanding of Enlightenment thinkers. The models developed in revolutionary France aimed at the unification of society into a single nation—with sovereignty, the force legitimising the authority of the state, now derived not from God, but from the people. As a result, the sovereign should speak in a single voice. This was the way the concept was understood in France, where society was to oppose any authority not derived from its election. The nation should be conscious of its existence, but equally consolidated. For this to be achieved, it was necessary to eradicate all differences present and to centralize the state through the elimination of regionalisms. Consequently, all separateness deviating from a national core shaped at the cultural centre was to be liquidated. Janusz Tazbir wrote:

---

[2] Andrzej Walicki, "Koncepcje tożsamości narodowej i terytorium narodowego w myśli polskiej czasów porozbiorowych," *Archiwum Historii Filozofii i Myśli Społecznej* 38 (1993), p. 219.

[3] Zbigniew Fras, *Galicja* (Wrocław, 2000), p. 9.

(…) the ideal of this epoch was the eradication of all regionalisms and differences, including linguistic, so our luminaries of the Age of Light advanced a demand for the denationalization of not only the Ruthenians, but the Jews as well.[4]

The Polish Enlightenment activist Stanisław Staszic articulated this demand most clearly:

(…) henceforth they speak in Polish, let them in this tongue take up their upbringing and in the same conduct their religious rites and learning.[5]

In the case of Poland, Warsaw fulfilled the function of the national centre. If the sovereign was to be the Polish nation, as the subject ruling the state—in the literal sense, via parliamentary (Diet) representation—then all ethnic groups had to resemble each other as closely as possible. As a result, the Ruthenian gentry could in no way be perceived as a separate nation, and were supposed to remain Polish. The Ruthenian peasantry, like the Polish peasants, were not taken into consideration at this time at all.

In the final years of the Polish state, it had been possible to introduce a series of solutions aimed at social integration. The best example of these is the activity of the Commission of National Education, as well as the Constitution of the 3rd of May 1791.[6] New solutions to such matters could not exist within the southern Polish lands which had been within the borders of Austria since 1772. Nonetheless, Enlightenment Polish thinkers viewed Ruthenians as a whole, as yet not dividing them (despite the existence of the new Polish-Austrian border) into Ukrainians (beyond the Zbruch River) and Galicians. The cultural separateness of the Ruthenian people was noted, but in the desire to "unify the Polish nation" it was necessary to bring them closer in a restrained way, but under no circumstances through violent religious and linguistic polonisation.[7] Hugo Kołłątaj—a head of the Commission of National Education—claimed that:

The sciences are taming the savagery of those lands, learning is bringing denomination to denomination and people to people. Nothing more is needed than for mathematics to be widely adopted in Rus' and then we will soon know that they will eagerly adopt our calendar. If dissidents

---

[4] Janusz Tazbir, "Tradycje wieloetnicznej Rzeczypospolitej," in *Inni wśród swoich*, ed. Wiesław Władyka (Warsaw, 1994), p. 13.
[5] Stanisław Staszic, *Pisma filozoficzne i społeczne*, ed. and introd. Bogdan Suchodolski, vol. 1 (Warsaw, 1954), p. 303, quoted in Tazbir, "Tradycje wieloetnicznej," p. 13.
[6] Michał Jagiełło, *Narody i narodowości. Przewodnik po lekturach*, vol. 1 (Warsaw, 2010), p. 10.
[7] Andrzej Walicki, *Idea narodu w polskiej myśli oświeceniowej* (Warsaw, 2000), p. 94.

[Protestants] have adopted it, then why should Uniates of the Ruthenian rite not want the same? This is a matter of such little importance that only a stubborn jackass could have an issue with it. And here the government should direct its efforts and teachings, for Rus' holds the closest in its rite the differences in calendar. Let us teach Latin to those who are to be consecrated as Ruthenian priests, let us provide a common education in the seminaries in which a cleric is educated under a single staff for the Latin and Ruthenian cloth, let us organise a joint gathering of teachers at academies both of the Ruthenian and the Latin rite, of secular Ruthenian priests as equally Basilians, only let there be forged a common brotherhood in these teachers, let their sweet character constitute a model for pupils from seminaries and schools, and then one can be sure that with time both the priests and the whole people will be the same.[8]

In turn, the future leader of insurrection Tadeusz Kościuszko, in hoping to persuade Ruthenians to merge [Uniate] Ruthenians with the Poles, but most importantly to differentiate them from the adherents of the "Muscovite religion," critically examined the question. Already in May 1789 he wrote in a letter to Michał Zaleski:

(…) incorporate all of their holy days with ours, let there be but a single calendar, and to try so that the Uniate priests could conduct Mass in Polish. (…) Accustom them ['unenlightened people'—here the Ruthenian populace—A.Ś.] to the need for the Polish language, let all their services be in Polish. In time the Polish spirit will enter into them.[9]

However, when the time of the greatest trial he was to face arrived— the war with Russia of 1794— Kościuszko simply called upon the Uniate bishop in Chełm for the priesthood to help win over the people to fight against the enemy. He asked for the priests to edify the people in a patriotic spirit:

I herein call upon you, Bishop, for the love of God, the love of the people and the love of the Fatherland, for you to explain our goal in simple terms so that every man can understand that the current war has been undertaken for the good, in the interests of, and for the happiness of everyone, that we want no one to oppress anyone, that we have sacrificed our life for the Fatherland in order to regain all of it, all her freedom and independence (…) Bishop! Your Holy character gives you access to the heart of the people, speak to them, teach them to love the fatherland, to despise tyrants and advise them to join in arms with the Poles for their own good and to help liberate our land. The fate of your lot, the

---

[8] Hugo Kołłątaj, *Listy Anonima i Prawo polityczne narodu polskiego*, vol. 2, eds. Bogusław Leśniodorski and Helena Wereszycka (Warsaw, 1954), p. 159.
[9] „List T. Kościuszki do M. Zaleskiego," Brest-Litovsk, May 1789, in *Pisma Tadeusza Kościuszki*, selection, comments, and introd. Henryk Mościcki (Warsaw, 1947), p. 45.

priests of the Greek rite, was harmed under the rule of injustice. Poles, free Poles, will rectify your fate and that of those who show themselves eager in service to them.[10]

After the partitions of Poland and its fall in 1795 up until the November Uprising of 1830 there were not a lot of factors among the inhabitants of Galicia that impacted the development of Polish national consciousness. One may talk of a heritage cultivated by the gentry for the state tradition of Old Poland, an opposition to the policy of Germanisation of the Habsburg monarchy, or finally, cultural differences of language, customs, etc. As Antoni Knot wrote: "Polishness lasted within the gentry by the force of tradition—while patriotic feelings were not fuelled by any central idea."[11] The conscious forging of Polish national identity, particularly among the non-gentry social strata, could occur as a result of patriotic education. In Galicia this could not develop on a broader scale because after 1772 the southern Polish lands were already under Austrian rule. Events such as the work of the Great Diet of 1788–92, the war over the constitution, or the Kościuszko Uprising in 1794 motivated Galician society to a limited degree to active involvement.[12] A more broadly known exception here could be the Greek Catholic priest Michał Harasiewicz, who together with Wawrzyniec Surowiecki edited the daily *Dziennik Patriotycznych Polityków* [The Daily of Patriotic Politicians] in Lviv from 1792 to 1798.[13] This publication was the official organ of the Association of Patriotic Poles, headed by Walerian Dzieduszycki, another known descendant of a boyar family and a patriotic activist during the final period of Poland's existence. Besides covering current affairs (including the military course of the insurrection itself), the daily contained feature columns, literary news, and extracts from Polish literature.[14] It is significant that Michał Harasiewicz after some time ceased his patriotic work for Polishness and became an Austrian loyalist committed to the policy of Germanisation in Galicia.[15]

---

[10] „List do Porfiriusza Ważyńskiego, biskupa chełmskiego, prezesa Komisji Porządkowej Chełmskiej w Srzedzinie," camp at Połaniec, 7 May 1794, in *Pisma Tadeusza Kościuszki*, p. 110–11.

[11] Antoni Knot, *Dążenia oświatowe młodzieży galicyjskiej w latach 1815–1830* (Wrocław, 1959), p. 11.

[12] Ibid., p. 6.

[13] Fras, *Galicja*, p. 81; Marian Tyrowicz, *Prasa Galicji i Rzeczypospolitej Krakowskiej 1772– 1850. Studia porównawcze* (Cracow, 1979), pp. 15, 34–35, 55, 81.

[14] Ibid., pp. 77, 174; Jerzy Jarowiecki, *Dzieje prasy polskiej we Lwowie do 1945 roku* (Cracow–Wrocław, 2008), pp. 23–24.

[15] Maurycy Dzieduszycki, "Przeszłowieczny Dziennik Lwowski," *Przewodnik Naukowy i Literacki* 3, no. 1 (1875), p. 41; Jan Lewicki, *Ruch Rusinów w Galicji w pierwszej połowie wieku panowania Austrji (1772–1820)* (Lviv, 1879), pp. 16, 20–23.

Participation in Polish independence activities at the end of the eighteenth century was taken up, if at all, by representatives of the gentry desiring a return to the lost state, or wishing quite simply for the freedoms and rights they had enjoyed in the Poland of old. Kosciuszko's attempts to engage the peasants, especially among the Ruthenian population, did not bring any major results. Polish patriotism did function as a value in Galicia, but it was chiefly centred on the nationally conscious part of society.

Galician Ruthenians during the Napoleonic Wars

The Napoleonic Wars offered Poles great hopes of gaining independence. The real answer to these operations were Jan Henryk Dąbrowski's Polish Legions in Italy, where Ruthenians as well as Poles served. And how did they get there? In 1797, besides volunteers from the former Polish Army, Dąbrowski managed to recruit to the new Polish formation prisoners-of-war from the Austrian army defeated by the French, and here were both Polish and Ruthenian recruits from Galicia. This group constituted up to eighty per cent of the legionnaires.[16] Jan Pachoński wrote that Ruthenians, Lithuanians, and Prussians within the legions were "undoubtedly an element more or less Polonized."[17] Considering the education conducted in the legions, the dissemination of democratic ideas, and finally, an evaluation of the subsequent involvement of the legionnaires on the field of battle, one may state that they were certainly far from indifferent to the question of Poland's independence. However, this was often the result of the awareness-raising work that was conducted in the legions themselves.

The situation was different in the Austrian partition, where Poles, and particularly Ruthenian peasants, were indifferent to national matters. The situation during the Duchy of Warsaw's war with Austria can serve as an example of the lack of clear national (Ruthenian) feelings among the Ruthenian population of Galicia at the time. As Vadym Adadurov makes clear, in 1809, the national-state question was of no interest to either the ordinary rank and file Greek-Catholic clergy or

---

[16] Zbigniew Moszumański, "Trening militarny żołnierza w aspekcie historycznym," in *Trening militarny żołnierzy*, eds. Andrzej Chodała, Jarosław Klimczak and Andrzej Rakowski, vol. 10 (Szczytno, 2006), p. 20.

[17] Jan Pachoński, *Oficerowie Legionów Polskich 1796–1807*, vol. 1: *Korpus oficerski Legionów Polskich 1796–1807* (Cracow, 1999), p. 42.

the Ruthenian peasants.[18] The Ruthenian populace, at this time devoid of an intelligentsia besides the upper echelons of the Greek Catholic Church, did not express any national or political feelings whatsoever. The hierarchy of the Greek Catholic Church in Galicia, taking a position of loyalty in relation to the monarch, was against any anti-Austrian movements[19]. This consequently included any Polish military operations, which were treated as revolutionary in nature. Here evidence can be seen in the work of the Metropolitan of Galicia and Austrian privy councillor Antin Anhelovych, entitled *Notes of an Austrian Patriot on Several Foreign Newspaper Articles* [*Uwagi Patryoty austryackiego nad niektóremi artykułami gazet zagranicznych*], which was distributed in several languages across Galician government offices, and even reached the Duchy of Warsaw.[20] It is difficult to see anything in it about Ruthenian national feelings. Loyalist motifs are more easily perceived. In general, the Lviv of the day was only to a small degree inhabited by Ruthenians. Bronisław Pawłowski wrote:

> Ruthenians as such were at the time, despite the agitation of Anhelovych and his aide Harasevych, extremely few in number, even amongst the clergy, which probably used the Ruthenian language in its daily activities, in contacts with ordinary people and the services for the rite, yet official state administrative matters such as oaths were conducted in Latin or German, and if neither of these were known, then in Polish, never in Ruthenian. Only contemporary events and appropriate agitation on the part of those two leaders were to change them into the 'Tyroleans of the East.'[21]

The anti-Polish (in effect treated as "anti-revolutionary") activities of Anhelovych were, however, weakened by the patriotic youth of Lviv, which invested its hope in the army of the Duchy of Warsaw. When the metropolitan suggested that churches pray for Napoleon's defeat, he received as a gift a picture with his likeness in a bishop's chasuble, yet dangling under the gallows.[22]

The majority of Galicia's non-gentry Ruthenian population, the mentioned Anhelovych aside, remained, however, rather indifferent to

---

[18] Vadim Adadurov, "Halyts'ki rusyny u kontseptsiiakh pol's'koï polityky Frantsiï ta Avstriï 1805–1812 rokiv (do postanovky pytannia)," *Ukraïna v mynulomu* no. 9 (1996), p. 57.
[19] Marian Mudryj, "Kwestia tożsamości wśród ruskich elit politycznych w Galicji," *Prace Historyczne* 144, no. 2: *Kształty galicyjskich tożsamości*, ed. Adam Świątek (2017), pp. 260–263.
[20] For more on the topic see Bronisław Pawłowski, *Lwów w 1809 r. z 20 rycinami w tekście* (Lviv, 1909), pp. 20–21.
[21] Ibid., pp. 23–24.
[22] Ibid., p. 33.

the political events of the time. Józef Białynia Chołodecki, who compiled a calendar from the period of the Duchy of Warsaw based on *Gazeta Lwowska*, did not note any "patriotic" behaviour on the part of Ruthenians. This was in stark opposition to the attitudes prevalent among the Polish populace with regard to the Napoleonic Wars.[23] The question of Polish patriotism bypassed the illiterate rural population, and it was Ruthenians who first and foremost made up their numbers. This situation created the conviction among Polish military authorities that there were no national differences between the Ruthenian and Polish peasants. Hence all inhabitants of Galicia, regardless of ethnic origin, were treated as citizens of the former and future independent Polish state. Rite and denomination were not considered—as was the case later—to be an indicator of nationality. This is borne out by the proclamation of General Aleksander Rożniecki, issued the day before the Duchy of Warsaw's forces entered Lviv in 1809. An officer addressing the Lviv municipal council assured them that the appeal by the Chief Commander of the Polish Army "should result in calm for individuals of all estates and denominations."[24]

Nevertheless, Ruthenians must have found themselves in the Polish army, for the gentry fought against the partitioning powers and here there were equally members of the Ruthenian nobility, and with them often the local peasants subject to them.[25] Let us briefly examine the participation of East Galicians in the army of the Duchy of Warsaw led by Józef Poniatowski. Already on 20 May 1809—that is, after the capture of Sandomierz and Zamość, both situated in so-called New Galicia—an appeal was made in Ulanów urging the inhabitants of Galicia to join the Polish army. The forces of Michał Ignacy Kamieński and Aleksander Rożniecki moved in the direction of Lviv to make this possible. The entry into Lviv of the Polish troops commanded by Piotr Strzyżewski at the end of May 1809 was met with widespread celebration. The town was illuminated and the church bells pealed. A similar reception was experienced in other towns of old Galicia. Michał Jackowski—a participant in the battles—wrote to convey the mood of the province's inhabitants:

---

[23] Józef Białynia Chołodecki, *Lwów w czasie wojen Napoleona Wielkiego w latach 1809–1814* (Lviv, 1927), passim.
[24] "The appeal of Rożniecki to the inhabitants of Lviv, Żółkiew, 28 May 1809," in Pawłowski, *Lwów*, pp. 74–75.
[25] Cf. Andrzej A. Zięba, "Tożsamość etniczna jako obiekt manipulacji politycznej: Przypadek Rusinów łemkowskich XVIII–XX w. (część pierwsza)," *Rocznik Ruskiej Bursy* (2007), p. 65.

> Everywhere we were greeted with the same zeal and enthusiasm; from
> every small town the inhabitants would come out to meet us together
> with Jews and their Ten Commandments.
> From old Galicia masses of children came running to us.[26]

Many local noblemen, along with their units composed on the
whole of their own peasants, joined the Polish army. The ranks of the
Duchy of Warsaw's army were sometimes augmented by the inclusion of prisoners-of-war—Galician peasants serving in the Austrian
army. Such a situation occurred after the Battle of Horodenka, where
the prisoners-of-war captured—chiefly inhabitants of Galicia earlier
forced to serve in the Austrian armed forces—added manpower to the
Polish army.[27] It is impossible that this army did not include Ruthenians. Yet we must ask whether the Ruthenian peasants went to fight
out of a sense of Polish patriotism or they were compelled to do so?
The gentry, including the Ruthenian nobility, most certainly went willingly to fight. An example of a Ruthenian nobleman who fought during the Moscow campaign was the earlier mentioned Józef Matkowski,
an artillery engineer.

The period of the Napoleonic Wars was not to bring any noticeable
political changes in Polish-Ruthenian matters, as the Ruthenian question did not exist at all in a political dimension. That said, this was to
be exceedingly important for another reason. First and foremost, the
Duchy of Warsaw, organized on the basis of French revolutionary order, was to be the most impressive realisation of the political thinking
of the Enlightenment in terms of forging a civil society, one centralized
and as homogeneous as possible. The introduction of *departments* instead of the former lands and voivodeships was planned. Hugo Kołłątaj
wrote in 1810:

> And so parts of Poland, intent on returning one day to its whole, can
> be organized even in wartime: for the change of the names of these
> parts allows one to happily forget about all their previous discord
> and age-old anarchy: so no one will be a Lithuanian, a Volhynian,

---

[26] Michał Jackowski, "Pamiętniki podpułkownika, byłego dowódcy brygady jazdy Michała Jackowskiego 1807–1809," in *Pamiętniki polskie*, selection Ksawery Bronikowski,
vol. 1 (Przemyśl, 1883), p. 285.

[27] Jarosław Dudziński, "Działania Piotra Strzyżewskiego w Galicji Wschodniej w czasie
wojny polsko-austriackiej w 1809 roku," *Roczniki Humanistyczne. Historia* 55, no. 2 (2007),
pp. 154–59. More on the volunteers from Eastern Galicia—including the Vistula Legion,
in which many prisoners-of-war who were inhabitants of Galicia served—has been
dealt with by the chronicler Józef Reitzenheim in "Galicya. Wyjątek z pamiętników Józefa
Reitzenheima," in *Pamiętniki polskie*, selection Ksawery Bronikowski, vol. 2 (Przemyśl,
1884), pp. 186–87.

a Podilian, a Kievan, a Ruthenian, etc. anymore, but everyone will be Poles.[28]

These ideas proclaimed in Warsaw or Paris did not coincide with the actual relations in force in Galicia. The Ruthenian leaders, and therefore the Greek Catholic hierarchy, were at this time not as much against becoming Poles as they were expressing their loyalty to the Austrian authorities—in a similar manner, in fact, to a part of the Polish elite (including representatives of the Roman Catholic Church). Michał Baczkowski, researching the participation of Polish volunteers in the Austrian army for the period 1772–1815, wrote that beginning from 1796 the Austrian army was financially supported not only by Polish landowners but also by the Greek Catholic bishop of Lviv Piotr Bielański [Petro Biliansky] and other Ruthenians.[29]

This situation intensified, particularly after Napoleon's defeat at Leipzig in mid-October 1813. The Austrian army was especially supported at this time by the three Catholic churches in Galicia, which was the result of the actions of the hierarchs, including the Uniate bishop of Przemyśl, Mykhailo Levytsky. As Baczkowski writes, donations were given by 127 Roman Catholic priests, 17 Greek Catholic, and 2 Armenian clergymen, as well as by deacons and the parishes of all these three denominations.[30] A proof of support for the partitioning powers was also the joy publicly expressed on learning of Napoleon's defeat. On 22 April 1814 *Gazeta Lwowska* noted that on 17 April the alumni of the Greek Catholic seminary, "infused with patriotism, loyalty and appreciation" for the Austrian monarchy, gave thanks for victory in their prayers, illuminated the seminary and tower on which they hung in addition loyalist banners in Latin and German, and on the following day conducted a Holy Mass of thanks.[31]

During the first decades of Galicia's existence, the contours for a future Polish-Ruthenian conflict were slowly emerging. We can look for its roots in the varied degrees of national consciousness among the representatives of both ethnoses, and the accompanying different stances taken by the respective Polish and Ruthenian political elites. Gentry political activity at this time was an aspiration to see a return of their

---

[28] Hugo Kołłątaj, *Uwagi nad terazniejszem położeniem tey części ziemi polskiej, którą od pokoiu tylzyckiego zaczęto zwać Xsięstwem Warszawskim* (Leipzig, 1810), chapter 5, pp. 65–66 [page numeration in the limits of the chapter].

[29] Michał Baczkowski, *W służbie Habsburgów. Polscy ochotnicy w austriackich siłach zbrojnych w latach 1772–1815* (Cracow, 1998), pp. 98–99.

[30] Ibid., p. 102.

[31] "Wiadomości kraiowe," *Gazeta Lwowska* no. 32 (22 Apr. 1814), p. 1. Cf. also: Chołodecki, *Lwów*, pp. 28–29.

former rights and freedoms as well as the gaining of independence. As for the Greek Catholic Church hierarchy, which did not yet have a national point of reference, their standing in society could only be secured through Austrian government support. This difference in relation to the existing authorities, treated by some as temporary yet by others as ensuring protection, was to accentuate itself in subsequent years, impacting, on one hand, the development of a Ruthenian nationality based on a loyalist program towards Austria, while on the other hand causing a divergence in the political interests of Poles and Ruthenians. However, this in no way discouraged Polish patriots from continuing to treat the Ruthenian populace as a part of the Polish nation itself, and to continue attempts to draw Ruthenians into undertakings for independence whenever such an opportunity arose.

Ruthenian Participation in the November Uprising

The Galicia of the second and third decades of the nineteenth century was to witness an increasing Germanization of public life, particularly in the educational system. Nonetheless, there had grown up new generations raised on the traditions of armed struggles for independence from the period of the Napoleonic Wars, while from the 1820s onwards Romantic works—about which I have written earlier—started to appear, whose role in the formation of Polish national consciousness cannot be overestimated. However, it was to be the November Uprising that for Galicia and its inhabitants constituted the main stimulus for a broader awakening of patriotic feelings. As Anna Wróbel wrote: "The year 1831 brought with it an 'explosion in Polishness' in Galicia. News of the November Uprising resounded like proverbial thunder on a sleeping society."[32] This is confirmed by memoirs. Józef Reitzenheim wrote that if there was already talk among certain inhabitants as to what should be done and where opportunities to fight would arise, "no one had thought about an initiative in the Congress Kingdom."[33] In turn, Andrzej Józefczyk concluded that "in fact one can reckon Polish life in Galicia from this uprising onwards. During the uprising, Polish youth felt themselves to be Poles."[34] The memory of the Kościuszko

---

[32] Anna Wróbel, "Od 'Galileuszy' do Polaków. Wejście do polskiej inteligencji przedstawicieli ludności napływowej i mniejszości w Galicji w XIX w.," in *Inteligencja polska XIX i XX wieku. Studia 5*, ed. Ryszarda Czepulis-Rastenis (Warsaw, 1987), p. 174.
[33] Reitzenheim, "Galicya," p. 198.
[34] Andrzej Józefczyk, *Wspomnienie ubiegłych lat (Przyczynek do Historyi Spisków w Galicyi)* (Cracow, 1881), p. 14.

insurrection and the victorious war of 1809 against Austria still lived on among the inhabitants of Galicia, but the province had been deprived of access to the Polish state for almost sixty years when the Uprising broke out in 1830. The youngest generation, brought up during the times of the absolutist governments of Austria and intense Germanisation, had to first discover their Polishness in order to take up arms.

Stefan Kieniewicz wrote that:

> At a still earlier stage in the crystallisation of Ukrainian, Belarusian, Lithuanian national awareness—even amongst the enlightened 'awakeners,' not mentioning the ordinary masses—the example of Poles standing up to fight against tsarism still did not (in 1831) arouse the opposition of the enlightened inhabitants of the so-called provinces, who did not feel themselves to be one hundred percent Polish. On the contrary, it encouraged emulation.[35]

News about the outbreak of the November Uprising reached the capital of Galicia around 5 December 1830. After the initial disbelief over the outbreak of a Polish-Russian war, a stand had to be taken—with a resulting national self-definition. The mood in the Lviv of the day is characterised by the diary kept by Józef Reitzenheim. He wrote about the involvement of priests from all three denominations, including the Greek Catholic clergy, in the independence actions. He noted:

> Catholic priests as always, and so also now, have shown themselves to be loyal sons of the fatherland. (...) From the other Catholic denominations it is the Armenians who stand out the most, less so the Uniate priests.[36]

The outbreak of the Uprising galvanized the young the most, including the students of the Greek-Catholic seminary in Lviv,[37] and also the students of Lviv University. Several thousand people from Galicia took part in the November Uprising, including every fourth student of Lviv University and 150 secondary school pupils.[38] These included Poles as

---

[35] Stefan Kieniewicz, "Powstanie listopadowe na tle ruchów rewolucyjnych w Europie," in *Powstanie listopadowe 1830–1831. Geneza, uwarunkowania, bilans, porównania*, eds. Jerzy Skowronek and Maria Żmigrodzka (Wrocław–Warsaw–Cracow–Gdańsk–Łódź, 1983), p. 285.

[36] Reitzenheim, "Galicya," p. 201.

[37] Iaroslav Hlystiuk, "Diial'nist' students'kykh tovarystv hreko-katolyts'koï dukhovnoï seminariï u Lvovi (1849–1914)," *Visnyk Lvivs'koho universytetu. Seriia Istorychna* special no.: *Lviv. Misto, suspil'stvo, kul'tura*, vol. 6: *Lviv–Krakiv. Dialoh mist v istorychnii retrospektyvi*, eds. Olena Arkusha and Marian Mudryi (2007), p. 247.

[38] Zbigniew Fras, *Demokraci w życiu politycznym Galicji w latach 1848–1873* (Wrocław, 1997), p. 17. A list of ascertainable surnames on the basis of several sources and studies

well as Ruthenians. The latter also supported the insurgents and/or approved of the struggle to rebuild the state. Markiian Shashkevych himself, the future Ruthenian Triad activist involved in awakening Ruthenian national awareness, wanted to go to Zamość to take part in the uprising. Ultimately, he did not go, but he was to remain influenced by Polish culture for several years. His biographer points out that Shashkevych wrote in Polish before starting to write in Ruthenian at the beginning of the 1830s.[39] It was not only Shashkevych who was drawn to the uprising, but also another later eminent "awakener" of Ruthenian national consciousness—Mykola Ustyianovych.[40] This illustrates the strong influence of Polish culture and the great impact that the Uprising had on them.

At a time when the so-called Ruthenian question did not exist as a political problem, Ruthenians would go to fight in solidarity with their Polish neighbours. This is borne out by the recollections of Marcel Drohojowski of Czorsztyn, who recalled that when he was studying at Lviv University, there was accord between the Uniates and the Latins, and at the moment of the uprising both sides set off together to the Congress Kingdom to fight for Polish independence.[41] A detailed list of students who stopped attending classes at Lviv University was compiled by Karol Lewicki, who studied the question of student participation in the November Uprising. He established a list of 177 names of likely insurgents—considered likely because no one clearly stated to the university authorities the reasons for their leave of absence. Lewicki quotes in his work the edict of the Lviv province of 2 May 1831 that listed 423 persons who had escaped to the Polish Kingdom. In both of these lists we can note a series of names pointing to Ruthenian provenance. We shall name only those who were Ruthenian for certain, the priests of the Greek Catholic seminary. The author wrote:

> They [the Ruthenian clergy—A.Ś.] were drawn together with their Polish colleagues to the Polish question and swelled the ranks of Galician volunteers speeding to fight for freedom; still clearly emphasizing their subsequent feelings following the uprising's collapse when they entered

---

was provided by Zygmunt Zborucki in his work, *Lwów w dobie powstania listopadowego (Szkic historyczny w 100-letnią rocznicę powstania 1830/31)* (Lviv, 1930), pp. 21–25.

[39] Mykhailo Tershakovets', "Do zhyttiepysu Markiiana Shashkevycha," *Zapysky Naukovoho Tovarystva imeni Shevchenka* 105, vol. 5 (1911), pp. 111–14.

[40] Marceli Handelsman, *Ukraińska polityka ks. Adama Czartoryskiego przed wojną krymską* (Warsaw, 1937), pp. 62–63.

[41] Marceli Drohojowski, „Pamiętnik," ZNiO, sygn. 13129 I, p. 186, Quoted after: Mieczysław Adamczyk, "Społeczno-gospodarcze położenie ludności unickiej diecezji przemyskiej w latach 1772–1848," *Przemyskie Zapiski Historyczne* 4–5 (1986–87), p. 114.

into secret unions in order to work to serve a single idea: casting off the shackles of the partitioners and gaining independence.[42]

Amongst these alumni were Jan Gwozdecki [Ivan Hvozdetsky], Jacek Krwawicz [Iatsko Krvavych], Grzegorz Szaszkiewicz [Hryhorii Shashkevych], and Teodor Wercholaz [Fedir Verkholaz]. The Austrian authorities searched among university youth for a certain Jan Uszcza-kiewicz [Ivan Ushchakevych], a student in the second year of law at Lviv University, the son of the Greek Catholic parish priest at Hłomcza (Sanok district). Karol Lewicki supposed that Ruthenians studying philosophy at Lviv University for the years 1830–31 could have also taken part in the uprising. Based on archival sources, he listed the following first-year students: Mikołaj Błoński [Mykola Blonsky], Eustachy Czaykowski de Berynda [Ostap Chaykovsky de Berynda], Włodzimierz Makarewicz [Volodymyr Makarevych] (who, however, most probably did not spend time in the Kingdom of Poland), and Hipolit Soniewicki [Ipolyt Sonevytsky] (appearing in the sources also as Soniewiecki), absent however from the university already from September 1830, and finally Justyn Studziński [Iustin Studzynsky], who officially was to have left to be with his family on 14 March 1831 to Shmankivtsi near Chortkiv. From among the students of the second year of philosophy, Lewicki mentions Jan Artymowicz [Ivan Artymovych] and Teofil Kozłowski [Teofil Kozlovsky].[43] These names, however, should not be treated as representing confirmed insurgents.

In addition, the young Mikołaj Tur-Przedrzymirski [Mykola Tur-Pzhedzhymirsky],[44] a landowner from Galicia, took part in the battles of 1831, as did the Greek Catholic landowner Jan Fedorowicz [Ivan Fedo-rovych], later a deputy at the constitutional assembly (Kremsier Parliament) in 1848.[45] Nevertheless, some Galician Greek Catholic clergy (particularly the hierarchy) were indifferent towards the uprising, not recognizing the Polish insurrection as their cause. There were also instances of open hostility towards the insurgents. The future metropolitan, Spyrydon Lytvynovych, wrote a poem at the time entitled *Aryia*, in which he cheered on the Russian general of Ukrainian descent Ivan Paskevych (who brutally suppressed the November Uprising) and forecast doom for the Poles.[46] Yet, one should not be surprised by such at-

---

[42] Karol Lewicki, *Uniwersytet Lwowski a powstanie listopadowe* (Lviv, 1937), p. 85.
[43] Ibid., pp. 83, 90, 97–98.
[44] Tomasz Pudłocki, *Iskra światła czy kopcąca pochodnia? Inteligencja w Przemyślu w latach 1867–1939* (Cracow, 2009), p. 419.
[45] Zborucki, *Lwów w dobie powstania*, p. 32.
[46] Ibid., pp. 32–33, footnote 18.

titudes and stances, if only because the neighbouring Uniate Church in Russia, in the Western Region of the Russian Empire—in opposition to many Roman Catholic clergy in this westernmost part of the Russian Empire—officially did not assist the insurgents, and even condemned their actions. For example, the Uniate bishop of the Lithuanian diocese Iosafat Bulhak [Jozafat Bułhak] condemned "the Warsaw revolution" in December 1830, which cooled the zeal of the lower clergy. Only in a former part of Galicia—the voivodeship of Lublin—were efforts undertaken to collect money for the uprising among the faithful of the Uniate Church.[47]

The November Uprising did not champion the Ruthenian cause on its standards. Nonetheless, it did play a significant role in the sense that it forced the Polish elite, particularly those in exile, to reflect over the reasons for the defeat. Almost all (Polish) political parties in France, Belgium, and England had to contend with the Ruthenian problem, which had yet to be comprehended in a social context. A realisation was just dawning that no fight for Polish independence would be successful without the participation of the lower social strata, and in the eastern part of Galicia these were chiefly Ruthenians.

The Ruthenian Question in the Political Thought of the Great Emigration

The November Uprising aroused the hitherto less active inhabitants of Galicia—in comparison to the Congress Kingdom—to conspiratorial acts. This related equally to Poles and Ruthenians. The initiator of the conspiracies in the 1830s and 1840s, as well as the designator of subsequent socio-political trends, was the post-November emigration in France, which through its emissaries was to influence the intelligentsia in Poland itself.[48] It is therefore worthwhile paying some attention to the views of the Polish political elites in exile—views expressed equally in political brochures and literary works, which were to strongly influence conspiratorial actions in Poland.

Here one should mention that the shaping of the conception of Rus' as an integral part of the Polish state, and the notion of fraternity between Poles and Ruthenians as members of the same nation, were

---

[47] Władysław Zajewski, *Powstanie listopadowe 1830–1831* (Warsaw, 1998), pp. 144, 149, 152.
[48] Zbigniew Fras, "Rola emigrantów w życiu politycznym Lwowa i Krakowa w 1848 roku," in *Galicja w 1848 roku. Demografia, działalność polityczna i społeczna, gospodarka i kultura*, eds. Andrzej Bonusiak and Marian Stolarczyk (Rzeszów, 1999), pp. 27–28.

forged at this time primarily by those post-November émigrés who had arrived in Western Europe from the so-called Western Region, the lands taken by the Russian Empire as a result of the partitioning of Poland. These were primarily nobles and intellectuals deeply rooted in Polish culture and coming from the Lithuanian lands (later referred to in the subject literature as *gente Lithuani, natione Poloni*, yet whose identity was more territorially than ethnically motivated in its nationalism). This was to result in Ruthenians being perceived in an analogous manner. Ruthenians were considered just as Polish as Lithuanians. The process of "empowering" the Polish nation by the Lithuanian nobility had a long-standing tradition, beginning with the Polish-Lithuanian union. Here is not the place to discuss more broadly the notion of the so-called *gente Lithuani, natione Poloni*, which has already been covered by an array of research, but what is important to point out are several questions. First and foremost, the term *gente Lithuani* covered both the nobility from ethnic Lithuania and the territory of modern-day Belarus. The nobility, conscious of the differences between the Grand Duchy of Lithuania and the Polish Crown, were to maintain this awareness in the nineteenth century after the partitions themselves. They felt an affiliation to a common Polish culture but also a close connection with the historical tradition of Lithuania.[49] Many famous Polish patriots have emphasized their "Lithuanianness": Tadeusz Kościuszko, Adam Mickiewicz, Joachim Lelewel, Ignacy Chodźko, Józef Ignacy Kraszewski, Bolesław Limanowski, and finally—many years later—even Józef Piłsudski himself, who called himself a Lithuanian.[50] However, with the passing of subsequent decades of the nineteenth century, the *gente Lithuani* element was to be increasingly less emphasized, with only an attachment to one's local homeland remaining. Without Mickiewicz, Chodźko, Kościuszko, Czartoryski, and many more, there never would have developed the myth of the Commonwealth of Three Nations. Both émigré writers and politicians associated with various political camps, as well as the members of varied cultural and literary organizations, created such a profile for the post-partition state.

In December 1831 the Association of Lithuanian and Ruthenian Lands [*Towarzystwo Litewskie i Ziem Ruskich*], headed by Cezary Plater, with Leonard Chodźko as secretary, was formed in the emigration. A public notice appeared on 20 August 1832 informing those in-

---

[49] Here a certain dividing line will be, according to Ryszard Radzik, the January Uprising of 1863, which forced the necessity of a choice of Polishness in its most modern understanding—encompassing the entirety of society. See ibid., p. 60.

[50] Antonina Kłoskowska, *National Cultures at the Grass-root Level* (Budapest, 2001), p. 129.

terested of the creation of an organization affiliating émigrés from the eastern lands of former Poland. Above the text, the Vytis coat-of-arms of Lithuania was proudly flanked by the standards of the Ruthenian and Lithuanian voivodeships, and above them was placed the emblem of the Polish Eagle. The thinking behind the association was to integrate the inhabitants of Poland of old under the name of a Polish nation comprising various elements. Therefore, the announcement explained:

> And Lithuanians with Ruthenians have founded the Lithuanian-Ruthenian Association to show to the world that Rus' and Lithuania share the fate of Poland, that there is no Poland without Lithuania and Rus' and that Rus' and Lithuania are Poland.[51]

In another place in the announcement it is recalled that regardless of provenance, "we are all Poles."[52] Many well-known individuals were involved in the organization. Besides the already mentioned Plater and Chodźko, there was also Mickiewicz, Słowacki, and Lelewel. However, the association was to cease its activities already in 1834. Although it was not to last long as an organization, it still constitutes one of many examples of Polish émigré thought.

In contrast, Tadeusz Krępowiecki, a representative of the Polish Democratic Society [*Towarzystwo Demokratyczne Polskie*], was hostile in his assessment of any form of particularism in Poland. In 1834, on the pages of *Postęp*, he accused past generations of not leading the country to unification at a time when Poland required and requires a "dictatorship of thought" which would erase the very names of Lithuanians, Samogitians, or Ruthenians. For it was they who had led to the parcelling of the former state, and Poland should arise within its pre-1772 borders.[53]

Yet the matter was seen differently by the well-known democrat and Lithuanian historian Joachim Lelewel. In 1836, he said in Brussels:

> The national whole depends on unity and total cohesion. A Ukrainian, a Kashubian, those from Little and Great Poland, a Lithuanian, a Podilian, a Samogitian, a Mazurian, a Volhynian and whatever son of the land of the former Commonwealth, is a Pole and in this single name do we perceive our wholeness and unity.[54]

---

[51] Cezary Plater, Leonard Chodźko, *Towarzystwo litewskie i ziem ruskich* (Paris, 1832), LNNBU, fond 9: Okremi nadkhodzhennia, spr. 2295: Zbirka vidozv, oholoshen', statutiv tovarystv, vypysky z hazet ta in., p. 151.

[52] Ibid.

[53] Jagiełło, *Narody*, p. 15.

[54] Joachim Lelewel, "Manifest Polaków znajdujących się w Belgii," in [Joachim Lelewel], *Polska. Dzieje i rzeczy jej rozpatrywane przez Joachima Lelewela*, vol. 20 (Poznań, 1864), p. 224.

16. An illustration from he leaflet printed by the Association of Lithuanian and Ruthenian Lands, which shows the standards of the lands of the Polish- -Lithuanian Commonwealth

He also tried to prove that brotherhood is a common thing in history and that even the languages of the Poles, Lithuanians, and Ruthenians merge into a single tongue. Lelewel believed that "the Polish nation had never refused brotherhood to its neighbours, and perhaps with the progress of the ages and the liberation of peoples a mutual fraternity would be found in them."[55]

We can therefore see two approaches to the Ruthenian question, both later present in Polish political thought. One conception respected the distinctiveness of peoples and regions in accordance with the slogans of Romanticism. That said, however, it was virtually impossible, at that time, to even conceive that there could exist independent Lithuanian and Ruthenian nations separate from the Polish in the lands of former Poland. The second republican current appealed to the ideology of the Enlightenment, refusing to accept any regional differences whatsoever, although it observed them and emphasized the urgent need for their eradication. Both visions, however, were united by the conviction that Poland was to arise within its former borders, and therefore all diffe-rences needed to be made uniform within the framework of a national community.[56] Both currents were to play an important role in the shap-ing of political thought of Polish conspirators in Galicia directed toward ethnic Ruthenians.

These ideas, the main vehicle for which was the huge literary output of émigré poets and writers, fell on fertile ground on reaching Galicia. The local youth avidly read (often in secret) this literature, frequently

---

[55] Ibid., p. 226.
[56] See also Joanna Nowak, *"Gente Ruthenus, natione Polonus.* Rusini w refleksji Wielkiej Emigracji," *Sprawy Narodowościowe. Seria Nowa* 23 (2003), p. 46.

revolutionary in content, emanating from the emigration. Translating these émigré postulates into real action was, however, extremely difficult if not impossible. It was easy to talk within émigré circles in France and Belgium about the necessity of eradicating the differences between Ruthenians and Poles, and the need for them to become a single nation. However, the denominational and linguistic differences, not to mention the social differences dividing the two peoples, were not evaluated, or at least not sufficiently considered. These ideas were consequently at odds with the reality in which they were to be realized.

Émigré politicians exerting a sizeable influence on the population living under partition were not able to foresee those differences between Poles and Ruthenians, which were soon to reveal themselves in Galicia. One of the few émigrés[57] who drew attention to the "distrust and possibly even hatred that existed between the gentry and the peasantry in Rus'" was Michał Czajkowski (later known also as Mehmed Sadyk Pasza—an agent of the Hôtel Lambert political grouping, who converted to Islam and organized an Ottoman Cossack Brigade to fight against Russia). He emphasized in his article "A Few Words about Ruthenians in 1831" ["Kilka słów o Rusinach w roku 1831"],[58] published in the emigration in 1839, that the outburst of Cossack uprisings in Ukraine had been provoked by the actions of the Polish gentry. However, he did not negate any blame on Khmelnytsky but underlined that he wanted equality within the nation and a strong monarchical authority in Poland, of which Czajkowski himself was an adherent. Nonetheless, he did make it clear that Poles and Ruthenians are "the children of a single mother" and that there still existed among the Ruthenian people an attachment to the Poland of old. He gave examples of this, including the utterances of Ruthenian peasants, and also the behaviour of a 92-year-old Orthodox priest who was to have blessed the November Uprising insurgents and the author of the above-mentioned text. Czajkowski signed his text off with the assurance that "there is the force for an uprising within the peasantry of Rus'."[59]

In turn, in 1843 another émigré, Teofil Wiśniowski, undertook an attempt to outline the future political order in Central Europe, postulating the rise of some form of Slavic federation. This assumption, as with many analogous concepts, was derived from the ideas of Johann Gottfried von Herder, very popular at that time, which envisioned a new and peaceful Slavic epoch following the passing of the Latin and

---

[57] Joanna Nowak writes more about Czajkowski's views. Ibid., pp. 50–51.
[58] Michał Czajkowski, "Kilka słów o Rusinach w roku 1831. Zapomniany artykuł Michała Czajkowskiego," ed. Józef Weniger, *Ruch Literacki* 5, no. 10 (Dec. 1930), pp. 314–17.
[59] Ibid., p. 317.

German eras. Wiśniowski conjectured in his analysis that in addition to the merger of the Czechs, Moravians, Slovaks, and also Serbs:

> Poland (...) and Rus', which have been linked for so long by history, would become a single state. Without such a union, all nations would never obtain a self-contained nature, and would never reach an important position in world history.[60]

Not only were Wiśniowski's great Slavic ideas not to see fruition, but his conviction about the historical union of Poles and Ruthenians was also to be brutally crushed in his own biography. In 1846, when he was involved in preparing a national uprising, it was to be two Ruthenian peasants who were to turn him over to the authorities. He was sentenced to death by hanging by the Austrians. Wiśniowski's death was to quickly take on a mythical character and was often referred to in political pamphlets from the period of the Spring of Nations revolutions of 1848 in order to emphasize the need for Polish-Ruthenian brotherhood.[61]

Few in the emigration made anything of the ethnic (and also national) differences between Ruthenians and Poles. At most, only some would appreciate the social import of the backwardness of the rural population, including here the Ruthenians. Democratic circles drew attention to the need to implement a range of social policies such as property rights, the abolition of serfdom, the elimination of social estates, etc. It was understood that the peasantry—whether Polish or Ruthenian—could only be involved in a fight for independence if it saw a realistic possibility for these ideas to be realized.

Some émigrés appreciated the importance of the religious differences that divided the Ruthenian population from the Polish. Hence the desire for the Uniate clergy to be particularly involved in the national issue.[62] Here it is worth recalling a little-quoted proclamation of the Polish National Committee [Komitet Narodowy Polski] entitled "The Most Reverend and Reverend Priests, Pleasing to God, of the Eastern Orthodox Church" ["Przewielebni i wielebni, nam w Bogu mili prawowiernej

---

[60] Teofil Wiśniowski, "Panslawizm czyli Wszechsłowiańszczyzna," *Pismo Towarzystwa Demokratycznego Polskiego* 3 [1843], p. 207.

[61] See for example the poem that is the alleged confession of Wiśniowski: "Spowiedź Teofila Wiśniowskiego," LNNBU, fond 5: Zbirka rukopysiv, avtohrafiv, hramot i dyplomiv biblioteky Natsional'noho zakladu im. Ossolins'kykh u m. Lvovi, op. 1, spr. 6807/III: Archiwum Darowskich. „Miscellanea historyczno-polityczne 1794–1877," k. 413–420. Another interesting document held at the Darowski archive is Wiśniowski's alleged address to the Polish people. See "Ludu polski!," LNNBU, fond 5, op. 1: Rukopysy, spr. 6807/III, p. 425.

[62] Por. Bolesław Łopuszański, *Stowarzyszenie Ludu Polskiego (1835–1841). Geneza i dzieje* (Cracow, 1975), p. 220.

Cerkwi wschodniej Kapłani!"], by Joachim Lelewel. In the name of his political camp he wrote:

> We are appealing to you as to God's servants, to whom Christ's vineyard has been entrusted; as to those born on Ruthenian and Polish land, who influence the conscience of the sons of Poland and Rus'. We appeal to you having been authorized by our [supporters to struggle] for the freedom of Poland, for freedom [in general].[63]

Lelewel proceeded to list all the differences between the believers of both denominations (e.g., those concerning the calendar and holy days), but he made it clear that they should not "split or weaken fraternal love, arouse hate, disturb mutual peace, for there are all the teachings of the Saviour."[64] He rhetorically asked the clergy if he who "kindles discord" (having in mind the Russian tsar), is not at times a "cat amongst the pigeons." He reminded the reader that both rites had lived in harmony in the former Poland, with the only conflicts that arose being those fomented by the Jesuits. Finally, he asked for a prayer for Poland, referring in this to the intercession of the Holy Mother as well as Saint Cyril, Saint Methodius, and Saint Volodymyr.

From among the émigré leaders it was Prince Adam Jerzy Czartoryski, standing at the head of the Hôtel Lambert grouping, who was particularly engaged in the Ruthenian question (first and foremost in the lands under Russian and not Austrian control). In one of his speeches delivered on 29 November 1845, he advised his colleagues to pay attention to the Ruthenian question. His words speak of the broadly understood notion of "the Ruthenian nation" and of Poles descended from the Ruthenians:

> There are in our country millions of inhabitants against whom some of us have unjustified prejudices; removing those prejudices, curing oneself of them, is just and necessary. Ruthenians have suffered the severest persecution of our tyranny, while they have in many places displayed a constancy worthy of martyrs. The heart of everyone should now extend out to them in the strongest way. More than one of us is descended from them, and we should not forget that our ancestors were amongst them. Let us respect therefore their rites, their customs, their original tongue, one so close to our own. After all, our literature has taken up their traditional songs and has been enlivened for that.
>
> Ruthenians as equally Lithuanians are our brothers and a single nation; they equally groan under a foreign yoke; here there are not differences, the matter is mutual, the fraternal feeling should be one, and

---

[63] Joachim Lelewel, "Przewielebni i wielebni, nam w Bogu mili prawowiernej Cerkwi wschodniej Kapłani!," in Lelewel, *Polska*, pp. 482–83.
[64] Ibid., p. 483.

a singular aim harnessed with all strength: the liberation of all equally. Our history has blended us for centuries; mutual obligation, noble impulses, friendship, justice have joined these kin into a single people; mistakes, blame lying on both sides, fatal misunderstandings destabilizing those beautifully free-willed bonds; but the ancient memories and tales have not lost their force; the mistakes shall never be repeated, and joint suffering, joint interests and the singular hope of freedom in a harmonious brotherhood should now join us in a bond firmer than ever. It is important to convince us and them of this important truth.[65]

The paradox is that the views of Czartoryski, the most conservative politician among all those in emigration, touch on the questions of the differences and divisions between Poles and Ruthenians, yet this was lacking in the thinking of the Polish National Committee or the Polish Democratic Society, which tried to place the emphasis in their political programs on the resolution of social questions.

In summary, although certain émigré politicians did not always appreciate the importance of the differences between Poles and Ruthenians, they most certainly did not envisage Rus' not being a part of any future Poland. Polish political activists were still motivated by the motto from the time of the Kościuszko Insurrection: "freedom, unity, independence." This is also why Ruthenians always appear in the deliberations of the émigrés as a part of the Polish nation. It should once again be emphasized that usually the term "Ruthenian" was still understood at the time to be an inhabitant of Rus' and not a Ruthenian in the ethnic or national sense. This helped to create the myth of the Commonwealth of Many Nations, which de facto was understood as a "commonwealth of the inhabitants of many territories." Émigré writers and politicians created a model of the Polish nation as one comprising Poles (also Lendians), Lithuanians, and Ruthenians. The latter of the three were perceived at most as the Ruthenian nobility rather than an actual Ruthenian ethnic or cultural community. Those in turn who placed their hopes in social changes which were to benefit the lowest social strata (the abolition of serfdom and land rights), also believed that Ruthenian and Polish peasants would jointly fight for the liberation of Poland. The assumptions developed in the emigration were later confronted by the reality of things only in the minds of those who travelled from Western Europe to Galicia and the Stolen Lands (Eastern territories of Poland which were taken by Russia and not included in Congress Poland in 1815) to organize a future uprising, and by those local conspirators imbued with the ideology radiating from distant Paris or Brussels.

---

[65] [Adam Czartoryski], *Mowy Xięcia Adama Czartoryskiego od roku 1838–1847* (Paris, 1847), pp. 93–94.

Galician Conspiracies

The job of organizing a new independence uprising following the defeat of the November Uprising was undertaken by emissaries from émigré circles. They searched for those willing to engage in subversive activities in Galicia, which was not difficult, for the Austrian area of partition had been settled by around ten thousand November insurgents from other parts of the Polish lands. The 1830s and 1840s were to be a period marked by the formation of secret associations and conspiratorial organizations. These were joined, in addition to the former insurgents mentioned above, by both the Polish and Ruthenian population of Galicia.[66] Secret groups could count first and foremost on the representatives of the young generation who were yet to sort out their lives, and who were full of zeal for the ideas emanating from the Great Emigration as well as from patriotic works—works uplifting, inspiring, and at the same time revelatory, particularly for the young inhabitants of Galicia, of the values of the lost fatherland of their ancestors, and with inspirational ideas for the reconstruction of the world according to a new and more just order. Andrzej Józefczyk wrote that:

> The young had by then already rid themselves of the remains of bar life, they no longer hung around beer cellars and cafes, and it appeared that there was something of more substance occupying their thoughts. During a period of disasters, the ideas of the young take on a more serious hue. And the overflowing jails, the word-of mouth news about some who were tyrannized and others who were imprisoned, became the reasons for pondering and investigating the causes of all this. A mass of pamphlets, newspapers, and forbidden works urgently sought by the police were to fall upon the Lviv cobblestones, and while the servants of the government, who saw their own demise in the collapse of order, basked in the glory of one conspiracy uncovered, ideas and thoughts matured to organize another.[67]

Through revolutionary literature the representatives of the younger generation combined democratic slogans with ones advocating independence, which not only shaped their views but first and foremost imbued them with the desire to implement them. Polish literature was to be often reprinted or simply copied by hand. A large role in the propagation of works of this type was played by the Ossolineum in

---

[66] Włodzimierz Borys, "Wyprawa J. Zaliwskiego i polskie organizacje spiskowe w Galicji w latach 1832–1835," in *Społeczeństwo polskie i próby wznowienia walki zbrojnej w 1833 roku*, eds. Władimir Djakow, Stefan Kieniewicz, Wiktoria Śliwowska and Feodosij Steblij, (Wrocław–Warsaw–Cracow–Gdańsk–Łódź, 1984), p. 83.

[67] Józefczyk, *Wspomnienie*, p. 15.

Lviv together with Lviv printers, who were as inclined to do so out of a desire for profit as from any patriotic sentiment.[68] Reprints of *Books of the Polish Nation and Polish Pilgrimage* and Adam Mickiewicz's patriotic poems, Kazimierz Brodziński's *On the Nationality of Poles* [*O narodowości Polaków*] were especially often produced and distributed, as well as Joachim Lelewel's work *On the Three Polish Constitutions 1791, 1807, 1815* [*O trzech konstytucjach Polaków 1791, 1807, 1815 r.*].[69] Andrzej Józefczyk recalled that:

> The leaflet was soon to appear in countless copies; bookshop keepers provided everything that had just come out in France, including émigré materials, they paid a high price for almost every letter. Emigration became (…) the political church, from whence articles of faith came into Poland. (…)[70]

Klemens Mochnacki recalled how, through following the "adapting" of literature from the French Revolutionary period as well as historical works on the subject of Spain and Portugal, he became convinced that:

> The ignorance of the common people was the mainstay of despotism and the cause of poverty. In projecting this on [the situation in] Poland, I have come to the conclusion that Poland will not gain independence and that the ordinary people will not be free of serfdom and will not be enlightened. With such a conviction, I returned to Lviv in order to complete school and I started to act in the spirit that I had developed for myself and disseminated among the young. (…) My first thought was to involve myself with the young and prepare them for political life, to the awakening of the Polish spirit and to devote my property and life to the achievement of independence.[71]

This inspiration was sufficiently strong that Mochnacki decided to use the contributions he obtained to purchase literature and establish a library, and then to lend books to the young people. Covert activities usually, but not only, involved the buying and lending of books, the organization of meetings, and the conducting of academic, literary, or even political discussions.

At this time Klemens Mochnacki together with his brother Józef also organized sightseeing tours in the district of Przemyśl from the Bieszczady Mountains, through Cracow, to the Tatry Mountains, where

---

[68] Stefan Kieniewicz, *Konspiracje galicyjskie (1831–1845)* (Warsaw, 1950), p. 109.

[69] Borys, "Wyprawa J. Zaliwskiego," pp. 102–3.

[70] Józefczyk, *Wspomnienie*, pp. 19–20.

[71] Klemens Mochnacki, *Pamiętnik spiskowca i nauczyciela 1811–1848*, ed. Antoni Knot (Cracow, 1950), p. 10.

other conspirators joined from the district of Jasło. This was recalled by Andrzej Józefczyk as well. In the course of the journey the youth contemplated field conditions conducive to conducting a guerrilla campaign and engaged in discussion with the highland population on subjects as varied as Poland and the need to eradicate serfdom.[72]

This zeal to organize an uprising, the willingness to engage in social work in the countryside, as well as a fascination with conspiratorial actions, were born first and foremost in school. Youthful ambition, a lot of free time, the lack of far-reaching plans for the future, as well as an unstable life situation made such an initiative possible. There were no better conditions for such actions (not that this was to mean that they were easy) than at school, where mutually influential young people assembled and undertook illegal forms of national life.

There was equally no lack of young people willing to act, and it should be remembered that the conspiratorial centres chiefly came into existence in urban environments, near schools, university, or seminaries. While patriotic motives prompted enrolment in conspiratorial activity, demands for social change also constituted a reason.[73] Finally, this transfer of emphasis from a desire to rebuild the former nobility--oriented Poland to the construction of a new society characterized by citizen equality and a freeing of oneself from feudal duties theoretically increased the conspirators' chances of obtaining greater social support. However, the problem was how to reach and subsequently convince the addressees as to the relevance of the slogans proclaimed.

The flaws of the first movements, such as the Union of Twenty-One [*Związek Dwudziestu Jeden*] or the Union of Unknowns [*Związek Bezimiennych*], as well as in the expeditions of Józef Zaliwski, were not only that they represented modest forces that would be powerless in any clash with the armies of the partitioning powers. First and foremost, they failed to encourage broader masses of the society to conspiracy, without whom no fight had any chance of success whatsoever. This required an awakening of national consciousness in society, particularly among its lowest strata.

Ryszard Herman characterized the problem of a lack of national feeling in the following extract:

> The nobility was the only genuine Polish element, with the exception of a small handful of burghers. A shelter for the migrants could only be found in the houses of the nobility. The rural gentry were on the whole

---

[72] Cf. ibid., pp. 11–14; Józefczyk, *Wspomnienie*, pp. 24–26.
[73] Hryhorii Herbil's'kyi, *Peredova suspil'na dumka v Halychyni (30-i – seredyna 40-kh rokiv XIX stolittia)* (Lviv, 1959), p. 124.

without higher education. It was good that they had maintained their affiliation to the fatherland after several decades of government-sponsored Germanisation. The ordinary people were not a nation: for it was merely riff-raff without any sense of patriotic worldview; these were people involved in agriculture and nothing more; not only having no concept as to what a nation was, but they had had instilled into them by the government a hatred of Poles, and to all who did not dress as they did, and whom they called in general 'Lach,' adding a certain disgust in their pronunciation of this phrase. The emigration wanted to liberate Poland by means of this unruly mass, having imagined that by freeing it from serfdom and ensuring it had its own land, which it had hitherto only known through renting its labour to the gentry, that through this possession of material means it could be roused to revolt.[74]

The question of essential social changes was further examined by the Union of the Friends of the People [Związek Przyjaciół Ludu], created in 1833. The leaders of the organization decided to issue three proclamations: to the gentry, to the serving classes, and to the peasants.[75] The leadership of the Union included individuals who in the future were to play an important role in the "conspiratorial history" of Galicia: Ignacy Kulczyński, Teofil and Hugo Wiśniowski. Two plans were also developed for the as yet still non-independent state: one as a centralized republic, and one as a federal republic, comprising in equal status the lands of former Poland, with Rus' included.[76] Anyone could become a member of the Union, regardless of their estate or ethnic provenance.[77] There exists the conjecture that the secret organization formed out of Przemyśl school circles in 1832 and known as the Society of Scholars [Towarzystwo Uczonych] was connected with the organization. Both Poles and Ruthenians belonged to it. Among the most active members of the association were Kazimierz Józef Turowski and the Ruthenian student Mykola Kmytsykevych [Mikołaj Kmicikiewicz] and his brothers Iuliian [Julian], Teofil, and Lev [Lew], as well as the Ruthenian poet Anton Luzhetsky [Antoni Łużecki]. However, the group did not possess a clearly developed political program. After its detection, the members were not subject to notable reprisals.[78] The Academic Associa-

---

[74] Henryk Bogdański, "Notaty do pamiętnika Ryszarda Hermana" (Lviv, 1868), LNNBU, fond 5, op. 1, spr. 3535/III, p. 8.

[75] Kieniewicz, Konspiracje galicyjskie, pp. 92–93.

[76] Borys, "Wyprawa J. Zaliwskiego," pp. 83–90.

[77] Feodosij Steblij, "Polskie spiski lat trzydziestych XIX w. a społeczeństwo ukraińskie w Galicji," in Społeczeństwo polskie, pp. 106–7.

[78] Herbil's'kyi, Peredova suspil'na dumka, pp. 124–25; Jan Kozik, The Ukrainian National Movement in Galicia 1815–1849, ed. and introd. Lawrence D. Orton, trans. Adrew Gorski and Lawrence D. Orton (Edmonton, 1986), p. 43. Kozik mentions more in his work about

tion [*Towarzystwo Akademickie*] functioning at Lviv University cooperated with the Union of Friends of the People including the *gente Ruthenus, natione Polonus* Jan Sielecki [Ivan Seletsky]. He was especially known because of his poem titled "Lviv Cheers" ["Wiwaty lwowskie"], which criticized the Austrian bureaucracy.[79]

Smaller secret organizations also operated in Galicia, though often merely of a Philomath [the Philomath (lovers of knowledge) Society was founded by Adam Mickiewicz in 1817—Ed.] or Philarets (lovers of virtue) character. Just such an organization was the Association of Antiquity [*Towarzystwo Starożytności*] founded in 1834 by the later eminent historian Karol Szajnocha, at the time a Lviv secondary school pupil. It attracted German and Ruthenian youth, but the organization was soon discovered by the authorities.[80]

When examining the participation of Ruthenians of Polish nationality in Galician conspiracies, we have to pay special attention to the greatest concentration of conspiratorial Ruthenian youth in the post-November period—at the Greek Catholic seminary in Lviv. Up until 1848 it was not yet associated with the Ruthenian national movement, although those who were to subsequently stir the Ruthenian nation were to come exactly from here and it was here that they were recruited. This school, like others in the larger towns of Galicia, was in the 1830s a Greek Catholic centre for the blooming Polish cultural life of the time. Klemens Mochnacki was to write about the seminary in the post--November period:

> The so-called Ruthenian movement in the seminary was large. The prevalent mood and the cleverest [of its representatives] supported [the cause of] Poland and these were numerically in the majority, although there also were opponents, at the head of whom stood Markiian Shashkevych, who were fervent Muscovite supporters. There were also those who had no affiliation whatsoever.[81]

Conspiratorial acts were being carried out at the seminary as early as 1831; something borne out by the inspection ordered by the Metropolitan Mykhailo Levytsky as well as the denunciations relayed to Vienna

---

Mykola Kmytsykevych's not extensively developed plans to create a Polish-Ruthenian federation, but for this conspirator Ruthenian interests mattered first and foremost. Ibid., pp. 29, 45–46.

[79] Włodzimierz Borys, "Do historii ruchu społeczno-politycznego studentów Uniwersytetu i młodzieży rzemieślniczej Lwowa w latach 1832–46," *Przegląd Historyczny* 54, no. 3 (1963), p. 420. An author uses another version of surname: Solecki [Soletsky].

[80] Kieniewicz, *Konspiracje galicyjskie*, p. 106.

[81] Mochnacki, *Pamiętnik*, p. 11.

by Father Symeon Pidliashetsky, the parish priest from Karliv. On the basis of both, an investigation was conducted in 1834, which found that the seminarians had been reading illegal literature.[82] It is worth quoting a fragment of a letter by the Ruthenian cleric Mykhailo Gerovsky, shocked by the scale of the matter, to his brother Iakiv, a professor at Lviv University:

> Here at the monastery school things are happening that have never happened before and which cannot possibly happen again; just as soon as something is reported to the government we are all miserable. The matter is as follows: Poles (Galicians—'*konwityści*' [inhabitants of the boarding school—A.Ś.]—of the Latin rite) receive here Parisian propaganda—revolutionary principles—and they gather together in the monastery school with '*Cewiliści*' [in the meaning of students of law—A.Ś.] of various calibre, and '*Medyciniesi*' [medical students—A.Ś.], and all the great big Polish bruisers debate, chewing over political affairs (with revolution constantly in their minds), and they bring various banned books, leaflets which refer to these revolutionary principles, while the '*konwiktyści*' Poles still read and, endlessly shouting, [and raising] clamour against the Emperor. Besides theological books there are: La Mainais [Félicité--Robert de Lamennais, a French Catholic priest, political theorist and Adam Mickiewicz's friend – A.Ś.], [Jerzy Samuel Bandtkie] *The History of the Polish People* [*Dzieje narodu polskiego*] etc., various other booklets of a similar content— *Das höchste ihr Prinzip ist Volkssouveränität* [Their Highest Principle Is Independence for the Nation], but the Emperor and religion mean nothing for them, and they are supposed to be priests of some sort. Oh, woe will befall our country someday!! We Ruthenians have fallen in a singular way, *ale Boh bat'ko, ne daimo sia!* [but the Lord is the father, we shall prevail!—A.Ś.] They wanted to draw us to them, but they didn't succeed, for we were able to work out the way things moved and none of us Ruthenians can be drawn in, we, as Pastoralists, will look over them and we expect that during the course of our existence none of us will they delude… Now they hold the greatest contempt for us, they darken our name before superiors, and if they only could, they would devour us Ruthenians to a man (…).[83]

We can enumerate the dozen or so Uniate seminarians connected with the Polish conspiracy at the seminary in 1833: Dezydery Hreczański [Hrechansky], Michał Gadziński [Mykhailo Gadzynsky], Józef Konstantynowicz [Iosyf Konstantynovych], Romuald Krzyżanowski, Teodor Kulczycki [Kulchytsky], Michał Minczakiewicz [Mykhailo Mynchakevych] (the brother of Filemon Minczakiewicz [Fylemon Myn-

---

[82] Kyrylo Studyns'kii, "Pol's'ki konspiratsïi sered rus'kykh pytomtsiv i dukhovenstva v Halychyni v rokakh 1831–1846," *Zapysky Naukovoho Tovarystva imeni Shevchenka* 80, vol. 6 (1907), pp. 55–56.

[83] Ibid., p. 61.

chakevych]), Sylwester Miejski [Sylvester Meisky], Dymitr Mochnacki [Dmytro Mokhnatsky], Klemens Mochnacki, Józef Ochrymowicz [Iosyf Okhrymovych], Michał Pokiński [Mykhailo Pokynsky], Jan Sielecki, Cyryl Słoniewski [Kyrylo Slonevsky], Hipolit Stańczak [Ipolyt Stanchak], as well as Benedykt Kuszczykiewicz [Venedykt Kushchykevych] and Iwan Szmelc [Ivan Shmelts] from the Lviv Latin seminary. Later other colleagues/associates were to join. The first leader was Sielecki, to be followed by Krzyżanowski. The group's activities involved secret meetings at the abodes of the various seminarians during which political topics were discussed, books read, articles written, and funds collected from donations for the purchase of books, etc.[84] One of the discussions involved the question of the future shape of any subsequent Polish state. Romuald Krzyżanowski stated at the time that Ruthenians should not be turned into Poles. Yet it was agreed that the most suitable form for any state would be a federation, encompassing the lands of the Polish-Lithuanian Commonwealth.[85]

The members were bound by a statute obliging them to act in the name of implementing democratic slogans such as: making the social estates equal, a republican form of governance, civil liberties, etc. The conspirators swore "in the name of God and Jesus Christ, the first martyr for freedom," while holding a sword to their breast. Each of the members swore to maintain the society's secrets even on pain of death. This regulation was, as Bogusław Łopuszański informed, totally upheld. When one of the clerics, Hipolit Stańczak, fearing being exposed and unmasked, decided to leave the organization, another conspirator was entrusted to poison him. The sentence was not actually carried out. But even if we were to try to adopt a contemporary perspective, such a form of conspiratorial action amongst a group of future priests would arouse astonishment.

It was not only seminary students who conspired, teachers were involved as well. Mochnacki gives the example of Father Mikołaj Hordyński [Mykola Hordynsky] and a certain Tarczyński [Tarchynsky].[86] The former, as a catechist of the Greek Catholic seminary—as Krajewski writes—"was obliged to disseminate there the spirit and principles of the association." Thanks to his authority and standing, "he easily drew in many clerics, to the common good of the national question."[87] He

---

[84] Józefczyk, *Wspomnienie,* p. 61; Łopuszański, *Stowarzyszenie Ludu,* p. 130–33; Steblij, "Polskie spiski," pp. 108–10.

[85] Steblij, "Polskie spiski," pp. 109–10.

[86] Mochnacki, *Pamiętnik,* p. 11. Cf. equally: Józefczyk, *Wspomnienie,* p. 49.

[87] Józef Krajewski, *Tajne związki polityczne w Galicyi (od r. 1833 do r. 1841)* (Lviv, 1903), p. 26.

was one of the members of the district association of the Eastern Galician cell of Association of the Polish People, founded in 1835, while his
organizational talents lent themselves well to his conspiratorial activities at the seminary. He was recalled by another conspirator—Henryk
Bogdański:

> Hordyński's job was the dissemination and upholding of the associa-
> tion's principles at the Ruthenian seminary. An enlightened man, gentle,
> strongly taken by the need for national action and capable in all, and es-
> pecially in those subordinate to him, to instil an attachment, respect and
> trust for his person—he was to gain many adherents among the clergy
> for our common aims.[88]

Hordyński's activities were to result in his being removed in 1837
from his position as seminary catechist, something which had been
under consideration from the very beginning of the 1830s.[89] Later he
became a priest at the parish of Kulykiv, and subsequently the parish
priest in Batiatychi. However, in 1841 he was arrested for conspiratorial
acts and had his nobility revoked, while a few years later the bishop of
Przemyśl banned him from performing any priestly duties.[90]

The potential of the youth at the Lviv Greek Catholic seminary was
so promising that activists of the Association of the Polish People decided to incorporate the said conspiracy as a section of their international
organization. Initially in 1834 Jan Sielecki, a seminarian and later law
student at Lviv University (and simultaneously a member of the secret
Academic Society), introduced a number of the seminarians to the organization.[91] Later more were brought in by Father Hordyński.[92]

Among those who were sworn in was Michał Minczakiewicz
[Mykhailo Mynchakevych], later one of the more active members of
the "Ruthenian Triad" that was to operate in tandem at the seminary.[93]
The "Ruthenian Triad," with Markiian Shashkevych as the head, had
as its aims the education of the Ruthenian population and the creation
of a literary Ruthenian language based on the Ukrainian models and
vernacular. The conspiratorial circles and the "Ruthenian Triad" were
divided, however, by their vision of the future. And even though—
as Bogdański wrote—"the spirit of unity with Poland was still not

---

[88] Henryk Bogdański, *Pamiętnik 1832–1848*, ed. Antoni Knot (Cracow, 1879), p. 71.

[89] Łopuszański, *Stowarzyszenie Ludu*, pp. 85, 88–89, 134–35.

[90] Karol Lewicki, "Hordyński Mikołaj," in *PSB*, vol. 9 (Wrocław–Warsaw–Cracow, 1961),
p. 623.

[91] Herbil's'kyi, *Peredova suspil'na dumka*, p. 125; Bogdański, *Pamiętnik*, p. 37.

[92] Bogdański, *Pamiętnik*, pp. 71–72.

[93] Steblij, "Polskie spiski," p. 107.

undermined,"[94] the differences between *gente Rutheni, natione Poloni* and Shashkevych must have been sufficiently pronounced at the seminary that the former even wanted to drown the leader of the opposite camp, though ultimately this course of action was abandoned. The conspirators also mutually warned each other of those Ruthenians who could possibly inform on them.[95]

The clerics from the Uniate seminary were to *de facto* terminate the group's activities in 1835, following their graduation. However, they mutually pledged to continue conspiratorial acts in the field, and this they also did. Some of them were to continue their activities in the Association of the Polish People, and when this group folded some entered the ranks of a new conspiratorial group called Sons of the Fatherland [Synowie Ojczyzny], a branch of Young Sarmatia, created through the participation of several members of the Association of the Polish People (Klemens Mochnacki, among others, joined the Sons of the Fatherland on the advice of Henryk Bogdański).[96]

Conspiratorial acts came with consequences, however. Following Hordyński's removal from the seminary, the Church authorities conducted a series of searches in the clerics' rooms. Volodymyr Borys wrote that "Metropolitan Mykhailo Levytsky [Michał Lewicki] in Lviv and Ivan Snihursky [Jan Snihurski], bishop of Przemyśl, made every effort to suppress the spirit of rebellion and revolution that had crept into the minds of their pupils".[97] Even though they did not find enough incriminating proof, they expelled all those suspected of conspiracy: Józef Balka [Iosyf Balka], Bazyli [Vasyl] Hrab, Piotr Kuliczkowski [Petro Kulychkovsky], Benedykt Kuszczykiewicz, Leon Maciliński [Lev Matsilynsky], Dymitr Mochnacki, Bazyli Siokała [Vasyl Siokala], Teodor Strzelbicki [Fedir Strelbytsky], Jakub Szwedzicki [Iakub Shvedytsky], and Antoni Ziniewicz [Antonii Zinevych]. Kuszczykiewicz moved at this time to the seminary in Przemyśl where, together with the son of a Greek Catholic priest, Marcjan Łapczyński, and Ludwik Wilhelm, he founded a new organization called The Union of Free Galicians" [*Związek Wolnych Haliczan*] named colloquially "Free Galicians" or "The Galician" [*Haliczanka*].[98] The organization's aim was the

---

[94] Bogdański, *Pamiętnik*, p. 72.

[95] Łopuszański, *Stowarzyszenie Ludu*, pp. 254–55.

[96] Feodosii Steblii, "Ukraïntsi i poliaky Halychyny v 30-40-kh rr. XIX st. Poshuky politychnoho partnerstva," in *Polska – Ukraina. Historia, polityka, kultura. Materiały międzynarodowej konferencji naukowej*, ed. Stefan Zabrowarny (Szczecin–Warsaw, 2003), pp. 44–45; Steblij, "Polskie spiski," p. 110. Mention of this organization has also been made by Józefczyk, *Wspomnienie*, pp. 53–54; Bogdański, *Pamiętnik*, p. 155.

[97] Borys, "Do historii ruchu społeczno-politycznego studentów," p. 423.

[98] Mochnacki, *Pamiętnik*, p. 16.

abolition of the nobility, "material equality," giving land to the peasants, and in the face of opposition to put the "aristocracy to the sword"—in other words, proposing the employment of any means necessary to realize their ideals. This organization also maintained contact with the Young Sarmatia assembly.[99] Through the persuasive skills of a certain Ferdynand Tirman, the conspirators rejected their hitherto held beliefs and disbanded their exceptionally aggressive union. Subsequently they were accepted into the earlier mentioned Sons of the Fatherland.[100]

The clerics Jan Ochrymowicz [Ivan Okhrymovych], Michał Kotowicz [Mykhailo Kotovych], Kajetan Stankiewicz [Kaietan Stankevych], Izydor Winnicki [Vynnytsky] and Michał Proskurnicki [Mykhailo Proskurnytsky] were "to fall" while making copies of the propaganda letter *A Letter to the friends of the people* [*Łyst do pryjateliw myru*], written in Ruthenian. The remainder completed the seminary and in accordance with the resolutions of the conspiracy were to continue patriotic-democratic activities in their own parishes. Bolesław Łopuszański determined that only Krzyżanowski and Hreczański were to continue their actions on a broad scale.[101] The latter, beset by various problems in his subsequent parishes as well as having fallen out with his former friend Ochrymowicz, decided in 1838 to turn himself over to the authorities and reveal all the conspiratorial activities at the seminary.[102] Many former conspirators, already working in parishes, were sentenced to prison terms of between one and three years following the subsequent investigations.[103]

The conspiratorial activity of the youth from the Lviv Greek Catholic seminary was strongly inspired, at least from a certain moment onwards, by the Association of the Polish People, which from 1835 had started to briskly develop across the territory of Eastern Galicia. This organization realized the importance and necessity of drawing Ruthenians into the conspiratorial movement and the need to work among the peasant population of Eastern Galicia.

Besides the already mentioned Hordyński and the students of the Lviv Greek Catholic seminary connected with the association through their own organization, other Ruthenians were also active in the Association of the Polish People. The organization was divided territorially into twenty-two districts, each of which had its own headman and

---

[99] Herbil's'kyi, *Peredova suspil'na dumka*, p. 131; LNNBU, fond 5, op. 1, spr. 3535/III, p. 13.

[100] Józefczyk, *Wspomnienie*, pp. 72–73.

[101] Łopuszański, *Stowarzyszenie Ludu*, pp. 136–40.

[102] Stanisław Schnür-Pepłowski, *Z przeszłości Galicyi (1772–1862)* (Lviv, 1895), p. 387.

[103] Łopuszański, *Stowarzyszenie Ludu*, pp. 140–43.

members. District thirteen undoubtably had a Ruthenian character. The headman was Klemens Mochnacki, and members included the Greek Catholics Piotr Kuliczkowski and Bazyli Hrab. In district fourteen an important role was played by Kasper Cięglewicz, who taught seminarians democratic principles and how to conduct partisan warfare. In turn, in Henryk Bogdański's district, the already mentioned Dymitr Mochnacki was to be found.[104] In 1835, conspirators from the Przemyśl conspiratorial organization, earlier created by Henryk Bogdański, and with the Uniate cleric Józef Konstantynowicz at its head, were to join the association.[105]

Ruthenians concentrated in the Association of the Polish People wanted to reconstruct the organization in such a way that it incorporated the demands of its Ruthenian members. There was even broached at the time the idea of expanding the name by an additional element so that it would then read: The Association of the Polish and Ruthenian People. This idea was to be ultimately rejected at the General Assembly.[106] Finally, the Ruthenian Circle was to emerge from the Association, being in effect a *gente Rutheni, natione Poloni* organ. Its members wanted to remain Ruthenians yet at the same time fight for a Poland federal in character. They stood in opposition to the adherents of Muscovy. The Greek Catholic parish priest in Medyka, the earlier mentioned Józef Łoziński, who belonged to the organization, proposed the introduction of Latin script to Ruthenian so as to differentiate it from the Russian language. This idea, like the Ruthenian Circle's proposal to introduce the Gregorian Calendar into the Greek Catholic Church's rite, was not to be implemented.[107] The Association of the Polish People was itself to collapse after a few years of activity. First, those Lviv activists of liberal tendencies broke away to form the Universal Confederation of the Polish Nation [*Konfederacja Powszechna Narodu Polskiego*], and then in 1839, following numerous arrests and the execution of the Association's leader Szymon Konarski, the organization came to an end.

Galician Agitators

Apart from the Ruthenians connected to the Association of the Polish People, there were outstanding agitators, who as well as being inspired by the slogans of "freedom" to the peasants, also carried out their own

---

[104] Ibid., pp. 91, 138.
[105] Bogdański, *Pamiętnik,* p. 41; Łopuszański, *Stowarzyszenie Ludu,* pp. 184–85.
[106] Kieniewicz, *Konspiracje galicyjskie,* p. 104.
[107] Łopuszański, *Stowarzyszenie Ludu,* pp. 230–32.

propaganda activities—most often directed at the Ruthenian peasant-ry[108]. Here it is worth mentioning again Kasper Cięglewicz and Julian Horoszkiewicz, Piotr Kotkiewicz [Petro Kotkevych], and first and fore-most, Ignacy Kulczyński.[109]

The initiator of all the propaganda directed at the Galician peas-antry was Ignacy Kulczyński from Volhynia. He had participated in the November Uprising, and following the revolt's collapse, had settled in 1830–31 in the Austrian area of partition. In 1833, he joined in the preparations for Józef Zaliwski's expedition [this émigré officer tried to initiate a Polish uprising in the Congress Kingdom], and following the creation of the Association of the Polish People, he was to act as intermediary between the General Assembly and Szymon Konarski, the leader of the association in Volhynia and the Vilnius area. He was to conduct agitation work in the villages of the Zolochiv district, draw-ing attention first and foremost to the need to give the people land and abolish serfdom. For propaganda purposes, he used materials from the emigration, as well as writing his own, including the extremely impor-tant booklet *On Scholarly Aristocracy and Popular Lectures* [*O arystokracji naukowej i popularnych wykładach*]. This was a project for the complete reconstruction of feudal society and the building of a new social order by the common people.[110] Kulczyński shot himself immediately after his address was discovered by the police.[111] A similar fate was to meet another agitator and conspirator, Piotr Kotkiewicz, who on being ar-rested for his activities committed suicide in prison.[112]

As Volodymyr Borys noted, it was Kulczyński who encouraged Cięglewicz and Horoszkiewicz, younger than he was, to write in Ru-thenian. Julian Horoszkiewicz, the son of a court official, on joining the conspiracy had his lithography lessons paid for by Kulczyński, who subsequently commissioned him to make a copy of an anti-feudal

---

[108] See more: Marian Tyrowicz, „Próby wciągnięcia wsi wschodnio-galicyjskiej do kon-spiracji demokratyczno-rewolucyjnej (1833–1839)", *Rocznik Naukowo-Dydaktyczny* no. 35, *Prace Historyczne* 5 (1970), pp. 133–44.

[109] Kotkiewicz born in Borschiv was probably of Ruthenian origin. Marian Tyrowicz indi-cates that he was the son of a servant in the manor, responsible for the pond. Ignacy Kulczyński was certainly a Pole of origin. Ibid., pp. 136, 139.

[110] Włodzimierz Borys, "Z dziejów walk o wyzwolenie narodowe i społeczne w Galicji w pierwszej połowie XIX w.," *Przemyskie Zapiski Historyczne* 4–5 (1987), pp. 229–30.

[111] Włodzimierz Borys, "Galicyjski okres w życiu Ignacego Kulczyńskiego (w świetle ar-chiwaliów lwowskich)," *Przegląd Historyczny* 68, no. 1 (1977), pp. 129–30.

[112] Steblij, "Polskie spiski," p. 112. Cf. also: Tyrowicz, "Próby wciągnięcia wsi wschodnio--galicyjskiej," p. 138; Włodzimierz Borys, "W kręgu rewolucyjnym Szymona Konarskie-go, Piotra Kotkiewicza i Ignacego Kulczyńskiego," *Przegląd Historyczny* 66, no. 3 (1975), pp. 461–62.

poem written in Ruthenian and entitled "Dumka".[113] Horoszkiewicz
had earlier experience of conspiratorial actions. He had worked on
arousing the national consciousness of peasants in his home village of
Lopatyn in the years 1834–35. When he moved to Lviv in 1836, Ignacy
Kulczyński acquainted him with Kasper Cięglewicz and other conspirators. It was then that Horoszkiewicz was to broaden the scope of his
activities. He wrote in Ruthenian, using the Latin script, *The Letters to
Friends of Peace*, comprising several letters to "friends." A separate copy
of this work is preserved at the Lviv National Vasyl Stefanyk Scientific
Library of Ukraine, but described as the Cięglewicz's work.[114] In these
letters, the author describes the fate of an imprisoned giant whom he
had the opportunity to see. This giant was searching for joy and freedom, but he was bound and locked away in the dark. This story is told
over the course of five letters and it is only in the last that the author
reveals who the suffering hero is:

> (…) the Polish nation that had for a long time and numerously inhabited
> the land has now succumbed to three emperors: the Muscovite, our Aus-
> trian, and the Prussian. This nation lived for centuries as a single family,
> in harmony, in happiness and according to God's laws, and even if to-
> day it proclaims its faith in three rites (the Roman Catholic or as we call
> it the Polish, the Greek Catholic or Ruthenian and Uniate), it has always
> believed in a single God, has been loved by Him because it respects His
> commandments which state 'As I have loved you, that ye also love one
> another (…).[115]

Further on he explains to the reader that before the partitions, Poles
and Ruthenians lived as brothers, for they knew no serfdom. At the
initiative of the authorities, the clergy were to spread discord amongst
the nations. And here not only nationally but first and foremost on the
social plane:

> (…) they set the peasants at odds with the masters, the lords were
> bought by orders, money and imperial grace, and then they came with
> fire and sword to take Poland. The good-natured Poles shed their blood
> in vain, with the price of which they had hoped to buy us out of lordly
> and imperial captivity, the cheated world did not join together, did not

---

[113] Borys, "Z dziejów walk," pp. 224–25.
[114] Kasper Cięglewicz [!], "Wskazówka dla nauczycieli ludu ruskiego" (Lviv, 1840 [!]),
LNNBU, fond 5, op. 1, spr. 2972/I [in point of fact this is: Julian Horoszkiewicz, "Łysty do
pryjateliw myru"].
[115] [Julian Horoszkiewicz], "Łysty do pryjateliw myru, 1837," in *Społeczeństwo polskie*,
p. 667; Bolesław Łopuszański, "'Wskazówka dla nauczycieli ludu ruskiego' Kaspra Cięglewicza (z literatury chłopomańskiej pierwszej połowy XIX w.)," *Rocznik Muzeum Etnograficznego w Krakowie* 5 (1974), p. 250.

17. *The first page of the Julian Horoszkiewicz's manuscript*
The Letters to Friends of Peace

save itself. The emperor tricked us through his priests, [saying] that the Poles want more restrictions for the peasants, and they believed these persuasions and thought that every Pole is the enemy of the peasant.[116]

Besides his examination of rural reality, Horoszkiewicz tried to also recall Poland and its multi-ethnic character:

Some people died, others became accustomed to captivity, forgot that it had all been a single Poland, a single nation, one Polish world of three beliefs, that everyone loved each other as brothers, Ruthenians with Poles, that they should live as one family, as a family in separation does not forget and loves each other (…).[117]

The Letters end with a clear appeal: "Down with tsarist and lordly bondage." The author appeals for all to join together "to take up the sword, the scythe, and the knife!" He places great hope that such teachings would be spread further. This democratic-revolutionary interpretation was to hold sway for the years up to the Revolutions of 1848, though with time Horoszkiewicz's radicalism was to decrease. But Horoszkiewicz's role was not to end with the writing of *The Letters* In 1837, having learned the art of lithography, he bought the appropriate equipment and started to reproduce his agitational works.[118] One of Horoszkiewicz's works was *Dumka*, produced in several dozen copies. He was arrested and imprisoned for his activities. He was sentenced to 12 years in prison in Kufstein, but Emperor Ferdinand I reduced him to 6 years in prison.[119] In the jail, where he was imprisoned in 1840, he took to writing poetry.[120]

Yet, it was to be Kasper Cięglewicz who was to go down as the strongest both in the conspiratorial acts and in

18. The Kufstein prison.
An illustration drawn by Julian
Horoszkiewicz in 1844

---

[116] [Horoszkiewicz], "Łysty," p. 668; Łopuszański, "Wskazówka dla nauczycieli ludu ruskiego," p. 251.

[117] [Horoszkiewicz], "Łysty," p. 668; Łopuszański, "Wskazówka dla nauczycieli ludu ruskiego," p. 252.

[118] Steblij, "Polskie spiski," p. 115.

[119] Tomasz Szubert, "Polscy więźniowie w twierdzy Kufstein w XIX wieku," *Śląski Kwartalnik Historyczny Sobótka* 60, no. 4 (2005), p. 449.

[120] Two of them, *Czużyna* and *Moja najmylijsza* of 1840, were published years later in a collection of literary works. See *Album lwowskie*, ed. Henryk Nowakowski (Lviv, 1862), pp. 120–22.

the general history of the *gente Rutheni, natione Poloni* formation of the 1830s and 1840s. Yet today, his identity constitutes a problem for historians. Researchers are divided into those who view him as a Pole, and those who see him as a Ruthenian of Polish nationality. It was Bolesław Łopuszański who first highlighted the matter, though he was not to provide an answer as to who the revolutionary was.[121]

Kasper Cięglewicz was born in Horodenka in Galician Podilia in 1807 into a family of civil servants. He finished school in Sambir and Lviv, and subsequently the faculties of philosophy and law at Lviv University. In 1833, he took up employment in the Sambir courts, where his conspiratorial adventure was to begin, one that was to last a dozen or so years. He proclaimed democratic slogans from the very beginning of his conspiratorial acts—including an idealisation of the peasantry, antinoble statements and sentiments, but first and foremost an appeal for Polish-Ruthenian fraternity.

Cięglewicz wrote works of poetry in Ruthenian in which he criticized the relationships of serfdom, blaming the partitioning powers for these.[122] Ryszard Herman, a school friend, recalls him thus:

> Kasper Cięglewicz, a pure republican of steadfast soul, despite not belonging to the Union, was nonetheless active as an agitator especially amongst the Ruthenians, and this through writing poetry and prose sometimes in Polish, other times in Ruthenian, and yet always universally respected.[123]

As Feodosii Steblii notes, ten of Cięglewicz's Ruthenian poems came into being under the influence of Ignacy Kulczyński.[124] In any event, these works were to resonate for a long time within social memory, especially given that *Tygodnik Illustrowany*, in recalling the deceased Cięglewicz in 1886, noted:

> He was a folk poet given the full entirety of the word. His Ruthenian *dumkas* to this day are on the lips of the peasants of Galician Podilia, some of them being real pearls of folk poetry. Many of these have been drowned in the flood of folk songs—while those which print has immortalized and which at present honest memory is bringing to light testify to the extraordinary talent of the lyricist.[125]

---

[121] Łopuszański, "'Wskazówka dla nauczycieli ludu ruskiego'," p. 240, footnote 3. Unequivocally he was considered a Ruthenian by, among others: Zygmunt Zborucki, *Proces studentów samborskich (1837–1839)* (Lviv, 1927), p. 31.

[122] Łopuszański, *Stowarzyszenie Ludu*, p. 159.

[123] LNNBU, fond 5, op. 1, spr. 3535/III, p. 12v.

[124] Steblij, "Polskie spiski," p. 113.

[125] "Korespondencya," *Tygodnik Illustrowany* no. 201 (6 Nov. 1886), pp. 295, 298.

During the communist era, Maria Janion pointed to the significance of this type of propaganda poetry, calling Cięglewicz "the creator of the folk agitation song."[126]

Besides writing poetry, Cięglewicz edited appeals and political texts, both in Polish and Ruthenian. For years he was unequivocally viewed as a typical representative of *gente Ruthenus, natione Polonus*. Only Julian Horoszkiewicz, his friend and comrade in conspiratorial activities, recalled in his memoires that he was in fact a Pole, as his parents had not been of the Greek Catholic rite. This very fact in relation to matters of national consciousness, though key, should not in itself determine a man's designation as Ruthenian or Polish, especially as religious matters, although appearing widely in Cięglewicz's poetry, were rather secondary for him personally. He thus could have potentially thought of himself as a Ruthenian. His later behaviour during the Revolutions of 1848, however, does somewhat negate this, when he, given the development of events, had to finally answer the question (fully understanding the political consequences resulting from this) as to whether the Ruthenian nation existed or not. It was then that his path diverged from that of Horoszkiewicz, who was prepared to continue reconciling his two identities, not resigning from either of them.

In reality, it is difficult to classify Cięglewicz as a Ruthenian. It is rather better to see him as a Pole who only instrumentally declared his alleged Ruthenianness. His father, Mateusz Cięglewicz, was a Roman Catholic, while his mother, Katarzyna Abrahamowicz, was of the Armenian Catholic rite.[127] Living within Ruthenian circles, he had learnt to speak Ruthenian fluently, which enabled him to use it at will later on in life,[128] when he undertook agitation amongst the Ruthenian peasantry. And thus Henryk Bogdański was to recall him (incidentally considering Cięglewicz to be a Ruthenian):

Cięglewicz, (...) in possessing perfect Ruthenian, being a Ruthenian, and having taken it upon himself to help the émigré Piotr Kotkiewicz, the poet and Ruthenian folk writer, also known as Chodkiewicz , set off amongst the Ruthenian peasants and under his own steam (...) started to disseminate propaganda amongst them with the aim of explaining the forms of government oppression they suffered and to acquaint them with the concepts of land ownership and freedom from serfdom. With this aim in mind, and to make it easier for him to rub shoulders with the

---

[126] Maria Janion, "Pieśniarz czerwonoruski," *Życie Literackie* no. 37 (19 Sep. 1954), p. 4.

[127] See for more: Franciszek Wasyl, *Ormianie w przedautonomicznej Galicji. Studium demograficzno-historyczne* (Cracow, 2015), p. 85.

[128] Julian Horoszkiewicz, *Notatki z życia*, ed. Henryk Wereszycki (Wrocław–Cracow, 1957), p. 116.

peasantry, he took up blacksmithing and practiced the craft in the Zolochiv district. He adopted a nomadic lifestyle. The main areas of their
activities were the districts of Zhovkva and Zolochiv: rumours about
them spread from village to village, but they were not discovered, for
a secret can be long kept among the peasants; they kept silent about
everything from their lord and from anyone dressed in an urban manner, but among their own they would display themselves openly.[129]

The first of Cięglewicz's pamphlets, written jointly in 1835 with
Kulczyński, was Proclamation to the Ruthenian People.[130] The authors
set themselves the goal of teaching democracy to the Ruthenian people,
hence we read of the need to choose national representatives from
among the particular groups whose interests they are going to represent. Up until then the people were to be controlled by the will of the
emperor or king regardless of whether they wanted it or not. Government officials represented the will of the ruler or the noble estate, but
not of the whole nation. Therefore, the agitators perversely appealed:

> Nations! Take the example from the emperors and kings and resolve the
> matter as they would themselves, for the whole magnitude of your task
> is to drive them out, just as in general the essence of being a king is for
> nations [in the sense of peoples] to be kept in serfdom. This is how our
> enemies teach us what we are to do to act against them![131]

Cięglewicz and Kulczyński also undertook the topic of the historical position of Ruthenians and the genesis of their connection with the
Poles. This was to have occurred after the Polish king took Rus' and
designated himself a Ruthenian prince. Obviously here the matter refers to Casimir the Great. Later the Ruthenian nobility were brought
into the Diet, appearing there in the name of Rus'. Admittedly the lot
of the Ruthenian peasants (in the same way as for the Polish peasantry)
was not to improve after this change, but there were to be more noblemen to draw the king's attention to Rus' and its affairs. Following this
line of argument, Cięglewicz and Kulczyński explained that the incorporation of Rus' could not be the reason for the deteriorating situation
of the Ruthenian populace. The authors simultaneously attempted to
show the historical significance of the historic fraternity of Poles and
Ruthenians:

---

[129] Bogdański, *Pamiętnik*, p. 140.
[130] Kyrylo Studyns'kii, "Pol's'ki konspiratsiï sered rus'kykh pytomtsiv i dukhovenstva
v Halychyni v rokakh 1831–1846," *Zapysky Naukovoho Tovarystva imeni Shevchenka* 82,
vol. 2 (1908), pp. 129–33; [Kasper Cięglewicz, Ignacy Kulczyński], "Odezwa do ludu ruskiego, [1835]," in *Społeczeństwo polskie*, p. 660.
[131] [Cięglewicz, Kulczyński], "Odezwa", p. 660.

We have lived in brotherhood with the Poles for five hundred years, we have known joy and sorrow with them, as a nation together we have lived life and together we have suffered. The life lived has been equally for us as for the Poles an identical series of events, whether one of happiness or adversity. And from just such brotherhood it has resulted that the heart of our nation [people] has grown with that of the Polish nation, that together we feel that the blood was as of two twins, that the souls of both nations became a single one.[132]

This booklet was to remain in circulation for several years. By 1835 it was already known to the police in the Stanyslaviv district, and within a year it had been distributed all over Galicia. In 1837, it was found in the possession of a member of the Association of Friends of the People, the former Lviv seminarist Cyryl Słoniewski, in Sniatyn.[133]

Cięglewicz wanted, among other routes, to reach the peasantry through their teachers at schools. At the end of the 1830s, finding himself in the village of Nakvasha in the Zolochiv district at the manor house of Karol Hubicki—someone who had a conciliatory approach towards Ruthenians—Cięglewicz prepared the so-called *Recommendations for Teachers of the Ruthenian Population* (an informal name, also used were the Polish equivalents of *Instruction...* and *Pointers...*).[134] Researchers struggled for a long time to establish which of the pamphlets known at the time was the said *Recommendations*, for on none of the preserved printed editions is this name visible, though other source texts have mentioned it under just such a heading. For example, Bolesław Łopuszański considered this document to be the earlier cited allegorical *The Letters to Friends of Peace* by Horoszkiewicz, which were preserved in a copy from 1840, yet published in its time incorrectly by Ivan Franko as a work by Cięglewicz. An edition of these letters as the alleged "Recommendations" was produced by Łopuszański on the pages of *Rocznik Muzeum Etnograficznego w Krakowie* [The Cracow Ethnographical Museum Annual].[135] As was later ascertained,[136] the actual *Recommendations...* was a document preserved at the Ukrainian Central State Historical Archive in Lviv, and published by Volodymyr Borys in 1968 as *An Appeal to the Peasants* [*Wydozwa do selan*]. The documents *The Letters* and *Recommendations...* were published with an additional appendix in 1984 in an annex to the volume *Polish Society and the Attempts to Renew the Armed Struggle*

---

[132] Ibid., pp. 660–61.
[133] Łopuszański, *Stowarzyszenie Ludu*, pp. 172–74.
[134] Fras, *Demokraci*, pp. 45–46.
[135] Łopuszański, "'Wskazówka dla nauczycieli ludu ruskiego'," pp. 239–56.
[136] Steblij, "Polskie spiski," pp. 113–15.

in 1833 [Społeczeństwo polskie i próby wznowienia walki zbrojnej w 1833 roku].[137]

Cięglewicz started his *Recommendations...* with a critique of the clergy, blaming them for propagating the notion that the Scriptures deem monarchical power to be derived from God. The author of the work claimed, however, that it cannot be the case that God had wanted the lot of the peasant to be bad. He explained that it was the emperor who ordered the clergy to deceive the peasantry in relation to laws legitimising his authority and power, for which the priests received money. As a consequence, Cięglewicz recommended that the people believe the Holy Scriptures themselves and not what the priest decided to advance as an interpretation. He called the clergy Pharisees, exactly like those who had led to the death of Christ himself. He confirmed that in the countryside nothing could be done without a priest's participation but "those who are in our countryside are tsarist agents, assassins, and spies."[138]

Zygmunt Zborucki suspected that the strong criticism Cięglewicz levelled against the Uniate clergy was the result of the formation of a separate Ruthenian national movement based on the alumni of the Uniate seminary in Lviv. They were no longer to display Polonophile sentiments, although at this time there was in operation at the same seminary another secret conspiracy of students of a pro-Polish orientation.[139] We can agree with Łopuszański, who drew attention to the mistake made here in attacking the Greek Catholic clergy. For it was chiefly they (i.e., the seminarians) who were involved in conspiratorial activities among the Ruthenian population and it was from their ranks that a series of patriots of the Polish idea were recruited.[140]

Cięglewicz was to explain to the peasants that the differences in rites came from the Jesuit snub to the Ruthenian rite, while calling the Latin rite—Polish. For earlier no one had been bothered by religious relations. He also explained that Ruthenians became Poles not because the Ruthenian nobility had adopted the Latin rite but because they had become a part of Poland, "for Rus' is a part of Poland, a sister, a twin that for five hundred years has grown close to Poland. In the manner that a Mazovian is a Pole, so we equally are Poles."[141] He also spoke of the partitions and the national liberation struggle conducted by the

---

[137] *Społeczeństwo polskie,* pp. 663–79.
[138] [Kasper Cięglewicz], "Instrukcya dla nauczycieli ludu ruskiego, [1837–1838]," in *Społeczeństwo polskie,* p. 674.
[139] Zborucki, *Proces studentów samborskich,* p. 34.
[140] Łopuszański, *Stowarzyszenie Ludu,* p. 164.
[141] [Cięglewicz], "Instrukcya," p. 661.

nobility. He emphasized that it was impossible to gain freedom without the participation of the peasantry. He said:

> (…) Again the Poles will seize the scythe, the axe, the flintlock and sabres against the tsars, but they will drive the lords and magnates out together with the tsar, and therefore this war shall succeed and Poland shall be free.[142]

The *Recommendations...* were to consequently become a weaving together of the liberation program with a revolutionary one, which according to Polish agitators was to result in both wide-sweeping social changes as well as the attainment of Polish independence in a fatherland of Poles and Ruthenians, with both peoples understood as a part of a single, greater nation.

He also questioned the rule of the emperor over man. Here he quoted fragments from the New Testament which were to refute the emperor's right to power. He confirmed the peasants in the conviction that the emperor, lord, and priest is but a single hand, and that none of them had the right to rule over the peasantry. He gave the example of a certain Ms. Chrząstowska from the Tarnów district, who was to have revoked the serfdom of her peasants and who for this had been sent to prison, where she still remained.

The Poles, according to Cięglewicz, had already risen up against the king and emperor three times: during the Bar Confederation, under Kościuszko, and during the November Uprising. During the two years 1830–1831, the insurgents had wanted to introduce the principle of equal rights for the peasants and had desired that the countryside join in the struggle for mutual goals (both independence and social ones), but—as Cięglewicz explained to the peasants—the countryside was unaware of this. He summed up his own story by reminding Ruthenians that: "and so you Ruthenian peasants are yourselves Poles—you rule, and then it will happen that people say 'Here the Poles shall rule.' For you are Poles."[143] In order to convey in the simplest terms the idea of the Polish nation being one composed of not only ethnic Poles but also Ruthenians and Lithuanians, he tried to refer to Poles as Mazurians (i.e., Mazovians) and consequently avoid the ambivalence in the understanding of the word *Polak*:

> You know, brothers, that this land and earth is Poland. Poland is composed of three main nations [peoples], that is of the Mazovians, the Lithuanians, and the Ruthenians. They are a trinity in a single nation, and in

---

[142] Ibid., p. 662.
[143] Ibid., p. 676.

the same way that a Mazovian is a Pole, and a Lithuanian is a Pole, so then is a Ruthenian a Pole.[144]

Recommendations... was to play a very important role, for it was a manifesto of a national-social nature, interpreting the social reality in Galicia and teaching the peasants history and the significance of Polish-Ruthenian brotherhood. It also instructed "teachers of the Ruthenian people" not to overlook any fragment of the proclamation and to truthfully convey the contents to the peasants. *Recommendations...* was to enjoy widespread popularity and was passed on further by those who felt the need to spread propaganda among the Ruthenian populace. Henryk Bogdański bears witness to the popularity of the work and also to Cięglewicz's activities as an agitator. He notes:

> (...) Kasper Cięglewicz and Ignacy Kulczyński, had many adherents and perpetrators of their acts, which they conducted in the Ruthenian half of the country on a large scale, but they did not run a separate close-knit association, for they considered their actions as the duty of each and every existing political body, which is why they did not give any specific name to their agreement, which would have set them apart from other unions.[145]

Apart from *Recommendations...* there were other appeals directed to the peasantry that alluded to the ideas of Polish-Ruthenian fraternity and at the same time emphasized democratic slogans. Here it is worth mentioning *A Proclamation to Brethren* [*Odezwa do braci*], written in Ruthenian in Latin script. Composed of thirteen questions and answers, it postulated the gaining by Poland of independence within its pre-partition borders, and the universal fraternity of its inhabitants regardless of the differences dividing them. At the same time it criticized the landlords, while emphasizing the contribution of the Liakhy [Poles], who were meant to be the friends of the peasants.[146]

If one is to believe Bogdański, then one plot among the Ruthenians was to take on a *quasi*-associational character. In Pomoriany the local manorial bookkeeper, the Ruthenian Antoni Kruszelnicki [Antonii Krushelnytsky], presented Cięglewicz's *Recommendations...* to the local conspirator Jan Gudziak, more than likely equally of Ruthenian provenance. This young rebel adapted the work and called it *Teachings for the People*. In this he called for an armed struggle for social and national freedom. Together with supporters of this idea, he formed an associa-

---

[144] Ibid.
[145] LNNBU, fond 5, op. 1, spr. 3535/III.
[146] Łopuszański, *Stowarzyszenie Ludu*, pp. 176–77.

tion called the Aid Association [*Towarzystwo Pomocy*], which was to be the rural branch of the Association of the Polish People for the eastern part of Galicia. Although the organization was never to have any written statute or other regulations, Gudziak took oaths from his comrades and obliged them to disseminate *Teachings for the People* in any way possible, without the need to account for the results obtained.[147] As a hallmark of allegiance, a black bone button worn on the right side of the hat and the password "Palmo" (more than likely from the Ruthenian word *pal'ma*—palm) was used. The leader of the conspiracy himself was to change his place of residence many times, something that drew the attention of the authorities. He finally arrived in Stanyslaviv, where he entered a higher school to cover his tracks; there he was to spread his propaganda, including among those peasants serving in the border guard and army. One of the members of the covert operation recruited, then betrayed, Gudziak, and he was given ten years' imprisonment in Špilberk.[148] His former colleague Antoni Kruszelnicki was also arrested.

Many young people were involved in agitation. Cięglewicz, while in Sambir, was able to recruit several pupils and students into the Association of the Polish People. Michał Popiel [Mykhailo Popel], the son of a Greek Catholic nobleman near Sambir, recruited for the democratic and Polish idea by Kasper Cięglewicz in 1835, founded an autodidactic organization, which two years later was to transform into a conspiracy called the Society of Ruthenian Participants and Pupils, with slogans for the abolition of serfdom and the brotherhood of Poles and Ruthenians.[149] Popiel outlined his organization's program in the poem "A Ruthenian on a Feast Day" ["Rusyn na praznyku"—in the sense of being at a church feast], running to 306 lines.[150] In its introduction, this work criticized the subjugation of the peasants, encouraged the overthrow of the existing social order, but also spoke out against the Austrian bureaucracy. The final part of the work emphasized how in times of old the Ruthenian and the Liakh lived in such harmony that they formed a single Polish nation, and therefore they should love each other. The differences between Poles and Ruthenians were to have been the result of the fact that centuries earlier one went to fight, while the other

---

[147] Bogdański, *Pamiętnik*, pp. 178–79.

[148] Marian Tyrowicz, "Gudziak Jan," in *PSB*, vol. 9, pp. 137–38. See also for more on the Gudziak conspiracy: Łopuszański, *Stowarzyszenie Ludu*, pp. 174–76.

[149] Bogdański, *Pamiętnik*, p. 139; Stefan Kieniewicz, "Popiel Michał," in *PSB*, vol. 27 (Wrocław–Warsaw–Cracow–Gdańsk–Łódź, 1983), pp. 563–64.

[150] Ivan Franko came to the elderly Popiel in the village of Cherhava near Sambir, and obtained a copy of the poem with the intention of publishing it in the newspaper in accordance with the original in the Latin script.

worked the fields, and afterwards the former started to live at the expense of the common people. He explained the current difficult situation as a result of the country finding itself under foreign domination. For Popiel there was to be only one solution to the problem:

> We shall cut down the German invaders
> And live to see happy times.[151]

Popiel's organization was to be officially founded on 7 May 1836, and he himself determined its main principles. He managed to bring young Poles and Ruthenians into the ranks.[152] The group's activities started with secret meetings where revolutionary publications were read and lectures given. Consequently, the organization conducted primarily self-education and activities raising patriotic consciousness. At the first meeting, it was decided that gatherings were to take place twice a week. Three judges were selected to help the leader, and they were entrusted with evaluating the works written by the association's members. This activity was not only to help express patriotic feelings but also had a practical goal—improving the participants' knowledge of the Polish language. After two weeks, elections for a new leader and judges were to take place. Meetings of this type did not necessarily meet the revolutionary expectations of Kasper Cięglewicz, or the action-focused needs of the impassioned Benedykt Sobecki, a post-November Uprising émigré who lived at this time in Sambir. Under their influence, the organization was soon to change from an autodidactic circle into a conspiratorial unit. They started to practice drill with a Polish command on the municipal meadow. With this aim in mind, an instructor was found—a teacher of the French language, a certain Mr. Hermanowicz [Harmanovych]. He constitutes a fairly interesting example of a Ruthenian of Polish nationality, as he was the son of a Greek-Catholic parish priest, who during the Napoleonic wars had fought in all of its campaigns, achieving the rank of warrant officer. He became an officer in the Polish Kingdom and joined the fight in the Polish-Russian war in 1830. Following the collapse of the uprising, he settled in Sambir, and years later started to train the local youth in drill, presumably knowing Popiel and his colleagues' real intentions. The boys practiced fighting with long sticks, and they also had their own standard and trumpet with Polish emblems.[153] In addition, Stefan Kieniewicz established that the

---

[151] Stefan Kieniewicz, "Rusyn na praznyku' i dalsze jego losy," in *Problemy wiedzy o kulturze. Prace dedykowane Stefanowi Żółkiewskiemu*, eds. Alina Brodzka, Maryla Hopfinger and Janusz Lalewicz (Wrocław–Warsaw–Cracow–Gdańsk–Łódź, 1986), pp. 327–29.

[152] Łopuszański, *Stowarzyszenie Ludu*, pp. 207–8.

[153] Zborucki, *Proces studentów samborskich*, pp. 10–12.

school boys commemorated the anniversary of the outbreak of the November Uprising with songs, drew anti-government symbols on walls, as well as conducted patriotic agitation work in Sambir and its environs.[154] The young people's zeal was to be weakened somewhat by the approaching school holidays, and they scattered across the local villages. Even though the leaders of the conspiracy ordered agitation to be conducted in these rural areas, the organization in fact simply died. Cięglewicz, together with the former theology student Jan Szymański, both equally involved in conspiratorial actions, wanted to reorganize the Sambir group and divide it into smaller circles. This was achieved later by Dobrzęcki, a Sambir court intern, with the persuasion of Cięglewicz—despite opposition from Popiel himself. But it was already too late for the organization to revitalize itself. It would more than likely have collapsed of its own accord had it not been for the betrayal of the young conspirators in February 1837 by one of the pupils. They were arrested, and a police case was conducted against them. During the investigation, several members of the Sambir conspiracy were found to possess Polish literature, including Mickiewicz's *Book of the Polish Nation and the Polish Pilgrimage* as well as various revolutionary publications.

Popiel and other Ruthenian comrades explained themselves during the interrogations by stating that as Ruthenians they could not have supported the Poles, as the Ruthenian people differed from the Polish nation.[155] This was, however, merely a ruse to help them avoid any consequences. Popiel's connection to Polishness is borne out by his later political activity. Despite their explanations, the leader of the conspiracy was sentenced to thirteen years' imprisonment, which was to be finally reduced to four. He was to serve his sentence at the fortress in Špilberk.

Great spirit was displayed by another boy, also a Ruthenian to his core, Józef Berechulski [Iosef Berekhulsky], who with immense involvement broadened the society's agitational activities in his village. Even though he had been beaten by his interrogators, he denied everything during the trial, not wanting to betray his colleagues. After the interrogations, he ended up in hospital in a terrible condition, after which he was sentenced to twelve years. Other boys received sentences of ten and eleven years.[156]

---

[154] Kieniewicz, "'Rusyn na praznyku'," p. 329.
[155] Zborucki, *Proces studentów samborskich*, pp. 12–17; Łopuszański, *Stowarzyszenie Ludu*, pp. 207–16.
[156] Zborucki, *Proces studentów samborskich*, pp. 27–28.

Subsequent attempts to set up societies in Sambir were undertaken; these bearing the names "Sent" and the Society of Scholars, but as they were not detected by the Austrian police, and consequently no information was held on them in political files, we know little about them.[157]

The arrests among the Sambir organization's membership were to lead the police also to the main ringleader Kasper Cięglewicz. Together with him were arrested—as Andrzej Józefczyk recalls—Ignacy, Kasper's brother, and the Ruthenian theology student Filemon Minczakiewicz.[158] Cięglewicz was able to escape from prison thanks to two friends—Julian Horoszkiewicz and Karol Dłużewski—who sent him an Austrian official's uniform (3 June 1837).[159] He had the possibility to travel to France, but he declined the opportunity and continued his agitation in the countryside of the districts of Zhovkva and Zolochiv.[160] As Józefczyk writes:

> (...) knowing the Little Russian language fluently, he went to the Ruthenian people and started propaganda work of his own accord with no recourse to the association and even against its will. In his talks to the people he exposed the sources of their captivity, while his songs in *Noworocznik Poznański* [The Poznań New Year Book] were to offer cheer until the yoke itself was cast off.[161]

The slogans proclaimed by Cięglewicz were passed along among the peasantry until eventually they reached the authorities, and in 1839 he was again detained, and sentenced once more in May 1840 and given twenty years' imprisonment (the highest possible penalty in Austrian legislation, not counting the death penalty) in Kufstein. At the same time a search was ordered at the home of Horoszkiewicz, at the time a clerk for a Lviv bookkeeper, and a double bottomed chest was discovered. Hidden in it was a lithographic machine for printing Horoszkiewicz's and Cięglewicz's Ruthenian poetry and leaflets. And in this manner both friends, the main agitators for the ideas of a Polish-Ruthenian brotherhood, ended up in jail.[162]

A similar fate was to meet another Ruthenian of Polish nationality—Dymitr Czubaty [Dmytro Chubaty]—operating in Ternopil. He was arrested four times for conspiratorial activities, beginning in 1836.

---

[157] Aleksander Kuczera, *Samborszczyzna. Ilustrowana monografja miasta Sambora i ekonomii samborskiej*, vol. 2 (Sambor, 1935), p. 316.

[158] Józefczyk, *Wspomnienie*, pp. 42–43.

[159] Ibid., pp. 47–48; Zborucki, *Proces studentów samborskich*, pp. 31–32.

[160] Zborucki, *Proces studentów samborskich*, p. 32.

[161] Józefczyk, *Wspomnienie*, p. 48.

[162] Schnür-Pepłowski, *Z przeszłości*, pp. 384–85; Józefczyk, *Wspomnienie*, p. 49; Zborucki, *Proces studentów samborskich*, pp. 37–38; Szubert, „Polscy więźniowie," p. 449.

He was famous for founding, together with Alojzy Zgierski and Robert Chmielewski, an emissary of the Central Command of the Polish Democratic Society in France, the secret organization "Democratic Poland" [*Polska Demokratyczna*] in Ternopil. He was to recruit to his secret organization Tytus Przysiecki, Tomasz Chołodecki, Seweryn Wszelaczyński, Bolesław Zienkiewicz, and others. His propaganda was directed chiefly to Ruthenian artisan youth and the rural population. First and foremost, he proclaimed revolutionary slogans and smuggled in illegal literature from France. He was finally arrested by the Ternopil starost along with his colleagues.[163]

Father Bazyli Hrab, a former conspirator from the Lviv Greek Catholic seminary, was to also act independently, though now in his capacity as a priest for the Greek Catholic parish in Potelych near Rava-Ruska. It is also worth recalling the Union of Men [*Związek Mężów*] — an organization set up in the Rzeszów district in 1835 chiefly by Czechs but also containing in its ranks Poles and Ruthenians (Bazyli Kawski [Vasyl Kavsky] and Mikołaj Mikietewicz [Mykola Mikytevych). The leader of the organization was Jakub Fischer, a graduate of the University of Prague. What is interesting is the organization's radical program arising out of cooperation with the Tarnów branch of the Association of the Polish People, one which envisaged revolution and the subsequent creation of a Slavic state with Prague as its capital. The "Union of Men" was eradicated as a result of a denunciation in 1835 and its leaders arrested.[164]

The Conspirators' Legend

Many Ruthenians participated in the conspiracies of the 1830s. Some are known to us because they were arrested, and the subsequent traces of activity are noted down in court and government acts or merely in the recollections of fellow prisoners. Wacław Czaplicki included in his memoirs an interesting list of all those jailed for conspiratorial acts, beginning with 1833 and ending in 1862. Here we can find figures such as: Kasper Cięglewicz, Dymitr Czubaty (twice), Michał Popiel, Michał Gadziński, Romuald Krzyżanowski, Teodor Kulczycki, Sylwester Miejski, Michał Minczakiewicz, Jan Ochrymowicz, Michał Pokiński, Jan Gudziak, Benedykt Kuszczykiewicz, Marcjan Łapczyński, Mikołaj Hordyński, Bazyli Konstantynowicz, Aleksander Lipiński, and

---

[163] Marian Tyrowicz, "Czubaty Dymitr," in *PSB*, vol. 4 (Cracow, 1938), p. 371; Kieniewicz, *Konspiracje galicyjskie,* p. 185.

[164] Łopuszański, *Stowarzyszenie Ludu,* p. 172–76.

Klemens Mochnacki.[165] A host of other surnames which have a decidedly Ruthenian ring to them are to be found in the index, but a lack of other sources means that we are unable to unequivocally establish their ethnic origin.

The very fact that conspirators, and here Ruthenians of Polish nationality, were arrested was to make quite an impression on Galician society. This is borne out by the recollection of such events in the memoirs of individuals often unassociated with the conspirators themselves.[166] In this way legends came into being of the men themselves as well as the popularization of the notion of conspiratorial struggle for an independent and democratic Poland, as something dreamed of by both Poles and Ruthenians. The greatest icon of his day was Kasper Cięglewicz. Aleksander Morgenbesser wrote with great solemnity about this agitator:

> Cięglewicz, *gente Ruthenus, natione Polonus*, a man of many talents, born into poverty, finished law studies all on this own, and entered into service at the finance office, where he became an ingenious assistant, even receiving a nomination to be a municipal assessor in Jarosław, when he was suddenly imprisoned and kept under police arrest. For it had come to light that Cięglewicz was the propagator of ideas to wrench Poland and Ruthenia away from Austria, out of which an independent Polish state would be formed, and that he would often leave Lviv secretly and spread these aspirations among the Ruthenian populace, and that in a similar spirit he had written instructions for teachers of the Ruthenian language, and these had spread throughout the countryside, inciting the people to revolt against Austria. (…) He was physically an impressive figure of exceptional abilities, with a great fortitude of spirit, who did not distinguish in Galicia between the two patriotisms—the Polish and the Ruthenian—and out of these had forged a single joint patriotism under the name of Poland.[167]

Here it is worth drawing attention to the fact that Cięglewicz was for the inhabitants of Galicia not only a model Polish patriot. His legend was so powerful that he constituted the worst sort of spectre to haunt the Austrian police. When Morgenbesser was interrogated for his conspiratorial involvement, Hoch the legal advisor accused him of taking

---

[165] [Ferdynand M. Władysław Czaplicki] Autor "Powieści o Horożanie," *Pamiętnik więźnia stanu* (Lviv, 1862), pp. 311–32.
[166] The conspirators at the Uniate seminary in Lviv, as well as the youth conspiracy in Sambir, and also Horoszkiewicz and Cięglewicz, are also recalled by Aleksander Morgenbesser, *Wspomnienia z lwowskiego więzienia*, ed. Rafał Leszczyński (Warsaw, 1993), pp. 34–35.
[167] Ibid., pp. 41–42.

Cięglewicz as a model, and warned that he could meet with a similar fate.[168] But it was not only the author of the *Recommendations...* who was to grow to heroic dimensions in diary accounts, but equally all who were like him. As Zbigniew Fras correctly noted:

> These were not merely a local national school, propagating Polishness, teaching language and the history of the fatherland, popularizing the poetry of bards. Conspiratorial acts and the later martyrology of its participants was to also affect the shaping of specific personality models. Such features and traits as courage, sacrifice, and patriotism were to become important merits and virtues enhancing social prestige.[169]

Yet one needs to remember that not simply activity in various types of conspiratorial organizations manifested the "patriotism" of the Ruthenians of Polish nationality mentioned. Some involved themselves in the "Polish" matter in a different way, as Feodosii Steblii pointed out years ago. Here it is worth mentioning the subsequent painter and sculptor Jan Wendziłowicz [Ivan Vendzylovych], who in 1834 took part in the printing of various types of illegal publications (Polish and Ruthenian) at the Ossolineum; or to recall the earlier mentioned Society of Scholars in Przemyśl, which also included Ruthenian members. There the question of Poland's rebirth was also of fundamental interest.[170]

Conspiratorial activities continued in Galicia despite numerous arrests and the liquidation of a series of secret organizations. In the 1840s Edward Dembowski, the future leader of the Cracow uprising in 1846, and the subsequently known conspirator Julian Goslar were to begin their activities in Galicia. Both agitated among the Polish and Ruthenian peasantry, particularly in the area of the environs of Sambir. Goslar even went as far as to translate his revolutionary texts into Ruthenian so that he could have access to local peasants.[171] The largest conspiracy was established in Lviv at the turn of 1845 and 1846. The main goal was to start a new national uprising. The agitators enlisted several hundred (up to 600) inhabitants of Lviv for cooperation, mainly students and craftsmen. On the basis of police files, Volodymyr Borys mentioned in this number also the Ruthenians: a 26-year-old tailor apprentice Teodor Hanas [Fedir Hanas] or a 19-year-old apprentice Konstanty Babycz [Konstiantyn Babych].[172]

---

168 Ibid., p. 48.
169 Fras, *Demokraci*, p. 28.
170 Steblij, "Polskie spiski," p. 110.
171 Herbil's'kyi, *Peredova suspil'na dumka*, pp. 148–53.
172 Borys, "Do historii ruchu społeczno-politycznego studentów," p. 428.

Ultimately, however, the uprising in Lviv did not break out because of the arrest of the conspirators (among them Teofil Wiśniowski, condemned to death), and in Podgórze, the Austrian army shot the leader of the rebellion, Dembowski. But it is important to draw attention to the increased radicalisation of slogans as time progressed. The matter of liberating Poland sometimes became secondary, with priority reserved for demands for general social change and revolution; or national independence was used as a means to achieve these very goals.

The many years of agitation conducted in the countryside, initially directed to motivate the peasantry to fight for an independent Poland, were finally transformed into revolutionary propaganda. Although the peasant uprising of Jakub Szela in 1846 erupted as a result of political, social, economic and especially natural (disasters) factors, it is important to remember that the grounds for the removal of the feudal order had been well prepared by the actions of radical agitators[173]. As we know, during the Galician slaughter peasants killed about 1,000 noblemen and destroyed about 500 manors in the western part of Galicia. The Polish nobility suffered the greatest loss in the Tarnów district, although some disturbances were noted also in Eastern Galicia. The most impressive event took place at the manor house in Velyka Horozhanna. The local Greek Catholic priest, a certain Horodysky, having learned about the insurgents' preparations in the court of Ferdynand Czaplicki, was to advise the village heads from the surrounding villages to report the matter to the Austrian commander in Drohovyzh. A commander advised them to let the peasants trap the plotters until the army reached their destination. This attempt eventually ended with a clash in which the insurgents suffered defeat.[174] The Ukrainian historian Herbilsky drew attention to the circulation of a proclamation written in Ruthenian from the beginning of March 1846 on the border of the Stryi and Sambir districts. This was addressed to the Ruthenian peasantry, and they were encouraged to join the Polish-Ruthenian fraternity and support Jakub Szela's peasant uprising.[175] However, the Ruthenian peasants did

---

[173] Currently, Polish historiography draws attention to four causes of rebellion: poverty in Galicia, agitation of Polish revolutionaries, the use of peasants by the Austrian bureaucracy, and behind-the-scenes activities of foreign powers, especially Russia. See: Krzysztof Ślusarek, "Zanim nadeszła rabacja. Uwagi na temat sytuacji społecznej na wsi galicyjskiej w latach czterdziestych XIX wieku," in *Rok 1846 w Krakowie i Galicji. Odniesienia, interpretacje, pamięć*, eds. Krzysztof K. Daszyk, Tomasz Kargol and Tomasz Szubert (Cracow, 2016), p. 25.

[174] The events in Velyka Horozhanna were described by Ferdynand M. Władysław Czaplicki in the novel *Powieść o Horożanie* (Lviv, 1862). After ten years, the next edition was published: *Rzeź w Horożanie i pamiętnik więźnia stanu* (Cracow, 1872).

[175] Hryhorii Herbil's'kyi, *Rozvytok prohresyvnykh idei v Halychyni u pershii polovyni XIX st. (do 1848 r.)* (Lviv, 1964), p. 26.

not join the Szela uprising, and noblemen in Eastern Galicia (maybe with the exception of the Sanok district, Przemyśl district and part of the Sambir district) did not meet with any misfortune in 1846. Among others, Andriy Zayarnyuk has tried to find an answer to the question why the Ruthenian peasants did not rise against the Polish nobility. He wrote that "it is possible that the Polish revolutionaries were more concerned with the Ruthenian peasants than with their Polish counterparts, whose participation in the uprising [Polish uprising of 1846 – A.Ś.] did not seem so problematic."[176] Following this lead, one might suspect that the democratic agitation of Polish revolutionaries among peasants in Eastern Galicia has succeeded and attracted them to the Polish cause, or at least did not oppose them to it. It would indeed be a phenomenon, but the events of the following years showed that the Ruthenian peasants were not influenced by Polish agitation (they still trusted the Austrian officials and the Greek-Catholic clergy above all). Recently, Krzysztof Ślusarek proposed a new thesis to consider. This author speculates that the genesis of the Galician slaughter was primarily the sum of two factors: "firstly a growing feeling of injustice due to the lack of changes in the legal situation of peasants and an inability to prove their rights in conflicts with the landlords (lengthy procedures); and secondly, the unprecedented poverty of the peasants due to natural disasters."[177] Following this lead, we can suspect that the Ruthenian peasantry probably did not take part in Jakub Szela's rebellion because Eastern Galicia, unlike Western Galicia, had not experienced natural disasters. Therefore, they had no reason to take revenge on the nobility for lack of help.

Regardless, it should be said that the rebellion of Polish peasants influenced the reorientation of the attitude of the Polish gentry toward Galician peasant affairs in general. The distrust of the nobility towards the Polish peasantry in the following years also moved to the Ruthenian peasantry, although the latter did not take part in any anti-feudal rebellion. Andriy Zayarnyuk makes an interesting observation:

> Among the long-lasting effects of 1846 on the Polish and Ruthenian discourses in Galicia was Polish fear of peasants and of social reform, the particular codification of everything plebeian and populist, and the transposition of these codes onto the Ruthenian movement.[178]

---

[176] Andriy Zayarnyuk, *Framing the Ukrainian Peasantry in Habsburg Galicia, 1846–1914* (Edmonton–Toronto, 2013), p. 32. See also: Marian Mudryj, "Nieznana rewolucja. Wydarzenia 1846 roku w Galicji w historiografii ukraińskiej," in *Rok 1846 w Krakowie i Galicji*, p. 271.
[177] Ślusarek, "Zanim nadeszła rabacja," p. 37.
[178] Zayarnyuk, *Framing the Ukrainian Peasantry*, p. 376.

In summary, some attempts to make conscious Poles out of the Ruthenian (and also Polish) peasantry fell completely short of the lofty ideas proclaimed by Polish patriots both in the country and abroad. The Galician slaughter of 1846 appears to have cured many Ruthenian-Polish agitators of proclaiming a radical anti-noble political program. During the period of the Revolutions of 1848, both Julian Horoszkiewicz and Kasper Cięglewicz were much more subdued in their outlooks, with the notion of Polish-Ruthenian brotherhood being created in a different fashion. Volodymyr Borys even considered that:

> (…) the evolution of the socio-political views of these two activists went so far to the right that from, and after, 1848 one can speak about them as conservatives, so drastically had they departed from the basis of many of their views from youth, those that corresponded with the period of Romanticism.[179]

Many Ruthenians participated in the conspiracies of the 1830s and 1840s. They joined their Polish peers in fighting against a partitioning power and system which in their view was the reason for the disadvantaged position of the Galician rural population. Many Ruthenians conspired for the Polish idea because of its link with democratic slogans (at a time when the idea of a separate Ruthenian nationality had yet to develop), while others had a genuine sense of patriotic obligation and duty. The first group, schooled by their experience of fighting the partitioner, would with time step back from supporting Polish national interests and engage in the development of their own sense of nationhood. Here it is worth mentioning at least Vasyl Podolynsky, a member of the Sons of the Fatherland, an activist during the revolutions of 1848, but on the side of the so-called "Saint George's party".[180] The latter group believed in the idea of Poland—a fatherland of Poles and Ruthenians—and were to cultivate this vision right up until the revolutions of 1848, when there appeared at last an opportunity to manifest it openly on the political plane.

---

[179] Borys, "Z dziejów walk," p. 224.
[180] Steblij, "Polskie spiski," p. 117.

Chapter IV
Gente Rutheni, Natione Poloni during the Revolutions of 1848

The Presentation of Polish and Ruthenian Demands to the Austrians

The events of 1848 represented a turning point in the history of Galicia, not merely in the political sense but also with regard to identity. During this period, representatives of the emerging Ruthenian nation outside of the intelligentsia began to appear on the political stage that had only just become accessible to the Gaflician elites. Ruthenians were, for the first time, able to present their own political demands. At the same time the revolutions of 1848 brought about conditions in which members of the *gente Rutheni, natione Poloni* were for the first time able to create a political entity tasked with the realization of their demands, resulting in the establishment of the Ruthenian Sobor. Save for historiographical references, this occurrence has almost completely disappeared into the margins of Polish historical discussion.[1] Recently this matter has aroused the interest of the Ukrainian researcher Marian Mudry, who is at the time of publication preparing a monograph about the organization.[2] The Ruthenian Sobor is proof that *gente Rutheni, natione Poloni* brought a tangible political camp into existence, albeit not an exception-

---

[1] On the subject of the Ruthenian Sobor see especially: Piotr Stebelski, "Lwów w 1848 roku. Na podstawie aktów śledczych," *Kwartalnik Historyczny* 23 (1909), pp. 544–45; Stefan Kieniewicz, *Czyn Polski w dobie Wiosny Ludów*, Biblioteka Historyczna (Warsaw, 1948), p. 85; Jan Kozik, *The Ukrainian National Movement in Galicia 1815–1849*, ed. and introd. Lawrence D. Orton, transl. Andrew Gorski and Lawrence D. Orton (Edmonton, 1986), passim; Jan Kozik, "Stosunki ukraińsko-polskie w Galicji w okresie rewolucji 1848–1849. Próba charakterystyki," *Prace Historyczne* 54: *Z dziejów współpracy Polaków, Ukraińców i Rosjan* (1975), pp. 35–37; Bernadetta Wójtowicz-Huber, *'Ojcowie narodu'. Duchowieństwo greckokatolickie w ruchu narodowym Rusinów galicyjskich (1867–1918)* (Warsaw, 2008), pp. 55–56.
[2] Marian Mudryi, "Rus'kyi sobor 1848 roku. Orhanizatsiia ta chleny," *Ukraïna. Kul'turna spadshchyna, natsional'na svidomist', derzhavnist'* 16: *Iubileinyi zbirnyk na poshanu Ivana Patera* (2008), pp. 107–26; Marian Mudryj, "'Jesteśmy rozdwojonymi członkami jednego ciała'. Do pytannia pro vidnosyny mizh Holovnoiu Rus'koiu Radoiu i Rus'kym Soborom 1848 roku," *Zapysky Naukovoho tovarystva imeni Shevchenka* 265: *Pratsi Istorychno-filosofs'koï sektsiï* (2013), pp. 54–80; Marian Mudryj, "Rus'kyi sobor 1848 roku. Istoriohrafichnyi ta dzhereloznavchnyi ohliad," *Visnyk Lvivs'koho universytetu. Seriia knyhoznavstvo, bibliotekoznavstvo ta informatsiini tekhnolohiï* 8 (2014), pp. 193–206.

ally strong one. This representation of Ruthenians of Polish nationality would not have emerged as a separate body had it not been for the creation of the very first national Ruthenian organization, the Supreme Ruthenian Council, to which the Ruthenian Sobor stood in opposition. 1848 opened a completely new chapter in the history of Galicia, particularly for Ruthenians, who were for the first time able to voice their national demands and vocally identify as a legitimate nation. The contemporary observers of these changes were aware of their significance. Chroniclers placed great store on the year 1848 as the date that the Ruthenian national movement came into being.[3] News of the revolutions breaking out in Palermo, Paris, Vienna, Berlin, Pest, and in Milan itself reached Galicia from January 1847 up to March 1848. The Galician elite were motivated to act because the Hungarians had issued a petition demanding the creation of a nation state within the framework of the Austrian monarchy, the abolition of serfdom, and the introduction of constitutional freedoms. When the unpopular chancellor Metternich was forced to resign under pressure from protesting crowds in Vienna on 15 March 1848, the inhabitants of the larger Galician towns reacted almost immediately with unrest and protest; even the emperor's agreement to the formation of constitutional governments, creation of the National Guard, and press freedoms had little effect. Already by March 18 the Eastern Galician gentry, viewing themselves as the natural choice to lead Galician society, had decided to address the Austrian authorities in a letter. It was not possible, however, to establish a united front. Few noblemen were prepared to give up on serfdom without imposing tenancy on the peasants or obtaining high levels of compensation for the lands for which the peasants were granted property rights.[4] The initiative was taken up at the time by the democratic circles in Lviv, namely the intelligentsia and the bourgeoisie. A well-known Lviv journalist of the Greek Catholic rite, Jan Dobrzański, was asked to compose the letter to the emperor. He, with the help of a few others, edited the missive on the night of March 18. Soon after, the letter was translated into German and delivered to the editorial office of *Dziennik Mód Paryskich*. The next day, crowds of Lviv inhabitants rushed to the newspaper's offices to sign the petition. Among them were representatives of almost every social estate (with the exception of the peasants), nation, and denomination, including landowners and Ruthenians concentrated around the

[3] See for example Aleksander Morgenbesser, *Wspomnienia z lwowskiego więzienia*, ed. Rafał Leszczyński (Warsaw, 1993), p. 67.

[4] Marian Stolarczyk, *Działalność Lwowskiej Centralnej Rady Narodowej. W świetle źródeł polskich* (Rzeszów, 1994), p. 64.

figure of Aleksander Fredro. Stefan Kieniewicz has estimated that up to 12,000 signatures in total were collected.[5] Among the thirteen demands outlined in the petition were "the guaranteeing of Polish nationality, and so the removal of all the limitations standing as a hindrance to its free development, the introduction of Polish as a language in schools, the courts, and government offices," the implementation of a separate administration, the establishment of a diet with representatives of all estates, the organization of a National Guard, and the abolition of serfdom.[6]

In order to get these points across to the non-Polish-speaking population, the petition was also translated into Ruthenian and printed in both Cyrillic and Latin script.[7] However, it is important to note that these demands did not touch upon any national interests of the Ruthenian population whatsoever; indeed, the Ruthenian translation of the demand for a guarantee of the rights of the Polish nation and the Polonization of the school system and administration can be seen as thoroughly paradoxical. This problem was immediately spotted by Leon Sapieha, who considered himself to be Ruthenian because of his place of birth. His secretary, Julian Horoszkiewicz, a *gente Ruthenus, natione Polonus*, recounted a conversation he had with him at the time:

> When I told him what the petition said, that we demand Polish as the language in schools and administration, he noted, "this is becoming foolish, as Ruthenians are demanding the same for the Ruthenian language." I was taken aback by the statement and pointed out that every educated person in eastern Galicia uses Polish in the family; Ruthenian priests speak Polish in church; Ruthenian seminarians have always belonged to patriotic associations and Polish conspiratorial circles; Ruthenian priests come from the Polish gentry, for which the ability to marry constituted the reason; the peasants to a man understand and in the majority speak Polish, so for whom would there be a need for Ruthenian schools?
>
> "All of this might be true and sufficient," said the prince, "if the German language ruled over us, but given that today we demand Polish as the primary language, then it is obvious that for the Ruthenians this would be an affront if these same freedoms were not bestowed on the Ruthenian tongue." The discussion continued in this vein, but the prince stubbornly explained his rationale from the vantage point of this being a Ruthenian land in which Ruthenians were at least entitled to equal

---

[5] Kieniewicz, *Czyn Polski*, p. 75.
[6] "Najjaśniejszy Panie", LNNBU, fond 76: Kolektsiia Pavlikovs'kykh, op. 3: Arkhiv Pavlikovs'kykh, spr. 276: Zbiór materiałów dotyczących wydarzeń politycznych w Galicji 1848 r., 1847–1849, pp. 26–26v.
[7] Cf. ibid., pp. 27–27v and 28–28v.

rights which—as it seemed to him—they would most certainly demand if such petitions came from Polish quarters.[8]

Leon Sapieha's words would be proven correct barely a month later, even without the help of the partial inclusion of Ruthenian interests in the new petition of April 6. The overlooking of Ruthenians resulted in a lack of enthusiasm for the Polish undertakings on the part of the Greek Catholic Church hierarchy, which had adopted a loyalist position in relation to the monarchy and offered little support to those calling for democratic change. The contingent of Polonized Ruthenian elite approved of the demands for political reconstruction of the state and supported the actions undertaken by the Lviv democrats. Even though Ruthenians (excluding Jan Dobrzański) did not take part in the drafting of the petition, they were present in the delegation that addressed Franz Stadion, the governor of Galicia. Alongside Aleksander Fredro and Leon Sapieha were other *gente Rutheni, natione Poloni*, including Jan Dobrzański, Cyryl Curkiewicz [Kyrylo Tsurkevych], the government official Samuel Leligdowicz, and the Greek Catholic priest Onufry Krynicki. There were also Protestants and Jews included in the delegation. Under Stadion's balcony, as Aleksander Batowski noted, "the crowd swelled and rose to 20,000 people."[9] Support for the demands, along with the issue of an amnesty for all political prisoners, was met most enthusiastically in Lviv. The petition was sent on to other towns in Galicia where it was signed by more people still.

A National Committee was organized on March 20, which while not legalized by Stadion was at least recognized by him as the instrument that would create the National Guard. It was composed of Lviv's democratic elite, including Jan Dobrzański, Leszek Dunin-Borkowski, Tomasz Kulczycki, Aleksander Fredro, and Father Onufry Krynicki.[10] Similar organizations began to be founded in other Galician towns based on the model of the Lviv National Committee. This organ was to become the political representation of the nation in a similar way to how this had come about in Hungary, and would bring about the realization of the demands listed in the petition. From its very inception it aimed to win over all ethnic groups to allow for the implementation of the necessary changes. Julian Aleksander Kamiński made such an appeal in one of the Committee's documents:

---

[8] Julian Horoszkiewicz, *Notatki z życia*, ed. Henryk Wereszycki (Wrocław–Cracow, 1957), pp. 236–37.
[9] Aleksander Batowski, *Diariusz wypadków 1848 roku*, ed., introd. and footnotes Marian Tyrowicz (Wrocław–Warsaw–Cracow–Gdańsk, 1974), p. 93.
[10] Stolarczyk, *Działalność*, p. 69.

Love each other Masurians, Ruthenians, Germans, and Jews, let language not divide you, for it is one land that nourishes you, a single law all shall serve. Let language, differences in faith or dress not divide, give each other your hand in a sign of brotherhood and come together while ceasing the oppression of one by another. The avarice of the Jews shall disappear for they will be your brothers. (...)
Ruthenian brothers! The Masurian is your brother, do not sever the close tie of blood bonds. Speak your language, preserve your customs and freedoms, for these differences should never divide us; for from a single cutting have grown both of these branches and the strong boughs that constitute the one Polish nation.[11]

The governor of Galicia soon noticed the strength of the National Committee and immediately set about weakening it. On March 22 Florian Ziemiałkowski and Józef Dzierzkowski were arrested together with a series of other particularly active individuals, causing violent protests in Lviv and other Galician towns. Under the pressure of these demonstrations, Stadion released the detainees.

Finally, on March 26 the "petition delegation" composed of 34 members set off from Lviv to Vienna. On the way they stopped off in Przemyśl, Rzeszów, Tarnów, Brzesko, Bochnia, and Cracow, in each town meeting with enthusiastic inhabitants and welcoming further numbers, including peasants, into their delegation. Its composition ultimately reflected an array of social estates and denominations. Among the members were Cyryl Wieńkowski [Kyrylo Vienkovsky] and Father Onufry Krynicki, both Ruthenians of Polish orientation.[12] As Marian Stolarczyk wrote:

(...) the petition expressed the notion of compromise articulated by people of various beliefs, nationalities, and language, in the face of the Russian danger and the possibility of a return to autocratic government in Austria. This petition revived the Polish spirit, restoring the significance of human brotherhood which was supposed to find its manifestation in freedom, namely the obtaining of freedom by the Polish nation.[13]

Seventeen years after the defeat of the November Uprising, dreams about autonomy once again became realistic without the need for

[11] Julian Alexander Kamiński, "Co to się stało we Lwowie?," TsDIAU, fond 474: Kolektsiia dokumentiv pro pol's'ki povstannia 1830–1831 ta 1848 rr., op. 1, spr. 15: Vidozvy, zvernennia i proklamatsiï pol's'kykh i ukraïns'kykh suspil'no-politychnykh, students'kykh ta relihiinykh tovarystv i orhanizatsiï u m. Lvovi periodu revoliutsiï 1848 roku, pp. 29–31.
[12] "Protokół Obrad Deputacyi polskiej sporządzony przez F. Ziemiałkowskiego zacząwszy od 29 marca tj. przybycia do Krakowa do 16 kwietnia tj. odjazdu części Deputacyi do Lwowa", TsDIAU, fond 93: Zemialkovs'kyi Florian 1817–1900 rr., op. 1, od. zb. 5: Protokoly narad pol's'koï deputatsiï u Krakovi ta Vidni, pp. 5–6.
[13] Stolarczyk, *Działalność*, p. 76.

bloodshed. The matter of Polish independence was openly discussed at the meeting of the petition committee, as Florian Ziemiałkowski noted in his report.[14]

In Vienna, under pressure from the representatives of the Cracow National Committee, as well as émigrés and activities of the National Central Committee from Poznań, a new petition was drafted on April 6.[15] In the introduction it was emphasized that the "ultimate goal" of Polish aspirations was a sovereign Poland. It strove not simply for the emergence of Galicia within the framework of the Habsburg Monarchy as an independent province, but also for its unity with Congress Poland under Austrian tutelage. All of this was to occur as a result of expected war between Austria and Russia. Included also in the petition were points on the implementation of education in national languages, i.e., in Polish and Ruthenian. This was certainly the work of Cyryl Wieńkowski and the direct result of his presence in the delegation. He argued not only for the equal treatment of Greek and Roman Catholics as well as Polish and Ruthenian as languages, but also for equal treatment of the various social classes in the name of the greater good which, under Wieńkowski's understanding, constituted a nation.[16]

The inclusion of the point on Polish and Ruthenian education was undoubtedly progress in relation to the previous petition. The authors were making efforts to meet the educational needs of Ruthenians. However, it soon became apparent that these initiatives did little to win favour with the Greek Catholic hierarchy in Galicia. Florian Ziemiałkowski noted that the representatives of Galicia sent to Vienna were unaware of this, writing in his diary on April 7:

> We also discussed our Ruthenians. Wieńkowski assured us that our Ruthenians have no sympathies with Russia, they only frighten Germans and Poles with this notion in order to bargain a few freedoms and a guarantee as such of their nationality. Now when Poles have genuinely taken the public move to fraternize as brothers with Ruthenians there is not only no danger of them linking up with Russia, but even the hope that Ruthenians will kindly grow to like us.[17]

---

[14] TsDIAU, fond 93, op. 1, od. zb. 5, pp. 8–9.

[15] "Podanie Polakow z Galicyi i Krakowskiego złożone w Wiedniu u stop tronu Jego Cesarskiej Mości," 6 Apr. 1848, LNNBU, fond 76, op. 3, spr. 276, p. 40; Marian Zgórniak, *Za Waszą i naszą wolność* (Warsaw, 1987), p. 34.

[16] TsDIAU, fond. 93, op. 1, od. zb. 5, pp. 16–17, 20.

[17] Ibid., spr. 6: Shchodennyk Zemialkovs'koho F. – chlena i sekretaria deputatsiï vid pol's'ko-shliakhets'kykh kil Halychyny u Vidni, p. 28. In the printed version of *Scho-dennyk* (Florian Ziemiałkowski, *Pamiętniki*, part 2: *1848*, (Cracow, 1904) p. 54–55) there is another citation of the last part of Ziemiałkowski's statement: "Now when Poles have

Missing from Ziemiałkowski's entry was any relevant insight into the Ruthenian question, possibly the result of simply too much trust in Wieńkowski, who through his involvement in the development of events and democratic activities created the impression that the Ruthenian intelligentsia held similar views to his own. For this very reason the Ruthenian question was not the primary focus of the petition, as is demonstrated by Ziemiałkowski's report from the petition commission in Vienna.[18] The greatest controversy among the delegation members was caused by the matter of the abolition of serfdom, which had been proclaimed by the petition of March 19. Unable to reach an agreement, it was finally decided that a future diet would regulate the matter.[19]

The Linking of the Ruthenian Question with the Peasantry

The peasantry was a dangerous topic during the revolutions of 1848, as it was feared that the peasants might be used — as with the uprising of 1846 — against the Polish political movement. There was a deep concern that imperial civil servants could once again rouse the peasantry against the nobility. For Polish democratic activists it was obvious that the peasant question had to be dealt with before the Austrian side decided to take matters into their own hands. On the night of 5 April 1848, Wiktor Heltman formulated an address to the landed classes in which he called for the waiving of serfdom for Easter, which fell on April 23 (April 11 according to the old calendar). However, only a few decided to adhere to the appeal.[20] Two of the first landowners to revoke peasant service on their estates were Adam Czartoryski and Władysław Sanguszko. Other owners followed their example, but in total their number was a mere hundred.[21] Galician democrats placed great score on the revocation of serfdom, as they saw it as the condition *sine qua non* to enable the peasantry's involvement in national matters. At the same time, the Austrian administration were trying to convince the peasantry that it was the emperor alone who had the right to repeal serfdom; thus,

---

genuinely taken the public move to fraternize as brothers with the Ruthenians there is not only no danger of them linking up with Russia but even the hope that Muscovite Ruthenians will kindly grow to like us." In the original there was no information about "Muscovite Ruthenians" but only about Ruthenians – by implication – Galician Ruthenians, which changes the sense.

[18] Ibid., od. zb. 5, pp. 26–27.

[19] Ibid., spr. 4: Shchodennyk (frakhmenty), p. 10.

[20] Zgórniak, *Za Waszą*, p. 35.

[21] Stolarczyk, *Działalność*, p. 71; Kieniewicz, *Czyn Polski*, p. 83.

those landowners who had "revoked" the practice on their estates had no jurisdiction to enforce such a policy. The democrats consequently undertook a two-pronged campaign, attempting to convince more landowners to renounce serfdom while trying to demonstrate to the peasantry that it was the Polish lords in their magnanimity who had voluntarily agreed to this. They made use of the press, and in particular *Dziennik Mód Paryskich*, which in subsequent April issues advanced the case for the abolition of serfdom in various ways. The published articles were addressed to both the landowners and the "beloved peasant brothers."[22] Of special interest is the poem allegedly written by a Ruthenian peasant residing near the Medobory (Podilski Tovtry) mountain range, and published on April 8:

Let God reward you, oh Lords!
for this divine decision:
Calling brothers brothers
we shall be unharmed![23]

The author addressed unity and brotherhood, writing: "the unity of compatriots—the unity that is the anchor of our prosperity, who from among the Poles would not enlist beneath this standard of salvation?"[24]

At the same time, activities were undertaken to raise awareness in the East Galician countryside. This was chiefly conducted by Kasper Cięglewicz, who under the pseudonym "Baltazar Szczucki" or "Baltasar Shchutsky" produced a number of appeals to the Ruthenian population. Imprisoned since the end of the 1830s, he was released as a result of the amnesty granted on 31 March 1848 and immediately set to work.[25] He wrote his works in Ruthenian, though often in the Latin script. Of particular importance is his significant address dated 26 March 1848 and entitled *To my Brothers, the People of Galicia* [*Do moich bratej ludu Hałyckaho*].[26] Cięglewicz also published this in Cyrillic.[27] The

---

[22] *Dziennik Mód Paryskich* no. 17 (22 Apr. 1848), pp. 134–36.

[23] "Głos ludu z Podola," *Dziennik Mód Paryskich* no. 15 (8 Apr. 1848), pp. 120–21.

[24] "Słów kilka o wychowaniu wiejskiego ludu," *Dziennik Mód Paryskich* no. 16 (15 Apr. 1848), pp. 125–26; "Głos ludu z Podola," *Dziennik Mód Paryskich* no. 15 (8 Apr. 1848), pp. 120–21.

[25] Władysław Tadeusz Wisłocki, Zofia Horoszkiewicz, "Cięglewicz Kasper Melchior Baltazar," in *PSB*, vol. 6 (Cracow, 1938), p. 71.

[26] [Kasper Cięglewicz] Baltazar Szczucki, *Do moich bratej ludu Hałyckaho*, ([Lviv] Buchach, 1848). See also: [Kasper Cięglewicz] Baltazar Szczucki, *Do moich bratej ludu Hałyckaho*, LNNBU, fond 76, op. 3, spr. 276, pp. 29–30.

[27] [Kasper Cięglewicz], *Do moyh bratei liudu Halytskoho!*, ibid., fond 9: Okremi nadkhodzhennia, spr. 2295: Zbirka vidozv, oholoshen', statutiv tovarystv, vypysky z hazet ta in., p. 159.

author deliberately used the Julian Calendar, so it should be correctly dated April 7—that is, the day after Heltman's appeal.

Cięglewicz tried in his address to shatter the widespread myth that the nobility would "(…) loot, burn your villages, killing and conducting other atrocities on [their subjects]."[28] Not only did he try to convince the peasants to stop believing such rumours, but he sought to demonstrate that the masters and peasants were brothers, and what is more that Ruthenians were equal to Poles. He argued the latter point by noting that the name for Poles is derived from the word for field [Polish *pole*]:

> Brothers! Do not believe these hypocrites after all, the Poles are your brothers, born on the same land, for you yourselves are Poles and who-ever calls you differently is mistaken. The word Pole has its origin in the Slavic for "field", from plots, and there are more fields and plots here with us than other nations have, and therefore we are known by other nations as Poles.[29]

Besides raising awareness among the Ruthenian peasantry on the matter of their identity, the primary objective of the appeal was to convince the people that it was the nobility, having gathered on 18 March 1848 in Lviv, who had submitted the application to the emperor for the abolition of serfdom.[30]

Kasper Cięglewicz was not alone in stirring up the countryside in order to win the Ruthenian peasantry over to the Polish national cause. Two days after issuing the first appeal, Jan Karol Cybulski produced another, writing under the pseudonym "Ivan the Smith of Tovmach [to-day Tlumach,] Kavetsky." The adoption of Ruthenian surnames written in the language of the ordinary people was a means of gaining greater credibility in the villages, though it was as much a ruse to convince the intended audience that they were being championed by their own people.

The appeal *To my Ruthenian Brothers!* [*Do moich Bratej Rusyniw!*], dated 28 March (though certainly produced later) sought to make the peas-ants aware of the fact that the Austrian administration was deliberately deceiving them by suggesting that the landowners who had initially abolished serfdom did not have any right to do so:

> (…) when a good and rich master [i.e., nobleman] immediately abol-ished this burdensome serfdom, the peasants already began their re-volt against him: "the master had no right to abolish serfdom, do not

---

28 [Cięglewicz] Szczucki, *Do moich bratej*, p. 1.
29 Ibid.
30 Ibid., p. 2.

believe the Poles, for this is betrayal—they want to instigate revolt against the Emperor." And so the peasant became confused (…). Elsewhere something else was said. For example, where the master was poor or impoverished and thus was unable to immediately free you [from serfdom] for he had nothing to sow [the field] with; there the estate manager would say: "See you poor little things, for [other] people serfdom has been abolished while you still labour, so do not believe the Poles, be patient a little longer, and when the emperor himself liberates you, then you will know that neither we nor our children will have to work off the yoke of serfdom" (…).[31]

Cybulski, in a similar way to Cięglewicz, attacked the rumours that Poles had planned an attack on the *tsisar* [emperor] and had taken to plundering the countryside. In addition, he tried to make the peasants aware that the abolition of serfdom would happen for certain, but only thanks to the will of the Polish masters "for it is their property."

If it were not for "(…) the Poles, not for the Lachs as you call them, then you would be with your German administrators and in 200 years you would not be free."[32] Cybulski concluded his address by pointing out that Poles and Ruthenians had already lived together for centuries and that any injustices the peasants had known at the hands of the masters would be completely compensated for by the abolition of serfdom.[33]

In reality, the process was not as simple as the Galician democrats had announced to the Ruthenian peasants. The contingent of landowners who were not inclined to revoke serfdom without compensation had it in their vested interests to direct the matter to the emperor for evaluation. Stadion decided to quickly take advantage of the delay and unwillingness on the part of many landowners, announcing on April 22 that by the order of the emper-

19. The cover of Kasper Cięglewicz's Dialogue of a Masurian and a Ruthenian

---

[31] [Jan Karol Cybulski] Iwan Kawećkyj, *Do moich Bratej Rusyniw!* (Tłumach, 1848), p. 2, TsDIAU, fond 474, op. 1, spr. 15, pp. 27–29.

[32] Ibid., p. 3.

[33] Ibid., p. 4.

or serfdom would be abolished on May 15. The document was pre-dated April 17. This was a severe blow to the Lviv democrats in their efforts to win over Ruthenians, therefore recourse was made to propaganda. The Lviv activists had to try to prove to the peasants that it was the masters who had repealed serfdom and not Austrian government officers, although in most cases the throwing off of the yoke of serfdom was only to take place after the Austrian law came into force. The propaganda took the form of leaflets, small poems, and other simple literary forms which were more accessible to the rural population.

Kasper Cięglewicz argued in one of the leaflets that the Polish gentry had wanted to abolish serfdom during the ratification of the Constitution of the Third of May (1791), but the partitioning powers had forbidden this. He also tried to explain the origins of the gentry, arguing that their lineage could be traced to the Cossacks who had distinguished themselves through their courage and received land from the king as thanks. Hence the Potocki lived in Potok, the Dzieduszycki in the Didushychi lands, and the Borkowski family in Birky. Cięglewicz deliberately listed names that were well known in Galicia. In his historical reckoning, the "Cossacks" had fought in defence of the land, while the peasants had cultivated it and therein incurred no costs whatsoever. The situation of the common people had deteriorated only under the partition rule of Russia and Prussia, which had incited Maria Theresa to join in the division.[34]

Often the peasant imagination was more effectively stimulated by literary works than leaflets, particularly those distinguished by a simplicity of expression. An interesting example is the literary dialogue by Szczucki in which a Polish peasant (Masurian) and a Ruthenian (Rusin) head for Lviv as a result of the founding of the National Central Council. Striking up a conversation, they speak of how the lord had freed them from serfdom, yet how later a civil servant who had come to the village claimed that it was he who had freed the peasants from serfdom, and not the masters:

The Masurian:
(…) Well, you must know, you yokel, that our master has presented us with his land, so… *(the Ruthenian interrupts)*

The Ruthenian:
And our master, God bless him, has also given us land.

---

[34] Baltazar Szczucki, *Widkie sia wziała slachta, pany, panszczyzna i piddani*, LNNBU, fond 76, op. 3, spr. 280: Zbiór różnych materiałów dotyczących wydarzeń społeczno-politycznych 1848 r., pp. 71–72b.

The Masurian:

So here's how it was after our master had given us his land: some official, petty bureaucrat, turns up from the district council or some such and starts carrying on like he'd given us the plots himself. And so our master has it out with this paper pusher that this just isn't the case, and he's not going to let this clerk mess up the image of the Emperor himself, for now the Emperor's made it big time getting pushed up the ranks to king, and for this very reason he doesn't lay a hand on anything that is not his, because... *(the Ruthenian interrupts)*

The Ruthenian:

Yes, yes, yes – we've had the same sort of fuss, it was exactly the same between the estate commissar and the master, it almost came to fisticuffs. Alas, but how clever they think they are now—when the master presented us with the land, the officials from the *cyrkuł* [*Bezirk*, district – A.Ś.]) wanted to make the peasant look a right Charlie. They wanted us to buy into the idea that it was not the masters but they themselves, the clerks, who had handed the land over to us. (...)

The Masurian:

Oh, you're not telling porkies, my old mucker! Get an earful of this: when our master had that terrible run in with them there officials from the *cyrkuł*, he said then, he did, to all who had gathered around (a crowd): Listen brothers! Just to put your minds at rest that it was no one else but me who out of total free will gave over the land to you, you shall go to Lviv to the National Council and there you'll be convinced of the worth of the words I speak now. (...)[35]

This sort of publication was not only designed to convince the peasants that they had known favour not from Austria but from their own landlords, but even more so to draw them onto the side constituting the Galician political movement.

Lviv agitators set the goal of not only winning the support of the Polish peasantry but also the Ruthenian rural population. Therefore, these leaflets and appeals present a picture of good relations existing between Ruthenian and Polish peasants (systematically referred to as Masurians, as Ruthenians and Masurians were to be two parts of the Polish nation). The stakes were extremely high. It was understood within Polish democratic circles that the peasants in Galicia did not yet have a developed sense of national identity, but without doubt it was the Greek Catholic clergy that commanded the greatest respect and wielded the greatest authority in rural areas. Therefore, much pressure

---

[35] [Kasper Cięglewicz] Baltazar Szczucki, *Rusin i Mazur. Dyalog przez Bałtazara Szczuckiego* (Lviv, 1848), pp. 4–5.

was placed on raising peasant awareness, an initiative that could only be carried out by people who could function in both cultures, Polish and Ruthenian, and who were committed to the Polish national idea. Cięglewicz and Cybulski, the authors of numerous leaflets directed towards the ordinary Ruthenian people, were two figures who embodied such characteristics.

Ruthenians in the Central National Council

In the meantime, members of the petition delegation began to return to Lviv, unable to wait indefinitely in Vienna for the realization of demands they had put to the emperor. The monarch had promised to favourably address the Galician delegation's demands,[36] but ultimately passed them on to his ministers in Vienna. Thus the matter was further delayed until May 29, when the prime minister, Franz von Pillersdorf, announced that the majority of the demands would be addressed in the constitution of April 25.[37]

This time-saving manoeuvre allowed the Austrian governor in Lviv to act. In the hope of gaining the support of the Galician landowners, Franz Stadion betrayed his earlier statements and decided to again assemble the estate diet, composed exclusively of landowners. However, this was a body with extremely limited powers, which shattered the plans to create an autonomous Galician Diet where every social stratum would have been represented. Hoping to oppose the plans of the Galician Austrian authorities, a meeting was called on April 14 at the editorial offices of Dziennik Mód Paryskich, in which it was decided to create a political body to represent the interests of Galicia's inhabitants: the Central National Council.[38]

The press organ of this newly formed organization was to be the journal Rada Narodowa [National Council] (later reshaped into Gazeta Narodowa [National Gazette]), which would not only act as a mouthpiece for public opinion but would guarantee the realization and development of the demands laid out in the petitions of March 18 and April 6. Among those instrumental in the paper's launch were the most dedicated activists of the revolutions of 1848, including the Greek Catholic Father Onufry Krynicki, the Basilian Mykola Ustyianovych, as well as the relatively unknown Antym Nikorovych, quite possibly also

---

[36] Stolarczyk, Działalność, pp. 77–79.
[37] Zgórniak, Za Waszą, p. 34.
[38] Stolarczyk, Działalność, pp. 87–90.

a Ruthenian.[39] Marian Stolarczyk has been able to establish that the Central National Council together with its district "branches" (the so-called District National Councils) had 170 members.[40] Today it is difficult to ascertain how many of these individuals were of Ruthenian origin, as we do not have at our disposal sources pointing to their identity or even denominational affiliations. That being said, Ruthenians were undoubtedly present in this initiative. It is worth mentioning those members who proved most active: Father Onufry Krynicki (a participant at the inaugural meeting of April 14),[41] Michał Obuszkiewicz [Mykhailo Obushkevych], Denys Zubrytsky, and the doctor of law Cyryl Wieńkowski. The minutes of the Central National Council meetings shed light on a series of other surnames of those involved in the organization. The minutes from the meeting of 21 April 1848 mention a certain Teofil Ostaszewski, who suggested that the Council's meeting be moved to a private flat where the Ruthenian Anastazy Kotowski [Anastasii Kotovsky] was chosen as treasurer.[42] Jan Kozik has established that during the initial sittings, held in a variety of locations, Ruthenians of different political persuasions and with little to no Polish affinity participated in the meetings. In Stanyslaviv the following priests were active: Bazyli Lewicki [Vasyl Levytsky], Jan Mogielnicki [Ivan Mohylnytsky], Jan Łękawski [Ivan Lenkavsky], Michał Gadziński [Mykhailo Gadzynsky], Mikołaj Piotrowski [Mykola Piotrovsky], Jan Iradajski [Ivan Iradaisky] and Aleksy Nawrocki [Oleksii Navrotsky]; in Berezhany: Teofil Pawlikow [Teofil Pavlykiv], Anton Leżohubski [Anton Lezhohubsky], Sylwester Leżohubski [Sylvestr Lezhohubsky], Bazyli Lityński [Vasyl Litynsky], Teodor Dżułyński [Teodor Dzulynsky], Hipolit Kaszubiński [Ipolyt Kashubinsky], J. Kwasnycki [I. Kvasnytsky], Bazyli Petrowicz [Vasyl Petrovych], Lew Połowy [Lev Polovy], Łopuszański [Lopushansky], Niżankowski [Nyzhankivsky], and Grzegorz Sawczyński [Hryhorii Savchynsky][43]. For a brief time, Uniate clergy also operated in each

---

[39] "Prospekt," LNNBU, fond 5: Zbirka rukopysiv, avtohrafiv, hramot i dyplomiv biblioteky Natsional'noho zakladu im. Ossolins'kykh i m. Lvovi, op. 1: Rukopysy, spr. 5792/III: "Rok 1848. Dokumenty, autografy, listy XIX w.", p. 11.

[40] Stolarczyk, *Działalność*, pp. 99–100.

[41] Franciszek Smolka, *Dziennik Franciszka Smolki 1848–1849 w listach do żony*, ed. and introd. Stanisław Smolka (Warsaw–Lublin–Łódź–Cracow, 1913), p. 267 (Entries for the years).

[42] *Protokoły posiedzeń Rady Narodowej Centralnej we Lwowie (14 Apr.–29 Oct. 1848)*, eds. Stefan Kieniewicz and Franciszka Ramotowska, prepared for printing Adam Gałkowski [et al.] (Warsaw, 1996), pp. 25–26.

[43] Jan Kozik, *Między reakcją a rewolucją. Studia z dziedziny ukraińskiego ruchu narodowego w Galicji w latach 1848–1849* (Cracow, 1975), p. 39. (In the English edition of Kozik's work there is no list of Greek Catholic priests. Cf. Kozik, *The Ukrainian National Movement*.)

council, at least until a ban was imposed on 12 May 1848 by Hryhorii Iakhymovych on the governor's recommendation.

It is important to note that there was no shortage of representatives of landed families with Ruthenian roots in the Central National Council, albeit ones who were completely Polonized, such as Leon Sapieha or Antoni Golejewski.[44] Of course, many representatives of the Polish landed gentry in Eastern Galicia as well as members of the intelligentsia considered themselves to be Ruthenians only because of where they lived.[45] Many family lines were descended from boyar families, yet when the matter concerned identity they in no way differed from the Polish landed gentry, families who had been Polonized and Latinized for ages[46].

Neither the Ruthenians working alongside Polish democrats nor the Galician landed gentry that cited its Ruthenian origins were, however, a representative force for Galician Ruthenians in general, and in particular they were not legitimate partners for the Greek Catholic elites concentrated around the Cathedral of St. George in Lviv. In fact, it was the Uniate clergy, as Bernadetta Wójtowicz-Huber wrote in her monograph, that had taken on the role of "fathers of the [Ruthenian] nation" which was forming at this time.[47] For Ruthenian nationality had not been an "Austrian invention" but had, in the words of Kieniewicz, grown "under the influence of the spirit of the times from its own ethno-cultural foundations, with only the policies of the partitioning powers turning it against Poland."[48]

On Stadion's initiative the Uniate clergy, with the bishop of Przemyśl Hryhorii Iakhymovych, at its head, wrote their own petition to the emperor on 19 April 1848 in which they expressed their loyalty to the throne

---

A list of those selected to the National Council in Berezhany of 19 April 1848 names, among others, Father Kaszubiński and Teofil Pawlików. See in: "Lista członków Rady Narodowej w Brzeżanach", LNNBU, fond. 5, op. 1, spr. 5792/III, p. 27.

[44] Cf. Batowski, *Diariusz*, pp. 148–52.

[45] Cf. Maciej Janowski, *Polska myśl liberalna do 1918 roku* (Cracow, 1988), p. 115; Michał Jagiełło, *Narody i narodowości. Przewodnik po lekturach*, vol. 1 (Warsaw, 2010), p. 25.

[46] Another point of view on the identity of the landed gentry in Eastern Galicia is presented by Marian Mudryi. He also counts Galician landowners as *gente Rutheni, natione Poloni* (cf.: Marian Mudryj, „Adam Świątek, *Gente Rutheni, natione Poloni. Z dziejów Rusinów narodowości polskiej w Galicji*, Cracow 2014, Księgarnia Akademicka, ss. 512, il. Studia Galicyjskie 3" [review], *Kwartalnik Historyczny* 123, no. 4 (2016), pp. 859–60). Stefan Kieniewicz wrote about the intentional adherence to the Ruthenians by Leon Sapieha. For Sapieha, the priority was not to divide Galicia, so during the Slavic congress in Prague, "he joined the Ruthenians." Stefan Kieniewicz, *Adam Sapieha 1828–1903* (Warsaw, 1993), p. 17–18.

[47] Wójtowicz-Huber, *'Ojcowie narodu,'* p. 10.

[48] Kieniewicz, *Czyn Polski*, p. 84.

and renounced cooperation with Polish activists. They demanded only concessions on matters of culture and language, distancing themselves from any political claims. Jan Kozik argued that the petition was drawn up because the offer extended to Ruthenians by the Central National Council had not been satisfactory. The discussion at the Council session of April 14 ended with a motion to develop special appeals to the Ruthenians and consistories, but in a later letter nothing more than a general guarantee of legal equality was envisaged. As revealed by the minutes of the Central National Council meeting,[49] the discussion of the appeal to Ruthenian priests was conducted by Dobrzański, Fredro, Ustyianovych, and Father Onufry Krynicki, the latter of whom was the main supporter of maintaining an accord between the Roman and Greek Catholic clergy.[50] However, only after the drafting of the Ruthenian petition on April 19 was Seweryn Smarzewski's proposal for equal status for the Ruthenian language in schools, the courts, and consistories ratified at the session of the Central National Council on April 24.[51] This ratification had come far too late.

This did not mean, however, that there was a lack of cooperative initiative or of willingness to understand Ruthenian interests on the Polish side. Such intentions may be clearly seen, for instance, in the article "From the National Council to Ruthenian Brothers" ["Od Rady Narodowej do Braci Rusinów"] from the first issue of *Rada Narodowa*:[52]

> For centuries two mighty boughs of a single powerful tribe have grown next to each other in Poland: Poles and Ruthenians—peoples in mixed residence, joined by equality in customs as well as numerous family bonds, praising God at the same altar—ostensibly harmonious and favourably inclined toward each other they, nonetheless, partially foster hostile feelings which are mutually hidden. To eradicate these [negative] feelings with full force, rooting them out remains one of our main tasks. Hence, we Poles call out to you brother Ruthenians. Be of aid to us in this undertaking that is favourable to people and God. We consequently extend a fraternal hand—take it with the same open heart with which it is given. If we do not know each other well enough then let us be acquainted. If we have affronted each other, then forgive us. Let equality everywhere and in all things be our emblem and goal. Our intentions are sincere, let yours, oh brothers of ours, become the same. If you see, if you notice any obstacle to this universal reconciliation, expose it openly. We shall eagerly take all comments on board. We shall try to remove the

---

[49] *Protokoły posiedzeń*, p. 1.

[50] Marian Tyrowicz, "Krynicki Onufry," in *PSB*, vol. 15 (Wrocław–Warsaw–Cracow, 1970), p. 463.

[51] *Protokoły posiedzeń*, p. 27. Cf. also: Kozik, *The Ukrainian National Movement*, pp. 335–36.

[52] *Rada Narodowa* no. 1 (19 Apr. 1848), p. 2.

causes of any justified accusations, while the unjustified we shall not fail to explain.[53]

It is impossible for this text to have been written after the announcement of the petition on April 19 (in fact, it was written the very same day), for its tone is not confrontational. It constitutes a genuine appeal for joint cooperation between Poles and Ruthenians. Possibly the proclamation was inspired by the growing tension observed in Lviv, but it is most certainly not a reply on the part of Central National Council circles to the petition of the Ruthenian clergy. The appeal continues:

> To you we are appealing, to you the Fathers of the people, spiritual pastors of both the Latin and the Greek rite—to you, oh you, the leading consistories, who wish to become guides on this meritorious road.
> Alongside us, utilize those strengths which the notion of a higher education has bestowed upon you in order that the intended deed be done. Give an example to the entrusted peoples of our solicitude for unity and equality in every way and at every position, while the people will know with their heart to support each other through mutual aid. And God's blessing will manifest itself as brotherly love, in which henceforth will lie only the prosperity and might of the nations.[54]

Cooperation with the Ruthenians was understood as an essential element in the gaining of independence. There was hope that in the near future Poland would rise again in its pre-partition form. The address given by Seweryn Celarski illustrates this hope. Delivered during the morning service of April 25, Celarski prayed, "Almighty God! We beseech you to bestow on Poland, Rus', and Lithuania a long and glorious life, blessed be your people (…)."[55]

A week later, during the meeting of the Central National Council, the member Piotr Wasilewski appealed "to make the Ruthenian nation tangible, by adopting the lion as its coat of arms and calling it the Ruthenian-Polish nation."[56] From this moment onwards, *gente Rutheni, natione Poloni* were to become the political representatives of the Ruthenian population in Galicia. This aspiring to forge out of Ruthenians, Ruthenians of Polish nationality, while out of the landed gentry and Eastern Galician intelligentsia the elite to rule over the lands of former Rus', later found its advocate in the personage of the "red prince," Adam Sapieha. The Greek Catholic hierarchy and the Galician Uniate clergy were not to display any interest in this sort of "offer." Father Onufry

---

[53] Ibid.
[54] Ibid.
[55] *Protokoły posiedzeń*, p. 28.
[56] Ibid., p. 41.

Krynicki was one of the few Uniate clergymen who spoke out on the Polish side, and he adopted only this cause and not any other national or political perspective. When Bishop Franciszek Ksawery Wierzchlejski read out the profession of faith of the Polish clergy of the Latin rite at a secret session on 1 May 1848, Canon Onufry Krynicki demanded that "in the minutes of the National Council it be noted that as a solitary conscious priest of the Greek rite he had joined in the profession of faith of the Latin clergy."[57] Such cases were infrequent, but they did occur.

Meanwhile, at a meeting organized at the chapter house of St. George's Cathedral on May 2, the Ruthenian petition committee transformed itself into the Supreme Ruthenian Council, in opposition to the Central National Council, with the mandate of representing the Ruthenian population. One of the demands advanced by the council was the division of Galicia into two parts: the Polish west and the Ruthenian east. The creation of a separate Ruthenian political organ was an even greater shock for the activists of the Central National Council than the petition of April 19 had been. The majority of those in the Central National Council—which was, in accordance with its principles, meant to represent all Galicians regardless of ethnic origin—saw in the establishment of the Supreme Ruthenian Council a desire on the part of the Austrians to divide the inhabitants of Galicia with the aim of weakening the Polish political movement.

With the creation of the Supreme Ruthenian Council and with the Greek Catholic clergy becoming the political elite of Galician Ruthenians, those *gente Rutheni, natione Poloni* connected to the Central National Council had to act politically. First, this would guarantee them the leadership role among the Ruthenian population within the Austrian area of partition, and second, it would prevent the development of Ruthenian political thought from taking a "separatist" direction in relation to the Poles. From its inception, this new political camp was etched into the Galician activist landscape, with the Lviv democrats desperately trying to hamper any escalation of events. With this goal in mind, a delegation of the Central National Council visited Bishop Iakhymovych and tried to persuade him not to succumb to the Austrian administration, but instead cooperate with the Polish committee. Two Ruthenians, Father Onufry Krynicki and Cyryl Wieńkowski, also participated in the talks. Furthermore, Wieńkowski attended the meeting of the Supreme Ruthenian Council, reporting at length to the Polish committee on May 4. He spoke to his compatriots, convincing them that the Poles had absolutely nothing against the development of the

---

[57] Ibid., p. 42.

Ruthenian movement, and would even support it.[58] However, his arguments were unable to break through the nascent political circles of the St. Georgians which were at the time beginning to crystallize.

The rise of the Supreme Ruthenian Council, the national character of which robbed the Central National Council of its claim to be the sole representative of Galician society as a whole, resulted in divergences in opinion within the ranks of the Central National Committee. Several positions were created at the time within the Polish camp. Stefan Kieniewicz drew attention to the two main political currents regarding the Ruthenian question: the first envisaged negating the existence of such a body as the Ruthenian nation (the existence of a Ruthenian tribe was accepted, in so much as it was incorporated into the composition of the Polish nation), while the second foresaw a challenge with the St. Georgians over leadership of the Ruthenian population in Galicia, in which the *gente Rutheni, natione Poloni* were to stand against the St. Georgians as representatives of Ruthenians.[59]

Some Ruthenians of Polish nationality were not entirely convinced that the St. Georgians would gain anything politically. The position of the landowners and intelligentsia was so strong that there was no way to predict that the Greek Catholic clergy would become a leading force among the Ruthenian population of Galicia. This relationship is very well illustrated by a fragment of Michał Popiel's letter of 13 May 1848 to Wiktor Rozwadowski:

> Having spent several days in Lviv arguing with Ruthenians, I departed with a dry throat and worn out lungs for Sambir, and crossed myself three times [exorcising myself from] the committee of St. George and half of the Ruthenian seminarians; I did not want to torment those survivors of this wretched affair who dreamed of power they did not have, about might and the state on the Moon.[60]

The petition of April 19 and the establishment of the Supreme Ruthenian Council on May 2 sent shockwaves through the ranks of the activists of the revolutions of 1848, with the possible exception of Leon Sapieha, who—so it appears—prophetically foresaw the futher course of events. In the Polish daily press the articulation of Ruthenian demands caused reverberations. For example, the daily *Dziennik Mód Paryskich* ran the article "Ruthenian Terror" on May 13, in which an

[58] Batowski, *Diariusz*, pp. 162–67, 172–74.
[59] Kieniewicz, *Czyn Polski*, p. 85.
[60] "List Michała Popiela do Tadeusza Rozwadowskiego," 13 May 1848, ZNiO, sygn. 7939/II (MF 2107): Archiwum Rozwadowskich. "Korespondencja Wiktora Rozwadowskiego z lat 1848–1852. Listy od różnych osób," p. 133.

attempt was made to prove that the causes of the commotion were the grievances concerning the social burdens of serfdom and the lack of liberty for the peasantry. According to the author, the feudal past had led to the Ruthenian population's hostility towards the Poles. He reassured his readers that if only the linguistic demands were met and the opposition to Ruthenian "schools" was lifted, then "the organization of Ruthenian resistance nurtured by the Ruthenian clergy would also collapse, and with this the clergy would lose their political influence which so amorally serves them."[61]

Besides the press coverage, concrete political steps were also taken. Already at the session of the Central National Council on May 5, the deputy Brunon Rogalski appealed for "a unity of Ruthenian love and brotherhood."[62] The very next day at a secret session it was decided that the selected members of the Central National Council were to make a proclamation explaining "the relationship and our desires concerning it."[63]

The resulting proclamation was officially read out and subsequently discussed at the meeting of 7 May 1848. It came out in print in *Rada Narodowa* on May 15. Central to the proclamation was the statement that "the rights of the Ruthenian nation are as holy and inviolable for it [the Central National Council – A.Ś.] as are its own." At the same time, it was stated that the "Ruthenian nation cannot have any other needs than those held by the Polish nation—these same are today both the yearnings and the aims."[64] Besides this appeal, a separate "energizing, unifying, convincing" appeal was drafted by Piotr Wasilewski. As Aleksander Batowski recalled, both were published in *Rada Narodowa*, and then edited in Ruthenian and distributed on separate sheets in Lviv.[65]

The Ruthenian voice also rang out at this time, although this voice was different from that of the St. Georgians. Although we do not know the names of the authors of the so-called *Ruthenians' Petition* [*Adres Rusinów*][66] of 11 May 1848, it is likely that they were *gente Rutheni, natione Poloni* as well as democrats working to maintain unity between Poles and Ruthenians—quite possibly those same ones who had participated in political acts and activities in March and April, and who had then joined the Ruthenian Sobor. The notion of writing the *Ruthe-*

---

[61] "Strach ruski," *Dziennik Mód Paryskich* no. 20 (13 May 1848), p. 163.

[62] *Protokoły posiedzeń*, p. 46. Cf. ibid., p. 47, footnote A.

[63] Ibid., p. 48. Only Poles were chosen for the task: Smarzewski, Smolka, Tadeusz, and Piotr Wasilewski.

[64] "Manifest do Rusinów," *Rada Narodowa* no. 16 (10 May 1848). Cf. *Protokoły posiedzeń*, p. 50, footnote 1.

[65] Batowski, *Diariusz*, pp. 182–83.

[66] *Adres Rusinów* ([Lviv, 1848]).

nians' Petition had presumably come to the fore on May 9. Batowski noted that at Józef Puzyna's home:

> (...) a private assembly of Ruthenians (100 people attended) had a discussion about the interests of the Sobor of hardline Ruthenians at St. George [The Supreme Ruthenian Council – A.Ś.], who had been placed in opposition by Stadion and who had handed over the petition of 27 points to Vienna, signed chiefly by priests and non-gentry, excluding all who *stricte* did not designate their denomination. The proceedings were presided over by [Ludwik] Stecki—there were a lot of us non-Ruthenians such as [Józef Bonawentura] Załuski, [Walerian] Ustrzycki and others. It was agreed to go to the National Council to enquire what was to be done in case unity with this anti-national brotherly party (Stadion's) could never be reached.[67]

The meeting constituted the initiation of the political organization of *gente Rutheni, natione Poloni*. The same day, another meeting took place at the Hall of the Society for the Teaching of Music in Galicia and continued until late into the evening. Here Denys Zubrytsky – at that time still cooperating with the Poles – addressed an audience of mainly peasants. His speech was met by loud applause. The manifesto, along with the petition to the Ruthenian brothers, was also read out. They were interrupted, according to Batowski's account, by frequent applause and shouts of "Long live the Ruthenian brothers, long live the Poles! Long live the National Council!"[68] The Ruthenians' Petition exceeded expectations.

The Lviv National Vasyl Stefanyk Scientific Library of Ukraine has in its possession two copies of the *Ruthenians' Petition*: one print copy held in the Rare Books Department,[69] and one in manuscript form held in the Manuscript Department.[70] Neither copy includes any signatures. The petition was undoubtedly read out at the meeting of the Central National Council on May 12. Batowski recalled that at this meeting, Zubrytsky first addressed the peasants, then the Ruthenian committee members who had prepared the *Ruthenians' Petition*, and then Wincenty Petrowicz, a medical doctor with a PhD in Art, "announced that they desired unity, that they are Poles equal with us but of the Ruthenian tribe; that they suffer the fatherland's one misery, one auspiciousness, and that they are prepared to shed blood for it, etc."[71]

---

[67] Batowski, *Diariusz*, p. 185.
[68] Ibid., p. 186.
[69] *Adres Rusinów.*
[70] *Adres Rusinów*, LNNBU, fond 76, op. 1: Rukopysy biblioteky Pavlikovs'kykh, spr. 254 Materiały do dziejów 1848 r. w Galicji, p. 44.
[71] Batowski, *Diariusz*, pp. 190–91.

The *Ruthenians' Petition* was written in Ruthenian and Polish, with both versions almost identical in content. This was without doubt designed to play a propagandistic role, aimed at convincing Ruthenians about the correctness of recent actions on the part of the democrats and to dissociate the Ruthenian population from the actions of the St. Georgians. The introduction announces:

> On the 19th of April a request was made to Your Excellence under the heading of "a petition of the Ruthenian people," which we here attach. Several dozen persons signed it, as is known, yet no one was publicly called for doing so. Consequently we, the undersigned, consider this appeal [here the matter concerns the petition of the St. Georgians – A.Ś.] to be solely the emanation of an association of individuals and not of the whole nation.[72]

This document is significant in that it proves that *gente Rutheni, natione Poloni* participated in political counter-offensive action. Here the matter does not concern world outlook, tradition, or nationality. This constituted the beginning of the political rivalry between Ruthenians of Polish nationality and the St. Georgians over who would lead the Ruthenian population in Galicia. The authors of the petition, in understanding not merely the strength of their opponent but also the validity of many of the St. Georgians' demands of April 19 that had been omitted from the March petition, wrote that they agreed with seven of the points in the St. George petition. Demands were made for equal treatment of denominations and nations through the introduction of Ruthenian as a language into all levels of the educational system, as well as its use in state administrative matters in government offices. The authors of the *Ruthenians' Petition* signed off by stating that the petition of March 18 and its revision on April 6 already embraced these demands—a statement which was, however, not completely true. It was simultaneously noted that the "Ruthenians" had dissociated themselves from several points of the petition of April 19, namely the commendation of former governance and the demand for a division of Galicia. The justification for their position is of particular significance:

> For we consider the country inhabited by us jointly with the Poles to be a fatherland—the Poles, with whom we have inseparable links of history, family, and customs that bind, we consider to be our brothers, and it is with them that we desire to share the lot of our common homeland.[73]

The press quickly addressed the new petition. The weekly chronicle of *Dziennik Mód Paryskich* related on May 13 that:

---

[72] *Adres Rusinów.*
[73] Ibid.

Ruthenians on their part, no matter how they stood on the petitionary points of the St. George petition, were outraged over its introduction, which was prejudiced and dissented from the common matters of the nation— and in fraternal reply to this noble outrage many members of the gentry of long-standing Ruthenian origin such as J. Puzyna, L. Stecki, Szumlański, A. Golejewski, J. Dzieduszycki and others openly engaged in the Ruthenian question. The result of this was several Ruthenian gatherings at J. Puzyna's house that had a character of public assemblies, for they were gathered not from a single priestly caste but from all the social estates, brought together by the matter of unity. At these gatherings, with the participation of two members of the St. George 'Ruthenian Council' Messrs Wieńkowski and Wysłobocki, it was decided to stand against this petition of St. George, and with this decision the rightful demands of Ruthenian nationality were supported against all the assaults threatening to splinter the century-old bond held by Rus' with Poland, as well as the vocal support for national unity. On Thursday this petition was publicly signed in many towns. We expect the most favourable of outcomes after this initial and open move in the name of brotherhood and equality.[74]

This was to be the first public political declaration by *gente Rutheni, natione Poloni*, which made it clear that they intended to follow and share their common homeland with the Poles. As stated in the minutes of the Central National Council of 12 May 1848:

The Ruthenian delegation understands that those who on the 19th of April filed the petition in the name of Ruthenians did not act in the spirit of the Ruthenian nation. Ruthenians provoked by this submitted a new petition [The *Ruthenians' Petition* of the 11 May 1848 – A.Ś.], confirmed by numerous signatures in which, demanding national rights, they proclaim that although the Ruthenians are a tribe, as a nation they always wish to be Polish. Further they realize that the club set up under the name of the Ruthenian Council [the Supreme Ruthenian Council – A.Ś.], and its members, not chosen by the nation, does not hold this trust. Ruthenians do not want to separate themselves from Poles or to create a separate Council because the National Council has their trust. They demand from the Council that they select four of those who are members, incorporate them into their circle, and designate a separate Department for Ruthenian Affairs.[75]

New members were accepted into the Central National Council;[76] however, the demand for the creation of the aforementioned Council

---

[74] "Kronika tygodniowa," *Dziennik Mód Paryskich* no. 20 (13 May 1848), p. 164.

[75] *Protokoły posiedzeń*, p. 53.

[76] According to the publisher of the Minutes, the said individuals were future members of the Ruthenian Sobor. See ibid., p. 54, footnote 2.

department was never realized. Instead, a separate political entity was created: the Ruthenian Sobor.

The Creation of the Ruthenian Sobor

The majority of Polish scholars are of the view that the Ruthenian Sobor came into being on 23 May 1848, when the first electoral meeting was held. However, the very fact that the organization was founded implies earlier stages of conception.[77] In one of Zubrytsky's letters to Yakiv Holovatsky, dated May 20, Zubrytsky informs Holovatsky that "an association of pseudo-Ruthenians has been set up, composed of apostates from our denomination, but we would not wish to have anything to do with them."[78] The Ukrainian historian Marian Mudry notes in his article that in the minutes of the Supreme Ruthenian Council from May 12, mentions can be found of a secret meeting that had taken place in which delegates from the "other Ruthenian Council" together with the *Ruthenians' Petition* were accepted.[79] We might trace the date of the Sobor's establishment to this meeting called on May 9 of Józef Puzyna's editorial committee, which two days later would compile the *Ruthenians' Petition*. Mudry mentions that *gente Rutheni, natione Poloni* were still present at the meeting of the Supreme Ruthenian Council of May 2. In turn, a day later, information appears in the documents of this organization relating that the "Polish National Council" is called the "Polish-Ruthenian Council," something that the Supreme Ruthenian Council was unable to accept, hence the Central National Council had to also appoint a separate "Polish-Ruthenian Council."[80] The Ruthenian Sobor could have been created during the petition committee meeting of May 9, although at that time, as the press report reveals, "several Ruthenian assemblies possessing the real colouring of public gatherings," were not yet called the Ruthenian Sobor.

On 23 May 1848 an electoral meeting of the organization at the Skarbek Theatre in Lviv took place. Here Kasper Cięglewicz was selected as the head of the organization.[81] This selection was undoubtedly earned by his conspiratorial activities in Eastern Galicia in the 1830s, which he paid for with a jail term in Kufstein, only returning after the amnesty of

---

[77] Cf. Stebelski, "Lwów," p. 545; Henryk Wereszycki, *Pod berłem Habsburgów. Zagadnienia narodowościowe* (Cracow, 1986), p. 143; Wójtowicz-Huber, *'Ojcowie narodu'*, p. 55.

[78] Quoted after: Kozik, "Stosunki ukraińsko-polskie," p. 35, footnote 28.

[79] Mudryj, "'Jesteśmy rozdwojonymi członkami jednego ciała'," p. 57.

[80] Ibid.

[81] Marian Mudryi, "Rus'kyi sobor 1848 roku. Orhanizatsiia," p. 108.

ȢСТАВЪ СОБОРȢ РȢСКОГО.

§. 1. О Цѣли.

Цѣль Соборȣ Рȣского єсть: чȣвати надъ народностію
рȣскою и причинятися до єи свободного розвитья, а при
томъ ȣдержовати згодȣ и одность съ миромъ соплеменною
народности вспольнои нашеи отчины.

§. 2. Предсѣдатели.

Члены обирают бользеньствомъ голосовъ предсѣдателя
и двохъ намѣстниковъ. Предсѣдатель завѣдаєтъ въ Ȣрядѣ
черезъ 14 днѣ, послѣ которыхъ, коли созволятъ члены,
опять на немъ же можетъ быти потвердженый; тоже ти-
читься и намѣстниковъ.

§. 3. О Членахъ.

До пріймȣ на члена постановлено слѣдȣюще:

а) Штобы быти конечне родȣ рȣского, а то обохъ ки-
вѣданъ греческого и латинского.

в) А при пріймѣ мати за собою бользеньство голосовъ
всѣхъ членовъ Собора.

20. The statute of the Ruthenian Sobor

1848. He fulfilled his position for a fortnight, after which the Ruthenian Sobor was reorganized.[82]

The organization had its own statute, and from August its own press organ, *Dnewnyk Ruskij*. In the first issue the short statute of the Ruthenian Sobor was published. In a mere three paragraphs it enumerated the aims of the organization, its structure, and the conditions for membership. The organization's aim was "to keep watch over the Ruthenian nation and enable its free development while maintaining accord and unity in peace with our brotherly nation"—that is, the Poles. The Sobor board was composed of one "representative" and two "governors." Two conditions had to be fulfilled in order to become a member of the organization: to belong to the "Ruthenian race," regardless of Greek or Latin rite, and to gain the support by vote of all the other members upon joining.[83] The list of those who belonged to the Sobor can be found in the *The Proclamation of the Ruthenian Sobor* [*Widozwa Soboru Ruskoho*] of 8 June 1848, preserved at the Central State Historical Archive in Lviv.[84] Here 64 surnames are visible (some of them in their Ruthenian

---

[82] Ibid.

[83] "Ustav' Soboru Ruskoho," *Dnevnyk' Ruskii* no. 1 (18 [30] Aug. 1848), p. 2.

[84] *Widozwa Ruskoho Soboru*, TsDIAU, fond 474, op. 1, spr. 15, p. 48.

variants), with a short annotation detailing each person. It is worth listing them here:

Baczyński Gabriel [Bachynsky Havryil], a citizen of Lviv
Bawankiewicz Jan [Bavankevych Ivan], a citizen of Lviv
Cięglewicz Kasper, a writer
Cybulski Jan Karol, a landowner and a writer
Czyrniański Emilian, adiunct of the Technical Academy
Dąbczański Antoni, court counselor in Lviv
Father Dolnicki Wiktor [Dolnytsky Viktor]
Dzieduszycki Aleksander [Dzedushytsky Oleksander], a landowner
Dzieduszycki Julian, a landowner
Dzieduszycki Włodzimierz [Dzedushytsky Volodymyr], a land-owner
Dziedzicki Joachim [Dzedzytsky Yoakym], an assessor
Dziedziniewicz Rościsław [Dzedzynevych Rostyslav], an office worker
Golejewski Antoni, a landowner
Horoszkiewicz Julian, an office worker
Jabłonowski Ludwik, a landowner
Jabłonowski Józef [Iablonovsky Iosyp], a landowner
Jabłoński Henryk [Iablonsky Henryk], a student
Jaciewicz Sylwester [Iatsevych Sylvestr], a lawyer
Kapczyński Teofil [Kapchynsky Teofil], a lawyer and Ph.D. student
Kokurewicz Michał [Kokurevych Mihail], a lawyer
Komarnicki Bolesław [Komarnytsky Boleslav], a landowner
Komarnicki Ignacy [Komarnytsky Ihnat], a writer.
Komarnicki Ludwik [Komarnytsky Ludvyk], a doctor of law and
    a lawyer
Korczyński Aleksander [Korchynsky Oleksander], a student
Korczyński Michał [Korchynsky Michail], a lawyer
Korostyński [Korostynsky], a writer
Father Krynicki Onufry, a doctor of theology and a canon
Krynicki Teofil, a seminarian
Father Krzyżanowski Romuald
Kuczyński Emilian [Kuchynsky Omelian], an office worker
Kulczycki Jakub [Kulchytsky Yakiv], a doctor of a law and an assessor
Lewicki Bazyli, an office worker
Łękawski Konstanty, a writer
Łodyński Antoni [Lodynsky Antin], a citizen of Lviv
Łodyński Hieronim [Lodynsky Ieronim]
Łodyński Onufry [Lodynsky Onufriy], a citizen of Lviv and an office
    worker
Męcinski Jan [Mentsynsky Ivan], an engineer
Mrozowicki Stanisław [Mrozvytsky Stanislav], a student
Polański Teodozy [Polansky Teodor] a doctor of a law and a lawyer
Petrowicz Wincenty [Petrovych Vincent], a doctor of medicine
Piątkiewicz Rościsław [Piontkevych Rostyslav], an assessor
Pogłodowski Zenon [Poglodovsky Zenon], an assessor
Popiel Michał, an officer in the Appellate Court in Lviv

Pruski Jan [Prusky Ivan], a writer
Przyłęcki Stanisław [Pshylentsky Stanislav], a writer
Raczyński Stefan [Rachynsky Stepan]
Sawczyński Zygmunt, Ph.D. student
Smereczański [Smerechansky], a secretary of the Credit Union
Statkiewicz Grzegorz [Statkevych Hryhorii], an officer
Stecki Ludwik, a landowner
Szemelowski [Shemelovsky Teodor], a doctor of a law and a lawyer
Szumlański Antoni [Shumlansky Anton], a landowner
Szumlański Stanisław [Shumlansky Stanislav], a landowner
Telichowski Mikołaj [Telikhovsky Mykola], a lawyer and a citizen
    of Lviv
Tustanowski Michał, a doctor of a law and a lawyer
Wieńkowski Cyryl, a doctor of a law and a lawyer
Witoszyński Ignacy [Vitoshynsky Ihnat], a seminarian
Wysłobocki Hieronim [Vyslobotsky Heronym], a doctor of a law and
    a director of the Credit Union
Zachariasiewicz Jan, a writer
Zarzycki Maksymilian [Zazhytsky Maksym], a lawyer and a citizen
    of Lviv
Zarzycki Karol [Zazhytsky Karol], a student and a citizen of Lviv
Zawadzki Józef [Zavadsky Iosyp], a landowner
Zawadzki Władysław, a landowner and a writer
Zwierzchowski Edgar [Zviezhkhovsky Edgar], a landowner

The list contains a dozen or so landowners whom it would be rather difficult to classify as Ruthenian; Antoni Golejewski is one such example. The members of the Ruthenian Sobor were chiefly representatives of the intelligentsia: writers, lawyers, graduates of and clergy from the Greek Catholic seminary, government clerks, doctors, as well as—as some members described themselves—"citizens of the city of Lviv."

The authors emphasize in the proclamation that the aim of the Ruthenian Sobor is to watch over the Ruthenian nation, to foster its free and independent development, to run schools in the Ruthenian language at the lower and upper levels, and to support the Greek Catholic clergy given its poor material situation. This last point was a gesture towards the Uniate clergy who saw their protection contained within the ranks of the Supreme Ruthenian Council. In the proclamation of the Ruthenian Sobor it is emphasized, however, that the St. George Council is an exclusively ecclesiastical representation, and consequently cannot involve itself in matters other than those concerning religion and the Greek Catholic Church. The proclamation explained that the Ruthenian Sobor represented all social estates, including clergy as well as those from other social classes. In addition, it announced the establishment of the Sobor's press organ, *Dnewnyk Ruskij*.[85]

While the proclamation of June 28 was rather informative in character, *The Proclamation of the Ruthenian Sobor to the reverend Spiritual Leaders* [*Widozwa Soboru Ruskoho do wełebnych dusz Prowidnykiw*], unfortunately undated, was already an attempt to win the Greek Catholic clergy over to their side.[86] In the introduction to the publication, the authors expressed their expectations that the clergy would deliver "that goodness and joy of the soul which the world is unable to provide."[87] They then attempted to prove that to sever the two boughs of "our most pleasant homeland" of Ruthenians and Poles would be in vain, for their union was formed from divine will "and what God in his wisdom has joined let no man in bad ineptitude undo." Furthermore, it was underlined that the Ruthenian Sobor, as a representation of various estates, focused on the education of Ruthenians, the confirmation of the freedoms of the Ruthenian nation, and the granting of rights equal to those of the Poles. The proclamation concluded with a call for brotherhood and unity because "a tree split at the trunk goes to waste and with time dries out." The text was carefully written with a religious message, one which was convincingly conveyed. Nevertheless, the proclamation did not generate much resonance even though it was published and circulated by *Gazeta Narodowa*.[88] On the one hand, this lack of success for the conciliatory Sobor resulted from its mandate of moderation. It was indeed a body that tried to conciliate various elements, something reflected in its carefully worded rhetoric. A calm and rational voice of this kind, at a time when fierce verbal rivalry between those declaring themselves as Poles and Ruthenians raged, would ultimately go unheard. In addition, as Marian Mudry notes, the Ruthenian Sobor often attracted those for whom "Ruthenianism" was but an element in their vision, which is also why the organization did not engage in any broader undertakings.[89]

---

[85] Ibid.

[86] *Widozwa Soboru Ruskoho do wełebnych dusz Prowidnykiw*, LNNBU, fond 76, op. 3, spr. 276, p. 94.

[87] In the original: "oczikujemo toho dobra, i toho duszy wesila, kotoroho nam świt daty ne może".

[88] *Gazeta Narodowa* no. 78 (29 Jul. 1848) (insert).

[89] Mudryi, "Rus'kyi sobor 1848 roku. Orhanizatsiia," p. 108.

Widozwa Ruskoho Soboru.

Wozlubyszy iskrenniaho twojeho, jako sam sebe.

Bratia Rusyny!

Duch zmyłowania Bożoho, Duch wilnosty, sstupyw meży Narody Europy, prodersia do nedawno smutnych zahorod naszych — Hrud' Rusyna nawykła tylko do wostennnia i domhy widziła — Rozraduwała sia ćusza Jeho u hozi po dowhyj toż — błahosławluczy welykie Imia Jeho w totim welykym dari hotoryj nam dnes zdaau. — Nyni z ciłym świtom pospiszajemu do wilnosty, a toje wynysuno konstytucyi nadanuj nam z natchninia Bożoho cześez Najjaśnijszaho Cisara Korola naszoho Ferdynanda I. — Konstytucya tota ułatwiaje nam nym wyrobłaty i uhrazaty nasu mowu, wprowadzowaty ju w żytie i daty jej takie sianowysho, na jakim wże stojat nyni bratni jazyki susidiw naszych.

Rusyny! dnes budyt sia narodnist ruska, bo duch Bożyj sstupyw na zemlu i zriwnau jak narody tak i ludy z soboju. —

W namirenju — tuju narodnist wozdwyhnuty, zawiazało sia wi Lwowi dwa sobrania pid nazwoju: „Rada narodowa ruska" (Swiatojurska) — i „Sobir ruskij" —

Perwuja składajucza sia po najbirszoj czasty z Prewełebnych świaszczennykiw, ne może sie skuteczno zapowuwaty czym innym, tohmo diłamy cerkownymy i czestnoju praćoju o spasenju nebesnym. — A nasz Sobir składajuczyj sia ne tohmo z wełebnych otciw duchownych, ale także zo wsich ynczych stanuw, posianowyw, — nemynujuczy także prawednoho namirenja Ruskoi Rady, zamiatysia wsimy potrebamy ruskoho naroda. — Wtyjmysty bude wychodyty dennyk Ruskoho Sobora kotoryj opici naszoho Myra Swiatych nazuw poruczajemo —

I widomo czyniuno pered Hospodom Bohom, myrom chrestyjańskim i cilym świtom, szczo namirenjem naszym jest:

Czuwaty nad narodnosteja ruskoju, pryczyniaty sia do jej swobodnoho i nezawysłaho rozwytku, proswiszczaty nasz narid; pidnosyty jeho do uczastnystwa w sprawach ciłoho naroda, — zaprowadyty szkoły tak nyzszi jako i wyzszi w jazyci ruskim; — nauczyty jeho używaty na dobro nadanych jemu swobod konstytucyjnych; — czuwaty nad prawamy i dobrom ciłoho naroda; — wspraty i wozdwyhaty pysmennyctwo nasze ruskie własnym naszym i majethom, nakonec staraty sia, hiłko w syłach naszych bude, o połipszenje doly duchowenstwa ruskoho, aby mohło tak wysokom swomu powołanyju bez pereszkody widpowidaty — prytiimete wsim utrzymanoho wsemy syłamy zhodu i jednist z narodom wspilnoho naszoho oteczestwa, — szczoby burja nerjadu i kołotni, taja pozina strasznyj waju, szczo derewa z horinniom wyrywaje, i wsio z zemleju riwnaje, ne popsuwała tych mołodych litorostej, kotory ne dawno wzemlu naszu światu czas wittknuw, —

W totum namirenju podalysmo wże supliku dnia 11. Maja b. r. do tronu naszoho Monarchy. —

Taja jest myłyji bratja Rusyny! — nasza spowid, naszoho sumlinia i perekonanja zerkało, nasza wira; — tuju dorohoju budem postupaty, wid neji ne damo sia niczym widwesty, — jako i wid tuho perekonania, że neja tohmo iduczy, w zhodi i sojedneniju bratnym, do spasenyja naszoho diijty potrafymo. —

Wzywajuczy uładno wsich czestnych i świtłych Rusyniw, szczoby nas w naszych dobrych i szczyrych namirenyjach wspiraty. — Poneże oświaszczenyje luda, narodnist ruska, szczastie myra i dobro naszoho kraju jest naszym naston. —

Wi Lwowi dnia 5. Czerwca 1848. r.

DIYSTWYTYLNYI CZLENY RUSKOHO SOBORU.

Baczyński Hawryił Ohpirał M. Lwa.
Baranskiewicz Juan Obyrał. M Lwa.
Cerepkiewicz Kasper Pysmeunyk.
Cybulski Juan Korol Posodult Zemi. Pysm.
Czyrniański Eustian Adjunkt Akad. Tech.
Dybczański Anton Sowdnyk C. K. Sadu Szlach. Lw.
X. Dolnicki Wiktor.
Dziedaszycki Alex Posid. Zem.
Dzieduszycki Julian Lasil. Zem.
Dziednozycki Władysław Posid Zem.
Dziedzicki Joachim Uried. C. K. Fisk.
Dziedzimiowicz Rostysław Uried.
Gabiewski Anton. Posid Zem.
Horaczkiewicz Julian U ied.
Jabłonowski Ludwyk Posid. Zem.
Jabłonowski Jozyp. Posid. Zem.
Jabłonski Hrorys Aktiwok.
Jerawicz Sylvester Praktyk.
Kaneczyński Teofyl praw Dent. Philozofyi.
Kokurewicz Mickaił. praw.
Komarnicki Bolesław Posid. Zem.
Komarnicki Jan Lysm.
Komarnicki Ludwyk Dr. P. Adwokat kraj.
Koreczyński Alexander Akademik.
Koreczyński Mickaił praw.
Korniłyński Pysm.
X. Krynicki Onufryi Dr. S Teologii, Kryłoszan,
Krynicki Teofil Alum. Seminarii.
X. Kryżanowski Romuald.
Kuczyński Emilian Uried.
Kulczycki Jakob Dr. Praw. i Uied. C. K. Fisk.
Lewicki Bazyli Uried. K.

Łykawski Konstanty Pysm.
Łodynski Antin Obyw. M. Lw.
Łodynski Hermogen P. Z.
Łodynski Onufryi. Obyw. M. Lw. Uied. K.
Męciński Juan Technik.
Mroszowicki Stanisław Akad.
Polański Teodory Dr. Praw. Adwok. Kraj.
Petrowicz Winceaty Dr. Med. —
Figlkiewicz Rostysław Uried. C K. Fisk.
Pogładowski Zenon Uried. C. K. Sad, S Lw.
Papiri Mychuił Sowdnyk C K. Appell.
Puski Juan Pysm.
Przątycki Stanisław Pysm.
Raczynski Stefan.
Sawczyński Zyhizmund Drat Filoz.
Smerecewski Sikre. Tow. Kred. —
Statkiewicz Hrehory C. K. Uried.
Steczi Ludwyk. Posid. Zem.
Szrudowicz Dr. Praw. Adw Kraj
Szumlański Anton Posid. Zem
Szumlański Stanisław. Pos. Zem.
Telischewski Mykołaj Prawn. Obyw. M. Lw.
Taszkowski Mychaił Dr. Praw. Adw. kraj.
Wronkowski Kyryl Dr Praw. A pukt C. K Fisk.
Wdoxsynski Hermogen D° Praw. Dyrekt. Tawar. kredyt
Zachariasiewicz Juan Pysm
Zaręcki Marijan Praw Obyw. M. Lw.
Zaręcki Karol Akad Obyw. M. Lw.
Zawadzki Jozyp. Posi . Zem.
Zawadzki Władysław Posid. Zem. Pysm.
Zwierzchowski Edyar. Posid. Zem.

Czujemo sia obowiazanymy wytowmaczyty sia prynyniszm Bratiam naszym Rusynam ze zbraku typiw kerylłycłch w Drukarniach Lwiwskich nemożem maty pryjemnosty pysm naszych do Was w tych typach drukowaty — a to tak dowho poki sobi ne sprowadymo z zahranyci. —

21. The Proclamation of the Ruthenian Sobor

The Political Views of *Gente Rutheni, Natione Poloni* Activists

The political programme of those *gente Rutheni, natione Poloni* assembled within the Ruthenian Sobor was based on opposition to the creation and activity of the Supreme Ruthenian Council. The year 1848 marked the establishment of a political movement for those nationally-oriented Galician Ruthenians. This undoubtedly constituted a period of breakthrough, and although Ruthenians did not yet feel themselves to be a "consolidated" nation, the political power base had developed upon which the growth of the movement depended over the course of subsequent years.

Gente Rutheni, natione Poloni experienced a certain internal discomfort in the light of such a situation. On the one hand, as a result of a common past, denomination, and blood bond, they were linked directly to the Ruthenian ethnic group. On the other hand, the burgeoning political Ruthenian elite had announced demands that were completely at odds with the aspirations of the Polish elites in Galicia. The only solution for the *gente Rutheni, natione Poloni*, unwilling to relinquish their "Polishness," was to attempt to maintain the peace between Poles and Ruthenians within the Austrian area of partition. This was to be accomplished by appealing to the popular refrain of "brotherhood," by negating radical acts on the part of their compatriots, and by making recourse to the centuries-old traditions of Poland.

Julian Horoszkiewicz, who was soon to become one of the main figures in these circles, reminded his readers in *A Letter to Ruthenian Brothers* [*Łyśt do bratiw Rusyniw*] that Poles and Ruthenians are:

> A single family; our mother Poland is undivided, the same field nourished us, the same lot we have experienced— to the confusion of him who sows discord among us! The fisherman muddies the water when he fishes in the pond, and so there are people among us who want to set us arguing against each other. They falsify pure truth in order to fulfil within our discord their imbroglio. (...)
>
> But the Lord's light shone on us, the fraternal hearts were warmed and melted into a single body. Let peace reign! Reach for happiness! Do not believe falsehoods and hypocrisy! Arm in arm we are all together! We are all brothers born, children; and God, who reigns in the heavens, blesses us with peace, and the evil shall cease that divided Rus' from the Poles. The Pole and the Ruthenian are children of a single Poland; we have the same enemies and they set us against each other, but brothers, let us leave this behind! Ruthenians are the children of a single Poland! In the coming hour you shall know those who wore shackles for your freedom and who spilt their blood, then certainly you will raise your

hands to the heavens, and with your pious heart you will say: Glory to them, glory! Glory![90]

Gradually, from the time the national movement among Galician Ruthenians was taking shape, *gente Rutheni, natione Poloni* ceased to be merely an example of a specific type of identity and became the believers in, and proclaimers of, a concrete political concept. This does not mean, however, that they felt confident in these choices. This unease is well illustrated by Father Teofil Pavlykiv, initially a member of the Berezhany National Council and the author of the *To Peasant Brothers* [*Bratyje seliany*] proclamation, in which he addressed the constitution and the abolition of serfdom. This proclamation was read out at the session of the Central National Council on 25 May 1848, and the Council decided to publish it at the expense of the Berezhany National Council. Later Pavlykiv changed his political views, entering a decanal Ruthenian Council and becoming its secretary.[91]

Pavlykiv's publication was more than likely an inspiration for another Ruthenian of Polish nationality, Michał Popiel, who took yet another route in the search for self-identification. He began his political involvement as a conspirator in the 1830s, joining the ranks of the Ruthenian Sobor during the Revolutions of 1848 and becoming a conservative during the times of autonomy. Preserved in the Lviv Central State Historical Archive is a printed document dated May 25 and catalogued as Michał Popiel's *Announcement to All Ruthenians in the Sambir National Council on May 25 [13], 1848 A.D.* [*Ohłaszenyje Mychaiła Popela do Wsich Rusyniu wo Samborskoj radi na 25 (hreczysk. kal. 13) maja 1848 r. po Chr.*][92] It begins in a similar way to Pawlikow's text, opening with the vocative address: "Peasant brothers!". This appeal was directed towards the rural population and, like those earlier proclamations and appeals mustering support for emancipation, was aimed at raising awareness of freedom in the peasantry. It sought to communicate that the former liege relations had not been derived from the attitude of the gentry but rather from the fact that this was a "global" phenomenon by nature. Following the example of other declarations made in 1848, it tried to convince the readers that it had been the landowners who had revoked serfdom and not the Austrians. The author also hoped to unify the Ruthenian population, explaining what Poland was, who Poles and Ruthenians

---

[90] [Julian Horoszkiewicz], *Łyst do bratiw Rusyniw a peredwsim do tych, szczo pidpisały proźbu do Cisara 11ho Maja 1848*, TsDIAU, fond 474, op. 1, spr. 15, pp. 25–26.

[91] *Protokoły posiedzeń*, pp. 68–69.

[92] *Ohłaszenyje Mychaiła Popela do Wsich Rusyniu wo Samborskoj radi na 25 (hreczysk. kal. 13) maja 1848 r. po Chr.*, TsDIAU, fond 474, op. 1, spr. 15, pp. 3–6.

were, and finally what constituted Ruthenian identity. He presented himself as a Ruthenian peasant baptized into the Uniate rite, just like the intended audience of his proclamation. This was an undertaking designed to win over the Greek Catholic rural population, before this feat was accomplished by the political activists of the St. George party and the Uniate clergy. This is well illustrated by the following excerpt:

> I am contemplating our people. Our great-great-grandfathers inhabited this great and beautiful land from these mountains right up to Moscow, from sea to sea, and they named this country with one name: Poland and Rus'. There is no Poland, there are no Poles, but there are Masurians, Silesians, Lithuanians, Ruthenians, Ukrainians, Volhynians, Podilians, Highlanders etc.
>
> This land inhabited by all the brotherly generations, and in which they harmoniously lived under a single authority like brothers in a hut — this entire land was known and is called in books and letters Poland, while all of those peoples are called Poles or Ruthenians, as you like.
>
> And so you see how the orchard is beautiful when next to the pear the apples blossom, the cherry, the peach, and the plum. And where is the orchard? The orchard is composed of apple trees, pear, plum, and cherry trees. And if someone wanted to name them nevertheless, then would it not be that the apple trees are the apple trees and the pears the pears? But we speak of all types of trees by a single word: an orchard. It follows only to say, let them not refer to Poland, we have no need of Poles, for now we shall have there Masurians, here Ruthenians, there Lithuanians, there Volhynians, and all born brothers. And where are the Poles? There are no Poles. And where are the Poles? We can be Poles or Ruthenians as you choose.[93]

Later in the proclamation, Popiel explains to the peasant that there is no difference between those from different rites and denominations and that one's religious rite in no way determines nationality:

> And is there not a single Lord above us? After all our Ruthenian rite comes from Tsarhrad [Constantinople], a Greek city, while the Latin rite comes from Rome, a Roman city, one faith, one God. And where is the Pole, and where is the Ruthenian? We are all brothers, all Christians. (...) whoever was born in this Polish Ruthenian land is the true Ruthenian and Pole.[94]

Here it is worth emphasizing that in the face of rivalry between the two national committees the Polish and Ruthenian — a struggle began between these two movements for the national consciousness of the rural population. The Polish side stirred fervour in a meticulous way.

---

[93] Ibid., pp. 2–3.
[94] Ibid., pp. 3–4.

Not only were things written in Ruthenian, but even the form of the appeal was tailored to the recipient. Often recourse was made to biblical stories with parallels drawn with village life, such as the juxtapositioning of particular ethnic groups with species of tree growing in a single orchard constituting the allegorical Poland. However, the matter at heart was not simply one of national awareness. The phantom of the peasant revolt of two years earlier could return and resume its haunt, bloodily cutting short the gains of the Revolutions of 1848. The abilities of the partitioning powers were mobilized to prevent defeat, particularly since Austrian government officials in Eastern Galicia had started to win over peasants, as reported by the minutes of the meetings of the Central National Council. For example, at the session of May 21 the creation six days earlier of the "Austrian-Constitutional Association" in Stanyslaviv was noted. Its aim, as is recorded in the minutes, was to:

> Bring about catastrophes similar to that of (…) 1846, and [it] had already started its activities in the mountains through the assuming and embodying in itself of financial inspectors (…)—and behind their undertakings with Hutsuls, village headsmen, and elected assemblies, it employs a host of means and forms of persuasion and adorns them with black-and-yellow ribbons.[95]

In turn, at the session that occurred a day later, information came from the Przemyśl Regional Council that the peasants had circulated among themselves a new leaflet from the *Gubernium* on the subject of serfdom. 1848 saw not only a struggle between the Polish democrats and Austrian propaganda, but also a rivalry in securing the national feelings of the Ruthenian peasant, in whom it was hoped an affinity with Polish nationality could be aroused.

The Problem of Recognizing the Ruthenian Nation

A major problem facing the representatives of the *gente Rutheni, natione Poloni* was that the Church hierarchy stood at the head of the Ruthenian movement. The implications of this leadership were not taken sufficiently seriously by the members of the Central National Council, where various social estates and classes participated in the organization's activities. In commenting on this state of affairs, Aleksander Batowski wrote:

---

[95] *Protokoły posiedzeń*, p. 64.

Those who were there at the gatherings [of the St. George Council – A.Ś.] agreed that it was a purely clerical party, acting in a hierarchical, anti-nationalist spirit, as Franciszek [Leszczyński], a doctor of law, defined well: a party having serfdom in view, that is *popokracja* [priestocracy; from the word *pop*: Uniate or Orthodox priest – G.T.] pro-clerical. For it is composed exclusively of priests, with a bishop at the helm, and according to the statute which has still to be finally adopted, composed of Ruthenians preserving the [Uniate] rite. It excludes numerous Ruthenian noblemen, born here and having never denounced their origins, but who through age-old relations have entered into Polish nationality and who deeply love the joint homeland; the numerous academic youth and those from the seminary; those following the progress and spirit of the time seeing the desire of the National Council and nobly thinking not to praise this apostate, to break away from them and to form a third intermediary party with the most fervent desire to join our petitions, our aspirations, and our Council.[96]

The initial underestimation of the force of the demands proclaimed by the Uniate clergy meant that not everyone in the Central National Council was able to accept the notion of creating—to use Batowski's wording—an "intermediary party," even among those who emphasized their Ruthenian origins. Conservative circles feared any admission that a Ruthenian nationality existed whatsoever. For example, Józef Puzyna, a landowner and member of the Central National Council who traced his lineage back to the Ruthenian princes, considered himself a Ruthenian in provenance but was critical not only of the Supreme Ruthenian Council, but initially even of the very concept of the Ruthenian Sobor which—when it was finally constituted—proclaimed the existence of the Ruthenian nation. Puzyna saw these organizations as a setback to the centuries of work undertaken to fuse Poles and Ruthenians into a single nation. This sentiment is expressed in the words of Aleksander Batowski, a firsthand observer of the events connected with the formation of the Ruthenian Sobor:

Puzyna Józef, a good citizen of the Chortkiv district, the former commander of Polish artillery, and a direct descendant of the Ruthenian princes, was against the tendencies present within the then Galician-Ruthenian Sobor, and wanted to clearly oppose or protest against it in conjunction with the rest of our good Ruthenian gentry, which together with him have worked exclusively so that it could merge with the Polish nation as an inseparable part of a whole family. When the discussion had lasted for a long time and it was my turn to speak, I brought this to the Council's attention, which put the discussion aside. I was advised to see those gentlemen the following day and to suggest to them

---

[96] Batowski, *Diariusz*, pp. 179–80.

that for the moment no one should summon up opposition, which for the cause in general and namely for the National Council, constituted irredeemable damage; secondly, to ask them to attempt to understand the committee, i.e., the Ruthenian Sobor, in its desire to undertake an act of its own declaration of political faith, while the Council was informed about its successful outcome by me.[97]

The landed gentryman Puzyna was not alone in questioning the right to recognize the Ruthenian ethnicity as a nation. Many other leading activists of the Revolutions of 1848, including those who considered themselves to be Ruthenians, expressed a similar view, whether at the Slavic Congress in Prague or in publications on the "Ruthenian question" which appeared extensively in 1848. Some reluctantly and uncertainly added their signatures to certain documents and proclamations on the matter of the Ruthenians. These sceptics foresaw that the assertion of the existence of a separate Ruthenian nation would lead to a schism in the society of former (and consequently any future) Poland. As an example, Ludwik Jabłonowski noted:

The next day, having entered the academy, I found in the anatomical theatre several graduates and priests of our former circles [Galician conspiratorial circles – A.Ś.] (Krzyżanowski, Krynicki, Mochnacki, Dolnicki, Hordyński), signing on the slab a petition to their brother Poles. Although the intentions were most noble, I did not like the very idea of a petition, for it recognized a difference between the Ruthenians and Poles, which hitherto had never occurred to any of us. Once such a certainty is accepted, it would take hellish labour to open the gate.[98]

However, other voices rang out within *gente Rutheni, natione Poloni* circles, though rarely among the landed gentry. Cyryl Wieńkowski published a fairly extensive article in *Gazeta Narodowa* devoted to Ruthenian nationality. He tried to prove the existence of a Ruthenian nation and a Ruthenian language, separate from Polish. At the same time he criticized a part of his circle, pointing out that due to the Latinization and Polonization of their families they had in fact lost their "Ruthenianness":

I could easily enumerate here many such Ruthenians who are already characterized as Ruthenian by their names, yet who would be offended if they were to be called Ruthenians. And I will gladly admit that between such Ruthenians and Poles no difference in terms of nationality is to be noted.[99]

---

[97] Ibid., p. 180.
[98] Ludwik Jabłonowski, *Złote czasy i wywczasy. Pamiętnik szlachcica z pierwszej połowy XIX stulecia*, introd. Stanisław Wasylewski (Poznań, 1928), p. 192.
[99] Cyryl Wieńkowski, "Sprawy krajowe," *Gazeta Narodowa* no. 60 (8 Jul. 1848), p. 2.

Arguments about "Ruthenian nationality" were to break out within *gente Rutheni, natione Poloni* ranks in the subsequent months, a conflict which forecasted the end of the formation. However, in May and June 1848 there was still belief in the success of a "third party."

Ruthenians at the Slavic Congress in Prague

A chance for the Ruthenian Sobor and its political circles to obtain the leading role in Ruthenian society was through domination of the Supreme Ruthenian Council. Such a possibility could be realized, as Jan Kozik argues, in the potential joining of the Ruthenian Sobor with the opposition organization.[100] On 29 May 1848 Antoni Dąbczański approached the Supreme Ruthenian Council with a proposal to amalgamate both organizations. The proposal reasoned:

> A nation without a people educated in religion cannot exist. Therefore we are the split members of a single body (…) because we, like you, live on Ruthenian land and were born to Ruthenian parents.[101]

There was, however, no political motive on the side of the Supreme Ruthenian Council to agree to a union with the Ruthenian Sobor, which was seen as subordination to the Central National Council.

This matter was readdressed at the Slavic Congress in Prague, an initiative meant to quell Ruthenian separatism in Galicia. Instigated by the Austrian authorities, this congress aimed to promote Austro-Slavism. It was a move particularly directed against Prussia, which was conducting anti-Slavic undertakings in the Frankfurt parliament.

The representatives of several Slavic nations inhabiting the lands of the Austrian Empire were invited to attend the congress, including Poles and Ruthenians. An invitation was sent to the Central National Council, which on May 20 selected its delegates by vote; another was sent to the Supreme Ruthenian Council, which nominated its three representatives.[102] For the Ruthenians this constituted a marvellous opportunity to demonstrate in an international forum that they were, in fact, a separate nation from the Polish, while for the Poles it was a chance to win over the Ruthenians and to establish an accord with them. These intentions can be seen in the minutes of the Polish-Ruthenian sessions

---

[100] Kozik, "Stosunki ukraińsko-polskie," p. 35.
[101] Quoted after: Mudryj, "'Jesteśmy rozdwojonymi członkami jednego ciała'," p. 65, footnote *.
[102] Stolarczyk, *Działalność*, pp. 140–44.

and the findings of Władysław Wisłocki, the author of a monograph on the subject of the Slavic Congress in Prague.[103]

The congress had its official opening on 2 June 1848 and ended ten days later; however, the delegates from Galicia had arrived in Prague somewhat earlier. An array of well-known Galicians were among the participants. It is worth examining the document attached to the second set of minutes for the proceedings of the Polish-Ruthenian section. Next to the surnames of those who attended is a letter representing the provenance of the participant. Hence, we have the following abbreviations: R. (Ruthenian), M. (Masurian), W.P. (Wielkopolanin [Grand Duchy of Poznań]), and L. (Lithuanian). There is no use of the letter P, as the minute-taker had presumably decided in advance that all the members of the Polish-Ruthenian section were citizens of the already non-existent Poland. The names present demonstrated that the congress participants represented various peoples of a single nation. Galicians were deemed Ruthenians of a varied "Ruthenian element." Ruthenians were noted to constitute 21 members of the section, while in truth only eight were declared "non-Polonized" Ruthenians.[104] The remaining thirteen were: Gabriel Baczyński, Kasper Cięglewicz, Jan Dobrzański, Julian Dzieduszycki, Adam Gorczyński, Juliusz Kossak, Jerzy Lubomirski, Zenon Pogłodowski, Józef Puzyna, Leon Sapieha, Ludwik Stecki, Stanisław Szumlański, and Władysław Zawadzki.[105] Over the subsequent days they were also joined by the *gente Ruthenus, natione Polonus* Zygmunt Sawczyński, who had been sent to Prague along with Cięglewicz, Szumlański, and Zawadzki by the Ruthenian Sobor.[106] However, in the case of a few of the aforementioned individuals, this admission of "Ruthenianness" was slightly overdone. Some even went as far as to state that this had been their first opportunity to present themselves as Ruthenians. An interesting piece of information concerning the identity of Juliusz Dzieduszycki can be found in his family diary, which speaks of the congress in Prague in passing:

[In 1848] (…) arrived Juliusz Dzi[eduszy]cki with [Zenon] Pogłodowski to Vienna as delegates of the Polish-Ruthenian Committee [the Ruthenian-Polish phrase was crossed out – A.Ś.], acting in opposition to the St. George Committee. Generally at this time several Dzieduszyckis

---

[103] Władysław Tadeusz Wisłocki, *Kongres Słowiański w 1848 r. i sprawa polska* (Lviv, 1927), p. 38.

[104] Wisłocki mentions the following names: Ivan Borysykevych, Hryhorii Hynylevych, Mykhailo Kulmatytsky, Benedykt Litynsky, Ivan Pavlivsky, Yuriy Voloshchak, Oleksandr Zaklynsky.

[105] Ibid., pp. 53–55 (alphabetical list of section members).

[106] Ibid., p. 56. Wisłocki writes also about others who took part in certain sessions.

1. Baczyński Gabriel z Galicyi. R.
2. Bakowski Marc. Teofil z Królestwa. M.
3. Bakunin Michał Rossyanin
4. Berwiński Rychard z Poznańskiego W. P.
5. Borynkiewicz Jan z Galicyi. R.
6. Brandys Wojciech z Poznańskiego W. P. Gal.
7. Brzozowski Ignacy z Galicyi
8. Buchwald Felix z Galicyi M.
9. Celarski Serweryn z Galicyi M.
10. Chłędowski Ludwik z Galicyi M.
11. Chojecki Edmund z Ukrainy. M.
12. Cieglewicz Kaspar z Galicyi R.
13. Cybulski Wojciech z Poznańskiego W. P.
14. Dzieduszycki Julian z Galicyi R.
15. Dobrzański Jan z Galicyi R.
    15. Giniewicz Grzegorz z Galicyi R.
16. Gorozyński Adam z Galicyi M.
17. Graconowski Franciszek z Galicyi M.
18. Grzybowski Witalis z Galicyi W. P.
19. Helcel Antoni z Galicyi. M.
20. Homulacz Eduard z Galicyi. M.
21. Horoch Kalixt z Galicyi. M.
22. Huppen Apolinary
23. Janiszewski z Poznańskiego W. P.
24. Kochanowski Adam z Galicyi M.
25. Kossak Juliusz z Galicyi R.
26. Kottula Andrzej z Szlaska
27. Kowalski Bazyli z Galicyi R.
28. Krainski Maurycy z Galicyi M.
29. Kulik z Galicyi M.
30. Kulmatycki Michał z Galicyi. R.
31. Libelt Karol z Poznańskiego W. P.
32. Libynski Benedykt z Galicyi R.

22 a-b. List of Polish and Ruthenian participants of the Slavic Congress in Prague

34 33. Lubomirski Jerzy z Galicyi. M.
34. Łącki Bolesław z Poznańskiego. W. P.
35. Łukaszewicz Lesław z Galicyi. M.
36. Magdzinski Teofil z Poznańskiego W. P.
37. Malisz Karol z Galicyi. M.
38. Midowicz Józef z Galicyi. M.
39. Milowadów Olimpi z Galicyi Rossyanin
40. Moraczewski Jędrzej z Poznańskiego W. P.
41. Pawłowski Jan z Galicyi. R.
42. Bogtodowski Zenon z Galicyi. R.
43. Potulicki Kazimirz z Poznańskiego W. P.
44. Purkinie Jan z Szlaska Pruskiego
45. Puzyna Józef z Galicyi. R.
46. Sapieha Leon z Galicyi. R.
47. Sawczynski Zygmund z Galicyi. R.
48. Sieminski Lucyan
49. Stabłowski Leon z Galicyi. R.
50. Stalmach Pawet z Szlaska
51. Stecki Ludwik z Galicyi. R.
52. Sydów Ludwik z Gniezna W. P.
53. Szumlanski Stanisław z Galicyi. R.
54. Szynglarski Felix z Galicyi. M.
55. Walewski Antoni z Galicyi. M.
56. Wisniowski Alojzy z Galicyi. M.
57. Wołoszczak Jerzy z Galicyi. R.
58. Zaklinski Alexander z Galicyi. R.
59. Zaleski Konstanty ze Żmudzi. L.
60. Zaremba Erazm z Królestwa. M.
61. Zawadzki Władysław z Galicyi. R.
62. Zaleski Józef z Królestwa. M.
64 63. — Potocki
65. — Kluczak
66. —

including Juliusz, Kazimierz, Włodzimierz, Alexander and Edmund deemed themselves to be Ruthenians.[107]

It became clear at the very beginning of the congress that the primary objective of the Polish delegates was achieving harmony and reaching an accord with the Ruthenians. During the second session Karol Libelt, a political and social activist from Poznań, was chosen to chair the proceedings, and he gave a speech outlining the need for Slavic accord. He assured the Ruthenians that there were no longer any Liakhs [Poles]: "they are the same as you, for the same are your aspirations and the very same are the goals."[108]

Gente Rutheni, natione Poloni played a dual role in the face of clashes. They tried to act as Ruthenians, yet all of their interests were directed towards the Poles. However, from the minutes recorded it appears that their intentions were abundantly clear. For example, when the discussion turned to the creation of a Polish commission during the sixth session, the Ruthenian Ivan Borysykevych proposed that the Ruthenians not attend. This caused Dzieduszycki to react, claiming that the Supreme Ruthenian Council were representing 15 million Ruthenians at the congress, and consequently they were obligated to join with the Polish section in order to represent all the lands of Rus' (understood as a part of former Poland).[109] Finally, it was determined that a general Galician commission would be established, composed of two divisions, a Polish and a Ruthenian. In the Ruthenian division sat Borysykevych, Hynylevych, Zaklynsky, Voloshchak, Leon Sapieha, Dzieduszycki, Pogłodowski and Kasper Cięglewicz. In addition to the Polish division of the Galician commission, a separate Polish commission was also created, composed exclusively of Poles.[110]

One of the most noteworthy sessions of the congress was the meeting of the Ruthenian division held on June 4, which concerned the matter of Galicia's division into two parts. With a vote of four against two the following terms were adopted: the division of Galicia into two national parts; the introduction of the Ruthenian language as a language for administrative use with the option for government replies to be written in Polish; the creation in Eastern Galicia of Ruthenian schools (at the request of the majority, Polish schools were to be also permitted);

---

[107] "Diariusz rodzinny (kalendarium)," ZNiO, sygn. 6725/I (MF 2490): Maurycy Dzieduszycki, "Zapiski. Pamiętnik z r. 1846, chronologia domu Dzieduszyckich 1844–1857, statystyczne dane o Towarzystwie Jezusowem (1845), Przepowiednie Wernyhory i o. Marka," p. 71.

[108] Wisłocki, *Kongres*, p. 52 (minutes of the second session).

[109] Ibid., p. 76 (sixth sitting).

[110] Ibid., p. 81 (sixth sitting).

the creation in all parts of the country of a national guard—Polish in the west and Ruthenian in the east; and the establishment of joint central authorities for both regions. Three delegates of the Supreme Ruthenian Council—Ivan Borysykevych, Hryhorii Hynylevych and Oleksiy Zaklynsky—took part in the sitting, and all of them voted in favour of the project. Standing in opposition were the delegates of the Ruthenian Sobor, Leon Sapieha and Julian Dzieduszycki. Zenon Pogłodowski initially voted in favour, but after consultation with colleagues withdrew his vote the next day and stood in opposition to the project to divide Galicia. It was therefore ultimately impossible to resolve the matter, and its resolution was consequently put off until the summoning of the Galician Diet.[111] Nonetheless, as soon as it became known that the project for a division of Galicia had been voted through, Leon Sapieha, presiding over the Ruthenian division of the Galician commission, began to receive threats.

Matters became particularly heated during the eighth sitting on 6 June 1848 during a vote to select a committee whose task was to present a manifesto to the emperor and enumerate the points and conditions for a union of Slavic peoples. With this goal in mind, the formation of a commission was proposed which could stipulate Polish interests and compare and collate them with the aspirations of other sections. At this time Borysykevych also demanded recognition for Ruthenian and not only Polish nationality. This caused an animated discussion on the subject of the definition of a nation and the status of Ruthenians. The often emotive words of the Polish-Ruthenian section allow us to understand their complex sense of identity. Jan Dobrzański explained:

> I am also a Ruthenian, but there is a huge difference between a single people and a nation itself. We, Ruthenians, are not a nation, we try to be a nation. Poles help us in this endeavour; let us not split the questions for they are closely connected with each other.[112]

Dobrzański saw Ruthenians as a part of a greater collective, the Polish nation. He did not rule out its distinction in the future, but these suggestions should be treated as a conscious acquiescence in an outcome that he did not believe could ever come about.

In turn, Libelt considered that if Ruthenians were recognized as a separate nation, similar demands would quickly pour in from Lithuanians and Masurians. Ruthenians should decide if they would rather stand with the Poles or the Russians. He emphasized that Poles desired the

---

[111] Ibid., pp. 92–95 (the publication of the Galician Ruthenians).
[112] Ibid., p. 105 (minutes of the morning session of June 6).

restoration of Poland, but one reconciled with Rus'. The arguments of Hynylevych and Erazm Zaremba in support of a separate Ruthenian nationhood were unacceptable to the other side. Even Kasper Cięglewicz, writing in Ruthenian and presenting himself as a Ruthenian in his extensive work on the Ruthenian past, adopted a supercilious position in relation to a people that he had allegedly represented up to this point. He emphasized, among other things, that the Ruthenian language was uncouth, "less rich than ours," and accused the Ruthenian gentry of being "guilty of adopting a rite that was at the time progressive."[113] He concluded his aggressive statement by saying: "It would be a disgrace and harm for the Ruthenian to tear himself away from Poland. I am myself a Ruthenian but for that no less a Pole." Borysykevych retorted to Cięglewicz that the Ruthenian gentry no longer existed, and there remained only the Ruthenian people who spoke in Ruthenian and who wished to become an independent nation.[114]

Despite the tense atmosphere, it was finally possible to reach a compromise between the Poles and Ruthenians on internal Galician matters, such as the issue of language in schools or official administrative documents.[115] On the afternoon of June 7, the two divisions of the Galician Commission, the Ruthenian and the Polish, debated this issue. Ultimately the Ruthenians withdrew their demand for the division of Galicia, leaving the decision to a future diet. As Wisłocki suspected, this was more than likely done under pressure from the Czechs, who had drawn attention to the fact that any realization of this demand would only help the Austrian bureaucracy. After extensive discussion, seven points were adopted:

1. There is to be language equality in the administration of the country. Despite the dominance of one language in one part of the country, the use of the minority tongue is to be permitted.
2. The nature of all forms of schooling, including tertiary education, should reflect the majority in a given place. In secondary schools both languages are to be compulsory.
3. The national guard in all areas will have officers with a Polish or Ruthenian command, with a joint badge in the form of the Polish and Ruthenian coats-of-arms placed side-by-side.

---

[113] Ibid., p. 107.

[114] Ibid. The lack of homogenization in *gente Rutheni, natione Poloni* circles is apparent here. Kasper Cięglewicz was identified with someone else, and Zygmunt Sawczyński with someone else again. The first considered himself to be a Ruthenian, the second actually was. The problem of the significant differences within *gente Rutheni, natione Poloni* circles has recently attracted the attention of Danuta Sosnowska, *Inna Galicja* (Warsaw, 2008), p. 78.

[115] Cf. Oleh Turii, "Hreko-katolyts'ka Tserkva i revoliutsiia 1848–1849 rr. u Halychyni," in *Rok 1848. Wiosna Ludów w Galicji. Zbiór studiów*, ed. Władysław Wic (Cracow, 1999), p. 82.

4. There is to be joint central authority and a diet, with correspondence conducted with interested parties in the language of the addressee.
5. There is to be equality for both denominations in their rights, and for the clergy in terms of finance and status.
6. The constitution is to ensure equality between Poles and Ruthenians in "humanitarian, political and denominational rights."
7. The question of the division of Galicia is to be resolved by a legislative diet.[116]

This was an act of good will on both sides, fulfilling the majority of the Ruthenian demands while at the same time respecting the Polish notions of the integrity of the former Polish lands. Libelt proudly announced:

> We have drawn up conditions of accord and unity between the brothers of a single mother, alike in provenance. For us they will be a source of joint solace and honour if only we preserve the great rule of Christian love, the negligence of which is not pleasant to us.[117]

These demands, however, were to remain only on paper. If these points had been accepted in the country, then the divergence in the political interests of Poles and Ruthenians might have been quelled, while the very formation of *gente Rutheni, natione Poloni* might have gained status and significance after such a success. In reality, the conflict between the sides only increased, and any return to the state of affairs that had existed prior to the revolutions of 1848 seemed more and more unlikely. Feodosii Steblii called this agreement "the only example of a judicious Polish-Ukrainian compromise,"[118] and it is difficult not to agree with this statement.

Another act of good will was the inclination expressed by Jerzy Lubomirski, the well-known Slavophile, to supplement Helcel's proposal to condemn the partitions of Poland by mentioning Rus'. He emphasized that the affairs of Poles and Ruthenians were inseparable and consequently the brother people must not be forgotten. Lubomirski's initiative spurred the counterargument that if mention was made of Rus', then one should recognize Lithuania, Samogitia, and other lands as distinct. Cięglewicz again claimed that Rus' was a part of Poland. Lubomirski's opponents either did not understand his perspec-

---

[116] Wisłocki, *Kongres*, pp. 110–12, 191–93.

[117] Ibid., p. 122 (the minutes of the tenth sitting of June 8, at 08:00).

[118] Feodosii Steblii, "Ukraïntsi i poliaky Halychyny v 30-40-kh rr. XIX st. Poshuky politychnoho partnerstva," in *Polska – Ukraina. Historia, polityka, kultura. Materiały międzynarodowej konferencji naukowej*, ed. Stefan Zabrowarny (Szczecin–Warsaw, 2003), p. 54.

tive, or simply feared compromise. In vain the prince attempted to convince them "that we are searching for sanctification and justice for the future of Rus' so that it will also believe favourably in our intentions."[119]

Upon his return from the congress, Jerzy Lubomirski ensured that the Central National Council ratified the agreement reached in Prague as quickly as possible. The Supreme Ruthenian Council was largely responsible for the resulting debacle, as they did not accept the compromise reached.[120] Thus the only moment over the course of the revolutions of 1848 in which the Poles and Ruthenians (as well as Ruthenians of Polish nationality) met in compromise came to nought. Later, given the conditions at home, there was quite literally no possibility of implementing the measures agreed to in Prague, even though many expressed a willingness to do so.

The Activities of the Ruthenian Sobor

Even after the Slavic Congress and the failure to realize an agreement, the Ruthenian Sobor remained active. Among the documents that have been preserved, the inauguration speech of Julian Horoszkiewicz from the meeting of 15 June 1848 is particularly significant. This speech can be treated as a political manifesto of the Ruthenian Sobor, although in form it is a literary morality work penned in a lofty tone. The author devotes his extensive introduction to the peoples who "through a route of tears, and roads of blood reached (…) the temple of the only God, of his true glory and his eternal gifts of truth and love."[121] He is referring, of course, to the Ruthenian people, with whom Horoszkiewicz identified totally:

> And our people, our Ruthenian people, had its bards and its martyrs who suffered greatly both the enormous labour of the people and the maintaining of freedom for their own, and they paid for this with cruel martyrdom and the spilling of sincere blood on this the altar of the highest glory. Its martyrdom was great, its suffering long and painful and extracted not only through the suffering of individual brothers but as a result of the persecution and oppression of the whole clan.[122]

---

[119] Wisłocki, *Kongres*, pp. 127–31 (the minutes of the eleventh Polish and Ruthenian section of June 9 at 08.00).

[120] Stolarczyk, *Działalność*, pp. 151–53.

[121] Julian Horoszkiewicz, *Mowa Juliana Horoszkiewicza na pierwszem publicznem posiedzeniu zboru ruskiego we Lwowie dnia 15go Czerwca 1848* ([Lviv], 1848), p. 1.

[122] Ibid., p. 2.

MOWA

JULIANA HOROSZKIEWICZA,

na pierwszem publicznem posiedzeniu zboru ruskiego

we Lwowie dnia 15go Czerwca 1848.

Przez długie wieki wspólnym losem wszystkich narodów był ucisk i ciemnota. Zuchwalstwo, samolubstwo i pycha przewodniczyły myśli, kierowały duszą, władały wolą wielkich ludów, przekazując potomności tylko swoje przekleństwo a ich politowanie. — Przez długie wieki przewaga rozumu i pierwszeństwo umysłowej potęgi, w świątyni wiary i światła osadziły chytre bóstwo własnych celów, a uczyniwszy szczytem swojej nauki i końcem mądrości tylko pokorę i pocieszenie w niewiadomości, niewinne a wolne z przyrody dzieci świata, wiodły na upodlenie, sposobiły na ciche ofiary kajdan występnych posiedzicielów, samodzierzców władzy. Ciemną i głuchą i krwawą była kolej przodków naszych żywota, a w tej ciemności tylko niewidomy palec Boży jak skry przyszłych wieków zaognienia, rzucał z kolebki swojej w różne świata strony dzieci prawdy i cnoty, które spełniając swoje wysokie przeznaczenie, niosąc w ustach swoich Boski dar światła, wolności, braterstwa, szły po cierniach męczeństwa na krzyż, na stos palny, na hak dla odkupienia ludzkości! — Drogą łez i drogą krwi dobijały się ludy do świątyni jedynego Boga, jego prawdziwej chwały i jego odwiecznych darów prawdy i miłości. Wolność i światło, które dzisiaj coraz dzielniej swoje promienia w doli rodu człowieczego roztacza, zdobyte było dłu-

23. Julian Horoszkiewicz's inauguration speech
at the first meeting of the Ruthenian Sobor

This suffering was to have been imposed on the Ruthenians by the Muscovites, the Turks and the Tatars. Tellingly, the author claims that "the most painful oppression was the one that came from the fraternal hand" — that is, the Polish hand. He proclaimed that the only cause for this oppression was the difference of rite. However, despite "the humiliation and suffering the indomitable Ruthenian spirit survived. (…)

The spirit of our bards of the Dnister, the Boh [Southern Bug], and the Dnipro."[123] In the new political reality prophesied by Horoszkiewicz, the world would see the "always noble tribe of Ruthenians." Further on he explains to Poles that Poland will collapse because of the faults of their "fathers." The situation had already changed—the actions of contemporary Poles convinced the Ruthenians of their "noble desires." However, Horoszkiewicz still emphasizes that there are also Poles who oppress and hate Ruthenians. Juxtaposed with these individuals he presents examples of Ruthenian devotion to their Polish brother, including taking part in battles or serving time in prisons. The most interesting part of Horoszkiewicz's speech is that which concerns the Greek Catholic clergy. He explains to Poles that they should not be surprised by the views held by some of the clergy, for the cause of these actions (contrary to the expectations of Polish democrats) is the very difficult financial situation which "arouses in them the fear of former injustice."[124]

Of equal importance is another section of Horoszkiewicz's address to the Ruthenians, in which the author solemnly calls upon his compatriots, at the hour of the dawn of freedom, "to maintain accord among all the nationalities. For Ruthenians, Poles, Armenians and Jews should fuse into a single mass."[125] Any opposite scenario would result in the Ruthenian idea collapsing in the same way Poland imploded as a result of the approach it adopted towards Rus'. Finally, he explains that this oppression was a feature of times past, and that this was noticeably less prevalent than had been the case in France or Germany.

It does not follow to treat Horoszkiewicz's words as an attack on Poles, but rather as an attempt to arouse in the Ruthenian listener or reader (as the speech was published) the impression or conviction that he is being addressed by a Ruthenian intellectual, one conscious of historical wrongdoings. Horoszkiewicz begins from the same position as the St. Georgians, but he differs in the conclusions he draws. The "bloody" Polish-Ruthenian relations he leaves to history while trying to convince his audience of the present-day need for cooperation between Ruthenians and Poles. He argues that the two peoples should aspire together to obtain a joint independence, and not work in opposition to each other. In this way he is criticizing the St. George camp as hindering attempts towards a mutually beneficial agreement:

> Therefore they sin, oh how badly they sin, our brothers who base themselves on the past, inciting in the Ruthenian people the notion that Poles

---

[123] Ibid., p. 3.
[124] Ibid., p. 4.
[125] Ibid., p. 5.

wish to damn and exterminate Ruthenians. Such an approach is an affront to our aims, to the honourable Ruthenian blood and the nobility of our nationality.[126]

In concluding his appeal, Horoszkiewicz directs attention to the foreign element by claiming that the partitioning power is a far worse enemy. He calls for the freedom to use Ruthenian and protection against the prospect of future generations speaking the language of the partitioner. Although Horoszkiewicz's piece is not a political programme, it would still constitute the ideological manifesto of the *gente Rutheni, natione Poloni* assembled in the Ruthenian Sobor.

The Sobor cooperated with the Central National Council,[127] but it was never reduced to a puppet of the organization. This is evident in the appeal read out at the sitting of the Central National Council on the "unacceptable behaviour of certain individuals in relation to awakening Ruthenian nationality." It was recommended that it be printed along with the Council's reply. On June 29 the Ruthenian Sobor issued another proclamation entitled *To Brothers Ruthenians* [*Do bratej Rusyniw*], which criticized those individuals who in the name of Ruthenian nationality presented demands in a way that ridiculed the organization.[128]

When the Supreme Ruthenian Council were collecting signatures for the petition to Vienna concerning the division of Galicia, Ruthenian Sobor activists on July 25 decided to write a petition of contrary wording and set about gathering signatures to send it to the emperor. The Ruthenian Sobor managed to acquire 577 signatures, a number which hints at the scale of Sobor influence and its support.[129] According to Franciszek Smolka the petition of the St. Georgians was signed by as many as 15,000 Ruthenians in Galicia.[130] Although this figure is not confirmed by any sources, and while the *gente Rutheni, natione Poloni* accused the St. Georgians of inflating numbers,[131] this in no way changes the fact that the extent of the influence exerted by the Sobor nationally

---

126 Ibid., p. 7.
127 *Protokoły posiedzeń*, p. 93.
128 *Do bratej Rusyniw* ([Lviv], 1848).
129 "Wysokyje Sobranie!," *Dnewnyk Ruskij* no. 3 (1 [13] Sep. 1848), p. 1.
130 Smolka, *Dziennik*, p. 22 (Letter to his wife, Vienna, 29 Aug. 1848).
131 See "Wysokyje Sobranie!". The author wrote: "A few days ago the news abroad, emanating from the so-called Ruthenian Council in Lviv, was that a request had been made to the imperial majesty in the name of the whole Ruthenian nation, to which many thousands of signatures have been added, with the aim of dividing Galicia into two separate political entities. The petition, preparation and requests were entirely secret, for no one in our country knew anything whatsoever about it and even more so, no one was called to sign. The entirety of this undertaking is shrouded in some sort of fog of darkness. On the one hand, the abundance of signatures therein speaks of their genuineness, while on the

was still minor. The collection of these 577 signatures would turn out to be the most significant political achievement for Ruthenians of Polish nationality.

It was likely at this time that the *Petition of the Inhabitants of Galicia* [*Adress mieszkańców Galicyi*] was compiled, in which the province's inhabitants "ever so humbly beseeched" the emperor not to divide the country into two parts. This demand was accompanied by the request that jurisdiction over such matters be granted to any National Diet (Sejm) formed in the future.[132]

At the sitting of the Central National Council held several days later on July 29, the members decided to "take steps to make the metropolitan [Mykhailo Levytsky – A.Ś.] sign the petition against the division of Galicia." A delegation composed of Kazimierz Krasicki, Tadeusz Wasilewski, Adam Lubomirski, Leon Sapieha, Aleksander Fredro, and Aleksander Batowski was sent to Levytsky.[133] Batowski described the meeting between the delegation and the metropolitan in detail.[134] During the meeting the delegates, believing that the metropolitan would side with the St. Georgians because he resided at the Univ Monastery, asked him whether he knew about "various innovations, journalistic arguments, the splitting of the inhabitants into Ruthenian and Polish nationalities, the agitation of the people by the clergy, and the Ruthenian Sobor and the new project for the division of the province."[135] The metropolitan answered all of these questions in the negative, and Batowski noted that there was something in the metropolitan's words that suggested "the influence and spirit of Iakhymovych over him, or simply his own aversion to Poles."[136] Levytsky anticipated the Poles treating the Ruthenians disparagingly and separating from them of their own accord. He did not support the Greek Catholic clergy's involvement in politics, but conceded that the time had come in which the clergy no longer listened to him, for which he blamed the Polish side. He stated that he did not read *Dziennik Narodowy*, and that in the content of *Zoria Halytska* he did not perceive any underlying hostility in relation to

---

other every good soul can be strongly convinced that this request did not originate from the will of the entire Ruthenian people of Lviv."

[132] *Adress mieszkańców Galicyi*, ([Lviv, 1848]).

[133] *Protokoły posiedzeń*, p. 139; Batowski, *Diariusz*, p. 261. Cf. Turii, "Hreko-katolyts'ka Tserkva," p. 86; Oleh Turii, "Ukraïns'ke dukhovenstvo i natsional'no-politychna borot'ba v Halychyni pid chas revoliutsiï 1848–1849 rokiv," *Ukraïna. Kul'turna spadshchyna, natsional'na svidomist', derzhavnist'* 9: *Iubileinyi zbirnyk na poshanu Feodosiia Stebliia* (2001), pp. 167–68.

[134] Batowski, *Diariusz*, pp. 274–83.

[135] Ibid., p. 277.

[136] Ibid.

Poles, and if that were the case then "don't praise them, but reprimand them." After hearing Levytsky's answers to the delegation's questions, Wasilewski finally presented the metropolitan with the petition against the division of Galicia. When asked whether he would sign it, Levytsky, having read it thoroughly, reportedly refused, because for him it made "no difference whatsoever if there was one or two gubernias."[137] The delegates then attempted to show him that there was no point in dividing lands that had been joined for centuries; that it would bring about discord; that Ruthenian kings had ruled Poland, and senators from Rus' had taken their seats in the senate; that the Ruthenian language was being supported, proof of which was the Stauropegion Institute printing press. However, the metropolitan was of the view that Ruthenians owed all their freedoms, liberties, and civilization to the Austrians. Eventually Leon Sapieha pulled out the Ruthenian Sobor's petition written in German, and proposed that the metropolitan sign this document if he does not want to sign the first. As Batowski noted, Levytsky knew nothing about the Ruthenian Sobor, so Sapieha explained to him that he himself "came from a Ruthenian-Lithuanian family and that he belonged to the Ruthenian Sobor." Despite this, the metropolitan did not sign the Ruthenian Sobor's petition, arguing that it in no way differed from the first petition. It then came out that he had already signed the St. Georgians' petition over the division of Galicia. Nothing would convince the metropolitan that it was an Austrian plot. Finally, Sapieha showed the head of the Greek Catholic Church "the Sobor's membership diploma and a paper in the Ruthenian dialect [intended] for the rural population".[138] This most likely concerned *Dnewnyk Ruskij*, which was probably in the organizational stage at this time; the first issue would be published the following August.[139] The metropolitan liked the idea, but did not want to belong to any organization:

> He again put on his glasses and read attentively, and upon finishing said: "Now this is good, I'm full of praise and wish you gentlemen success, but I myself do not wish to belong to this for I have no need of it. I do not belong to the St. George Council as this is not for me. I shall take the paper and read it and support it if it is good, but it is not becoming of my office for me to become a member as such."[140]

Levytsky also did not accept the charges levelled against the behaviour of certain Uniate clerics, including that of the Przemyśl bishop, Iakhymovych. Finally, having paid his compliments to the delegates he

---

[137] Ibid., p. 278.
[138] Ibid., p. 281.
[139] *Dnewnyk Ruskij* no. 1 (18 [30] Aug. 1848).
[140] Batowski, *Diariusz*, p. 281.

took his leave. This account was presented the next day at the forum of the Central National Council.[141]

Dnewnyk Ruskij

The periodical *Dnewnyk Ruskij*, the press organ of the Ruthenian Sobor, commenced its activities in August 1848.[142] The instigator of the project was Jan Wagilewicz, known for his literary work in the 1830s in the framework of the Ruthenian Triad. Behind Wagilewicz's reputation lay the legend of the aborted *Rusalka Dnistrovaia*, the first ever Ruthenian almanac in Galicia, most of the circulation of which had been confiscated due to censorship. Wagilewicz, as the author of a textbook on Ruthenian grammar and as a scholar of Ruthenian history and culture, was the natural frontrunner for the role of editor of this new journal that would provide a platform for the *gente Rutheni, natione Poloni*. Wagilewicz had functioned for several years within Polish circles, to which he was introduced by Józef Dunin-Borkowski. Already in 1843, Denys Zubrytsky wrote of the former cofounder of the Ruthenian Triad as "the outcast Vahylevych, completely Polonized and wandering among the Poles feeding on fantastic dreams."[143]

Wagilewicz quickly set to work in the forum of the Ruthenian Sobor, of which he had become a member. As Julian Horoszkiewicz noted:

> In the very first days Wagilewicz presented a proposal for the establishment of a publication by the Sobor, designed to enlighten the nation and communicate the aspirations of those assembled. He presented the need for this publication to be printed in the Latin script in order to, as he said, enable Rus'—aspiring as it was to constitutional freedoms and for centuries connected with the civilization of the West—to decisively sever everything that could assimilate it with Russia. Efforts were immediately undertaken to publish the journal under the title *Dnewnyk*, and Wagilewicz was to be its editor.[144]

---

[141] *Protokoły posiedzeń*, p. 147.
[142] Kozik, "Stosunki ukraińsko-polskie," pp. 35–36; Marian Tyrowicz, *Prasa Galicji i Rzeczypospolitej Krakowskiej 1772–1850. Studia porównawcze* (Cracow, 1979), pp. 21, 142; Jerzy Jarowiecki, *Dzieje prasy polskiej we Lwowie do 1945 roku* (Cracow–Wrocław, 2008), pp. 44–45; Wójtowicz-Huber, *'Ojcowie narodu'*, p. 55, footnote 93; Myroslav Romaniuk, Mariia Halushko, *Ukraïns'ki chasopysy L'vova 1848–1939*, vol. 1: *1848–1900* (Lviv, 2001), pp. 27, 159–61; Oleksandr Sedliar, "'Dnevnyk Ruskii'," in *Entsyklopediia L'vova*, vol. 2, ed. Andrii Kozyts'kyi (Lviv, 2008), p. 101.
[143] Quoted after: Marceli Handelsman, *Ukraińska polityka ks. Adama Czartoryskiego przed wojną krymską* (Warsaw, 1937), pp. 83. See also: Jan Kozik, *Ukraiński ruch narodowy w Galicji w latach 1830–1848* (Cracow, 1973), p. 215.
[144] Horoszkiewicz, *Notatki*, p. 291.

The editorial offices were located in Lviv, on 11 Szeroka Street [today Kopernyka Street], in the premises at 2/4.[145] *Dnewnyk Ruskij* was to be published weekly, in Ruthenian, in two versions: one in Latin and one in Cyrillic script. A unique set of all nine published issues has been preserved in the Rare Books Department of the Lviv National Vasyl Stefanyk Scientific Library of Ukraine.[146] The journal, despite its serious aspirations, was not to enjoy much popularity outside of Lviv, something that Father Walerian Kalinka lamented a whole decade after its collapse.[147]

24. *Jan Wagilewicz*
[Ivan Vahylevych]

The texts that appeared in *Dnewnyk Ruskij* often took on the political programme of Ruthenians of Polish nationality. In the first issue the editor-in-chief printed the "Program", in which he informed the readership of the Ruthenian Sobor and its goal: the implementation of accord and peace between Poles and Ruthenians within the scope of a common homeland.[148] Included in this same issue was "An Appeal of the Ruthenian Sobor to Its Brothers" ["Vozvanie Ruskoho Soboru do svoikh bratov"]. In this piece, the history of Rus' was laid out, in which it was painted as enjoying freedoms under the rule of the "co-tribalist" (in the original: *soplemennyky*) Poles, only to suffer for 70 years after being dismantled and shared between Russia and Austria—as had happened to the Poles. Only now the situation was ripe for change. For it was possible to foster the development of Ruthenian nationality through, for example, the Ruthenian language in the school system, which the Ruthenian Sobor had taken it upon itself to support. Later in this appeal

---

[145] Sedliar, "'Dnevnyk Ruskii'," p. 101.

[146] Numbers 1–5 and number 9 are in Latin script, numbers 6–8 in Cyrillic. The authors of a guide to Lviv newspapers, on the basis of Ivan Franko's statement that no more than 10 issues of "Dnewnyk Ruskij" were produced, are of the view that one more issue was published. However, to date this has not been located, which leads one to believe that only nine issues were produced. Cf. Romaniuk, Halushko, *Ukraïns'ki chasopysy*, p. 161.

[147] Waleryan Kalinka "Konspiracya dzieci we Lwowie," in Waleryan Kalinka, *Pisma pomniejsze*, part 2 (Cracow, 1894), p. 195. The author wrote: "A circle of well-meaning Ruthenians, wanting to enlighten the deceived ordinary people, started to publish in a good--natured spirit a Ruthenian paper, *Dnewnik*, but this journal did not even reach the people, as it was hardly read outside of Lviv and soon collapsed."

[148] Ivan Vahylovych', "Program"," *Dnevnyk" Ruskii* no. 1 (18 [30] Aug. 1848), p. 1.

the members of the organization extended words of peace and accord to the Ruthenian clergy and the serfs and peasants, whose wretchedness was to finally end.[149]

Besides the "Program" and "An Appeal," also included in this issue was "A Proclamation of the Ruthenian Sobor to the Venerable Priests" ["Otozva Soboru Ruskoho do velevnykh" Sviashchennikov"] of 13 August 1848, in which the goals of the Sobor were once again presented to the Uniate clergy. They encouraged them to teach that both Poles and Ruthenians came from the same stem or root, and urged them not to drive a wedge between the two peoples.[150] While "A Proclamation" was aimed at winning over the Uniate clergy, the article "The Distinguished Gathering!" ["Wysokie Sobranie!"], likely penned by Julian Horoszkiewicz, mercilessly took to task those who wanted to drive a wedge between Poles and Ruthenians." It is worth quoting the author's straightforward statements:

> And to you the enemies of freedom! And to you the children of darkness and discord, this is my advice to you: stop inciting two brotherly peoples, stop antagonizing the family! The Pole and the Ruthenian often would argue among themselves, but chiefly against a third party that stood between them. You ask the Podolian meadow, the banks of the blue Boh [Southern Buh] River, you ask the Swedish graves, they will tell you, they will teach you how slippery and how dangerously you stand. Listen to the old songs: they will tell you how we fought the Vlachs, the Swedes, the Muscovites, the Turks and Tatars and all who came to us with lies. The old glory still rings across the Ruthenian lands, young blood still flows in the breasts; the family will argue and die but the crow that will not take the bones of the enemy to the land that spawned them does not deserve its pay. Our Holy Land is rich; Ruthenians and Poles are famed for hospitality, but how might one play host in another's cottage?[151]

Even more noteworthy is Cyryl Wieńkowski's pronouncement, published in the fourth issue of *Dnewnyk Ruskij*. He confided to his readers that he had obtained a letter from a certain Ruthenian of Stanyslaviv, who had had the nerve to threaten him and attempt to teach him. Wieńkowski, emphasizing that he had been elected in the name of the Ruthenian people to the constituent assembly in Warsaw, sought to prove that he was a Ruthenian, and claimed that from the time of

---

[149] "Vozvanie Ruskoho Soboru do svoikh bratov"," *Dnevnyk" Ruskii* no. 1 (18 [30] Aug. 1848), pp. 1–2.
[150] "Otozva Soboru Ruskoho do velevnykh" Sviashchennikov"," *Dnevnyk" Ruskii* no. 1 (18 [30] Aug. 1848), pp. 2–3.
[151] "Wysokyje Sobranie!," *Dnewnyk Ruskij* no. 3 (1 [13] Sep. 1848), p. 1.

25. The masthead of the journal Dnevnyk' Ruskii

his conspiratorial activities in 1834 his outlook on the world had never changed. His Ruthenian "confession of national faith" reads as follows:

> Alas, I did not become a Ruthenian, however much the black-and-yellow [the heraldic colours of Habsburg Austria – A.Ś.] author of the foul letter imagined such, but the awareness of my nationality and my position as a Ruthenian is within me and is as old as my notion about my very self.[152]

Another crucial text, "An Appeal to the Ruthenian Intelligentsia" ["Wozwanie do intelligencii ruskoji"], appeared in the fifth issue of September 27. The anonymous author informed the Ruthenian reader that the aim of the Ruthenian Sobor was the establishment of equal legal, language, and religious rights with the Poles, reached in the spirit of accord and unity. Hence *Dnewnyk Ruskij* also, as the organ of the Sobor, appealed to the "educated countrymen" to involve themselves in public enlightenment. The publication requested that they not turn their backs on the Poles, for among them were friends and brothers. At the same time, several members of the clergy were subjected to criticism, with the Przemyśl bishop Iakhymovych maligned above others.[153] In a subsequent text that appeared in the same issue, entitled "Something about the Sextons" ["De szczo o diakach"], greater attention was directed towards the problems of the Greek Catholic clergy, particularly the material situation of the clergy and the Greek Catholic Church in general. The Ruthenian Sobor offered to stand in defence of their interests, even at the Diet sessions in Vienna.[154]

Although the basic purpose of *Dnewnyk Ruskij* was to inform readers about the activities and work of the Ruthenian Sobor and to publish its

---

[152] Kyryl M. Wienkowskij, "Oswidczenije," *Dnewnyk Ruskij* no. 4 (8 [20] Apr. 1848), p. 13.

[153] "Wozwanie do intelligencii ruskoji," *Dnewnyk Ruskij* no. 5 (15 [27] Sep. 1848), pp. 17–18.

[154] "De szczo o diakach," *Dnewnyk Ruskij* no. 5 (15 [27] Sep. 1848), p. 18.

proclamations and other papers of a political nature, space was also al-
lotted for texts more generally journalistic in style. An article appeared
in four consecutive issues entitled "Discourse on Rus' and Its Political
Situation" ["Słowo o Rusy i jej polityczeskom stanowyszczy"], the au-
thorship of which was indicated only by the initials F.H. Framing his
argument with a history of Rus', the author reminded his readers of its
centuries-long connection with Poland and the contemporary situation
of Ruthenians themselves.[155] Besides the political content, reviews of
upcoming Ruthenian works were published, such as those of the Polish-Ruthenian brotherhood bard Tymko Padurra in the ninth issue, as
well as various other poetic works. The fourth issue included the poem
"To the Martyrs of [the Fight for] Freedom of 1847" ["Muczennykam
wolnosti z r. 1847"], while the seventh contained the piece "Dumka
in Steppe" [Dumka w stepach], in which it was emphasized that the
strength of the Ruthenians in conjunction with the Poles would help
in the fight against the Muscovites. The St. Georgian circle was particularly hostile towards *Dnewnyk Ruskij*, as there was a blatant anti-
-St. Georgian polemic in the pages of the journal.[156]

The Breakup of the *Gente Rutheni, Natione Poloni* Camp

Besides questioning and scruntinizing the activities of the clergy af-
filiated with St. George's Cathedral, *Dnewnyk Ruskij* criticized its own
"gaps." Kasper Cięglewicz fell out of favour due to his refusal to consider Ruthenians as a separate nationality, a position he made clear at the
Slavic Council in Prague. In his famous work *The Red-Ruthenian Cause*
[*Rzecz czerwono-ruska*]), published at the turn of September in Lviv, he
presented his view of Ruthenians as part of a greater whole, that of the
Polish nation.[157] This was the first treatise on the question of Ruthenian nationality to appear in *gente Rutheni, natione Poloni* circles. Certain
politicians in Galicia had long awaited Cięglewicz's thesis. As early as
August 29, Franciszek Smolka had written in a letter from Vienna to his
wife that it would be good if someone prepared a work on Ruthenians
to have up his sleeve for when the Ruthenians broached their demands
in the House of Lords.[158] Cięglewicz's work answered this call, and was
met by Smolka with great praise. On September 6 he appealed to his

---

[155] F. H., "Słowo o Rusy i jej polityczeskom stanowyszczy," *Dnewnyk Ruskij* no. 6–9 (1848).
[156] Tyrowicz, *Prasa Galicji*, p. 21.
[157] Kasper Cięglewicz, *Rzecz czerwono-ruska 1848 roku* (Lviv, 1848).
[158] Smolka, *Dziennik*, pp. 22–23.

wife to produce a German translation of the treatise so that the Ruthenian question could be presented in a wider political forum.[159] Not long afterwards, in accordance with this plan, a German-language issue of Cięglewicz's work appeared.[160]

Cięglewicz's booklet centred on the assertion that "Poland from the Oder [!] to the Dnipro contained three main peoples: the Masurians, the Ruthenians, and the Lithuanians."[161] The Polish language which was used by all three ethnic groups had come about, according to Cięglewicz, because the languages of the Poles and Ruthenians "rubbed off" on each other; Cięglewicz identified the central

26. *The cover of Kasper Cięglewicz's brochure* Red-Ruthenian Cause *(Vienna, 1848)*

part of Galicia as the place where this "friction" had occurred. He considered Ruthenian to be "rural" and uncouth, yet necessary. Because of its lack of linguistic refinement and its backwardness, this language should not, according to the author, become an instrument for education.[162] In writing these words Cięglewicz had to explain why he himself had hitherto used the Ruthenian language, if only in reference to his folk songs. He admitted without mincing his words that he wished to "influence its spirit," a task in which he confessed he had not succeeded. He criticized in passing Cyryl Wieńkowski, who tried with figures such as Józef Puzyna to demonstrate at meetings that the Ruthenian language was not simply a dialect of Polish, and that the Ruthenian population wanted to speak and write in Ruthenian. Cięglewicz argued that, complicit in the Austrian scheme, the St. Georgians wanted to introduce Ruthenian in all areas, a language which they themselves had rarely used. He singled out Bishop Iakhymovych, who never used to write in Ruthenian, as well as Michał Popiel, Julian Horoszkiewicz, and their colleagues, who eventually did use Ruthenian as a language. He would later write that the Polish and Ruthenian languages were so

---

[159] Ibid., pp. 28–32.

[160] Kasper Cięglewicz, *Die roth-reukischen Angelegenheiten im Jahre 1848* (Vienna, 1848).

[161] Cięglewicz, *Rzecz czerwono-ruska*, p. 1.

[162] Ibid., p. 2.

similar to each other that Ruthenian peasants who did not know Polish were able to understand the residents of Lviv, who in turn could understood Ruthenians perfectly despite not speaking Ruthenian. From this he developed the conviction that there was no real need for any special treatment of the Ruthenian language. Cięglewicz also criticized Wieńkowski's belief that Cyrillic was a "national Ruthenian" treasure which should be preserved. He saw this choice of alphabet as an unnecessary strengthening of relations with Russia. In a later part of the text he attempted a historical proof to demonstrate that Poles and Ruthenians together formed the society of former Poland, noting that kings such as Michael I (Michał Korybut Wiśniowiecki) and various dignitaries (he enumerated the Chodkiewicz, Żółkiewski, Ostrogski, Potocki, Sapieha and Czartoryski noble families) had been Ruthenian. He tried to quash the opinion that the Greek Catholic rite determined nationality, which was the argumentation of the St. George camp. Cięglewicz stated that a change in denomination on the part of the Ruthenian nobility in no way meant that this social stratum became deprived of its nationality. Speaking of the demand for a division of Galicia into two parts, he underlined that this was an initiative of the clergy, while "the whole of the more enlightened part of Red-Ruthenians did not want this division."[163] The crux of Cięglewicz's work comes at the end of the booklet, when the author emphasizes that his aim is to stop his compatriots making the mistake they were forced to make through the Ruthenian Sobor's publishing of *The Proclamation of the Ruthenian Sobor*. He chiefly criticized the demand put forward in this publication of establishing a lower and higher Ruthenian schooling system. He stated that even though he had signed the proclamation, he in no way agreed with this point; furthermore, he claimed that he had been at the time in Prague and consequently could not have personally contributed his signature. He also reacted negatively to the published speech given by Julian Horoszkiewicz from a Ruthenian Sobor meeting because of its claim "that in Poland a Ruthenian is exposed to political oppression." It was for this reason that Cięglewicz decided to leave the Ruthenian Sobor.[164]

The Red-Ruthenian Cause naturally sparked outrage among the *gente Rutheni, natione Poloni* concentrated around *Dnewnyk Ruskij*. In the third issue a critical account of Cięglewicz's work appeared, entitled "Some Explanations" ["Deszczo do izjasnenija"]. The anonymous author emphasized that a Ruthenian schooling system could not exist without higher institutions of education with classes conducted in Ruthenian.

---

[163] Ibid., p. 5.
[164] Ibid., pp. 6–7; Horoszkiewicz, *Notatki*, p. 320.

Regarding Cięglewicz's claim that his signature had been placed under *The The Proclamation of the Ruthenian Sobor* without his permission, the readers were left to judge as to whether his inclusion within the ranks of the Sobor had been such a good decision.[165]

One might conclude that Kasper Cięglewicz, being a Pole, albeit one deeply immersed in Ruthenian culture and language, was not able to place the interests of Ruthenians on the same level as those of the Polish nation. However, drawing such a conclusion would be an over-simplification. Cięglewicz's opinions demonstrate that two visions of *gente Rutheni, natione Poloni* were at this time in conflict. The first vision proclaimed that Ruthenians were a nation equal to Poles linked by the common homeland of Poland, whose independence both elements should fight for with an equal and combined force. Such an option was represented by, among others, the editorial board of *Dnewnyk Ruskij*, composed of figures such as Wagilewicz, Wieńkowski, and Horosz-kiewicz. The second vision acknowledged the existence of several ethnic groups, including the Ruthenians and the Masurians, but saw them constituting a singular, historically authorized nation of Poles.

The second option was eagerly embraced by Polish politicians in Galicia who dreamed of an independent Poland within the pre-partition borders. Many Ruthenians agreed with such a model as understood by *gente Rutheni, natione Poloni* and supported the concept. A good example is that of the Lviv provincial court counselor Antoni Dąbczański, known for his participation in the "Black Senate" in Lviv during the investigation and trial of Polish independence activist Józef Zaliwski and his colleagues in 1834. He had aided those arrested at the time by providing a modified translation of the testimonies, which saved many from the death penalty. The publisher of a selection of Dąbczański's re-collections wrote about him: "Even though Dąbczański himself was of the Greek Catholic rite he never for the whole of his life had any doubts that he was in fact a Pole."[166]

Dąbczański prepared a booklet for publication entitled *The Ruthenian Question Explained* [*Wyjaśnienie sprawy ruskiej*] soon after the publication of Cięglewicz's *The Red-Ruthenian Cause*. The text appeared in a Polish and German bilingual version in September.[167] In the introduction the author took on the Supreme Ruthenian Council, accusing it of being composed partly of Greek Catholic clergy and a handful of clerks and suburban sorts summoned for the "bestowing of significance." He explained to the reader that as a result of the petition of April 19 and the

---

[165] "De szczo do izjasnenija," *Dnewnyk Ruskij* no. 3 (1 [13] Sep. 1848), p. 2.
[166] [Antoni Dąbczański], *Antoni Dąbczański i jego pamiętnik (z portretem)* (Lviv, 1912), p. 10.
[167] Antoni Dąbczański, *Wyjaśnienie sprawy ruskiej* (Lviv, 1848).

policies of severing centuries-old links with the Poles, the Ruthenian intelligentsia together with the Greek Catholic gentry had set up the Ruthenian Sobor "clearly declaring that Ruthenians form a single body and setting for itself all kinds of labour in order to thwart all the calamities threatening the aspirations of Ruthenian society."[168] At the same time he also criticized the vain attempts undertaken by the Central National Council which had, according to him, engaged in unnecessary attempts to convince the Ruthenian clergy that the Council members were right. Dąbczański did not believe in the possibility of any change in the views held by the Greek Catholic clergy.

27. *Antoni Dąbczański*

On the subsequent pages of *The Ruthenian Question Explained* he took it upon himself to present his vision of the history of Rus', from the tenth century to the present day. Here he drew attention to the possession by the Polish state of the lands lying within the scope of Eastern Galicia, even under the rule of King Bolesław the Brave. He saw the rule of Ruthenian princes and Tatars as hindering progress, while the "recovery" of these lands by the Polish state in the fourteenth century bestowed on Ruthenians "rights totally equal with those of Poles." Later in his work Dąbczański described the benefits gained by Ruthenians under Polish rule. In turn, when analyzing his own times he concentrated on criticism of the St. Georgians, explaining that denomination did not determine nationality. Here he cited with approval the booklet by Cięglewicz described above.[169]

The next section of Dąbczański's work was devoted to language. The author, allegedly basing his argument on Nestor the Chronicler, set out to show the reader that Ruthenian and Polish were one and the same language. The relationship of Ruthenian to Polish is "like a dialect to an educated tongue."[170] Ruthenians themselves were responsible for the lack of "development" in their language, for they did not take care of its progress .

The peasant question is also presented in the booklet. The author tried to unmask the way in which the St. Georgians collected signa-

---

[168] Ibid., p. 4.

[169] Ibid., p. 18.

[170] Ibid., p. 19.

tures to support the demand for the division of Galicia. He states that the members of the Supreme Ruthenian Council asked the peasants: "Would you rather be a Pole or a Ruthenian?," when in reality the question should have been: "Would you rather belong to Poland or to Russia?" He attributed the collection of so many signatures on the petition to the illiteracy of the peasantry and the tactic of threatening them with the alleged return of serfdom and a renunciation of their religion at the hands of the Poles.[171]

Dąbczański concluded with an appeal to the youth at the Greek Catholic seminary in Lviv. He reminded the seminarians that they had always been connected with Poland and that they had willingly signed the petition of March 19, and emphasized that someone now wanted to separate them. He admonished them:

> (...) you have turned your gaze away, not without emotion, from the Polish nation in just the way a lover casts off his beloved at the wish of a parent.[172]

These texts were read and consulted by Dąbczański at his villa in Lviv, to which Ferdynand Cielecki, Dzierzkowski, and Batowski were invited. Batowski evaluated the work fairly coolly, but did see its worth as yet another act directed against the St. Georgians:

> There is little spirit in it, the historical facts are superficial, the lecture aloof. Timidity and two-stoolism ring through. Yet that willingness in the office to stand up against people of ill will aroused by Stadion and [Joseph Wilhelm] Eminger, who so incite and unite this most numerous people, is most commendable.[173]

Despite such a lukewarm evaluation, this work constituted a significant initiative in the discussion between Poles and Ruthenians. Various aspects of the conflict that had developed in Galicia were discussed at length over the course of forty pages. As the publisher commented on a section of Dąbczański's memoirs, his work could be considered an "opening statement and commencement to this dispute [Polish-Ruthenian – A.Ś.], calling into being violent attacks from the Ruthenian side."[174]

It is difficult today to establish which of the preserved letters, proclamations, or articles were in fact replies to Dąbczański's work. Without doubt, however, letters were penned among the Supreme Ruthenian

---

[171] Ibid., p. 34.
[172] Ibid., p. 40.
[173] Batowski, *Diariusz*, p. 324.
[174] [Dąbczański], *Antoni Dąbczański*, pp. 10–11.

Council activists denouncing the works of both Poles and Ruthenians of Polish nationality. Rare are booklets such as *A Ruthenian to the Poles* [*Rusin do Polaków*], written by a certain Fedko znad Pełtwy [Fedir from the Banks of the Poltva River], which enumerated the damage inflicted by Poles in the past, yet did so with the idea of respecting the separate interests of both nations and appealing for an accord.[175]

In the leaflets published by members of the Supreme Ruthenian Council there was no absence of criticism of those Ruthenians who had cooperated with the Poles. For example, Father Iosyf Krushynsky accused Father Aleksander Kmicikiewicz [Oleksandr Kmytskykevych] of the Kulykiv deanery of adopting from the Polish gentry, with whom he had cooperated, the worst of their vices.[176] Kmicikiewicz was also criticized for his inadequate knowledge of the Ruthenian language: "And finally Father Kmicikiewicz has clearly shown what an excellent Ruthenian is, if he can think that a Ruthenian can speak Ruthenian so badly."[177]

In turn, a broad disquisition on the separateness of the Ruthenian nation from the Polish can be found in Teodor Leontovych's lengthy article. He emphasized the existence of a brotherhood of Poles and Ruthenians, but citing the findings of Wacław Zaleski, he also drew attention to the differences between these two peoples. He did not view the creation of a common homeland as negative, but he had no desire to see in any future homeland a situation where one nation was to enjoy a relationship similar to that of the helots and Spartans.[178]

Iosyf Lozynsky, in his work *On the Change in Nationality in Relation to the Ruthenian Nationality* [*O zmianie narodowości pod względem na narodowość ruską*],[179] enumerated those criteria on which basis Ruthenian nationality could be characterized: generation, language, and rite. He agreed that Ruthenians were able to actively engage in politics during the times of old Poland, but they had not so much changed their nationality as betrayed it.[180] The *gente Rutheni, natione Poloni* were simply considered to be apostates of the Ruthenian nation. Lozynsky went on to analyze the question of change of rite in Rus'. According to him, it was religious conflicts that had in the past been the "bone of conten-

---

[175] Fedko znad Pełtwy, *Rusin do Polaków* ([Lviv, 1848]).

[176] Józef Kruszyński, *Odpowiedź na protest niby kleru ruskiego Dekanatu Kulikowskiego, rzeczywiście zaś podpisany przez Alexandra Kmicikiewicza, ogłoszony w Nrze 73 tak zwanego Dziennika Narodowego* ([1848]).

[177] Ibid., p. 3.

[178] [Teodor Leontowicz] L., *Odpowiedź na artykuł o nieistnieniu Rusinów umieszczony w Numerze 2gim Dziennika Narodowego* ([1848]), passim.

[179] Josyf Łozyńskyj, *O zmianie narodowości pod względem na narodowość ruską* (1848).

[180] Ibid., p. 2.

tion" between the Ruthenians and Poles. Lozynsky's work ended with an exhortation to love one's own nation and respect the other. The author emphasized here that each should be given its rightful property, which in this case meant the division of Galicia.[181]

Interestingly, it was Jan Zachariasiewicz, a member of the Ruthenian Sobor, who called for equal treatment of the Ruthenian nation, a rejection of the rhetoric referring to the tradition of Polish-Ruthenian unions, and a "lowering" of oneself to the people in order to rebuild a true "people's Poland." During the revolutions of 1848, he had written a noteworthy article entitled "Czech Policy and Ruthenian Nationality" ["Polityka czeska a narodowość ruska"], which he published in the Lviv paper *Postęp*. Excerpts from this article supplement the picture of the multitude of attitudes prevalent among the Ruthenian population in Lviv. Unlike other Ruthenians of Polish nationality, Zachariasiewicz did not shun troublesome questions, but attempted to solve them:

> Rus' has shared its lot with Poland. Everything that was under its governance was called Poland. Poland fell and with it collapsed everything that was under it. The government of former Poland became the strength of its nationalities. A future Poland will come into being not by the force of its nationality but by the strength of the idea of freedom and brotherhood, while Rus', in order to be at one with any arisen Poland, requires the drive of its nationality. A free Poland cannot come about at the expense of the Ruthenian nation; it cannot be a colonial Poland. Those times have passed, and whoever continues to live in them is a man of the past.

He spoke of the future of Poland:

> The future Poland is to be a peoples' Poland, for why should there be animosity for no reason among peoples sharing the same interests? Here lies the mystery of our inner split. Ruthenians fear the former Poland because of exploitation by the gentry, while the champions of the Polish gentry approach the Ruthenians as the apostles of unity and accord, persuading the people about the former times of excellence, which are for them a pure abstraction or a painful recollection. The people will not ascend to the memories of the past; we should lower these memories to them; discard for them the blessed delusions that we have acquired through history on the route of deceit and inhumanity.[182]

---

[181] Ibid., p. 5.
[182] Jan Zachariasiewicz, "Polityka czeska a narodowość ruska," *Postęp* no. 22 (8 Jun. 1848), p. 80–81, 84. Cf.: Czesław Kłak, "Literacka młodość Jana Zachariasiewicza," in *Z tradycji kulturalnych Rzeszowa i Rzeszowszczyzny. Księga pamiątkowa dla uczczenia X-lecia*

Zachariasiewicz's text is a moderate voice in the Polish-Ruthenian debate (and the simultaneous internal debate at the Ruthenian Sobor), refuting the interpretation that *gente Rutheni, natione Poloni* were merely Polonized Ruthenians or worse, tools in the hands of Polish conservative circles. Zachariasiewicz's demand for lowering oneself to the actual level of the people would find proponents, not among the gentry, but within the ranks of the democratic agitators composing minor works of propaganda.

Gutter Publications

The period of the revolutions of 1848 infected Galician society with enthusiasm, something especially visible in Lviv. This zeal enveloped not only political activists, but also poets, with Lviv streets overflowing with poetry on the subject of historical events. The content of these numerous leaflets and the wording that appeared on billboards, posters, in poems and printed fliers are worth examining in detail, as they constitute a fertile source for the history of this period. The "Poetry of the Revolutions of 1848" of interest here survived primarily in magazines and printed fliers, which have been preserved in large numbers at the Department of Rare Books of the Lviv National Vasyl Stefanyk Scientific Library of Ukraine. This poetry corresponded to the political demands of the democrats and propagated the idea of Ruthenian-Polish fraternity. The verses serve as appeals for unity and a resolution to all the questions troubling Galician society in 1848[183].

The poem *The Tale* [*Powiastka*], one of the most popular pieces written by a certain Boczkowski,[184] presented an example of a Polish peasant named Wawrzek and a Ruthenian named Havrylo, who "for a long time lived righteously, in harmony." They symbolize not only the rural population, but also represent an allegory of the Polish and Ruthenian peoples. The former idyll in which they lived gave way to arguments and disputes, particularly the arguments over "the cow," personifying in this poem the fatherland. The instigator of the dispute was none other

---

rzeszowskiego oddziału Towarzystwa Literackiego im. Adama Mickiewicza, eds. Stanisław Fry-cie and Stefan Reczek (Rzeszów, 1966), pp. 176–77.

[183] More about gutter publications in: Adam Świątek, "Rusyn, Polak to dwa tiła, szczo jedneho serdcia syła. Polska agitacja względem Rusinów galicyjskich w dobie Wiosny Ludów na przykładzie wybranych druków ulotnych," in *Druki ulotne w procesie komunikacji społecznej w XIX wieku (do 1918 roku)*, ed. Małgorzata Karpińska (Warsaw, 2018), p. 49–71.

[184] [Juwenal Boczkowski], *Powiastka* (Lviv, 1848).

than the devil himself. The brothers, "instead of fighting with Satan when needed, brawled over the cow, destroying their very selves." In the meantime the dogs—the allegorical partitioning powers—eat the cow, leaving the peasant with only the horns and its tail. The poem is accompanied by an illustration showing on the one side a Ruthenian peasant in a long black coat pulling the animal by its tail, and on the other a Pole in a russet coat dragging the cow by its horns. The work is not characterized by any textual or formal complication, but this was the intention of the piece—to reach the ordinary man. The extreme didacticism was aided by the illustration, which literally expressed the general meaning of the work.

Antim Lubowicz, utilizing farm animals as a metaphor for Ternopil, also presented his views in a fairy tale in verse entitled *The Hawk and the Hens* [*Jastrib i kury*].[185] The author expressed the lofty ideas of Polish-Ruthenian brotherhood, depicting in his work chickens with combs and without, to whom the cock-sage speaks:

Listen to old me, brothers
Here we are all of the same tribe
With a crest or without – we are all the same
Always hens, and not sparrowhawks

28. An illustration from the Boczkowski's leaflet The Tale
(Lviv, 1848)

---

[185] Antim Lubowicz, *Jastrib i kury* (Lviv, 1848), TsDIAU, fond 474, op. 1, spr. 18: Virshi pro pol's'kyi natsional'nyi rukh druhoï chverti XIX st., napysani pid vplyvom revoliutsiï 1848 r., vol. 1, p. 89–90.

The fairy tale ends with a moral address to both Galician communities:

> Let the Pole and the Ruthenian watch out
> What the old cockerel says
> Let them consider as hawks all
> Who bring discord

Not all the poems were naively moralistic. Some critically evaluated the past in order to draw the reader's attention to the possibility of creating a better future. Such was the goal of a piece by Franciszek Dydacki.[186] This work presents a dialogue between an Angel—whom one might view as a prophet or judge—with an Eagle and a Lion, that is with Poland and Ruthenia. The Lion (Ruthenia) complains that he has been a captive since the days of King Casimir the Great, kept in a state of slumber. Having awakened and discovered his strength, he now holds the Eagle in contempt. The Eagle (Poland) defends himself in the poem, casting the blame on Lucifer, who poisoned life in the country by employing the Jesuits, and who subsequently introduced the "two-headed eagle monsters,"—that is, the partitioning powers—to tear the state apart. According to the Eagle, these monsters are guilty of inciting the former feuds with the express goal of dividing Poles and Ruthenians. The Angel silences the disputers, showing them that they are brothers and that their quarrels are in vain at a moment when it is possible to fight for freedom. The Lion is afraid that in the future the Eagle will once again do him harm, which the latter denies by saying that "Sarmata [Polish nobleman – A.Ś.] does not sin a second time." The Angel finally calls upon them to come together in a union through which they will gain a common freedom, and having received the Angel's blessing the animals give each other their "hand." The verse is illustrated with coats of arms and an angel, as well as the figures of the Ruthenian and Pole in their characteristic national costumes.

In many poems, as either a main or secondary motif, the image of Poland appears as an explicitly Polish-Ruthenian-Lithuanian state. A good example is the poem *The Pole's Anthem* [*Hymn Polaka*] by an unknown author. The work starts as follows:

> Rule my nation in a single Trinity,
> Twins by fraternity joined three-fold;
> The honest Masurians and courageous Ruthenians,
> The loyal Lithuanians, Poland your holy authority![187]

---

[186] Franciszek Dydacki, [*Lew, Orzeł, Anioł*] ([Lviv, 1848]).

[187] *Hymn Polaka* (Lviv, 1848), TsDIAU, fond 474, op. 1, spr. 18, p. 43–44.

29. An illustration from the Franciszek Dydacki's leaflet
[Lion, Eagle, Angel] *(Lviv, 1848)*

The ideology of unity that characterizes the poetic output from the period of the revolutions of 1848 is not framed as a moral obligation or as the result of political tradition, but rather becomes a value in itself. In the poem *To All* [*Do wszystkich*], printed at Piotr Piller's printing house in Lviv, the anonymous author shows that unity is a weapon stronger than the sabre. However, as the sabres numbered so high, it was all the more necessary to combat the divisions between Poles and Ruthenians:

> Let the spirit of discord
> That has driven us backwards vanish!
> After all we are brothers, not nations!
> Whoever does not believe this, be away with him![188]

This poem was also published in Ruthenian at the Stauropegion Institute publishing house, though under different initials.[189] The publi-

---

[188] M.B., *Do wszystkich* ([Lviv, 1848]), ibid., p. 87.

[189] B.L., *Do wsich* ([Lviv, 1848]), ibid., spr. 19: Virshi pro pols'kyi natsional'nyi rukh druhoï chverti XIX st., napysani pid vplyvom revoliutsiï 1848 r., vol. 2, p. 98. The Ruthenian version differs from the Polish. The line "After all we are brothers, not nations!" has the completely opposite formulation in the Ruthenian version: "Because both nations are already brothers." In as far as the Polish version denies that Ruthenians are a nation, in the Ruthenian translation it is the brotherhood of the two nations that is emphasized.

cation of a work in both languages was a widespread practice in Lviv during the revoutions of 1848. This act was not merely a visible attempt to win over Ruthenians to the ideas propagated by Polish activists or the *gente Rutheni, natione Poloni*, but also to create the impression that Ruthenians themselves were writing for Ruthenians. This provided an opportunity to bring arguments over historical problems to an end, and subsequently to increase the possibility of realizing those goals considered common to both peoples.

M. W. Głoskowski's poem *To Brothers Ruthenians* [*Do bratej Rusyniw*] explained the misfortune of the joint history of the Poles and Ruthenians as the inability to live a harmonious and shared life.[190] He expressed his belief that the landowners' abolition of serfdom rendered it possible to improve relations between both nations. He emphasized that a Pole is not an executioner but a brother to Ruthenians, and that Ruthenians and Poles are the children of a single mother, destined in the future to amaze the world:

> A Ruthenian and a Pole are brothers born
> For ages back, since years of yore
> Together they've been famed and poor
> Together again they'll amaze the World
> If they'll love each other
> Like the sons of a single mother.[191]

The brotherhood of Poles and Ruthenians presented in the poetry was often presented as being demanded by Christ himself, as seen in Dymitr Koczyndyk of Sambir's poem *A Ruthenian to Ruthenians* [*Rusyn do Rusyniw*].[192] This was one of those works from the period of the revolutions of 1848 that enjoyed sufficient popularity to be referred to subsequently.[193] The author's main thesis is similar to that of other poems of this genre, both Polish and Ruthenian, and is conceptualized through these words:

> A Ruthenian, a Pole are two bodies
> Driven by the force of a single heart
> And he who says different
> Is our foe, one who beguiles us
> To our detriment

---

[190] M. Głoskowski, *Do bratej Rusyniw* ([Lviv, 1848]).

[191] Ibid., p. 2.

[192] Dymitr Koczyndyk, *Rusyn do Rusyniw* (Lviv, [1848]), TsDIAU, fond 474, op. 1, spr. 18, pp. 45–46.

[193] This was used by Julian Jakubowski as the motto for his book, *Zgoda. Poemat historyczny. Ruskiej braci poświęca Julian Jakubowski* (Lviv, 1874).

The value of the motherland, the "common mother," is conveyed in this type of poetry not only through literary metaphors but primarily by means of the image of a Poland paid for by sacrifice. This theme runs through the poem *The Resurrection* [*Woskresenije*] by the otherwise unknown Ruślan. The author invoked the image of Poles tortured by Russia and the post-November-Uprising exiles sent to Siberia. The suffering of years past would be avenged by divine retribution directed at Russia, which would enable Poles and Ruthenians to fight united against their enemies:

> Let us shake each other's hand
> Send us God's speed and aid!
> Unity, accord for centuries onwards
> And confusion to the enemy!![194]

But it was not simply former heroes who had fought for the fatherland who were put forward as models. Often these authors drew upon actual social tensions and summoned the memory of people who had recently died at the hands of the Austrian authorities or who had lost their lives or found themselves imprisoned for anti-state activities. One such man was Teofil Wiśniowski, a former insurgent and conspirator who entered this "canon of holy opponents" when he was hanged together with Józef Kapuściński on Execution Hill in Lviv in 1847 for organizing an uprising a year earlier.[195] Published in his honour was the poem *A Song about Wiśniowski* [*Piśń o Wyszniowskim*], in which the author, Henryk Jabłoński, describing himself as "Podolak from beyond the border," described how the hero wandered from village to

30. *Henryk Jabłoński's poem about Teofil Wiśniowski adressed to the Ruthenians*

---

[194] Ruślan, *Woskresenije* ([Lviv, 1848]), p. 4, TsDIAU, fond 474, op. 1, spr. 19, pp. 108–9.

[195] *Dwa wyroki śmierci w c. k. sądzie karzącym lwowskim wydane przeciw Teofilowi Wiśniowskie-mu i Józefowi Kapuścińskiemu* (Paris, 1847).

village and recounted how the Ruthenians and Poles were brothers and how their fatherland, Poland, represents a resurrection. Like other works from this genre, the poem employs a sacralization of national values with the martyrological element taken to an almost Christological dimension. The hero Wiśniowski in Jabłoński's verses, escorted by Austrian soldiers, manages to tell eyewitnesses: "We are all equal brothers, and Poland is a mother to us," and subsequently, according to the author, "he suffered a passion like Christ."[196] Wiśniowski's message, although its authenticity is uncertain, would nevertheless function as its own political testament. Jan Karol Cybulski translated the text into Ruthenian as Teofil Wiśniowski's final words to the Galicians, written down on 28 July 1847, several days before the conspirator's death. Cybulski relates Wiśniowski's words as follows:

> You should love each other like the sons of a single Mother, of the Motherland! And join together in fraternal accord in the way the boughs of an oak link together, and be strong like a fearless man, like the martyr of our lands, and create through your works a freedom and happiness that for centuries forth will be heard in future *dumkas*.[197]

Besides Teofil Wiśniowski, several works were devoted to those penalized at the fortress in Kufstein for their participation in the Galician conspiracies. On the strength of the amnesty of March 1848 the political prisoners started to return home, men enshrouded in the legend of the fight for independence. Several of these figures would become involved in the events of 1848 in Lviv, including Kasper Cięglewicz, the main propagator of the notion of Ruthenian-Polish brotherhood.[198] Celestyn Skomorowski [Tselestyn Skomorovsky], an author of the Ruthenian poem *In Honor of the Brothers Returning from Captivity (2 March)* [*Na czest' bratej powernuwszych z newoli (2go Bereznia 1848)*] welcomed those returning from imprisonment as "angels of peace," who were to carry "the cross of the fatherland."[199]

A prevailing theme in the majority of these works is the expression of joy felt at being free. This sense of freedom was bolstered by the abolition of serfdom and therefore the theoretical social levelling of the

---

[196] [Henryk Jabłoński] Podolak zza Kordonu, *Piśń o Wyszniowśkim* (Lviv, 1848), TsDIAU, fond 474, op. 1, spr. 19, p. 32.

[197] *Ostatni Słowa Teofyla Wyszniowskoho do Mury Hałyćkoho pysani dnia 28 Łypcia 1847 hoda po publykowanym dekreti*, trans. Jan Karol Cybulski (Lviv, [1848]), p. 2.

[198] [Stefan Mułkowski], *Kufstein. Więzienie stanu i dola Polaków w nim osadzonych* (Poznań, 1848), pp. 27, 73.

[199] [Celestyn Skomorowski] C….t.n. S….r….i, *Na czest' bratej powernuwszych z newoli (2go Bereznia 1848)* ([Lviv, 1848]), TsDIAU, fond 474, op. 1, spr. 19, pp. 99–100. Cf.: Kozik, *The Ukrainian National Movement*, pp. 347–48.

peasantry and gentry, as well as political relaxation on the part of the regime, which in turn raised hopes for further concessions and eventual independence. The authors of works such as *A Song of Joy* [*Piśń radosty*] or *To the Rural People* [*Do selskoho ludu*] wrote in a similar spirit.[200]

The division that existed among the Ruthenian intelligentsia would also be reflected in poetry. The acts of the Greek Catholic clergy were perceived as "separatist." Perhaps the most famous poetic work levelled against the St. Georgians was *The Song of the St. Georgian Apparitions* [*Pieśń o marach święto-jurskich*], in which an anonymous author compares the activities of the clergy to bloodthirsty apparitions. The poem reflects the mood prevalent among the Polish democrats in Lviv, disillusioned by the Greek Catholic Church's rejection of a joint front:

> You rejected the fraternal hand offered to you
> Your hearts crave the blood of your murdered brothers
> But, our dear brothers, you are familiar with the actions
> Of the enemies who are deprived of virtue, faith, and honour.

This poem struck a chord and prompted a swift response from Przemyśl in the work *The White Eaglet's Threat to the St. Georgian Apparitions* [*Groźba orlika białego świętojurskim maram*].[201] The Ruthenian author replied, in Polish, to the grievances of the "eaglet" (the Poles):

> Oh weak birdie! Dishonour of eagles,
> Do you know the strength of Ruthenian apparitions?
> Tremble, tremble before them for damnation
> You will receive as a gift in a single breath

This seemingly innocent and purely artistic fight through rhyme was in reality a way of propagating the concrete ideas of rival political currents. Poetry of this type, rarely referenced in historiography, draws attention to the nuances of the conflicts that flared up in Galicia in 1848. The vast number of poems written at this time, published as small leaflets mainly in Lviv, bears witness to the fact that they constituted, or were perceived to constitute by the authors themselves, a type of opinion-forming media for the people of Eastern Galicia. The fact that ephemeral texts called for Polish-Ruthenian fraternity proves that the realities left much to be desired.

---

[200] A.Ł., *Piśń radosty* ([Lviv, 1848]), ibid., p. 105; *Do selskoho ludu* ([Lviv, 1848]), ibid., p. 143.
[201] *Groźba orlika białego świętojurskim maram* (Przemyśl, [1848]).

The Echo of the Revolutions of 1848
in the Provinces

The main territory in which ideological options came up against each other was Lviv. The largescale involvement of its inhabitants in the course of events is testified by the source materials preserved, an array of printing materials that were chiefly produced in the region's capital. The situation in the provinces is, however, less well documented. The events that occurred in Lviv were echoed in provincial situations, enacted in smaller towns where local National Councils were formed. Involvement in the activities of National Councils was not unique to the capital; many local National Councils were well attended by Ruthenians.

Thanks to the correspondence between the district councils and the Central National Council as well as the appeals directed to Lviv, it is possible to grasp the relations of other regions and small Galician towns to the Ruthenian question. It should be noted that Lviv, as the arena for political strife and conflict, usually initiated activities in the provinces and not the other way round.

In Sanok, the Greek Catholic clergy of the town issued an appeal in the second issue of *Dnewnyk Ruskij* to the Sanok District Council. On behalf of the priests, the proclamation had been signed by Józef Wieńkowski [Iosyf Vienkovsky], a medical doctor. Besides emphasizing the links between Poles and Ruthenians, the author of the text pleaded for patience and moderation. He concluded that the two streams would diverge before again coming together, not so that one might displace the other but so that they could flow on together. This was how Józef Wieńkowski perceived the trajectory of Polish and Ruthenian relations.[202]

Besides appeals published in newspapers, there were other types of reports emanating from the countryside which communicated the events of the day. These were often first read out publicly before publication at the sittings of the Central National Council in order to notify the politicians in Lviv of potential threats. For example, the National Council of the Stryi Region informed the Central National Council about Ruthenian religious services not only conducted in a tone antagonistic to the Council and Poles in general, but also potentially capable of inciting the rural population to revolt. Such a service took place on

---

[202] Józef Wieńkowski, "Otozwa Swiaszczennykow hreczesko-sojedynenoho ispowidania zemły sianockoi do czestnoi rady obwodowoi sianockoi," *Dnewnyk Ruskij* no. 2 (25 Aug. [5 Sep.] 1848), pp. 1–2.

August 3 in Stryi. Details of the events were preserved in the Pawlikow-ski archives in Lviv with the following commentary:[203]

> (…) in our district the discord sown by the hand of envious bureaucracy is starting to sprout.
>
> The clergy of the Greek rite, who were members of our Council in greater number, have stopped attending the sittings in order to avoid persecution on the part of the Consistory, while the stability of the few who are still active has been strongly shaken.[204]

The author of the account described how several clergymen had arrived in Stryi and conducted a service during which a Ruthenian standard with the Archangel Michael was consecrated. Four speeches were delivered which criticized Poles for their forceful Polonization of Ruthenians and emphasized that the borders of Rus' ran from the San River to the Black Sea. The author wrote that the Ruthenian peasants listening to these words understood little and thus distorted the words. He claimed that some even wanted to go and beat up the Poles, taking the consecrated banner with them. A different tone is adopted in another personal reflection of a witness to the events, who more than likely was a Ruthenian of Polish nationality. He confides that:

> It is hurtful to recall those biting expressions of hate towards the brotherly tribe of Poles, who have for centuries shared everything with the Ruthenians, who in finding themselves in the same situation as Ruthenians strive for the same goal and who only see in a close fraternal relationship the means to break out of the helplessness into which hostile relations have plunged them. Sorrow grips the soul of a Ruthenian cherishing his land, staring at the deliberate premeditated severing of the fraternal bonds joining the two brotherly strands into one, and the same strivings for freedom. A democratic Poland, a people's Poland—and only such a Poland can exist today—cannot act in a hostile manner, it is to team up in eternal alliance with a democratic people's Rus'.'[205]

Although this excerpt expresses hope for an eternal alliance of Poles and Ruthenians, it is however filled with a sense of regret resulting from the deepening chasm between them.

The only attempt at an institutionalized form for propagating the idea of brotherhood among the ordinary, common people was the creation in May 1848 of the so-called Fraternal Association (Tovarystvo Bratej / Towarzystwo Braci). As Piotr Stebelski wrote:

---

[203] *Wolność, równość, Braterstwo. Rada Narodowa Obwodu Stryjskiego do Szanownej Rady Narodowej Centralnej*, LNNBU, fond 76, op. 1, spr. 254, pp. 83–86.

[204] Ibid., p. 83.

[205] Ibid., p. 84v.

(...) This was a clearly open organization with humanitarian and phil-
anthropic goals that aimed to raise the standard of education for rural
dwellers in particular, to make them conscious, create schools, broaden
learning and propagate a love of one's neighbour.[206]

The organization conducted long-range activities by delivering
speeches and printing leaflets, books and journals.[207] Years later Wiktor
Heltman recalled that the members of the Association, "like the Christian apostles of old, full of faith and hope, ran about the manor houses and villages, spreading words of harmony and Christian unity."[208]
Dominik Gębarzewski headed the Association, and Kasper Cięglewicz
was one of seven board members. He was likely the author of the appeals directed to the rural population. This organization also had its
own emissaries tasked with spreading the idea of fraternity in the provinces. One of these was Father Hipolit Bobek [Ipolyt Bobek], who tried
in vain to found Association branches in the Ternopil and Chortkiv
districts.

One of the Association's Ruthenian appeals, dated 30 September
1848, is preserved in Lviv. The role of the Poles is framed in an almost
messianic way, and the author warns the Ruthenian peasants against
those enemies who for eighteen years had frightened them with lies
about the Poles:

> Brothers! Whoever dishonours a Pole before you dishonours a Ruthe-
> nian, and whoever dishonours a Ruthenian dishonours a Pole. For Poles
> and Ruthenians are born brothers.

The appeal noted that the Association, comprised of Ruthenians and
Poles, had been created out of concern for the good of the people. It was
once again mentioned that the peasants owed their freedom and land to
the squires who had bestowed it upon them.[209]

Besides writing appeals and proclamations, the members of the Association were also involved in money collections[210] as well as cooperation with the Central National Council, sending them among other
things reports on the activities of the Greek Catholic clergy in rural
areas. This is mentioned in some of the minutes of the Central National
Council. That four delegates of the Association of Brothers were to sit

---

[206] Stebelski, "Lwów," p. 314.

[207] Zbigniew Fras, *Demokraci w życiu politycznym Galicji w latach 1848–1873* (Wrocław,
1997), p. 79.

[208] Wiktor Heltman, *Demokracya Polska na emigracyi. Wyjątki z pism* (Lepnitz, 1866), p. 299.

[209] *Widozwa towarystwa Bratej, do myłych bratej selaniu, aby swoi grunta namarnowały*,
LNNBU, fond 76, op. 3, spr. 280, pp. 76–77.

[210] Stebelski, "Lwów," p. 314.

on the Central National Council was decided on at its sitting of August 8.[211] Yet four days later, at the next sitting, it was decided to take control of the "enlightenment" of the people planned by the Association.[212] Finally, however, after protracted meetings on financial matters, the Association was allowed its autonomy.[213] The organization lasted until November 2, when it was dissolved by the authorities.

Individuals were also active in the provinces. The greatest achievements were seen in Sambir, and this was the work of the then 30-year-old Michał Popiel, who enjoyed national hero status as a result of his leading role in organizing the so-called Sambir conspiracy. Besides writing the aforementioned appeal (*Announcement to All Ruthenians in the Sambor National Council on May 25 [13], 1848 A.D.*.) and supporting the Ruthenian Sobor protest, he lobbied in Sambir among craftsmen and the minor gentry. He was also involved in founding a National Guard, but he himself was not interested in taking command of it. He also attended a National Council sitting in Sambir on May 25 when he announced that "from now on there is no lord, there is no peasant, we are all lords and we are all peasants." His activites guaranteed him victory in the election to the Imperial Diet in Vienna, at which point this *gente Ruthenus, natione Polonus* entered the world of serious politics.[214] Other Ruthenians also sat next to Poles on the Sambir National Council.[215]

Gente Rutheni, Natione Poloni at the Constitutional Diet in Vienna and Kroměříž

The year 1848 was to bring one more significant political change to Galicia. Following the second revolution in Vienna (May 1848) Emperor Ferdinand I established the Imperial Diet on May 16 that would pass the second successive constitution. The calling into being of an elected representative body with the ability to decide on the most important state matters created the possibility for legal political activity among the inhabitants of Galicia. Although absolutist government returned following the revolutions of 1848 and the defeat of the Hungarians in

---

[211] *Protokoły posiedzeń*, p. 147.

[212] Ibid., p. 150.

[213] Ibid., pp. 181–84.

[214] Stefan Kieniewicz, "'Rusyn na praznyku' i dalsze jego losy," in *Problemy wiedzy o kulturze. Prace dedykowane Stefanowi Żółkiewskiemu*, eds. Alina Brodzka, Maryla Hopfinger and Janusz Lalewicz (Wrocław–Warsaw–Cracow–Gdańsk–Łódź, 1986), pp. 331–32.

[215] Aleksander Kuczera, *Samborszczyzna. Ilustrowana monografja miasta Sambora i ekonomii samborskiej*, vol. 2 (Sambor, 1935), p. 348.

their war with Austria, at the moment the diet was formed huge hopes were aroused among Galicians that changes in the monarchy would also occur.

The Constitutional Diet began its work in Vienna on 22 July 1848, and brought matters to a close on 4 March 1849. Two-tiered elections were held to fill the seats of 383 parliamentary delegates. Together, Poles and Ruthenians could count on 108 seats at the Viennese parliament, which allowed them real influence on the politics of the whole monarchy and Galicia specifically.[216]

Among those selected at the time were three *gente Rutheni, natione Poloni*, two of whom had been known activists in the Ruthenian Sobor. Cyryl Wieńkowski was elected from the Iavoriv constituency of the district of Przemyśl, Michał Popiel from the Stara Sil constituency in the Sambir district, and the landowner and member of the local National Council Jan Fedorowicz from Ternopil.[217] There were also delegates who considered themselves to be Ruthenian as a result of their territorial origin and roots, such as Florian Ziemiałkowski or Aleksander Dzieduszycki.[218] As Stanisław Pijaj noted, it was difficult to determine the nationality of certain Ruthenians in the Constitutional Diet because "no one demanded of them a clear declaration of national affiliation."[219] While several other individuals could be included in the *gente Rutheni, natione Poloni* group because of their pro-Polish sympathies, such categorizaiton must be approached with caution as these figures would later undergo changes in various directions. For example, Julian Maciej Goslar, writing under the pseudonym Antoni Białkowski, took down information on two Ruthenian peasant delegates of the Constitutional Diet, who declared "We are Ruthenian-Poles." If one is to believe Goslar, Józef Dyniec [Iosyf Dynets], a peasant from Tartakiv, and the elected representative for Sokal, as well as Pańko Kozar [Panko Kozar] of Boianets, serving Zhovkva, also spoke thus of themselves.[220] Stanisław Pijaj wrote that Cyryl Wieńkowski, Jan Fedorowicz and Aleksander Dobrzański, supported in their election by the National Council in Sanok, failed to join the "Centrum" party where the Ruthenian delegates sat. The Poles

---

[216] Cf. Józef Buszko, *Polacy w parlamencie wiedeńskim 1848–1918* (Warsaw, 1996), p. 16; Stanisław Pijaj, "Posłowie ruscy w parlamencie wiedeńskim w latach 1848–1879," in *Ukraińskie tradycje parlamentarne. XIX–XXI wiek*, ed. Jarosław Moklak (Cracow, 2006), p. 99.

[217] Buszko, *Polacy w parlamencie*, pp. 347–53.

[218] Pijaj, "Posłowie ruscy," p. 106.

[219] Ibid., p. 95.

[220] "Nieznane listy Juliana Macieja Goslara z 1848 r.," [ed.] Jan Kozik, *Przegląd Historyczny* 66 (1975), p. 620.

created an "association" in Vienna which 42 delegates joined, including Cyryl Wieńkowski.[221] Father Mykhailo Hankevych also joined the Polish association of delegates and subsequently called on the Ruthenians to cooperate with the Poles.[222]

The leading figure in the ranks of the Ruthenians of Polish nationality was Michał Popiel. In Vienna, this Polish patriot and democrat shaped by Cięglewicz supported the candidature of his former mentor for the post of governor of Galicia, believing that he would effect positive change in the country. This idea would ultimately fail despite the fact that many people were convinced of his worth. At the plenum of the Imperial Diet, Popiel attempted to lay out his views on the subject of a Ruthenian-Polish accord and the peasant question. He saw the solution to both problems in the support of the Ruthenian peasantry and opposition to the Greek Catholic clergy entwined in St. Georgian circles. In a Vienna engulfed by revolution, Popiel easily found his compatriots from Sambir, both Poles and Ruthenians, and gained their support. But when discussion at the congress turned to winning over the Ruthenian peasantry, things turned out to be not quite as simple as he had forecast in the 1830s or during the revolutions of 1848. During the vote on compensation to be paid to landowners for the losses incurred as a result of the abolition of serfdom, Popiel stood against remuneration. His actions failed to win him supporters for two reasons: first, he was for the granting of freeholds to peasants yet was against any form of compensation for said freeholds; second, he supported the matter on the central level, which was taken to mean not supporting the demands for Galician autonomy. Popiel's work at the Diet was truncated by the outbreak of revolution in Vienna in October 1848 and the subsequent war with the Hungarians in the spring of 1849. In this way the political career of Michał Popiel was cut short. He settled in Sambir, and until the second election to the Galician Diet in 1867 he led a fairly quiet life as a government official, not even engaging in the insurgent battles of 1863.[223]

As much as Popiel continued to strive for social justice in the admittedly changed Constitutional Diet, hoping to lay the groundwork for a Polish-Ruthenian brotherhood in Galicia, the majority of the Galician delegates were instead preoccupied with a completely different matter derived from the so-called Ruthenian question—the division of Galicia

[221] *Protokoły Koła Polskiego w wiedeńskiej Radzie Państwa (lata 1867–1868)*, eds. and introd. Zbigniew Fras and Stanisław Pijaj (Cracow, 2001), p. 27.

[222] Pijaj, "Posłowie ruscy," p. 105.

[223] Kieniewicz, "'Rusyn na praznyku'," pp. 331–37.

into two parts. This division had the support of Bishop Iakhymovych and the political activists of St. George's Cathedral. Furthermore, there were the countless letters with the signatures of Ruthenian inhabitants which asked Vienna to divide the country; 200,000 signatures had been collected supporting the division by the beginning of 1849.[224]

The St. Georgians' demand was problematic in a broader context. As far as the political model for the entire monarchy was concerned, a single and fundamental difference existed between Poles and Ruthenians. The latter, in demanding the division of Galicia, supported a centralized state and remained loyal to the emperor. The Poles, however, wanted more far-reaching changes to the formation of the state in order to allow for the greatest possible autonomy for an undivided Galicia. These differing political aspirations on the Ruthenian and Polish sides resulted in strange behaviour. The Ruthenians supported anti-Polish acts, even backing the Germanization of the Galician school system — anything as long as it was not Polish. This surprised the Czechs, who initially viewed their dealings with the Ruthenians with favour. The Poles, anxious to avoid a division of the country, fiercely opposed the existence of Ruthenian nationality.[225] Jan Kozik attributed this situation in part to the popularity of the aforementioned works by Kasper Cięglewicz and Antoni Dąbczański, printed in Polish and German.[226] The question of the division of Galicia would finally be resolved on 25 January 1849 at the vote of the constitutional commission, established on 31 July 1848 and composed of three representatives from every nation. Three representatives were for division (including Iakhymovych), two abstained, while the rest voted to maintain the *status quo*. The work of the Constitutional Diet would not ultimately see fruition, as the emperor suspended it and he himself proposed a constitution which also did not include a division of Galicia. Subsequent attempts undertaken in 1849 by Iakhymovych were also thwarted by the governor of Galicia, Count Agenor Gołuchowski.[227] From the revolutions of 1848 onwards, the question of the division of the country was to become the foremost problem that divided Poles and Ruthenians.

---

[224] Kozik, *The Ukrainian National Movement*, p. 268; Jana Osterkamp, "Imperial Diversity in the Village: Petitions for and against the Division of Galicia in 1848," *Nationalities Papers* 44, no. 5 (2015), pp. 731–50.

[225] Kozik, *The Ukrainian National Movement*, pp. 275–77; Pijaj, "Posłowie ruscy," pp. 104–5.

[226] Kozik, *The Ukrainian National Movement*, p. 270–71.

[227] Ibid., pp. 275–82.

The End of Activities for the Ruthenian Sobor

Meanwhile, the Polish-Ruthenian conflict in Lviv had intensified from 1848. A significant series of events took place over the Feast of Corpus Christi on 22 June 1848. As Marceli Handelsman relates in an account based on Austrian and Ruthenian sources, the Greek Catholic Church gave permission for a ceremonial procession to take place in the city. The entourage was provided by the Lviv National Guard, who carried two standards—a Ruthenian and a Polish. Later these were placed in the townhall as proof of brotherly relations. It would appear that this was a gesture of friendship on the part of the Ruthenians towards the Poles, but the background to this event was more complex. Bishop Iakhymovych had initially counted on the National Guard refusing to participate in the celebrations, but he had been unable to gain permission from the Austrian authorities for the formation of separate Ruthenian Guard. The bishop's plans failed and the procession took place, but the Greek Catholic Church hierarchy considered it to be a "political demonstration."[228]

The impact of the deteriorating relations between Poles and Ruthenians could be seen in the ban on conducting services by Uniate clergy to mark the anniversary of the execution of Józef Kapuściński and Teofil Wiśniowski in Lviv; the repeated demands for the division of Galicia supported by the Greek Catholic hierarchy; the increasingly heated debate in the pages of the Polish and Ruthenian press; the raid on the Stauropegial Institute printing press, where *Zoria Halytska* was produced; agitation of the peasants; and finally, the idea to organize a congress of "Ruthenian academics." Jan Kozik wrote that the Ruthenian Sobor tried to send its members to this congress but was unsuccessful.[229] However, the blame for this may have lain with the non-Ruthenians within the ranks of the Ruthenian Sobor. A work entitled *The Ruthenian Question* [*Kwestya ruska*], admittedly published almost two decades after the revolutions of 1848, notes that "the Sobor, by a majority of votes in defiance of the sincere demands of the Ruthenian members [at the congress of "Ruthenian academics" – A.Ś.], did not take up participation."[230] On October 6 Antoni Golejewski, at the time the head of the Ruthenian Sobor, called a meeting at which the organization was dissolved, although many *gente Rutheni, natione Poloni* were supposedly against it. With the Sobor disbanded, representation of Ruthenians of

---

[228] Handelsman, *Ukraińska polityka*, p. 94.
[229] Kozik, "Stosunki ukraińsko-polskie," p. 44.
[230] [Bernard Kalicki], *Kwestya ruska* (Lviv, 1871), p. 44.

Polish nationality in Galicia was confined to a branch of the Central National Council.[231] The main advocate of this change, as Marian Mudry established, was Antoni Golejewski, a landowner and member of both organizations.[232] Therefore, the failure of the Sobor was brought about not by the Ruthenian representatives but the Polish landowning class who treated their Ruthenian provenance (often understood in a territorial sense) as purely instrumental. Maciej Kozłowski was correct when he wrote that "the sizeable participation in the work of the Sobor on the part of Polish aristocrats defining themselves as *gente Rutheni natione Poloni* (…) took away the Sobor's authenticity (…)."[233] If these landed gentry had been guided by their Ruthenianism, then they would not have treated the Sobor simply as a means for the realization of Polish and particularist interests, the result of which was the dissolution of the organization. Following the pacification of Lviv on 2 November 1848, the Central National Council was also finally disbanded, in sharp contrast to the Supreme Ruthenian Council, which was allowed to continue its activities. This was not simply a humiliating blow for the Poles, but above all it was a political decision which ensured the Supreme Ruthenian Council would become the sole representative of the Ruthenian population.

Gente Rutheni, Natione Poloni
and the Austro-Hungarian War 1848–49

It is not possible to examine the revolutions of 1848 without considering the Hungarian uprising of 1848–49. The Hungarians in their fight against the absolutist monarchy gave the Poles hope that they would gain independence either by fighting at their side or as a result of a general European conflict. Franz Joseph I's ascension to the Austrian throne in December 1848, despite the earlier agreement given by Ferdinand I to the Hungarians to form a government, resulted in armed conflict with the insurgents. Poles instinctively rushed to aid their southern neighbours. Polish generals Józef Bem, Henryk Dembiński and Józef Wysocki are well known for their involvement in the uprising, but ordinary volunteers also joined in the struggle, forming the three-thou-

---

[231] Ibid.

[232] Mudryi, "Rus'kyi sobor 1848 roku. Orhanizatsiia," p. 109.

[233] Maciej Kozłowski, *Między Sanem a Zbruczem. Walki o Lwów i Galicję Wschodnią 1918–1919* (Cracow, 1990), p. 41; Maciej Kozłowski, *Zapomniana wojna. Walki o Lwów i Galicję Wschodnią 1918–1919*, introd. Bohdan Skaradziński (Bydgoszcz, 1999), p. 56.

sand strong Polish Legion. A well-known Ruthenian and later Greek Catholic bishop, Julian Kuiłowski, also served in the unit of Henryk Dembiński in 1849.[234] The grandfather of the future political activist Stanisław Srokowski, Szymon Srokowski [Symon Srokovsky], also fought in the uprising.[235]

However, given the thousands of Galician recruits serving in the Austrian Army, was military support the only avenue available for those Poles who were aware of the situation? It is worth reflecting on the question of the national identity of any Galician recruit, who, as Michał Baczkowski demonstrated, was fairly indifferent to the nationalist rhetoric of the mid-nineteenth century. The many years of service meant that soldiers felt more attached to their regiments than to national values. The majority of the recruits displayed loyalty to the monarchy; part of them were purely concerned with their financial situation, though a small number remained who had developed national or political views. Soldiers recruited from the peasantry, who formed the basis of the army, were particularly indifferent to nationalist platforms. This explains why it was possible during the revolutions of 1848 for Polish or Ruthenian soldiers serving in the Austrian army to carry out their orders to crush the revolutions without any scruples whatsoever. The situation changed only slightly during the Hungarian campaign, when a number of these soldiers joined the Polish Legion of General Józef Wysocki.[236]

Indifference towards political events was not just characteristic of peasants serving in the army; such an attitude was also evident in the provinces. Andrzej A. Zięba drew attention to the fact that Polish conspirators addressed one of their appeals, entitled *A Voice of the World to the Ruthenian Brothers* [*Hołos świta do brati Rusnakiw*], written in Latin script, to those Ruthenians living on the Galician-Hungarian borderlands, and in particular the Lemkos. Not only did the attempt to draw the Lemkos population into military action fail, but they even helped the Russian army move against the Hungarians.[237] The Ruthenian peasants, both on the Galician side and on the Hungarian side

---

[234] Tomasz Pudłocki, *Iskra światła czy kopcąca pochodnia? Inteligencja w Przemyślu w latach 1867–1939* (Cracow, 2009), p. 419 and footnote 21.

[235] Andrzej A. Zięba, "Srokowski Stanisław Józef," in *PSB*, vol. 41 (Warsaw–Cracow, 2002), p. 238.

[236] Michał Baczkowski, "Galicjanie w armii austriackiej wobec wydarzeń lat 1848–1849," in *Galicja w 1848 roku. Demografia, działalność polityczna i społeczna, gospodarka i kultura*, eds. Andrzej Bonusiak and Marian Stolarczyk (Rzeszów, 1999), pp. 89–93.

[237] Andrzej A. Zięba, "Tożsamość etniczna jako obiekt manipulacji politycznej. Przypadek Rusinów łemkowskich XVIII–XX w. (część pierwsza)," *Rocznik Ruskiej Bursy* (2007), p. 77.

(present-day Slovakia), also helped capture volunteers heading beyond the Carpathians; meanwhile, the St. Georgians called on Ruthenians in Hungary to show their loyalty to the emperor.[238] This behaviour resulted in the leader of the Hungarian revolution, Lajos Kossuth, wanting to form units to stop the Ruthenians from capturing Galician volunteers in the Carpathian mountain passes.[239]

There are known examples of Ruthenians fighting side-by-side with Poles against the partitioning powers. According to the Austrian list of insurgents of 1850 that noted the surnames of emigrants from the Sanok district to Hungary, a group of 98 insurgents yielded representatives of all social estates, with no absence of Ruthenian-sounding surnames. Researching this group, Dora Kacnelson noted the presence of individuals such as Jurko Hyha [Iurko Hyha], a peasant from Radoszyce; Ilko Drahan, a servant from Smolnik; Hryć Kotyk [Hryts Kotyk], a peasant from Wola Michowa; Wasyl Soroka [Vasyl Soroka], a servant from Łupków; and Seńko Kostew [Senko Kostev] as well as Maciej Petryniuk [Matvii Petrynuk] and Fedor Petryniuk [Fedor Petrunyk], all servants from Smolnik.[240]

The Polish Legion was not the only manifestation of Poles' national feelings. Individual local "heroes" also appeared who aided the insurgents. In his memoirs, Bogusław Longchamps de Bérier described his Lemko "Ruthenian nanny":

> In [18]48 together with her husband, Łeś [Les'], and with the forester falconer, Semion Hułaj [Semen Hulai], she led insurgents across the border into Hungary. Once at the border itself she happened upon a dragoon, whose corpse was later found under a rock in a stream. How this happened, nanny did not tell, "for she was simply then too afraid" (...).[241]

It is not difficult to deduce who took the dragoon's life. Ruthenian support for the insurgents was also extended by certain members of the clergy. De Bérier's nanny reminded her charge of the parish priest, Father Hładyszewski [Hladyshevsky], who "in church spoke at length

---

[238] Eligiusz Kozłowski, *Legion polski na Węgrzech 1848–1849* (Warsaw, 1983), p. 53.

[239] Ibid., p. 70.

[240] Reference is made to the acts found at TsDIAU (fond 146, op. 7, spr. 3071, pp. 149–50). Names are mentioned by Dora Katsnel'son, "K istorii uchastiia Slavian k vengerskoi revoliutsii 1848–1849 gg. (Po materialam lvovskikh arkhivov)," in *Tsentral'naia i Iugo--vostochnaia Evropa v novoe vremia. Sbornik statei*, selection, ed., and introd. Iurii Pisarev (Moscow, 1974), p. 174. Dora Katsnel'son is also cited by Kozłowski, *Legion polski*, pp. 48–49.

[241] Bogusław Longchamps de Bérier, *Ochrzczony na szablach powstańczych... Wspomnienia (1884–1918)*, eds. Włodzimierz Suleja and Wojciech Wrzesiński (Wrocław–Warsaw–Cracow–Gdańsk–Łódź, 1983), p. 35.

then [i.e., the years 1848–49 – A.Ś.] and later in [18]63, for the souls of those who had fallen and for the well-being of the insurgents."[242]

Another well-known figure recurrent in the subject literature was Konstanty Łękawski, the son of a Greek Catholic priest from Stanyslaviv. He had already been involved prior to 1846 in conspiratorial acts in Galicia, and in 1848 he entered the ranks of the Ruthenian Sobor. In the face of the Hungarian revolution he made it across the Carpathians and fought as a lieutenant under the command of General Józef Wysocki. He subsequently escaped to Turkey, where he founded a branch of the Polish Democratic Society, in which Franciszek Sokulski and Zygmunt Miłkowski played an active role. After this episode Łękawski sailed to England, where he was a leader of the Polish community of Newcastle for twelve years.[243]

The Balance of the Events of 1848–49 in the Context of the Ruthenian Question

The involvement of the inhabitants of Galicia in the Austro-Hungarian War and later in the struggle against Russia was decidedly insignificant when one considers the possibilities these struggles presented. Years later Platon Kostecki lamented the lost opportunity, criticizing the older generation for the wasted chance of 1848:

> The Ruthenians screamed that the appeals to Vienna mentioned only the Poles, with nothing about the Ruthenians, that the Ruthenians' demands were deemed by the Poles to be distorted claims, delusions, and finally the unfortunate Mr. August Bielowski refuted the teaching that Rus' had ever existed anywhere whatsoever. As a result, when a party was formed within the Polish-Ruthenian bosom with a journal printed in the Latin script (while incidently having claimed it was written in some Church-Slavonic-Muscovite Ruthenian language), a party that sought unity with ultra-Ruthenians, they took the matter to be a ploy and trick, and the Latin letters in the journal were seen as a betrayal directed against Cyrillic Ruthenian nationality. Soon the Poles in Lviv understood what an obstacle to their plans—if they had any judicious plans—the Ruthenians constituted, and they went berserk. The gentry and townsfolk, one as blockheaded as the other and playing at being a guard around villages and towns, instead of following Bem with 1200 horses to Moscow, would pick fights with the Ruthenians, who then were only represented by the clergy, mocking them and taunting them. The gentry's dark

---

[242] Ibid.

[243] Peter Brock writes further about Łękawski, *Z dziejów wielkiej emigracji w Anglii* (Warsaw, 1958), pp. 114–15.

rebellion once again has fired from the grave with a flame but a flame without heat or clarity, and when the guard sabres and epaulettes are soon taken from the Poles, for the Ruthenians it adds to the sense of hate for their negation and the recording of an even more hellish derision.[244]

The defeat of the Hungarian revolution eradicated the chance for change in the monarchy. For a period of a dozen or so years, severe absolute rule was to return to the whole empire, Galicia included. The abolition of the majority of democratic organizations that had arisen in 1848, as well as the disappearance of almost every newspaper, made it impossible for activists within *gente Rutheni, natione Poloni* to continue their work. When twelve years later new possibilities appeared alongside Galician autonomy to express political ideas and views, there was no longer room on the political stage for the construction of an organization similar to the Ruthenian Sobor, as the national identity of Ruthenians was at a very different point than it had been in 1848. The rivalry of *gente Rutheni, natione Poloni* with the Greek Catholic clergy, who were viewed as national leaders and enjoyed support among the ordinary people, was already condemned to failure, a fact that Platon Kostecki aptly touches on while at the same time blaming the Poles for their patriarchal attitude towards the Ruthenians. Michał Jagiełło astutely delineated four ways of perceiving the so-called Ruthenian question at this time. It is worth citing them here in order to understand what drove the Polish elite in Galicia in the decades post-1848:

> (...) the first is that the Ruthenians yearn for "the spirit of Poland to inspire them"; the second, that "a Ruthenian truly living for the well-being of Rus" sees this only in unity with Poland; the third, that Poles know best which Ruthenian is "good" and which has already been "deceived" by the Austrian bureaucrats, or already by the Muscovites; and finally the last, that my Polish party and I know what is good for Rus' (Ukraine) and what is bad.[245]

None of the four approaches enumerated by Jagiełło could possibly arouse a positive response among Ruthenians. Furthermore, the views proclaimed by the Polish democrats could not reach the ordinary Ruthenian population or the clergy, who were the only elite among Ruthenians at this period.

---

[244] Platon Kostecki, „W sprawie ruskiej" [Lviv, 1863], LNNBU, fond 5: Zbirka rukopysiv, avtohrafiv, hramot i dyplomiv biblioteky Natsional'noho zakladu im. Ossolins'kykh u m. Lvovi, op. 1: Rukopysy, spr. 3063/II, p. 12. See also: Handelsman, *Ukraińska polityka*, p. 97.

[245] Jagiełło, *Narody*, p. 28.

An example of the discrepancy between the Polish conceptions about Ruthenians and the actual attitudes held by the Ruthenian population is the oft-quoted text produced by the Greek Catholic parish priest for the village of Wetlina, Vasyl Podolynsky [Bazyli Podolinski]. In *A Word of Warning* [*Słowo przestrogi*],[246] published in Sanok in 1848, the author deals critically with the acts undertaken by Poles under the guise of "becoming fraternal" with Ruthenians. He wrote of the inherent false-hood in the very notion of "fraternity":

> Everyone shouts out these days: "Harmony, unity and fraternity!" But the initiatives for such cannot even be seen in those who do the shouting. (...) They call out: "Oh, Ruthenian brothers!", but they defile the entirety of their classes and link them with the bureaucracy, forgetting that this is a fist thrown under the ribs, which is usually unwittingly returned.[247]

Elsewhere in his work Podolynsky accused the Poles of persuading Ruthenians to build a Poland, but failing to describe exactly what sort of Poland it should be outside of its encompassment of Polish, Lithuanian and Ruthenian lands. Podolynsky questioned how well Ruthenians would prosper in such a state. He added ironically, yet aptly:

> However much one may conjecture as to whether they will succeed in the same way as other Poles, this is under the condition that they deny their very selves and adopt both the speech and the names of Poles. And in this speculation lies the Gordian knot itself which alienates Rus' from Poland, not (...) simply in the very persuasive acts of the bureaucracy.[248]

As a priest in charge of a rural parish, Podolynsky recognized what the majority of Polish politicians of the time did not see: that it was impossible to model the world outlook of the Ruthenian population as a whole on the basis of the *gente Rutheni, natione Poloni* intelligentsia. He noted the treatment of the Ruthenian peasantry as *ignorami* in need of enlightenment, but pointed out that it was easier to defeat an army of one hundred thousand than to Polonize a single Ruthenian village. He argued that Poles were not even able to create Poles out of Polish peasants (Masurians), yet had set about shaping the consciousness of the Ruthenian peasantry. *A Word of Warning* also reprimanded those circles of *gente Rutheni, natione Poloni* who had left the countryside, becoming people of learning who did not know "the difference between themselves, all speaking Polish, writing in Polish," and warned readers not

---

[246] Bazyli Podolinski, "Słowo przestrogi" ed. Feodosii Steblii, *Zapysky Naukovoho tovarystva imeni Shevchenka* 228: *Pratsi Istorychno-filosofs'koï sektsiï* (1994), pp. 444–62.

[247] Ibid., p. 445.

[248] Ibid., p. 446.

to "be surprised that they have forgotten about the Ruthenians, for they have always considered themselves to be Poles, while in the countryside they saw people not as Ruthenians, but simply as peasants."[249] For Podolynsky that absence of a privileged Ruthenian stratum, one capable of leading the nation, posed no problem, as he believed that the world would rid itself of the aristocracy. He did, however, distinctly emphasize that:

> We want to be a nation and we shall unfailingly be one for the voice of the people is Divine, while we lack no patience for the future [times – A.Ś.], since we have been taught it well. A Ruthenian constantly thinks and thinks, and once the idea is transformed into an undertaking, he cannot be dissuaded or frightened off.[250]

Of particular importance in Podolynsky's text is the segment analyzing the political routes available to the Ruthenians. He enumerated four routes: purely Ruthenian, Polish-Ruthenian, Austro-Ruthenian, and Russian-Ruthenian. While the first route would see Ruthenians fight independently for autonomy, the other three would achieve freedom in combination with other national/state factors. The Polish-Ruthenian route did not imply the adoption of the *gente Rutheni, natione Poloni* agenda, but rather indicated a subsequent alliance with the Poles, as the construction of a federation of Rus' with Poland would only help Rus' achieve full freedom. In summary, Podolynsky's voice is not only a polemic against the Polish democrats, but also serves as evidence that the Ruthenians from the period of the revolutions of 1848 were articulating concrete political demands and had dreamed of their own visions of a future nation independent of Polish political thought. In the scheme of things, the political proposals formulated by *gente Rutheni, natione Poloni* circles after the defeat of the revolutions of 1848 would become secondary, yet did not completely disappear. Instead, they became accentuated as individual demands within various aspects of public life and realized when possible in the subsequent decades of the nineteenth century, though not without attempts to create a political camp assembling Ruthenians of Polish nationality.

---

249 Ibid., p. 449.
250 Ibid., p. 453.

Chapter V
Ruthenians
in the Period of Absolutism's Return

The Struggle for the Language of Instruction in Education

The revolutions of 1848 were not to bring to Poles the long yearned-for freedom. They also failed to construct an "accord" between Polish and Ruthenian activists (not counting *gente Rutheni, natione Poloni*, though here disagreements also existed with regard to recognising the existence of Ruthenian nationality). In addition, the collapse of the Central National Council meant that Polish democrats were unable to engage in any further political activity. They would "wake up" again only after the defeat of Austria in the war with Piedmont and France in 1859 and in the face of constitutional transformation of the state in 1860–61. In the period of neoabsolutism, Polish conservatives, mostly landowners, would strengthen their position. Nonetheless, the years 1848–49 did result in Galician society being politically activated. It was then that the generation born during the first decades of the nineteenth century was to experience their political initiation. It would be difficult to conceive of any better conditions for the crystallization of political outlooks and the forging of those principles that were to constitute the basis for future activity.

At the same time, the birth of the Ruthenian national idea initiated a period of struggle for the full emergence of Ruthenian nationality — and here chiefly in those areas of life where influence could be exerted on the national consciousness of the Ruthenian populace, that is education, language, literature, religion, and politics as a whole.

Embedded between two cultures, the Polish and Ruthenian, the Ruthenians of Polish nationality were an obstacle to the "nationalizing" of the Ruthenian population in Galicia. Simultaneously, as representatives of the Greek Catholic urban intelligentsia (though not all), they constituted too weak a grouping for Ruthenians as a whole to view them as representatives of the nation. Their possibilities were therefore restricted to certain areas of activity, where their vision of a harmonious life led by Poles and Ruthenians could find realization. Such an area was education, where the world outlooks of children and the young were shaped. An opportunity to act presented itself here with changes in Austrian educational directives. The abandonment of the German character of education in Galicia following the 1848 revolutions raised questions on the direction the education of the young generation was to take. The "struggle for the soul" was to start almost from the very beginning, with the initiative being taken by Ruthenian activists.

Bronisław Łoziński wrote:

> (...) in the secondary schools of Eastern Galicia all means, including even those illegal in nature, were used to exert pressure, to orchestrate a return to the Greek Catholic rite of those pupils whose parents, although coming from Ruthenian ancestors, considered themselves to be Poles and adhered to the Latin rite.[1]

Łoziński cites an example from 1851, when several inhabitants of Sambir complained to Emperor Franz Joseph on his Galician visit that pupils who did not wish to return to the Greek Catholic rite were experiencing difficulties in attending school.[2]

At this time there quite possibly did not exist quite so much mutual distrust between the teaching staff of the two nationalities, but there did exist pressure to care for the furthering of one's own national culture. The *gente Ruthenus, natione Polonus* Euzebiusz Czerkawski recalled in his memoirs the attempt to create joint instruction in Polish and Ruthenian as a comparative method designed to achieve "a closer coming together of both nations." However, as he wrote: "except for Przemyśl there were neither teachers predisposed nor willing enough to undertake such an experiment."[3] This is borne out by the fact that a bicultural model of education did not enjoy much support among social activists from either side. The question of language in schools consequently assumed the character of a political dispute.

At that time, Agenor Gołuchowski, who was appointed in 1849 as viceroy, favored Polish interests in Galicia, although he was accused of betraying Polishness. He was an Austrian loyalist who resigned from independence plans, but at the same time he tried to Polonize Galicia, he cared for its economic development and believed that the province would receive autonomy in the future. Therefore, he tried to stop all centrifugal factors (among them – development of the Ruthenian national movement).

Following the revolutions of 1848, the language struggle in the school system was to become an important factor in the Polish-Ruthenian rivalry in Galicia as a whole. This matter is significant for two rea-

---

[1] Bronisław Łoziński, *Agenor hrabia Gołuchowski w pierwszym okresie rządów swoich (1846–1859)* (Lviv, 1901), pp. 166–67.

[2] Ibid., p. 167.

[3] Quoted from: ibid., p. 171.

sons: first, instruction of Ruthenian children and youth in Polish could continue to maintain the *gente Rutheni, natione Poloni* formation, and second, the chief defender of Polish as the language of instruction in schools was one of the best known assimilated Ruthenians—the earlier mentioned Euzebiusz Czerkawski. In the 1850s he was a secondary school inspector in the Lviv district as well as for Bukovyna, and subsequently for the Free City of Cracow.[4]

In the wake of the revolutions of 1848 it was possible throughout the Habsburg Monarchy to conduct classes in national languages on the basis of appropriate rulings by the authorities of the given crown land. This was part of the entire educational reform project for secondary and higher schools within the monarchy as a whole.[5] In one of the rulings (2 September 1848) it was recommended that the "national language" be introduced into public schools, and in another the conduct of classes at secondary schools and at Lviv University in Polish, with the stipulation that the Ruthenian language should be eligible, as it developed, for the same rights as Polish.[6] In 1848, Polish was introduced as the language of instruction into Galician secondary schools, with those not knowing Polish being able to use German. German as the language of the partitioning power was to continue to be used at the academic secondary school in Lviv.[7]

The protest launched by the Supreme Ruthenian Council at the Ministry of Education was soon to result, in January 1849, in the return of German as the language of instruction for all secondary schools in Galicia, with the intention that it would be replaced in the future by Ruthenian, which soon afterwards was to become a compulsory subject for all secondary schools in the eastern part of Galicia. Subsequent decisions of the Ministry of Education were to limit the influence of Polish in Eastern Galicia. From 1850, only religion continued to be taught in Polish. This unfavourable period for the Polish language was to be terminated only with the imperial letter issued for secondary schools (9 December 1854), reiterated by a rescript of the Ministry of Education (16 December 1854), which ordered teaching to be in "the language understood by the pupils," while making German a compulsory

---

[4] Antoni Knot, "Czerkawski Euzebiusz," in *PSB*, vol. 4 (Cracow, 1938), p. 334.

[5] Stanisław Kot, *Historja wychowania. Zarys podręcznikowy*, vol. 2: *Wychowanie nowoczesne (od połowy w. XVIII do współczesnej doby)* (Lviv, 1934), p. 268.

[6] Zygmunt Zborucki, *Euzebiusz Czerkawski i galicyjska ustawa szkolna z 1867 r.* (Lviv, 1927), p. 5.

[7] Jarosław Moklak, *W walce o tożsamość Ukraińców. Zagadnienie języka wykładowego w szkołach ludowych i średnich w pracach galicyjskiego Sejmu Krajowego 1866–1892* (Cracow, 2004), p. 25.

subject.[8] Declarations thus formulated may be interpreted variously, but they did provide the possibility for a change in the *status quo*. Ultimately, the teaching of Ruthenian to Polish youth in Eastern Galician schools was imposed in 1856.[9]

During this period, it was the secondary school inspector Euzebiusz Czerkawski, in desiring a Polonization of schools in Galicia, who was to provide direction to the policy of the governor of Galicia Agenor Gołuchowski. He was entrusted in 1857 with the first task of inspecting the state of schooling in the eastern part of the country and issuing reports on the subject. Gołuchowski perceived a threat in the development of Russophile attitudes among Ruthenian teachers, particularly among the ranks of religious instruction teachers (catechists). Yakiv Holovatsky was considered the instigator here, who from 1848 as a professor held the position of head of the Department of Ruthenian Literature and Language at Lviv University. Known for his activity in the Ruthenian Triad in the 1830s, he was, with time, to change his outlook and became a Russophile.[10] As Euzebiusz Czerkawski was to show in his report, the Ruthenian clergy delivered sermons to the people not in their own tongue but in Church Slavonic, and this resulted "in the gradual though inevitable complete assimilation of this dialect with the Russian language, something already openly propagated by Ruthenian publications (*Zoria Halytska* and *Simeina Biblioteka*), as well as by Father Holovatsky at the department itself."[11]

The Czerkawski–Holovatsky dispute was in no way a strictly personal conflict, for in point of fact it neatly etched the rivalry between the two routes that could be taken by the Ruthenian population in their quest for national self-determination. Czerkawski's outlook did not so much illustrate his hostility towards Ruthenians (after all he himself was a Ruthenian), as it was directed against the development of Russophilism. Gołuchowski did not conduct his policy in such a way to enhance Ruthenian culture, but he came out in opposition to the Pan-Slavic tendencies then prevalent. The promotion of Orthodoxy and the reliance of Galician Ruthenians on Russia were equally perceived as threats to Eastern Galicia of being taken away and incorporated into the Russian Empire. Given this tendency towards Orthodoxy and Russia within Galician Ruthenian culture, Polish political and educational

---

[8] Ibid., pp. 25–28.

[9] Łoziński, *Agenor hrabia Gołuchowski*, p. 171.

[10] For more on the subject of Holovatsky see: Włodzimierz Osadczy, *Święta Ruś. Rozwój i oddziaływanie idei prawosławia w Galicji* (Lublin, 2007), pp. 135–59.

[11] Quoted from: Łoziński, *Agenor hrabia Gołuchowski*, p. 181.

activists aware of this problem tried to halt such a development. This alternative, however, was viewed as pulling Ruthenians in the direction of Polish culture. Despite the experience gained from the revolutions of 1848, there was still no acceptance on the Polish side for the notion that a separate Ruthenian national culture could indeed develop without connection with the Poles. Hence *gente Rutheni, natione Poloni* such as Euzebiusz Czerkawski attempted to integrate their compatriots with the Poles not so much with the aim of Polonization but simply to prevent their

31. Euzebiusz Czerkawski

Russification. Czerkawski's attitude had to arouse opposition in Ruthenian circles, but there were also those who were in agreement with his argumentation. Czerkawski, in his recollections preserved in Bronisław Łoziński's copy, wrote:

> My attitude aroused many Ruthenians against me, for there were among them those who considered official Russian as their real written language, seeing Ruthenian as merely a folk dialect, whose use in a written form was to be indecent defeatism. For it was not desired to distance oneself from the allegedly common trunk, regardless of the fact that the elements of folk language conceal within themselves the notes of ideas and feelings, and in general linguistic gems are conceived in completely new conditions. Despite this, many teachers were persuaded by me and followed my instructions.[12]

Czerkawski's report, enhanced by the words of Gołuchowski, was presented to the Minister of Education, Leopold von Thun, on 12 March 1858. It demanded the removal of Holovatsky from the department (the candidate for the post was another highly regarded teacher, also *gente Ruthenus, natione Polonus*—Zygmunt Sawczyński; though this change was never to happen); the official adoption of the Latin script for the Ruthenian language; teaching to be conducted in Polish in the lower secondary schools until such time as Ruthenian had developed, which was only to be taught in higher secondary schools; and finally the stan-

---

[12] Wypisy z "Pamiętnika" Euzebiusza Czerkawskiego, Archiwum Uniwersytetu Jana Kazimierza we Lwowie. Personalia 425, Biblioteka Jagiellońska (subsequently: BJ), sygn. 10065 IV: Bronisław Łoziński, "Materiały warsztatowe do książki *Agenor hrabia Gołuchowski w pierwszym okresie rządów swoich (1846–1859)*, Lwów, 1901", p. 256v.

dardization of the calendars, which constituted a "division between Poles and Ruthenians while at the same time representing something convergent between the Galician Ruthenian Pan-Slavists and Russia."[13]

Czerkawski's demands, despite Thun's partial agreement, were not to be accepted by the minister but with one exception — the introduction of the Latin alphabet for the Ruthenian language. This was soon to occur and became the cause of the "alphabet war."

"The Alphabet War"

The suggestion that Ruthenians should use the Latin alphabet was in no way a new project. Even when Poland was still in existence, the Cyrillic alphabet had been gradually replaced by the Latin one, which bore witness to the blending of Ruthenian and Polish culture over many centuries. In the modern era, as Stanisław Stępień claimed, both languages — Polish and Ruthenian — were still sufficiently similar to each other that the replacement of the Cyrillic by Latin letters in Ruthenian texts enhanced their communicative ability, particularly if the matter concerned individuals unfamiliar with the Cyrillic alphabet. This referred equally to official administrative texts, as well as to the ecclesiastical, where priests made recourse throughout a service to hand-written fragments, in Latin script, of the Ruthenian *Sluzhebnyk* [Service book].[14]

A knowledge of Cyrillic was to enjoy a renaissance only with the end of the eighteenth century, i.e., from the time of Austrian state support for the Uniate Church in Galicia, manifested by the creation of the Studium Barbareum in Vienna (1774), and then the General Greek Catholic Seminary in Lviv (1783). These schools produced several dozen Uniate clergymen annually. This was not to affect priests, who would still use the Latin script when writing their sermons. The small number of Ruthenian intelligentsia worked in a similar way when composing their texts. The Latin script was the order of the day even in Przemyśl, which up until the revolutions of 1848 had remained the most flourishing Ruthenian centre and most actively involved in the development of the Greek Catholic Church and national Ruthenian life. The clergymen

---

[13] Łoziński, *Agenor hrabia Gołuchowski*, pp. 182–83. Czerkawski wrote at length in his memoirs about the need to introduce the Latin alphabet and calendar. See BJ, sygn. 10065 IV, k. 255v–256v.

[14] Stanisław Stępień, "Spory wokół języka i alfabetu Ukraińców galicyjskich. Druki ukraińskie wydane alfabetem łacińskim w Przemyślu w XIX i XX wiekach," in *Do dzherel. Zbirnyk naukovykh prats' na poshanu Oleha Kupchyns'koho z nahody ioho 70-richchia*, vol. 1, ed. Ihor Hyrych et al. (Kyiv–Lviv, 2004), pp. 190–91.

at the Przemyśl cathedral wrote their sermons employing Latin letters, and even the choir performing there in 1829 sang the liturgy from texts copied out in the "Polish" alphabet. This was made all the more the case by the fact that across the entirety of Galicia (with the exception of the Stauropegion Institute in Lviv) there was no printing house employing Cyrillic typeface.[15]

The undefined status of the Ruthenian language meant that in the 1830s, and particularly in the 1840s, several positions on the future fate of the language and its alphabet crystallized among the enlightened strata of Galician Ruthenian society. One of the most important issues was that the folk language differed significantly from the Church Slavonic used during church services. Several options were proposed: the use of the Cyrillic Russian alphabet reformed under tsar Peter I (bringing Ruthenian closer to Russian itself); remaining with Church Cyrillic; the creation of a new alphabet, reflecting the language of the people but on the basis of Cyrillic; and finally, choosing the Latin alphabet, which from the end of the 1850s was the option that the *gente Rutheni, natione Poloni* most fervently supported, with Euzebiusz Czerkawski at the head.

The rivalry between the various positions was to manifest itself chiefly in the subsequent publication of grammar textbooks for the Ruthenian language, though finally also with primers and catechisms, as well as other forms of printed matter. It is not true that the use of Latin script was from the very inception of the so-called "alphabet war" something inspired by Polish "factors." These joined into the melee when things were already well developed.

Let us recall that at this time—more or less when the Ruthenian Triad had disbanded its literary activities—the Greek-Catholic priest Iosyp Lozynsky wrote in the Lviv *Rozmaitości* the famous article "On the Introduction of the Polish Alphabet to Ruthenian Writing" ["O wprowadzeniu abecadła polskiego do piśmiennictwa ruskiego"].[16] *Rozmaitości* was edited at this time by a nationally-known Ruthenian of Polish nationality—Mikołaj Michalewicz [Mykola Mykhalevych].[17]

---

[15] For more see ibid., pp. 194, 196.

[16] Józef Łoziński, "O wprowadzeniu abecadła polskiego do piśmiennictwa ruskiego," *Rozmaitości* (Lviv) no. 29 (19 Jun. 1834), pp. 228–30.

[17] Mikołaj Michalewicz was a Ruthenian nobleman from Kopychyntsi in the Husiatyn district. He obtained an education at a Basilian school, subsequently becoming a private tutor for Aleksander Fredro. He then managed the Lubomirski library in Przeworsk, studied in Vienna, worked at the Ossolinski Institute, became a professor of Polish language and literature at Lviv University, and finally in 1827 was offered the editorship of *Gazeta Lwowska* and its supplement *Rozmaitości*. He held this position for eight years until the

The magazine he headed was one of the best cultural-social journals to have emerged prior to the revolutions of 1848, and one which had an impact on the intellectual development of the inhabitants of Galicia.[18] Iosyp Lozynsky, who had attended Michalewicz's university lectures, was to cause a storm in Ruthenian intellectual circles with his article, and numerous retorts by opponents. For he wrote that:

> (...) the Ruthenian language, not yet having a written form, has the free-
> dom to designate for itself such an alphabet which would be the most
> apt in expressing its sounds and the most efficient in its development;
> such an alphabet is the Polish alphabet.[19]

Here the author of the article was concerned first and foremost with maintaining continuity in the literary tradition initiated by Wacław Za-leski (Wacław of Olesko), who had transcribed the songs of the Ruthe-nian people using the Latin script.[20] Furthermore, Lozynsky considered that it would be much easier for children to grasp the "Polish ABC" than Russian Cyrillic. As Stanisław Nabywaniec wrote, Lozynsky was of the view that thanks to the Latin alphabet, Ruthenian as a language would have a chance to find a prominent place in Slavic literature and through this in European literature.[21] One of Michalewicz's biograph-ers concluded that this bold step resulted in his former student not be-ing offered an extension of his contract as editor, for Lozynsky was not a popular figure with the authorities. The entire print run of his Ruthe-nian language textbook — written in the Latin script — was confiscated. Michalewicz, being responsible for the publication of Lozynsky's text, lost his job in 1835 and only returned to journalism in the years 1840–44 as an employee of the *Lwowianin* [Leopolitan].[22]

---

end of 1834. It is of interest to note that he unsuccessfully applied in the 1830s to become the censor of Ruthenian books. Antoni Knot, "Michalewicz Mikołaj," in *PSB*, vol. 20 (Wro-cław–Warsaw–Cracow–Gdańsk, 1975), p. 571.

[18] For more on the subject of *Rozmaitości* see: Wilhelm Bruchnalski, *Historya Rozmaitości. Pisma Dodatkowego do Gazety Lwowskiej 1817–1848 i 1854–1859* (Lviv, 1912).

[19] Łoziński, "O wprowadzeniu abecadła," pp. 228–30.

[20] Cf. Marceli Handelsman, *Ukraińska polityka ks. Adama Czartoryskiego przed wojną krymską* (Warsaw, 1937), p. 86.

[21] Stanisław Nabywaniec, "Ksiądz Józef Łoziński – człowiek pogranicza," in *Dwa pogra-nicza. Galicja Wschodnia i Górny Śląsk. Historia – problemy – odniesienia*, eds. Zdzisław Bu-dzyński and Jolanta Kamińska-Kwak (Rzeszów, 2003), pp. 124–25.

[22] Stanisław Wasylewski, "Mikołaj Michalewicz. Redaktor Gazety Lwowskiej 1827–1834," in *Stulecie Gazety Lwowskiej 1811–1911*, vol. 1, part. 2: *Życiorysy*, ed. Wilhelm Bruchnalski (Lviv, 1911), pp. 1–13. Danuta Sosnowska drew a completely opposite conclusion from the failure to extend Michalewicz's contract: that by supporting Cyrillic he was stigma-tized. Wasylewski's version, however, seems more likely. Cf. Danuta Sosnowska, *Inna Galicja* (Warsaw, 2008), p. 48.

Despite the fact that Lozynsky's article came in for criticism from other Ruthenian intellectuals (Iosyp Levytsky and Markiian Shashkevych[23]), the author continued to develop his line of thought. In 1846 he prepared a grammar of the Ruthenian language which taught the language through the use of Latin letters, for as the author explained, "with the aid of the Latin alphabet we come closer to those Slavs who already use Roman characters and with it to the entirety of civilized Europe."[24] He also published a work on the subject of the Ruthenian wedding, containing among other things a series of Ruthenian songs that accompany engagements and nuptials.[25] The entire work was published exclusively in the Latin script. However, in the period in question the matter of what alphabet Ruthenians used was not as controversial as it was to become following the revolutions of 1848. As Jan Kozik wrote, Lozynsky was to continue with the practice of printing Ruthenian works in Latin script. This researcher noted eight such instances for the years 1821–34 and 76 up to 1857. Furthermore, the demand for the Ruthenian language to have the Latin alphabet was an issue that the Greek Catholic bishop of Przemyśl, Ivan Snihursky, was aware of, and it was he who even encouraged Lozynsky to publish a text presenting such a proposal in order—through the reaction to the article—to test public opinion on the subject.[26] This consequently meant that at the time the Church hierarchy itself was far from being opposed to the concept.

The transcription of Ruthenian songs into the Latin script was not controversial up to the publication of Lozynsky's article—it is worth recalling the earlier mentioned works by Wacław Zaleski or Ignacy Żegota Pauli, as well as those of Stepan Petrushevych[27]—but the fact that this Ruthenian decided to use the Latin script in his own language was to cause instantaneous criticism.

Neither Lozynsky's textbook nor his article represented anything exceptional. They concerned matters which had hitherto aroused no particular controversy within common Polish-Ruthenian territory. The notion of using an appropriate alphabet had up until then passed off without an ideological comment (the choice of letters resulted from practical possibilities or simply from the level of one's knowledge), yet in the face of the development of Ruthenian nationality (i.e., the

---

[23] On the subject of the polemic with Lozynsky see: Stępień, "Spory," pp. 199, 202 and Nabywaniec, "Ksiądz Józef Łoziński," pp. 125–27.

[24] Józef Łoziński, *Grammatyka języka ruskiego (mało-ruskiego)* (Przemyśl, 1846), p. 9.

[25] J[osyf] Łozynśkyj, *Ruskoje wesile* (Przemyśl, 1835).

[26] Jan Kozik, *The Ukrainian National Movement in Galicia 1815–1849*, ed. and introd. Lawrence D. Orton, transl. Andrew Gorski and Lawrence D. Orton (Edmonton, 1986), p. 88.

[27] About works written by Ruthenians using Latin script see: Stępień, "Spory," pp. 202–3.

creation of intellectual elites) the matter started to become a dispute national in character. The question of alphabet was, from the times of the revolutions of 1848, one of the fundamental issues that separated not so much Ruthenians from Poles as the followers of the 'St. George party' from the *gente Rutheni, natione Poloni*. The examples of poetry from the period of the 1848 revolutions cited in earlier chapters, the proclamations of the Ruthenian Sobor or of *Dnewnyk Ruskij*, as well as the choices made by individuals identifying themselves with those circles of Ruthenians of Polish nationality, vividly depict the problem of the Polish-Ruthenian conflict within the context of the alphabet used. Obviously not all Greek Catholic clergy transferred immediately to Cyrillic from the Latin alphabet, or decided to drop Polish, but from 1848 the question of the choice of language and alphabet was to become an element in discerning "true" Ruthenians from their "Polonized" compatriots. Despite the clear manifestation of a Polish-Ruthenian conflict, with the quieting down of politically-motivated disputes Ruthenian documents were to appear in the Latin script right up until the end of the 1850s, when the debate over the alphabet flared up in earnest.

In 1859, on the initiative of Minister of Education and Religion Leopold von Thun, a commission on the matter of the alphabet was to be assembled. The primary defenders of the use of Latin script for Ruthenian were two eminent *gente Rutheni, natione Poloni* who sat in the Galician Diet: the deputies Euzebiusz Czerkawski and Zygmunt Sawczyński. Czerkawski, in his article "Latin Script in the Ruthenian Language" ["Łacińskie czcionki w języku ruskim"], wrote about the advantages for Ruthenians of using Latin script in helping disseminate Ruthenian literature in the world.[28]

Thun, in order to stop the Ruthenian side from treating efforts to introduce the Latin script as an activity solely designed to Polonize the Ruthenian language through the use of an alphabet, proposed the inclusion of new letters for the Ruthenian alphabet as written in Latin script in place of some of those used in the Polish alphabet (for example the consonant clusters: *szcz, sz, cz*). Czerkawski prepared his project taking into consideration this idea; he also incorporated the proposal of the Czech linguist Jozef Jireček, who in transcribing the sounds of Ruthenian syllables used a Latin alphabet employing not Polish but Czech letters to render the sounds (č, š, ž, etc.).[29]

---

[28] Euzebiusz Czerkawski, "Łacińskie czcionki w języku ruskim," *Dodatek Tygodniowy przy Gazecie Lwowskiej* no. 24 (18 Jun. 1859), pp. 99–102; no. 26 (2 Jun. 1859), pp. 109–12.
[29] Joseph Jireček, *Über den Vorschlag das Ruthenische mit lateinischen Schriftzeichen zu schreiben. Im Auftrage des k. k. Ministeriums für Cultus und Unterricht* (Vienna, 1859).

The matter was to be ultimately decided on 8 May 1859 at a sitting of a special state commission called for that purpose by the Ministry of Education and Religion. The twelve-member commission comprised Ruthenian clergymen and intelligentsia, Euzebiusz Czerkawski (alone in such company), and Jireček, together with Austrian government civil servants. Even though the Czech's proposal was far from the Polish concepts, the Latinization of the alphabet was rejected. The main critic, the former chairman of the Supreme Ruthenian Council, Mykhailo Kuzemsky, saw the project as an attack on the national rights of the Ruthenian people. What is interesting is that those Ruthenians in the commission who were connected in some way with education displayed an interest in the gradual introduction of Latin script to Ruthenian textbooks. As Bronisław Łoziński has it, votes for the implementation of such a Latin alphabet were received from—in addition to the two Austrian government officials—the headmaster of the secondary school in Sambir, Father Tomasz Polański, as well as the headmaster of a Lviv secondary school, Ambroży Janowski.[30] Jireček finally relented, and this dissuaded Minister Thun from taking any further action. Thun agreed with Czerkawski about the need to stop the Ruthenian language from becoming more similar to Russian, but the attempt to change the alphabet was abandoned.[31] The Ministry approved the Ruthenians' right to their own literary language, its introduction to parish and folk schools, and also as a compulsory subject in secondary schools. School textbooks could be printed in Cyrillic, but the use of the "civil" Russian script was forbidden. The relevant ministerial rescript was sent to the Governor's Presidium on 25 July 1859.[32]

In practice, however, it was not the Cyrillic used by Galician Ruthenians that was victorious but the Russian "civil" script introduced by Peter I. Only church texts were printed in Cyrillic. In all other cases, Russian letters were employed. Latin script was used in those areas where the knowledge of Cyrillic letters was poor.[33] In exceptional situations, Latin letters were permitted for use in Ruthenian schools.[34] The *gente Rutheni, natione Poloni* continued to use them, men such as Platon Kostecki, as well as Polish writers and poets like Leon Eugeniusz

---

[30] Łoziński, *Agenor hrabia Gołuchowski*, p. 187.

[31] Ibid., p. 190; Moklak, *W walce o tożsamość Ukraińców*, p. 36.

[32] Renata Dutkowa, "Polityka szkolna w Galicji 1866–1890," in *Nauka i oświata*, eds. Andrzej Meissner and Jerzy Wyrozumski (Rzeszów, 1995), pp. 40–41.

[33] Stępień, "Spory," pp. 209–10.

[34] "Reading and writing by means of Latin letters is to be undertaken in Ruthenian folk schools, in as far as Polish language is a subject of instruction there, and in the teaching of reading Polish texts may be used." "Rzecz urzędowa," *Gazeta Lwowska* no. 182 (11 Aug. 1859), p. 725.

Węgliński or Tymko Padurra, who came from Russian-ruled Ukraine. The Latin alphabet was also used for practical purposes in government offices, the best example being—and this already in the era of autonomy—how Ruthenian deputy contributions were noted down in Latin script shorthand during the sessions of the Galician Diet.

The functioning of the Ruthenian language in the first half of the nineteenth century, not based at that time strictly on its own alphabet or standardized grammar, reflected in many ways the process that the evolving Ruthenian nation was passing through. The use of the Latin alphabet allowed two ethnoses to function within a single, written, cultural environment. The introduction of separate forms of notation was to result in the separation of both literatures. It is therefore not surprising that the chief users and at the same time defenders of Ruthenian use of the Latin script were those in a dilemma between their Ruthenian roots and an acquired Polish state-national consciousness—the *gente Rutheni, natione Poloni*.

Rivalry for Equal Status for the Ruthenian Language

The beginning of the 1860s was to present another possibility for Ruthenians of Polish nationality to manifest their ideas. The question of equal status and rights for the Ruthenian language was to return. On 5 September 1859, the emperor nominated Hryhorii Yakhymovych as Greek Catholic Metropolitan of Lviv; the nomination was approved by the pope on 23 March 1860. National considerations decided these matters, for Yakhymovych was to be the actual guardian of not merely the Greek Catholic Church but also of Ruthenian nationality, which was viewed as being persecuted by the Poles. Emotions were fuelled in the Polish-Ruthenian conflict by the fact that at this time in the Stauropegion Institute the exclusive album *Galician Dawn as an Album for the Year 1860* [*Zoria Galitskaia iako al'bum" na god" 1860*] was published. This publication, over five hundred pages long, contained literary works of Ruthenian writers and poets, including Yakiv and Ivan Holovatsky, Ivan Naumovych, Mykola Ustyianovych, and many others.[35] This was the first undertaking of its kind depicting Ruthenian national culture, and in addition it was dedicated to the Greek Catholic hierarch Hryhorii Yakhymovych.[36] The name of the album is an obvious reference to the

---

[35] *Zoria Galitskaia iako al'bum" na god" 1860* (Lviv, 1860).
[36] Dmitrii Věntskovskii, *Grigorii Iakhimovich" i sovremennoe russkoe dvizhenie* (Lviv, 1892), pp. 70–73.

Ruthenian journal *Zoria Halytska*, which had been published in Lviv from 1848 to 1857. Here it is worth recalling that this journal twice changed its orientation and the language in which it was published. Up until 1851 it was a newspaper Ruthenian in character. Up to 1854 it appeared in Russian and adopted a Russophile orientation. It was again a Ruthenian organ in its final years. The publication of the album in 1860 proved to be of exceptional significance. Since the album made references to the Russophile period of the newspaper's activity while also suggesting its earlier service to the Ruthenian culture in Galicia, there were concerns that Galician Ruthenians—in the same way as their newspaper—were heading in the direction of Moscow.

The album's publication evoked ardent opposition on the part of Platon Kostecki, who soon produced an extensive review and, in point of fact, a criticism of the Russophile aspect of the policies of the 'St. Georgian party.' The article appeared in the Lviv monthly *Przegląd Powszechny* at the end of 1860. In an exposé the author argued that it was the Poles who had awakened Ruthenian literature, which was able to freely develop up until 1848 thanks to some Polish literary figures. From that moment onwards, Platon Kostecki blamed Ruthenians for their cultural orientation toward Russia (visible in their assimilation of the alphabet, emphasising the unity of all lands of Rus', etc.) and he unequivocally condemned any non-Polish-oriented route of development for Ruthenians. He commented on the situation in the following manner:

> Unfortunately, Ruska Matytsia published its handiwork [here the matter concerns *Zoria Halytska*—A.Š.] in this supposedly Ruthenian, but in actuality administrative Russian language—if something of that ilk can be called a language; this language was taught and, in part, is still taught to the Ruthenian youth in normal and secondary schools; this language is being fostered in seminaries; and in this language Ruthenian letters are taught at Lviv University. And it has reached the stage whereby even sermons are delivered from the pulpits in this language even though the people understand nothing. And we have reached the point where Galician Ruthenians, though not all, with amazing zeal have become the very propagators of influences against which Dnipro Rus' fights with its most precious blood and intellect.[37]

The author wanted in this way to show Ruthenians that their countrymen beyond the Zbruch River were fighting against Russian dominance while they were, at the same time, turning their gaze

---

[37] Platon Kostecki, "Zorja Galickaja jako album na god 1860. Recenzya," *Przegląd Powszechny* (Lviv) no. 97 (22 Nov. 1860), p. 3.

towards Russia. He also reminded them that the album was, in accordance with the publisher's promises, to appear under the Ruthenian title: *Zoria Halytska na rik 1860*, but that it was changed into Russian. Platon Kostecki did not conceal his outrage. He posed the following questions:

> Who forced Bohdan Didytsky [the editor in chief of the journal — A.Ś.] [to promote the idea] that a Ruthenian child, born on Ruthenian land, nourished by Ruthenian labour, raised on the money of Ruthenians, be christened in the Muscovite faith, that most terrible enemy of Rus', under whose knout groan 12 million Ruthenians?[38]

Kostecki also reminded the readers in his review that Bohdan Didytsky, as editor of *Zoria Halytska*, had initially acted in support of the development of Ruthenian nationality, but later had become a Russophile. Kostecki was unwilling to accept this, particularly given that he himself had edited the newspaper from December 1854. He also considered that thanks to him it had gained some renown, as he had found for it "young Ruthenian strolling lyre players." If one is to believe Platon Kostecki, the paper's switch to a pro-Russian orientation also caused a backlash among other authors who had submitted their texts for the album. Kostecki's attitude itself already shows us the role played by *gente Rutheni, natione Poloni* at this stage in the development of Ruthenian identity. One may even state that as the popularity of the idea of Pan-Slavism and the Russophile current increasingly gained advocates, it was the *gente Rutheni, natione Poloni* — individuals like Platon Kostecki — who acted as the catalyst in the development of national tendencies among Ruthenians. They spoke out against Russian and Pan-Slavic influences in Galicia, while concurrently believing in the in-

32. *The masthead of the newspaper* Zoria Halytska *under the editorship of Platon Kostecki*

---

separable bonds that linked the Ruthenian people with the Poles. And the latter had for decades treated Ruthenians of Polish nationality first and foremost as an equal partner in discussion. In this way it was possible for the national movement to develop as long as it did not head towards Russophilism (or was not treated as such). Kostecki's polemic with Didytsky was still seen in the nineteenth century as the beginning of an intensive struggle of *gente Rutheni, natione Poloni* with the Russophile current.[39]

It is worth recalling that at this time the notion of Poles supporting Ruthenians in their national development, but in brotherhood with Poles and in opposition to the Russophiles, found increasing coverage in Galician newspapers. Halina Kozłowska-Sabatowska wrote that:

> The slogan of brotherhood with the Ruthenians, openly proclaimed in *Czytelnia dla Młodzieży* and radiating from *Dziennik Literacki*, was subjected to a practical test during the period of patriotic demonstrations. It came through unscathed, if the model based on the principle of *gente Rutheni, natione Poloni* was not questioned, that is when Ukrainian youth cooperated with the Polish youth in pre-insurrection organizational work, and then in the uprising itself, considering these to be common undertakings. Departures from this rule would be treated as treason and result in instigations by the conservative St. George party.[40]

Platon Kostecki's text entitled "The Ruthenian Fragment" ["Fragment ruski"], published in the periodical *Czytelnia dla Młodzieży* in 1861, may serve as an example. Here the author criticizes the members of the 'St. George party' who " spew fire and brimstone against the Poles and Poland," and he attempts to prove that it was no one else but the Poles who supported Ruthenian literacy and undertook the Ruthenian theme in the pages of their tomes. He even gave the examples of Adam Mickiewicz, Juliusz Słowacki, Józef Bohdan Zaleski, Henryk Rzewuski, "Bodzantowicz" (pseudonym of Kajetan Suffczyński), Józef Ignacy Kraszewski, and Józef Dzierzkowski. Meanwhile—according to Platon Kostecki—these self-same Ruthenians did not care about their own language, as proof of which may serve the figure of Metropolitan Antin Anhelovych, who allegedly burnt non-Uniate Ruthenian books.[41] Kostecki simultaneously referred to his own criticism of the Russophile current contained in his review published one year earlier.

---

[39] See: *Encyklopedyja powszechna*, vol. 7: *Den.–Eck.* (Warsaw, 1861), p. 891.

[40] Halina Kozłowska-Sabatowska, *Między konspiracją a pracą organiczną. Młodość Tadeusza Romanowicza* (Cracow, 1986), p. 54.

[41] Platon Kostecki, "Fragment ruski," *Czytelnia dla Młodzieży* 2, no. 1 (2 Jan. 1861), pp. 3–5.

It was not just Kostecki who spoke out. Bernard Kalicki's historical outline "Recalling the Joining of Rus' to Poland in the 14ᵗʰ Century" ["Przypomnienie połączenia się Rusi z Polską w wieku XIV"] appeared in the above mentioned *Czytelnia dla Młodzieży*. The text, in a clear and lucid manner, informs the reader about the might and greatness of Poland, in what was quickly to become a close brotherhood of "nations of various tribal provenance." There is no need to summarize the entire article. We shall cite merely the most relevant of the author's conclusions: "in the name of common national thought, in the name of freedom and faith, in the name of protection and aid, our fatherland gave its hand of fraternity to Lithuania, Rus', Crownland and others"; "Red Ruthenia has belonged from the oldest times to Poland"; "from the benevolent royal hand came many documents ensuring countless benefits for various towns."[42] Of course, the author did not omit that out of the grace of King Casimir III the Great came not only castles but also churches, including St. George's in Lviv. His bitterness towards the overseers of this Uniate temple was in this case clearly palpable.

These texts convey to us the atmosphere of rivalry surrounding Ruthenian identity at the beginning of the second half of the nineteenth century. The desire was to halt the Russophile direction being followed by the Uniate Church or at least to influence the 'St. George's party,' whose head was Metropolitan Yakhymovych. On the other hand, the conflict incited anti-Polish sentiments among Ruthenians, and behind this process stood an archbishop who was unwilling to compromise and who rose, at that time, to the position of the leader of the Galician Ruthenians.

However, to return to the matter of the album and the start of Yakhymovych's ministry as metropolitan, we should mention why this clergyman intentionally delayed his installation in Lviv. He did so as a result of the failure, in his opinion, to maintain the principles of equality for both nations in Galicia with regard to language. Twice, on 21 and 23 September 1860, he addressed the emperor on the matter. He asked for Franz Joseph I *ex officio* to forbid discussions on the subject of the Ruthenian language as such that would have legal force in Galicia.[43]

The second time, together with other Ruthenians (clergymen and civil servants/government officials), he sent a petition to the throne in the name of the Ruthenian population. In this he included five demands:

• To annul the ministry's order introducing a new grammar and to leave Ruthenians their language and grammar;

---

[42] Bernard Kalicki, "Przypomnienie połączenia się Rusi z Polską w wieku XIV," *Czytelnia dla Młodzieży* 2, no. 8 (11 Mar. 1861), pp. 58–60.

[43] Věntskovskii, *Grigorii Iakhimovich"*, pp. 70–73.

- To introduce Ruthenian as the language of instruction to those urban schools where not two thirds but just the majority of children are Ruthenian;
- For Ruthenian to be treated as a compulsory subject in the secondary schools of Eastern Galicia;
- For Ruthenians to be allowed to use the Ruthenian language when addressing matters in government offices and the courts;
- That those applying for administrative posts have a knowledge of Ruthenian in its written and oral form.[44]

These were admittedly not excessive demands. The metropolitan himself did not demand the division of Galicia into a western and eastern part. Rather, he simply stood up for the rights of the Ruthenian language guaranteed by the power of Austrian law. However, the address by the clerics caused a reaction not only in Polish circles, but also among Ruthenians of Polish nationality.

This situation was to repeat itself at the time of constitutional changes at the turn of 1861. It should be noted that October 1860 gave Galician residents hope for change. Agenor Gołuchowski, as the new interior minister of Austria, developed the October diploma, which assumed federalization of the state. The Poles counted on autonomy in Galicia. On 4 January, that is just after the issuing of the October diploma, the Polish elites in Galicia sent a petition to the throne demanding the creation of a Galician Diet with wide ranging powers. Simultaneously they appealed for the introduction of Polish as a language for administration and schooling. They also spoke out on the subject of equality for the Ruthenian language, though here fairly enigmatically. When on 11 January 1861 another delegation (this time Ruthenian) arrived in Vienna with the new Lviv metropolitan, Hryhorii Yakhymovych, at the head, which—besides assuring the loyalty of Galician Ruthenians to the throne—was also to demand a special position for the Ruthenian language in Eastern Galicia, critical voices appeared in the Polish press. In one of the issues of *Przegląd Powszechny* from this period we can find a text praising the first petition (of 4 January) for "the national principle *gente Mazurus, Ruthenus aut Judaeus, natione autem Polonus* was to find the most ardent support in this petition."[45] It was also emphasized that this petition represented the voice of all Galician inhabitants of Mazurian, Ruthenian, or Jewish origin, who stood for the principle of national

---

[44] Ibid., p. 73.
[45] "Przegląd dzienników wiedeńskich," *Przegląd Powszechny* a supplement to no. 13 (29 Jan. 1861).

unity, while Yakhymovych's deputation was, at least for the author of the text, not even the general Ruthenian voice but merely the outlook of specific circles connected with the Lviv Greek Catholic hierarchy. These views were particularly shared by the *gente Rutheni, natione Poloni*.

Teodozy Golanik [Teodosii Holanyk], Dymitr Koczyndyk, Platon Kostecki, and Hieronim Łodyński assembled a Ruthenian protest against the petition to the throne drawn up by the St. George deputies and handed it personally to the ministry in Vienna.[46] This was to clarify the statements of the Greek Catholic clergy, presenting them as not being representative of the people and only representing the stance of St. George's Cathedral in Lviv. The document was drawn up in two languages—Polish and Ruthenian—and dated 22 February 1861. It was emphasized in the protest that Yakhymovych's demands did not reflect what Ruthenians really believed and what they actually needed. The authors, in describing themselves as entrusted to act as the full representatives of the Ruthenian population of Galicia, wrote:

> The undersigned citizens of the Ruthenian soil linked by blood and provenance with the Ruthenian people, bound through denomination and past, living amongst this people and with these folk sharing from the cradle to the grave the same lot, cannot accept that dignitaries of the consistory of our rite on the strength of their clerical office have the right to present the demands and needs of the people, which they lead in a spiritual capacity, on matters secular. For standing on the hierarchical ladder without family and social ties at the base, amongst which the lower orders of our clergy live and work, they are restricted within their specific oligarchic circle, with the crown of the national tree being without boughs, trunk or roots they do not hear from on high the pulse of national life, they do not see the national currents of the times which pass by their headquarters at St. George's and which lead the Ruthenian people on other salutary routes to other loftier goals displayed through fraternity and accord.[47]

In a further section of the petition the *gente Rutheni, natione Poloni* reduced Yakhymovych's demands to a laboured spiel about the shape of the letters and signs "of rural notice boards (...) as if the well-being and happiness of a nation depended on such." As Ruthenians they defended their compatriots, proclaiming that:

> (...) the Ruthenian nation has yet to have fallen so low for matters as trifling as the shape of letters and the inscriptions of rural sign posts to

---

[46] *Protest Rusinów przeciw adresowi do tronu podanego przez deputację świętojurców*, ([Lviv], 1861), LNNBU, fond 45: Arkhiv Didushyts'kykh, op. 1: Rukopysy biblioteky poturyts'koï Didushyts'kykh, spr. 201.

[47] Ibid., p. 1v–2.

be elevated to the heights of national tasks deemed fit to draw the attention of Your Excellency.[48]

But the crux of the entire protest did not depend solely on negating the validity of the St. Georgian demands, but also involved repudiating the significance of Yakhymovych and his supporters as a political option. *Gente Rutheni, natione Poloni* did not want the representatives of the 'St. George's party' to claim the right to speak out in the name of the whole nation for themselves alone. They considered political and not spiritual circles to be entitled to speak.

In protest, the authors cited the document that had already been drawn up in Cracow on 31 December 1860 but handed to the state minister in Vienna by the deputation on 4 January, considering it to be a representative voice for both Galician denominations. We shall recall the most important matters therein touched on. We read in the document:

> With this intent we have the honour to present to Your Excellency that the inhabitants of our land, both peoples joined by voluntary union centuries back, the Poles and Ruthenians, who despite the lot that befell the entirety of what once was their Polish fatherland, have not abandoned and will never abandon the eternal historical rights of their nationality, ones that can never be obsolete, a nationality based on an act of divine providence. For us the said divided trinity of Poland will always be simply one and the same person of our former mother (…).[49]

Further on appeared a warning about the possible division of the Austrian zone of partition into smaller parts and the creation of separate parliaments for each of them. It was proposed that Polish as the national language could be used also "for internal [use] across all the dicasteries of the country in the treatment of public matters" because "Polish is rich, flexible, and has developed through many centuries of practice to the highest degree in all the branches of literature." At the same time, however, a hope was expressed that "the Ruthenian language will immediately have bestowed upon itself all the rights reflecting its worth."[50] The argument for the equalising of languages appeared in the document but was so enigmatically presented that it was possible in advance to predict that it would be impossible to implement. But this was not to be the most important matter in this document. The most important was the appearance before the Austrian minister of state of the authors as representatives of a harmonious community—the Polish

---

[48] Ibid., p. 2v.
[49] *Czas* no. 4 (5 Jan. 1861), p. 1.
[50] Ibid.

nation divided by the partitioning powers in the eighteenth century and composed of two "clans," once joined in union.[51] Hence the emphasis that was placed on the necessity for a single National Diet instead of two parliaments for both parts of Galicia.

The authors of the later protest (of 22 February), with Kostecki at the head, were to recall the document of the Galician deputation, "We Ruthenians, together with our delegates, entered with a thousand of our signatures, which we ceremoniously and totally confirm." And the situation from 1848 was to repeat itself when the *gente Rutheni, natione Poloni* again made use of a petition designed to question the influence of the Ruthenian clergy. At the end of the document, in the two languages, Polish and Ruthenian, the authors urged people to sign the protest. The role of organizer was here taken by Platon Kostecki, at whose dwelling in the Market Square in Lviv the deputation met.[52] A group headed by the State Diet deputy Teodor Szemelowski was to make the trip to Vienna to present the proposals of Ruthenians of Polish nationality.[53] En route to the Austrian capital the delegation stopped off in Cracow, where they were welcomed with full honours. The Cracow correspondent for the Lviv *Głos* [Voice] wrote:

> Immense crowds of Cracovians waited for the Ruthenian brothers at the railway station. On the train's arrival the station reverberated from the cries of a joyous fraternal welcome. One of those present spoke to the delegation in the Ruthenian dialect, while Mr. Lodynsky of Miliatyn expressed thanks in Polish. They departed to new cries of "Long live the Ruthenians!"[54]

At the same time the press underlined that the Uniate deputation had been welcomed by no one but the Cracow police.[55]

---

[51] The press gave examples of the approval among Ruthenians for the petition delegation. Cf. J.K., "Z pod Janowa," *Przegląd Powszechny* no. 11 (24 Jan. 1861), p. 3. It was written: "Here in our district the entire Ruthenian intelligentsia, curiously along with the Greek Catholic priest, sincerely applauded the deputation's demands under the leadership of Mr. Smolka, with the single exception of one man who sowed monstrous lies amongst the people that our deputation had gone to His Magnificence with a request for the reinstatement of serfdom (…)."

[52] LNNBU, fond 45, op. 1, spr. 201, p. 5.

[53] For more on the deputation: Marjan Mudryj, "Dylematy narodowościowe w Sejmie Krajowym galicyjskim (na przykładzie posłów formacji *gente Rutheni natione Poloni*)," in *Ukraińskie tradycje parlamentarne XIX–XXI wiek*, ed. Jarosław Moklak (Cracow, 2006), p. 63 and footnote 7; Stanisław Pijaj, "Posłowie ruscy w parlamencie wiedeńskim w latach 1848–1879," in *Ukraińskie tradycje parlamentarne*, pp. 110–11.

[54] "Korespondenye 'Głosu'," *Głos* no. 50 (1 Mar. 1861), p. 1.

[55] Cf. ibid.; "Przegląd dzienników wiedeńskich," *Przegląd Powszechny* no. 7 (15 Jan. 1861), p. 1.

The *gente Rutheni, natione Poloni* cannot be accused of only acting in the Polish interest, for some of them can be seen as real defenders of matters Ruthenian, though in union with the Poles. Evidence of this can be served by the figure of Platon Kostecki, who, at the beginning of January 1861, published in *Przegląd Powszechny* the famous article "Lviv University" ["Uniwersytet Lwowski"]. Here he totally criticized the policy of Germanization, particularly in the context of the university in the region's capital—Lviv. He demanded at the same time that lectures be conducted at the university in Polish and Ruthenian.[56] He concluded his text—to put it mildly—with a display of his immense impatience over the current situation. Kostecki threatened:

> (...) the days of police violence, custody and presumptuousness are numbered. The sense of one's own worth is aroused, we shall not let it slumber or take fright, for our fathers are watching us, the world is watching, our children are watching, our homeland. Patience would no longer be a virtue but a crime, a disgrace![57]

Platon Kostecki was to pay for this display of social courage, for the article was deemed to incite social unrest and ended with the author in a court case. The minutes of the court sessions were published in the press.[58] They wanted to sentence Kostecki to two years' imprisonment, but he was ultimately only sent away for two months—and it was to be this two-month period that ensured him legendary status. It also provided the opportunity for him to create his famous compilation *Poems* [*Poezyi*], out of which came not only the idea of Polish-Ruthenian-Lithuanian brotherhood, but also the Russian (Pan-Slavist) threat.[59]

One may say that Kostecki's "daring to stand out" came at the wrong time—a period of centralizing policies in the Austrian monarchy. At this time, on 26 February 1861, the new minister of internal affairs (after the dismissal of Gołuchowski) Anton von Schmerling issued the initiative to reduce the competencies of planned national diets in favour of Vienna. This change meant for Poles the loss of hope for the federalization of the monarchy and the autonomy of Galicia. At the same time there was also announced a return to the educational status of December 1848, and this meant giving up on any hope for its Polonization.[60]

---

[56] [Platon Kostecki], "Uniwersytet lwowski," *Przegląd Powszechny* no. 2 (3 Jan. 1861), p. 2.

[57] Ibid.

[58] "Sprawozdanie z ostatniej sądowej rozprawy...," *Przegląd Powszechny* no. 86 (10 Sep. 1861); no. 87 (12 Sep. 1861); no. 88 (14 Sep. 1861); no. 91 (21 Sep. 1861); no. 92 (24 Sep. 1861); no. 94 (28 Sep. 1861).

[59] Platon Kostecki, *Poezyi* (Lviv, 1862).

[60] Renata Dutkowa, *Polityka szkolna w Galicji. Między autonomią a centralizmem (1861–1875)* (Cracow, 1995), p. 41.

The language question in education, the matter of alphabet, and at the same time the equality of Poles and Ruthenians in Galicia were temporarily resolved by the memorandum issued by the Ministry of State on 13 March 1861. This presented Ruthenians with freedom in the shaping of their own language and literature, although "with especial consideration for the folk language." This was in point of fact a victory for the adherents of Cyrillic in Ruthenian, and therefore the representatives of the 'St. George's party.' Those who supported the use of the Latin script, and who often were *gente Rutheni, natione Poloni*, were to lose their patron—the Austrian minister of internal affairs Agenor Gołuchowski—who was replaced by Anton von Schmerling. This change meant that the loyalist orientation of Ruthenians was to gain in

33. The cover of Zygmunt Sawczyński's book The Languages of our Country's Eastern Part *(Cracow, 1861)*

significance. The conflict over the alphabet was to unequivocally end in the imperial rulings on Ruthenian writing of 10 April 1861, announced in the directives of the Ministry of Justice on 21 April 1861. This made it obligatory for the national authorities to accept correspondence written in Cyrillic.[61]

Yet, this was in no way to bring an end to the conflict between Ruthenians and Poles, especially Ruthenians of Polish nationality, waged within the public sphere over language. On the strength of the decisions, Ruthenian was to become the language used in administration. The next area of realization was to be the education system, one that had hitherto been dominated by German as a language.

Władysław Sanguszko, Franciszek Smolka, as well as Adam Sapieha sent a petition to Anton Schmerling, the minister of state, in which they demanded a national diet with legislative powers, as well as the establishment of independent national institutions and the introduction of Polish as the language of instruction into schools as well as government

---

[61] Moklak, *W walce o tożsamość Ukraińców*, pp. 38–39.

offices with the "Ruthenian language being granted rights appropriate to its stage of development."[62] A supporter of the introduction of Ruthenian into schools was, on the Polish side, Adam Sapieha.

Spyrydon Lytvynovych was chosen to go with the delegation and their project to the Imperial Council in Vienna, although on the condition that he guarantee his loyalty in relation to the Poles.[63] This cordial gesture on the part of politicians with a pro-Ruthenian sentiment was to soon prove insufficient, and this as a result of the Ruthenian representatives in the Imperial Council: Bishop Lytvynovych and his supporter Antin Mohylnytsky. They believed that the Imperial Council and not the Galician Diet should make decisions about educational matters in Galicia. Soon the *gente Rutheni, natione Poloni* Teodor Szemelowski and Mikołaj Zyblikiewicz were protesting against the transference of Galician matters to the Imperial Council.[64] The former presented himself as "a Ruthenian by family and rite" and warned against "a foreign protector who stands up for the Ruthenians and protects them but on the basis of the right of the destitute," for Poles and Ruthenians who sit side by side are able to manage their own problems splendidly and here "at home," that is at the forum of the Galician Diet. Here he pointed out that in 1848, foreign protection had merely resulted in the "splitting of brotherly tribes." He proclaimed:

> The fact is that for centuries Ruthenians and Poles have lived together and have created a common political whole, that they have shared joy and sorrows, that they have jointly taken part in wars of religion, for freedom and the law, and that for centuries they have known no dualism. They—almost all of them—have used the Polish language as their literary language.[65]

Szemelowski considered that on this basis all problems would be equally resolved by Poles and Ruthenians themselves, without the participation of third parties. For if the matter concerned the desire on the part of Lytvynovych to introduce another language than the state one to the secondary and university educational system, then Szemelowski "in the name of Ruthenians" wanted to protest against this, arguing that the Galician Diet had established that both Polish and Ruthenian were to be the languages of instruction.[66]

---

[62] Paweł Sierżęga, "Obchody rocznicy unii lubelskiej na terenie Galicji w 1869 roku," in *Działalność wyzwoleńcza*, ed. Jadwiga Hoff (Rzeszów, 2001), p. 147.

[63] Dutkowa, *Polityka szkolna w Galicji. Między*, p. 42.

[64] *Czas* no. 147 (29 Jun. 1861), pp. 1–2.

[65] Teodor Szemelowski's statement see: *Czas* no. 148 (2 Jul. 1861), p. 2.

[66] Ibid.

On 26 July 1861 the Ministry of State issued a decree sanctioning the delegation's demands, although it was made clear that the introduction of the second language—Galician (Ruthenian)—into schools would only take place if the children spoke it fluently. The Diet's passing of the resolution was to provoke considerable emotions. Its main opponent was Henryk Schmitt. In his pamphlet published in Lviv at the time he agreed theoretically with the equal treatment of Poles and Ruthenians but at the same time questioned whether Ruthenians were in fact a nation. He considered them a Polish branch, with their language a mere dialect, an offshoot of Polish.[67]

This opinion was far from isolated, and in fact reflected not only the views of a sizeable portion of Polish society, but also expressed the views held by some Ruthenians of Polish nationality. We should draw attention to that fact that in this very same year another deputy of the Galician Diet, Zygmunt Sawczyński, wrote the book *The Languages of our Country's Eastern Part* [*Języki wschodniej części kraju naszego*].[68] This was its own form of polemic with the demands emanating from Ruthenian circles at this time, but simultaneously it broke with the view held in Polish public opinion that Ruthenians constituted no more than one of the Polish tribes.[69] Sawczyński, as opposed to Schmitt, primarily emphasized the elements of national differences between Poles and Ruthenians in Galicia, though in general he considered it a historical necessity for them to forge together into a single state entity—in the way the Italian tribes had constituted the Roman nation. Sawczyński wrote:

> In Polish history, in Polish literature; in general in the entirety of Polish education, three elements have flowed together: next to the Polish element the Ruthenian and Lithuanian have adhered as if they were individual tones in a chord or factors in a mathematical product; and as more modern philological criticism, having accepted the view that the epics known to the world as Homeric were composed by various bards, cannot more closely determine which were the [poems'] original parts or to whom they should be attributed: equally history would find itself in trouble if it were to designate from what today is called Polish each of the elements that make up the composition of Polish historical life, and what it would follow to assign.[70]

---

[67] Cf. Henryk Schmitt, *Kilka słów bezstronnych w sprawie ruskiej* (Lviv, 1861).

[68] Zygmunt Sawczyński, *Języki wschodniej części kraju naszego* (Cracow, 1861).

[69] Marian Mudry analysed Sawczyński's leaflet in more detail, emphasising that the views expressed by him resulted in them being opposed by nationalist activists, and consequently had an impact on the development of Ruthenian nationality. Mudryj, "Dylematy narodowościowe," pp. 65–67.

[70] Sawczyński, *Języki wschodniej części*, p. 35.

Therefore, it was the *gente Ruthenus, natione Polonus* who were to contribute to the failure of their own language in education. The problem of the lack of loyalty among some Ruthenians of Polish nationality can serve as an example. Some, like Platon Kostecki, fought for Ruthenian to be the language of instruction at university. Others, like Zygmunt Sawczyński, helped with the total Polonization of all levels of the educational system.

In summary, at this stage it was the opponents of a Ruthenianization of schools who were victorious for, as Jarosław Moklak writes, "Polish was announced to be the mother tongue of Ruthenians."[71] This state of affairs was only to start to change in April 1863, when a ministerial resolution making Ruthenian the language of instruction for certain subjects at the academic secondary school in Lviv came into effect.[72] Yet, at this time Galician society was experiencing completely different events which were to portend other scenarios for the Ruthenians— ones not linked to the grace or disfavour of the partitioning powers—the eruption of the January Uprising.

---

[71] Moklak, *W walce o tożsamość Ukraińców*, p. 48.
[72] Ibid., p. 50.

Chapter VI

Beneath the Standard of the Eagle, the Angel, and the Vytis Coat-of-Arms... The January Uprising

The Situation Prior to the January Uprising

Before we confront the events of 1863–64, we must go back in time in order to present the context of the first national uprising that strove for the reconstruction of a Polish-Ruthenian-Lithuanian state. First and foremost, the Crimean War of 1853–56 aroused renewed hope in Polish politicians both within the country and abroad. For it was then that it became obvious that the Viennese order was not invincible, and that the partitioning powers could stand in opposition to each other. This was to result in fresh interest in the participation of Ruthenian/Ukrainian lands in the revival of the Polish state. The émigré faction concentrated around Prince Adam Czartoryski was most actively involved in the attempts to incite the region's inhabitants to take up arms against Russia. His agents in this part of Europe as well as other émigré activists often contemplated the place of Rus' and its inhabitants in any upcoming struggle for independence as well as in any future state.

Adam Mickiewicz, residing in Turkey in 1855, called for abandoning religious divisions and advocated instead the coming together of various ethnic and religious elements with the goal of creating a single Polish nation.[1] Michał Czajkowski, in relating in particular Mickiewicz's arrival amidst the legions that were being formed on Turkish territory, referred to him as "the great Statesman of Poland, Lithuania and Rus', the great Slavic Statesman."[2] Those assembled were to have exclaimed: "together with Adam Mickiewicz, to Rus', to Poland, to Lithuania— given that we've got Adam Mickiewicz."[3] Mehmet Sadyk Pasha himself, in assembling the units, created, among others, Ukrainian Cossack contingents. The battle against Russia was not envisaged in any other way than taking place in Rus' with the participation of its inhabitants.

---

[1] Joanna Nowak, "*Gente Ruthenus, natione Polonus*. Rusini w refleksji Wielkiej Emigracji," *Sprawy Narodowościowe. Seria Nowa* 23 (2003), p. 51.
[2] Michał Czajkowski, *Kozaczyzna w Turcyi. Dzieło w trzech częściach* (Paris, 1857), p. 122.
[3] Ibid., p. 123.

Within such a constellation the image of Mickiewicz was to assume an almost apostolic status within the concept of a multi-ethnic nation. This is borne out by his own words. Before his death in 1855 he wrote:

> (…) the most effective way of preparing Poland for its rebirth is to destroy the causes of its very fall, which means the joining together and fraternity of all the various races and religions of our fatherland.[4]

It was impossible to defeat Russia — the strongest of the partitioning powers — without the participation of the Ruthenian people, which was being absorbed by the culturally akin Russians. The anti-Russian slant in the deliberations over the Ruthenian nation was also presented by many other well known individuals. Zygmunt Krasiński considered, for example, that:

> Poland received the order to save ten Slavic peoples from this deadly influence. The example of such torment should influence them and draw them towards a divine future.[5]

Only a few were able to accept the distinctiveness of the Ruthenians as a separate nation, but they could not imagine the existence of a future Poland without them, and in principle without Rus'. For example, Henryk Kamieński believed that Ruthenians are a nation that has not yet been fully formed, a "younger nation" on which Poland historically had a huge civilizational influence. He also believed in a common future for the Poles and the Ruthenians.[6] These ideas were to permeate Galicia's territories, as they had in the 1830s and 1840s, and the Polish independence movement's activists concerned with the national cause accepted them as their political program.

The Hôtel Lambert's views were shared by Julian Horoszkiewicz, a *gente Ruthenus, natione Polonus*, who set about outlining the reasons for the failure of the Polish-Russian war of 1830–31. In his booklet *Family Council* [*Rada familijna*], published in Paris in 1861, he delineated Poland's historical mistakes up until the November Uprising and also the conspiracies that were organized after it ended. Horoszkiewicz criticized the Polish aristocracy but also the democrats and, in his conclusion, the Ruthenian "separatists" and thus the [entire] Ruthenian national movement. He conceded that in fact both the Poles and the

---

[4] *Adama Mickiewicza wspomnienia i myśli z rozmów i przemówień*, collected and ed. Stanisław Pigoń (Warsaw, 1958), p. 263.
[5] Zygmunt Krasiński, "O stanowisku Polski z Bożych i ludzkich względów," in Zygmunt Krasiński, *Pisma filozoficzne i polityczne*, ed. and comments Paweł Hertz (Warsaw, 1999), p. 119.
[6] Nowak, "*Gente Ruthenus*," p. 53.

Ruthenians existed, but that it had become possible to merge these two elements as a single people only thanks to Poland. At the same time, he provided a catalogue of historical and linguistic evidence that Polish-Ruthenian unity existed.[7] At that time one can see a gradual convergence in Horoszkiewicz's views with those he polemicized against during the Revolutions of 1848, when he differed with Cięglewicz particularly about the question whether a Ruthenian nation exists. In *Family Council* Horoszkiewicz focused attention on the need for the close amalgamation of Rus' and Poland in view of the Russian threat, and he emphasized the unbreakable bonds of blood and the superiority of Polish civilization, which he deemed worthy of emulation. He had but one conclusion: "Rus' as Rus' can only exist with Poland."[8]

34. The coats-of-arms of Poland, Lithuania, and Rus' at the building of the Polish Higher School founded by Prince Adam Jerzy Czartoryski in 1849 at 80 boulevard du Montparnasse in Paris

How did the ideas proclaimed on the Seine correspond with the reality in the country itself? Before the January Uprising, in contrast to the November Uprising of 1830, the inhabitants of Galicia were in possession of a far more developed national consciousness. The three decades which had witnessed the experience of the Polish-Russian war of 1830–31, political agitation, conspiracies, the expansion of Romantic

---

[7] [Julian Horoszkiewicz], *Rada familijna* (Paris, 1861), pp. 60–68.
[8] Ibid., p. 71.

literature, the events of the Revolutions of 1848, and finally a change in generation, had been sufficient for the development among the young of Polish patriotic feelings. Nevertheless, the revolutionary zeal of the 1830s had already long faded, and in its place new concepts for the struggle for an independent homeland had developed. It is incorrect to believe that no conspiratorial acts were undertaken in Galicia before the January Uprising, although these were undertakings far more restrictive in scale than had been the case during earlier decades. That said, we encounter several examples of "Polish-Ruthenian brotherhood" among young people, as well as Polish attempts to forge cooperation between both nations in the fight against Russia.

The greatest shock in pre-uprising Galicia was the discovery and police arrest on 17–18 April 1858 of youths from the dormitories of the Stauropegial Institute. Subsequently a search was conducted at the Dominican secondary school as well as of the Greek Catholic Theological Seminary. The Austrian press fuelled speculation of a secret circle, accusing the young people detained of wanting to destroy the Uniate rite and the desire to become part of Orthodoxy, all this being the result of their fascination with Pan-Slavism. In reality, the conspiracy had no Russophile orientation whatsoever but was solely a striving for independence and was completely harmless for Austrian rule. The chief party accused was the Uniate Paweł Paszkowski [Pavlo Pashkovsky], a private teacher at the dormitory. As Stanisław Schnür-Pepłowski wrote:

> (...) [Paszkowski], having intended—as he claimed—to devote himself to a military career, would read with especial interest works of a military and historical content and under the influence of this type of literature combined the notion of organizing a secret union with the aim of liberating Galicia from Austrian rule, as well as the creation of a sovereign Polish--Ruthenian state.[9]

One needs to look for the organization's beginnings in the spring of 1857, when Paszkowski, having become acquainted with Aleksander Daniłowicz [Oleksander Danylovych], a student at the teaching seminary who claimed to trace his lineage to the Sobieski family, started agitating among secondary school pupils and recruited more people for the conspiracy. A statute was drawn up, officers were appointed, a plan for the upcoming campaign devised, and further recruitment activities were conducted, counting on the formation of a five-thousand strong troop within seven months that was to take over Lviv and defeat the

---

[9] Stanisław Schnür-Pepłowski, *Obrazy z przeszłości Galicyi i Krakowa (1772–1858)*, part 2: *Dziatwa Apollina* (Lviv, 1896), p. 397.

Austrian army. After the holidays the conspirators' zeal, as was often the case in similar youth organizations of this time, started to wane. Daniłowicz decided to rejuvenate the organization during Easter of 1858, signing up new individuals and taking oaths of loyalty. Nevertheless, Paszkowski's and Daniłowicz's conspiracy was exposed by an informer and the perpetrators arrested. The organization's plans had no chance of success. The members—already during the trial—revealed on which forces they had intended to base their patriotic struggle. According to Schnür-Pepłowski, Paszkowski had at midnight summoned forth the devil at Chortivska Skelia [The Devil's Rock], while on the eve of St. John's Day he had searched for fern/bracken flowers in the forest, while Daniłowicz deluded his younger associates into believing he had obtained superhuman power thanks to certain secret properties. Schnür-Pepłowski noted, not without irony, that:

> By means of various spells he promised his comrades that he would open the arsenal door for them, would make them invisible, and even give them the possibility of killing their opponent at a distance, even of a hundred miles. This last practice was to occur by means of a spike thrust into something—none too fragrant.[10]

The methods of combat presented by the police were certainly designed to show the Lviv conspiracy as a childish game, one of no danger whatsoever for the monarchy. However, this aside, Daniłowicz's and Paszkowski's activities indicate that the struggle for an independent Poland still affected the school-aged young and pupils of various denominations and provenance.[11] Here one should add that Paszkowski, thanks to his youth conspiracy, had acquired almost legendary conspiratorial status and immediately after his release in 1862 was to again work at the Stauropegial Institute dormitory, equally involving himself in "illegal" activities. As Halina Kozłowska-Sabatowska wrote: "as a result of his Ruthenian provenance, place of employment and contacts— he aspired to expand among Ukrainian youth those activities which proved the existence of a sense of community with Poles."[12] Paszkowski, popular as he was, could possibly have played an iconic role for Polish-Ruthenian fraternity a year later during the January Uprising. This conspirator, however, was to poison himself, as Stanisław Schnür-Pepłowski speculated, out of "unrequited love."[13]

---

[10] Ibid., p. 399.
[11] Halina Kozłowska-Sabatowska also mentioned the conspiracy and Pawłowski, *Między konspiracją a pracą organiczną. Młodość Tadeusza Romanowicza* (Cracow, 1986), p. 45.
[12] Ibid., p. 63.
[13] Schnür-Pepłowski, *Obrazy z przeszłości*, part 2, p. 400.

This was not the only initiative aimed at bringing Polish-Ruthenian brotherhood to life. It is worth recalling the activities of Prince Adam Sapieha, the son of Leon and the nephew of Adam Jerzy Czartory-ski's wife Anna. During the revolutions of 1848 he tried to improve relations between the two nations. As Stefan Kieniewicz writes, Adam Sapieha had contact with Ruthenians since childhood at the family estate in Krasiczyn and he knew the Ruthenian language, allegedly promising the Ruthenian peasants a compromise in linguistic matters during the elections to the Galician Diet in 1861. He looked on the Polish-Ruthenian conflict not through a nationalist prism but viewed it within its social and religious context. He believed all problems would disappear once agreements would be reached between the nobles and the peasants and the Uniate clergy with the Roman Catholic one. For this to happen, however, he considered it necessary to cut Ruthenians off from the influences of the St. George party. However, in wanting to persuade Ruthenian political activists to cooperate, he needed to be sure that there was something to offer them in return. He approached, among others, Prince Adam Czartoryski in Paris, in order for him to persuade the landed gentry in Galicia to agree to concessions in the field of language. Czartoryski, himself a supporter of involving Ruthe-nians in the struggle for Poland, encouraged his brother-in-law to work on fostering the Ruthenian intelligentsia and extending influence over the Greek Catholic Church. He shied away, however, from the gentry adopting the Uniate rite. He counted on being able to create a conservative intellectual environment among Ruthenians. Sapieha took Czart-oryski's views to heart and tried to implement them, as indicated by the initiatives he undertook. For example, he cooperated with Poles among the Greek Catholic clergy: Jan Woliński [Ivan Volynsky], M. Zarzycki [M. Zarytsky], and Michał Borysiekiewicz. These were corresponding members of the Economic Society, which Sapieha headed. This organization was half agricultural in character, but also semi-conspiratorial. In November 1862 Sapieha organized in Berezhany a gathering of Greek Catholic priests on whom he could rely to send a petition to the pope to bring the Uniate Church to order. Eighty-six signatures were gathered, though ultimately the petition was never sent.[14]

Polish patriotic sentiments in Galicia were to escalate, particularly with the news emanating from beyond the border. These called for a closing of ranks and strenuous work to prepare for armed struggle, to commence when the moment arose.[15] The idea of propagating the no-

---

[14] Stefan Kieniewicz, *Adam Sapieha 1828–1903* (Warsaw, 1993), pp. 352–59.
[15] Kozłowska-Sabatowska, *Między konspiracją*, p. 47.

tion of a brotherhood of all peoples and social estates across the lands of the former Poland was most clearly understood in Warsaw. Books and magazines reached Galicia, followed finally by proclamations, which were reprinted or simply passed from hand to hand to subsequently shape the ideological views of the intelligentsia within the Austrian area of partition. For example, Józef Białynia Chołodecki recalled that in mid-1861, a leaflet *Proclamation [Posłanie]* written by the inhabitants of Warsaw that called for national unification in order to gain independence, was found in Galicia. It made it clear that all the blame lay with the partitioning powers, recalling among other things:

> They are wiping out our native tongue, they sow mistrust among us, setting the peasantry against the gentry, the Christian against the Jew, the Ruthenians against the Poles, and yet we are all the children of a single mother, for we are all brother Poles.

There was an appeal here for:

> Our brothers in Lithuania and Rus', for ages freely joined to Poland, let them reject the instigations of the Muscovites and the Germans, attempting to drive a wedge between them and their compatriots (...).[16]

The *Proclamation*, whose content was aimed at inciting the reader against the partitioning powers, was published in German in Wrocław in *Schlesische Zeitung* [Silesian Newspaper] (1862, no. 322, 13 July), while in Galicia a reprint of the proclamation was prepared by the Lviv-based *Głos* (1861, no. 161, 16 July), but the entire print run was confiscated and the editor, Zygmunt Kaczkowski, imprisoned after a quick trial under the accusation of conducting a "crime against the state."[17] Despite its confiscation, the *Proclamation* circulated in Lviv as a printed leaflet.[18]

Similar views were also expressed in the Galician press. Kazimierz Olszański, in his research on the subject, pointed out the significant role played by *Gazeta Narodowa* on the eve of the Uprising in propagating the "axiom of Polish politics of the day," as if the Ruthenian-Ukrainian lands were an integral part of the former Poland and all separatist movements were directed against Poles.[19] This accounts for the critical

---

[16] The appeal content cited after: Józef Białynia Chołodecki, *Do dziejów powstania styczniowego. Obrazki z przeszłości Galicyi* (Lviv, 1912), pp. 19, 23.

[17] Ibid., p. 25.

[18] See for example ibid., p. 32. Józef Bem of Zaliztsi, interrogated at the time, claimed that "he knew about *Posłanie* having bought it in Lviv from some Jew or other for 10 Guldens (...)."

[19] Kazimierz Olszański, *Prasa galicyjska wobec powstania styczniowego* (Wrocław–Warsaw–Cracow–Gdańsk, 1975), pp. 233–34.

depiction of the role played by the St. George camp. One of the articles, published at the end of August 1862, whose author—unfortunately unknown—signed himself as *Gente Ruthenus, natione Polonus*, emphasized that there was no Ruthenian nation, for there were merely Polish citizens of the Latin and Slavonic rite. The differences were accentuated, yet the treatment of these differences as having their basis in indicators of a difference in nationality were strongly opposed.[20] After the outbreak of the January Uprising the tendency to deny the existence of a Ruthenian nationality was to wane somewhat, while at the same time the union of Poland, Lithuania, and Rus' as a counterweight to Moscow was emphasized more strongly.[21]

As had been the case earlier, other activities were undertaken beside merely directing addresses to the urban intelligentsia, including actions targeting the national consciousness of Ruthenian peasants (obviously accentuating Polish self-identification). Here one should mention that Bogusław Longchamps de Bérier's mother, Wanda, née Dybowska, had written, among other things, short stories drawn from Polish history, but published in Ruthenian and directed at the inhabitants of the village of Sokilnyky. She was arrested for her Polish patriotic acts.[22] Similarly Kornel Ujejski, who leased the village of Zubra, undertook educational work among the ordinary people and—as mentioned in the accounts of his biographer—"he educated several peasants," including a certain Maślanka.[23]

The dissemination of certain ideas was one problem. Another and far more significant one was convincing the intended recipients of their worth. Wishing to achieve the restoration of an independent state within its former borders required finding a way to engage the former inhabitants of the eastern lands in the pursuit of this goal. Consequently, the Ruthenians' distinctiveness was acknowledged, but only under the condition of involving them in the reconstruction of the Commonwealth—this time a Commonwealth of Three Nations. Hence one of the uprising's fundamental symbols—embroidered onto the standards, engraved on seals, and printed on appeals—was a shield with the emblems of the three nations: Poland's eagle, Lithuania's Vytis [charging

---

[20] *Gazeta Narodowa* no. 47 (28 VIII 1862), Quoted after: Olszański, *Prasa galicyjska*, pp. 233–34.

[21] Ibid., p. 235.

[22] Bogusław Longchamps de Bérier, *Ochrzczony na szablach powstańczych... Wspomnienia (1884–1918)*, eds. Włodzimierz Suleja and Wojciech Wrzesiński (Wrocław–Warsaw–Cracow–Gdańsk–Łódź, 1983), p. 33.

[23] Kazimierz Wróblewski, *Kornel Ujejski (1823–1893). W dodatkach garść listów Ujejskiego, Szajnochy i Bohdana Zaleskiego* (Lviv, 1902), pp. 170–71.

knight], and Ruthenia's Archangel Michael. It is important to remember that during the November Uprising the insurgents marched under the standard with the eagle and the Vytis, but in 1846 the insurgents in Cracow proclaimed that their fatherland was ethnically and historically homogeneous.[24] This does not mean, however, that the Poles involved in the uprising immediately recognized the existence of a Ruthenian nation or that an independent Ruthenian state was possible. According to the proclaimed federal concept, Rus' was envisaged as being at most a self-governing land federated (meaning that it was strictly linked) with Poland and Lithuania. However, before everything else it was expected that as allies, the Ruthenians would take part in the joint struggle with the invaders.

This new conception of a federation rather than a unitary structure was constructed on the basis of a tradition of the Union of Lublin of 1569, and it drew even more on the unfulfilled Treaty of Hadiach of 1658. This was to be expressed for the first time in such a way in 1861 on the lands of the former New Galicia, in the Lublin lands then part of the Kingdom of Poland. In 1861 in Horodło the Congress of the Commonwealth Unity of the Two Nations took place, which assembled a crowd of ten thousand people to mark the 448th anniversary of the concluding there of the Polish-Lithuanian union. The procession saw Greek Catholic and Roman Catholic clergy march together, while there was no absence of Jews among those gathered on the day. A mound was erected to commemorate the event, but the Russian authorities quickly ordered it to be razed. However, the jubilee celebration did see a repeat of the act of Union. Kazimierz Gregorowicz [Kazymyr Hrehorovych]— a witness to the events and from a polonized Ruthenian family from Ukraine—noted down in his memoirs:[25]

> We, the undersigned delegates from all the lands and voivodeships of pre-partition Poland, on this day gathered in Horodło on the four hundred and forty-eighth anniversary of the union of Lithuania with Poland, do swear by this very act, evidenced by our own signatures herein given, that a union joining all the lands of Poland, Lithuania and Rus' we do herein renew on principles of the total equality of the three national-

---

[24] Tadeusz Łepkowski, "Ojczyzna historyczna a etniczna w XIX i na początku XX w.," in Tadeusz Łepkowski, *Rozważania o losach polskich* (London, 1987), p. 62.

[25] On Gregorowicz and his innovative federal views for the time, ones incorporating Rus, see Wiesław Śladkowski, "Idee federacyjne Kazimierza Gregorowicza," *Annales Universitatis Mariae Curie-Skłodowska. Sectio F. Historia* 51 (1996), pp. 63–73; Wiesław Śladkowski, "Pod znakiem Orła, Pogoni i Michała Archanioła. Idee unijne i federacyjne w dobie powstania styczniowego," in *Unia lubelska. Unia Europejska*, ed. Iwona Hofman (Lublin, 2010), pp. 132–42.

ities combined and of all denominations, coming together in the closest of unions to labour for the extrication of our joint fatherland from its present-day decline until such time that full independence is achieved.[26]

Following the reading out of the act, a speech emphasizing the significance of the event and reflecting the spirit of encouraging Poles, Ruthenians, and Lithuanians to work for the recovery of a common homeland was given. We also know the content of the proclamation prepared for this occasion by Apollo Korzeniowski, the father of the writer Joseph Conrad. Here we read:

> We call on the three united nations to heartily adopt our proclamation, in the way their ancestors adopted the appeal for the Horodło assembly, and we hope that our voice will sound favourably with everyone who loves the Fatherland.[27]

The Ruthenians of the Lublin lands were far more Polonized than the Greek Catholics of Galicia. This affinity with Polishness was to have tragic consequences a dozen or so years later during the course of the tsar's eradication of the Uniate Church in the regions of Chełm and Podlachia. How Polonized the Ruthenians in the Lublin area were can be shown best by the example of the Ruthenian Basilian priest Stefan Laurysiewicz [Stepan Lavrysevych], who not only involved himself in the organization of the celebrations but also gave a famous speech after the church ceremony. Gregorowicz was to describe the event as follows:

> After the Mass, Father Laurysiewicz delivered an extremely beautiful sermon. The message was lofty and poetic, he recalled the torment and pain of the Old Testament prophets bewailing the fall of Jerusalem. The political aspect of his speech may be summarized as follows: let Poland not forget about Rus' and let Rus' not forget about her sister Poland. Many mistakes had been committed in the past by both sides. Poland had overly abused its advantage, while Rus' had sought alliance with the Muscovites. Let us give up on the excesses of the past and commence a new era, one aimed towards obtaining joint independence.[28]

His sermon calling for national unity because Poles and Ruthenians were linked by a common faith, tradition, and history was widely known. He published it in Lviv in 1861 and it was distributed through-

---

[26] Kazimierz Gregorowicz, *Zarys główniejszych wypadków w województwie lubelskim w r. 1861*, introd. and ed. Wiesław Śladkowski (Lublin, 1984), p. 98.

[27] [Apollo Korzeniowski], *Bracia Polacy, Rusini i Litwini!*, Archiwum Narodowe w Krakowie, zesp. 29/1571: Archiwum Franciszka Piekosińskiego, F 93: Archiwum galicyjskich organów Rządu Narodowego 1863, p. 213.

[28] Gregorowicz, *Zarys główniejszych wypadków*, pp. 97–98.

*35. Father Stefan Laurysiewicz during the holy mass on the occasion
of the 448th anniversary of the Union of Horodło, 1861*

out various regions of Galicia.[29] Because of it, many Ruthenians took part
in the commemorations, as Wacław Lasocki recalled in his memoirs:

> (…) Father Laurysiewicz, a Ruthenian, went to the trouble of gathering
> as many Ruthenians as possible and not merely from within the borders
> of the former Polish Commonwealth but from Dnipro Ukraine.[30]

This was to also have unfortunate consequences. Father Laurysiewicz was forced to flee to Galicia and subsequently to Bulgaria as
a result of his activities. Ultimately, he managed to make it to Cracow,
where he took over the Greek Catholic parish in St. Norbert Church
on Wiślna Street. He was also involved in the January Uprising, after
the collapse of which—in 1864—he died. His position as parish priest
was taken over by another *gente Ruthenus, natione Polonus*—Józef
Czerlunczakiewicz.[31]

The Horodło celebrations are important for another reason as well.
The visual representation of the Archangel Michael representing Rus'

---

[29] Eugeniusz Niebelski, *Duchowieństwo lubelskie i podlaskie w powstaniu 1863 roku i na zesłaniu w Rosji* (Lublin, 2002), pp. 86–87, footnote 225.

[30] Wacław Lasocki, *Wspomnienia z mojego życia*, vol. 1: *W kraju*, prepared for print by
Michał Janik, Feliks Kopera (Cracow, 1933), p. 371. Cf. also: Niebelski, *Duchowieństwo*,
pp. 89–90, footnote 232. Lasocki made a mistake with the dating of these events, claiming
that the celebrations took place in 1862.

[31] Tadeusz Filar, "Miejsce społeczności ukraińskiej w XIX i XX-wiecznym Krakowie do
1918 roku," *Krakowskie Zeszyty Ukrainoznawcze* 1–2 (1992–93), p. 445.

alongside the Vytis coat-of-arms of Lithuania and the Polish Eagle appeared there for the first time.[32] Gregorowicz considered the hitherto absence of this symbol to have been a mistake of the past.[33] The January Uprising insurgents were to go to battle with this symbol in 1863, so that the three nations together would overcome the enemy and build the Commonwealth in a new three-member federal construct.

The Attempt to Include Ruthenians in the January Uprising

As Jarosław Demiańczuk, one of only a few researchers[34] involved in the question of the relationship of Galician Ruthenians to the revolt of 1863, wrote:

> The Central Committee, from the moment the January Uprising broke out, acting as the provisional National Government, viewed "Ruthenians" on the basis of the Union of Lublin; that is, they recognized Lithuania and equally Rus' to be a component part of a new, to be liberated, Commonwealth. The democratic convictions of this committee's members together with the deep-felt desire among the whole of the patriotic part of Polish society to rectify the mistakes of the past meant that the attitude towards "Ruthenians" was a most positive and accommodating one. The matter of how the conditions for the coexistence of both nations in a state of mutual understanding was to be legally formulated in the future following victory.[35]

Consequently, the Provisional National Government [*Tymczasowy Rząd Narodowy*] attempted to cooperate with the Ruthenians. Rus was addressed in its entirety in official correspondence, with no specific addresses being made separately to Galician Ruthenian youth. Here the

---

[32] Wacław Lasocki wrote: "The symbol of Rus', the Archangel Michael, was placed before the assembled, added to the coats of arms of Poland and Lithuania and in this matter the three-emblem coat of arms was created." Lasocki, *Wspomnienia*, vol. 1, p. 371.

[33] Kazimierz Gregorowicz, *Z jakich powodów zmieniony został herb państwa polskiego. Odczyt miany podczas obchodu 23-letniej rocznicy horodelskiego zjazdu dnia 10 października 1884 r. w Paryżu* (Paris, 1884), p. 19.

[34] The first to write about this was Franciszek Rawita-Gawroński, *Rok 1863 na Rusi*, vol. 1: *Ruś Czerwona i Wschód* (Lviv, 1902). During the interwar period the matter was investigated by Jarosław Demiańczuk, "Ukraińcy galicyjscy wobec powstania styczniowego," *Biuletyn Polsko-Ukraiński* 6, no. 3 (17 Jan. 1937), pp. 29–32. After the Second World War the question of Ruthenian participation in the uprising was analysed by Piotr Łossowski and Zygmunt Młynarski: Piotr Łossowski and Zygmunt Młynarski, *Rosjanie, Białorusini i Ukraińcy w powstaniu styczniowym* (Wrocław, 1959). Three years later another work appeared, but this time, of academic value for it was written purely in the spirit of communistic propaganda: Tadeusz Książek and Zygmunt Młynarski, *Udział Rosjan, Litwinów, Białorusinów, Ukraińców w powstaniu styczniowym (1863–1864)* (Warsaw, 1962).

[35] Demiańczuk, "Ukraińcy galicyjscy," p. 29.

matter referred first and foremost to all the lands under Russian control. The very fact of addressing Ruthenians could be inspiring. Just two weeks after the outbreak of the uprising, on 5 February 1863, the Provisional National Government issued the proclamation *To the Ruthenian Brothers!* [*Do Braci Rusinów!*], in which it was proclaimed that "the struggle for the independence and freedom of Poland, Lithuania and Rus" had begun. It was announced:

> Ruthenian Brothers! Your lands have for so many centuries shared the joys and woes with the rest of the Commonwealth, and today should resound to the cries of freedom! On your land, in your realms, the blood spilled will bring victory to the uprising! Under the barrows of your steppe the tsarist forces shall find their graves, and the scythes of yours and the Lithuanians' at one with the Polish will be victorious in bringing independence and freedom to Poland, Lithuania, and Rus'.
>
> In unity and unwavering, fearless and determined battle we shall find the guarantor of victory. And to this battle, Ruthenians, we call on you! Your tardiness, sluggishness, may result in the moment of general happiness being delayed. Don't be responsible for stopping the rebirth of a common fatherland![36]

It must be noted, however, that the above address did not honour in any particular way just Ruthenians. Analogical versions were issued in parallel *To the Lithuanian Brothers* [*Do braci Litwinów*] and *To the Polish Brothers of the Judaic Creed* [*Do braci Polaków wyznania mojżeszowego*], manifesting a desire to recruit for the fight not merely the ethnic Polish part of society under the partitions.[37] It is also worth remembering that for the first few months of its duration the seal of the uprising was still just the Eagle and the Vytis coat-of-arms. The Archangel Michael was only to officially appear in May 1863, even though the design for its inclusion in the coat-of-arms had actually come about in January.[38] However, the Archangel Michael on the uprising stamp was of no use to the Galician Ruthenians. First of all, they did not feel themselves to be

---

[36] "Komitet Centralny Narodowy jako tymczasowy Rząd Narodowy do Braci Rusinów," in *Wydawnictwo materyałów do historyi powstania 1863–1864*, vol. 1: *Księga pamiątkowa 25-letniej rocznicy powstania styczniowego* (Lviv, 1888), pp. 40–41; "Do Braci Rusinów," in *Dokumenty Komitetu Centralnego Narodowego i Rządu Narodowego 1862–1864*, prepared for print by Dawid Fajnhauz, Stefan Kieniewicz, Franciszka Ramotowska [et al.] (Wrocław, 1968), pp. 44–45.

[37] Michał Jagiełło, *Narody i narodowości. Przewodnik po lekturach*, vol. 1 (Warsaw, 2010), p. 53.

[38] Iurii Shtakel'berg, "Nekotorye rezul'taty izucheniia sfragistiki Pol'skogo vosstaniia 1863–1864 gg.", in *Tsentral'naia i Iugo-vostochnaia Evropa v novoe vremia. Sbornik statiei*, eds. Vladilen Vinogradov, Dmitrii Markov and Il'ia Miller (Moscow, 1974), p. 293.

inhabitants of Ukraine, which it symbolized, and secondly, they were not interested in the "Polish uprising."

The best indication of the Ruthenian population's relations to the insurrection are the accounts preserved. The mood in Eastern Galicia, not even a full month after the outbreak of the uprising, was commented on by Zygmunt Kaczkowski in a letter sent to the Hôtel Lambert:

> The mood among the rural populace, especially in Rus', is the worst. Cordons of peasants, who join up eagerly, stretch out, maintaining guard across villages of their own will. Ruthenians have completely gone quiet for the moment as a political option. A dualism has occurred in them: some are known as St. Georgians, i.e., a purely Austrian party, others as the Ukrainian party which they understand as the aspirations of Kyivan Ruthenians. The latter renounce the former and say that in their own time they will create an uprising in conjunction with Ukrainians, a revolt with the program: "If a Polish nobleman sides with us then all the better, if not then he'll be done for." In as far as it seems they would prefer the latter—and for that reason their agitation together with that of the St. Georgians brings about a single result among the peasants. In certain places they have provoked the peasants to act against the gentry from Poland to such a degree that on getting the nod they are prepared to attack the landowners when they have not yet even crossed the thresholds of their estates. The government keeps this agitation on a short leash and even though it cannot vouch for sporadic incidents it does not allow, without due reason, for any movement to arise.[39]

Kaczkowski's letter talks of two milieux within the ranks of Galician Ruthenian intellectual elites. The Austrian loyalists were one, yet these increasingly sympathized with Moscow with the passing of time; while the other were Ukrainophile populists who distanced themselves equally from Russia and from Poland. At this time the interests of the second group were represented by the Progressive Ruthenian Community [Hromada] in Galicia as well as by its press organ—the biweekly social-literary journal Meta [Goal], founded in 1863 and produced under the editorship of Ksenofont Klymkovych.[40]

Jarosław Demiańczuk, in researching the attitude held by these milieux in relation to the uprising leaders, characterized, on the basis of one of the articles published in Meta, the conception of the Polish-Russian war as viewed by the Ruthenian population as a war of two

---

[39] "Zygmunt Kaczkowski do Hôtelu Lambert w Paryżu, Lwów, 19 Feb. 1863," in Galicja w powstaniu styczniowym, eds. Stefan Kieniewicz and Ilia Miller (Wrocław–Warsaw–Cracow–Gdańsk, 1980), p. 23.

[40] Jerzy Jarowiecki, Dzieje prasy polskiej we Lwowie do 1945 roku (Cracow–Wrocław, 2008), p. 183; Rawita-Gawroński, Rok 1863, vol. 1, p. 302.

hegemonies for control of a third nation, i.e., the Ruthenians. Such an interpretation of the policy pursued by the Polish authorities was not to bode well for Ruthenian involvement in the struggle.[41]

But this was not the only voice to be heard in *Meta*. Articles encouraging the broad cooperation of Poles and Ruthenians also appeared, as well as ones creating a good atmosphere for Polish-Ruthenian brotherhood at this hour of trial which was the war of 1863. Those who functioned in both cultures—Polish and Ruthenian—were to play the role of liaisons between the two nations as had been the case during the conspiracies of the 1830s or the revolutions of 1848. This time it was to be the intelligentsia who came from beyond the border, from the Ukrainian lands comprising tsarist Russia, who had the greatest impact. It is worth mentioning here figures such as: Stanisław Żukowski, Mikołaj Zagórski, and first and foremost Leon Syroczyński and Paulin Święcicki. Not only did they speak Ruthenian, but they also had conspiratorial experience gained during student activities at Kyiv University.[42]

Leon Syroczyński, the author of two articles published in *Meta*, is of note among those publishing in this Ruthenian paper, and consequently gained renown among its readership. In the first of his texts, on the subject of the significance of Kyiv University for the Ukrainian nation, he wrote that the Poles, in issuing the *Golden Charter* [Złota hramota / Zolota hramota] (the document proclaiming the abolition of serfdom and property rights), had bestowed on Ruthenians the rights they had sought for centuries. He also emphasized that Ruthenians could join together with the Poles, to which the editorial board of *Meta* added its reservations, underlining that it was Poland which needed Rus' and not Rus' that needed Poland.[43]

It was not only Syroczyński who tried to convince Ruthenians to cooperate with the Poles. Paulin Święcicki, another arrival from Ukraine who while still studying at Kyiv University had attempted to forge conspiratorial links with the Ukrainians there, also undertook this task. He came to Galicia before the January Uprising and under the pseudonym of "A Pole from Ukraine" wrote about the uprising and the activities of the National Committee, including articles about the future federal structure of Poland. In his view Ukraine would be able to choose the

[41] Demiańczuk, "Ukraińcy galicyjscy," p. 30.

[42] Stepan Trusevych, *Suspil'no-politychnyi rukh u Skhidnii Halychyni v 50-70-kh rokakh XIX st.* (Kyiv, 1978), p. 107.

[43] Cyryl Studyński, "Powstańcy polscy z r. 1863 w redakcji ukraińskiej 'Mety'," *Ziemia Czerwieńska* 3 (1937), p. 82.

route it wished to follow—whether with Poland or without it—following victory over Russia. Despite this he encouraged fraternity between Poles and Ruthenians, recalling at the same time the *Golden Charter*.[44] These views were not, however, to be heard.

In as far as it was difficult to convince the Ruthenian intelligentsia in Galicia to fulfil their "patriotic" duty (patriotic in relation to the idealized Commonwealth of the Three Nations), a more promising policy on the question of Ruthenians in Ukraine was employed. The above mentioned *Golden Charter*, addressed to the Ruthenian rural population in Podilia, Volhynia, and central and eastern Ukraine, was published in 1863. It was a beautiful document with golden letters, a depiction of the Archangel Michael in the upper vignette, and text directed to the peasantry both in Ruthenian and Polish (there were also different versions of this document, with text exclusively in Ruthenian, and text exclusively in Polish). Seven points declared the annulment of all obligations of serfdom as well as the distribution to the peasantry of land farmed by landed peasants or other land supplied by the National Treasury, in exchange for participation in the uprising.[45] This address to the Ruthenian peasantry through the *Golden Charter* recalled the methods employed by the conspirators in Galicia in the 1830s. Young insurgents would travel from village to village and read out the text of a proclamation written in Ruthenian, exposing themselves to being handed over, arrested, or physically attacked.[46] However, what was most important is that they challenged the social order. In offering them land and the abolition of serfdom, they hoped Ruthenian peasants could be won over for the uprising. However, as Vasyl Shchurat noted: "in 1863 the Ukrainian nation still remembered the Polish promises of 1830, which they had equally not believed. And since 1830 they had had thirty years to convince

---

[44] Trusevych, *Suspil'no-politychnyi rukh*, pp. 109–10.

[45] "Hramota sel'skomu narodu / Hramota dla ludu wiejskiego," in *Wydawnictwo materyałów do historyi powstania 1863–1864*, vol. 3: *Dokumenta do historyi powstania 1863/64. I. Galicya*, collected and ed. [Jan Stella-Sawicki] Pułkownik Struś (Lviv, 1890), pp. 36–39; For more on the subject of various versions of the *Złota hramota*, published also in Lviv by *Gazeta Narodowa* and *Goniec* [Messenger], see "Złota Hramota," in Stefan Kieniewicz, *Powstanie styczniowe* (Warsaw, 2009), pp. 755–56 (fourth annex).

[46] One such scene was noted down by Jan Stella-Sawicki in his memories. He recalled how 21 young men, the majority of whom were students of Kyiv University, travelled around the villages of the Kyiv region proclaiming the document's contents. The peasants were to remain, however, unmoved (with the exception of the village of Olenivka). The small insurgent unit was finally to be encircled at Soloviivka, and later was defeated by peasants. A number of the young men were killed, and some others were arrested and subsequently exiled to Siberia. See: [Jan Stella-Sawicki] Pułkownik Struś, *Szkice z powstania 1863 roku* (Cracow, 1889), pp. 84–85.

themselves that they had been justified in not believing them."[47] This Ukrainian scholar emphasized that if one were to collate the promises made from both uprisings one would not see any progress whatsoever in regard to concessions for Ruthenians. He ironically pointed merely to the change in the colour of the letters from black to gold and summed up the entirety of Polish efforts by employing the Polish adage: "A Pole is wise after the event."[48] There is indeed a lot of truth in this for bar the rhetoric and symbolism, no practical concessions in relation to Ruthenians were actually declared. And this concerned equally the Ukrainian lands as well as Galicia. The greatest proof of Polish guardedness in relation to Ruthenians in the context of the eventual handing over of land to the peasants is the fact that nothing whatsoever was done in Galicia to win over the peasantry to fight.

The boldest statement for a general call up of the peasantry appeared in Lviv in the 5 July 1863 issue of *Gazeta Narodowa*, where an article proclaimed that commanders had been found in the Polish Kingdom who were leading the common people.[49] It was noted that it was necessary to find the right approach to the common people because "the common people do not understand the speeches and decrees of government, they understand only deeds." Stefan Kieniewicz wrote that this declaration must have aroused anxiety (particularly among the landed gentry), for a week later there was to appear in *Gazeta Narodowa* another text on the very same topic proposing a curtailment, i.e., controlling the levy in mass.[50] Ultimately, given the constant recollection of the revolt of 1846, in no way was anyone prepared to employ the Ruthenian peasantry in armed engagement during the January Uprising.

However, the fundamental goal of the insurgent leadership was not Austrian-ruled Galicia but Russian-ruled Ukraine. On 8 April 1863 a meeting took place between General Edmund Różycki and Colonel Zygmunt Miłkowski along with General Józef Wysocki, during which an attack on Right-Bank Ukraine from Galicia was planned. The date for the outbreak of the uprising in Rus' was scheduled for 8 May. However, Józef Wysocki's expedition was to ultimately occur much later, already after the collapse of the uprising in Ukraine, while the promised support from Galicia was not to make it across the eastern border of

[47] Vasyl Shchurat, "Zolota hramota z 1863 r. i nezolota z 1830 r.," in Vasyl Shchurat, *Na dosvitku novoï doby. Statti i zamitky do istoriï vidrozhennia Hal. Ukraïny* (Lviv, 1919), p. 70.
[48] Ibid., p. 73.
[49] "Obecne położenie sprawy polskiej," *Gazeta Narodowa* no. 120 (5 Jul. 1863), p. 1.
[50] Stefan Kieniewicz, *Sprawa włościańska w powstaniu styczniowym* (Wrocław, 1953), p. 346.

the Habsburg Empire. Wysocki's undertakings ended in failure.[51] The failure to engage Galicia in military action in Ukraine was the result of the awful conspiratorial organization in operation in the area of the Austrian partition.

Several uncoordinated groups involved in conspiracy and support for the insurgency had operated in Galicia up until the outbreak of the uprising. Lviv circles saw cooperation between Adam Sapieha, Franciszek Smolka, and Florian Ziemiałkowski (on 15 January 1863 they formed the Eastern Galician Committee), while in Cracow there was Cezary Haller, Leon Chrzanowski, and the *gente Ruthenus, natione Polonus* mentioned earlier: Mikołaj Zyblikiewicz. Stefan Kieniewicz summarized their views on the uprising: they were in agreement with the decision taken by the conspirators in Warsaw for an insurrection in the Russian zone of partition, and they were prepared to support this revolt, but when the matter concerned the possible expansion of the uprising to Galicia they were not as inclined to support the notion as a result of the spectre of the events of 1846. It is no surprise, therefore, that they were reserved in their approach to the founding, already in 1862, of an institution gathering the bodies willing to organize an uprising — The Galician Chief Council, operating in two branches in Cracow and Lviv. The Council had been subordinated to the National Central Committee in Warsaw from the autumn of 1862, but the politically most active Galician activists were in no hurry to support this organization as well as the uprising itself when it did finally erupt in January 1863.[52] The legal forum that was the Galician Diet could also do little. After the outbreak of the uprising, the Galician Diet was closed on 30 January 1863 and was only to be called to meet again in 1865 following the lifting of the state of siege imposed on 24 February 1864.[53]

However, initial support for the insurgents did in fact start to come from Galicia two weeks following the outbreak of the January Uprising. Insurgent Lviv youth, the so-called "first Galician legion," crossed the border on 30 January but withdrew after failing to encounter the enemy.[54] The first properly organized insurgent unit from Eastern

---

[51] Andrzej Wroński, "Powstanie styczniowe na Ukrainie," in *Powstanie styczniowe 1863–1864. Wrzenie, bój, Europa, wizje*, ed. Sławomir Kalembka (Warsaw, 1990), pp. 378–79, 385.
[52] Kieniewicz, *Powstanie styczniowe*, pp. 301–4; Jerzy Zdrada, "Rząd narodowy wobec udziału Galicji w powstaniu styczniowym 1863–1864," in *Galicja a powstanie styczniowe*, eds. Mariola Hoszowska, Agnieszka Kawalec and Leonid Zaszkilniak (Warsaw–Rzeszów, 2013), p. 14.
[53] Irena Pannenkowa, *Walka Galicji z centralizmem wiedeńskim. Dzieje rezolucji Sejmu galicyjskiego z 24. września 1868. W 50. rocznicę uchwały rewolucyjnej* (Lviv, 1918), p. 31.
[54] Kieniewicz, *Powstanie styczniowe*, p. 503.

Galicia was formed by Adam Sapieha in March 1863 (young people from Western Galicia had already in February 1863 taken part in the Miechów expedition). Four hundred well-armed men set off to the region of Zamość, but after ten days and several skirmishes they returned to Galicia, where they were interned by the Austrians. Subsequent attempts at military expeditions from Galicia, in which Ruthenian youth could have taken part, were to end without notable successes.[55] Among those who took part in the preparation and organization of the insurgent units was the Greek Catholic Henryk Rewakowicz, though he was ultimately not to fight himself.[56]

The cause of the Galician failures in attempts to support the insurgents in Congress Poland was due to very poor organization and the lack of a universally accepted leadership. Adam Sapieha, standing at the head of the "white" circles in Eastern Galicia, did not recognize the command of the National Council in Warsaw. A similar situation existed following the arrest of Sapieha in July 1863, when the Committee of Eastern Galicia reorganized itself and changed its composition (including, among others, the former Ruthenian Sobor member and landowner Antoni Golejewski).[57] This organization was dissolved by Izydor Kopernicki, who had been delegated by General Edmund Różycki on 1 October 1863.[58] In any case, the Lviv conspiracy did little in joining up with the uprising, and certainly failed in the recruitment of Ruthenians to fight for the cause. The matter was somewhat different in the second centre of command in Cracow, where in July 1863 there was a meeting of the National Government with the political representation of Ruthenians from Eastern Galicia, with the aim of becoming acquainted with Ruthenian demands for possible cooperation with the Poles given an up-

36. *Father Stefan Laurysiewicz*

---

[55] Ibid., p. 482.
[56] Krzysztof Dunin-Wąsowicz, "Rewakowicz Henryk Karol," in *PSB*, vol. 31 (Wrocław–Warsaw–Cracow–Gdańsk–Łódź, 1988–89), p. 170.
[57] Kieniewicz, *Powstanie styczniowe*, p. 617.
[58] Otton Beiersdorf, "Galicja wobec powstania styczniowego," in *Powstanie styczniowe 1863–1864*, p. 409.

rising.[59] This meeting was organized by the National Government commissar Władysław Majewski with Stefan Laurysiewicz, the Greek Catholic parish priest of St. Norbert's Church, who had only recently been the organizer of the well-known Horodło anniversary celebrations in 1861. Father Adam Słotwiński, who was present at this meeting, recalled that representatives of the National Government turned up from the Polish side, while the Ruthenian delegation was headed by Yulian Lavrivsky.

We can partially reconstruct the Ruthenian demands on the basis of Słotwiński's critical speech, which he was to have given after listening to Lavrivsky. The priest's statement is sufficiently telling, for it betrays the approach of the Polish side to these demands. Słotwiński said:

> What, my good sirs, (…) you are demanding from the National Government the Ruthenian lands for yourselves, language, schools and parish matters? All this is too early. Today the National Government does not have an inch of land free and cleared of Muscovites. What can someone who has nothing give you? National rights are not so easily obtained! History tells us that they are gained through blood, property and the sacrifices of entire generations, and not through language at a green baize table. Set up Ruthenians regiments with the standards of St. Michael, defend Podlachia, Brest, Zhytomyr, and your Bug River etc., your rite and religion, which the Muscovites want to destroy, and to cause a schism, jointly with the Poles drive out the Muscovite — our joint enemy, and when we are at last alone no brother does harm to another. If Ruthenian is a better language than Polish, the poetry more sublime in your language, then we all shall be educated on these. The Poles will not disturb your rite or homestead fire but will join in mutual matrimony and become a singular link in the common chain.[60]

Słotwiński's speech met with the approval of Władysław Majewski, who concluded the meeting after hearing it. Consequently, no agreement was reached at all. However, a new person who was to be responsible for recruiting Ruthenians for battle was appointed.

The crisis that consumed Polish conspiratorial organizations in Galicia was to end in the autumn of 1863. By government decree (9 November), the National Government Department was called into being for the Austrian area of partition (1 December). Władysław Majewski was nominated commissar, with Colonel Jan Sawicki (pseudonym

---

[59] Marian Mudryj, "Powstanie styczniowe a środowisko *gente Rutheni, natione Poloni* w Galicji," in *Powstanie styczniowe. Odniesienia, interpretacje, pamięć*, ed. Tomasz Kargol (Cracow, 2013), p. 72.

[60] Adam Słotwiński, *Wspomnienia z niedawnej przeszłości*, part 1: *1860–1871* (Cracow, 1892), p. 117.

Struś) appointed military organizer.[61] It was he among others who, on behalf of the insurgent authorities, was to encourage Ruthenians to take part in the insurgency.[62]

Struś, even prior to taking up the post, established contact in August 1863 with Ruthenian youth in Galicia when he was the chief of staff for the commander of the Ruthenian lands General Edmund Różycki, wanting to create from among these young people a unit that would cross over into Congress Poland and engage in battle.[63] He wrote the following about his motivation for taking up the task:

> (...) I decided to get closer to the Ruthenians, being convinced that it was merely a lack of tact and brotherly love that had made any hitherto understanding with them problematic. I wanted to gain support for the uprising among Ruthenian youth at any price, I wanted to create a Ruthenian unit which would cross over into the Lublin lands and leave their mark as the children of Rus', as adherents of the self-same rite as the ordinary people, being convinced that from the very moment Polish and Ruthenian blood were to flow in a single stream, when the tears of Polish women mingled with those of Ruthenian women, when a Polish woman plunged into mourning meets with a pained Ruthenian mother, misunderstanding will give way, hands will be extended in greeting, and the blood of the children and the tears of the mothers will bring the fathers closer and join them together in the name of the marvellous moments of a beautiful past, ones unblemished by discord and in the name of a future based on common freedom, liberty and equal rights.[64]

However, reality offered a stark contrast, for the romantic dreams of Struś and other insurgents were not necessarily shared by the Ruthenian elites in Galicia. The Ruthenians presented Struś with two demands. The first concerned organizational questions for the unit:

> (...) the unit was to comprise only Ruthenians of the eastern rite, the officers were to be Ruthenians: soldiers by choice, clothing for the unit is to be folk in character according to the pattern that we ourselves provide, the command has to be Ruthenian, while the commander has to be a pure-blood Ruthenian and selected with our agreement.

---

[61] Kieniewicz, *Powstanie styczniowe*, p. 704.

[62] For more on Jan Sawicki: Stefan Kieniewicz, Maria Domańska-Nogajczyk, "Stella-Sawicki Jan," in *PSB*, vol. 43 (Warsaw–Cracow, 2004–5), p. 354.

[63] Demiańczuk, "Ukraińcy galicyjscy," p. 30.

[64] "Udział Galicyi w powstaniu 1863–1864. Wyjątek z pamiętników pułkownika Strusia," in *Wydawnictwo materyałów do historyi powstania 1863–1864*, vol. 2: *Pamiętnik Pułkownika Strusia, moje notatki, Bentkowski, z pamiętnika dla moich wnuków Deskura, wspomnienia z roku 1863 S. Duchińskiej* (Lviv, 1890).

The second demand concerned the future: the guarantee on the part of the National Government of the free development of the Ruthenian language and Ruthenian nationality and also for the "number of schools in Rus' to equal the needs of the people and that instruction in these schools be in Ruthenian."[65] Colonel Struś was to accept without reservation the first mentioned conditions. The final set of demands, completely unexpected, was to thwart any plans for cooperation. Jan Stella-Sawicki related the Ruthenian statement of the Progressive Hromada's representative:

> (...) given that we as a nation have no nobility, for in its entirety all the gentry of our blood have been polonized, and yet for the needs of the functioning of a healthy society such a class is necessary, we demand that the National Government promise us to force the gentry residing in Rus' to send their children to Ruthenian schools and to raise them in such a way that they will with time create a Ruthenian nobility: one as educated as the Polish and yet organically and warmly merged into our nation and not into yours.[66]

Although it was not possible to recruit Ruthenians to fight in 1863, this did not mean that the idea of fighting for a Commonwealth of Three Nations stopped being propagated. This was driven by the principle that given the inability to agree on a joint front in fighting the partitioning power, then after victory was achieved Poles perforce, due to their being in control, would establish their own order in the country. Undoubtedly this was how the high command of the uprising thought. There was yet another problem that dissuaded Ruthenian youth from joining the struggle—the relatively limited involvement of Galician Poles themselves in the uprising. Financial support, aid, and arms were provided, and insurgents hidden, but the actual number of soldiers sent from Galicia to fight the Russians was small. There was also a lack of Ruthenian leaders interested in selling the concept. It could hardly have been any different when the Polish elites themselves did not call for participation in the battles. Possibly the only person from among the Ruthenians of Polish nationality who was brave enough to speak out was Mikołaj Zyblikiewicz, though not in the context of participation in the armed struggle but in opposition to the repression being carried out by the Austrian authorities. In November 1863 he appeared at the forum of the Imperial Council in Vienna, where in a fiery speech he enumerated those acts directed against the Galician conspirators. Although he criticized the conduct of the authorities (surveillance, searches, sealing

---

[65] *Wydawnictwo materyałów*, vol. 2, p. 68.
[66] Ibid., p. 69.

the borders, etc.), it was in fact a blow directed against the Habsburg monarchy.[67] Zyblikiewicz, as a member of the Galician elites, was not to involve himself directly in the uprising although—which one should give him credit for—he was at least brave enough to condemn counter-measures against it. Yet, this was completely insufficient when one considers the involvement of Ruthenians, the Ruthenian elites, or Galicia as a whole—as a part of a former and future Poland—in the uprising. Colonel Struś, writing in January 1864 to the plenipotentiary commissar of the National Government, characterized the situation in the Austrian area of partition:

> There are noble individuals who have great significance in the country, and the rest of the people follow them as long as they are at the forefront. (…) A paralyzed urban element; a patriotic youth of the sort exemplified by the academic youth of Cracow simply doesn't exist. And this is the current state in Eastern Galicia.[68]

Given that this was the attitude of Polish society in Galicia, there is no need to ponder why the Ruthenians on the whole were resistant to Polish activities or to the central idea of an uprising in general. This situation was not to change noticeably right up to the very end of the January Uprising, although certain glimmers of hope did appear at the beginning of 1864.

On 20 January 1864 the Progressive Ruthenian Hromada in Lviv issued an appeal that was presented the next day to the plenipotentiary commissar for Eastern Galicia.[69] The memorandum demanded:

> (…) for the National Government as the rightful heir of pre-partition Poland to stop considering Rus' as a component part of the Polish state, to give up its historic rights to Rus', maintaining them only for Moscow, and for the Polish nation to help in the development of Ruthenian nationality, while a liberated Rus' shall enter into a federation with Poland, to which the Hromada is to prepare Ruthenians at a time more or less distant, and perhaps even a future generation will assume this obligation.[70]

---

[67] "Mowa posła Mikołaja Zyblikiewicza w Radzie państwa, Nov. 1863," in *Wydawnictwo materyałów*, vol. 3, pp. 214–16.

[68] "Wódz naczelny ziem ruskich [J. Stella-Sawicki] do Komisarza pełnomocnego Rządu Narodowego, Jan. 1864," in *Wydawnictwo materyałów*, vol. 3, p. 270.

[69] This appeal, as Demiańczuk established (Demiańczuk, "Ukraińcy galicyjscy," pp. 30–31), did not survive. Its contents can only be surmised at on the basis of the reply to it.

[70] "Rząd Narodowy, Sekretaryat Rusi do Wydziału wykonawczego Rządu Narodowego na Rusi (Odpis dosłowny z odpowiedzi Rządu Narodowego na odezwę Postępowej Gromady Rusińskiej we Lwowie, wystosowanej na imię Komisarza pełnomocnego)," in *Wydawnictwo materyałów*, vol. 3, p. 368.

The Ruthenian proposal was not linked to any practical offer of participation in the uprising but did create a favourable atmosphere for possible future cooperation. The National Government decided to reply to the Hromada's appeal, delegating Colonel Struś to the task. The insurgent authorities respected the Ruthenian nationality's right to develop, expressed recognition as a result of the Hromada's approach to the Government, but at the same time attempted to convince Ruthenians of the broad character of the uprising, intended to construct a multinational Commonwealth. The divergent manner in which the Ruthenians understood the policy of the insurgent authorities there was described:

> A significant difference between the concepts of the Hromada and the opinion held by the National Government was in the fact that the Hromada reads the present national insurgent movement as an exclusively Polish movement, and the Polish element in Rus', the uprising there and the local provisional government are considered a phenomenon alien to the internal life of Rus'; while at the same time the National Government reads the present-day movement as a genuine manifestation of the needs and interests of the three fraternal peoples that constituted the former Polish Commonwealth. (...) in the Ruthenian land the citizens of Rus' are Ruthenians and Poles, whoever is neither a Ruthenian nor a Pole belongs to the invaders. To consider Poles to be invaders, as an alien element, would be a historical and social falsehood. Five hundred years of joint history, the Polish blood that for whole centuries was shed in the defence of Rus', the similarity in the languages, out of which each was moulded on the model of the other, so far so that present-day literary and conversational Polish unquestionably carries features of Ruthenian influence, as does Ruthenian those of Polish, the most excellently coined political notions of equality and the Ruthenian entitlement to their language at the Diet and in legislation, finally the telling social fact of the holding by Poles of huge estates in Rus' and the intelligent significance of the Polish element both in former and present-day life in Rus'—these are things that only in bad faith or prejudice could refute the Polish element the right to citizenship in Rus'.[71]

In analysing the political thinking of the National Government in the Ruthenian context we can conclude that they wished to achieve two goals: to convince Ruthenians that they were not a part of the Russian nation, and to justify the presence of Poles on Ruthenian lands through the many centuries of cultural-state bonds with Rus'. The accumulating mutual aversions of Poles and Ruthenians to each other are also mentioned. The authors of the declaration list as reasons for the escalating animosity, among others, "the coalition of Ruthenian desires with

---

[71] Ibid., pp. 369–70.

the base intentions of the invader," that is of the partitioning powers (the Russophile threat existing among Ruthenians is emphasized here). Polemics were also conducted with the Hromada's views that the insurgent authorities in Rus' were not the political representation of this land, because no one had legitimized their status. It was argued that it would be possible to accuse the Hromada of the very same. It was emphasized here that:

> All three joined nations find themselves in that unhappy generation that they do not have a normal representation and in such extraordinary circumstances he who acts in the real interests of his country with respect for its faith, tradition, language, customs, independent development, who gives everything for this life and property and through his sacrifice gains genuine respect in the world, he and he alone in the present state of things is the true representative of the fatherland. On this basis the National Government, not through imposing and appropriation, but with a genuine fatherly and fraternal mind, considers itself to be the representative of the rightful interests and aspirations of Poland as equally Lithuania and Rus'.[72]

Further, the National Government letter took on an explanatory tone. It was explained to the Hromada that Ruthenians were linked to Poles by the Act of the Union of Lublin. Only Poland was able to guarantee Rus' equality in rights and independence, something the partitioning powers could not guarantee. At the same time, it debated with the Hromada's demand that Poles renounce their rights to Rus', for something else was shown by the five-hundred-year tradition of common ties. An example was to have been the "Polish element" present in Rus', "the intellectual and material force" of this land, and at the same time the main political factor. Without this "element" Rus' could have fallen prey to Russia. In response to the Hromada's plea that Poland wrongly insisted on the pre-partition borders separating itself from Ukraine beyond the Dnipro, the retort was that it was necessary to maintain the legal state which had been violated by Europe at the end of the eighteenth century that allowed for the partition of Poland. The borders from the year 1772 were for the National Government a guarantee of the equal existence of Rus', and not its division. The insurgent authorities also stood for the autonomy of each of the lands of any future independent state, an autonomy that Rus' would not receive from Russia, which desired to turn Ruthenians into Russians. In the thinking of the National Government, the announcement of state integrity guaranteed the safety of Rus'. The fact that the future shape of the state

---

[72] Ibid., pp. 371–72.

should be determined by a representation of the nations following victory over the partitioning powers was also emphasized. They opposed the policy proposed by the Hromada, which would have decided immediately on the future status of its lands.[73]

In essence the document sent by the National Government to the Hromada was a criticism of it. The hope was expressed that Ruthenian society, in opposition to the Hromada, "will not waiver in standing in the defence of a common fatherland."[74] Finally, the fundamental principles of National Government policy in relation to Rus' were underlined:

I. The Polish nation and the National Government consider Rus to be a land joined to Poland on the basis of religious, national, political, and civil equality. It further recognizes Ruthenian nationality to have the right to an independent and separate development on the basis of self-government democratic in principle. Poles inhabiting Rus' are considered in the same way as Ruthenians to be Ruthenian citizens, though in this they do not cease to be citizens of a common fatherland, i.e., one combined from Poland, Lithuania and Rus. The equality in rights proclaimed by the National Government satisfy the principle of a federation if such a principle turns out to be a practical one.

II. The National Government, as the legal heir of the pre-partition government of the Commonwealth, basing itself on historical right in this singular scope and spirit, considers Rus' to be linked to Poland and Lithuania on the basis of equality in rights regarding religious, national, political, and civil matters. The right to rule over Rus' in the meaning of its religious, national, political, and civil enslavement is rejected by the National Government, is opposed, and will never be realized by it, for the right to enslavement is a fundamental contradiction.

III. The authority legislated by the National Government in Rus' regards the National Government to be the rightful national authority as equally Ruthenian as Polish for it was established for the good of both nationalities and functions in the common interest. It should in no way be the expression of a single class but has to express the needs and aspirations of all the inhabitants of Rus' and to be an organ for the obtaining of its independence in combination with Poland and Lithuania.

IV. Poland, Rus and Lithuania should combine in their efforts and sacrifice to remove the yoke of foreign domination. (…) The National Government with open arms welcomes to the ranks of its staff all Ruthenians who undertake common work for the good and joint happiness of the Ruthenian and Polish fatherland (…).[75]

---

[73] Ibid., pp. 374–82.
[74] Ibid., p. 383.
[75] Ibid., pp. 383–84.

Franciszek Rawita Gawroński summarized the attempts at a compromise between the Hromada and the Polish authorities by noting that as no offer of a rapid involvement of the Ruthenian population in the battles was forthcoming, the National Government did not attempt to conclude an agreement.[76] It is also unknown whether the Lviv Hromada reacted at all to the National Government's response. The fact remains that no Ruthenian unit was ever formed.

Ruthenians in the January Uprising

Although attempts of military cooperation with the representatives of Galicia's Ruthenians failed, this does not mean that individuals did not take part in armed insurgent battles. Twenty-five units were sent in total from Galicia, of which thirteen were from Eastern Galicia. In total the Austrian area of partition mustered 5,200 insurgents.[77] Among these were also Ruthenians; although we do not know their exact number. Several attempts at studying the social composition of the insurgent army have been completed but hitherto there has yet to appear a statistical study covering recruits from the entirety of the former Polish lands.[78] The problem here is first and foremost the lack of data—the card index running up to 25,000 names of January Uprising insurgents compiled by Edward Maliszewski was destroyed by fire during the Second World War.[79] Consequently, research is only possible on individual units or based on a different type of sources.

Nevertheless, we do know of cases, admittedly only a few, of representatives of the Ruthenian ethnic group who wanted to fight for an independent Poland. As Piotr Łossowski and Zygmunt Młynarski wrote half a century ago: "undoubtedly here the example of Poles leaving Galicia in numbers to join the ranks of the insurgents played a part as did a series of other, individual factors."[80] These instances are worthy of attention, particularly since Ruthenian youths often shared the views of their Polish colleagues with whom they sat at the same school desk. The situation that took place in Lviv, and which was recounted years later by Zygmunt Miłkowski, is characteristic:

[76] Rawita-Gawroński, *Rok 1863*, vol. 1, pp. 307–11.

[77] Trusevych, *Suspil'no-politychnyi rukh*, p. 100.

[78] Stefan Kieniewicz, "Z problematyki badań nad społeczną historią 1863 roku," *Prace Historyczne* 78: *Struktury, ruchy, ideologie XVIII–XX wieku*, ed. Halina Kozłowska-Sabatowska (1986), pp. 61–67.

[79] Krzysztof Dunin-Wąsowicz, "Próba analizy składu społeczno-zawodowego oddziału powstańczego z 1863 roku," *Kwartalnik Historyczny* 70, no. 4 (1963), p. 873.

[80] Łossowski, Młynarski, *Rosjanie*, p. 202.

At that time the first Galician Diet was functioning. The members, Poles and Ruthenians, among whom besides Uniate priests were to be found a few Ruthenian peasants, knew what was happening in town. Namely they knew about the day and the hour of the march out of the first insurgent unit. What they did not know is what the authorities would do about this. This sorely worried them. Some sensed a street battle, barricades, etc., horrors. Others envisaged the bombing of the city. Anxiety gripped them especially on the designated day, during which all were present at the gathering, bar only a few. When the appointed hour was near, the rostrum was taken by Włodzimierz Cielecki, a speaker on the matter of reform needed in the shoeing of horses. He delivered his speech despite the house, whose attention had been taken by events elsewhere. They pricked up their ears to catch any sounds from outside; eyes were riveted on the doors in case they were to open and one of those not present was to appear with some news or other. They waited—they waited—they waited to the end. The doors opened, [Ivan] Karpynets entered, the member for Chortkiv—he entered, took off his cap—on his entrance the speaker fell silent, silence reigned in the chamber, the members followed the slowly approaching Karpynets, who stopped in the middle of the room, raised his hand and in a clear gesture waved his hand and said:

–Well!…our Ruthenians have gone…

The peasant, predisposed to anti-Polish patriotism, had seen the unit march away and in it, besides Poles in confederate caps, had glimpsed Ruthenians in sheepskin caps (…). This scene put the peasant off his stride, having only recently converted to the idea of Poles as his enemy.[81]

We do know a number of the Ruthenian insurgents by their surname. Here it is worth mentioning a few figures. The example of Józef Daniluk, an employee of the Stauropigial Institute printing house in Lviv and later a socialist activist, is of special interest. He organized an insurgent group comprised of young Ruthenian craftsmen, with whom he joined the unit commanded by Major Józef Władysław Rucki.[82] There were also several Ruthenians in Marcin Borelowski's unit, in which there served individuals drawn from the territories of Galicia. They included Mikołaj Sawicki [Mykola Savytsky], the son of a Ruthenian Uniate cantor who died at the Battle of Sowia Góra near te village of Batorz, and Dymitr Procajłowycz [Dmytro Protsailovych], fighting in it as well (b. 1847 in the Zhovkva district), who also took earlier part in the skirmishes at Panasówka.[83] In the latter there also participated

---

[81] Zygmunt Miłkowski, *Sprawa ruska w stosunku do sprawy polskiej* (Lviv, 1902), pp. II–III (88–89).

[82] Marian Tyrowicz, "Daniluk Józef," in *PSB*, vol. 4 (Cracow, 1938), pp. 410–11.

[83] *Pamiątka dla rodzin polskich. Krótkie wiadomości biograficzne o straconych na rusztowaniach, rozstrzelanych, poległych na placu boju, oraz zmarłych w więzieniach, na tułactwie i na wygnaniu*

another Ruthenian, the baker Teodor Dyniak [Fedir Dyniak], as well as Teofil Merunowicz, known later for his journalism and diet work; who was wounded at the Battle of Radyvyliv. The Austrians arrested him for insurgent activities and imprisoned him for three years at the fortress in Kufstein.[84] Twenty-year-old Klemens Srokowski [Klyment Srokovsky], the father of the future Galician Diet member, Konstanty Srokowski, also fought in the uprising.[85]

One also has to remember that the insurgent units were chiefly reinforced by young people, including students from Lviv as well as Cracow, where many Ruthenians went to study. Andrzej A. Zięba gives two characteristic examples: Włodzimierz Lewicki [Volodymyr Levytsky] of Volytsia Komarova in the Zhovkva district, who fought in Erazm Skarżyński's unit, as well as Emilian Palatyński [Emiliian Palatynsky], born in Liadske in the Stanyslaviv district, who produced gun powder explosives for the insurgents. His family members Zygmunt [Zygismund], Jan [Ivan], and Aleksander [Oleksander] Palatyński [Palatynsky] were also involved in the uprising.[86]

In attempting to determine the social estate of the small number of young people of Ruthenian origin known to us who took part in the uprising, we come to the conclusion that besides young people of school or university backgrounds, the most numerous group were artisans, the petty bourgeois, and representatives of an array of rural freelance trades. It is worth recalling, here citing Magdalena Micińska, Klemens Puza [Klyment Puza], who was a tailor in Nowy Żmigród in the district of Jasło,[87] as well as Dominik Terlecki [Dominik Terletsky], who had previously worked as a smith on military convoys for the Austrian army.[88] Other researchers such as Piotr Łossowski and Zygmunt Młynarski noted in their work the following: Andrzej Hawryluk

---

Syberyjskiem, 1861–1866 r. ze źródeł urzędowych, dzienników polskich, jak niemniej z ustnych podań osób wiarygodnych i towarzyszy broni, part 2, collected and ed. Zygmunt Kolumna [Aleksander Nowolecki], introd. Bogdan Bolesławita [Józef Ignacy Kraszewski] (Cracow, 1868), p. 244; Antoni Barowicz, Marcin „Lelewel" Borelowski. Rękodzielnik – pułkownik (Rzeszów, 1913), p. 101; Dunin-Wąsowicz, "Próba analizy," p. 884.

[84] Jerzy Zdrada, "Merunowicz Teofil," in PSB, vol. 20 (Wrocław–Warsaw–Cracow–Gdańsk, 1975), p. 455.

[85] Andrzej A. Zięba, "Srokowski Konstanty," in PSB, vol. 41 (Warsaw–Cracow, 2002), p. 231.

[86] Andrzej A. Zięba, "Inne 'Tamte światy'," in Rzecz o roku 1863. Uniwersytet Jagielloński wobec powstania styczniowego, ed. Andrzej A. Zięba (Cracow, 2013), pp. 86, 98, footnotes 28–29.

[87] Magdalena Micińska, Galicjanie – zesłańcy po powstaniu styczniowym. Zesłanie w głąb Cesarstwa Rosyjskiego – Działalność księdza Ludwika Ruczki – Powroty (Warsaw, 2004), pp. 644–45.

[88] Ibid., p. 787.

[Andrii Havryliuk], a twenty-six-year-old smith from the Ternopil district sentenced to four years of prison unit service by the Austrians; his twenty-year-old brother Józef Hawryluk [Iosyf Havryliuk], also a blacksmith, was sentenced similarly as his brother; Mikołaj Hulik [Mykola Hulyk], a labourer from Galicia, was sentenced to two weeks' arrest; the coachman Gabriel Hykawy [Havryil Hykavy], who fought in Robert Sienkiewicz's unit at Porytsk [today Pavlivka] and Peretoky; the carpenter Jan Sawańczuk [Ivan Savanchuk] of Lviv, who fought at Tuchapy, Radyvyliv, and Porytsk and was arrested and imprisoned in Lviv following his withdrawal to Galicia. These authors also cite individuals of unknown social origin: Michał Mirojew [Mykhailo Miroiev] (arrested and imprisoned in Lublin), Mikołaj Sawicki and Antoni Kulmatycki [Anton Kulmatytsky], who was to end up in Arkhangelsk after the January Uprising. A certain Morosko, a political émigré who was sentenced to two years imprisonment by the Austrians for his involvement in the uprising, is also known.[89]

A number of those insurgents attempting to force their way through from Congress Poland were detained at the Austrian-Russian border. This was the case with the journeyman M. Malowany [M. Malovany], Michał Michałowski [Mykhailo Mykhailovsky], and Józef Makowski [Iosyf Makovsky]. Others were detained in turn just as they returned to Galicia either during the course of the uprising or after its collapse. Such was the fate of the lackeys serving at Lviv manor houses: Stefan Hrehory [Stepan Hrehory] and Wasyl Karpiak [Vasyl Karpiak]; and other Ruthenians such as Fedek Maśluk [Teodor Masliuk] of Horodok, Maksym Jakymowycz [Maksym Iakymovych] of Brody, Julian Papirnyk [Iuliian Papirnyk] and Filip Petrycki [Pylyp Petrytsky] of Ianiv [today Ivano-Frankove], as well as Piotr Hetmańczuk [Petro Hetmanchuk] of Sokal.

Another group was unable to even engage in combat as they were apprehended by the Austrian military police during the process of forming units or when crossing the border. Jan Humeniuk [Ivan Humeniuk], a servant from Krynica, was arrested in the forest where one of these units was being organized, while others such as Wasyl Dorosz [Vasyl Dorosh], Józef Hankewycz [Iosyf Hankevych], Michał Dmiszek [Mykhailo Dmyshek], along with many more, were apprehended on the border itself.[90]

Not everyone supported the uprising by fighting. We should mention *gente Ruthenus, natione Polonus* Konstanty Łękawski, a political émi-

---

[89] Łossowski, Młynarski, *Rosjanie*, pp. 202–4.
[90] Trusevych, *Suspil'no-politychnyi rukh*, pp. 113–14.

gré in Newcastle, who—on the instruction of Joseph Cowen, a propagator of Polish independence—was sent in April 1863 to Constantinople. As an agent of David Urquhart, a member of the British political opposition and founder of the so-called Committees for Foreign Affairs, he was to act there for the realization of Prince Władysław Czartoryski's plan. This plan envisioned military aid for the Circassians in revolt against Russia, which would weaken Russia as a partitioning power on a second front and increase the chances of victory for the January Uprising insurgents. The plans to supply arms ultimately failed, when in April 1864 Łękawski sailed for Spanish Malaga. There he dreamed up further visions of a simultaneous attack on Russia, Prussia, and Austria, and even taking the war to the Pacific, but by then the uprising had already been suppressed.[91]

There were also those who supported the insurrection financially or by some other means, including Jan Fedorowicz, the son of a Ruthenian priest and a participant in the November Uprising. Although he declined to directly participate in the fighting, he did send the insurgents three and a half thousand gulden.[92] Tomasz Polański should also be mentioned. During the course of the January Uprising he did not inform on those pupils of the Rzeszów secondary school he headed who had left its walls, while later he protected them from repression by the Austrian authorities.[93] In one of his articles, Andrzej A. Zięba also mentions the Uniate Józef Dietl, who was the son of a German civil servant, Franciszek, and a noblewoman from Eastern Galicia, Anna née Kulczycka [Anna Kulchytska], a Ruthenian of Polish nationality. The well-known professor, later mayor of Cracow, organized medical aid for the insurgents when he was a member of the Medical Council, something he was to pay for later by losing his departmental job at the Jagiellonian University.[94]

News about the uprising not only reached the towns but also the countryside. In a manner similar to earlier conspiracies, plans were afoot to agitate and involve the peasantry, both Ruthenian as well as Polish. The Austrian authorities placed peasant guards on watch in border villages to stop the influx of insurgents to Galicia. In addition, they used landless peasants to capture Polish soldiers.[95] Jan Stella-Sawicki wrote about the situation in the Galician countryside:

---

[91] Peter Brock, "Joseph Cowen and the Polish Exiles," *The Slavonic and East European Review* 32, no. 78 (1953), pp. 66–67.

[92] Ibid., p. 104.

[93] Tadeusz Śliwa, "Polański Tomasz," in *PSB*, vol. 27 (Wrocław–Warsaw–Cracow–Gdańsk–Łódź, 1983), p. 282.

[94] Zięba, "Inne 'Tamte światy'," pp. 83–84.

[95] Trusevych, *Suspil'no-politychnyi rukh*, p. 102.

The peasants of the two nationalities, Polish and Ruthenian, who inhabit Galicia differ from each other only in terms of language, only certain customs separating one nationality from the other are merely an artificial state of affairs maintained by the Austrian authorities and Muscovite rubles, by means of which agents of this state try to gain themselves friends especially among the priests and journalists, maintained by a part of the exalted youth who fail to comprehend that they are merely an instrument in the enemy's hand as much for us as for others, and that the development of nationality cannot proceed in any other way than through the development of independence and personal liberty.

The landless peasants in Galicia had not developed as a class during the period of our uprising to undertake joint action; the bloody brook which divided the peasantry from the gentry had not completely dried up though at least the peasant no longer obstructed national work, while in some places they even actively aided it. There were many examples of betrayal, spying, opposition: peasant sentries caused much trouble, but one cannot keep an ignorant people responsible [for their actions], those who were continually instigated by various instigators.[96]

The insurgents were not met with hostility everywhere on the part of the Polish and Ruthenian inhabitants of Galician towns and villages. The Central State Historical Archive of Ukraine in Lviv has preserved lists of those Galicians arrested in particular districts for participating in or aiding the January Uprising. These records, admittedly not stating the nationality of those arrested, do allow us on the basis of surnames and places of origin to conjecture as to the ethnic group the given individuals belonged to. For example, the court in Przemyśl was to oversee the case of Wasyl Miśko [Vasyl Misko] of Trójca and Jurko Ciż [Iurko Tsyzh] of Święte. In turn the following individuals were sent to Stanyslaviv: Fedor Karabyn [Fedir Karabyn] of Khryplyn; Dymitr Glembicki [Dmytro Glembytsky] of Lazarivka; Wasyl Szmerluk [Vasyl Shmerluk] of Tustan; Kosma Dulenczuk [Kozma Dulenchuk] of Kuty; Wasyl Stefaniszyn [Vasyl Stefanyshyn] of Vistova; Ołena Owczar [Olena Ovchar] of Lysets; Iwan Czerwak [Ivan Chervak] of Bortnyky; Pańko Chinczak [Panko Khynchak] of Pniv; Tymko Chominiec [Tymofii Khomynets] of Pidpechery; Wasyl Srebrny [Vasyl Sribny] of Nadvirna; and Harasim Dubiszczak [Harasym Dubyshchak] of Pniv. Those tried in Zolochiv included: Wasyl Dydyk vel Kucharzów [Vasyl Dydyk vel Kukhariv] of Byshiv; Tymko Kubrak [Tymofii Kubrak] of Zahiria; and Semen Humeniuk of Synkiv. In Sambir was: Iwan Hołojda [Ivan Holoida] of Pyniany; Hryń Jurciów [Hryn Iurtsiv] of Stynava; Semion Kluczyszyn [Semen Kluchyshyn] of Opoka; and Iwan Kohut [Ivan Kohut] of

---

[96] [Jan Stella-Sawicki] Pułkownik Struś, *Moje wspomnienia (1831–1910). (Rosja, Polska, Francja)*, ed., introd., and footnotes Eugeniusz Barwiński (Lviv, [1921]), pp. 76–77.

Kostalyn.[97] There are significantly more surnames in the aforementioned document which suggest Ruthenian provenance. We are also able to determine the ethnic affiliation of those arrested from the Ruthenian sound of the first names, or in the case of Poles those names consistently written in Latin or German. If the matter concerned an individual of non-Ruthenian provenance, then it would not be written as Ivan but as Johannes, in the manner Poles were noted down.

Many Ruthenians paid heavily for their participation in the January Uprising, either through losing their lives, exile, or arrest. Some, such as Iwan Didyk [Ivan Didyk], Jan Gruszkiewicz [Ivan Hrushkevych], Iwan Hordij [Ivan Hordy], Antoni Kulmatycki, Mykoła Maślak [Mykola Masliak], Iwan Paszkowski [Ivan Pashkovsky], Klemens Puza, Tymisz Sotnyk [Tymofii Sotnyk], Dominik Terlecki [Domynyk Terletsky], Edward Wołoszyński [Edvard Voloshynsky], or the Kowszewicz brothers, Jan and Konstanty [Ivan and Konstantyn Kovshevych], were sent to Siberia, with the brothers losing their estate.[98] It is interesting that some of them, despite exile, persisted in their Polish patriotic activities. Antoni Kulmatycki was such a rebellious soul. His brave deeds during the insurrection, his exile, and his subsequent propaganda activities during exile were recalled by Bolesław Limanowski in his memoirs:

> He was a true original and even to a degree a historic figure. Born in Eastern Galicia, he was the son of a Uniate priest. Once during a journey, he recounted to me his entire story. As a young boy, a servant, he set off on some foreign trip with some academic or other. They became friendly and he was to influence his intellectual development. They visited Slavic countries and Italy; under the influence of this researcher he acquired a critical mind and views, particularly anti-clerical ones. In 1863 he was drawn to a group which crossed over into the Polish Kingdom. The band was defeated and Kulmatycki taken prisoner. When [General Ksaverii] Chengery, spoke to the assembled Galician prisoners-of-war "Why have you taken it upon yourselves to enter a foreign country?" —Kulmatycki proudly retorted, "It is you who have taken it on yourselves to enter, for we are in our own country."[99]

Kulmatycki was subsequently sent to Arkhangelsk to units of jailed insurgents, where he aroused other prisoners against the authorities. For this he was sentenced to several years hard labour in Siberia, where

---

[97] "Spysky uchasnykiv povstannia, zasudzhenykh viis'kovym sudamy v mm. Zolochevi, Peremyshli, Riashevi, Ternopoli ta n.," TsDIAU, fond 102: Kolektsiia dokumentiv pro pol's'ke povstannia 1863-1864 rr., op. 1, spr. 28.

[98] Cf. Trusevych, *Suspil'no-politychnyi rukh*, p. 114; Micińska, *Galicjanie*, pp. 224, 370–72.

[99] Bolesław Limanowski, *Pamiętniki (1835–1870)*, introd. Adam Próchnik (Warsaw, 1957), p. 411.

his "haughty" attitude manifested his continued defiance. He was once chained to the walls in a dark cell and fed only a piece of bread and water in order to humiliate him. After a week the governor came to see him, and the following exchange was to have taken place:

> – Are you all so cocky back there in Galicia? The governor asked.
> – What?—called out Kulmatycki—I'm the most mediocre of the lot, all the Galicians there are even freer spirits than I am.[100]

Freed by the governor of backbreaking work, he nevertheless did not cease his agitation, now directing his efforts towards inciting the soldiers. As Limanowski writes:

> Kulmatycki (...) would continue to speak to the soldiers in his own form of Russian, one composed of Russian, Ruthenian and Polish words, that they were slaves, that they were not worthy of the name people, and that without any resistance they allowed themselves to be kicked around.[101]

His courage gained the respect of the soldiers and he did not complain of his relations with them. He is, however, one of only a few Ruthenian insurgents whose fate and views were to be reported in such detail in recollections and diaries.

The limited number of accounts of Ruthenian insurgent acts confirms the assumption that in fact their number was not too large. The idea of a three-partition and three-nation uprising had no chance of success, all the more so given that the lofty ideas and symbols of the uprising did not find many sympathisers among non-Poles, who were expected to take up arms in an uprising in the name of their fatherland that was not theirs. There were additional critical voices among Ruthenians over the uprising. For example, Ostap Levytsky published in 1863 a satirical pamphlet on the January insurgents entitled *The Escapees*, signing it: "Ostap Kovbasiuk, *gente Ruthenus, natione* also *Ruthenus*."[102]

One should also mention Bohdan Didytsky's poem "We Shall Dance!" ["Będziemy tańczyć!"], which was circulating in Lviv. As Ostap Sereda notes, it was supposed to be a reply to the hitherto undiscovered poem by Platon Kostecki entitled "Do You Want to Dance?" ["Wy chcecie tańczyć?"].[103] Kostecki in his work rebuked Ruthenians for planning

---

[100] Ibid., p. 412.
[101] Ibid.
[102] [Ostap Levytsky] Ostap Kowbasiuk, gente Ruthenus, natione także Ruthenus, *Uciekinierzy, poemat à la „Konrad Wallenrod"* (Lviv, 1863). Cf. Studyński, "Powstańcy polscy," p. 69.
[103] Ostap Sereda, "'Ruś będzie tańczyć!' 'Rus'ki baly' u L'vovi iak faktor pol's'ko-ukraïns'kykh vzaiemyn u Halychyni kintsia 40-kh – 60-kh rokiv XIX st.," *Visnyk*

to organize, immediately after the outbreak of the uprising, two dances for Ruthenian youth; something the poet saw as a tactless smiting of Polish national feelings at the very moment of the outbreak of the revolt. Didytsky's poem was cited by Marian Mudry in his essay on the subject. The first two verses are worth quoting:

> To dance again, again are we, young Rus',
> For pure in heart and conscience are we,
> With a mind as sharp as the Dnipro's waters
> From which the enemy shadows of the Poles flee
>
> Rus' will dance for it has such valour ·
> And enough mercy that in polonized Lviv
> For the ills and martyrdom endured
> To the wrath of the Poles the reply is in dance![104]

The works of Ostap Levytsky and Bohdan Didytsky best convey the attitudes of the Ruthenian intelligentsia to Polish insurgent activities. The total defeat of the January Uprising was to eradicate any dreams the Polish elite had harboured of independence. Together with the collapse of the 1863 revolt, the hope for the incorporation of various *gente* into a single *natio* through the construction of a Commonwealth of Poland, Lithuania, and Rus' also finally died. Nonetheless, an echo of the insurrection and its symbolism was to still return. The significance within such a context of the total defeat of the January Uprising was noted by Franciszek Bujak, who in 1908 wrote:

> Right up until the epoch of the January Uprising Poles had culturally controlled and represented the entirety of the area of the Commonwealth, standing by the position of a union of all the tribes inhabiting the Commonwealth under the umbrella notion of a uniform Polish political idea. The poetic output of Mickiewicz and the Ukrainian School, archaeological and historical research, the entirety of the area covered most clearly stated our position—a political one. Following the January Uprising the spiritual low and the very real depletion in strength for any cultural work which, on the one hand, had to quickly proliferate and become increasingly intensive, while on the other the ruthlessly hostile position of the Russian government in the annexed provinces, and the competing Ruthenian national movement in Galicia, growing in

---

L'vivs'koho uniwersytetu. Seriia Istorychna 6, special no.: *L'viv. Misto, suspil'stvo, kul'tura,* vol. 6: *L'viv–Krakiv. Dialoh mist v istorychnii retrospektyvi,* eds. Olena Arkusha and Marian Mudryi (2007), p. 323.
[104] Mudryj, "Powstanie styczniowe," p. 71; Marian Mudryi, "Sichneve povstannia ta seredovyshche 'rusyniv pol's'koï natsiï' (*gente Rutheni, natione Poloni*) v Halychyni," in *Galicja a powstanie styczniowe*, p. 139.

strength year by year, made it impossible for us to culturally and politically take control and represent the remains of the Commonwealth beyond that which constituted ethnographic territory and this constituted the greatest, irrevocable defeat which the second half of the nineteenth century was to cook up for us as a consequence of the partitions and the collapse of the state.[105]

37. The coat-of-arms used by the insurgents during the January Uprising of 1863. Postcard „Boże zbaw Polskę" from 1903

Paradoxically the defeat of the January Uprising, and with it the failure to materialize the ideas of a tri-axial Commonwealth in which *gente Rutheni, natione Poloni* could have most comfortably found their place, resulted in the popularization of the motif of Polish-Ruthenian-Lithuanian unity in spite of the fact that no such unity existed in actuality. The coat-of-arms depicting the emblems of Poland, Lithuania, and Rus' was to permanently dominate public and private life across the entire area of the Polish lands. The Eagle, the Vytis coat-of-arms and the depiction of Archangel Michael from the uprising of 1863 appeared on monuments, gravestones, in book illustrations, magazine plates, and pictures, and finally could be found embossed on items of everyday use such as tableware or jewellery. Kazimierz Chłędowski was to describe Tadeusz Romanowicz, a well-known social and political activist in Galicia and a former insurgent:

> (…) dressed in the Polish style, in a black nobleman's tunic with a great silvered buckle clasping a leather belt, on which boldly embossed is the coat of arms of Poland, Lithuania and Rus' *en relief*.[106]

The collapse of the uprising ended the Romantic dreams of liberating the state—a Polish-Ruthenian-Lithuanian state. The slogans carried on the standards for the years 1863–64 remained only the symbols of

[105] Franciszek Bujak, *Galicya*, vol. 1: *Kraj, ludność, społeczeństwo, rolnictwo* (Lviv–Warsaw, 1908), pp. 85–86.
[106] Kazimierz Chłędowski, *Pamiętniki*, vol. 1: *Galicja (1843–1880)*, ed. Antoni Knot (Cracow, 1957), p. 168.

values cultivated by Polish society prior to the partitions but ones impossible to resurrect.

The period of positivism thrust onto Polish society a revision of the forms of struggle for the realization of dreams of independence. The Polish intelligentsia were particularly interested, given the situation in Galicia and the increasingly marked ethnic conflict, to preserve hitherto cordial relations between Poles and Ruthenians. The maintenance of the said unity, brotherhood, bond, or union—as these links were variably called—was desired chiefly by those who represented bicultural Galician society, that is by the Ruthenians of Polish nationality, though not just exclusively by them. The social activities of those who could be most clearly identified as *gente Rutheni, natione Poloni* were characterized by the propagation of cordial existence among Poles and Ruthenians and the cultivation of Poland with a clear reference to the role played by Rus' in its history and cultural achievements. Their activity, not revolutionary-romantic but positivist, was to intensify from the 1860s and 1870s onwards.

Galician Ukrainophiles and Ukrainian Poles Guarding Polish-Ruthenian Brotherhood

The idea of a federation was not abandoned following the collapse of the January Uprising. In fact, the numbers of those who supported the notion increased. Federal concepts, behind which lay the conviction for the necessity of cooperation among Poles, Lithuanians, and Ruthenians, were especially propagated in Galicia in the second half of the nineteenth century by Poles coming from Ukraine. They included January Uprising insurgents, the sons of noble families, students of Kyiv University, domestic tutors/teachers, and finally writers and poets. Constituting an ethnic minority among the Ruthenian population of the southwestern provinces of the Russian Empire, they often had the most excellent command of both the Ruthenian and Polish languages. As inhabitants of Ukraine they were fully aware of its history, culture, and traditions, and first and foremost knew the real threat emanating from Russia itself.

Some of them, brought up on romantic ideals, involved themselves in building a brotherhood between Poles and Ruthenians after their arrival in Galicia, often publicising their activities in Ruthenian. Seeing Russia as a mortal enemy, they worked especially against Russophile tendencies while supporting the, in effect, opposite current—the national populist tradition among Ruthenians, although they did not envisage any greater political development among the ordinary people themselves.[107] A group of individuals who were to later immerse themselves in the question of Rus especially strengthened the Galician intelligentsia. They included Tymko Padurra, Paulin Święcicki, Leon Syroczyński, as well as the later Polish nationalists Zygmunt Miłkowski and Franciszek Rawita-Gawroński. The fruit of their activities were, among others, publications in journals and other similar texts, though first and foremost they initiated a discussion on the history of Rus' and the future of its inhabitants.

An important voice in the discussion was that presented in Leon Syroczyński's *Word to Word* [*Słowo do słowa*], published in Lviv in 1865 in Ruthenian in Latin script, which he signed as Łewko Czornyj. The clear influence of his colleague Platon Kostecki is visible here. Syroczyński, appearing as a Ruthenian, criticized the Germanization and Russification of Ruthenians, while recalling at the same time the magnificence of the former Polish-Lithuanian-Ruthenian union. This state had collapsed because Poles and Ruthenians had had common enemies. The author protested in his leaflet against the demands for the division of Galicia into two parts and called for Ruthenians to join with Poles in the way their forebears had so willingly done in ages past.[108] Kyrylo Studynsky pointed out that the leaflet brought about the opposite result to that intended:

> With the leaflet *Word to Word* Syroczyński decisively ended the role of the sower of peace in the Galician lands. For instead of improving Ukrainian-Polish relations it was to dig an even greater chasm and to sow a new suspicion among the Ukrainian circles within which Syroczyński moved.[109]

Paulin Święcicki was another figure who was active in the Polish--Ruthenian field. As Kyrylo Studynsky wrote: "He created an outlook for himself of a crystallized idea of a federation of Ukraine and Poland, of a fraternal union of two free nations."[110] In an attempt to bring together the Polish and Ruthenian nations, many works were published under Ruthenian pseudonyms: Danyło Łozowskyj, Pawło Swij, Paulin Stachurski, Zorian, Polak z Ukrainy [a Pole from Ukraine], etc.[111] He in

---

[107] Cf. also: Włodzimierz Osadczy, "Galicyjski mit unii polsko-litewsko-ruskiej," in *Unia lubelska. Unia Europejska*, ed. Iwona Hofman (Lublin, 2010), p. 172.
[108] Studyński, "Powstańcy polscy," pp. 85–89. Mudry also writes about it in his "Powstanie styczniowe," pp. 77–78.
[109] Studyński, "Powstańcy polscy," p. 90.
[110] Ibid., p. 91.
[111] Ibid.

no way ceased activities he had earlier embarked on following the January Uprising. He directed his first steps towards the Ruthenian theatre in Lviv. In 1864 the Besida society in Lviv obtained a licence to produce plays in Ruthenian[112]. Among the plays produced were the works of Ukrainian dramatists, adaptations of Polish and foreign works, as well as texts written, translated, or adapted by Paulin Święcicki, who on instruction from the theatre's management also adapted the works of such eminent playwrights as Shakespeare, Molière, Aleksander Fredro, Józef Korzeniowski, and Taras Shevchenko. Święcicki even acted on theatre stage for a short period under the stage name of Danyło Łozowskyj. He was undoubtedly one of the most active participants in Ruthenian theatre at the beginning of its renewed existence. Soon, however, he left the institution as a result of conflict with the management.[113]

Święcicki did not manage to use the theatre to propagate the ideas of the Polish-Ruthenian brotherhood that he advocated. He was to continue his writing within the Ukrainophile current and publishing in the Ruthenian journal *Nyva* [*Field*] under the name "Pawło Swij." In one of his novels, *As It Once Was* [*Kolys bulo*], he emphasized the harmonious relations between the Cossacks and the Polish gentry. The enemies of this union, according to him, were external forces—for example the Tatars.[114]

Święcicki was soon to establish his own journal—*Sioło*. He published in this journal devoted to "Ukrainian-Ruthenian folk matters" texts both in Polish and Ruthenian, but with the latter written in the Latin script. The material covered history, culture, and literature. Cossack themes were discussed, as were the works of Shevchenko, the poems of Polish poets such as Józef Bohdan Zaleski on Ukraine, and reprints of interesting articles by, for instance, Jan Wagilewicz. After Wagilewicz's death the extensive "Posthumous Recollections" ["Wspomnienie pośmiertne"] was published, in which his deeds in literary and social areas, not forgetting obviously his editorial work for *Dnewnyk Ruskij*, were enumerated.[115]

Antoni Serednicki, a researcher of *Sioło*, characterized the periodical's objective:

---

[112] More about the Ruthenian theatre in Galicia see: Stanisław Schnür-Pepłowski, *Teatr ruski w Galicji* (Lviv, 1887) and Stepan Charnets'kyi, *Istoriia ukraïnskoho teatru v Halychyni. Narysy, statti, materialy, svitlyny* (Lviv, 2014).

[113] Schnür-Pepłowski, *Teatr ruski w Galicji*, pp. 11–15.

[114] Sereda, "Ruś będzie tańczyć!", p. 480.

[115] "Jan Wagilewicz. Wspomnienie pośmiertne," *Sioło* no. 1 (1866), pp. 79–88.

The journal called for the fight for a free Ukraine, for the rights of the Ukrainian nation and separation from Russia, to combat the mistaken notion that the Ukrainian language was but a dialect of Russian, it gave information about Western European interests in Ukraine. It critically evaluated the hostility between Poles and Ukrainians as well as countered the conservative views of certain Poles on the subject of Ukraine. The editor-in-chief (...) considered that to resolve the matter of the Ukrainian nation involved the granting to it of the rights it deserved and the normalising of relations between Poles and Ukrainians.[116]

The journal was consequently an initiative designed to maintain the coming together of Poles and Ruthenians and to help "the national development of the people of Ukraine-Rus'—for it was the harbinger of better days for the future."[117] In one of the issues, an article was published entitled "The Ruthenian-Ukrainian Question" ["Sprawa rusko-ukraińska"], in which there appeared a proposal for the normalization of relations between Poles and Ruthenians. The author wrote that Poles held Ruthenians in contempt, while there existed the necessity to recognize the existence of the "Ruthenian-Ukrainian nation," its language, etc. Reference was even made to events of the past that were to prove the distinctiveness of the Ruthenian lands within the expanse of the Polish state. This allowed the conclusion to be drawn that the "decree of the National Government of 1863 speaking of Rus' as the third component part within the Polish Kingdom was not a whim."[118] Although the text talks of concessions to Ruthenians and the recognition of their rights, it nevertheless did not see any possibility whatsoever of Rus' existing beyond Poland itself. On the question it posed of how "to settle the relationship between Rus' and Poland," it answered, "on the basis of Ruthenian autonomy and the political unity of Rus' with Poland."[119] The publication of this text betrays the main underlying message the editorial board wanted to convey: to prove that Ruthenians (Ukrainians) are a separate nation from the Russians and consequently from the Poles themselves. Thus, they then have the right to develop their culture, language, and other aspects of their nationality, but there are no statements made as to the necessity for an independent Rus'. Rus'--Ukraine ultimately should be—as the author wrote—an autonomous part of an independent Poland, as the third part of its components.

---

[116] Antoni Serednicki, "Polsko-ukraińskie pismo 'Sioło'," *Nad Odrą* no. 1–2 (2007), p. 13.
[117] [Paulin Święcicki], "Słowo wstępne," *Sioło* no. 1 (1866), p. iv.
[118] W.K., "Sprawa rusko-ukraińska," *Sioło* no. 3 (1867), p. 141.
[119] Ibid., p. 156.

These were the views coinciding with those proclaimed by certain *gente Rutheni, natione Poloni* during the Revolutions of 1848 and which should have constituted a part of the National Government's program in 1863. According to the text's author, Ruthenians were a legitimate nation but this did not exempt them from a loyalty to Poland as a state designed on federative principles. These ideas most obviously found adherents neither on the Polish side nor among the Ruthenians. The editorial board of *Sioło*, after having published four issues and unable to find a sufficient number of subscribers and the funds to maintain its publication, ceased the journal's activities in 1867.[120]

This was not, however, the only manifestation of Święcicki's activities. He was equally involved in the work of the Prosvita Ruthenian Society, which also attracted others who considered themselves *gente Rutheni, natione Poloni*, such as Teofil Merunowicz and Volodyslav Fedorovych, who were chairmen of the association for the years 1873–77.[121] Later Święcicki was to be the first teacher of the Ruthenian language in the higher classes of the Lviv Academic Gymnasium.[122] According to Ivan Franko, it was Święcicki who started the use of the ethnonym "Rus'-Ukraine," popular indeed in later decades among the Galician-Ukrainian elites.[123] Poles like Święcicki and Syroczyński coming from Ukraine constituted a breath of fresh air for the subsequent fate of the notion of a Polish-Ruthenian brotherhood—one which had seemed a lost cause following the defeat of the January Uprising. They extended the life of this idea albeit in a new guise, and created a conducive climate that gave hope for its realization. Marian Mudry in his later publications emphasized the significance of this group. He writes:

> Both Poles and Ukrainians were able to find in the publications of Święcicki views reflecting their moods and convictions (...). At the same time his ideas were to become an important stage in the history of the *gente Rutheni, natione Poloni* as they modernized its ideology and broadened its social base. Święcicki's idea combined *natione Poloni* with Ruthenians in an unclear federation alongside the notion of Polish-Ukrain-

---

[120] The financial problems of *Sioło* were mentioned in the fourth edition of the journal: "Od redakcji," *Sioło* no. 4 (1867), pp. i–iii.

[121] Sereda, "Ruś będzie tańczyć!," p. 482.

[122] AV, "Lwów oczami Ukraińców," *Kultura* (Paris) no. 9 (107) (1956), p. 140.

[123] Ostap Sereda, "Pavlyn Svientsitsky u suspil'nomu zhytti Halychyny. Do istorii pol's'koho ukraïnofil'stva," *Ukraïna. Kul'turna spadshchyna, natsional'na svidomist', derzhavnist'* 15: *Confraternitas. Iubileinyi zbirnyk na poshanu Iaroslava Isaevycha* (2006–7), pp. 483–85; Ievhen Nakonechny, *Ukradene im'ia. Chomu rusyny staly ukraïntsiamy*, introd. Iaroslav Dashkevych (Lviv, 2004), p. 275.

ian equality, enabling a defence against the Russian threat, the idealising of ordinary Ukrainian people, the motif of aid for Ukrainians threatened with total Russification, and the use of the Latin script for the publication of Ukrainian literary works.[124]

---

[124] Mudryj, "Powstanie styczniowe," p. 76.

Chapter VII
Gente Rutheni, Natione Poloni in Power

Gente Rutheni, Natione Poloni in the Imperial Council in Vienna

The neo-absolutist governments in Austria connected with, as Józef Buszko christened it, the "annihilation of parliamentarianism" were short-lived and transitional in character. They collapsed following the military defeats in the wars with France and Piedmont in 1859 and with Prussia in 1866. The October Diploma of 1860, drafted by Agenor Gołuchowski, and subsequently Anton von Schmerling's February Patent of 1861 were decisive in the reformulation of the state. The latter document, a fundamental act in scope, differed significantly from the federalist proclamations contained in the October Diploma, but nonetheless envisaged the creation of legislative organs, including a central body in Vienna as well as regional diets allocating delegates to the Imperial Council. This two-tier parliament would comprise a House of Lords (*Herrenhaus*), in which seats were allocated as a result of inherited titles, clerical office, or imperial nomination, as well as a House of Delegates (*Abgeordnetenhaus*), consisting of 343 members selected by the newly opened regional diets.[1] From 1867 the Imperial Council was an exclusive organ of the Austrian side of the monarchy, and the number of deputies in the House of Deputies was reduced to 203, among whom there were 38 selected by the Galician Diet and 5 from Bukovyna. In 1873 the number of members of the Imperial Council was increased to 353, and thus the number of delegates from Galicia rose to 63 and from Bukovyna to 9. The next increase in the number of delegates—up to 425—occurred in 1896. For this entire period the electoral statute would remain curial. This statute was only abolished in 1907, simultaneously raising the number of parliamentarians to 516.

The creation of the Imperial Council and the subsequent elections enabled the existence of activists on the Galician political stage who were not only of varied political orientation, but also of various nationalities and social estates. Researchers have undertaken several investigations

---

[1] Józef Buszko, *Polacy w parlamencie wiedeńskim 1848–1918* (Warsaw, 1996), pp. 38–39.

into the number of Ruthenian and Polish delegates who sat on the parliamentary benches in Vienna, but such inquiries have been doomed from the outset, as it is difficult to ascertain the national affiliation of many of them.[2] Furthermore, the identity of some remains undefined, while others may have changed their affiliation. Nonetheless, in following the subsequent parliamentary terms and the surnames of the then-delegates to the Imperial Council, we are able to pinpoint several whose *gente Rutheni, natione Poloni* affiliation we can state with certainty. In the House of Lords, Ruthenians of Polish nationality only held seats twice. During the course of the sixth parliamentary term (7 October 1879 – 23 April 1885) Mikołaj Zyblikiewicz was named a lifelong delegate, while in 1900 Julian Kuiłowski, the Greek Catholic metropolitan, also secured a seat as a *virilist* to the House of Lords for the ninth parliamentary term (27 March 1897 – 7 September 1900).

In turn, *gente Rutheni, natione Poloni* delegates were present for almost half a century, from the start of the first term in 1861 right up until the year 1907 and the end of the tenth parliamentary term. These delegates included Tomasz Barewicz (for a part of the second term, 1867–70), Euzebiusz Czerkawski (for a part of the second term, the third to seventh, and a part of the eighth, 1869–93), Julian Czerkawski (a part of the fifth term and the sixth, 1873–77, 1879–85), Teofil Merunowicz (ninth and tenth terms, 1897–1907), Tomasz Polański (second term, 1867–70), Zygmunt Sawczyński (a part of the second term, the third and fourth terms as well as a part of the seventh term, 1867–79, 1885–91), Teodor Szemelowski (first term, 1861–65), and Mikołaj Zyblikiewicz (first term, a part of the second term as well as the third to fourth terms, 1861–79)[3]. As many as five delegates from this political formation sat on the benches of the Imperial Council during the second parliamentary term of office (1867–70). The longest serving member of the Austrian parliament was Euzebiusz Czerkawski, who served for seven terms in total. After Czerkawski's death in 1896, Teofil Merunowicz took over his parliamentary duties for another two terms, until 1907. It is worth examining certain undertakings of this group within the parliamentary forum, and also in the Polish Circle [*Koło Polskie*], which arose in Vienna in the 1860s.

The first elections to the Imperial Council in Vienna took place in 1861, and the newly appointed parliament contained several Ruthe-

---

[2] Stanisław Pijaj, "Posłowie ruscy w parlamencie wiedeńskim w latach 1848–1879," in *Ukraińskie tradycje parlamentarne. XIX–XXI wiek*, ed. Jarosław Moklak (Cracow, 2006), pp. 99–102.

[3] Na podstawie: Buszko, *Polacy w parlamencie*, pp. 345–440.

nians eager to cooperate with Poles, as well as Ruthenians who considered themselves to be Polish (such as Mikołaj Zyblikiewicz and Teodor Szemelowski of Sambir). Ruthenians of Polish nationality also strengthened the recently founded Polish Circle (25 delegates), the chair of which was held by Kazimierz Grocholski, Florian Ziemiałkowski, and then Mikołaj Zyblikiewicz from the 1870s.[4] The second term (1867–70) saw the selection of only three Ruthenian delegates, but four *gente Rutheni, natione Poloni*: Father Tomasz Barewicz, Tomasz Polański, Zygmunt Sawczyński, and Mikołaj Zyblikiewicz, later joined by a fifth, Euzebiusz Czerkawski. Ruthenians of Polish nationality were also supported by adherents of this orientation, including Kazimierz Grocholski, Florian Ziemiałkowski, Ludomir Cieński, Włodzimierz Baworowski, and Stanisław Polanowski.[5] Two other Ruthenians were later invited to join the Polish Circle: the government clerk Ivan Chachkovsky [Jan Czaczkowski] and the peasant Vasyl Makovych [Wasyl Makowycz].[6] As Stanisław Pijaj wrote:

> (…) the concentration within the Polish Circle of the majority of the Ruthenian delegates allowed one to claim that the club had a general Galician profile and that Ruthenian representatives could indeed be found there.[7]

The *gente Rutheni, natione Poloni* deputies, considering themselves to be the genuine representatives of Rus', were tasked with discrediting their political opponents. This took the form of attacks on the St. Georgians, who increasingly presented Russophile attitudes. For example, at the session of the Polish Circle of 10 July 1867 a resolution was passed to grant the editor of the daily *Die Debatte* [The Debate] information needed to write an article about Iakiv Holovatsky, which would alert the government of the "need to remove this dangerous man."[8] Florian Ziemiałkowski's public announcement two months later at the Polish Circle sitting of 22 September 1867 suggested that steps had been made towards this initiative.[9] A press discussion on the subject was also conducted at the forum of the Imperial Council. Stanisław Pijaj has recalled, among other things, Zygmunt Sawczyński's and Tomasz

---

[4] Pijaj, "Posłowie ruscy," pp. 110–12.
[5] Stanisław Pijaj, *Między polskim patriotyzmem a habsburskim lojalizmem. Polacy wobec przemian ustrojowych monarchii habsburskiej (1866–1871)* (Cracow, 2003), p. 151.
[6] Pijaj, "Posłowie ruscy," p. 115.
[7] Ibid., p. 116.
[8] *Protokoły Koła Polskiego w wiedeńskiej Radzie Państwa (lata 1867–1868)*, eds. and introd. Zbigniew Fras and Stanisław Pijaj (Cracow, 2001), p. 77.
[9] Ibid., p. 81.

Barewicz's dispute with Father Ivan Hushalevych concerning the representation of the Ruthenian people.[10] This is the best proof of the willingness among *gente Rutheni, natione Poloni* politicians sitting in the Viennese parliament to assume the leadership of Ruthenians in Galicia. The struggle with the St. Georgians conducted in the salons of Vienna and Lviv did not go unnoticed in Polish circles. Kazimierz Chłędowski recalled the activity of one of the Ruthenians of Polish nationality:

> He [Zygmunt Sawczyński – A.Ś.] gave several most excellent speeches at the Viennese Imperial Council, often engaging in blows with the St. George party and expertly refuting the accusations and arguments of Fathers Lytvynovych and Pavlykiv.[11]

The influence of the St. Georgians during the first term of the Imperial Council remained steady throughout the subsequent two terms (1870–71 and 1871–73). Only one of the ethnic Ruthenians sitting on the benches of the Viennese parliament elected not to join the Polish Circle. From 1870 onwards, a tendency was visible in the Polish political camp to support within Ruthenian circles Ruthenian national populists against the Russophiles, resulting in the election of Iuliian Lavrivsky, an advocate of compromise, to the Imperial Council. Lavrivsky, connected in his youth to the Ruthenian Sobor, guaranteed that he would steer Ruthenians away from Moscow and towards the Poles; he himself could be labelled a Polonophile, rather than a Ruthenian of Polish nationality.[12] Following Lavrivsky's death, Stepan Kachala, a national populist supported by the Poles, took over the appointment of this position in the subsequent elections until the fifth term (1873–79). His election to the Imperial Council as the delegate for the second curial election district Tarnów–Bochnia was made possible by Jerzy Czartoryski. His task was not an easy one, for in cooperating with the Poles he found himself in the federalist camp that sought a federation within the monarchy, while his compatriots, the St. Georgians, supported the German centralists.[13] The argument over the character of the monarchy, which had raged for several decades in the Habsburg state, would also affect Polish-Ruthenian relations in Galicia. Various camps interpreted the monarchy as either a federation that could grant autonomy to individual lands or as a centralist state managed by the bureaucratic

---

[10] Pijaj, "Posłowie ruscy," p. 116, footnote 113.

[11] Kazimierz Chłędowski, *Pamiętniki*, vol. 1: *Galicja (1843–1880)*, ed. Antoni Knot (Cracow, 1957), p. 222.

[12] See more: Jerzy Zdrada, "Ławrowski Julian," in *PSB*, vol. 18 (Wrocław–Warsaw–Cracow–Gdańsk, 1973), pp. 282–83.

[13] Pijaj, "Posłowie ruscy," pp. 117–21.

apparatus in Vienna. The Ruthenians, regarding Vienna as their protector, supported the centralist solutions; the Poles, aspiring towards provincial autonomy that would see them dominate politically, economically, and culturally, favoured federalist resolutions. In the face of these conflicting views, Polish politicians in Vienna sought to establish a joint front with the Ruthenians in the Imperial Council.

When discussions were being held in 1874 regarding the title and regulations of the circle of Galician deputies, a proposal was put forth that suggested naming this body the Polish-Ruthenian Circle. Such a name was meant to create the impression that the Circle did indeed represent the whole of Galicia. The inventor and main advocate of this title was Julian Czerkawski, who openly admitted his Ruthenian provenance. He was not afraid of taking the parliamentary oath in Ruthenian, an action that was criticized in the Polish press.[14] Stanisław Pijaj considers him to be the most distinctive member of the *gente Rutheni, natione Poloni* to belong to the Polish Circle.[15] This affiliation was demonstrated even in Czerkawski's victory in the by-election to the Imperial Council (in place of Florian Ziemiałkowski, who had resigned his seat), which he tellingly attributed to the support of the *Gazeta Narodowa* newspaper and its editor-in-chief and fellow Ruthenian of Polish nationality, Jan Dobrzański.[16] Julian Czerkawski was courageous enough to stand against the St. Georgians on the matter of the election of the deputy Pavlykiv, whom he accused of Russophilism. He expressed his fears and those of his circles in relation to the Russophile movement, underlining that he himself was "also a Ruthenian on the side of my great-grandfather's grandfather."[17] The Russophile threat was linked to support for Austrian centralism, and consequently these were considered by Poles as "two nightmares" in one, and this coming from a "brotherly" people. It then comes as no surprise that Czerkawski and the aforementioned Kachala stood against both of these tendencies. Nevertheless, Czerkawski's petition to change the name of the circle to reflect these dimensions would never fully materialize.

Aside from Kachala, another man in the Imperial Council allied himself with the Poles, though the nature of his identity raises many questions. Baptized in the Uniate rite, Volodyslav Fedorovych [Władysław

---

[14] Ibid., pp. 122–23.

[15] Stanisław Pijaj, *Opozycja w wiedeńskiej Radzie Państwa w latach siedemdziesiątych XIX w. (skład – organizacja – funkcjonowanie)* (Cracow, 2011), p. 154.

[16] Stanisław Pijaj, "Lwowskie wybory parlamentarne w 1873 roku," *Visnyk Lvivs'koho universytetu. Seriia istorychna* special issue: *Lviv. Misto, suspil'stvo, kul'tura*, vol. 8, part 1: *Vlada i suspil'stvo*, eds. Olena Arkusha and Marian Mudryi (2012), pp. 113–14.

[17] *Gazeta Narodowa* no. 50 (3 Mar. 1874), p. 1; Pijaj, "Posłowie ruscy," p. 123.

Fedorowicz] was a highly educated and propertied gentry man. Initially he had wished to fight in the January Uprising, but his father forbade him. After travelling extensively, he later took up the cause of Liberalism. Deferring to family tradition, he started to refer to himself as a Ruthenian. However, wanting to work within the political current of compromise, he joined forces with Iuliian Lavrivsky. For four years (1873–77) he was even the chairman of *Prosvita*, though he chose to give up the post. In 1879 he was elected to the Imperial Council in Vienna, where he entered the Polish Circle. He was considered by the Poles in the Circle to be a Ruthenian, while Ruthenians at home regarded him as a Pole because of his participation in the Polish political camp.[18] Volodyslav Fedorovych's membership in the Polish Circle in Vienna was not considered unusual by the Poles. The essence of action for the Polish faction at the Council was to work in a spirit of agreement with the "Polish historical-political national conception," while the Circle itself would function as "a supra-ethnic structure," in the words of the scholar Harald Binder.[19] The presence of such a figure in the Polish Circle, however, was in no way used to further the idea of Polish-Ruthenian understanding. It is reasonable to suggest that he was perhaps the last member of the Imperial Council who, in attempting to join the Polish and Ruthenian cultures, could actually have played a role in bringing Ruthenians closer to Polishness. The small group of *gente Rutheni, natione Poloni* who sat on the benches of the Imperial Council from the 1880s onward would become, as Stanisław Pijaj writes, "increasingly anachronistic with the passage of time, while the majority of its membership referred to themselves as Poles."[20] Meanwhile, from the seventh term (1885) the Ruthenian delegates in the House of Lords completely distanced themselves from Polish political concepts, dividing themselves into Russophiles, Ukrainophiles, and "pro-government." The fact that not a single Ruthenian entered the Polish Circle is a testament to this aversion. Although the pro-Polish Ruthenian conservative (but not Russophile) politician Oleksander Barvinsky attempted to strike an agreement between the two camps in 1895,[21] his actions had little in common with attitudes of a *gente Rutheni, natione Poloni* nature.

---

[18] Stefan Kieniewicz, "Fedorowicz Władysław Walenty," in *PSB*, vol. 6 (Cracow, 1948), p. 390.

[19] Harald Binder, "Ukraińskie przedstawicielstwo w austriackiej Izbie Posłów, 1879–1918," in *Ukraińskie tradycje*, p. 131.

[20] Pijaj, "Posłowie ruscy," p. 126.

[21] Binder, "Ukraińskie przedstawicielstwo," pp. 133, 160–61.

Ruthenians of Polish Nationality in the Galician Diet

A similar process was observed in the case of Galician parliamentarianism. The establishment of the Galician Diet with its headquarters in Lviv had a significant effect on the development of a national consciousness among Ruthenians, enabling this group to present its political demands, and subsequently to fight for their realization. It would be difficult to conceive of better conditions for the creation of a nation. Ruthenians finally had the ability to publicly speak out about their own affairs, to present themselves as a nation, and to influence the conditions in which they had come to live. The initial organization into delegate groupings, and subsequently parties, was clear proof that the Ruthenian nation existed and was trying to realize its political demands. This situation was to become especially problematic for Ruthenians of Polish nationality, who were torn between their Ruthenian roots and Polish national interests. The Polish-Ruthenian political conflicts simply did not allow anyone to remain "on the fence," as had been possible prior to the establishment of the Diet. John-Paul Himka believes that towards the end of the 1860s the *gente Rutheni, natione Poloni* were already forced to make a choice.[22] For the most part, the *gente Rutheni, natione Poloni* politicians chose to take the Polish side. The Polish deputies to the Galician Diet needed Ruthenians of Polish nationality to act not only as experts on Ruthenian matters and language, but also to serve as proof that Ruthenians could be Poles. It is therefore all the more important to examine their views during the political disagreements in the Diet.

On 26 February 1861 the National Statute for Galicia was proclaimed, in which the jurisdiction for the Galician Diet was set out. It was to consist of 141 deputies elected in four curiae: from the great estates (44); the chambers of commerce (3); the large towns (23; from 1896 – 26, while from 1900 – 31); as well as from communities of lesser property (74). In order to become a deputy from the first curia it was enough to gain fifty votes, while the fourth demanded an entire eight thousand. In addition, seats in the Galician Diet were taken by *virilists*—the bishops of the three denominations and the rectors of both (Cracow and Lviv) universities.[23]

For the duration of each of the ten parliamentary terms of the Galician Diet, which lasted up until the outbreak of the First World War,

---

[22] John-Paul Himka, "The Greek Catholic Church and nation-building in Galicia, 1772–1918," *Harvard Ukrainian Studies* 8, no. 3–4 (1984), p. 437.
[23] Stanisław Grodziski, *Sejm Krajowy Galicyjski 1861–1914, T. 1–2*, introd. Marian Małecki (Cracow, 2018), pp. 68–74.

their episcopal status secured the positions in the Diet of the Greek Catholic archbishop of Lviv, the bishop of Przemyśl, the Greek Catholic administrator for the Lviv diocese (from 1870–76), and the Greek Catholic bishop of Stanyslaviv from 1885 onwards. From time to time, seats were also held by those Ruthenians who served as the rectors of Lviv University, as was the case for Hryhorii Iakhymovych (1861), Iakiv Holovatsky (1864), and the *gente Ruthenus, natione Polonus* Euzebiusz Czerkawski (1866, 1876, 1877, and 1887). Another Ruthenian of Polish nationality, Emilian Czyrniański, also held a seat as rector of the Jagiellonian University. Ruthenian deputies of a national populist or Russophile orientation were, on the whole, selected from the fourth curia and were either Ruthenian peasants or Uniate priests; far less frequently were they secular members of the intelligentsia, as this gap in the social hierarchy of the Ruthenian population was filled by *gente Rutheni, natione Poloni*. They were elected during each term of the Galician Diet.[24] The majority of Ruthenian deputies of Polish nationality were neither peasants nor clergymen, but representatives of the intelligentsia, often academics or learned people.

Among the most famous deputies of this orientation was Mikołaj Zyblikiewicz (first to fourth terms and a part of the fifth until his death, 1861–87), who was speaker of the Diet during the years 1881–86. Other well-known Ruthenians of Polish nationality include Euzebiusz Czerkawski (second to fifth terms, 1867–89), Dymitr Koczyndyk (part of the second term, 1868–69), Teofil Merunowicz (part of the fourth term as well as the fifth to ninth terms, 1881–1913), Father Tomasz Polański (second term, 1867–69), Michał Popiel (second to fourth terms, 1867–82), Zygmunt Sawczyński (part of the first term as well as the second to fourth terms, 1865–82), Konstanty Srokowski (tenth term, 1913–14), as well as the Szemelowski brothers, Julian (third term, 1870–76) and Teodor (first term, 1861–67). It is also important to mention Father Tomasz Barewicz (second term, 1867–69), who was selected for the Diet from the Stanyslaviv electoral district in 1867. The latter gave a fiery speech on February 2 of the same year at a pre-election sitting, in which he stated:

> Being a Ruthenian in origin and by denomination, knowing exactly what constitutes the main and specific feature of a Ruthenian, born in Rus' and raised there, and with that being acquainted with Muscovite values, I can boldly state that a Ruthenian differs even more from a Muscovite than from a Czech or a Serb (…).

---

[24] Cf.: Ibid., vol. 2: *Źródła* (Warsaw, 1993), pp. 142–224.

And further:

> If Poles have maintained friendly relations with Ruthenians for so many centuries, then now their approach cannot be any different. Therefore, with the common good in mind, in no other way than hand in hand does it follow for us Ruthenians to behave in relation to the Polish nation; for only in this way can we obtain our goal, the goal set out for us by Divine Providence.[25]

Chłędowski wrote of Barewicz that:

> (…) he was almost as much a Ruthenian as Sawczyński, who considered both nations to have been in brotherly relations for centuries and agreed with Poles on all national matters and did not court the St. Georgians. Such Ruthenians were increasingly fewer in number.[26]

Barewicz was, however, strongly criticized for his political activities and views by differently thinking Ruthenians. Father Mykhailo Zubrytsky recalled in his autobiography that Barewicz, as the director of the gymnasium in Drohobych, admonished him for speaking in Ruthenian. He noted: "We Ruthenians did not like him for the fact that he served the Poles."[27]

The activities of the *gente Rutheni, natione Poloni* on the parliamentary benches, which scholars such as Marian Mudry and Jarosław Moklak have addressed, will be briefly discussed at a later point. We will first examine those moments in which the presence of Ruthenians of Polish nationality was the most noticeable. The greatest number of *gente Rutheni, natione Poloni* deputies sat in the Diet during the first to fifth terms, during the years 1861 to 1889. They exerted a genuine influence in the 1860s, 1870s, and 1880s, particularly because Mikołaj Zyblikiewicz held the position of speaker at certain sessions of the fourth and fifth parliamentary election terms. Only in 1889 did the power of the *gente Rutheni, natione Poloni* begin to

38. *Mikołaj Zyblikiewicz*

---

[25] A special supplement to *Gazeta Narodowa* no. 31 (7 Feb. 1867), pp. 1–2.

[26] Chłędowski, *Pamiętniki*, vol. 1, p. 285.

[27] Mykhailo Zubryts'kyi, „Avtobiografia," in Mykhailo Zubryts'kyi, *Zibrani tvory i materialy u tr'okh tomakh*, eds. Frank E. Sysyn et al., vol. 2: *Materialy do biohrafii*, ed. Vasyl Sokil (Lviv, 2016), p. 66.

decline. During this year, only a single *gente Ruthenus, natione Polonus,* Teofil Merunowicz, won a parliamentary seat. He was the longest serving Ruthenian of Polish nationality in the Galician Diet, having been elected six times from 1881 to 1913, to the end of the ninth term. After Merunowicz, only Konstanty Srokowski was elected to the Diet during the tenth term (1913–14), which was interrupted by the First World War. With the exception of Merunowicz, Michał Popiel, and Mikołaj Zyblikiewicz, who were all elected from the fourth curia, *gente Rutheni, natione Poloni* were usually able to take up seats on the basis of selection from the third curia or even the first. They were thus elected by urban populations and large landowners, chiefly from Lviv and Ternopil, but also from Chortkiv, Drohobych, Rzeszów, Przemyśl, Sambir, Stanyslaviv, and Stryi.

It should be noted that these aforementioned individuals were not alone in declaring their Ruthenian provenance. The designation *gente Rutheni, natione Poloni* was also adopted by Poles, namely Eastern Galician landowners. Some had boyar ancestors in their distant past, though by the nineteenth century these were completely Polonized and Latinized families. Nevertheless, in inhabiting Ruthenian territories they considered themselves to be Ruthenians, or at least believed it politically prudent to be so. They believed that this declaration of being Ruthenian legitimized their right to rule the eastern part of the land. Individuals who demonstrated this affiliation include: Leszek Dunin-Borkowski (first term and third term, and elected for the second term but refused the mandate); Aleksander Dzieduszycki (first term, up to 1865); Antoni Golejewski (deputy during the first to sixth parliamentary terms, during which he died); Kazimierz Grocholski (deputy during the first to fifth terms, deceased in 1888); and finally Adam Sapieha (a deputy for the first term, though he gave up his mandate in 1863 and then again for the second, third [until 1873], and fifth term); as well as his father, Leon Sapieha, who was the speaker for the Galician Diet for the years 1861–75 (a deputy for the first, second, third, and fifth terms). The nature of their "ostentatious Ruthenianness" is demonstrated by the famous parliamentary speech of Kazimierz Grocholski on 16 April 1866, when debate raged over the possible administrative division of Galicia into two parts.[28] When Father Iosyf Lozynsky claimed that Poles and Ruthenians were divided by hate, Grocholski replied:

> As a representative of this part of the country [i.e., Eastern Galicia – A.Ś.], as a Ruthenian — and I am proud of the fact that I am a Ruthenian — I will say that this is a falsehood and an untruth.

---

[28] Marian Mudry wrote more about Grocholski's attitude to the project, "Dylematy narodowościowe w Sejmie Krajowym galicyjskim (na przykładzie posłów formacji *gente Rutheni natione Poloni*)," in *Ukraińskie tradycje,* p. 80.

I feel in my heart and in my bosom that hate is most impossible, for one cannot hate the one who is hateful himself; it is true, Gentlemen, I am *gente Ruthenus, natione Polonus*, which you somewhat ironically voice here, but I do not consider you all only as *gente Ruthenos, natione Polonos!*

You say, Gentlemen, that you are representatives of the Ruthenian nation; but I am sorry, for you are representatives of the land of the kingdom of Galicia and Lodomeria, and not of the Ruthenian nation. You were chosen not only by those who adhere to the Greek Catholic Church, by also by adherents of the Latin Church, as you were selected by Israelites; you are representatives of the country and not of a given nationality.[29]

This effectively conveys the aspirations of the Eastern Galician land-owners to take the leading role in running the Ruthenian part of Galicia, including rule over the Ruthenian population. On the one hand, such an approach results from the tradition of authority historically exercised by a privileged social estate in Poland, allowing landowners to represent the lands on which they lived, while on the other hand it stems from an unwillingness to recognize the separateness of a Ruthenian nation. Grocholski not only considered himself to be a Ruthenian as a result of his place of residence, but he also considered Ruthenian deputies of a national populist orientation to be Poles. He considered himself and those in Galicia who were similar to him to be part of a single Polish nation, composed of various ethnic groupings.

Grocholski's statement was obviously a reckless attempt to prove to the body of Ruthenian delegates that they were of Polish nationality, but it nevertheless raises the question whether there was ever truly an opportunity to spur an examination of national consciousness among Ruthenian parliamentary representatives. In his article on the activities of *gente Rutheni, natione Poloni* delegates during the first years of the Galician Diet, Marian Mudry asks whether the number of deputies of this orientation could have increased due to the inclusion of Ruthenian deputies of other political leanings. He suggested that one such *gente Ruthenus, natione Polonus* might have been Iuliian Lavrivsky, who already during the course of the Revolutions of 1848 had deserted the Supreme Ruthenian Council for the Ruthenian Sobor. He justified this choice by the later conciliatory and pro-Polish orientation of his political views, particularly in 1869, when he initiated a Polish-Ruthenian compromise.[30] Nevertheless, Lavrivsky never fully moved over to the

---

[29] *Stenograficzne sprawozdania z trzeciej sesyi Sejmu Krajowego Królestwa Galicyi i Lodomeryi wraz z Wielkiem Księstwem Krakowskiem w roku 1865–1866*, vol. 2: *Posiedzenie 41–80*, p. 1618.

[30] The Sapieha–Lavrivsky agreement of 1869 guaranteed, as the price for Ruthenians giving up on the notion of a division of Galicia, that Ruthenian would obtain the status of

Polish camp. One individual who did do so was the second term deputy Father Tomasz Polański (not to be mistaken with the Przemyśl Greek Catholic bishop Toma Poliansky), who considered both nations to be divided only by a language dispute, and spoke out for the "union of Poland with Rus'."[31] There is little to report concerning his activities in the Galician Diet, though a mere month after the election of 1867 he was to become a delegate to the Imperial Council in Vienna (second term of the Council, 1869–70).[32]

The peasants afforded certain opportunities for the shaping of a Polish national consciousness, although the national question had been almost completely alien to them during the course of parliamentary canvassing. This state of affairs was eloquently captured by Prince Leon Sapieha, the first speaker of the Galician Diet, in his memoirs:

> National questions have absolutely no significance among the peasantry. They do not comprehend words such as "Pole" and "Ruthenian," as these only designate a difference in rite: A Pole goes to a Roman Catholic church, while a Ruthenian to the Greek Catholic temple. They also do not grasp the animosity of one denomination towards the other. For most of the feast days a Pole will attend a Ruthenian service as willingly as a Ruthenian will go to a Roman Catholic church.[33]

The peasants mainly kept the company of priests at the Diet. This interaction was culturally and religiously conditioned, as the priest was the main authority in rural society. Furthermore, the peasants had no reason not to believe the priests in the Diet, particularly as they themselves had little knowledge on many of the matters discussed during the subsequent parliamentary sessions.[34] Those who gained the peasant

---

the second national language, bilingual instruction would take place in elementary schools, a Ruthenian secondary school was to be opened in Lviv, Ruthenian classes would be founded in secondary schools in Berezhany, Przemyśl, Sambir, Stanyslaviv, and Ternopil, minutes and sittings at the Galician Diet would be conducted in Ruthenian, while Ruthenian associations and societies would receive grants to support their activities. Cf. Marian Mudryi, "Sproby ukraïns'ko-pol's'koho porozuminnia v Halychyni (60-70-i roky XIX st.)," *Ukraïna. Kul'turna spadshchyna, natsional'na svidomist', derzhavnist'* vol. 3–4: *Zbirnyk naukovykh prats'* (1997), pp. 87–89; Mudryj, "Dylematy narodowościowe," p. 74; Ivan Monolatii, *Razom, ale, maizhe okremo. Vzaiemodiia etnopolitychnykh aktoriv na zakhidnoukraïns'kykh zemliakh u 1867–1914 rr.* (Ivano-Frankivs'k, 2010), pp. 502–3.

[31] Jerzy Zdrada, "Wybory do galicyjskiego Sejmu Krajowego w 1867 r.," *Rocznik Biblioteki Polskiej Akademii Nauk w Krakowie* 9 (1963), p. 77.

[32] Tomasz Pudłocki, *Iskra światła czy kopcąca pochodnia? Inteligencja w Przemyślu w latach 1867–1939* (Cracow, 2009), pp. 111–12.

[33] Leon Sapieha, *Wspomnienia (z lat od 1803 do 1863 r.)*, introd. Stanisław Tarnowski, ed., introd., and fragments of a correspondence Bronisław Pawłowski (Lviv–Warsaw–Poznań, [1914]), p. 256.

[34] Zdrada, "Wybory do galicyjskiego Sejmu," pp. 80–81.

votes were primarily the Ruthenian intelligentsia, particularly priests, or the Polish deputies. Some of the latter were indeed able to gain the support of the Ruthenian peasantry. Kazimierz Chłędowski wrote that Antoni Golejewski, a former member of the Ruthenian Sobor and one of the leaders of the utilitarian camp (so-called "Mamelukes", loyal to Austria and opponent to the far-reaching autonomy of the province) in the second half of the 19th century, was:

> (…) a man none too educated but possessing much common sense and a knowledge of the country's needs; courageous, voicing his opinion without reservation, without recourse to anyone else, and having huge influence on those peasant deputies from Rus' who had not entirely sold out to the St. Georgian clique. Anyone who did not succumb to his persuasions would have had to have been a Ruthenian with an extremely "black palate."[35]

A similar role was played by Stanisław Polanowski (second to seventh terms, 1867–98), who as the owner of property at Huta in the Sokal district was most influential among peasants and priests in Rus'. Chłędowski recalled that the outcome of elections in the Zhovkva, Belz, and Kamianka Strumylova [Kamianka-Buzka] districts could chiefly be attributed to him.[36] It is worth considering what these Polish lords ruling over Ruthenian peasants stood to gain. The question of language had become somewhat paradoxical; as Leon Sapieha's account demonstrates, often Ruthenian peasant deputies would complain that "when the masters speak in Polish we understand, but when our priests speak we understand nothing."[37] The language of the Ruthenian elites, influenced by the Russophile attitude of the Uniate Church and the desire to imitate the Russian language, had in time distanced itself from the language of ordinary Ruthenian people. This tendency in the Uniate Church would only be broken later by Archbishop Sylvestr Sembratovych. The language question soon became a political matter differentiating Ruthenian and Polish deputies (as well as *gente Rutheni, natione Poloni*) in the Galician Diet.

The Language Problem in the Galician Diet

Even before the January Uprising, the problem of using the Ruthenian language had arisen during the very first sitting of the Galician Diet

---

[35] Chłędowski, *Pamiętniki*, vol. 1, p. 284.
[36] Ibid.
[37] Sapieha, *Wspomnienia*, p. 256.

in 1861, on April 15[38]. The Ruthenian deputy Father Hryhorii Hynylevych had proposed that only finance officers and secretaries who were
fluent in both languages be selected. There was a desire on the Polish
side to create divisions in appeals of this sort. Father Sofron Vytvytsky
proclaimed:

> A Ruthenian loves his fatherland, let yourselves be aware of this, I re-
> peat heartily... (applause). (...) Let us do and speak openly (applause),
> we do not want a split. Some of you gentlemen say that a Ruthenian is
> a simpleton (hissing), that a Ruthenian is an enemy of Poland (every-
> one shouts out "no"). I apologize, for I may not have expressed myself
> appropriately—I am no diplomat.
>
> We worry about our plight just as Poles do, but with that difference
> that you've only had to worry for a hundred years while we have for
> five hundred, so be sure that the history of your heroes is noted down
> in all of our memories. What pains you pains us also—so only the equal
> rights of the people who work for us, worked and will work (applause),
> need to be supported—but stratagem and tricks ... (one cannot hear for
> the applause) let unity command us... (applause).
>
> A Ruthenian is a good man, he genuinely loves his homeland—what
> has happened as a result of misunderstandings, it follows to judge those
> who sow disagreements, but for the lack of education... (applause)
>
> My heart is pained, I have grown up among the people (applause)...
> I proclaim unity and reconciliation and I have been filled with hope that
> we shall welcome and greet it sincerely.
>
> This reconciliation is a duty to be fulfilled before the Lord and we are
> obliged by our offspring to do so (raucous applause).[39]

This discussion over language quickly turned into a dispute of a national populist character. Father Antin Mohylnytsky demanded that
the Polish deputies demonstrate that they were brothers and genuine
friends of the Ruthenians, and that the love, unity, and freedom proclaimed in 1848 were not merely words but also deeds.[40] Bishop Spyrydon Lytvynovych put an end to the disagreement, asking that the ceremonial moment not be ruined, and then offering thanks to God and the
emperor.[41] During the reading of Golejewski's petition to the throne,
a dispute once again erupted when Antin Petrushevych pointed out
that the petition spoke of a single nation and not of two: Polish and Ru-

---

[38] See more: Kazimierz Karolczak, "Sprawy narodowościowe w Galicyjskim Sejmie Krajowym w latach 1861–1873", in *Galicyjskie dylematy. Zbiór rozpraw*, eds. Kazimierz Karolczak and Henryk Żaliński (Cracow, 1994), p. 32.

[39] *Sprawozdania stenograficzne z posiedzeń Sejmu Krajowego galicyjskiego we Lwowie odbytych
od dnia 15. do 26. kwietnia 1861 r.*, pp. 12–13.

[40] Ibid., p. 13.

[41] Ibid., p. 14.

thenian. Finally, Father Vytvytsky proposed that the petition be composed both in Polish and in Ruthenian.[42]

During the subsequent sitting on April 16, another problem arose concerning the compilation of parallel minutes in both Polish and Ruthenian.[43] It was postulated also that everything that Diet's speaker Leon Sapieha would say in Polish, the vice-speaker bishop Lytvynovych would repeat in Ruthenian, but there was no agreement from the Polish side for it. Amidst the fervour of debate it was suggested that the Ruthenian deputies "understand Ruthenian, but not Polish."[44] At the time, the entire chamber agreed to such a solution.[45] However, the subject was again broached at the next sitting on April 19. The Ruthenian deputies amicably demanded that the minutes be read out in Ruthenian as well. At the time none of the *gente Rutheni, natione Poloni* reacted, but the Eastern Galician landlords expressed their opinion most decisively. The deputy Leszek Dunin-Borkowski protested against the proposal, but what was especially important in his appearance at the Diet was his refusal to acknowledge Ruthenian as a separate language. He emphasized: "I said it is a dialect and that is my internal conviction."[46] Support came from Prince Adam Sapieha, who publicly explained the reality of the language situation in Galicia: "I refute that any of these gentlemen do not understand Polish, for I know that those who most heartedly deny their knowledge of the language indeed speak Polish in private.'[47] This time it was not so easy for the Ruthenians, and they were outvoted. The minutes would be henceforth read out in Polish.

These parliamentary discussions are significant in that they illustrate the climate of Polish-Ruthenian relations on the eve of parliamentarianism in Galicia. Palpably problematic was the lack of recognition of equality between Poles and Ruthenians as well as the disavowal of Ruthenian national identity as something separate from Polish nationality. Ruthenians demanded equal treatment of their language even though they themselves knew Polish well. The Poles' fervent denial of the very existence of Ruthenian as a language (notoriously referring to it as a "dialect") was echoed in their rejection of the existence of the Ruthenian nation.

The next dispute occurred when the Galician Diet had resumed its work following the January Uprising. In the course of the third session

---

[42] Ibid., pp. 16–17.

[43] Ibid., pp. 24–25.

[44] Ibid., p. 26.

[45] Ibid., p. 28.

[46] Ibid., p. 46.

[47] Ibid., p. 47. About this sitting see also: Mudryj, "Dylematy narodowościowe," p. 70.

of the first parliamentary term, at the fifth sitting on 30 November 1865, Ruthenian deputies complained that Polish had become the language of administration, even though the land was Galician and not merely Polish. Iosyf Lozynsky saw the division of the land into an eastern Ruthenian half and western Polish half as a solution to the discord.[48] This naturally engendered opposition on the part of Polish deputies, whose words were only heeded by those Ruthenians of Polish nationality. The deputy Leszek Dunin-Borkowski tried to argue in an unusually long speech that there was in fact but a single nation, one composed of various parts, including a Ruthenian element. The same could be said in regard to language, as Polish was the academic language and for this reason fulfilled the function of being the national language. Leszek Dunin-Borkowski in this manner chose to deny the Ruthenian language those rights enjoyed by Polish.[49] This decision has been characterized by Marian Mudry as "censoring Ukrainian-Polish relations," a move that would elicit a massive reaction in Galician society.[50] The results of this speech were twofold: Dunin-Borkowski closed the ranks of those non-pro-Polish Ruthenians against himself and the parliament's Polish deputies, while the Polish position hardened in relation to Ruthenians. Given these conditions, the *gente Rutheni, natione Poloni* were forced to take sides, and often they would take the Polish position.

As the situation developed over the next few years, the Poles did not move closer to *gente Rutheni, natione Poloni* as a result of the latter's insight into Ruthenian matters. Ruthenians of Polish nationality increasingly adopted the views of Polish deputies, gradually denying their own roots or the will to fight for their cultivation. During the course of the first parliamentary term, an unequivocal national problem arose in Galicia. The resulting dispute divided Polish and Ruthenian members of parliament. The idea of a brotherhood of Poles and Ruthenians, fought for during the uprisings and proclaimed in the conspiratorial political programs and the verses of poems and leaflets, had simply no ground to exist in the face of political practice. In a Galicia of Poles and Ruthenians there was no place for a third option such as that put forth by the representatives of *gente Rutheni, natione Poloni*. Nevertheless, their struggle during the subsequent years of the Galician Diet will constitute the focus of this chapter.

Let us turn first to the sitting of 20 December 1865, when the Ruthenian deputy Antin Petrushevych introduced a motion for the recogni-

---

[48] *Stenograficzne sprawozdania z trzeciej sesyi Sejmu Krajowego Królestwa Galicyi i Lodomeryi wraz z Wielkim Księstwem krakowskiem w roku 1865–1866*, vol. 1: *Posiedzenie 1–40*, pp. 57–59.
[49] Ibid., pp. 59–64.
[50] Mudryj, "Dylematy narodowościowe," pp. 71–72.

tion of Ruthenian as an official language for Galician Diet sessions.[51] The reading of the motion was planned for 16 January 1866. As Jarosław Moklak has noted, Petrushevych cleverly presented the fate of the Ruthenian language, which was the exclusive language of Rus' up until the times of Casimir the Great, and had remained, despite the Latinization of the land, an administrative language until the close of the seventeenth century. He stated that thanks to the actions of Austria, Ruthenian had functioned as the language of instruction at Lviv University from 1787 to 1808; that during the revolutions of 1848 it was deemed to be the equal of Polish; and that the imperial certificate establishing the Galician Diet was written in Polish and Ruthenian, proving the emperor's willingness to recognize the Ruthenian language as an official language for parliamentary use. Petrushevych's motion was particularly opposed by Leszek Dunin-Borkowski, the representative of a Polonized landed family from Red Rus' who considered himself to be a Ruthenian. On January 19 this landowner introduced his own motion to recognize Polish as "the language of the Diet as a whole." He argued that both languages had come from the same root and had mutually influenced each other. He supported this point by enumerating Ruthenian families who had adopted Polish as their own language. Mikołaj Zyblikiewicz also stood against the publication of resolutions in Ruthenian, noting that if the basis of the sessions was a Polish report then an act announced in Ruthenian could at best be a translation.[52] The rest of Zyblikiewicz's conversation with one of the Ruthenian deputies is documented. When this deputy accused him of being Ruthenian but not speaking Ruthenian, Zyblikiewicz replied:

> (…) yes, I am a Ruthenian or descended from Ruthenians, so what is it you want from me? To stop chatting to you in Polish, for me to speak like [Mykola] Kovbasiuk or like… [Mykhailo] Kuzemsky in Ruthenian? I'm *gente Ruthenus, natione Polonus.*[53]

Nevertheless, as Irena Homola noted, Zyblikiewicz ultimately voted like the other Ruthenians.[54] This discourse demonstrates the general

---

[51] *Stenograficzne sprawozdania galicyjskiego Sejmu krajowego z roku 1865. 14. posiedzenie 3ciej sesyi Sejmu galicyjskiego dnia 20. grudnia 1865*, p. 188. See also Karolczak, "Sprawy narodowościowe," pp. 33–34

[52] Jarosław Moklak, "Spór polsko-ukraiński o język obrad sejmu galicyjskiego (1865–1866). Wnioski Antona Petruszewycza i Aleksandra Borkowskiego. Przyczynek do kształtowania się nacjonalizmów w Galicji Wschodniej," *Biuletyn Ukrainoznawczy* 9 (2003), pp. 42–47.

[53] [Ignacy Baranowski], "Pamiętniki Ignacego Baranowskiego (1840–1862)," ed. Adam Wrzosek (Poznań 1923), p. 299.

[54] Irena Homola-Dzikowska, *Mikołaj Zyblikiewicz (1823–1887)* (Wrocław–Warsaw–Cracow, 1964), p. 35.

tendency for Ruthenians of Polish nationality not to allow for a Ruthenianization of political life.

The marginalizing attitude of Poles towards Ruthenians was manifest in even the most trivial of matters. This attitude was also embodied to an extent by individual Ruthenians of Polish nationality, who most often stood on the Polish side, opposing Ruthenian demands and in doing so refuting their own past, often in an absurd manner. One such instance came in response to the Ruthenian deputy Mykhailo Kurylovych's introduction of a motion on 30 December 1865 that proposed financial support for the secondary school in Buchach, at the time privately funded by Mikołaj Potocki. This Basilian institution, in operation since 1754, was the only secondary school from 1848 onwards in which Ruthenian was the language of instruction. The Polish deputies, among them the *gente Ruthenus, natione Polonus* Zygmunt Sawczyński, a graduate of this very school and subsequently a teacher at it, spoke against state support for the school.[55]

Another situation unfolded during the sitting of 22 March 1866, when Father Iakiv Shvedsytsky proposed the introduction of Ruthenian as the language of administration for the city of Lviv. Father Iosyf Lozynsky even went as far as to call Lviv a Ruthenian town and the heart of Rus' under the threat of Polonization. Another deputy questioned Polish rights to Lviv, claiming that they had expired along with the first partition of Poland.[56] On the other side, the *gente Ruthenus, natione Polonus* Teodor Szemelowski stood up in defence of a "Polish Lviv." Speaking "as a Ruthenian, as a deputy for the city and as a former inhabitant of Lviv," he challenged the right of Ruthenian deputies from the rural electoral districts to put forward motions suggesting the introduction of Ruthenian in the city's administrative affairs. He substantiated his decision with a concrete example, citing his acquaintance with the Lviv Ruthenian deputies Michał Dymet [Mykhailo Dymet], Hilarion Szwedzicki [Ilarion Shvedsytsky], Jan Towarnicki [Ivan Tovarnytsky] and Grzegorz Tustanowski [Hryhorii Tustanovsky], who in presenting the statute in no way appealed for the introduction of Ruthenian as the language of administration. He argued:

> How can one impose another language, which Ruthenians themselves have inherited from their fathers and from their great-grandfathers?

---

[55] Jarosław Moklak, *W walce o tożsamość Ukraińców. Zagadnienie języka wykładowego w szkołach ludowych i średnich w pracach galicyjskiego Sejmu Krajowego 1866–1892* (Cracow, 2004), pp. 51–52.

[56] For a broader analysis of the Ruthenian deputies' input, see Mudryj, "Dylematy narodowościowe," p. 73.

They cannot renounce this inheritance on the basis of an appeal by rural representatives, and therefore such an official language for administration cannot be imposed on them.

I state again and again that it is only the Polish language as such that is a national language and that is refined. (…) After all, Ruthenians have been using this language for centuries without any hindrance and I claim that we Ruthenians have a better command of the Polish language, as an educated tongue, than we do of Ruthenian.[57]

The affiliation of Lviv Ruthenians to Polish rather than Ruthenian nationality was addressed by Mikołaj Zyblikiewicz at the session on 12 April 1866, when a discussion developed concerning funds for the Ruska Besida theatre in Lviv.[58] As a member of the budget commission, Zyblikiewicz opposed the funding. He argued that such an initiative was not the desire of the Ruthenian members of the Lviv Municipal Council, as they considered their language to be Polish and therefore "the literary language." After Ruthenian deputies complained that he had supported the restoration work on the Wit Stwosz altar at the Church of St. Mary's in Cracow because it was a Polish monument, Zyblikiewicz became so upset that he emotionally addressed those assembled in the chamber. He emphasized that the altar was not simply a Polish monument, but a valuable work of art. To fund the Ruska Besida theatre, on the other hand, would open up "one more centre for the sowing of discord and hatred." Here he betrayed his ethnic provenance, denouncing the Ruthenian deputies:

My loyalty in this respect—however much you gentlemen may find it amusing—is wholly to Rus'; to those who call themselves the representatives of Rus', I have none at all. Why? Because to this day, they have yet to do anything for the good of Rus', for the good of this land. What have they done instead? They have worked to spread animosity and discord, plunging classes of the population into eternal hatred, and yet they still wish to use the crudest of means to obtain their goals.[59]

Both of these situations show us the specific nature of the social position held by *gente Rutheni, natione Poloni* deputies. They themselves belonged to the intelligentsia, a social stratum reached through an education that privileged the achievements of Polish science and Polish literature; subsequently, they simply did not view Ruthenian culture with

---

[57] *Stenograficzne sprawozdania z trzeciej sesyi Sejmu Krajowego Królestwa Galicyi i Lodomeryi wraz z Wielkiem Księstwem Krakowskiem w roku 1865–1866*, vol. 2: *Posiedzenie 41–80*, p. 1288.
[58] See Mudryj, "Dylematy narodowościowe," pp. 75–76.
[59] *Stenograficzne sprawozdania z trzeciej sesyi Sejmu Krajowego Królestwa Galicyi i Lodomeryi wraz z Wielkiem Księstwem Krakowskiem w roku 1865–1866*, vol. 2, p. 1471.

parity, believing it belonged in the countryside and not in the library. They treated the Ruthenian language in a similar fashion. Those who wished to make a national tongue out of the "the language of peasants" were considered troublemakers, demanding rights for themselves but in effect kindling conflict in a Polish-Ruthenian society in Galicia that had—according to them— lived harmoniously thus far.

Several salient issues divided the *gente Rutheni, natione Poloni* deputies from the remaining Ruthenian deputies. First and foremost, these were individuals who had made a career for themselves via administrative or academic avenues. For such people, it was impossible—not to mention illogical—to return to what they perceived to be a "lower culture," the representatives of which were the Ruthenian peasantry, the clergy, and a scattering of intellectuals. Encased within the ranks of the Galician Polish elite, they were unable to understand or recognize that deputies who spoke Ruthenian during parliamentary sessions could represent the land in the name of the Ruthenian people. They believed that a country could only be ruled by an elite class, be they Polish, Ruthenian, or German; if someone had socially advanced to this group, then they had the right to rule. As the elite in power was Polish, the Ruthenians of Polish nationality did not wish to differentiate between the two nationalities of Galicia. Instead, they believed that as long as the land was undivided, then it should have a single representation. At this point, the status of the Ruthenians as a nation and the status of their language would overlap. During the Revolutions of 1848, Ruthenians of Polish nationality considered themselves to be a Ruthenian nation merged with the Poles. This attitude was already divisive at the time, playing out within the Ruthenian Sobor. Two decades later, however, no representative of *gente Rutheni, natione Poloni* was to speak of the Ruthenian people as even a fledgling nation. The nation was singular and Polish, encompassing Ruthenians. However, this rhetoric was devised not by Ruthenians of Polish nationality, but by the Polish landed gentry. The former would adopt it in moments of conflict with Ruthenian deputies. The language debate followed a similar pattern. For the *gente Rutheni, natione Poloni* in the intelligentsia, Ruthenian was the language of the ordinary people; while such members knew the language, they were unable to use it intellectually or academically, or to converse with other representatives of the elites. Hence Ruthenian was considered a branch of Polish, the broadly understood language of science and literature. The *gente Rutheni, natione Poloni* would spend the subsequent years defending this status quo and refuting the rights of the Ruthenian language. Though Ruthenians of Polish nationality did often emphasize that they wished Ruthenian might develop into a language of science, in time they stopped believing this.

Gente Rutheni, Natione Poloni
Deputy Attitudes in the Period of Political Changes in the Monarchy

A robust representation of *gente Rutheni, natione Poloni* deputies in the Galician Diet during the 1860s coincided with the reconstruction of the Habsburg monarchy. As a result of the defeat in the war with Prussia in 1866, Austria had lost its significance within the German Confederation, with its very future as a multi-national state plunged into doubt. Under such conditions the opportunity for the absolutist government to continue diminished, particularly given the separatist aspirations of Hungary. The reconstruction of the monarchy in the spirit of Austro-Hungarian dualism, discussions over the situation in Galicia, the passing of the December Constitution in 1867, and finally the establishment of autonomous institutions such as the Galicia's Provincial School Board [*Rada Szkolna Krajowa/Kraiova Shkil'na Rada*] within the Austrian area naturally created an opportunity for the removal of politicians of various political leanings and nationalities. This was likewise a very significant period for the political choices of *gente Rutheni, natione Poloni* deputies at the Galician Diet, who took stances on exceptionally important matters, particularly in the context of disputes on national issues between Poles and Ruthenians. In this way, they decided the fate of their national self-designation.

In addition to Russophilism, Ruthenians of Polish nationality saw another dangerous tendency in the Ruthenian deputies: Austrian loyalism, which was by nature contrary to Polish aspirations for autonomy. However, this was a somewhat different brand of loyalism than that which characterized those Polish deputies strengthening the centre or right side of the House. The main difference was that Ruthenian loyalists advocated a central authority strengthened through the monarchy and a division of Galician territory; the Polish, on the other hand, only supported a strong Austria under the condition that it reinforced autonomic authority in the country and preserved the integrity of Galicia. It is likely that the pro-Austrian policy of Ruthenian deputies targeted the Polonizing policy of Polish deputies, as well as the dominance of Poles in the country's leadership.

Several episodes in the Galician Diet effectively illustrate the differences between the *gente Rutheni, natione Poloni* deputies and other Ruthenians. In one of his articles, Marian Mudry cites the confrontation of 13 March 1866 between Zygmunt Sawczyński and Iuliian Lavrivsky, two Ruthenians of different political and national persuasions, and both former members of the Ruthenian Sobor.[60] When the desire was voiced to suspend the teaching of general history and Polish literature at St. John Girls' School in Cracow, Sawczyński accused the Austrian authorities of weeding out Polishness, calling Austria "a fatherland issued by fiat, a stepmother." Lavrivsky disagreed, emphasizing that Ruthenians considered Austria a mother, not a stepmother. Total Ruthenian loyalty to Austria was manifested by the end of March 1866, when a discussion took place concerning the new, more autonomous governance model for Galicia and the creation of the office of a *de facto* minister for Galician Affairs in Vienna. On 27 March 1866 the deputy Mykhailo Kuzemsky criticized the Polish demands and spoke out in the name of the Galician-Ruthenian people, deeming them a party against the parties and a nation against the nation. Szemelowski claimed, however, that he was not going to refute the accusations, for they did not exist. In other words, he suggested that there was no Polish-Ruthenian conflict, as there had been no anti-Polish sentiment up to this point among the inhabitants of towns and civil servants of Ruthenian provenance.[61]

A key event for Galician politicians was the discussion of the petition to the emperor following the defeat in the Austrian-Prussian War of 1866. After the failure of the January Uprising, the Polish-raised political elite, predominating at the time over the independence-orientated democrats, saw an opportunity to increase Galicia's autonomy while strengthening their own authority in the country. Around this time a famous petition to emperor Franz Joseph I was passed by Galician Diet on 10 December 1866, closing with the statement: "We stand with you, Your Majesty, and we wish to stand with you" ["Przy Tobie, Najjaśniejszy Panie stoimy i stać będziemy"]. The appeal proposed no action that would weaken the monarchy, which the initiators (Galician conservatives, among them "Mamelukes") believed would reinforce the authority of the Polish landed gentry in Galicia and ensure the continued Polonization of the province. The petition found opponents not only among democratic politicians due to its failure to engage in open confrontation with the monarchy, but also among Ruthenians, albeit for different reasons. It was important for the Ruthenians that the petition emphasized that the representatives of Galicia were not solely Poles. In their own separate address, they called for the assurance of equality between Poles and Ruthenians.[62] Voices of opposition were also raised

---

[60] Mudryj, "Dylematy narodowościowe," p. 74.
[61] Ibid., p. 75.
[62] The Ruthenian address was read out by Anton Dobriansky. See *Sprawozdanie stenograficzne z 4 sesyi Sejmu Krajowego Królestwa Galicyi i Lodomeryi, wraz z Wielkiem Księstwem Krakowskiem w roku 1866*, pp. 128–29.

against the Ruthenian appeal, including that of the deputy Zyblikie-wicz, who publicly emphasized that he himself was a Ruthenian of the Uniate rite. At a session of the Galician Diet, he said:

> It follows to solemnly state that not all Ruthenians are on his side; and that I am a Ruthenian and I am convinced that possibly more Ruthe-nians stand behind me than behind the authors of this appeal. As a Ru-thenian, I renounce this appeal in my own name and in that of my fellow believers, and for this I have decided to speak.[63]

In as far as Zyblikiewicz proudly claimed that the majority of Ru-thenians stood behind him, Teodor Szemelowski made an even grander claim when commenting on his compatriot's speech. He argued that Ruthenians, among whom he counted himself, considered this to be a mere utterance of one political faction. Taking issue with the desig-nation "leader of the Ruthenian nation" casually contrived by deputy Kornel Krzeczunowicz, he denied that any leader of the Ruthenian na-tion existed in the Diet or in the Ruthenian party itself. He likened it to deeming the half a million Jewish inhabitants of Galicia a nation. He also emphasized that for the eastern part of the land, even if the en-tire annexed territory were to be divided in half, even then the dep-uties represented the property of the great estates, the towns as well as the rural folk, rather than "the pastoral circle which imposes itself on the representative of the land and Ruthenians."[64] In this way he denied the Ruthenian deputies' right to represent Ruthenians, though a mo-ment later he tried to expose the real aspirations of these deputies:

> (…) these gentlemen here pretend to be loyal and true, while in news-papers it is announced that they are one nation with the Muscovites and that they may be schismatics; is this not hypocrisy?[65]

In order to prove to the Ruthenian deputies that prior to the parti-tions Poles and Ruthenians had not been feuding, he suddenly began to address the assembly in Ruthenian, eliciting laughter from his com-patriots. As Marian Mudry wrote:

> "The raucous applause and general merriment" in the parliamentary chamber reflected irony not only in relation to the speaker but to the *gente Rutheni natione Poloni* formation in general.[66]

---

[63] Ibid., p. 149.
[64] Ibid., p. 150.
[65] Ibid.
[66] Mudryj, "Dylematy narodowościowe," p. 88.

Ruthenians of Polish nationality did not lose their significance in the Galician Diet after this episode, continuing to occupy their deputy benches. They used their authority and power to achieve goals in line with their political orientation, and therefore strove to bring the Ruthenian part of Galician society closer to Polishness through a legal and not merely rhetorical route.

Resolutions on Language and on the Creation of the Provincial School Board of December 1866

As a result of the reconstruction of the monarchy, certain branches of government were transferred to individual lands, one such branch being education. A Provincial School Board was established in Galicia. This initiative was criticized by the Greek Catholic clergy, who had, in a similar fashion to the Roman Catholic hierarchy, previously exercised control over the school system. Those who supported the establishment of a Provincial School Board were accused of wresting the school system away from Church care and handing those powers transferred from Austria to Polish bodies in Galicia.[67] From the very outset Ruthenian deputies interpreted these changes as a deterioration in the national schooling situation. They feared that the creation of the Provincial School Board, along with the introduction of Polish as a language into secondary schools, would invite a hegemony of the Polish nation over the Ruthenian, as mentioned by the deputy Hryhorii Hynylevych during a sitting of the Galician Diet.[68] Florian Ziemiałkowski reacted vigorously to the Ruthenian argument that "there are no Polish deputies, there are no Ruthenian deputies, (...) there are only national deputies," for he himself considered that, in representing Stanyslaviv, he was a Ruthenian deputy. He also did not agree that the composition of the Provincial School Board would in any way limit Ruthenian rights. He based his speeches on the decades-old reports compiled by Euzebiusz Czerkawski, which showed that a Russophile threat existed among

---

[67] Renata Dutkowa, "Polityka szkolna w Galicji 1866–1890," in *Nauka i oświata*, eds. Andrzej Meissner and Jerzy Wyrozumski (Rzeszów, 1995), p. 142; Renata Dutkowa, *Polityka szkolna w Galicji. Między autonomią a centralizmem (1861–1875)* (Cracow, 1995), pp. 31–32.

[68] The original is as follows: "Namirenie komisyi edukacyjnoj oczewydno stremłyt, a osobenno jesły także uwzhladnymo druhu czast' wnesenia szczo do jazyka wykładowoho, do toho, szczoby utorowaty dorohu do hegemonii naroda polskoho nad narodom ruskym. (...) Zawirte meni, moi panowie! narid ruskij daleko postupył, aby dał sia jako materjał do czużych ciłej upotrebyty." *Sprawozdanie stenograficzne z 4 sesyi Sejmu Krajowego Królestwa Galicyi i Lodomeryi, wraz z Wielkiem Księstwem Krakowskiem w roku 1866*, p. 369.

Ruthenians.[69] Ultimately the Ruthenian deputies left the chamber during the course of the debate, and the motion to create the Board ended favourably for its supporters.[70]

Around the same time, the question regarding the language of instruction in education arose. During the parliamentary session of 1865/1866 Adam Sapieha proposed a motion that called for an exact analysis of this matter. Action was not taken immediately, but a special commission was established and tasked with preparing a project for an act on national language. As Jarosław Moklak has noted, discussion on the degree of development of Ruthenian as a language had become an animated one at this time, resulting in unequivocal criticism from the Polish side.[71] The language legislative project was picked up by the National Council on 27 November 1866 and opened for debate in the commission for educational affairs. After broadening the project's scope, the commission presented it to the parliamentary sitting that took place on 31 December 1866. The presentation was met with much emotion, particularly from the Ruthenian side.[72] When deputies of *gente Rutheni, natione Poloni* came to the act's defence, a most interesting situation arose as Ruthenians from both national populist options stood opposed to each other.[73]

The preparation and drafting of the project were spearheaded by Euzebiusz Czerkawski. The project proposed that Polish would be used in secondary schools, with the exception of the four lower classes of the First Lviv (Academic) Secondary School, where Ruthenian would be used, as well as in the Second Secondary School in Brody, where lessons were to be conducted in German. In rural schools the language of instruction would be decided by the given parish authorities. In a school where both languages were used, the language of the minority of students would be offered as a compulsory class. Any future expansion of Ruthenian would be left to the decision of the Galician Diet. Ruthenian youth were permitted to be educated in Polish and Polish youth in Ruthenian but, as Jarosław Moklak has noted, this second option was fairly impractical.[74] Nevertheless, Euzebiusz Czerkawski

---

[69] Ibid., pp. 60–61.

[70] Dutkowa, "Polityka szkolna w Galicji 1866," p. 142.

[71] Jarosław Moklak, "Stanowisko posłów polskich *gente Ruthenus* i ruskich (ukraińskich) w Sejmie Krajowym galicyjskim wobec projektu ustawy o języku wykładowym w szkołach ludowych i średnich w 1866 r.," *Biuletyn Ukrainoznawczy* (2002), p. 31.

[72] Zygmunt Zborucki, *Euzebjusz Czerkawski i galicyjska ustawa szkolna z 1867 r.* (Lviv, 1927), p. 9.

[73] Moklak, "Stanowisko posłów polskich," pp. 28–29.

[74] Ibid., pp. 32–33.

and other authors of the act can be considered conscious advocates for the gradual Polonization, but not total Polonization, of Ruthenian youth. Czerkawski's inclusion in the commission was undoubtedly meant to strengthen the bonds between Poles and Ruthenians. The use of Ruthenian in secondary schools was not a closed issue, rather one postponed in terms of implementation to a future time by which the language would have appropriately "developed." Nonetheless, Czerkawski's project naturally invited disapproval on the part of national populist Ruthenian activists.[75]

The project was initially criticized by the deputy Iakiv Shvedsytsky[76] and then by Father Stepan Kachala.[77] Both emphasized that the promise of equality between languages had not been maintained; furthermore, they refuted the argument that there were neither teachers nor textbooks for Ruthenian, the lack of which resulted in the failure to recognize Ruthenian as being sufficiently developed. The very procedure for determining the language of instruction in a given school was also subject to criticism. As it stood, the introduction of Ruthenian into a school required the mobilization of 25 parents and the acceptance of their motion by the school, then the parish council, and finally by the Galician Diet, all of which could at various stages deny the request.[78]

Czerkawski's project was defended by Zygmunt Sawczyński,[79] who proclaimed that Ruthenian was the language of the lower strata of society. He asserted that the language of the intelligentsia in Galicia after 1848 had been Polish. According to him, Ruthenian had not been sufficiently developed to be used in the teaching of certain subjects. Golejewski added fuel to the fire by producing a petition from the inhabitants of the village of Latsky who did not want to be taught in Ruthenian.[80] Sawczyński and Czerkawski justified their position by referencing historical tradition. According to them, in 1340:

> Rus' sought, in union with its more powerful sister, protection for its very existence, while the Crown guaranteed it the right to maintain its Eastern rite as well as tribal and political separateness.[81]

---

[75] Zborucki, *Euzebjusz Czerkawski*, pp. 10–17.

[76] *Sprawozdanie stenograficzne z 4 sesyi Sejmu Krajowego Królestwa Galicyi i Lodomeryi, wraz z Wielkiem Księstwem Krakowskiem w roku 1866*, pp. 514–15.

[77] Ibid., pp. 522–28.

[78] Moklak, "Stanowisko posłów polskich," pp. 34–35.

[79] *Sprawozdanie stenograficzne z 4 sesyi Sejmu Krajowego Królestwa Galicyi i Lodomeryi, wraz z Wielkiem Księstwem Krakowskiem w roku 1866*, pp. 515–22.

[80] Ibid., p. 528.

[81] Moklak, "Stanowisko posłów polskich," p. 37.

The past achievements of the Ruthenian language were considered by Czerkawski to have arisen under the influence of Church Slavonic, and consequently embodied an underlying threat of Russification. Considering the lack of development in Ruthenian, Czerkawski saw only two alternatives: either Russification, the result of which he was already familiar with, or Polonization, which he preferred. Czerkawski summed up the entire discussion by citing his own roots and feelings:

> If (…) the Ruthenian element has not yet disappeared, then disappear it shall not. I do not feel that a Polish element would be so hostile that Ruthenian would not be able to develop alongside it. Gentlemen, in my veins flows Ruthenian blood, I am Ruthenian to the bone, and I do not share the fears of Father Kachala. Obviously, I expect that next to the Polish element and language the Ruthenian language will soon form and develop stronger than earlier.[82]

In reality, however, the act devised by Czerkawski did not give equal chances to his ethnic compatriots, and in fact allowed Poles to dominate the school system.

In summary, Euzebiusz Czerkawski, Zygmunt Sawczyński, and the Polish deputies managed to vote through the creation of the Provincial School Board (27 December 1866) as well as the language act (30 December 1866). Imperial sanction for both of these matters was obtained in Vienna on 25 and 22 June 1867, respectively.[83] These initiatives ushered in a new stage in the history of the Galician school system which saw not only the fight against illiteracy and the Germanization of education, but also support for the development of general education and for the struggle for identity among Galician youth.

The Galician Diet Resolution of 24 September 1868

While the language act and the Provincial School Board awaited imperial sanction, a series of significant disputes broke out concerning Galicia's position in relation to the political changes in the monarchy as a whole. Following the Austrian defeat at the hands of the Prussians, Hungary had gained for itself a position equal to Austria within the monarchy. In February 1867 the Habsburg state became the Monarchy of Austro-Hungary, as the emperor had reinstated the Hungarian constitution of 1848 to the Crown of St. Stephen and established the Hun-

---

[82] *Sprawozdanie stenograficzne z 4 sesyi Sejmu Krajowego Królestwa Galicyi i Lodomeryi, wraz z Wielkiem Księstwem Krakowskiem w roku 1866*, p. 532.

[83] Dutkowa, *Polityka szkolna w Galicji. Między,* pp. 51–52.

garian government. In light of these developments, discussion took place over whether to send those elected from Galicia to the Imperial Council, and if they were to be sent, what demands they should present to the partitioning power. While the Czechs encouraged the Poles to oppose the Austrians, the spirit of loyalism was ultimately victorious in Galicia, both among Poles and Ruthenians.

When Father Teofil Pavlykiv prepared an address to the emperor, in which loyalty was declared and at the same time he was asked to ensure equality of the Ruthenian nation in Galicia. Pavlykiv's initiative met with the critical reaction of the *gente Rutheni, Poloni natione* deputy Michał Popiel. He refused to the Ruthenian clerics the right to represent the entire Ruthenian nation and accused Pavlykiv of inciting hatred. Popiel was also supported by other Polish politicians, among others Florian Ziemiałkowski. In the end, Pavlykiv's application was rejected by the Galician Diet.[84]

On 1 March 1867 it was decided that the Galician Diet would send deputies to Vienna and that a petition would be presented to the throne. However, the petition was abandoned due to two factors: first, the threat incited by the conservative Agenor Gołuchowski that the Austrians would dissolve the Galician Diet and call new elections; and second, an awareness that the loyalist attitude of the Ruthenian deputies could allow them to become an instrument in the hands of the partitioning power. When on March 2 it came time to vote on the unconditional despatch of a delegation, those in favour were Ziemiałkowski's supporters, Polish and Ruthenian peasants, and (interestingly) Mikołaj Zyblikiewicz. Only 34 deputies of varying political orientations, including Zygmunt Sawczyński, voted against the motion. The results demonstrate that the attitudes of *gente Rutheni, natione Poloni* were not completely uniform, as Zyblikiewicz represented a far more loyalist perspective than that displayed by other Ruthenians of Polish nationality.[85]

The infamous act of 2 March 1867 was met with immense criticism throughout the land. The outrage expressed in the newspapers was picked up by their readers, particularly those of a democratic and independent viewpoint. Against this backdrop, the seeds of the famous resolution act were sown a year later. On 22 August 1868 Franciszek Smolka unexpectedly introduced a motion to withdraw the act of

---

[84] *Stenograficzne sprawozdania z 1. sesyi 2. peryodu Sejmu Krajowego Królestwa Galicyi i Lodomeryi wraz z Wielkiem Księstwem Krakowskiem z roku 1867. Posiedzenie 1-10*, (Lviv, 1867), p. 151. Cf.: Karolczak, „Sprawy narodowościowe," p. 34.

[85] Irena Pannenkowa, *Walka Galicji z centralizmem wiedeńskim. Dzieje rezolucji Sejmu galicyjskiego z 24. września 1868. W 50. rocznicę uchwały rezolucyjnej* (Lviv, 1918), pp. 56–68.

2 March 1867, which in practice meant the resignation of those deputies already sent to the Imperial Council.[86] This was to be the first step towards the long-term goal of obtaining those same rights within the monarchy that the Hungarians had enjoyed for a year. Smolka's demand was an exceptionally brave one. He did not anticipate, however, that his demand would gain an assembly majority in support. Paradoxically, Mikołaj Zyblikiewicz helped to bolster the feasibility of Smolka's proposal, despite the fact that he had been in favour of the conciliatory resolution of 2 March 1867. Zyblikiewicz proposed an amendment to Smolka's demand, which would ultimately become, as a result of assembly work, a separate draft of the resolution act.[87] Both drafts were discussed by a commission composed of nine persons, including Smolka, but also three Ruthenians: Mikołaj Zyblikiewicz, Euzebiusz Czerkawski, and Iuliian Lavrivsky. They, along with the remaining members of the commission save for Smolka himself, opted in favour of the Zyblikiewicz draft.[88] Smolka's controversial demand that asked for *de facto* Galician independence had no chance of passing through the Galician Diet, but Zyblikiewicz's balanced and autonomous proposal, which would send the deputies to advocate for the broad autonomy that all Galicians desired, was able to gain traction.

How did Ruthenian delegates of other political persuasions react? At the Diet sitting of 13 September 1868, the Ruthenians presented their own project for a petition to the emperor, written by the deputy Vasyl Kovalsky. They demanded a legal guarantee for equality of rights between the two Galician nationalities, implemented in education, administration, and through a reform of the electoral system which they viewed as discriminatory toward Ruthenians. The Galician Diet and the Diet's Executive [*Wydział Krajowy/Kraiovyi Viddil*] were cited as being institutions dominated by the representatives of a single (Polish) nationality. Kovalsky spoke out for a strengthening of the monarchy, and against reforms in the spirit of autonomy for Galicia.[89] The Polish part of the House was unable to understand the proposal as it was read out in Ruthenian, and thus the deputies Leszek Dunin-Borkowski and Józef Tyszkowski demanded it be translated into Polish. However, Mikołaj Zyblikiewicz requested that the proposal not

---

[86] *Stenograficzne sprawozdania z drugiego peryodu drugiey sesyi Sejmu Krajowego Królestwa Galicyi i Lodomeryi wraz z Wielkiem Księstwem Krakowskiem z roku 1868. Posiedzenie 1–34*, p. 4.

[87] Pannenkowa, *Walka Galicji*, pp. 102–10.

[88] Pijaj, *Między polskim patriotyzmem*, p. 207.

[89] *Stenograficzne sprawozdania z drugiego peryodu drugiey sesyi Sejmu Krajowego Królestwa Galicyi i Lodomeryi wraz z Wielkiem Księstwem Krakowskiem w roku 1868. Posiedzenie 1–34*, pp. 212–13.

be examined by the commission on which he sat, which was to discuss his project and that of Smolka, as he did not want to delay the compilation of the resolution act. Father Teofil Pavlykiv also employed a cunning strategy by demanding the immediate presentation of the demands to the commission without publication and presentation to the whole deputy chamber for review. He presumably was aware that following its translation into Polish, the petition would provoke the opposition of the Poles. Ultimately Pavlykiv's plan did not succeed, and the demand to have the project sent to the commission was rejected.[90] For the moment, the Ruthenians were at a standstill. When the discussion resumed at the session of 21 September 1868, Father Pavlykiv gave a speech in which he emphasized that he was neither in favour of the draft for the resolution written by the commission nor against it, even though it was not in agreement with the demands of Vasyl Kovalsky's petition. He also announced that Ruthenians would not take part in the debates surrounding the drafting of the act, and in a show of theatrics he left the chamber together with approximately a dozen deputies.[91] The non-participation of the opposition Ruthenians in resolution discussions merely gave Zyblikiewicz and his supporters free rein to close the matter as quickly as possible.

The commission's project, spearheaded by Mikołaj Zyblikiewicz, was passed on 24 September 1868.[92] The resolution did not contest the December constitution and therefore in no way questioned the character of the reconstruction of the monarchy. Instead, it was a legal struggle to change the law by means of the Diet introducing amendments to the constitution, demanding autonomy for the province in the same way as it had been achieved in Croatia from Hungary. Criticism within the act was chiefly levelled at the fact that the December constitution was an obstacle to Galicia's autonomous development. Several significant demands included determination on the part of the Galician Diet of the means by which Galician deputies were elected to the Imperial Council; the Council's forfeiture of the power to manage commercial and retail chambers and organs in Galicia; legislation in the area of banking, tertiary level education, criminal, civil and mining law, the police, judiciary, and administration; the allocation of funds from the state budget to cover expenditure on Galician administration; the appointment of a separate high court and court of cassation for Galicia; as well as a board responsible only to the Galician Diet "in matters of

---

[90] Ibid., p. 214.
[91] Ibid., pp. 350–51.
[92] Ibid., p. 523.

internal administration, public safety, national culture and justice, and a minister in the crown council."[93]

These were tall demands, but the majority of them would be met through the efforts of Galician deputies at the Imperial Council over subsequent years. A significant role was played by the so-called Resolutionist Club [*Klub Rezolucjonistów*] established by Prince Adam Sapieha, the aim of which was to fight for a separate Galicia in the spirit of the resolution act of 24 September 1868.[94] Members of this club completely opposed not only the democrats assembled in the National Democratic Association [*Towarzystwo Narodowo-Demokratyczne*] (founded by Smolka), but also the "Mamelukes" under the banner of Gołuchowski and Ziemiałkowski, who were political minimalists. There was no absence of *gente Rutheni, natione Poloni* among the Resolutionists, which included Zygmunt Sawczyński and Jan Dobrzański. Even though the activity of this group had already waned by 1870, individual deputies still acted in the spirit of the resolution both in the Galician Diet and Imperial Council, fighting until 1873 for the expansion of autonomy in Galicia.[95] A resolute majority of the Polish deputies concentrated around the Polish Circle began to strive towards the realization of the resolution, despite the dominance of the "Mamelukes" headed by Florian Ziemiałkowski.[96] In June 1869, Polish replaced German as the language of administration, the police, and the judiciary in the Austrian area of partition and was brought into use on place name signs outside of towns, although these signs could be in Ruthenian if this was requested by a given community. In 1871 a department for Galician affairs was created in the Austrian government with Kazimierz Grocholski acting as the first minister, while separate elections were introduced in 1873 in all the crown lands, including the Kingdom of Galicia and Lodomeria. In this manner, the Polonization and autonomization (although non-formal) of Galicia became a reality.

Such a course of events did not please the Ruthenian deputies in the Galician Diet, in which they constituted a minority. For this reason, there were numerous confrontations between Ruthenian and Polish deputies, but there were also cases of Ruthenians (not *Gente Rutheni, natione Poloni*), who tried to seek agreement with the Poles. First of all, Iuliian Lavrivsky and Ivan Levytsky should be mentioned here. The latter, according to Kazimierz Karolczak, even claimed that parliamentary

---

[93] Pannenkowa, *Walka Galicji*, p. 128.

[94] Stefan Kieniewicz, *Adam Sapieha 1828–1903* (Warsaw, 1993), p. 217.

[95] Cf. Zbigniew Fras, *Demokraci w życiu politycznym Galicji w latach 1848–1873* (Wrocław, 1997), pp. 197–206.

[96] Zbigniew Fras, *Florian Ziemiałkowski (1817–1900). Biografia polityczna* (Wrocław–Warsaw–Cracow, 1991), pp. 104–19.

disputes do not reflect the true relations between Poles and Ruthenians in Galicia, between whom there is no such mistrust and no quarrels. That is why he appealed for permission and found support on the Polish side – among others in the person of Adam Sapieha, whom he called "our prince."[97]

Anyway, the position of the Poles was much stronger than that of the Ruthenians in Galicia. This manifested itself especially in the field of education, where the *gente Rutheni, natione Poloni* played a significant role.

The *Gente Rutheni, Natione Poloni* on Galician Education

The Provincial School Board, created by the act of 27 December 1866, began its duties on 24 January 1868 after assembling all of the board members. Besides the government official Edward Gniewosz, the first board was composed of the Roman Catholic canon and gymnasium headmaster Łukasz Solecki, the Uniate clergyman Vasyl Ilnytsky, the member of the Galician Diet's Executive Oktaw Pietruski, as well as representatives from the world of scholarship and letters, including Juliusz Starkel, Father Eugeniusz Janota, Zygmunt Sawczyński, and Henryk Schmitt. School inspectors, including Euzebiusz Czerkawski, also sat on the Board. The Board secretary was Kazimierz Chłędowski, who described the institution's activities in his diaries.[98]

Due to its primarily Polish composition, the Provincial School Board was unable to gain approval from the Ruthenian deputies in the Galician Diet. Furthermore, the Polish deputies wanted it to be a fully autonomous entity, separate from the authority of the governor and subject exclusively to the Galician Diet, something which only increased opposition. The Board only became independent in 1888 under the governorship of Kazimierz Badeni, when a personal director was appointed for the Board, a role that was validated by Vienna and the emperor in 1890. Of greater interest, however, is the position of the Provincial School Board regarding the use of the Ruthenian language in education. The stance maintained by the deputies Sawczyński and Czerkawski may indeed prove that these two *gente Rutheni, natione Poloni* wished to Polonize the entire education system. Of course, it stands to recall the rationale behind this state of affairs. In Polish opinion, the level of development of the Ruthenian language in no way equalled that of Pol-

---

[97] Karolczak, „Sprawy narodowościowe," p. 36–37.
[98] Chłędowski, *Pamiętniki*, vol. 1, p. 274.

ish, and certainly not to the extent whereby the former could be used in school instruction at higher educational levels. What is more, Ruthenian had been subjected to Russian influence from the 1850s onwards.

Other Polish educators evaluated the degree of development of the Ruthenian language in a similar way. It is worth quoting the account given by Bolesław Adam Baranowski, a pupil at the Stanyslaviv secondary school, where the teaching of Ruthenian had been compulsory prior to the act of 1867. He wrote about the so-called "national language" which he was forced to learn:

> Earlier the entire class at secondary school—pupils of one and the other denomination—had to be instructed in so-called Ruthenian. I'm saying "so-called," for what the name itself contained was some kind of linguistic oddity, something most curious and which did not exist in real life. This was a strange mix of Old Church Slavonic forms with phrases taken from the folk Ruthenian tongue, but the forms and endings added on to a language used in the monastic/ecclesiastical literature of the Greek Slavonic rite were littered with a pronounced Russian terminology. Sources from which Ruthenian lessons could draw material simply could not be found (Wacław of Olesko, Żegota Pauli, Zorian [Dołęga-Chodakowski]); to flood school books simply with excerpts from Russian authors was not appropriate, or there was not the courage to do so.[99]

The author summed up his evaluation of the teaching of Ruthenian thus:

> I had to remember this detail, for we would often read in various Ruthenian journals how the great breakthrough in the history of Galician education during the year 1867 was the sanctioning of the Galician national act on the language of instruction and the announcement of the statute that led to the establishment of the Provincial School Board; that this was carried out only for the relative interests of the Polish population and as if it was only Polish society that benefited from this enormous change fought for by representatives of Polish nationality. So, the details cited above are a clear simplification of misleading information. The Provincial School Board has only just thrown out of schools the textbooks compiled by Holovatsky and authors of a similar ilk.[100]

A critical evaluation of the teaching of Ruthenian and the state of the language itself in the first half of the nineteenth century may appear to contain an element of chauvinism. The author, himself a teacher, evalu-

---

[99] Bolesław Adam Baranowski, "Kołomyjska Kreis-Hauptschule i gimnazjum w Stanisławowie," in *Galicyjskie wspomnienia szkolne*, ed. Antoni Knot (Cracow, 1955), pp. 247–48.
[100] Ibid., p. 248.

ated the degree of Ruthenian development as a language based on his observations at the time of his own education at school. The absence in Ruthenian of a common script and a literary corpus, the incorporation of Russian literary tradition, and the dislike of Ruthenians lay at the basis of the "Polonizing" policy of Czerkawski and Sawczyński in the Galician Diet and the Provincial School Board. This policy was a reaction to the real state of relations within the country. On the one hand it did to a degree block the development of Ruthenian schooling, while on the other hand it curbed Russian influences and gave thousands of pupils a chance to gain an education in the lexically richer Polish language.

Therefore, it comes as no surprise to learn that the Provincial School Board was subject to constant criticism on the part of the Ruthenians, who accused it of Polonizing Eastern Galicia. They argued that the Board had failed to adhere to the guarantee of Ruthenian instruction in seminaries and had made it difficult for secondary school teaching posts to be filled by Ruthenians, as for a long time Ruthenian was the language of instruction in only one academic secondary school in Lviv. Support in general was not forthcoming for the Provincial School Board as long as the question of language instruction in schools had not been comprehensively resolved.[101]

It is obvious that Ruthenians strove for their rights in education and that Poles stood in opposition to these demands, but it is still worth examining the position of those *gente Rutheni, natione Poloni* sitting on the Provincial School Board and in the Galician Diet. Zygmunt Sawczyński headed the Provincial School Board, eagerly assisted by Euzebiusz Czerkawski. As Renata Dutkowa has established, it was they—along with the speaker of the Diet for the years 1881–86, Mikołaj Zyblikiewicz—who most vehemently opposed the Ruthenian protests, "questioning the aspirations for a nation's right to equality when neither the language, national consciousness, nor cultural separateness are fully developed."[102] This fact forces us to consider the importance of this organization in the education process as a whole, as it exerted significant influence not only on schooling, but also on the formation of a people's national consciousness. It was evidently important for the Polish authorities to have the *gente Rutheni, natione Poloni* represented in a body that shaped the intellectual development of Galician society. Indeed, the representatives of this formation gave direction to the

---

[101] Dutkowa, "Polityka szkolna w Galicji 1866," pp. 144–45; Dutkowa, *Polityka szkolna w Galicji. Między*, p. 76.
[102] Ibid.

development of education in Galicia, gradually moving the Galician schooling system towards Polonization.

Zygmunt Sawczyński jointly formed the membership of the Provincial School Board for the 25 years of its existence; for this reason, he had a genuine impact on the development of schooling in Galicia. In 1868, under the auspices of the Provincial School Board, he was appointed along with Euzebiusz Czerkawski to a commission entrusted with the revision and writing of Ruthenian textbooks. For the years 1873–77 he headed a comparative commission tasked with overseeing Polish and German books designed for rural schools. In 1868 he co-founded the Pedagogical Society [*Towarzystwo Pedagogiczne*], an organization that assembled and represented Galician teaching circles, and from 1873 served as its chairman. In 1880 Sawczyński became an honorary member.

39. Zygmunt Sawczyński

He also wrote numerous pedagogical and academic articles for publication in the association's journal *Szkoła* [School].[103] The influence of this periodical on the development of Galician schooling was significant, as it appeared on a regular basis for the duration of the period of autonomy; its contributors were academics, educationists, teachers, writers, and politicians.[104] For a long time this journal was the only forum for the exchange of information on the subject of schooling in Galicia and broader innovations and solutions in education. The issue of patriotism was also not alien to *Szkoła*. The journal published an array of interesting pieces of advice and didactic solutions, with the aim of educating children and young people. This journal was subscribed to by an extensive group of teachers, and also broadened and promoted a specific vision of education. Though never explicitly stated, this vision promoted a strong spirit of accord between Poles and Ruthenians. Ruthenians of a conciliatory disposition such as Isydor Sharanevych wrote for the journal, and information was published about Ruthenian books

---

[103] For more on Zygmunt Sawczyński's activities see Elżbieta Głaz, "Zygmunt Sawczyński – pedagog, polityk i działacz oświatowy," in *Biografie pedagogiczne. Szkice do portretu galicyjskiej pedagogii*, eds. Czesław Majorek and Jerzy Potoczny (Rzeszów, 1997), pp. 41–58.

[104] *Szkoła* was published once a week for the period 1868–1908, and in 1867 and from 1909, once a month. Jerzy Jarowiecki, *Dzieje prasy polskiej we Lwowie do 1945 roku* (Cracow–Wrocław, 2008), pp. 154–55.

along with the obituaries of Ruthenian teachers. The journal's initial avoidance of confrontation was to diametrically change into a critical vantage point when viewing the Ruthenian movement following the assassination of Andrzej Potocki in 1908.[105]

Sawczyński finally became an active deputy in the Galician Diet, acting to strengthen the autonomy of the Galician school system. When the act on the language of instruction at the universities of Lviv and Cracow was discussed in 1868, he argued for Polish.[106] The shorthand minutes of this Galician Diet sitting reveal that Sawczyński did not advocate the Polishness of the university without reflection but solved the problem by taking his own identity into consideration. He spoke out "with a certain internal anxiety":

> My provenance on my father's side is Ruthenian; being a Ruthenian, it would appear consequently my duty to side with those gentlemen who at every opportunity stand up in the defence of Rus'. I have examined myself in this respect, and I have reached the conclusion as to which side I should be standing on, for having followed my own conviction for the entirety of my life I would not like to be a reckless imitator in this matter.[107]

Engaging in an internal dialogue with himself, Sawczyński realized that although he was a Ruthenian he was unable to agree to the introduction of Ruthenian as a language of educational instruction. In an unusually lengthy disquisition, he argued that Ruthenian as a language was not sufficiently developed for it to be imposed as a language of tuition. Only a language of scholarship such as Polish would be able to fulfil such a role, although he did not deny the potential for Ruthenian to develop into such a language in the future.[108] Another *gente Ruthenus, natione Polonus*, Father Barewicz, agreed with Sawczyński, and announced in Ruthenian in the Diet that the absence of this language at university in no way meant that it had lost the possibility to develop. As an example, he cited Italian, French, English, and finally Polish, which had developed as languages despite not being languages of scholarship

---

[105] More on the subject in Adam Świątek, "Problem patriotycznego wychowania ludu na łamach lwowskiej 'Szkoły' w czasach autonomii galicyjskiej," in *Czasopiśmiennictwo XIX i początków XX wieku jako źródło do historii edukacji*, eds. Iwonna Michalska and Grzegorz Michalski (Łódź, 2010), pp. 180–83.

[106] Zbigniew Fras, "Sawczyński Zygmunt," in *PSB*, vol. 35 (Warsaw–Cracow, 1994), p. 292.

[107] *Stenograficzne sprawozdania z drugiego peryodu drugiey sesyi Sejmu Krajowego Królestwa Galicyi i Lodomeryi wraz z Wielkiem Księstwem Krakowskiem z roku 1868. Posiedzenie 1–34*, p. 199.

[108] Ibid., pp. 199–203.

for centuries. He therefore suggested that the draft resolution should not be seen in any way as discriminatory against Ruthenians.[109] Sawczyński and Barewicz presented the position of the *gente Rutheni, natione Poloni* circles at the Galician Diet, which, judging by the applause following each speech, had earned the support of the Polish deputies. In the end the resolution was adopted despite Ruthenian protests, including that of deputy Kovalsky, but it was not to be sanctioned.[110]

The following year two Ruthenians of different orientations, Kovalsky and Sawczyński, would fall into conflict when Kovalsky proposed an amendment to the Provincial School Board that would ensure formal protection of the rights of Ruthenian nationality through the increased participation of Ruthenians in the Board's leadership. Speaking out, Sawczyński reiterated his difficult position as a Ruthenian but nevertheless opposed Kovalsky. He explained that those recruited to the Board were individuals who held public trust, and if they were to fulfil their duties inappropriately then there could be consequences, as reports on the functioning of the Council were transparent.[111] In reality, he did not want to implement any systematic solutions that would guarantee Ruthenians places on the Provincial School Board. The Board had a well-integrated team of a similar outlook, with the only Ruthenian besides himself being Father Vasyl Ilnytsky, his friend from their student days in Vienna.[112]

It was not only within the Provincial School Board that Zygmunt Sawczyński sought to avoid a Polish-Ruthenian division. He expressed a similar wish in regard to the teaching seminaries in Galicia. Jarosław Moklak has noted that in discussing the reorganization of the seminaries, Sawczyński deliberately avoided emphasizing nationality differences. Actual exigencies, and not the unequivocal regulation of the legislator, were to inform the decision of whether the language in a given seminary/college was to be Ruthenian or Polish. In this way the project was to ultimately demonstrate that both Ruthenian and Polish are languages of instruction, while the decision as to the selection of subjects taught in either language would be left to the Provincial School Board. This naturally stirred doubts among the Ruthenian contingent of the Galician political scene, but Sawczyński and his associates from the Provincial School Board were given in principle unlimited authority in this regard.

---

[109] Ibid., pp. 203–4.
[110] Władysław Koziebrodzki, *Repertorjum czynności galicyjskiego Sejmu Krajowego od roku 1861 po rok 1883*, vol. 1 (Lviv, 1885), pp. 69–70.
[111] *Stenograficzne sprawozdania z trzeciey sesyi drugiego peryodu Sejmu Krajowego Królestwa Galicyi i Lodomeryi wraz z Wielkiem Księstwem Krakowskiem w roku 1869*, p. 357.
[112] "Zygmunt Sawczyński," *Szkoła* no. 20 (20 May 1893), p. 254.

Czerkawski's argumentation that such a system employed in seminaries would lead to a "unity of the two tribes" was unconvincing for the Ruthenians, as they had no intention of taking a route that led ultimately to Polonization.[113] At this time Sawczyński was called to participate in a commission tasked with assessing the problem of teaching colleges, and three years later as a result of this engagement he visited the teacher training colleges in Ternopil and Stanyslaviv over the decision of the language of instruction at these institutions.[114] Finally in 1871 the status of Galician colleges was announced, which proclaimed the compulsory teaching of Ruthenian in colleges. However, when the matter was questioned by the Ministry of Education, it was decided that certain subjects would be taught in Ruthenian in the men's colleges in Lviv, Stanyslaviv, and Ternopil as well as in the women's colleges in Lviv and Przemyśl.[115] Furthermore, the director of the newly founded men's college in Lviv was to be none other than Sawczyński himself.[116] So-called exercise schools were also created within the colleges. These were normal educational establishments, except that they allowed future teachers studying at teacher training colleges to take part in actual teaching practice. The issue of language also arose in these institutions, and Sawczyński allegedly caused problems by preventing support for the Ruthenian exercise schools in Stanyslaviv and Ternopil. He explained in the Diet that there were simply no funds for this, though the Ruthenian delegates did not believe him. Jarosław Moklak has argued that the Provincial School Board on which Sawczyński sat prioritized exercise schools where instruction was in Polish. This did not mean, however, that Sawczyński failed completely to support his mother tongue. When a debate took place in 1874 concerning the language of instruction for an academic secondary school, Sawczyński, together with Adam Sapieha and Józef Szujski, was in favour of a gradual introduction of Ruthenian into the higher classes of secondary school (in 1867 Ruthenian had been only introduced to the lower elementary forms). He had in his activities the additional support of Euzebiusz Czerkawski.[117]

Euzebiusz Czerkawski, also heavily involved in the formation of national education, had spent a long time outside of Galicia following Gołuchowski's defeats of the 1850s. It was Gołuchowski himself who brought him from Graz in Styria and Carinthia, where he had worked

---

[113] Cf. Moklak, *W walce o tożsamość Ukraińców*, pp. 79–80.
[114] Fras, "Sawczyński Zygmunt," p. 293.
[115] Moklak, *W walce o tożsamość Ukraińców*, p. 81.
[116] "Zygmunt Sawczyński," *Szkoła* no. 20 (20 May 1893), p. 254.
[117] Moklak, *W walce o tożsamość Ukraińców*, pp. 128, 139–40.

since 1864, to Lviv. By 1868 Czerkawski, already a parliamentary deputy, also held the position of school inspector, a role he would maintain until 1871. He had organized the project that had led to the creation of the Provincial School Board, and was an advocate for the organization having the broadest possible jurisdiction.[118] Czerkawski was also the foremost defender of the Board: when in 1874 the Provincial School Board was accused at the Imperial Council of "acting against the interests of the state, of being a Polish institution not a Galician one, for it favoured Poles, proof of which was their numerical dominance on the Board, the appointing of chiefly Poles to secondary schools, and the oppression of Ruthenians both teachers and pupils," it was Euzebiusz Czerkawski who stood in defence of the Galician educational institution in the name of the Polish Circle. Upon his return to Lviv his speech was greeted by "university youth that gave [him] an ovation with a procession."[119] A year later he, together with Mikołaj Zyblikiewicz and others of the Provincial School Board, was again forced into defence at the plenary session of the Galician Diet.[120] Wiesława Duszkiewicz emphasized that the entirety of Czerkawski's political and educational activity was devoted to defending autonomous rights and the Polish language, fighting centralism and Germanization.[121]

As far as the Ruthenian language was concerned, Czerkawski, in a similar way to his *gente Rutheni, natione Poloni* colleagues, did not consider there to be a sufficiently large difference between Polish and Ruthenian as they had developed from a single root, while the many centuries of close proximity meant that "Poles and Ruthenians understood each other with ease, without prior learning or any kind of preparation."[122] However, it was the Polish language that Czerkawski saw to be European in stature, equal to the other civilized tongues of the continent. This did not mean that he did not value Ruthenian, for he was aware of its literary output in previous ages. However, in the current environment he, like Sawczyński, did not see a chance for Ruthenian to occupy a place among the so-called academic languages. He made his views known over the course of his work on the language act for the school system from 1866 to 1867.[123]

---

[118] Głaz, "Zygmunt Sawczyński," pp. 85–87; Wiesława Duszkiewicz, "Euzebiusz Czerkawski i jego poglądy na szkolnictwo średnie," in *Biografie pedagogiczne*, p. 35.

[119] Dutkowa, *Polityka szkolna w Galicji. Między*, pp. 93–94.

[120] Ibid., p. 98.

[121] Cf. Duszkiewicz, "Euzebiusz Czerkawski," p. 40.

[122] Euzebiusz Czerkawski, *Rozprawy i wnioski komisyi powołanej w roku 1879 przez galicyjską Radę Szkolną Krajową do zbadania sprawy gimnazyów* (Lviv, 1882), p. 81.

[123] Ibid.

Czerkawski was not only a defender of the Polish language in secondary schools, but also an adherent of its inclusion in tertiary education with the goal of countering the omnipresent German. In *Remarks
on the Learning of German in Secondary Schools and Realschule where Polish
and Ruthenian are the Language of Instruction* [*Uwagi o nauce języka niemieckiego w gimnazyach i szkołach realnych z językiem wykładowym polskim
i ruskim*], published in 1880, he did not reject the notion that a knowledge of German is necessary, but argued that thematic material could
not be taught in a language that had no "spirit." He also warned that
the teaching of "historical subjects" had to be conducted in one's first
language. He supported the teaching of German in schools, but not
teaching in German.[124]

When two proposals, a Polish and Ruthenian, appeared in 1867 at
the Galician Diet, both concerning the introduction of Polish in place
of German at Lviv University, Czerkawski found himself part of a petitionary commission set up to examine the subject. Reporting on the
commission's findings, he informed those assembled that the Ruthenians had referenced historical aspects but that "the petitionary commission as such did not feel itself to be empowered to address in detail
the motives cited by both petitions or to methodologically dismantle
them."[125] Even if this was not the singular voice of Czerkawski himself
but rather the collective voice of the commission, it still exposes the convergence in viewpoints among the *gente Rutheni, natione Poloni* with the
views of Polish deputies on the presence of Ruthenian at the university.
Czerkawski expressed a similar opinion in relation to other institutes
of higher education in Galicia. He primarily saw Polish as the language
through which teaching should be conducted.

At the second session of the second term of the Galician Diet (1868),
as discussion turned to the problem of the reorganization of higher
technical institutes, Czerkawski submitted a proposal for Polish to be
introduced as the language of instruction at the Technical Academy
in Lviv. This motion was supported by the other Polish deputies and
the *gente Rutheni, natione Poloni* Barewicz, Popiel, and Zyblikiewicz.[126]
A fierce discussion ensued over the failure to take Ruthenian into consideration in the statute when a relevant regulation had been prepared

---

[124] Euzebiusz Czerkawski, *Uwagi o nauce języka niemieckiego w gimnazyach i szkołach realnych z językiem wykładowym polskim i ruskim* ([Lviv, 1880]), pp. 1–9.
[125] *Stenograficzne sprawozdania z 1. sesyi 2. peryodu Sejmu Krajowego Królestwa Galicyi i Lodomeryi wraz z Wielkiem Księstwem Krakowskiem z roku 1867. Posiedzenie 1–10*, p. 118.
[126] *Stenograficzne sprawozdania z drugiego peryodu drugiey sesyi Sejmu Krajowego Królestwa
Galicyi i Lodomeryi wraz z Wielkiem Księstwem Krakowskiem z roku 1868. Posiedzenie 1–34*,
pp. 239, 341–42.

in 1869. Czerkáwski explained that the commission had deliberately not mentioned a second national language so as not to demand from future technical students additional demanding subjects. He explained that "if we overload this course with extravagant subjects then the whole of the institution will be disjointed at its core." He proposed that if a secondary language was introduced into the schools, it should not be compulsory.[127] Additional amendments were eventually incorporated to take into consideration Ruthenian, but the ratified statute never gained imperial sanction. In 1871 Czerkawski prepared another motion with the support of the other *gente Rutheni, natione Poloni* Zyblikiewicz, Sawczyński, and Szemelowski. He proposed the introduction of Polish as the language of instruction at the tertiary education level. He noted in article two that lecturers would be able to use Ruthenian with students if "this was needed."[128] Czerkawski presented his demands during a speech at a Diet sitting on 19 September 1871, and the motion was passed.[129]

Czerkawski also attempted to introduce Polish to Lviv University, raising a question to the Diet's Executive at the Galician Diet session of 29 August 1868 as to whether they intended to Polonize the university or to ultimately address the problems existing in this respect.[130] The ministerial directive of 5 June 1869 introduced Polish into government offices, including also in school administration, yet the language of instruction at Lviv University was to remain German. The matters did not resolve themselves immediately. The right to deliver individual lectures in Polish had been fought for, but the systematic solution to this issue would only come later. Similarly, Ruthenian deputies were simultaneously petitioning for lectures in Ruthenian.

At this time there was no practical reason to maintain a "German" university, as only three German language professors remained at the establishment, two of whom knew Polish.[131] The matter was to be regulated in 1879 through the introduction of Polish as the compulsory language of instruction at the university.

[127] *Stenograficzne sprawozdania z trzeciey sesyi drugiego peryodu Sejmu Krajowego Królestwa Galicyi i Lodomeryi wraz z Wielkiem Księstwem Krakowskiem w roku 1869*, p. 1068.

[128] *Sprawozdanie stenograficzne z rozpraw galicyjskiego Sejmu Krajowego. 1. posiedzenie 2. sesyi 3. peryodu Sejmu galicyjskiego z dnia 14. września 1871*, p. 4.

[129] *Sprawozdanie stenograficzne z rozpraw galicyjskiego Sejmu Krajowego. 5. posiedzenie 2. sesyi 3. peryodu Sejmu galicyjskiego z dnia 19. września 1871*, pp. 5–6.

[130] Stanisław Starzyński, *Historya Uniwersytetu Lwowskiego*, part 2: *1869–1894* (Lviv, 1894), p. 21.

[131] *Stenograficzne sprawozdania z trzeciey sesyi trzeciego peryodu Sejmu Krajowego Królestwa Galicyi i Lodomeryi wraz z Wielkiem Księstwem Krakowskiem w roku 1872*, pp. 383–84.

Simultaneously Czerkawski fought to have Polish subjects introduced into the law degree programs in Galicia. When the Ministry of
Education terminated the study of Polish law and instead introduced
German law and its history, Czerkawski tried to have Polish law reinstated as an academic subject. He courageously stated in his defence
of the course:

> I do not need to explain to what degree this ministerial move has of-
> fended everyone's sense of national being, and with it has also damaged
> learning; not only are the youth unable to study other subjects that be-
> long to the Law faculty, they are also unable to become acquainted with
> their own law.[132]

Several days later Czerkawski took a step further, submitting a proposal for the establishment of a Department of Polish History at Lviv
University. He explained his motion to the house:

> Nations that do not know their history or that do not have one are either
> primitive or puny peoples, ones who are nascent, unable to influence
> the common work of humanity that aims to fulfill the highest of tasks.
> Nations who have a history and forget [it] are condemned to death and
> oblivion.[133]

Czerkawski's initiative, first proposed in 1881, was quickly realized.
Imperial sanction for the creation of such a department was granted by
16 September 1882.[134]

Czerkawski continued his education crusade by addressing the matter of textbooks. In 1877 he motioned that four thousand guldens from
the national fund be used to fund "the writing of good textbooks in Polish for secondary schools." Paradoxically, this act of Czerkawski's was
informed by the fact that *Prosvita* had applied for a state subject grant
for Ruthenian books that same year. As Czerkawski confidently told
the Diet: "I imagine that this noble Diet will not refuse Polish textbooks
similar support."[135] This comment, and indeed the initiative itself, demonstrates the commitment of the *gente Ruthenus, natione Polonus* to ensuring that the state of Polish education was not any worse than that of

---

[132] *Stenograficzne sprawozdania z czwartej sesyi trzeciego peryodu Sejmu Krajowego Królestwa Galicyi i Lodomeryi wraz z Wielkiem Księstwem Krakowskiem w roku 1873–1874*, p. 70.

[133] *Stenograficzne sprawozdania z czwartej sesyi czwartego peryodu Sejmu Krajowego Królestwa Galicyi i Lodomeryi wraz z Wielkiem Księstwem Krakowskiem w roku 1881. Posiedzenie 1–29*, p. 645.

[134] Władysław Koziebrodzki, *Repertorjum czynności galicyjskiego Sejmu Krajowego od roku 1861 po rok 1883*, vol. 1 (Lviv, 1885), p. 342.

[135] *Stenograficzne sprawozdania z pierwszej sesyi czwartego peryodu Sejmu Krajowego Królestwa Galicyi i Lodomeryi wraz z W. Ks. Krakowskiem w roku 1877. Posiedzenie 1–15*, p. 178.

Ruthenian education. The matter was directed to the educational commission but was ultimately abandoned.[136]

Czerkawski and the rest of the Provincial School Board placed special emphasis on the teaching of national history. As the *gente Rutheni, natione Poloni* understood it, this was the history of Poland supplemented with events from the history of Rus'. Czerkawski outlined this historical understanding in his 1882 publication *The Theses and Deductions of the Commission Established in 1879 by the Provincial School Board to Research the Work of Secondary Schools* [*Rozprawy i wnioski komisyi powołanej w roku 1879 przez galicyjską Radę Szkolną Krajową do zbadania sprawy gimnazyów*]. In it he wrote:

> There is no need to add that the history of Rus', which for so many centuries shared the fate of the Polish Commonwealth, should be properly and exhaustively covered and that in particular the first period of its history constitutes a unique chapter; beginning with the joining of Rus' to Poland, it is an organic part of this common history.[137]

Two years later a textbook appeared which subscribed to this vision. On 3 September 1884 the Provincial School Board consented by means of a special resolution to using the book *An Outline of the History of Poland and the Rus' Lands Attached to It* [*Zarys historyi Polski i krajów ruskich z nią połączonych*] written by Anatol Lewicki, an author of Ruthenian provenance. Lewicki outlined his own philosophy and linguistic vision for the school system:

> I desired to instill in the young by word and deed the conviction that what was Ruthenian was Polish and *vice versa*: what was Polish was Ruthenian. For this reason, if only to avoid the division of the land into two halves I would have extended the obligation to teach Ruthenian in school to Western Galicia.[138]

Lewicki's plan did not succeed, but his textbook, written in the spirit of strengthening Polish-Ruthenian bonds, was revised many times and taught several generations of Poles and Ruthenians the joint history of Poland and Rus'. Thanks to its reprints, the textbook endured for many years as tangible proof of not only the presence of *gente Rutheni, natione Poloni* in Galician education, but also the shaping of notions of the past by the young generations living in the Austrian area of partition.

Perhaps the most important confrontation in Galicia regarding schooling occurred in the mid-1880s. Tensions and emotions were run-

---

[136] Koziebrodzki, *Repertorjum*, vol. 1, p. 273.
[137] Czerkawski, *Rozprawy i wnioski*, p. 58.
[138] Quoted from: Stanisław Bryła, *Język ruski w szkolnictwie* (Lviv, 1913), p. 13.

ning high in 1884 over the act on language of instruction in schools, largely due to the modifications suggested by deputy Iuliian Romanchuk.[139] He proposed that the language used in rural schools should be dictated by the number of inhabitants of each nationality in particular locations. In towns of over 12,000 inhabitants where the second nationality constituted at least 25% of society, the language of the minority was to be mandatory in one of the schools. This would prevent a situation in which local authorities would rule on language, a system that could potentially generate nationality-based conflicts. Romanchuk's proposal was directed to the school commission, which was charged with establishing the "criteria of determining 'the needs of a [given] nationality to establish schools with a specific language of instruction'; they questioned the use of the population number as the deciding criterion for the building of schools, and criticized the the proposal that would strip community authorities of the power to decide the language of instruction."[140] Interestingly, Teofil Merunowicz, one of the *gente Rutheni, natione Poloni* who was favourably disposed to Romanchuk's undertakings, took a stand in voting for the project.[141] The responsible commission drew up a report listing a series of faults in the project, though they had yet to decide on its fate. Romanchuk was the first to speak in its defence, followed by the Eastern Galician conservative Wojciech Dzieduszycki. The latter, referring to the Polish-Ruthenian-Lithuanian slogan of unity, took the position of maintaining harmony between Poles and Ruthenians in Galicia.[142] He believed that the establishment of schools with Ruthenian as the language of instruction would only result in division between Poles and Ruthenians, inviting subsequent demands for similar division in government offices, etc. He said:

> There is the danger that the land divides itself into two halves alien to each other, that society here in Rus' will mutilate itself terribly: the isolated gentry— the severed head—will lie down helplessly at the side of the blind torso of the common people, that drags itself, groping, to a certain doom.[143]

He attempted to prove the former inseparability of bonds:

---

[139] For more see: Moklak, *W walce o tożsamość Ukraińców*, pp. 149–78; Kieniewicz, *Adam Sapieha*, pp. 383–85.

[140] Moklak, *W walce o tożsamość Ukraińców*, pp. 152–54.

[141] Dariusz Maciak, *Próba porozumienia polsko-ukraińskiego w Galicji w latach 1888–1895* (Warsaw, 2006), p. 91.

[142] Moklak, *W walce o tożsamość Ukraińców*, pp. 152–59.

[143] *Stenograficzne sprawozdania z drugiej sesyi piątego peryodu Sejmu Krajowego Królestwa Galicyi i Lodomeryi wraz z Wielkiem Księstwem Krakowskiem z roku 1884*, p. 744.

(...) in the past whatever was Polish and Ruthenian-Lithuanian was inseparably joined; not only did the songs of the Polish poets but also the Ruthenian *dumka* ballads resound from sea to sea. This unity in difference was the most beautiful thing in our fatherland (...).[144]

Prince Jerzy Czartoryski then took the floor. While he believed that Ruthenians had the right to bring up their children in their own language, he questioned the logistical possibility of implementing the act. He proposed that the parishes look out for the best interest of both nationalities in choosing the language for schools, eliminating the need for Romanchuk's proposal. For this reason, he called for the dismissal of the proposed act.[145] The Ruthenian deputies reacted by appealing for the rejection of the commission's report and introducing an amendment to the act. Teofil Merunowicz, a supporter of Romanchuk, even decided to run at this moment for general speaker against the commission's proposal.[146] He was ultimately not selected, although the minutes he compiled at Diet sessions reveal his thoughts. In this booklet published both in Polish and Ruthenian, Teofil Merunowicz appeared confident in the successful outcome of the commission's work. He informed the reader that the majority of the Diet favoured the project, attributing the failure to pass the resolution to the need for a "thorough evaluation of the matter and an estimate of what has matured." He believed in the realization of the project, noting that "there is little doubt that the Diet will justly fulfill the wishes of deputy Romanchuk."[147]

The matter was again addressed during the next, third session of the Diet's fifth term in 1885. In the report submitted by the Diet's Executive on 30 November 1885 and developed in consultation with the Provincial School Board and local government bodies, a further element of debate over Romanchuk's project occurred. First it was argued that the current school system was in no way discriminatory to Ruthenians. What is significant is that Mikołaj Zyblikiewicz, a Ruthenian of Polish nationality, put his signature to the report.[148]

At the sitting of 4 January 1886, the Diet revisited Romanchuk's project. Euzebiusz Czerkawski, the *de facto* primary architect of the 1867 act, weighed in on the proposal. His telling speech revealed the rela-

---

[144] Ibid., p. 745.

[145] Ibid., pp. 745–47. Cf. Moklak, *W walce o tożsamość Ukraińców*, p. 159.

[146] *Stenograficzne sprawozdania z drugiej sesyi piątego peryodu Sejmu Krajowego Królestwa Galicyi i Lodomeryi wraz z Wielkiem Księstwem Krakowskiem z roku 1884*, p. 750. Cf. Moklak, *W walce o tożsamość Ukraińców*, p. 159.

[147] Teofil Merunowicz, *O czem radzono w Sejmie w roku 1884* (Lviv, 1884), p. 30.

[148] Jarosław Moklak has conducted a detailed analysis of the individual points of the report in his book *W walce o tożsamość Ukraińców*, pp. 162–69.

tionship of this Ruthenian of Polish nationality to many of the issues encompassed in the project. Firstly, Czerkawski referred to the notion of introducing systematic solutions to regulate the establishment of Ruthenian schools. As an example, he spoke of one school in Lviv where a Ruthenian class had been specially formed, in a sense going against "the campaign." If the number of Ruthenian pupils increased a school was to be established for them, although at the time only 120 students studied at the school, making for 30 pupils a class. On the one hand, Czerkawski supported Romanchuk's idea to guarantee by law the protection of the minority through an act ensuring the establishment of their own schools or parallel classes. On the other hand, however, he criticized the project for ideological reasons, citing particular misgivings over those places where the word "nationality" appeared, a significant hang-up given the deputy's provenance. His major qualm was with the section that spoke of the necessity to establish a Ruthenian school where "the second nationality constitutes a quarter of the population." He outlined his reservations in his address:

> The word "nationality" is a word that I cannot accept here. Language comes in conjunction with nationality, and we know, gentlemen, the outcomes of our country's history. I am not going to enter into whether these outcomes were good or bad, but it is certain that through the work of centuries, Polish civilization has been undeniably dominant. Even those inhabitants of this land who were Ruthenian adopted it, along with the language as well. Therefore, if we were to not have another criterion, only the one given here by Mr. Romanchuk, then the inhabitants of a certain town being of Ruthenian nationality but using Polish and standing on the ground of Polish civilization would view this situation as if they were the representatives of those who demand Ruthenian schools. I cannot take this position, for I stick to facts, and I demand that a difference in nationality not be perceived here, but only the actual state of the language used for social intercourse, which has been noted today through the national census, and which is to serve as the basis for the division.
>
> So Gentlemen, we shall see that those citizens of our land who to this day use Ruthenian in colloquial daily life, in certain relations of a higher significance, however, always adhere to Polish civilization. They demand that their children study through the medium of Polish, while they themselves in such circumstances use no other language than Polish. From this, one may conjecture this it is indeed a superior tongue and a language of education, proving that it ought to be used in higher education instead of Ruthenian.
>
> I am not saying here whether this is good; I have merely ascertained that there is in such a state of affairs a fact which cannot be refuted.[149]

---

[149] *Stenograficzne sprawozdania z trzeciej sesyi piątego peryodu Sejmu Krajowego Królestwa Galicyi i Lodomeryi wraz z Wielkiem Księstwem Krakowskiem z roku 1885/6*, p. 423.

Czerkawski found himself unable to agree to the project, which according to him would result in a national division in the school system. His proposal of a dozen or so years earlier was based on the premise of supporting a single, common form of education for all citizens of Galicia, and not distinct educational systems for two different nations in their own respective languages. Polishness and Ruthenianism constituted elements of his own identity, ones he could not imagine separating from each other. This outlook coloured his analysis of Romanchuk's project and informed his amendment of particular points.[150] Following several more speeches, the project was sent off to the educational commission with Czerkawski's proposals included. Three reports with various proposals for solutions were sent, but Czerkawski's proposals were rejected during the course of the Diet sessions. On 19 January 1886, the amendment was adopted which partly modified the act's legal status, specifically point five of the act. It introduced the regulation for the compulsory teaching of a second language in secondary schools, with the reservation this could be revoked at the request of the parents.[151]

Meanwhile, the deputy Teofil Merunowicz had published a report based on Diet work for the years 1885–86. He related various angry exchanges that had occurred during Diet sessions, tempering them slightly so as not to accentuate an already tense situation and the growing conflict with its national basis. Broaching the subject for the first time, he diplomatically stated:

> As is often the case when the matter relates to some undertaking between Poles and Ruthenians, at this time various deputies have exchanged sharp words. For it is known that the fiercest of arguments occur when two brothers quarrel.[152]

Romanchuk's demands and the subsequent criticism of his proposals in the Diet itself, although cited selectively by Merunowicz, were for the most part downplayed. Merunowicz sought to convince the reader that although boisterous and obstinately dogged discussion was taking place between Poles and Ruthenians, unity still reigned in Galicia. He emphasized the strong social bonds that existed between Poles and Ruthenians:

---

[150] Cf. ibid., pp. 424–31.
[151] Ibid., p. 811 and next. Cf. Władysław Koziebrodzki, *Repertorjum czynności galicyjskiego Sejmu Krajowego od roku 1883 po rok 1889 (sześć sesji piątego periodu)*, vol. 2 (Lviv, 1889), pp. 83–84; Moklak, *W walce o tożsamość Ukraińców*, pp. 173–77.
[152] Merunowicz, *O czem radzono w Sejmie w roku*, p. 20.

And so, like two brothers in the same cottage, in our land Poles and Ruthenians live together in inseparable unity. How many families like this
do we have where the father is Ruthenian and the mother is a Pole or
vice versa, and so the children follow one and the other in both rites and
nationality! And so, given the thousands of interrelations in parish and
daily life, can any division between Poles and Ruthenians be discerned
whatsoever? How many of those among us who consider themselves
to be Poles are of a lineage from great-grandfather to grandfather that
was Ruthenian in provenance, and how many Poles are there, particularly in Ruthenian villages, who talk, think, and feel themselves to be
Ruthenian?[153]

Merunowicz, framing his report as a conclusion to the debate on
Romanchuk's proposal, was in full agreement with the position taken
by the Diet. He explained the unwillingness among Polish members for
the division of schools into Polish and Ruthenian in certain towns:

Poles and Ruthenians have to learn identically, both jointly in Polish
and Ruthenian, so that from their very youth the conviction is instilled
in them that both the Polish and Ruthenian languages should be pleasant for all. The Polish and Ruthenian languages are to have equal status
in school, with all young people learning them together—and our Diet
is against the division of our children into separated Polish and Ruthenian schools. For in daily life, in the family, the parish, and in the land
as a whole, Ruthenians and Poles are so closely bound to each other, so
mixed that to separate them is impossible unless someone wished to
drag wives from husbands, brothers from their own sisters. Therefore,
there exists no fathomable reason for them to be separated in school.[154]

Later in his text Merunowicz quoted individual contributions made
during the course of the discussion. He went on to explain, however,
that "there was no doggedness whatsoever between the Poles and
Ruthenians." For Merunowicz the selection of a Ruthenian, Teofil
Berezhnytsky, as a member of the Diet's Executive was proof that the
deputies had the ability to arrive at compromises.[155]

Various viewpoints on school reform were disclosed during the
course of the debate on the matter of amendments. Two such viewpoints were exemplified in the attitudes of the *gente Rutheni, natione
Poloni* deputies Euzebiusz Czerkawski and Teofil Merunowicz. They
approached matters from similar premises, both desiring Polish-Ruthenian harmony, though they arrived at different solutions. Czerkawski believed concord between nations could only be reached through

---

[153] Ibid., pp. 20–21.
[154] Ibid., pp. 22–23.
[155] Ibid., p. 26.

a Polonization of the schooling system. Merunowicz was of the opposite view, pushing for compromises in favour of the Ruthenians. Various notions of this ilk arose among members of the *gente Rutheni, natione Poloni* at the Galician Diet on how relations between Poles and Ruthenians in Galicia should be arranged and managed.

Teofil Merunowicz's Political Activity

The *gente Rutheni, natione Poloni* were barely audible in the Galician Diet from 1889, the start of the sixth term of the Galician Diet. Until 1913, the only Ruthenian of Polish nationality among its members was Teofil Merunowicz, followed by Konstanty Srokowski during the short period 1913–1914, whose involvement in Ruthenian matters was negligible. The activity of this demographic within the Diet is therefore almost completely embodied in Merunowicz, the "veteran" of the Galician Diet and well-known journalist. Merunowicz had participated in the January Uprising, had proven particularly active during the 300-year anniversary celebrations of the Union of Lublin in 1869, and had served as a member of the Ruthenian *Prosvita* society. He held a seat in the Galician Diet from 1881 to 1913 and acted as a delegate to the Imperial Council in Vienna from 1896 to 1906. He also belonged to the so-called

"Circle of Peasant Deputies" [*"Koło Posłów Włościańskich"*] and the Polish Democratic Club [*Klub Demokratyczny*], which he left in 1898 when he moved to the Conservative Union [*Unia Konserwatywna*]. Only in 1907 was he subjected to the influences of the Eastern Galician conservatives, the Podolians, and entered into the anti-Ukrainian National Council [*Rada Narodowa*] in Lviv.[156] Until this point he had been a deputy of moderate and conciliatory views.

Merunowicz made his views on the Ruthenian question public, producing numerous leaflets reporting on Diet activities,[157] as well as socio-political

40. Teofil Merunowicz

[156] Jerzy Zdrada, "Merunowicz Teofil," in *PSB*, vol. 20 (Wrocław–Warsaw–Cracow–Gdańsk, 1975), pp. 455–57.

[157] Teofil Merunowicz, *Pismo do gmin wiejskich powiatu Lwowskiego* (Lviv, 1882); Teofil Merunowicz, *O czem radzono w Sejmie w roku*; Teofil Merunowicz, *O czem radzono w Sejmie krajowym w sesyi roku 1885 i 1886* (Lviv, 1886); Teofil Merunowicz, *Nad czem nasi posłowie*

works.[158] Merunowicz's publications were intentionally produced in both Polish and Ruthenian. They were often directed at the rural populace, incorporating a specific form of localized didacticism in the narrative.[159] Several of Merunowicz's works concerned the various problems experienced by the peasantry, but he devoted most attention to matters of economic development in the land itself, something he considered a priority for Galician society and the main subject of his policies.[160] He tried to draw attention away from national disputes, which, according to him, were detrimental to the realization of prosperity for the land as a whole. He defended himself against those who saw in him a tendency for compromise:

> My opponents criticize me for the fact that, though I am a Ruthenian by birth, I do not care to argue with Poles, and though I am a peasant deputy, I do not revile other social estates. This I do because I have seen in other countries, ones richer and happier than ours where there are also mixed nationalities living side by side (for example, the Czech lands), where everyone cares about improving the country above all else (…).[161]

Merunowicz denounced Galicia's backwardness in the treatment of its Jewish population, for whom he demanded, among other things, equality in rights so as to be on a par with the representatives of other nations.[162] He advanced himself as a supporter of Polish-Ruthenian accord in Galicia and remained true to this conviction until the end of his life. Appeals for unity, calls to ignore the "Ukrainian radicals," examples of the harmonious life shared by Poles and Ruthenians, and finally references to the traditions of Old Poland often filled the pages of his publications.

Merunowicz was not indifferent to the aversion displayed by his compatriots to Polish initiatives. He reviled in his publications those Ruthenian political activists of this period who advanced positions and views that were antagonistic towards Poles. Initially his greatest

---

w Sejmie radzili? (1886/7) (Lviv, 1887); Teofil Merunowicz, *Do wyborców kuryi IV okręgu wyborczego Lwów–Gródek–Jaworów słów parę od byłego ich posła do Rady państwa* (Lviv, 1900).

[158] Teofil Merunowicz, *Wewnętrzne sprawy Galicji. Spostrzeżenia i uwagi* (Lviv, 1876); Teofil Merunowicz, *Wolski czy Dobrzański? Głos wyborcy lwowskiego w sprawie kandydatur na krzesło poselskie w Radzie Państwa* (Lviv, 1877); Teofil Merunowicz, *Stańczyki a konserwatyzm polski* (Lviv, 1879); Teofil Merunowicz, *Wyniki samorządu w Galicji* (Lviv, 1916).

[159] Cf.: Teofil Merunowicz, *O wyborze posłów do wiedeńskiej Rady Państwa* (Lviv, 1885).

[160] More in Adam Świątek, "Ruś i Rusini w pismach społeczno-politycznych Teofila Merunowicza," in *Nowożytnicze Zeszyty Historyczne*, vol. 3: *O kształt Europy Środkowo-Wschodniej*, ed. Stanisław Witecki (Cracow, 2011), p. 132, footnotes 6–7.

[161] Merunowicz, *Do wyborców kuryi IV*, p. 18.

[162] Świątek, "Ruś i Rusini," p. 132, footnote 9.

criticism was levelled against the St. Georgians, whom he varyingly accused of pro-Austrian activity and being crypto- Russophiles. In his 1876 publication *The Internal Affairs of Galicia...* [*Wewnętrzne sprawy Galicji...*] he criticized the clergy for speaking in the name of the Galician-Ruthenian nation when "such a nation as a separate historical individuality had never existed."[163] Above all he denied their right to act as the representative of all Ruthenians, and particularly the Ruthenian peasantry, who had their own representatives in the Galician Diet. He also tried to prove that they should not even be considered the voice of the Greek Catholic clergy as a whole, citing the speech made in the Diet by the deputy Father Iosyf Zavadovsky in which he claimed that "a significant part of the Ruthenian clergy regard their political game to be charlatanism."[164] He also attempted to expose the political opportunism of the clergy from St. George's Cathedral, citing their loyalty to Austria and their stands at the Galician Diet against Poles and Jews, while they in turn worked together with the latter in the Imperial Council. What angered him more than anything was their pro-Moscow sympathies and their increasing alignment with Orthodoxy. He quoted an excerpt from one of the editions of *Slovo* [Word], a journal with a Russophile orientation, which stated:

> We, truly speaking, will last in the union with Rome for as long as our political interests require this.[165]

Merunowicz saw as especially dangerous the conversion to Orthodoxy of those Greek Catholic clergy with Russophile views, namely those who went to the Chełm lands and to Podlachia to help the Russian authorities introduce Orthodoxy in place of the local Uniate Church eradicated in 1874.[166] He did not restrict himself to criticizing misdeeds of this type, also seeking to uncover the causes of this process. He attributed this tendency to the poor financial situation of the Greek Catholic clergy in Eastern Galicia, who, unlike the Roman Catholic priests, also had to support families. He wrote:

> It is necessary for the soul to display strength and reject material aid from wherever it presents itself, when one cannot feed or clothe one's wife and children. So, one can in no way be surprised that the Muscovite recruiters strike with such force at this very point.[167]

---

[163] Merunowicz, *Wewnętrzne sprawy Galicji*, p. 88.

[164] Ibid., pp. 88–89.

[165] Ibid., p. 90.

[166] For more see: Włodzimierz Osadczy, *Święta Ruś. Rozwój i oddziaływanie idei prawosławia w Galicji* (Lublin, 2007), pp. 211–34.

[167] Merunowicz, *Wewnętrzne sprawy Galicji*, p. 97.

Merunowicz believed that increasing the remuneration received by the clergy (the so-called *congrua*) would solve this problem and ultimately curb their rate of conversion to Orthodoxy.

Merunowicz also took an unequivocal position with regard to the calendar used by the Uniates, which for him provided no benefits to the Ruthenian people. He polemicized with the prevailing opinion that this alternate calendar was a national Ruthenian monument, finally even pointing to the practical advantages resulting from a change in calendar, such as eliminating the need to organize two sets of religious holidays. He noted that such an approach would counter "Orthodox propaganda," "so that our people can isolate themselves from Orthodoxy with which they are already dangerously linked by a commonality in rites and liturgical language."[168]

Merunowicz relayed the fierce points of debate in the Galician Diet regarding Galician schooling to his electors. He also published works expressing his views on how people ought to be raised and educated. One such work was *The Civil Catechism for Poles and Ruthenians...* [*Katechizm obywatelski dla Polaków i Rusinów...*], in which he undertook to explain, in an accessible way, the basic foundations of society. He offered astute observations on concepts such as "family," "lineage," "citizen," and "society." Even within this framework, it was impossible to avoid addressing the question of national relations in Galicia. Merunowicz explained to his readers that Galicia was jointly inhabited by Poles and Ruthenians, who had formerly "governed themselves" separately, but who were distinct in that they derived their faiths from the two different Christian capitals. He claimed that the Poles and Ruthenians joined together out of necessity for protection from external threats, emphasizing that such unity was still needed as the threat still existed: "the strength of Poland and Rus' lies in unity, in separation these nations await certain doom."[169]

The publication of Merunowicz's *Civil Catechism* coincided with the peak period in the growth of Russophile attitudes among the Ruthenian population of Galicia. At this time, the Ruthenian intelligentsia found itself in a state of—to use the phraseology of Mykhailo Hrushevsky—"the psychology of despair." Danuta Sosnowska explained the gradual alignment of Ruthenians to a culturally stronger Russia and the Pan-Slavist and Great Russian movements as the result of an antagonistic attitude displayed to everything that was Polish, as well as a simultan-

---

[168] Ibid., p. 93.
[169] Teofil Merunowicz, *Katechizm obywatelski dla Polaków i Rusinów w Galicyi i w Krakowskiem* (Lviv, 1884), p. 15.

eous lack of belief in their own developmental potential.[170] Cultural closeness, common origin, a similar alphabet, and finally the Eastern rite resulted in the adoption on the part of the Ruthenian elite of a pro-Russian orientation. The Russification of the Ruthenian population of Galicia and the future possibility of the incorporation of this province into the tsarist state were viewed as deadly threats for the Polish elites in the Austrian area of partition, exceeding those of Polish-Ruthenian equality or the division of the land into two parts. This policy stemmed from fear of the expansion of the Russophile current among the Ruthenian population of Galicia, the most prominent example of which was the conversion of the Greek Catholic population of Hnylychky in the district of Zbarazh to Orthodoxy in 1881.[171] With this prospect looming, it was necessary to take action to lessen Russia's influence in Galicia. There was a danger that Moscow's policy, whether conducted within the current of Pan-Slavism or the ideology of a Great Russia, would result in a Russified national identity for Galician Ruthenians. The fears of the Polish political elites stemmed from actual events and the attitudes of known Ruthenians who worked towards the cultural accord of Ruthenians and Russians, if only through changes in language and liturgy. Secondary literature on the subject has frequently cited several key events as causes of Polish concern, namely the change in national orientation by the former Ruthenian Triad activist Iakiv Holovatsky vel Golovatskii, the abolition of the Union of Brest in Congress Poland, or the conversion at Hnylychky. The strength of the fears can be seen in Kazimierz Chłędowski's diary entry:

41. The cover of the Teofil Merunowicz's book The Civil Catechism for Poles and Ruthenians… *(Lviv, 1884)*

> (…) Poles fought with all means possible against this to prevent the Galician Ruthenian population from becoming Muscovites, so that the Little Russian language did not change into Russian itself, so that the Ortho-

---

[170] Danuta Sosnowska, *Inna Galicja* (Warsaw, 2008), p. 71.
[171] See especially Osadczy, *Święta Ruś*, pp. 246–55; Bernadetta Wójtowicz-Huber, '*Ojcowie narodu'. Duchowieństwo greckokatolickie w ruchu narodowym Rusinów galicyjskich (1867–1918)* (Warsaw, 2008), pp. 133–63.

dox service was not introduced in place of the Greek Uniate liturgy—all this was most natural. The St. Georgians, Muscophiles as they were known, attempted to make Ruthenians the complete equal of Russians, to erase all differences whatsoever that overlapped, particularly with regard to the language, customs, and religion of the Little Russian population in comparison with the Great Russian. (…) The Russian government and the Slavic Society in Russia most generously spent roubles on supporting Galician agitators, namely Orthodox priests, with the aim of strengthening this current (…).[172]

The Polish side favoured a strategic solution: instead of fighting with the Ruthenians, support them in a controlled way. The intention was to protect Ruthenians (and *de facto* Eastern Galicia) from Moscow and the growing Russophile tendencies. Teofil Merunowicz began to implement his solution with the support of Adam Sapieha[173]. This 1882 initiative represented quite possibly the final political attempt at organizing *gente Rutheni, natione Poloni* circles with the aim of "defending the Ruthenian question."[174] At the inaugural meeting of the party, the following policies were established:

1) Loyalty to Rus', not Muscovite but Ruthenian;
2) True loyalty to Austria resulting from the clear conviction that only within Austria could the Ruthenian element freely develop; a loyalty which did not require any external manifestation by means of banal, servile addresses of loyalty;
3) A decisive break with centralism in internal Austrian matters;
4) Loyalty to the union with Catholicism and consequently with Western civilization as opposed to Muscovite Byzantinism;
5) Ceasing efforts expended on fruitless argument and rabble rousing in the country, to be replaced with organizational work for the spiritual and material development of the interests of the Ruthenian people and society as a whole.[175]

On June 9, the organizers of the initiative also published a manifesto in the two languages, Polish and Ruthenian, entitled *To Galician Ruthenians Loyal to their Church and Nation!* [*Do Rusinów halickich wiernych swej cerkwi i narodowi!*]. The document declared that "those who proclaim to be the leaders of our Rus' merely sow discord among us and maintain endless dispute in the land, considering their own actions to be

---

[172] Chłędowski, *Pamiętniki*, vol. 1, p. 292.
[173] Kieniewicz, *Adam Sapieha*, p. 381–82.
[174] Marian Mudryi, *Ukraïns'ko-pol's'ki vidnosyny v Halychyni u 1867–1890 rr. Politychnyi aspekt. Dysertatsiia na zdobuttia naukovoho stupenia kandydata istorychnykh nauk* (Lviv, 1996), pp. 180–82 [unpublished work].
[175] *Gazeta Narodowa* no. 153 (7 Jul. 1882), p. 1.

the main aim."[176] According to Mudry, a total of 213 people signed the document, chiefly the clergy and peasants, as well as one sole Galician Diet deputy: Teofil Merunowicz. Mudry is of the view that all the signatures were obtained on the basis of personal contacts by the organizers. There was no other initiative of such scope in Ruthenian society. What is more, certain members of the clergy who signed the document were brought to account by the Lviv metropolitan consistory, resulting in their withdrawal of support.[177] Ultimately, the hopes rested on Merunowicz's undertaking would not be fulfilled.

Nevertheless, he continued to fight for Polish-Ruthenian accord, opposing the divisions between Poles and Ruthenians. He often defended this position in Diet sessions or in treatises published in brochures. In one such brochure he discussed the conflict that had arisen during the election period. Speaking of the election to the Imperial Council in Vienna, he emphasized that national criteria could not dictate voting, for the courts, government offices, and taxes were common to both nations. He recommended that one should not listen to those who:

> Wish to distinguish us from each other through election: the peasants from the townsfolk, the townsfolk from the peasants, the laymen from the clergy, the Ruthenians from the Poles! Let each of us, whoever has the happiness and honour of the country at heart, decide conscientiously to ensure that only honest, enlightened, hard-working, and capable deputies are sent to Vienna, for otherwise we shall not eradicate poverty from the land...[178]

In his election address of 1900, Merunowicz wrote that he did not want to travel to Vienna with those Poles and Ruthenians who go there "simply to bring up our domestic rows." He underlined that only the two nationalities could settle the conflicts that had arisen between them.[179] He decisively opposed the constantly reiterated demands for the division of the land into an eastern and western part, arguing that such an outcome would not result in what those who advocated it desired, for the Poles residing in Eastern Galicia would remain even after a division. In addition, he pointed out the huge costs of such an undertaking, even if one only took into consideration the need for a new governorship in Cracow.[180]

---

[176] The appeal was republished in, among others, *Czas* no. 152 (7 Jul. 1882), p. 2 and *Gazeta Narodowa* no. 153 (7 Jul. 1882), pp. 1–2.

[177] Mudryi, *Ukraïns'ko-pol's'ki vidnosyny*, pp. 181–82.

[178] Merunowicz, *O wyborze posłów*, pp. 15–16.

[179] Merunowicz, *Do wyborców kuryi IV*, p. 10.

[180] Ibid., p. 9.

Merunowicz's views were to evolve over the many decades of his parliamentary work, with the changes of the epoch reflected in his own life. However, his *gente Rutheni, natione Poloni* identity left an indelible mark on his political biography. This old-school Ruthenian and advocate of Polish-Ruthenian accord—an accord deemed in the programs of the Ukrainian parties in the Diet to be a "relic" of a passing age—was unable even at the moment of the shaping of Ukrainian national populist ideology to recognize Ruthenian nationality as distinct from Polish. Merunowicz's social and political work advocating for federation, for which he had fought in the January Uprising, began in the 1860s and spanned half a century. When he joined the January Uprising in 1863 or participated in the events to commemorate the 300-year anniversary of the Union of Lublin in 1869, he was one of many Ruthenians of Polish nationality based in the socio-political expanse of the Austrian partition who propagated ideas of this type. When the fate of Eastern Galicia hung in the balance in 1919, he was one of the last figures to publicly forward the opinions of the *gente Rutheni, natione Poloni*.

The Place of Rus' in the Programmes of Galician Polish Political Parties

The weakened influence of *gente Rutheni, natione Poloni* in Galician socio-political life was connected not only with its decreasing number of parliamentary seats but also with the changes occurring in political life at the end of the nineteenth century. *Gente Rutheni, natione Poloni* not only stirred opposition among Ruthenians of national populist leanings but also clashed with the Polish political pragmatism that resulted from these new realities. Almost no Polish political current that came into being in Galicia during the second half of the nineteenth century paid any attention whatsoever to the significance of *gente Rutheni, natione Poloni*. An examination of the activities of these political parties helps to elucidate the salient issues and trajectory of Galician political life at the close of the century.

The Western Galician conservative camp ("Stańczyk" party), concentrated chiefly in the environs of Cracow and around figures such as Paweł Popiel, Józef Szujski, Stanisław Koźmian, Ludwik Wodzicki, Walerian Kalinka, and Stanisław Tarnowski, was based on the notion of negotiating suitable relations with Austria and strengthening authorities in the Galician area[181]. It sought to abate national conflicts through

---

[181] On the beginning of this political group see: Lawrence D. Orton, 'The Stańczyk Portfolio' and the Politics of Galician Loyalism, *The Polish Review* 27, no. 1–2 (1982), pp. 55–64.

an improvement in relations with the Ruthenians, understood as a recognition of many of the Ruthenian claims. During the 1860s, with his attention focused on the creation of a future Poland in its pre-partitions form, Stanisław Tarnowski propagated a recognition of Ruthenian nationality "in a controlled manner." He wrote:

> Here in Galicia do not persecute but cultivate, nurture Ruthenian nationality, and strengthen it on the Dnipro, let it develop here in Lviv, and soon it will draw into itself the essences of Volhynia, Podilia and Ukraine (...) It will be Rus', but a Rus' fraternal to Poland and one devoted to a single cause. [182]

At the turn of the 1890s, this same Stanisław Tarnowski was already shaping his party by proclaiming the separateness of Poles and Ruthenians, placing faith in the fact that the neighbouring nationality would remain in union with the Poles as a result of its cultural proximity. Tarnowski's work of 1891, entitled *On Rus' and Ruthenians* [*O Rusi i Rusinach*] expresses this belief. Tarnowski laid out his intentions in the introduction to this work:

> We come from a single tribe, we speak languages so similar that without learning the other we can understand one another, we have the same faith though of a different rite, we live on the same land, and for centuries we have shared the same history. Yet, we are not the same as the Ruthenians, and they do not consider themselves to be the same as us. One can occasionally hear rumours of old feuds and mutual resentment between us. How, given a common provenance, a common faith and land, is there not trust and accord? Who is at fault? Who once did evil unto whom and to what degree? It is important to know and to carefully consider.[183]

On subsequent pages Tarnowski revealed to his reader the differences between Poles and Ruthenians. Absent from Tarnowski's discussion are the popular arguments that the Ruthenian language is but a dialect of Polish or that the Poles provided the Ruthenians with everything that was best in a common state. Tarnowski did not question the legitimacy of the Union of Brest but recalled that it "could have had more beneficial and permanent outcomes if we had taken care of matters more fervently."[184] In turn he wrote that the Polonized (in essence Latinized) Ruthenian gentry no longer cared about their Church or the Ruthenian

---

[182] *Przegląd Polski* 1 (1866), pp. 146–47, quoted from: Włodzimierz Osadczy, *Kościół i Cerkiew na wspólnej drodze. Concordia 1863. Z dziejów porozumienia między obrządkiem greckokatolickim a łacińskim w Galicji Wschodniej* (Lublin, 1999), pp. 191–92.

[183] Stanisław Tarnowski, *O Rusi i Rusinach* (Cracow, 1891), p. 3.

[184] Ibid., p. 14.

people, a fact that would later prove detrimental to Polish-Ruthenian relations. Tarnowski clearly emphasized in his book that Ruthenians had the right to call themselves a nation "given that the Lord created them Ruthenians" and "gave them their own language."[185] Nevertheless, he did criticize their separatist policies both in the times of Hetman Bohdan Khmelnytsky and from 1848 onwards. He pointed to the hostile actions of the Greek Catholic Church with Spyrydon Lytvynovych at its head, as well as those of Ruthenian deputies. However, seeking accord with Ruthenians, he referenced those initiatives in Galicia which would support Ruthenians while fostering harmony between both nations, such as the undertakings of Father Walerian Kalinka to found a dormitory for Ruthenian students.[186] In a mind-set characteristic of Cracow conservative circles, Tarnowski found no room to support notions such as *gente Rutheni, natione Poloni*; the focus was on bringing the two distinct nationalities of Poles and Ruthenians together in harmony within the territory of Galicia. Tarnowski's argument against Ruthenian separatism was that Red Rus' had been Polish since the Middle Ages, something that was, in his view, admitted even by Nestor the Chronicler.[187] He did not seek to "convert" the Ruthenians into Poles, but instead hoped to educate the Greek Catholic population so that the Galician inhabitants of both denominations could understand each other within a common Christian spirit. If not, then Russia would crush them as it had done in the 1870s to the Uniates in the Chełm lands and in Podlachia.[188]

Supporting the Ruthenian national aspirations was appealing to politicians in part because it offered the possibility of acquiring an ally against tsarist Russia. For this reason, the Cracow conservatives were often willing to adopt a compromise position in relation to the Ruthenian deputies.[189] These politicians considered the designs of Russia on Galicia to be a far greater threat than Ruthenian designs on the land in which they lived alongside Poles. The infringement of Russia on Galicia was evident in the expansion of Orthodoxy, manifesting itself, among other things, in the Orthodox Church's use of Greek Catholic clergy to destroy the Union in the Chełm lands and Podlachia.[190] The

---

[185] Ibid., p. 48.

[186] Ibid., p. 56.

[187] Ibid., p. 5.

[188] Cf. ibid., pp. 33–46, 67–68.

[189] Janusz Gruchała, *Rząd austriacki i polskie stronnictwa polityczne w Galicji wobec kwestii ukraińskiej (1890–1914)* (Katowice, 1988), p. 25; Janusz Wiśnicki, "Konserwatyści polscy w Galicji wobec kwestii ukraińskiej (1864–1914)," *Przegląd Humanistyczny* 43, no. 5 (356) (1999), pp. 48–49.

[190] Włodzimierz Osadczy, "Kler katolicki obu obrządków wobec polsko-ruskiej rywalizacji w Galicji Wschodniej w XIX i XX wieku," in *Prace Komisji Środkowoeuropejskiej*, vol. 7,

culminating point of this expansion into Galician territory was the conversion of the Uniate inhabitants of Hnylychky in 1881 to Orthodoxy, conducted on the initiative of a Galician Diet deputy, the Russophile Ivan Naumovych.[191] This was a time when the idea of "Holy Rus'" was becoming increasingly popular among a sizeable part of the Greek Catholic clergy. Many influential figures in the Uniate Church openly favoured a return to Orthodoxy. This was motivated not only by the sense of community with Russian Orthodoxy conditioned by history, but it also was the effect of Russian interference and financial backing. Galicia, the westernmost part of medieval Rus', remained outside the rule of its then heir—the Russian state. The Russophile moods rife among Austrian Galician Ruthenian elites aroused deep-rooted fears in Poles, who were worried not only by the abandonment of the Union on the part of Greek Catholics—a union which was after all the cultural "invention" of the Poland of old—but above all by the possible desire of Russia to annex Galicia in the future. Therefore, all Uniate moves to edge closer to Orthodoxy were closely monitored. A state civil servant from Zolochiv provided an interesting evaluation of this situation when he wrote to the governorship in Lviv:

> However, it is my duty to draw the attention of the High Presidium to the fact that as far as I am aware, the relations of the Ruthenian clergy in this district, accounting for a mere 20 per cent of priests, are genuinely and deeply bound to Catholicism and the Union, and they are far from any form of Ruthenian proselytism. The major part belonging to the old Ruthenian party *Slovo* certainly harbours schismatic desires, albeit secretly, while the so-called Ukrainian party of the new Ruthenians at *Dilo* sighs for the schism beyond the border, considering this schismatic religion, one unblemished by foreign Roman influences, as the most appropriate religion for Galician Rus'. The frequent correspondence sent by priests from the provinces to the Ruthenian dailies *Slovo* and *Dilo* are ample proof that the destructive element mutates among the Ruthenian clergy, fuelled by the attacks and criticism of the Ruthenian press on the Latin rite and the hatred of the Polish nation. If the Ruthenian clergy does not act openly (...) against the ideas of apostasy, if it has up to this point limited itself to correspondence (...) and confidential chats within its own circles (...) then for just this reason its pitiful material position has made it dependent on the Government (...). [192]

---

eds. Jan Machnik and Irena Stawowy-Kawka (Cracow, 2000), p. 83. The author writes that out of 51 clergymen who left Eastern Galicia for Congress Poland from 1866 to 1875, only two did not convert to Orthodoxy.

[191] Cf. Ibid., p. 29; Wójtowicz-Huber, *'Ojcowie narodu'*, pp. 133–63.

[192] "List starosty Złoczowa do Prezydium Namiestnictwa", Zlochiv, 24 Jan. 1882, TsDIAU, fond 146: Halytske namisnytsvo m. Lviv, op. 7, vol. 2, spr. 4005: Perepiska s ministrer-

A critique of Russophiles also appeared among Ruthenian intellectual circles of a national populist orientation, and hence in counterbalance positive opinions developed on the subject of the relationship with the Poles. This line of thought is exemplified by Ivan Levytsky's booklet entitled *The Ruthenian Movement in Galicia during the First Half Century of Austrian Rule (1772–1820)* [*Ruch Rusinów w Galicji w pierwszej połowie wieku panowania Austrji (1772–1820)*], published in 1879. In the introduction the author, a representative of the national populist current, condemned the Ruthenian Church elite for supporting Russophile tendencies and opposing everything Polish, while simultaneously defending what he deemed to be the positive influence exerted by the Poles on the development of Ruthenian nationality.[193]

This reorientation in political thinking, the result of the Cracow conservatives taking over the most important offices in the state and Diet, was met with disbelief on the part of Ruthenian politicians. The best example of such an attitude was the Ruthenian reaction to the funding of a dormitory for Greek Catholic pupils by the Resurrectionists in Lviv, and more precisely by the Order's provincial superior, Father Walerian Kalinka.[194] This act was a part of a broader policy conducted by the Roman Catholic Church aimed at maintaining the Union.[195] The aforementioned dormitory was framed as an initiative that supported the union of Churches and stood against the conflict engulfing Poles and Ruthenians. Kalinka stated at one of the conferences "(…) the Union is neither an exclusive Polish nor Ruthenian matter. It is a joint work, the joint legacy of the past (…)."[196] He explained in a separate booklet that the aim of the dormitory was:

> To instill in those Ruthenian children entrusted to us a deep love of Rome and of the holy faith, thoroughly connected to their nationality; gratitude to the Monarchy which has magnanimously granted rights to Ruthenians and Poles—an appreciation which already flows from Catholic principles themselves; and finally, fraternal goodwill for a kin-

---

stvam vnutrennikh del i greko-katolicheskoi konsistoriei ob antigosudarstvennoi agitatsii v propovediakh greko-katolicheskikh sviashchennikov, p. 60.

[193] Jan Lewicki, *Ruch Rusinów w Galicji w pierwszej połowie wieku panowania Austrji (1772–1820)* (Lviv, 1879), pp. 3–9.

[194] Jarosław Moklak wrote a separate article about the matter, "Spór o Internat Ruski we Lwowie," in *Poprzez stulecia. Księga pamiątkowa ofiarowana Profesorowi Antoniemu Podrazie w 80. rocznicę Jego urodzin*, ed. Danuta Czerska (Cracow, 2000), pp. 191–97. The article recalls the negative attitude of Stepan Kachala to the dormitory as an example of a broader reluctance on the part of Ruthenians towards Kalinka's ideas.

[195] Cf. Osadczy, "Kler katolicki," pp. 78–79.

[196] [Walerian] Kalinka, *Schyzma i unia. Dwie konferencje powiedziane w kościele P. Maryi w Krakowie, 16 i 17 Marca 1883 roku* (Lviv, 1883), p. 45.

dred nation in which it will be the destiny of these young people to live and work.[197]

However, this initiative was met with opposition from the Ruthenians. Kalinka already by 1884 had published a booklet in which he wrote about the attitudes of Poles and Ruthenians to the dormitory. The Poles praised Kalinka's initiative, with some believing that the Greek Catholic rite could be strengthened by "transforming Ruthenians slowly and gradually into Poles."[198] At the same time the author added that no one now "doubted that the dormitory would bring up its charges to be honest Ruthenians."[199] In turn the Ruthenians remained sceptical and even hostile towards the dormitory, for they saw it as a manifestation of some kind of Polish plot. As Kalinka wrote: "There were but a few who did not categorically reject us."[200] One of these few was Metropolitan Sylvestr Sembratovych, who supported the Resurrectionists' undertaking.

The question of the dormitory would soon be debated in the Diet. When proposals appeared during 1886–87 for financial support of the dormitory, Ruthenian deputies, and in particular Petro Linynsky and Mykola Antonevych, suspected that the real aim of such a subsidy was the Latinization and Polonization of Ruthenians.[201] The initiative was seen as an attempt to make Poles out of Ruthenians.[202] It is difficult to ascertain the thought process of the Polish deputies, though Walerian Kalinka, the initiator of this undertaking and a man connected with the Cracow conservatives, could not really be suspected of a deliberate plot to deprive anyone of their national identity. After all, he had defended himself against these exact charges from the Ruthenian side. But how did the *gente Rutheni, natione Poloni* react? Unfortunately, none of them spoke out in the Diet save for Mikołaj Zyblikiewicz, who was the speaker at the time. When deputy Linynsky made reference during his

---

[197] [Walerian] Kalinka, *Internat ruski XX. Zmartwychwstańców we Lwowie* (Lviv, 1881), p. 3.

[198] [Walerian] Kalinka, *Stosunek Polaków i Rusinów do internatu ruskiego XX. Zmartwychwstańców we Lwowie (Sprawozdanie odczytane na Walnem Zgromadzeniu Stowarzyszenia Opieki nad tymże Internatem, w marcu 1884)* (Lviv, 1884), p. 5.

[199] Ibid., p. 7.

[200] Ibid., p. 8.

[201] The matter was discussed at two subsequent parliamentary sessions of the fifth term. See *Stenograficzne sprawozdania z trzeciej sesyi piątego peryodu Sejmu Krajowego Królestwa Galicyi i Lodomeryi wraz z Wielkiem Księstwem Krakowskiem z roku 1885/6*, pp. 983–97; *Stenograficzne sprawozdania z czwartej sesyi piątego peryodu Sejmu Krajowego Królestwa Galicyi i Lodomeryi wraz z Wielkiem Księstwem Krakowskiem z roku 1886/7 od 9. Grudnia 1886 do włącznie 25. Stycznia 1887*, pp. 603–11.

[202] Dariusz Maciak, among others, has made reference to the dormitory affair, *Próba porozumienia*, p. 79.

long speech to historical evidence, drawing out the history of Polish-Ruthenian relations, Zyblikiewicz became exasperated and threatened several times to remove the speaker's right to address the house. A similar situation took place in 1884, when all the Basilian monasteries came under the jurisdiction of the Jesuits, resulting again in protests from the Ruthenians.[203]

The political success of the Stańczyks' policy ushered in the so-called "New Era," embodied by the accord reached in 1890 between Kazimierz Badeni and the Ruthenian national populist camp (National Council [*Narodna Rada*], established in 1885) represented by the deputy Iuliian Romanchuk.[204] Romanchuk delivered his famous speech on 27 November 1890 in which he emphasized the main principles that guided his political camp: loyalty to the Greek Catholic Church; loyalty to the Austrian state and the ruling dynasty; liberalism and support for the economic enhancement of the peasantry and burghers; and finally the conviction that the Ruthenian nation was one distinct from the Polish and the Russian.[205] He then spoke the important words: "We are neither *gente Rutheni, natione Poloni*, nor *gente Rutheni, natione Russi*, but we are *gente Rutheni* and *natione Rutheni*."[206] The Poles agreed to these principles in exchange for Ruthenian loyalty. They believed that this would weaken the influence of the Russophiles, whom they considered to be the greatest threat, while simultaneously abating the radicalism of Ruthenian deputies in the Diet.

Thanks to this conservative camp policy compromise, the Chair of Ukrainian History (officially it was called The Second Chair of Universal History, with special reference to the History of Eastern Europe) was established at Lviv University with Mykhailo Hrushevsky of Kyiv at its helm. Ruthenian was then introduced as the language of instruction at the Lviv University Faculty of Philosophy and Theology. Finally, Andrei Sheptytsky, a representative of the Polish landed gentry who

---

[203] Ibid., pp. 83, 88–89.

[204] Gruchała, *Rząd austriacki*, pp. 36–37; Czesław Partacz, *Od Badeniego do Potockiego. Stosunki polsko-ukraińskie w Galicji w latach 1888–1908* (Toruń, 1997); Maciak, *Próba porozumienia.*

[205] The original points of the program are as follows: "Perszyj: Narodnist ruska jest widrubna ne tilko wid polskoji ałe i wid rosyjskoji, druhyj: wirnist dla grecko-katołyckoji wiry, tretyj: szczo z perszoho wypływaje, ałe ne znaczyt, szczo stoit na tretim miscy: wirnist dla awstryskoji derzawy i panujoczoi dynastyi; czwerte: libereralizm [!], ałe liberalizm w tim zmyśli, szczo prenosym ustrij konstytucyjnyn nad absolutyzm; po piate: ekonomiczne piddwyhnenie selaństwa i miszczaństwa". See *Stenograficzne sprawozdania z drugiej sesyi szóstego peryodu Sejmu Krajowego Królestwa Galicyi i Lodomeryi z Wielkiem Księstwem Krakowskiem z roku 1890. Posiedzenie 1–29*, p. 1058.

[206] Ibid., p. 950.

had entered the Basilian order despite familial resistance, was elected metropolitan in 1900, and ultimately went on to become not only the head of the Uniate Church but of the Ukrainian movement in Galicia as a whole.

Given this new policy of Polish conservatives in relation to Ruthenians, the concept of a multi-ethnic nation gave way to the notion of supporting the Ruthenian national populist camp. On the one hand this created new possibilities to bring Ruthenians over to the Polish cause (but no longer to Polish nationalism) and laid the foundations for the idea of a new federation consisting of a union of separate and sovereign states connected to each other by tradition, which would become popular several decades later. On the other hand, the policy involved recognizing Ruthenians of a national populist orientation as a political partner, which completely destroyed the platform upon which the representatives of *gente Rutheni, natione Poloni* were standing, as they had always fought to be the representative of the Ruthenian population in Galicia and were treated as such by the Polish side. In addition, the recognition of the existence of Ruthenian nationality on the part of the Polish elite deprived those Ruthenians of Polish nationality of any basis for action.

Despite achieving initial success with the Stańczyk policy, the support for the Ruthenian national populist movement ultimately ended in failure. While it did slow the development of Russophile sentiments among Ruthenians, it also supported a national development among Ruthenians whose elite did not merely proclaim their separateness from Russians but from Poles as well. As Maciej Janowski points out, the design for the construction of an independent state based on ethnicity was already emerging among the Ruthenian political elites (increasingly referred to now as Ukrainian) in the 1890s, a decade earlier than a similar demand of establishing an ethnic Poland was formulated by Polish nationalists.[207] Janowski notes that Poles were shocked by the rapid development of national populist aspirations on the part of this second nation. They were particularly surprised by the sudden desire for separation of Ruthenians from Poles, this being all the more painful given the Polish involvement in Ruthenian national development during the final decades of the nineteenth century.[208]

According to Janowski, both Polish democrats and conservatives desired to cooperate with the Ruthenians. The Polish democrats hoped to

---

[207] Maciej Janowski, *Inteligencja wobec wyzwań nowoczesności. Dylematy ideowe polskiej demokracji liberalnej w Galicji w latach 1889–1914* (Warsaw, 1996), pp. 64–65.
[208] Cf. ibid.

deprive the Polish conservatives of their political significance through this cooperation with the Ruthenians. There was here a completely different understanding of the national space. While both Polish and Ruthenian politicians had many common goals, including remedying social problems in Galician society, the Polish democrats supported Ruthenian undertakings only under the condition that they renounce any pro-Russian orientation and the desire for Galician partition. As Maciej Janowski so clearly emphasizes, the opportunity to create a Polish-Ruthenian political formation, which would have maintained accord between the two nations, was not taken. Meanwhile, Ruthenian political formations were being founded which were even further removed from the Polish agenda. During this time the national conflict was mounting, rendering the 1890 Badeni–Romanchuk Accord empty words.[209]

Meanwhile the Eastern Galician conservative circles of the Podolians, desiring to maintain the ethnic *status quo* in relations in Galicia, ensured that the *gente Rutheni, natione Poloni* formation remained alive to a certain degree. The Podilian conservatives viewed the political activities of the Ruthenians at the Galician Diet completely differently than their Western Galician counterparts. They often denied the right of Ruthenian national populist activists to represent the interests of Rus', as they believed this role was rightfully their own. As Jarosław Moklak writes, the Podolians "often considered themselves to be Ruthenians, more strictly so than the Ruthenian gentry, and were guided by the *gente Ruthenus, natione Polonus* formation."[210] In their case, *gente Rutheni* was neither an indication of ethnic provenance nor the Greek Catholic rite, but was rather an element understood primarily in the territorial sense. Therefore, the Podolians considered themselves to be *gente Rutheni* as a result of living in Rus' and possessing estates. During a Diet session in 1869, Antoni Golejewski, a representative of this contingent, voiced his opposition to a subvention for the Ruthenian theatre in Lviv:

> We all are Ruthenians, even the honourable speaker—we are Ruthenian-Poles. Let us be content with the theatre as it is. For some faction or other that seeks accord with us yet wishes to distinguish itself as a different group of Ruthenians, we are unable to give a subvention to the amount of four thousand zloty. Obviously if these brothers of ours were to replace the so-called St. Georgians, abandon their former thinking and stop using Muscovite phrases, if they were to return to our way of thinking, then I myself would argue the case for such a subvention. But until

---

[209] Ibid, pp. 66–68. The author supplies a series of noteworthy examples of what Polish and Ruthenian politicians and publicists said, these being marked by a noticeable amount of aversion if not hatred.

[210] Moklak, *W walce o tożsamość Ukraińców*, p. 42.

then, no! Until we have proof that you, gentlemen, are not Muscovites, then I am unable to vote for any subvention for the Ruthenian theatre. [211]

Wojciech Dzieduszycki publicly made the circle's goals known in 1886 when he stated, "we want to be here [in Rus' – A.Ś.] considered Ruthenians, remaining always Poles."[212]

The existence of a Ruthenian nation as a separate being was categorically rejected. Scholars often illustrate this rejection with the sharp words of another important representative of East Galician landowner circles, Leszek Dunin-Borkowski. Borkowski frequently took to the Diet floor with explicit opinions on the subject of Ruthenian politicians' aspirations, reinforcing his denial of the existence of Ruthenian nationality. For example, when the Diet was debating on the language in the judiciary and administration in Galicia during its second session in 1868, he proposed that the Little Russian language (Ruthenian) be called the "Małopolski" [Little Polish] language.[213] Kost Levytsky noted that Borkowski would often repeat: "There is no Rus' at all; Rus' is Poland and what is not Poland is Moscow's!"[214] Speaking on the relations of the two nations during the debate about bilingual secondary schools in 1886, Emil Torosiewicz was to have said:

> Listening to the arguments in today's debate it would seem that the country is engulfed in feuding and dithering. Yet that is not the case; for the most fulfilling accord exists between the people. The customs of the people are one and the same. The Polish and Ruthenian languages are considered as one, while the Ruthenian population prefers to write letters and applications in Polish when they are to be submitted to district authorities, government offices and courts; only in the most exceptional cases will something be submitted in Ruthenian. (...) The most remarkable Ruthenians such as Sawczyński, Czerkawski, Zyblikiewicz are also the best of Poles! I can confidently state that in this country there are two denominations, but a single nation.[215]

According to Olena Arkusha and Marian Mudry, "up until the beginning of the twentieth century the Polish Eastern Galician aristocracy

---

[211] *Stenograficzne Sprawozdania z trzeciey sesyi drugiego peryodu Sejmu Krajowego Królestwa Galicyi i Lodomeryi wraz z Wielkim Księstwem Krakowskiem w roku 1869*, p. 1038. Cf. Ołena Arkusza, Marian Mudryj, "XIX-wieczna arystokracja polska w Galicji Wschodniej wobec ruskich (ukraińskich) aspiracji narodowych," *Krakowskie Pismo Kresowe* 4: *Galicja jako pogranicze kultur* (2012), p. 157.

[212] "Sesja Sejmowa," *Gazeta Narodowa* no. 3 (5 Jan. 1886), p. 3.

[213] *Stenograficzne sprawozdania drugiego peryodu drugiey sesyi Sejmu Krajowego Królestwa Galicyi i Lodomeryi wraz z Wielkim Księstwem Krakowskiem w roku 1868. Posiedzenie 1–34*, pp. 89–90.

[214] Kost' Levyts'kyi, *Istoriia politychnoï dumky halyts'kykh Ukraïntsiv 1848–1914 na pidstavi spomyniv* (Lviv, 1926), p. 105.

[215] "Sesja Sejmowa," *Gazeta Narodowa* no. 3 (5 Jan. 1886), p. 3.

was unable to believe that Ruthenians had doubts over the Polish character of Eastern Galicia (…). Eastern Galician conservatives were counting on the fact that the Polish-Ruthenian conflict would not take on
national dimensions and in doing so become a conflict between nations,
but rather remain at the level of religious, social, and ethnic oppositions
within the framework of a single nation and a 'common fatherland'."[216]
In spite of the policy of West Galician conservatives to compromise on
Ruthenian matters, the existence of a long ignored Ruthenian problem
would finally result in a sudden opposition to any form of compromise
with the Ruthenian national populist movement. The changes occurring
in the Eastern Galician countryside forced a resolute policy directed
against Ukrainian national populist political activists, i.e., those who
were combining the agricultural problem with the adoption of Ukrainian national populist and social activist slogans; slogans characterised
by a genuine radicalism. This unrest was widespread during the first
decade of the twentieth century, when several farmers' strikes swept
through Eastern Galicia. The Ruthenian peasants turned out not only
to protest against their own situation, but also to demand the division
of Galicia and the Ruthenian people's restitution of property from the
landlords. In order to maintain the Polish state of ownership in Galicia,
the Podolians reacted to this new reality by becoming warriors, drawing upon rhetoric of the unity of a nation of two rites and referencing
the beneficence shown by the Polish landed gentry to their Ruthenian
subjects.[217] It is therefore no surprise that the Podolians soon found
a common language with the National Democracy that was growing in
strength in Eastern Galicia from the beginning of the twentieth century.
The Eastern Galician conservatives were even prepared to support the
Russophiles in order to halt support by the Stańczyks for the Ruthenian
national populist camp. The Podolians were not only paralyzed by the
agricultural strikes organized in the Ruthenian countryside, but also
by the increasingly common call to "drive the Poles back over the San
River."[218] Given the prevailing circumstances, the instrumentality of
the *gente Rutheni, natione Poloni* (in the territorial sense) had diminished
for the Podolians. From their perspective, there was now a single aim:

---

[216] Arkusza, Mudryj, "XIX-wieczna arystokracja," pp. 160–61.

[217] Magdalena Semczyszyn, "Społeczno-polityczne postawy ziemiaństwa wschodniogalicyjskiego w świetle lwowskiej 'Gazety Narodowej'," in *Społeczeństwo, polityka, kultura. Studia nad dziejami prasy w II Rzeczypospolitej*, ed. Tomasz Sikorski (Szczecin, 2006),
pp. 11–20.

[218] For more on the subject see Artur Górski, *Podolacy. Obóz polityczny i jego liderzy* (Warsaw, 2013), pp. 20–29; Jacek Skwara, "Konserwatyści wschodniogalicyjscy – podolacy
wobec kwestii ukraińskiej w okresie namiestnictwa Michała Bobrzyńskiego 1908–1913,"
Rocznik Historyczno-Archiwalny 11 (1996), pp. 13–38.

to preserve their possession of estates and power over territory. This could only be achieved by two means: to either continue ignoring the demands of the rapidly developing Ukrainian national populist movement, or to fight it with the aim of subordinating the entire population of Eastern Galicia to the Podolians. The rapidly changing political climate at the turn of the twentieth century clarified the national divisions and left no place for groups with a two-tier identity. Jan Czerwiński, writing in 1891, illustrated the contemporary intolerance of these mixed demographics:

> What is a Germanized or Muscovite Pole, if such a thing can even be found? Certainly not a Pole, but a German or a Muscovite. And who are the Ruthenians that speak of themselves as being *gente Rutheni, natione Moscovitae?* They are Muscovites. Likewise, those who speak of themselves as *gente Rutheni, natione Poloni* are already on the strength of inexorable logic neither Ruthenians nor Poles. We have devastated the sacramental formula by which a true Ruthenian is first measured, one which has survived for centuries but which no longer reflects the truth, and have admitted to the national separateness of Ruthenians.[219]

In nineteenth-century Galician politics, a new framework for understanding the concept of "nation" arose. Paradoxically, it was not the National Democrats but the populists who were the first in Galicia to redefine the view of what constituted a nation. The political program of the Polish populists articulated in Bolesław Wysłouch's sketches supported the reconstruction of Poland, but within ethnographic and not historical borders. Wysłouch wrote that "the very existence of a twelve million person Polish ethnographic group is the permanent guarantee of our national being, while at the same time it is the actual basis of our national rights and their ethical-social sanction."[220] In "Program Sketches" ["Szkice programowe"] of 1886 he recognized the Polish nation to be an ethnographic notion. This outlook was based on the idea that a "nation" should not be understood merely as the noble strata but the society in general situated under the leadership of these strata. Above all, it argued that the concept of a nation should include its foundations—the peasants. It was this section of the population that would become the main force within this party.[221] Therefore the struggle of the populists to make the peasantry a decision-maker in political mat-

---

[219] [Jan Czerwiński], *O Rusinach i dla Rusinów* (Cracow, 1891), p. 4.

[220] [Bolesław Wysłouch], "Szkice programowe II (Narodowość)," *Przegląd Społeczny* 1, no. 4 (Apr. 1886), p. 258.

[221] Cf. Andrzej Walicki, "Koncepcje tożsamości narodowej i terytorium narodowego w myśli polskiej czasów porozbiorowych," *Archiwum Historii Filozofii i Myśli Społecznej* 38 (1993), pp. 224–25.

ters instead of allowing power to be held exclusively by elites helped to forge a new national model that broke with the political, upper-class national conception.[222] A nation was thus understood not as the product of the nobility, but derived from the people themselves. In this model, Polish territory was to comprise ethnically Polish lands, including: the Congress Kingdom excluding the northern part of the governorship of Suwałki; the western districts of the Hrodna province with Hrodna [Grodno], Białystok, and Bielsk; Western Galicia beyond the San River; the dukedom of Cieszyn; Spiš; the south-east part of Silesia; the Grand

42. Henryk Rewakowicz

Duchy of Poznań; as well as Eastern and Western Prussia.[223] There was no room for Lithuanian or Ruthenian lands, and plans to bring Lviv into the fold were abandoned. This was the result of a thorough repudiation of the noble tradition and of the entire legacy of the Union of Lublin, which Wysłouch rejected when considering the rights of the nation, because this very fact was a historical argument, and not a national one. The author of "Program Sketches" also criticized this mentality for its double-edged character; after all, Kyivan Rus' had a longer historical tradition than the Polish state. He was not convinced by arguments of the civilizing deeds carried out by the Poles in the East. Following this line of logic, he argued, the Polish lands ought to be returned to the Germans as a result of their colonization in the Middle Ages and accompanying economic development. In short, Wysłouch effectively severed any further route for the development of a multi-ethnic model of nationality. There simply could not be any *gente Rutheni, natione Poloni*, for, as he argued, "Democrats in Rus' have to be Ruthenians, while in Latvia—Latvians etc."[224]

Similar programs also found recognition in Ruthenian circles. Ivan Franko even advanced a proposal for the creation of a Polish-Ruthe-

---

[222] Andrzej Walicki, "Naród i terytorium. Obszar narodowy w myśli politycznej Dmowskiego," *Dziś* no. 7 (Jul. 2002), p. 23.

[223] [Bolesław Wysłouch], "Szkice programowe IV (Polska Etnograficzna. Nasze zadania narodowe)," *Przegląd Społeczny* 1, no. 6 (Jun. 1886), p. 403, footnote **.

[224] Ibid., pp. 400–1.

nian party, although it never came to fruition.[225] This was an initiative for cooperation based on an ordinary union of independent political camps, and was consequently completely different from what had been proposed earlier by those in favour of a Polish-Ruthenian brotherhood. Wysłouch also planned a Polish-Ruthenian People's Union for Galicia (Związek Ludowy Polsko-Ruski dla Galicji), but determined in 1889 that the cause was not sufficiently mature to succeed. In the same year the Lviv police confiscated the statute of this aborted organization, which was found in the office of Henryk Rewakowicz,[226] both a populist and a Uniate from a Ruthenian family. It was Rewakowicz who published a piece in *Nowa Reforma* expressing a willingness for agreement between Poles and Ruthenians over the resolution of the problems of the common people.[227]

Yet within the populist movement this vision of tolerance for the national needs of Ruthenians was short-lived, as there were populists who in no way shared Wysłouch's vision and who continued to treat Ruthenians with a sense of cultural superiority. Already in the first political program of the Supreme Council of the Polish People's Party [*Polskie Stronnictwo Ludowe*] in 1903, Galicia emerged as the "fatherland of the Poles" and an integral part of any future Poland. Ruthenians, on the other hand, were granted vaguely defined equality within the "historical federation of Poland, Lithuania, and Rus'."[228]

The ethnographic conception of nation was fully developed in the political program of the National Democrats. The idea of the Polish nation as a nation of the nobility and gentry was rejected in favour of an ethnic-peasant nation in Jan L. Popławski's article "Two Civilizations" ["Dwie cywilizacje"], published in *Głos* in 1886[229]. In the 1887 publication entitled "Means of Defence" ["Środki obrony"] the author proposed a change in the direction of Polish politics from an eastern (the so-called Jagiellonian concept) to a western orientation (the so-called Piast concept)[230]. Similar to Wysłouch's thinking, this shift meant forsaking Poland's interest in the lands of Rus' and Lithuania in favour

[225] Józef Hampel, *Chłopów polskich drogi do demokracji. Studia i szkice* (Cracow, 2008), pp. 34–35.

[226] Maciak, *Próba porozumienia*, p. 141.

[227] See Marian Mudryi, "Pol's'ki liberal-demokraty ta ukraïns'ke pytannia v Halychyni u 80-kh rr. XIX st.," *Visnyk Lvivs'koho universytetu. Seriia istorychna* 32 (1997), p. 108.

[228] Quoted from: Leonid Zaszkilniak, "Polsko-ukraiński spór o Galicję na początku XX wieku. Między świadomością historyczną a realiami," in *Narody i historia*, ed. Arkady Rzegocki (Cracow, 2000), p. 166.

[229] Jan L. Popławski, „Dwie cywilizacje," *Głos* 7 (1(13) Nov. 1886), p. 98–100.

[230] Jan L. Popławski, „Środki obrony III," *Głos* 41 (3(15) Oct. 1887), p. 634.

of regaining Silesia, Mazovia, and Pomerania and instilling in the local populations an awareness of their common provenance with Poles.[231]

In time Popławski abandoned support for the strong division of both national models in favour of strengthening the ethnic nation by espousing the historical noble/gentry tradition. Otherwise, he believed there was a risk of losing the political character of nationality. This rationale justified the right to expand into territories extending beyond the ethnographic borders of the nation in the spirit of national egoism.[232] Furthermore, the author argued that the many centuries of Polish cultural influence in the eastern lands had given Poles the right to rule over these territories.[233]

Popławski's ideas were further developed by Roman Dmowski, who claimed that in shaping the modern Polish nation, resistance should be shown to not only the partitioning powers but also to those national minorities hindering the creation of an integrated and homogeneous nation. He considered Polish policy in relation to national minorities to have always been characterized by excessive "magnanimity." Through this lens he viewed the "illusion of Polish-Ukrainian unity," the fruits of which were supposed to be the winning over of Ukrainians to one's own side. In the article "Half-Poles" ["Półpolacy"],[234] Dmowski demanded total solidarity with the nation, criticizing any policy of compromise and tolerance. He wrote that the race of "half-Poles" had to die.[235] As Andrzej Walicki claims:

> The national ideal of the "modern Pole" demanded an undivided national identity and undivided loyalty; those considering themselves to be Poles at the highest level yet Lithuanians at the local level—or Ruthenians in the ethnic sense, yet Poles in the political—were treated as a relic of a feudal past and ordered to side with monopolistic Polishness.[236]

For Dmowski, the boundaries of Poland were the Kingdom of Poland, the Kaunas [Kowno], Hrodna, Vilnius Governorate, part of the Minsk Governorate and Volhynia, the Grand Duchy of Poznań, Western Prussia (Pomerania) with Gdańsk, Upper Silesia, the southern strip of Eastern Prussia, Austrian Silesia with Cieszyn, and most importantly, Galicia in its entirety.[237] Given that the aim was trans-territorial national

---

[231] Hampel, *Chłopów polskich drogi*, pp. 24–25.

[232] Walicki, "Koncepcje tożsamości narodowej," p. 227.

[233] Walicki, "Naród i terytorium," pp. 25–26.

[234] Roman Dmowski, „Półpolacy," *Przegląd Wszechpolski* 11 (Nov. 1902), p. 801–5.

[235] Ibid., p. 805.

[236] Walicki, "Naród i terytorium," p. 30.

[237] Piotr Eberhardt, *Polska i jej granice. Z historii polskiej geografii politycznej* (Lublin, 2004), pp. 120–21.

uniformity, there was simply no room for any other nationalities except for Poles. As a result, National Democracy was to completely redefine the previous policies advanced in relation to Galicia's cohabitants. After a period of many years of support for Ruthenians, a party had emerged that fluctuated between denying their existence as a nation and inviting open conflict, all the while forcing those who considered themselves to be Ruthenians of Polish nationality to choose where their national loyalties lay.

The socialists, as a result of the progressive modernization in the larger urban centres of Galicia at the end of the nineteenth century, were not merely attempting to gain popularity on the nationality ticket. The chief problem was not the question of national self-determination or even—within the radical fraction—one's own state, but above all the notion of being for the individual. The most significant matter for this political group was the struggle against the ruling "feudal-capitalist" order, which actually opened up the perspective of cooperation between Poles and Ruthenians regardless of nationality divisions. Meanwhile, various individuals and various groupings under the auspices of the socialist camp approached the Ruthenian question differently. Bolesław Limanowski, despite understanding the changes in consciousness among Galician Ruthenians, was still of the view that the centuries-long tradition of coexistence would prevail over separatism. He believed that a program of autonomy could reconcile the differences, and that the reborn Poland would become "the Switzerland of the East."[238] This desire for separation was also criticized by Edward Abramowski, another Polish socialist based outside Galicia, who defined it as a manifestation of cowardliness and a diminishment of the soul, and even degeneration.[239] According to him:

> The fatherland is created evolutionarily; it is created by the history of human coexistence on the same lands; it is created through the interbreeding of blood and soul, through the experiencing of those very same cases of a collective life, those self-same battles, feelings, common hopes and joys, defeats and sorrows. (...) Therefore the peoples and tribes, even those speaking separate languages but who have interbred constantly throughout the centuries and generations and who have together experienced the same history, who have the same historical memories preserved in their blood, such people always have a single fatherland (...).[240]

---

[238] Walicki, "Koncepcje tożsamości narodowej," p. 226.
[239] Ibid.
[240] Edward Abramowski, "Pomniejszyciele ojczyzny," in Edward Abramowski, *Pisma publicystyczne w sprawach robotniczych i chłopskich*, ed. Konstanty Krzeczkowski (Warsaw, 1938), p. 272.

In another text Abramowski, considering the character of the Polish people, explained that Ukrainians (Ruthenians), Belarusians, and Lithuanians are not alien peoples but rather "brothers" as a result of their common past, fatherland, and language. He likened this to the various peoples inhabiting France and Germany who consider themselves to be French and Germans:

> (...) exactly as it was during the Commonwealth: a Lithuanian and a Ruthenian so in the same way a Mazovian or inhabitant of Great Poland consider themselves to be a single Polish nation; the Commonwealth was Polish-Ruthenian-Lithuanian and on its coat-of-arms next to the White Eagle there were the Lithuanian Vytis and the archangel of Ukraine. The Polish nation has always been composed of three peoples: the Polish, the Lithuanian (...) and the Ukrainian (that is Ruthenian).[241]

Abramowski drew a single conclusion: the borders of any future independent Polish state should remain as they had been before the partitions, while simultaneously emphasizing that without Rus' and Lithuania there could be no Poland.[242]

In turn, another socialist thinker from Congress Poland, Kazimierz Kelles-Krauze, expressed his hope that the nations of Poland strive to rebuild the former state. According to him, autonomy would appease the Lithuanians and Latvians while Ukraine would choose a federation with Poland so as to protect itself from Russia.[243] Such thinking, strongly grounded in Polish history, was to become a cornerstone of Józef Piłsudski's idea of a federation.

Even with this nuance of argument, there was simply no room in these ideas to support the *gente Rutheni, natione Poloni* model as the desired direction for Ruthenians. The priorities had shifted with socialism, so that emphasis was no longer on the nationality question but rather on the matter of mass capitalist exploitation and the relics of feudalism in Galicia. Furthermore, there was no desire among Ruthenian socialists to spearhead a new democratic Polishness. For Ruthenians, national ideas were linked with social issues, and through this the noticeable dominance of the lower strata in the structure of the Ruthenian nation. Socialist thinking saw in these societal strata the masses persecuted by feudal lords and capitalists, and so on Galician soil by Polish masters and Polish industrialists, the bourgeoisie, and the Jews.

However, this does not mean that there were simply no *gente Rutheni, natione Poloni* within the Ruthenian and Polish socialist camp.

---

[241] Edward Abramowski, "Ludność Polski," in Abramowski, *Pisma publistyczne*, p. 283.
[242] Ibid., p. 287.
[243] Walicki, "Koncepcje tożsamości narodowej," p. 227.

Certain individuals were captivated by these political ideas but found it difficult to reconcile both elements of their two-tiered identity. Józef Daniluk serves as an example of a figure from these two cultures who participated in the socialist movement and served it well, and who through participation in the January Uprising demonstrated his affiliation to Polishness as an ethnic Ruthenian. After 1863 he helped to found the Progressive Society of Lviv Printers [Towarzystwo Postępowe Drukarzy Lwowskich], was active for twenty years in the Campfire [Ognisko] organization of typesetters, and organized workers' strikes in Lviv. From 1873 he co-produced the illegal paper Czcionka [The Font] and edited Praca [Work], the mouthpiece of Galician socialists founded in 1878. It was this paper's editorial board, together with Daniluk and the editorial board of Robotnik [The Worker], that founded in 1892 the very first socialist party in the Austrian area of partition, the Galician Social Democratic Party [Galicyjska Partia Socjaldemokratyczna].[244] The journal edited by Daniluk was socialist in character, although he did not renounce the historical tradition, as he had fought for Poland during the January Uprising. This mélange of viewpoints was evidenced by the publication in Daniluk's Praca of an obituary of Karl Marx by the Ruthenian socialist Mykhailo Pavlyk, where he voiced his support for the reconstruction of Poland within its pre-partition borders, a viewpoint for which he had to soon leave the editorial team.[245] After various conflicts within Galician socialist ranks, Daniluk finally gave up his political involvement and concentrated on managing the Stauropegion Institute printing press in Lviv.[246]

Characterizing the main directions of Polish politics in the Austrian partition, Halina Kozłowska-Sabatowska identified three fundamental views on the Ruthenian question, the first being the traditional model of viewing the Ruthenians as a Ruthenian tribe melded with the Polish element ("the Jagiellonian Union model"), the second in which domination is imposed on the Ruthenians, while the third model, though finally granting Ruthenians various concessions, could not defuse the growing Polish-Ukrainian conflict.[247] As Maciej Janowski writes, it was to be the second option of the above three that prevailed over the others.[248] This can be attributed to the progressive democratization that

---

[244] Ignacy Daszyński, Pamiętniki (Cracow, 1925), pp. 67–68.

[245] Walentyna Najdus, Polska Partia Socjalno-Demokratyczna Galicji i Śląska 1890–1919 (Warsaw, 1983), pp. 66–67.

[246] Marian Tyrowicz, "Daniluk Józef," in PSB, vol. 4 (Cracow, 1938), pp. 410–11.

[247] Halina Kozłowska-Sabatowska, Ideologia pozytywizmu galicyjskiego 1864–1881 (Wrocław–Warsaw–Cracow–Gdańsk, 1978), p. 166.

[248] Janowski, Inteligencja wobec wyzwań, p. 90.

increased Polish chauvinistic tendencies. The widespread propagation of the national idea in its new guise sparked a growth in negative feelings between the representatives of both nationalities. Both the historical traditions, as well as the refrains of brotherhood and equality, gave way to national populist slogans proclaiming national interests. The nation was to be based primarily on its own ethnos, leaving no room for any fringe elements such as the "half-Poles," the *gente Rutheni, natione Poloni*. Simultaneously, a parallel process was taking place on the other side. As it was impossible for Ukrainians to fight for rights through legal channels such as the Galician Diet or the Imperial Council, more radical alternative methods began to gain popularity. A symbol of the escalation of this process was the assassination of the governor to Galicia, Andrzej Potocki, by Ukrainian student Myroslav Sichynsky in 1908, followed by the Polish-Ukrainian war a decade later. In the aftermath of these events, there was simply no possibility of a return to the previous state of affairs.

Chapter VIII
The Manifestation of Ideas

Gente Rutheni, Natione Poloni
in the Social Life of Galicia

The benches of the Galician Diet were not the only place where the ideas of *gente Rutheni, natione Poloni* had a chance to be voiced. Ruthenians of Polish nationality were equally active outside the political sphere, proving to be even more visible in public life.

In examining the titles of the Galician press from the period of so-called autonomy, one can find many Ruthenians of Polish nationality on editorial committees, while contemporary newspapers contain numerous articles written in accordance with this particular worldview. *Dnewnyk Ruskij* or *Sioło* were not the sole publications to forward this group's perspectives on Polish-Ruthenian relations. A notable newspaper was *Gazeta Narodowa*, which became a fertile creative environment for *gente Rutheni, natione Poloni*, and in particular for the views of one of its editors, Platon Kostecki. The seeds of *Gazeta Narodowa* were sown in 1848, when the newspaper *Rada Narodowa* first appeared in Lviv. The publication was initially connected to the Central National Council, but following its reissue in 1862 functioned as an independent paper of a democratic, and subsequently conservative-patriotic, orientation.[1] No other Galician newspaper employed as many well-known journalists of Ruthenian origin. The founder of this periodical was the Uniate Jan Dobrzański, who hailed from a Ruthenian family that had been Polonized for generations.[2] Jan Dobrzański had worked for seven years on the paper *Gazeta Lwowska*, leaving in 1848 and going on to edit the *Dziennik Mód Paryskich*. His experience placed him in the perfect position to establish his own publication, although he would only finish his work as editor in 1885.[3] Besides Dobrzański, another prominent Greek Catholic by the name of Henryk Rewakowicz worked for *Gazeta Narodowa*, having gained experience in 1856 on *Świt* and from 1858 on *Przegląd Powszechny*. Rewakowicz would later participate in the January Uprising and serve as the editor of *Kurier Lwowski* [The Lviv

---

[1] Halina Kozłowska-Sabatowska evaluated this journal critically, writing that "from out of flowery declarations there emerged superficiality of the program and flatness of the solutions." Halina Kozłowska-Sabatowska, *Ideologia pozytywizmu galicyjskiego 1864–1881* (Wrocław–Warsaw–Cracow–Gdańsk, 1978), p. 166.

[2] Anna Bańkowska, "Opowieść o Janie IV," *Rocznik Lwowski* (1995–1996), p. 146.

[3] Stanisław Wasylewski, "Dobrzański Jan," in *PSB*, vol. 5 (Cracow, 1939–1946), pp. 266–67.

Courier], in which representatives of the Polish People's Party published towards the end of the nineteenth century.[4] Another figure "of Ruthenian kin" involved in *Gazeta Narodowa* was Teofil Merunowicz, who was primarily involved in economic and financial matters. Until October 1875 he was also the editor responsible the journal *Ojczyzna* [Fatherland], published from 1874 to 1875 in Lviv, as well as the publisher of *Ekonomista Polski* [Polish Economist]. Similar subjects could be found in both of these journals, which focused on the need for economic reforms in order to strengthen Polish industry through the creation of strong companies rather than small commercial entities.[5] Besides Dobrzański, Rewakowicz, and Merunowicz, Tadeusz Czapelski [Tadeush Chapelsky] was loosely connected with *Gazeta Narodowa* through the contribution of articles, and later became the editor of *Kurier Warszawski* [The Warsaw Courier], *Kurier Codzienny* [The Daily Courier], and *Tygodnik Illustrowany* [The Illustrated Weekly] in Warsaw.[6] Franciszek Rawita-Gawroński wrote that "Mr. Tadeusz also took the Polish side. He was in every way a Ruthenian of the mould of Platon Kostecki and Jan Dobrzański."[7]

The most important figure at *Gazeta Narodowa*, however, was Platon Kostecki. He arrived at the periodical already having gained significant editorial experience. From 1854 to 1855 he worked on the Ruthenian newspaper *Zoria Halytska*, which shifted in character from its original Russophile profile established by Bohdan Didytsky and Severyn Shekhovych. Kostecki had started his career in the Polish press in 1854, cooperating with Jan Dobrzański's *Nowiny*, but he permanently associated with the Polish press in 1858 when he joined the editorial board of *Przegląd Powszechny*, the name of which soon changed to *Dziennik Polski*.[8] Kostecki then moved to *Gazeta Narodowa*. He would often speak out on the pages of *Gazeta Narodowa* on subjects connected with Rus' and Ruthenians. He advanced ideas that reflected his outlook, one moulded by his own two-tiered identity. However, as the political situation in the country changed, so did the faces of *Gazeta Narodowa*. Initially the newspaper attracted democratic activists, but as Magdalena Semczyszyn points out, from the mid-1880s *Gazeta Narodowa* was increasingly connected with the activities of

---

[4] Krzysztof Dunin-Wąsowicz, "Rewakowicz Henryk Karol," in *PSB*, vol. 31 (Wrocław–Warsaw–Cracow–Gdańsk–Łódź, 1988–89), pp. 169–72.
[5] Jerzy Zdrada, "Lwowska 'Ojczyzna' z roku 1875," *Rocznik Biblioteki Polskiej Akademii Nauk w Krakowie* 15 (1969), pp. 252, 271–72.
[6] Kazimierz Tyszkowski, "Czapelski Tadeusz," in *PSB*, vol. 4 (Cracow, 1938), p. 164.
[7] Franciszek Rawita-Gawroński, *Ludzie i czasy mego wieku. Wspomnienia, wypadki, zapiski (1892–1914)*, ed., introd., and footnotes Eugeniusz Koko (Gdańsk, 2012), pp. 30–31.
[8] Florian Ziemiałkowski, *Pamiętniki*, part 1 (Cracow, 1904), p. 26.

Eastern Galician conservatives. For this reason, the romantic and conciliatory tone that characterized Kostecki's articles started to give way in this newspaper to pieces in defence of the Polish stance and holdings in Eastern Galicia, and with this the confrontational position with regard to Ruthenian national populist activists.[9]

An examination of the biographies of other well-known Ruthenians of Polish nationality reveals that they operated within the framework of an array of institutions that had a significant impact on society. These organizations did not place the propagation of the *gente Rutheni, natione Poloni* worldview as their primary aim, but the very fact that so many eminent Ruthenians of Polish nationality involved themselves in the activities of these institutions speaks volumes about their commitment to Polish affairs. In becoming social authorities, they encouraged those similar to themselves to act. The patriotic zeal of even this handful of Ruthenians was at times greater than that of the ethnic Poles. This enthusiasm was often channelled through several recognizable institutions in Lviv.

For a long time, the Ossolineum, considered the most important academic institution for Poles in the Austrian area of partition, benefitted from the sizeable input of one particular Ruthenian. Ivan Vahylevych, who at the time was using the Polish version of his name, Jan Wagilewicz, was a proponent of Ruthenian nationality and a researcher of folklore, language, and Ruthenian history. Following his involvement in the activities of the Ruthenian Sobor and his editorial work at the pro-Polish *Dnewnyk Ruskij*, he had to search for a way of supporting himself solely among Poles. He found this at the Ossolineum Library. Thanks to the influence of the well-known historian August Bielowski, Wagilewicz became a copy editor for *A Dictionary of the Polish Language* [*Słownik języka polskiego*]. According to Leonid Zashkilniak, Wagilewicz was the author of 1,240 editorial corrections to the dictionary. When he lost his position at the Ossolineum, he was offered the job of municipal archivist.[10] He simultaneously continued his own research into Slavdom, contemporary history, and the history of Poland, as well as various issues to do with ethnology and literature. Zashkilniak notes that:

---

[9] Cf. Magdalena Semczyszyn, "Społeczno-polityczne postawy ziemiaństwa wschodniogalicyjskiego w świetle lwowskiej 'Gazety Narodowej'," in *Społeczeństwo, polityka, kultura. Studia nad dziejami prasy w II Rzeczypospolitej*, ed. Tomasz Sikorski (Szczecin, 2006), pp. 9–13.

[10] Rostysław Radyszewśkyj, "Przedmowa," in Jan Dalibor Wagilewicz, *Pisarze polscy Rusini wraz z dodatkiem Pisarze łacińscy Rusini*, preparation for printing and introd. Rostysław Radyszewśkyj (Przemyśl, 1996), p. 11.

Polish colleagues made use of his substantial erudition and good know-ledge of Slavic languages and varied historical sources in the prepara-tion of source works for publication such as *Monumenta Poloniae Histo-rica, Akta grodzkie i ziemskie...* and others.[11]

In collaboration with Bielowski, Wagilewicz published the Polish-language translation of *Nestor's Chronicle*, also known as the *Tale of Bygone Years* [*Kronika Nestora*]. In the same language he wrote a series of commendable historical texts. His work *Polish-Ruthenian Writers* [*Pisarze Polacy Rusini*] referred to Polish-Ruthenian relations, in which the author examined Ruthenian writers of the sixteenth to eighteenth centuries who published in Polish and in Latin.[12] He also began another work on a similar subject entitled *When Rus' and Poland Came into Exist-ence* [*Gdy Ruś i Polska istnieć poczęły*], although it was ultimately left un-finished.[13] Aside from his publishing activities, already in 1848 he was involved in talks with Maurycy Dzieduszycki and Kasper Cięglewicz to create an academic association dedicated to the commemoration of Poland "through its language and learning," so as to "one day resurrect the Polish nation."[14] His work in publishing and social initiatives as-sisted in the development of Polish academia.

Besides Wagilewicz, two other notable former members of the Ru-thenian Council, Julian Horoszkiewicz and Zygmunt Sawczyński, wrote for an array of publications. The former addressed his works, ones certainly not devoid of nationalistic feelings, chiefly to the youth. He published in *Dzwonek* as well as in separate books. He wrote about the most varied of matters in a non-specialist way: about coins, the Slavs, fashion and customs,[15] and also in general about the world, with particular attention devoted to duties in relation to one's homeland and Poland.[16] His output also included popular publications about Polish dance and national folk costume.[17] Yet, the most important of Julian Horoszkiewicz's texts was a brochure published under the pseudo-nym *Gente Ruthenus natione Polonus*, and subtitled *The Basis for Agree-ment within the Nation* [*Podstawa do zgody w narodzie*]. This publication

---

[11] Leonid Zaszkilniak, "Iwan Wahyłewicz (1811–1866)," in *Złota księga historiografii lwow-skiej XIX i XX wieku*, eds. Jerzy Maternicki and Leonid Zaszkilniak (Rzeszów, 2007), p. 73.

[12] Wagilewicz, *Pisarze polscy Rusini*.

[13] Zaszkilniak, "Iwan Wahyłewicz," p. 77.

[14] Aleksander Batowski, *Diariusz wypadków 1848 roku*, ed., introd. and footnotes Marian Tyrowicz (Wrocław–Warsaw–Cracow–Gdańsk, 1974), p. 308.

[15] [Julian Horoszkiewicz] J.H., "O monetach," *Dzwonek* 1 (1850), pp. 104–7; Julian Ho-roszkiewicz, "Słowianie," *Dzwonek* 2 (1850), pp. 110–13; Julian Horoszkiewicz, "Moda, zwyczaj i potrzeba," *Dzwonek* 4 (1851), pp. 132–35.

[16] Julian Horoszkiewicz, *Świat popularnie opisany* (Lviv, 1853).

[17] Julian Horoszkiewicz, *Taniec polski według dawnego zwyczaju* (Lviv, 1897); Julian Ho-roszkiewicz, *Strój narodowy w Polsce* (Cracow, 1900).

documented the state and needs of the formation represented by the author in the second half of the nineteenth century. The pretext for writing the brochure was the fortieth anniversary of the defeat of the November Uprising. The author began by informing his readers that the Polish-Russian war of 1830–31 was an event of historical significance for Poland, for it brought to an end the era of the knight within the nation's history. While acknowledging its mistakes, Horoszkiewicz viewed the war as a thing of beauty, an uprising of the gentry and intelligentsia, heavily influenced by the wording of the Constitution of May 3. In pondering the significance of

43. Julian Horoszkiewicz

the defeat, Horoszkiewicz predicted that the actions would be bear fruit only if the social estates were to be replaced by a nation, comprised of various peoples derived from diverse social strata.[18] Following this line of thought, he praised the agitators for conducting their activities in the post-January Uprising period in villages and the countryside, particularly in Galicia. He noted that:

> Agitation in the heart of the Ruthenian people (…) came from a single joint core, from a single predominant thought: Poland raised up by the people, a free people, and with the freehold to be the heir and master of this Poland.[19]

Insurgency also attracted the sons of Ruthenian clergymen as well as clerics from the Uniate seminars, members of *gente Rutheni, natione Poloni*. The author, in contemplating the lack of any real effects from this activity, that is, an opposite effect of turning the Ruthenian population against the Poles, explained that this had been the result of the reforms that liberated the peasantry from their former obligations. They had become the masters of Rus', for which they demonstrated their gratitude to the partitioning authorities by obeying them exclusively. Horoszkiewicz saw the genesis of the Polish-Ruthenian conflict in the activities of Austria.[20] This viewpoint represented a significant shift in perspective from an author who had three decades earlier almost been a revolutionary. He recalled that following the joining of Rus' to Poland,

---

[18] [Julian Horoszkiewicz] Gente Ruthenus natione Polonus, *Podstawa do zgody w narodzie* (Lviv, 1871), pp. 6–7.

[19] Ibid., p. 11.

[20] Ibid., pp. 14–15.

the will and desire to create an independent Ruthenian political entity had disappeared, the Ruthenian gentry had become Polonized, and the ordinary people had lost their Ruthenianism to the point whereby the word "Ruthenian" meant someone of the Greek Catholic rite and nothing more. Ruthenian as a language was used only because it was employed in Uniate Church business. According to Horoszkiewicz, "this constituted the entirety of his difference from Polishness, from being a Pole; therefore he was merely *gente Ruthenus, natione Polonus.*"[21] He was critical of the notion that Poles themselves had created the idea of Rus'—a Rus' admittedly fighting against Russia, but bolstering Moscow's interest in sequestering the Ruthenian lands from Polish spheres of interest. Horoszkiewicz argued that it would have been much easier for Russia to transform the nascent Ruthenian movement into a pro-Russian body. He also criticized the tradition of the January Uprising, particularly the emphasis on Rus''s independence as a separate political entity federated only with Poland. Here he referred to the former state tradition of Poland-Lithuania, and not that of Poland-Rus'-Lithuania. He dismissed as baseless the development of the Ruthenian movement in Galicia, and in particular the policies pursued by the St. George camp, as "Eastern Galicia is *de origine* a Polish land, the people there settled on being Polish."[22] He opposed the unconditional realization of the demands of the Ruthenian camp, and accused the Ruthenian priests of succumbing to Russian influences. Summarizing his argument, he presented a way in which the Ruthenian problem in Galicia could be resolved. He adopted as the cardinal principle the "reservation and safeguarding of national integrity," proposing a discontinuance of the Russification of the Ruthenian language as well as a curtailment of the flow of Russian literature into the Austrian area of partition. He identified the introduction of the Latin alphabet to Ruthenian as a helpful measure. Simultaneously, he proposed equal treatment and status for both languages in Galicia, so that in schools where pupils expressed such a desire, classes were to be conducted in the stated language. However, Horoszkiewicz's most important wish was for Ruthenians to publically state that they were Ruthenians, yet ones of Polish nationality, which would result in accord and harmony within the land.[23]

Horoszkiewicz's treatise was the product of a new political reality, in which the leading goal for Poles was no longer an independent fatherland but social consolidation within a Polish spirit, involving

---

[21] Ibid., p. 38.

[22] Ibid., p. 43.

[23] Ibid., p. 45–50. The author wrote: "If according to historical truth and ancient custom they utter that they are *gente Rutheni, natione Poloni,* freedom shall be general, accord total and the prosperity of the land broad and lasting" (p. 50).

the stemming of Ruthenian separatism, particularly if it was to lead to a movement in the direction of Russia. These goals had been earlier postulated by Horoszkiewicz, but now he proposed other methods for their realization.

Interestingly, the Horoszkiewicz brochure generated a critical reaction among the *gente Rutheni, natione Poloni*. In September 1871, Platon Kostecki in *Gazeta Narodowa* wrote a critical review of Horoszkiewicz's work (because of the pseudonym used by Horoszkiewicz, Kostecki did not know that he was the author). Kostecki admittedly appreciated the orientation of *gente Rutheni, natione Poloni*, which he himself professed, but he refused to accept the adoption of the Latin alphabet by the Ruthenians (Horoszkiewicz believed that this would stop the development of the Russophile orientation). Kostecki also criticized Horoszkiewicz for deprecating the fact that during the January Uprising Rus' was elevated to the rank of the third component of the Commonwealth (by adding Archangel Michael to the coat of arms), although this practice did not have historical (heraldic) justification. Kostecki believed that the ideological message of the National Government of the January Uprising remained very current. He claimed that the work of Horoszkiewicz, though rightly directed against the Russophiles, would undermine the Polish-Ruthenian agreement. Kostecki stood for the position of full equality between Poles and Ruthenians as two communities forming one society. Therefore, he espoused full rights for the development of Ruthenian education[24].

But over the years, Kostecki and his views became more and more isolated among the *gente Rutheni, natione Poloni*. Other *gente Rutheni, natione Poloni* not only became more and more Polonized, but also—consciously or unconsciously—furthered the Polonization of Ruthenians. The best example is Zygmunt Sawczyński, who held a Ph.D. in philosophy, published historical and pedagogical works. His articles on aspects of teaching were to grace the pages of many Galician journals, including *Szkoła*, the press organ of the Pedagogical Society that he himself had helped to found in 1868. In July 1873 he was elected president of the society, a position he held until his death. It was thanks to him that the society, being more or less a national forum for teachers, was able to maintain cordial relations for the entirety of his office with the Provincial School Board, which managed education nationally. Constituting a link between the two institutions, Sawczyński supported the Polonization of the school system. Despite his Ruthenian origins, he was an expert in the Polish language. He had not only opted for the

---

[24] P.K. [Platon Kostecki], "Literatura polityczna polska. W sprawie ruskiej," *Gazeta Narodowa* no. 292 (23 Sep. 1871), p. 1–2.

Polonization of the Germanized school
system while working on the National
Council, but he also was active initially as
a corresponding member, later serving on
the Language Commission established by
the Society.[25]

What Zygmunt Sawczyński did for
schooling, Jan Dobrzański, another joint
founder of the Pedagogical Society and
also a Uniate, was to do for Lviv theatre.
Together with his son Stanisław Dobrzański he essentially controlled the stage
from 1873 until 1886, with a short break
in 1883. As the biographer of "Jan IV" —as

44. Jan Dobrzański

he was called following his participation in the revolutions of 1848—
wrote: "Lviv is in his debt for totally eliminating the German stage, for
founding a drama school, as well as for the marvellous period in the
history of its theatre."[26] In the preceding decades, the Germanization
of the theatre had been ensured by its most generous benefactor. The
Lviv theatre was built in the years 1837–42 through donations from
the Stanisław Skarbek Foundation. This landed gentryman used imperial privilege, which made him a monopolist in the theatre branch.
Skarbek's support rested on the condition that performances were presented chiefly in German for four days a week, with performances in
Polish, French or Italian reserved for the remaining days.[27] This privilege, ensuring the dominance of German at the Lviv theatre, continued
until 1871. At this point, thanks to the efforts of Jan Dobrzański, it was
possible to relieve the Skarbek Foundation of the obligation to support
the German theatre.[28] The theatre would experience some of its best
years under the father and son team of the Dobrzańskis, who took over
its management from 1873.[29]

Apart from the theatre, Dobrzański was involved in one other
undertaking of immense importance for the development of national consciousness: the Sokół Gymnastic Society, founded in Lviv
in 1867. As the founder of the organization, Dobrzański was connected with it for many years; he served first as its director, and
then from 1871 until his death in 1886 as president and honorary

---

[25] Zbigniew Fras, "Sawczyński Zygmunt," in *PSB*, vol. 35 (Warsaw–Cracow, 1994),
pp. 290–94.
[26] Stanisław Wasylewski, "Dobrzański Jan," in *PSB*, vol. 5 (Cracow, 1939–1946), p. 267.
[27] Stanisław Schnür-Pepłowski, *Teatr polski we Lwowie (1780–1881)* (Lviv, 1889), pp. 174–75.
[28] Ibid., pp. 324–25.
[29] Ibid., pp. 365–411.

member.[30] The Association promoted the development of physical education among the youth, but also aimed to shape their morality and national spirit. It enjoyed enormous popularity among the young people of Galicia, and for a long time remained the only association with such a profile; its rival organization, the Ukrainian Sokil, was only founded in 1905. Both Poles and their Ruthenian neighbours were involved in the activities of the Polish Sokół. Platon Kostecki, who served as secretary from 1873–76, placed particular hope in the Sokół youth for the future struggle for the independence of a tripartite state.[31] Kostecki dedicated several poems to this institution,[32] one of which was entitled *At the Cornerstone-laying Ceremony at the Headquarters of the Gymnastic Association Sokół in Lviv on 1 June 1884* [*Na uroczystość założenia kamienia węgielnego pod gmach Towarzystwa Gimnastycznego „Sokół" we Lwowie dnia 1 czerwca 1884*].[33] In this poem, Kostecki brought together the past and future of Poles and Ruthenians, naturally presented in a collective spirit:

> With God and the fatherland a grain we do place
> Youngsters in penance that cornerstone hew
> Let our work by that silent monument grace
> For those who'll one day a wedding chorus imbue
>
> And we place in this stone a memento
> Etched in the tongue of Pole and Rus' too
> For in a single storm a rainbow of one
> God will see that all our future is together in the sun

The Polish and Ruthenian members of Sokół were to gain independence together:

> And the Archangel shall play a signal resounding
> And the Little Falcons will bravely outside go a-rushing!

Thanks in part to Kostecki, Sokół would become an arena for the realization of the construction of a Commonwealth of Three Nations. The question as to the numbers of other ethnicities besides Poles that

---

[30] *Księga pamiątkowa ku uczczeniu dwudziestej piątej rocznicy założenia Towarzystwa Gimnastycznego 'Sokół' we Lwowie* (Lviv, 1892), p. 168.

[31] *Przewodnik Gimnastyczny 'Sokół'* was to underline at a later date that Kostecki often defended Sokół activities in the press. See *Przewodnik Gimnastyczny 'Sokół'* no. 6 (Jun. 1908).

[32] Platon Kostecki, 'Projekt pomnika'. *Wiersz na cześć Jana Dobrzańskiego pracownika na polu obywatelskiem, literackiem i scenicznem, twórcy i głównego filaru 'Sokoła' i gmachu 'Sokoła'* (Lviv, 1886); Platon Kostecki, *Przy wręczaniu sztandaru od Polek na srebrne gody 'Sokoła' lwowskiego dnia 27 marca 1892 roku* (Lviv, 1892).

[33] Platon Kostecki, *Na uroczystość założenia kamienia węgielnego pod gmach Towarzystwa Gimnastycznego 'Sokół' we Lwowie dnia 1. czerwca 1884* (Lviv, 1884).

were involved in the organization's activities may only be answered when a work analyzing the social composition of the Sokół membership is undertaken. However, confirmation that Ruthenians were also involved in the Association's activities can be found in the example of the Sambir section set up in 1890 to mark the 500th anniversary of the town. As a specialist on Sambir wrote:

> As was typical and characteristic of the times in question, the first founders and members of Sokół were not only drawn from the most nationally aware Poles but also included Jews and Ruthenians, who saw in the reconstruction of an independent Poland their own happiness and material gain.[34]

A visualization of the idea that motivated the founders and initial members of the Sambir Sokół was its standard, produced somewhat later, in 1902. It depicted a coat of arms displaying in equal parts the emblems of Poland, Lithuania, and Rus' (The Archangel Michael), with an oval in the centre encircling the Virgin Mary and Child. On the sash was the inscription: "Until death comes, persevere with this standard. Take the insignia as a gift from the Polish women of Sambir."[35]

The Commemorations of the 300th Anniversary of the Union of Lublin in 1869

One type of public occasion in which Ruthenians of Polish nationality were particularly active was anniversary celebrations commemorating historical events. As long as those prominent *gente Rutheni, natione Poloni* lived and operated in the public forum, there was the need to manifest Polish-Ruthenian accord at the most important anniversary celebrations in Galicia so as to express the dream of fulfilling the federal idea of an independently aligned Poland, Lithuania, and Rus'.

Not only did the 300th anniversary of the Union of Lublin enter into the history of Lviv as the most important demonstration of the former and forthcoming Polish state's federal character, but it was also an important argument for discussions about federalization of the Habsburg Monarchy which was undertaken by Polish democrats in Galicia from 1867 (see chapter: *The Galician Diet Resolution of 24 September 1868*).

The official activities commemorating the Polish-Lithuanian state's former glory, as well as the union of Lithuanians and "Little Russians"

---

[34] Aleksander Kuczera, *Samborszczyzna. Ilustrowana monografja miasta Sambora i ekonomii samborskiej*, vol. 2 (Sambor, 1935), p. 366.
[35] Ibid., illustration after p. 364.

with the Poles, could not have taken place in tsarist Russia in the aftermath of the January Uprising. Only during the era of autonomy was it possible to stage such an event in Galicia, even though these types of occasions were often heavily censored and sometimes suspended entirely by the authorities. As the capital of the Austrian area of partition, the main political centre for Galician elites, and a city that straddled Polish and Ruthenian culture, Lviv was the ideal place for the organization of the 300th anniversary commemorations of the treaty, and also for the raising of a Lublin Union mound.[36] In terms of the message they propagated, these events were to be similar in character to those organized in 1861 in Horodło for the 448th anniversary of the Polish-Lithuanian union. The broad participation of Ruthenians at that event gave hope for a similar attendance in Lviv.

The idea of organizing a 300th anniversary commemoration of the Union of Lublin in Galicia was first hatched in France, as a result of deliberations over Ruthenian participation in any future national uprising as well as the opposition of Rus' to Russia.[37] Yet for the Polish political activists from Galicia and abroad, the Union of Lublin was a symbol of the might of the Commonwealth of Two Nations, which despite its multi-ethnic character had managed to become a significant political player in Europe. For the entire nineteenth century, the nationally conscious part of Polish society dreamed of regaining independence as a state with its former shape and boundaries, but this was not possible without the involvement of other ethnic groups who inhabited the territory of the former Polish-Lithuanian Commonwealth. In Galicia, it was the Ruthenians who were the target demographic. Consequently, from the beginning of the 1860s it became imperative to emphasize that the Union was Polish-Lithuanian-Ruthenian, and not merely Polish-Lithuanian. This position is clear in the numerous press articles that appeared before and during the anniversary celebrations.

---

[36] The matter of the celebrations in Lviv to commemorate the Union of Lublin has attracted much interest in both Polish and Ukrainian scholarship. See chiefly: Stanisław Schnür-Pepłowski, *Obrazy z przeszłości Galicyi i Krakowa (1772–1858)*, part 1: *Lwów i lwowianie* (Lviv, 1896); Paweł Sierżęga, *Obchody 200. rocznicy odsieczy wiedeńskiej w Galicji (1883 r.)* (Rzeszów, 2002); Marian Mudryi, "Aktyvizatsiia suspil'no-politychnoho zhyttia u 60-70-kh rokakh XIX st.," in *Istoriia Lvova*, vol. 2: *1772 – zhovten' 1918*, ed. Iaroslav Isaevych (Lviv, 2007); Markian Prokopovych, "Kopiec Unii Lubelskiej: Imperial Politics and National Celebration in Habsburg Lemberg," *Ece-urban* no. 3 (2008), accessed 1 Sep. 2019, http://www.lvivcenter.org/en/publications/ece-urban/; Marian Mudryi, "Ideia pol's'ko-ukraïns'koï uniï ta 'Rusyny pol's'koï natsiï' v etno-politychnomu dyskursi Halychyny 1859–1869 rokiv," in *Visnyk Lvivs'koho universytetu. Seriia istorychna* 39–40 (2005), pp. 134–47.

[37] Paweł Sierżęga, "Obchody rocznicy unii lubelskiej na terenie Galicji w 1869 roku," in *Działalność wyzwoleńcza*, ed. Jadwiga Hoff (Rzeszów, 2001), pp. 151–54.

In the 28 February 1869 edition of the Cracow *Czas*, it was written that:

> The Union did not bind the Kingdom of Poland, the Great Duchy of Poznań, Lithuania, and Galicia into a single body, but joined and will join Poland, Lithuania, and Rus' and their three peoples into a single national body. It did not thwart the partitioning of Poland, nor are the present-day political positions of each of the post-partition parts troubled by the joining in union of the three nations (...).[38]

Given the recurrent announcement of Ruthenian demands for the division of Galicia into an eastern and western part, the very existence of the Act of Lublin gave Polish politicians something approaching an unquestionable historical precedent on which to stand. It seemed to offer a proof that Rus' had joined with Poland on the power of former agreements, therefore refuting the need to partition these lands. It was announced that despite the collapse of the state resulting from the partitions, Poles and Ruthenians as a single political nation had demonstrated longevity that would last right up until the gaining of independence based on pre-1772 borders. Another article published in the aforementioned *Czas* noted:

> The Union of Lublin is presented to us as the fruit of two centuries of joint existence over the glorious epoch of the Commonwealth. It represents the underlying assumption of a great tripartite national body, of the whole future life of three nations increasingly politically, socially, spiritually, religiously and literally joining together, and having to rebuff a subsequent attempt at confinement and joint persecution as they share common glory and greatness. Strangely, no one is able to break that which has grown through freedom in captivity.[39]

Commenting critically on the idea of Ruthenian political demands, the author wrote:

> So the historical thread of the Union was not severed, yet in the absence of political raison d'être, faith and history served as the link. That is why only in the ranks of those indifferent to those two great properties of the nation are there those who stand against the tradition of unity; they are among us as they are among the Ruthenians. Those who repel history or who do not know the spirit of their ancestors, or those who betray their creed, fight against this historical as well as religious matter. Yet they are only able to stop this march of history, not to lead it forward. Therefore, the Union shall triumph and be reborn in spite of them, while the memory of the past three hundred years rises as a challenge [!] to revive its soul. It does not follow to mark this recollection with mean-

---

[38] "Kraków 27 lutego," *Czas* no. 48 (28 Feb. 1869), p. 1.
[39] "Kraków 25 maja," *Czas* no. 117 (26 May 1869), p. 1.

ingless words, or through a lively commemoration, but through deeds and life.[40]

The most important demand underlined in the article was not for the unreflective celebration of this historical act, but rather to convince contemporary Ruthenians to accept this celebration:

It is not for us among graves and ruins to commemorate historical triumphs, it is not for us to remove the purple mantle from our ancestors in order to cover our own rags, but it follows to revive their soul, rekindle in oneself the idea of union, for it was aptly said that "if you want to commemorate the Union then revive it with the Ruthenians."[41]

Of course, not everyone believed that the Ruthenian population of Galicia would take up this calling. The matter was critically addressed by the leading representative of Cracow Stańczyk circles, Stanisław Koźmian. Within the main publication of his political powerbase, *Przegląd Polski*, he wrote that the grand celebrations of the 300th anniversary of the Union did not improve the political position of the Poles, but rather revealed its weak points. For this reason, the Ruthenians did not join in celebrations commemorating the Act of Lublin. He argued:

The anniversary of the Union unilaterally celebrated, without the participation of Ruthenians and Ruthenian deputies, is in our eyes no longer an absurdity, no longer a fruitless demonstration, but a comedy unworthy of us and almost an affront from our lamentable position. What will such a commemoration prove, what will it achieve? Possibly that unpleasant fact for us that for three hundred years we have only managed to muster in the matter a comic presentation of this great political act, and that in this presentation, not being able to recruit any Ruthenian actors, we have been forced to dress ourselves up as Ruthenians.[42]

Stanisław Tarnowski echoed Koźmian's sentiments to a wider audience in the form of satire. In *Stańczyk's Portfolio* [*Teka Stańczyka*], Koźmian penned a fictitious letter from a young "political woman" named Aldona to her friend Malwina.[43] The author of the letter describes in earnest her own plans for the commemoration of the anniversary. She decides that during the church ceremony to mark the tricentenary, she will enter the temple in a black dress, tied with a red ribbon to symbolize martyrdom, with a thorny crown on her head and handcuffs on her wrists, which at the moment of the anthem being

---

[40] Ibid.
[41] Ibid.
[42] Stanisław Koźmian, "Przegląd polityczny," *Przegląd Polski* 1, no. 3 (13) (1869), p. 352.
[43] [Stanisław Koźmian, Józef Szujski and Stanisław Tarnowski], *Teka Stańczyka* (Cracow, 1870), pp. 36–38.

sung would be broken. She also confided that the priest had advised her against resting in a coffin in a white dress, from which she was to triumphantly rise up to symbolize the resurrection of Poland. She recounts further that a female friend, Kornelia, had asked her to engage two other friends in the plan so that the three of them together would symbolize the Commonwealth of Three Nations. Finally, on the advice of a certain general Kilof [Pickaxe], she became convinced that she herself could best convey the notion of a unified Commonwealth. Hence Poland, Lithuania, and Rus' would be symbolized by their coats of arms, sewn to her dress. She regales her addressee with details of the appropriate composition for the particular national elements in a broad *post scriptum* note. The whole pastiche ends with the words:

> Probably on this note I shall finish: I will fit the Eagle, Knight [Vytis] and Angel [Archangel Michael] on a single shield to the front, but if I were to have some good idea or other then I would share it, for it is not about me but the good of the country that's at stake![44]

Also satirized in *Stańczyk's Portfolio* were the Lviv democrats. Headed by Franciszek Smolka, this group understood the anniversary matter differently. Even though he was not an ethnic Pole (his father had been an Austrian officer from Silesia, while his mother was Hungarian), Smolka was a politician whose early career in the years following the revolutions of 1848 had been characterized by positive relations with Ruthenians; indeed, he decided to grant them a series of concessions.[45] Paweł Sierżęga described Smolka as being different among Lviv circles in terms of his attitude towards the Ruthenians. Amid his agenda to advance democratic changes while demanding the creation of a federation comprising the subjects of historic Poland, he also stated the need to recognize the Ruthenians as a separate nationality. He supported the Ruthenian demands for the introduction of Ruthenian into schools and government offices, a move that was questioned by a significant part of the Polish political scene.[46] For Smolka, fulfilling these Ruthenian demands in no way conflicted with Polish interests; he saw Poland as an independent state, within its former borders, where all social problems would be solved. Smolka and his circle wanted to preserve Polish-Ruthenian unity in both a national and societal sense. Following this line of thought, the Union of Lublin was revered as symbolic, as it proved that neighbouring nations could come together in good faith to pursue the higher ideal that was the well-being of the state and the legal equality of its subjects. For this reason, the commemorations of the Union of

---

[44] Ibid., p. 38.
[45] Prokopovych, "Kopiec Unii," p. 8.
[46] Sierżęga, "Obchody rocznicy unii lubelskiej," p. 160.

Lublin had a patriotic goal, rooted in tradition yet making recourse to current national and social problems. They were also, as Markian Prokopovych has interpreted the matter, a form of demonstration for "federalism of the Polish Commonwealth as an alternative to the centralized model of the Monarchy – rather than to question the very existence of the Monarchy altogether."[47]

The commemoration preparations began in April 1869 when a committee, several dozen strong, was formed with Franciszek Smolka at the head. On July 4, a 29-person organizational commission was established, comprising several representatives of Lviv's socio-cultural life, including the *gente Rutheni, natione Poloni* Platon Kostecki and Dymitr Koczyndyk.[48] The presence of these two men in the committee constituted an exception to the norm, as other politically active Ruthenians did not feel drawn to what they deemed to be a Polish initiative. In addition, Franciszek Smolka planned not only to exalt the act of the Union of Lublin, but in so doing turn the commemorations into an act of propaganda aimed against Russia and its act of partition, which may not have been to the taste of the Russophiles. He intended to prepare for the celebratory march on August 11 the flags of the Polish Crown's former south-eastern provinces, lands which were now considered part of Russia.[49]

One of the committee's main aims was to gain the support and participation of Galician Ruthenians in celebrating the Union. A separate commission of five men, including Henryk Schmitt and Karol Widman, was carved out of the committee, with the purpose of developing a consensus with the Ruthenians and incorporating them into the organizational process. An obstacle to the commission's work was the fact that Schmitt unconditionally viewed the Ruthenian nation as a Polish tribe, and strove for its close integration into the Polish nation. His motto, expressed in a book published several years later, was well known: "What God and history have joined, this Saint George shall not undo."[50]

---

[47] Prokopovych, "Kopiec Unii," p. 8–9.

[48] Sierżęga, "Obchody rocznicy unii lubelskiej," pp. 165–66.

[49] These intentions were met with an almost instant reaction. The Russophiles announced the organization of parallel celebrations to mark the 900th anniversary of the death of Princess Olha as well as marking the anniversary of Galicia's inclusion in Austria and the liberation of Red Rus' from Polish occupation. See ibid., p. 164.

[50] Henryk Schmitt, *Kilka słów bezstronnych w sprawie ruskiej* (Lviv, 1861). For the views of Schmitt in a leaflet outlining his position on the Ruthenian question, together with other texts where he debated with articles appearing in the Ruthenian publication *Slovo*, see Antoni Artymiak, *Lwowianin Henryk Schmitt (spiskowiec, powstaniec, bibliotekarz, publicysta, historyk, organizator szkolnictwa)* (Jędrzejów, 1939), pp. 46–49. See also: Stefan Kieniewicz, "Schmitt Henryk Leonard," in *PSB*, vol. 35, pp. 559–62 as well as the interesting (though not particularly good) play by Schmitt from the period of the revolutions of 1848

Recalling the concept for the reintroduction of the Latin script to Ruthenian and the replacement of the Julian Calendar with the Gregorian in the Greek Catholic Church a decade earlier, Schmitt saw the celebration of the Union of Lublin as the best possible opportunity for encouraging a different mentality.[51] However, his ideas were not to be realized, even though Schmitt returned to them in the 1870s with the help of the Ruthenian Anton Kobyliansky.[52] As Paweł Sierżęga has demonstrated in his article, all of the commission's efforts ended in a fiasco. The undertakings of Tadeusz Romanowicz and Teofil Merunowicz had the greatest chance of success, as they wished to cooperate with the Prosvita Society. They discussed the distribution and propagation of Ruthenian books and increasing literacy among the Ruthenian peasantry, hoping to encourage this part of the population to partake in the commemorations. Ultimately, however, their endeavour also ended in failure.[53] What is more, not only were the Ruthenians uninterested in the celebrations, they even went so far as to boycott them with a public protest; they published articles, hung posters, made announcements, and even moved to hold memorial services in Greek Catholic churches and to fly black flags in homes, although it ultimately did not come to this.

The most important document directed towards the Polish commemorations was the Ruthenian article of 18 July 1869 protesting the Union of Lublin anniversary celebration. Initially it was published in the Ruthenian *Slovo*,[54] later circulating as a separate leaflet published in both Ruthenian and German.[55] The piece argued that the Union of Lublin, which Ruthenians "resisted as much as possible," had constituted for Rus' an act of "imprisonment" on the part of the Poles. This was outlined through an extensive historical account provided further on in the text. The article ended with the ascertainment that this was not the first time that the Poles had expressed the desire to renew an

---

performed at the Ossolineum in Wrocław: Henryk Schmitt, "Niezgodni bracia. Tragedja w 5 działaniach," ZNiO, sygn. 5923/II.

[51] See Artymiak, *Lwowianin Henryk Schmitt*, pp. 117–18. For more on Schmitt's views on the Ruthenian question as contained in the leaflet *Kilka słów bezstronnych w sprawie ruskiej* see: ibid., pp. 48–49.

[52] Ibid., p. 118 (the author refers to Kobyliansky's letter of 20 Jul. 1876 written in Vienna, which before the Second World War was held at the National Ossoliński Institute in Lviv under the catalogue no.: 5916/II, and is currently held in Wrocław under the same number). Cf. Jarosław Moklak, *W walce o tożsamość Ukraińców – Zagadnienie języka wykładowego w szkołach ludowych i średnich w pracach galicyjskiego Sejmu Krajowego 1866–1892* (Cracow, 2004), p. 37.

[53] Sierżęga, "Obchody rocznicy unii lubelskiej," pp. 168–69.

[54] "Protest" halytskykh rusynov" protyv" prazdnovan'ia rochnytsy 'Uniy Liublynskoi' na Rusy," *Slovo* no. 58 (23 Jul. [4 Aug.] 1869), p. 1–3.

[55] For more on the subject read: Mudryi, "Ideia pol's'ko-ukraïns'koï uniï," pp. 140–42; Sierżęga, "Obchody rocznicy unii lubelskiej," pp. 181–82.

"accord" between nations. The author rebuked the initiators of the event, noting that instead of raising a mound on the High Castle in Lviv they would have been better off meeting at the Galician Diet to build accord through ensuring national rights and equality. This highly critical reaction to the events of 1569 was rooted in the belief that the Union had deprived Ruthenians of their national identity by means of assimilation, the *gente Rutheni, natione Poloni* themselves being proof of this phenomenon. It was not long before this article was met with an opposing polemic, first taken up on the pages of *Przegląd Polski*.[56]

The Lviv democratic circles did not give up, despite the Ruthenian resistance and the difficulties posed by the Austrian administration. They continued to propagate their noble idea in the press, as well as through various leaflets and flyers. One of the most interesting pamphlets of the time was Teofil Merunowicz's *Souvenir of the 300th Anniversary of the Union of Lublin 1869* [*Pamiątka 300 letniej rocznicy unii Lubelskiej 1869 roku*], published in Polish and Ruthenian in Latin script.[57] In this piece, Merunowicz set out to sketch a historiosophical vision of events from Poland's past. The Ruthenian edition was even supplemented with Platon Kostecki's well-known poem "Our Prayer", segueing perfectly into the commemorative mood of 1869. Merunowicz attempted to illustrate that the genesis of the Polish, Lithuanian, and Ruthenian cooperation had been forged centuries earlier, seeing the main cause for this confluence in the external threat posed by the Germans, Russians, and Tatars, who could not be defeated if faced alone.[58] He endeavoured to outline the whole process of Rus's unity with Poland, starting from the rule of Casimir the Great and even making reference to early

45. *The cover of Teofil Merunowicz's brochure* A Souvenir of the 300th Anniversary of the Union of Lublin 1869 *(Lviv, 1869)*

---

[56] "Kronika bibliograficzna," *Przegląd Polski* 1, no. 3 (13) (1869), pp. 522–23.

[57] Cf. Teofil Merunowicz, *Pamiątka 300 letniej rocznicy unii Lubelskiej 1869 roku* (Lviv, 1869); Teofil Merunowicz, *Pamiatka 300-litnoj ricznyci unii Lublińskoj 1869 roku* ([Lviv, 1869]).

[58] Merunowicz, *Pamiątka 300 letniej rocznicy*, p. 6.

Slavic times.[59] The main thrust of Merunowicz's thesis was to show that even though the Jagiellonians were no longer alive,

> (...) the Polish nation lives, Lithuania and Rus' live these nations are alive to this day, inseparably connected through the glory of times of yore, through the present-day pressure exerted by Muscovites and Prussians, through the trouble with Germans, and finally joined by the hope for better times to come (...).[60]

On the occasion of the anniversary, Merunowicz appealed to his contemporaries:

> If there are Ruthenians or Poles in our land who look askance at each other, and hold in their hearts some non-fraternal envy towards one another, then they should forget about all this on this day of celebratory remembrance and give each other their hand in accord, as our fathers did three hundred years ago in Lublin. (...) For if we are not to keep contact with each other, if we are not genuinely going to mutually support each other and work upon pulling ourselves out of our joint adversity, then our current enemies will crush us exactly as old Poland, Rus', and Lithuania would have been crushed if they had not stood side by side![61]

Merunowicz was not the only author who wrote about the Union with the intention of reaching a wider audience. At the time, a fairly large number of minor publications of this ilk began to appear. One such work was the aforementioned book *The Union of Lithuania with the Crown Achieved at the Lublin Diet of 1568–1569* [*Unja Litwy z Koroną dokonana na sejmie lubelskim 1568–1569*] by Henryk Schmitt, a German by origin who was involved in organizing the commemorations.[62]

The celebrations worried the authorities not only because of their symbolic character, but also because of the contemporary political context in which they were situated. As a result, obstacles were put in place by the Austrian administration as preventative measures. The police in Lviv, fearing the "provocation of a large part of the inhabitants both here in the capital [of Galicia – A.Ś.] as well as in the country as a whole," banned the commemorations in the name of public safety.[63] In response to this injunction, Smolka issued an appeal. Reprinted in the Galician press, his article expounded on the idea of the anniversary and the issue of the ban:

---

[59] Ibid., pp. 6–12.
[60] Ibid., p. 13.
[61] Ibid., p. 14.
[62] Henryk Schmitt, *Unja Litwy z Koroną dokonana na sejmie lubelskim 1568–1569. Szkic dziejowy* (Lviv, 1869).
[63] Sierżęga, "Obchody rocznicy unii lubelskiej," pp. 170–71.

> We have not been allowed to publicly and ceremoniously uphold in Lviv [the jubilee celebrations – A.S.] as we had desired. We can neither invite emissaries from the provinces nor guests from abroad, for we do not wish to expose them to any unpleasantness, and we are unable to organize the march. But if they have forbidden us in one place to celebrate that day together, then let the whole nation celebrate it, not in the way befitting such a lofty moment, but insofar as relations allow for it to be commemorated. For if the celebration loses its external brilliance, then let it benefit instead from a heightened spiritual concentration, let it grow in the sense that the celebrations will be everywhere that the feelings of freedom and fraternity reach.[64]

Though the celebration could not be organized in an official fashion, it could still take place in the city in a spontaneous form, even though Smolka had been forbidden from calling on the townsfolk to close up their houses and workshops and join in with those celebrating the jubilee. Despite the ban, the press eventually published a program of events.[65] As Stanisław Schnür-Pepłowski writes, three days before the celebrations Smolka had assured the authorities that "there is no intention of summoning a mass assembly during the mound-raising ceremony."[66] Unsurprisingly, the reality would play out completely differently. The commemorations were to take place unofficially, which caused no problems whatsoever and at least allowed the Polish inhabitants of Lviv to participate.

Stanisław Schnür-Pepłowski provided a detailed account of the commemorations in his book. The day of August 11, the three-hundredth anniversary of the act of Lublin, was rainy and overcast. The inhabitants of Lviv allegedly did not open their shops and craft workshops remained closed; instead, they went to the Dominican church for the celebratory service, which was to be attended by "a vast host of the public."[67] The sermon was given by Piotr Korotkiewicz, a national populist priest, who presented the history of the Union of Lublin to those assembled as an act through which Poland outstripped other nations by centuries. He called for a fraternal hand to be extended to the Ruthenians and for old wounds to be forgotten. Following the mass, those who attended joined in a "spontaneous" procession to Lviv Castle Hill, upon which the erection of the mound commenced after Smolka delivered a solemn address. The mound's foundation stone was emblazoned with the emblems of Poland, Lithuania, and Rus', with the inscription: "The free with the free, the equal with the equal – Poland,

---

[64] "Kronika miejscowa i zagraniczna. Kraków 31 lipca," *Czas* no. 173 (1 Aug. 1869), p. 3.
[65] Ibid.
[66] Schnür-Pepłowski, *Obrazy z przeszłości*, part 1, p. 79.
[67] Ibid., p. 79.

Lithuania, and Rus' united by the Union of Lublin on 11 August 1569."
Representatives of the Municipal Council took turns throwing earth
after Smolka had done so, followed by other delegations, with local city
residents partaking at the end. Several "fistfuls" of earth were intended
to be a national sacralization of the monument under construction, for
soil had been brought from the graves of famous Polish poets and national heroes such as Adam Mickiewicz, Juliusz Słowacki, General Karol
Kniaziewicz, Antoni Jan Ostrowski, as well as from Soloviivka, where
students of Kyiv University had fallen during the January Uprising.[68]
As Bolesław Limanowski mentioned in his memoirs, the earth for the
mound was brought in wheelbarrows, with around 30,000 people gathered around the monument as it took form. Franciszek Smolka, dressed
in a robe and a calpack hat with feathers, delivered a speech. His address was followed by those of Poznań delegate Ignacy Moszczeński
and a mysterious unknown peasant, whose inclusion might have been
an intentional and symbolic act.[69] The mound grew day by day, soon
becoming one of the most significant memorials for the inhabitants of
the former Polish lands.

*46. Franciszek Smolka places the foundation stone for the construction
of the Mound of the Union of Lublin in Lviv in 1869*

---

[68] Ibid., pp. 79–80.
[69] Bolesław Limanowski, *Pamiętniki (1870–1907)*, ed. Janusz Durko (Warsaw, 1958),
pp. 40–41.

Following the raising of the mound, a celebratory meal attended by around 100 people took place the next day in the restaurant on Lviv Castle Hill. The banquet was intended to reflect the cooperation of various nationalities in commemorating the Union of Lublin. Addresses were made by the representatives of various national and émigré groups: Karol Widman spoke for the committee, Michał Jolles spoke on behalf of the Jews, and Platon Kostecki delivered two poems for the Ruthenians, one in Polish and one in Ruthenian. Bolesław Limanowski recalled an excerpt of the latter:

> The slave driver's whip erases the Polish name
> But the nation alive shall always remain.[70]

The poet Krystyn Ostrowski gave an address as a representative of émigré groups, Father Tadeusz Chromecki spoke in the name of the exiled Polish clergy, and Tadeusz Romanowicz, Karol Groman, Mieczysław Darowski, Franciszek Smolka read out telegrams from Poland and abroad.[71]

Ruthenian participation in the organizational work for the commemorations was poor, and was restricted to the most active Ruthenians of Polish nationality in Lviv: Platon Kostecki, Teofil Merunowicz, and Dymitr Koczyndyk. It is impossible to establish how many Ruthenians actually took part in the celebrations. It is also difficult to gauge the interest of Ruthenians outside of Lviv in this event, although there was certainly some degree of curiosity; the list of telegrams published on the pages of *Czas*, which mentions the receipt of a letter from Poles and Ruthenians from a burghers' club (casino) in Stanyslaviv, suggests as much.[72]

Not all initiatives were geared towards procuring Ruthenian involvement; gestures were also made in a display of magnanimity towards the Ruthenian population in the name of the fraternal ideal. It was in this spirit that those gathered at the restaurant on Lviv Castle Hill gave donations to Prosvita, even though this organization ultimately did not take part in the commemorations.[73]

The construction of the mound and the ceremonial meal at the restaurant were not the only highlights of the commemorative program. The theatre in Lviv organized a robust artistic program that was extremely well attended. A fragment from *Superstition, or Cracovians and Highlanders* [*Zabobon, czyli Krakowiacy i Górale*] by Jan Nepomucen

---

[70] Ibid., p. 41.
[71] "Kronika miejscowa i zagraniczna. Kraków 13 sierpnia," *Czas* no. 184 (14 Aug. 1869), p. 2.
[72] Ibid.
[73] Schnür-Pepłowski, *Obrazy z przeszłości*, part 1, p. 81.

Kamiński opened the performance, followed by an excerpt from the opera *The Ukrainian Girl* [*Ukrainka*], with numerous allusions to the unity of Poland, Rus', and Lithuania. The performance closed with "a picture of living folk" entitled *Sigismund II Augustus on the Throne* [*Zygmunt August na tronie*], during which the anthem "Poland Is Not Yet Lost" ["Jeszcze Polska nie zginęła"] was sung; the Polish singers Filomena Kwiecińska and Aleksander Koncewicz then hummed the Ruthenian *dumka* "Over Podilia, Ukraine..." ["Nad Podilliam, Ukrajinoju..."], which the audience greeted with standing ovations.[74] This reaction was not surprising given that the *dumka* tells of the role played by Poland in the rousing of Rus':

> The Angel of our Polish Mother
> Open up the tumulus
> Live it up, oh Polish brother
> The steppe still plays for us![75]

This program, richly infused with the symbols of Polish-Ruthenian-Lithuanian unity, was, however, the reserve option. Initially there had been plans to mount a piece written especially for the occasion by Krystyn Ostrowski entitled *The Golden Anniversary* [*Złote gody*], with music by Wojciech Sowiński.[76] This play, bombastic in style and rife with patriotic references, would transport the audience to the times of Queen Jadwiga and King Władysław II Jagiełło, later to those of Sigismund II Augustus. The atmosphere of this drama as well as its ideological message can be gleaned from a few choice quotations. The first part of the play, the action of which takes place in a Lithuanian forest, is crowned by the cry of the heroines and the chorus:

> Let Lithuania, Rus' and the land of the Poles
> Bloom and blossom in fraternal accord
> God shall support us in this reward
> In which is hope and solace.[77]

Fraternal accord is realized through the marriage of Jadwiga and Jagiełło and the ensuing union between the states. A knightly chorus comments on this significant historical event:

> Let Poland with Lithuania in the crown of the Piasts,
> Grow in might for centuries all!

---

[74] Cf. ibid.; "Kronika miejscowa i zagraniczna Kraków 13 sierpnia," *Czas* no. 184 (14 Aug. 1869), pp. 2–3; Mudryi, "Ideia pol's'ko-ukraïns'koï uniï," p. 139.

[75] Schnür-Pepłowski, *Teatr polski*, p. 312.

[76] Krystyn Ostrowski, *Złote gody czyli unia lubelska. Hymn dziejowy (1569)* (Lviv, 1870).

[77] Ibid., pp. 14–15.

On their example, the Dnipro land,
 A fertile land with honey flowing,
Let it with children noble in stock hand
Along with the Poles a nation together emerging![78]

Peasants are also present in the scene, who already by now understand the threat emanating from distant Moscow.

For as long as the Dnipro's waves roar,
On the Turk, the Tatar, the Muscovite score
For one enemy are they:
Rus' and Poland forever one
In song, in heart, in blades in the sun,
Hurrah, with God as one![79]

In the play, the idea of a union able to defend Poland, Lithuania, and Rus' from external threat is as appreciated by the knightly estate as it is by the common people. King Władysław II Jagiełło states that he will do everything to unite the three peoples and secure the boundaries of their state:

I swear I shall join my people with this nation
For common liberation
So that Lithuania with Poland as one moves
Into the most distant generation!
To my faithful Rus' do I swear
Who yearns brotherhood with the Piasts as heir
To stand in defence from Muscovite hordes
And live united in labour and glory
I swear, oh Poland, as my faith is dear
As I desire the heavens open and near
To defend your borders and those given you by God
From the waves of the Dnipro to the Warta's banks of reeded rod![80]

The third and and final act of the drama depicts Sigismund II Augustus's establishment of the Union of Lublin. The shift in time is here of no relevance, for the whole play is subjected to conspicuous accentuation of the significance of unions concluded centuries ago. These events are sanctioned each and every time by the majesty of the cross. This was intended to emphasize the permanence of the treaties constituted. Along these lines, Sigismund II Augustus proclaims:

The Union of Lublin, today, under its standard
Your king and father does declare in this city

---

[78] Ibid., p. 21.
[79] Ibid., p. 22.
[80] Ibid., p. 22.

Rus', Poland, Lithuania, of towns and villages
Our Fatherland is an inseparable whole!

And so from this day with us until the final days
In adventure, happiness, a route of tears or glory?
And with the cross the three fraternal banners flutter:
The Archangel, the Vytis and our Eagle white![81]

Krystyn Ostrowski's play was far from being a great dramatic work, but it was able through its nimble form to reach those seeking an inspirational artistic experience associated with these commemorations. However, the work was ultimately banned by the Austrian police, and could not be performed as part of the celebrations.[82] This did not stop the play from being published a year later in a print run of 1500 copies, with the income derived from its sales across Galicia being donated to the construction of the mound. A letter from French émigrés (including Ludwik Nabielak and Agaton Giller) on the subject of the Union was included in the slim volume.[83]

The Lviv Union of Lublin celebrations were the most elaborate of any Polish town, and were met with a good deal of interest on the part of its inhabitants. But as Paweł Sierżęga outlined in his research on the subject, other towns in Galicia attempted, admittedly with varying degrees of success, to organize local anniversary celebrations. Sierżęga gives the example of Przemyśl, where an attractive spectacle was organized after sunset; a theatrical performance with audience participation took place on illuminated and decorated barges that sailed up and down the San. The event was accompanied by music and Polish and Ruthenian songs. In Łańcut, 250 peasants came to town to attend a ceremonial church service. The Ruthenian population also took part in events organized in Dukla and Podkamień to mark the occasion.

The Church, both the Roman Catholic and above all the Greek Catholic, kept its distance from the jubilee events. Nevertheless, there were still cases of Uniate clergymen taking part in the commemorations. Holy Masses to mark the jubilee were conducted in the churches in Rava-Ruska and Rozdil, while Uniate clergy took part in the Roman Catholic service in Holohory. In Veldizh, masses were held in both denominations, which included the singing of "God Thou Hast Poland" ["Boże coś Polskę"] in Polish and "Peace Be upon You, Brethren" ["Myr wam bratia"] in Ruthenian.[84]

---

[81] Ibid., pp. 28–29.
[82] Schnür-Pepłowski, *Obrazy z przeszłości*, part 1, p. 81.
[83] Ostrowski, *Złote gody*, pp. 31–32.
[84] Sierżęga, "Obchody rocznicy unii lubelskiej," pp. 184–85, 193–98.

Although conducted in certain places with panache, the Union of Lublin commemorations generally did not achieve their basic aim, which was not so much the winning over of the Ruthenian population as persuading the Ruthenian elites to accept their part in the legacy of the Union. Despite *gente Rutheni, natione Poloni* participation in what was clearly an undertaking of interest to them, the celebrations nevertheless failed to bring about the desired political effects. What is more, this narrow representation of the Ruthenian population in the form of Ruthenians of Polish nationality was often not taken seriously because of their views. This attitude is demonstrated in Kazimierz Chłędowski's opinion of Kostecki, Smolka, and the idea of raising a mound in general. He wrote:

> Platon [Kostecki] has placed the union of Poland with Rus' on an even more idealized pedestal. It appears to him that those who are creating the Union Mound at Lviv Castle Hill are in fact laying the foundations for a future understanding between both nations. Meanwhile this mound is a mound of shifting sands, with this fundamentality accepted only by Smolka and a handful of idealists, to which Kostecki also belongs. Smolka's obsessive idea was this mound, which they started to raise to commemorate the union of Poland with Rus'. The work continued, supported only by the meagre funds gathered by ideologists such as Smolka; later no one gave any money to the project, for Ruthenians simply laughed at this Polish fantasy, as the mound did nothing to touch their hearts. However, Smolka was stubborn, and for years directed a sizeable part of his income to raising this mound of sand, even to the detriment of his own children. Just as soon as he's in Lviv he will use any free moment to go to Castle Hill, take a wheelbarrow and take sand from mound to mound. He's laughed at, mocked, but Smolka is not going to give up (…).[85]

Rather than diminishing, the gap between Poles and Ruthenians only increased as differences deepened, the best example of which was the failure of the compromise suggested by the deputy Iuliian Lavrivsky at the Galician Diet. He had proposed cooperation between Ruthenian and Polish deputies at the forum of the Imperial Council in exchange for language concessions which never materialized.[86] Additionally, the propaganda that was intended to make Ruthenians conscious of their connection with the Poles caused the opposite effect in Ruthenian intellectual circles. As Marian Mudry has noted, it was at this very moment that the Ruthenian publishing market came to life as a result of a series of publications on the "Ruthenian town of Lev I [Danylovych]."[87]

---

[85] Kazimierz Chłędowski, *Pamiętniki*, vol. 1: *Galicja (1843–1880)*, ed. Antoni Knot (Cracow, 1957), pp. 278–79.

[86] See Sierżęga, "Obchody rocznicy unii lubelskiej," p. 191.

[87] Mudryi, "Aktyvizatsiia suspil'no-politychnoho zhyttia," p. 233.

Yet the propagation of the ideas of the Union of Lublin was not to end with the close of the anniversary celebrations. The mound would remain under construction for many more years. In 1871 Smolka brought representatives of other Polish lands to Lviv, managing to achieve what he had been unable to do two years earlier. A ceremonial congress and a repeat processional march to Lviv Castle Hill took place, this time in national costume. The invited delegates brought soil from other places of significance for Poles: from the Kościuszko, legendary prince Krak, and his daughter Wanda Mounds in Cracow, the cemeteries of those exiled to Siberia, the Powązki Cemetery in Warsaw, and the battlefields of Racławice and Radyvyliv. Delegates made official presentations of "Great Poland soil" and "Cracow soil" in Lviv. Despite the fact that with each passing year Polish-Ruthenian relations were changing, Smolka remained true to his ideals. He said during the meeting at the mound:

> (…) this mound is to be a monument to a fact, the most splendid in our history: nations of varied provenance, enemies for centuries, having come close then fused into a single political whole in order to defend their joint interests, in order to jointly enter onto the road to civilization and progress.[88]

Although the mound was conceived as being a visible sign of the federative idea and a permanent point on patriotic trails and pilgrimages to Lviv, it was never regarded as seriously as other similar commemorative sites. Though the Kościuszko Mound in Cracow took a mere three years to erect, the Lublin Union Mound took a quarter of a century to build, with its creator paying a huge amount to see its completion through when its funding had dried up.[89] The mound eventually merged into the Lviv cityscape, and with time the controversy around it stopped fanning the heated emotions of the 1860s. It continued to commemorate the significance of the Union of Lublin, but only for Poles.

In addition to the mound, other events were organized for the commemorations: plays were performed, speeches were delivered, and leaflets and brochures were produced. Jan Matejko created a noteworthy work of art on Ruthenian themes, marking the beginning of a preoccupation with the idea of Polish-Lithuanian-Ruthenian fraternity that would become a feature of his art.[90] Matejko's *The Union of Lublin* was exhibited in Cracow, Lviv, Vienna, and Paris, where he was

---

[88] Schnür-Pepłowski, *Obrazy z przeszłości*, part 1, p. 83.
[89] Ibid., p. 84.
[90] For more on Matejko's relationship to the Union of Lublin and his painting, see Adam Świątek, *'Lach serdeczny'. Jan Matejko a Rusini* (Cracow, 2013), pp. 34–38 and 98–103.

awarded the French Legion of Honour for the composition in 1870. This success roused such interest in the piece that the organizers of the commemorations decided to purchase the work from the artist. On 6 October 1874 a special committee was set up in Lviv, Platon Kostecki among its members, with the purpose of collecting donations for the purchase of the canvas. The committee considered the work to be an excellent propaganda tool in the promotion of the occasion and all that it represented. Concerning the painting, the committee noted:

> One of the brightest moments in the past history of our nation is the moment when Poland, Rus', and Lithuania swore everlasting love and faith to God the Almighty. One of the greatest works of modern art is the painting by our compatriot Matejko, *The Union of Lublin*, depicting the momentous oath-taking by King Sigismund Augustus and the representatives of the three nations (...).[91]

The committee members collected contributions in all parts of Galicia, conducted street collections, and directed the income from cultural events towards purchasing the painting, which Matejko had valued at 30,000 guldens.[92] The lists of those paying subscription contributions were published for three years (1874, 1875, and 1876) by the newspaper *Dziennik Polski*. List no. LXX reveals that Ruthenians also took part in these collections:

> (...) Ignacy Czerkawski [Ihnati Cherkavsky] of Berezhany sent the sum of 122.77 [guldens] from a performance by the municipal theatre directed by T. Romanovych [Teofila Romanowicz], representing half of the takings, with a polite letter in which, speaking on behalf of the Berezhany audience, he sincerely thanks Mrs. Romanovych for the willingness with which she supported the cause so extolling the country, raising with the same that in all the productions of this Ruthenian theatre the lofty ideal of the unity of both nations as conveyed by the Union of Lublin emanates.[93]

Following the actual purchase of the painting, there was heated discussion as to where it should hang. Initially the plan was to place it in the building of the Galician Diet, but it ultimately went to the Ossolineum. The artist was made an honorary citizen of the city of Lviv. Shortly after the Union of Lublin anniversary celebrations, Matejko

---

[91] [Public notice], ZNiO, sygn. 17094/II: Papiery dotyczące obrazu Jana Matejki *Unia Lubelska* w Zakładzie Narodowym im. Ossolińskich we Lwowie, p. 131.

[92] We read in the artist's letter that the picture was sold for 20,000 złoty with a further ten thousand to be possibly paid at a later date. See „List Jana Matejki do M[ikołaja] Zyblikiewicza," Cracow, 7 Jun. 1876, ZNiO, sygn. 17094/II, p. 181.

[93] *Dziennik Polski* no. 155 (9 Jul. 1876). Mention of the sending of half of the box office revenue from the Ruthenian theatre's performances can also be found in no. 86 (14 Apr. 1876).

decided to found a special scholarship "for two students devoted to art, one a Pole and one a Ruthenian,"[94] and more precisely "for a Ruthenian pupil of the Uniate rite, and the other for a Pole of the Roman Catholic denomination."[95] Although the history of this scholarship has not been broadly researched, one may conclude on the basis of materials preserved by the Society of Friends of the Fine Arts in Lviv that apprentices of the fine arts from both religious rites applied for the scholarship until at least 1888, though the small number of Uniates interested in the award did pose a problem.[96]

The Jubilee celebrations, while successful to a degree, demonstrated that it was not possible to instil in the Ruthenians a sense of a joint history with the Poles. Various financial and propagandistic initiatives directed towards Ruthenians had little effect, while even the active participation of *gente Rutheni, natione Poloni* during the organization of the Jubilee failed to persuade the Ruthenian population of Galicia to support the event.

Kazimierz Chłędowski has argued that with the end of the 1860s there were increasingly fewer Ruthenians of Polish nationality, while more common among Poles was the image of a "malicious Ruthenian," and therefore of an individual with anti-Polish leanings.[97] As a result, animosity grew on both sides. That being said, the immense effort and amount of work that went into the upholding of the Union of Lublin commemorations in Galicia firmly cemented the notion and significance of the events of 1569 in the Polish national tradition. Although Ruthenians grew more distant from Poles, the latter increasingly made themselves aware—partly thanks to the celebrations—of the significance of the Union of Lublin, and demanded the persistence of these

---

[94] [Jan Matejko], *Listy Matejki do żony Teodory 1863–1881*, ed. and preface Maciej Szukiewicz (Cracow, 1927), p. 94 (Letter XLI, 30 Sep. 1869).

[95] Marian Gorzkowski, *Jan Matejko. Epoka od r. 1861 do końca życia artysty*, eds. Kazimierz Nowacki and Ignacy Trybowski (Cracow, 1993), p. 53.

[96] Cf. "List Jana Matejki do N.N. w sprawie przesłania obrazów do Towarzystwa Przyjaciół Sztuk Pięknych we Lwowie," Cracow, 10 Jun. 1870, ZNiO, sygn. 12038/II: Autografy różnych osób z lat 1663–1910. Lit. M., p. 107; "Pismo Towarzystwa Przyjaciół Sztuk Pięknych we Lwowie w sprawie dwóch stypendiów ufundowanych przez Matejkę," Lviv, 22 Nov. 1870, Muzeum Narodowe w Krakowie. Oddział Dom Jana Matejki w Krakowie (subsequently: MNK, DJM), sygn. IX/2921; "List Towarzystwa Przyjaciół Sztuk Pięknych we Lwowie do Jana Matejki w sprawie wybrania stypendysty," Lviv, 9 Dec. 1887, ZNiO, sygn. 7527/II: "Papiery Towarzystwa Przyjaciół Sztuk Pięknych we Lwowie. Akta Sekretariatu. Kopiariusz z lat 1886–1891," pp. 163–64; "List Towarzystwa Przyjaciół Sztuk Pięknych we Lwowie do Jana Matejki w sprawie wybrania stypendysty," Lviv, 24 Nov. 1888, ZNiO, sygn. 7527/II, pp. 415–16.

[97] Chłędowski, *Pamiętniki*, vol. 1, p. 284. Cf.: Anna Wróbel, "Od 'Galileuszy' do Polaków. Wejście do polskiej inteligencji przedstawicieli ludności napływowej i mniejszości w Galicji w XIX w.," in *Inteligencja polska XIX i XX wieku. Studia 5*, ed. Ryszarda Czepulis-Rastenis (Warsaw, 1987), p. 186.

bonds between the three nations of historical Poland. Yet, in doing so, they refused to hear of the existence of a separate Ruthenian nation, preferring to live in a reality constructed in their own imagination from a Polish view of the country's past. This was evidenced through subsequent anniversary celebrations of historical events in which the *gente Rutheni, natione Poloni* were as actively involved.

The Commemorations of the 200th Anniversary of the Relief of Vienna in 1883

A revival in the organization of historical anniversaries was brought about by the 200th anniversary of the relief of Vienna in 1883. As Paweł Sierżęga wrote, the impulse was provided by the parades in Vienna which had not sufficiently taken into consideration the Polish role in the victory over the Turkish threat; John III Sobieski, the actual victor, was rendered a secondary figure.[98] Sierżęga has devoted an entire study to the commemoration of the relief of Vienna, though this chapter shall concentrate on only two of the aspects which resonate with the subject at hand. The diminishment of John III Sobieski's role is significant, because within the social consciousness of the inhabitants of Galicia there existed a conviction that John III Sobieski was a Ruthenian. Alongside King Michael Korybut Wiśniowiecki, John III Sobieski was often used as an example to show that, aside from the Polish dynasties of the Polish Piasts and the Lithuanian Jagiellonians, Poland had been also ruled by kings with Ruthenian roots. John III Sobieski did in fact have Ruthenian roots, for his mother, Zofia Teofila [Sofiia Teofila], was from the Daniłowicz [Danylovych] boyar line. Furthermore, he could count as his ancestors Ruthenians from the Dąbrowski [Dobrovsky], Paniowski [Paniovsky], Malczycki [Malchytsky], Drohojowski [Drohoiovsky] and Lipski [Lypsky] families. Adding to his Ruthenian provenance was the fact that he had been born in Rus'—in Olesko, which was situated in Eastern Galicia.[99] Therefore, he was often regarded as the "Ruthenian King," and his rule was seen to represent the participation of Rus' in the Commonwealth of Two Nations. In the words of Jan Matejko:

> (...) our hero king was a Ruthenian, and having lived for a long time in Olesko, Zhovkva, Lviv etc., was often moved when recalling those places. (...) This great Ruthenian king, having so much love in his heart for the land, was at the same time the pride of Poland, a fatherland common to us all.[100]

---

[98] Sierżęga, *Obchody 200. rocznicy*, p. 25.
[99] Otto Forst de Battaglia, "Ze studjów genealogicznych nad epoką Jana III Sobieskiego," *Miesięcznik Heraldyczny* 12, no. 9 (1933), p. 135.
[100] Gorzkowski, *Jan Matejko. Epoka*, p. 239.

The well-known *gente Rutheni, natione Poloni* who actively participated in this jubilee took it upon themselves to emphasize the Ruthenian origin of the King of Poland, hoping to bolster the image of Polish-
Ruthenian brotherhood in Galicia.

The organizational committee for the commemorations was established on 22 March 1883. Jan Dobrzański chaired the meeting, and
Adam Sapieha was chosen as the committee head. The executive committee contained several Ruthenians of Polish origin, including Euzebiusz Czerkawski, Jan Dobrzański, Platon Kostecki, Teofil Merunowicz,
Zygmunt Sawczyński, and a Greek Catholic priest expelled from Pratu-
lin in the lands of Lublin, Adolf Wasilewski. They were later joined
by Sylvestr Sembratovych, the Greek Catholic archbishop of Lviv,
and Ivan Stupnytsky, the Greek Catholic bishop of Przemyśl, along
with the Basilian order provincial Father Klemens Sarnicki [Klyment
Sarnytsky].[101] It is difficult to imagine a better gathering of *gente Rutheni,*
natione Poloni in one place, or a group of Ruthenians more set on Polish-
-Ruthenian cooperation. Although it was later decided to appoint a nar-
rower, 12-person "permanent committee," Mikołaj Zyblikiewicz's participation ensured the continued representation of Ruthenians of Polish
nationality.[102]

As had been the case during the commemorations of the Union of
Lublin, there was much concern as to how the celebrations would be
perceived by the Ruthenians. During the meeting of 21 April 1883, the
committee adopted a series of resolutions concerning the matter. It
was agreed, among other things, that "both languages are to be used
in publications and acts relating to the celebrations," that the episcopal and archepiscopal ordinariates of all three denominations were to
be invited to attend along with the Jewish religious communities, that
a historical work would be composed that would explain the "global
significance of the relief of Vienna" and that would be published in
Polish and Ruthenian along with other European languages, and that
a colour picture of John III at Vienna would be produced to be distributed as a memento, accompanied by an explanation in both Polish and
Ruthenian. The committee also supported a petition of the Pedagogical
Society calling for every school to contribute to the commemorations.
The organizers hoped that further celebrations would be organized and
supported at the local level.[103] Seweryna Duchińska's "Song in Honour

---

[101] Cf.: "200 letnia rocznica odsieczy Wiednia," *Gazeta Narodowa* no. 68 (24 Mar. 1883),
p. 3; "Komitet jubileuszowy dla uczczenia 200-letniej rocznicy odsieczy Wiednia," *Gazeta
Narodowa* no. 96 (28 Apr. 1883), p. 2; Sierżęga, *Obchody 200. rocznicy*, pp. 26–27.
[102] Sierżęga, *Obchody 200. rocznicy*, p. 44.
[103] "Komitet jubileuszowy dla uczczenia 200-letniej rocznicy odsieczy Wiednia," *Gazeta
Narodowa* no. 96 (28 Apr. 1883), p. 2.

of John III Sobieski" ["Pieśń na cześć Jana Sobieskiego"] was published in an attempt to reach the youth. The poem included the following rousing stanza:

> And if the trumpet was to call us to fight
> And the heart was permeated with sorrow all through
> Spread out your arms from the heavens
> And embrace Poland, Lithuania, and Rus'.
> The beams of a common house rebuilt
> And throw yourself into an array of ways
> Yet the stream of grace, oh John the Great
> And through your deeds God's release to us stays.[104]

It was also important for the jubilee organizers that the Ruthenian king was not only remembered by Poles but also by the Ruthenian population of Galicia. To ensure this, they established a competition to write a work entitled *The History of John III's Rule and His Times* [*Dzieje panowania Jana III i jego czasy*]. Not only were Józef Szujski and other prominent historians invited to join the competition jury, but so was Anatol Lewicki, a Ruthenian of Polish nationality. In describing the activities of the Lviv committee and its Cracow counterpart, Sierżęga wrote that their aim had been "on the one hand the integration of local societies, while on the other the shaping of the historical and national consciousness; the latter would become the priority."[105]

How were these initiatives viewed by Ruthenians outside of the *gente Rutheni, natione Poloni* orientation? Sierżęga gives the example of the local commemorative committee in Ternopil, where members of the Ruthenian intelligentsia were invited to participate in the organizational work; Oleksander Barvinsky, Petro Levytsky, and Lev Shekhovych all declined to participate. The Ruthenian press also took a critical stance on the subject of the celebrations, pegging them as "purely Polish national manifestations."[106] Yet a folk pilgrimage comprising Polish and Ruthenian peasants was organized by Roman Catholic Father Stanisław Stojałowski, who came from a Greek Catholic family.[107] On 10 September 1883 peasants took part in a funeral mass at the Wawel Cathedral for John III and those who had fallen at Vienna. During the course of the ceremony, two Polish peasants and two Ruthenians held a laurel wreath with a ribbon on which it was written "The Polish

---

[104] Seweryna Duchińska, *Pieśń na cześć Jana Sobieskiego* (Lviv, 1883), quoted after: Sierżęga, *Obchody 200. rocznicy*, p. 34, footnote 38.
[105] Ibid., p. 40.
[106] Quoted from: ibid., p. 81.
[107] Andrzej Kazimierz Banach, *Młodzież chłopska na Uniwersytecie Jagiellońskim w latach 1860/61–1917/18* (Cracow, 1997), pp. 52–55.

and Ruthenian people on the 200th anniversary." After the service, the organizer of the pilgrimage spoke, reminding those assembled that among those fighting at Vienna were the knights of Poland, Lithuania, as well as Rus', which Sobieski "had loved particularly." Stojałowski considered "adhering to a unity of faith and national togetherness" to be a duty of the fatherland.[108]

The main celebrations took place the following day. After the mass held at the Wawel Cathedral, artefacts from the relief of Vienna were put on display at the National Museum in the Cloth Hall [Sukiennice]. The Diet speaker, Mikołaj Zyblikiewicz, opened the exhibition with a rousing speech. He then met with district council deputies at the Barbican in Cracow. He commended the peasants who had attended the commemorations for understanding the importance of the event.[109] The Ruthenian aspect was present throughout; Zyblikiewicz emphasized that:

Rus' should be especially grateful to King John III, for it was he who freed her from the incessant raids of Tatars and Turks.[110]

The Cracow celebrations took on another dimension of significance, as they coincided with the 25th anniversary of Jan Matejko's illustrious artistic career.[111] The event organizers knew that he had been working for some time on a painting commemorating the relief of Vienna. They expected him to gift the finished piece to the nation, as he had done in 1882 with the work Prussian Homage [Hołd Pruski]. Matejko did indeed present the work to the nation in a symbolic sense, ordering it to be sent to Rome as a gift for the Pope. He said that "Europe will remember Poland, the bulwark of Christendom!"[112] He wanted the gift to be presented by a delegation sent to the Vatican, composed of representatives of all the areas of partition and estates including Poles as well as Ruthenians. Stanisław Tarnowski recalled that "the benefactor himself, Matejko, most righteously demanded the participation of the peasantry of both rites: a Pole and a Ruthenian," which is why the artist was joined by the alderman of Krzeszowice near Cracow, Karol Rusek, and by a Ruthenian peasant, Iur Dobosh [Jur Dobosz] of Jurowce, near

---

[108] "Kronika miejscowa i zagraniczna. Kraków 11 września," Czas no. 206 (12 Sep. 1883), p. 3.

[109] "Uroczystość dwuchsetletniej rocznicy zwycięstwa Jana III pod Wiedniem," Czas no. 206 (12 Sep. 1883), pp. 1–3.

[110] Ibid., p. 3.

[111] For the jubilee program see: "Program zbiorowy uroczystości dwusetnej rocznicy zwycięstwa króla Jana III pod Wiedniem oraz Jubileuszu Matejki, tudzież zjazdu literatów i artystów od d. 11 do d. 16 września 1883," Czas no. 204 (8 Sep. 1883), p. 3.

[112] Stanisław Serafińska, Matejko. Wspomnienia rodzinne (Cracow, 1955), p. 529.

Sanok.[113] Matejko believed that the trip would inspire these peasants to tell others about the event that the painting celebrated—the relief of Vienna—and its importance to both peoples. While still at the Holy See, Matejko encouraged the peasants:

> (…) to remember and repeat to your own people what you have seen and heard, that they should take to heart the truth: that Sobieski's struggle was the exact same as it is today, the very same struggle and battle for duties, with victory possible only through unity. And since peasants are the most numerous, they will have a significant role in [the forging of] this unity.[114]

Despite initial criticism in the press, news of Matejko's magnanimous initiative was eventually met with approval in national publications.[115] In this way Matejko put his own unique stamp on the commemoration of John III Sobieski, in propagating the Polish participation in the defence of the Christian world from Islam and—of the most interest to us—in making the Polish and Ruthenian peasantry historically conscious.

The idea of a Polish-Ruthenian brotherhood was even more vigorously promoted in the eastern part of the country. Celebrations started on September 11 in Lviv Cathedral with a memorial service for John III Sobieski and those who fell during the relief of Vienna. The mass brought together representatives of the national authorities, including Euzebiusz Czerkawski, deputy chairman of the central events committee. The cathedral itself was festively decorated, adorned with ornaments prepared especially for the occasion; a contemporary account noted that "the Great Altar and balconies around the chancel were enveloped in black cloth upon which were embroidered the coats of arms of Poland, Lithuania, and Rus'."[116] In another nod to the common Polish-Ruthenian-Lithuanian heritage, a poem by Platon Kostecki that had been written especially for the occasion was distributed along with a translation of a Ruthenian *duma* done years earlier by the Greek Catholic priest Ivan Hushalevych [Jan Guszalewicz].[117] Kostecki had

---

[113] Stanisław Tarnowski, *Matejko* (Cracow, 1896), pp. 273–74.

[114] Ibid., p. 284.

[115] Cf.: "Ostatni dar Matejki," *Tygodnik Illustrowany* no. 44 (3 Nov. 1883), p. 274; *Nowa Reforma* no. 208 (14 Sep. 1883); *Djabeł* no. 18 (22 Sep. 1883). It is important to draw attention to Tarnowski's extensive accounts from the journey to Rome: Stanisław Tarnowski, "*Sobieski pod Wiedniem* Matejki," *Przegląd Polski* 69 (1883), pp. 470–75; Stanisław Tarnowski, "Obchód wiedeńskiej rocznicy," *Przegląd Polski* 70 (1883), pp. 24–35; Stanisław Tarnowski, "Oddawanie Ojcu Ś. Leonowi XIII daru narodowego z obrazu Matejki," *Przegląd Polski* 71 (1884), pp. 122–43.

[116] "Jubileusz we Lwowie," *Dziennik Polski* (Lviv) no. 208 (12 Sep. 1883), p. 2.

[117] Platon Kostecki, *W dwusetną rocznicę odsieczy Wiednia* (Lviv, 1883); Ivan Hushalevych, *Vospomynan'e posviashchenno Ioannu III Sob'eskomu koroliu pol'skomu, osvoboditeliu Vĕdnia*

even published both works the previous day in *Gazeta Narodowa*.[118] The Ruthenian aspect of the celebrations was also emphasized by Euzebiusz Czerkawski, who in the name of the central events committee welcomed those who had come to Lviv town hall for a session devoted to John III Sobieski. The *Gazeta Lwowska* reported that this last part of the Ruthenian-oriented proceedings was well received.[119] *Gazeta Narodowa* printed Czerkawski's address in its entirety, in which we can find this excerpt:

> The Polish Commonwealth was not strictly a uniform state, but on the principles of freedom and equality it combined in itself by means of a fraternal bond various tribes and denominations, connected in joint national labour. The uniting of Poland, Rus', and Lithuania into an organic whole sanctified by formal accord only that which had existed for centuries—what was at the core in the very blood of the nation in possibly far broader dimensions, for it was inspired by the spirit of freedom, love and accord, of notions inseparable from the essence of the Polish nation.
>
> The said nations confirmed this unity not only in a long political life, but what is more, through the blood shed on the field of battle, in repelling the raids of Turkish and Tatar formations. Most rightly the Ruthenians demand their part in the glory won through the Viennese victory. Together with Poles and Lithuanians, they paid for the defence of the present-day Austrian capital, of Christendom, and civilization with their blood, having at their head a leader and king in whose veins flowed Ruthenian blood, and at his side a man who as a priest of the Ruthenian Church magnificently served the common fatherland.[120]

Later in his speech Czerkawski recalled how for ages the "germs of feuding" had sprouted in society; that being said, he emphasized that any division of society into parts would not constitute redemption for any of the sides. He concluded his speech by saying that "mutual understanding and good will finally overcome, although possibly slowly, all difficulties." He also expressed his wish for the "blood jointly lost at Vienna to finally become a symbol of unity."[121]

---

ot' Turkov' dlia 12 verenia 1663 v den' dvokhsotlĕtneho iubileiu prasdnovannoho 11 i 12 veresnia 1883 vo Lvove ([Lviv, 1883]).

[118] "Wspomnienie poświęcone Janowi III Sobieskiemu królowi polskiemu, oswobodzicielowi Wiednia od Turków dnia 12. września 1683 r., w dzień dwusetletniego jubileuszu, święconego 11. i 12. września 1883 roku we Lwowie (Dosłowny przekład dumy ruskiej)," trans. Jan Guszalewicz, *Gazeta Narodowa* no. 206 (11 Sep. 1883), pp. 1–2; Platon Kostecki, "W dwusetną rocznicę odsieczy Wiednia," *Gazeta Narodowa* no. 206 (11 Sep. 1883), pp. 2–3.

[119] "Sobiesciana. Uroczystości lwowskie," *Gazeta Lwowska* no. 208 (12 Sep. 1883), p. 2.

[120] "Obchód jubileuszowy we Lwowie," *Gazeta Narodowa* no. 208 (12 Sep. 1883), p. 2.

[121] Ibid.

The next day another memorial mass was held at the cathedral, after which the crowds headed to the Lviv market square in order to take part in the unveiling of a marble commemorative plaque on the Korniakt Palace where Sobieski had lived. There Platon Kostecki recited on bended knee the final fragment of his poem in honour of John III, and went on to place a wreath from the editorial board of *Gazeta Narodowa* with the inscription "Honour to the Past! Faith in the Future!"[122] As Paweł Sierżęga has established, the town house in which Sobieski lived was also decorated with a banner proclaiming national unity, emblazoned with the national emblems of Poland, Lithuania, and Rus'.[123]

Ultimately, neither the emphasis on national unity, the participation of Ruthenians in the Battle of Vienna, the Ruthenian provenance of the king, nor the pro-Ruthenian speeches by Euzebiusz Czerkawski and Platon Kostecki were able to garner any favour or support in Ruthenian socio-political organizations. Overall, the reaction to the jubilee celebrations on the part of organizations such as the Ruthenian Council was largely negative. This is not to say, however, that all Ruthenians distanced themselves from the events. For example, the Ruthenian inhabitants of Zhovkva, who were invited by the local organizing committee, only resigned from participation in the celebrations after they were advised to do so by their compatriots in Lviv.[124] The situation was different in the Greek Catholic Church, which followed the example of Bishops Sembratovych and Stupnytsky and took part in similar commemorations, especially in Zhovkva.[125] Paweł Sierżęga has included a table in his book listing the towns in which memorial masses to commemorate the relief of Vienna were held in Roman Catholic and Greek Catholic churches. He notes that the Uniate Church took part in commemorations in Borshchiv, Bohorodchany, Bibrka, Brody, Berezhany, Buchach, Budaniv, Burshtyn, Busk, Khyriv, Chortkiv, Drohobych, Horodenka, Iahilnytsia, Jarosław, Iavoriv, Ozerna, Kalush, Kamianka[-Strumylova], Kolomyia, Kosiv, Krakovets, Kuty, Leżajsk, Melnytsia, Mykolaiv, Nadvirna, Olesko, Otynia, Pidhaitsi, Pomoriany, Przemyśl, Rava, Rohatyn, Rudky, Sambir, Sanok, Sasiv, Sieniawa, Skala[-Podilska], Skalat, Stare Misto, Stryi, Sniatyn, Ternopil, Turka, Tysmenytsia, Ulashkivtsi, Ustrzyki Dolne, Zaliztsi, Zagórz, Zbarazh, Zolochiv, and Zhuravno.[126] Fifty-five towns in total saw the 200th anniversary celebrated in Uniate

---

[122] Ibid.

[123] Sierżęga, *Obchody 200. rocznicy*, p. 108.

[124] "Kronika miejscowa i zamiejscowa. Dnia 8. sierpnia," *Gazeta Narodowa* no. 180 (9 Aug. 1883), p. 3.

[125] Cf. the jubilee program: "Kronika miejscowa i zamiejscowa. Dnia 3 sierpnia," *Gazeta Narodowa* no. 176 (4 Aug. 1883), p. 3. Por. Sierżęga, *Obchody 200. rocznicy*, p. 111, footnote 21.

[126] Cf. ibid, pp. 122–32, table 1.

churches. This success presumably derived from the pro-Polish currents that ran through the Greek Catholic hierarchy at this time. Adam Galos wrote that amid all the Polish commemorations of historical anniversaries, it was this one that saw the greatest Ruthenian participation.[127] This merely confirmed in Ruthenians of Polish nationality the appropriateness of their actions, encouraging them to participate in subsequent anniversary commemorations. Nevertheless, no other jubilee was to generate such involvement on the part of the Uniates, despite the wishes of the *gente Rutheni, natione Poloni.*

The 400th Anniversary Commemorations of the Death of Saint John of Dukla in 1884

The next large-scale opportunity for a manifestation of Polish-Ruthenian brotherhood arose in 1884, with the commemoration of the 400th anniversary of the death of the Blessed (he was canonized in 1997) John of Dukla. This Bernardine was not only the honoured patron of Lviv, but had also defended the city from the designs of the Cossacks and Tatars in 1648. On 19 June 1884, the Lviv city council elected a 12-person special committee under the chairmanship of the city mayor, Wacław Dąbrowski. This committee was tasked with scheduling an eight-day events program, which would later be ratified at the council sitting of July 10.

Before long, these outwardly religious celebrations took on a political character.[128] Platon Kostecki immediately began to advertise the Blessed's commemoration on the pages of *Gazeta Narodowa*, with the paper proclaiming that John "was and is the patron of Poland, Rus', and Lithuania, and for Lviv a benefactor many times over and a defender before God himself."[129] Kostecki edited the life of the Blessed for publication in the paper, including his miraculous saving of Lviv from the Cossacks.[130] Presumably Kostecki was also the author of the subsequent texts and accounts that appeared at this time in *Gazeta Narodowa* portraying the harmonious life of Poles, Ruthenians, and Lithuanians.[131]

---

[127] Adam Galos, "Obchody rocznicowe na prowincji zaboru austriackiego," in *Studia z dziejów prowincji galicyjskiej*, ed. Adam Galos (Wrocław, 1993), p. 105.

[128] See Adam Świątek, "Patron Polski, Litwy i ... Rusi? Rzecz o lwowskich obchodach czterechsetnej rocznicy śmierci Jana z Dukli w 1884 roku," *Rocznik Przemyski. Historia* 51, no. 3 (2015), pp. 79–104.

[129] "Kronika," *Gazeta Narodowa* no. 157 (9 Jul. 1884), p. 2.

[130] [Platon Kostecki] P.K., "Jubileusz błog. Jana z Dukli," *Gazeta Narodowa* no. 154 (5 Jul. 1884), p. 2; no. 156 (8 Jul. 1884), pp. 1–2.

[131] Cf. *Gazeta Narodowa* no. 157 (9 Jul. 1884); no. 158 (10 Jul. 1884); no. 159 (11 Jul. 1884); no. 160 (12 Jul. 1884); no. 161 (13 Jul. 1884).

For example, on July 10 there was an account of missionary celebrations organized by the clergy of the Greek Catholic rite in Ozeriany, in the district of Borshchiv. In this article, the author enthusiastically recounts the meeting with a certain canon by the name of Father Kostecki [Kostetsky]. The canon praised Prince Leon Sapieha, who was present at the ceremony, as "the descendant of the Lithuanian-Ruthenian dukes." A toast was raised by one of the priests to "the prosperity of Poland, Rus', and Lithuania," and a guest from Lithuania made a speech in the spirit of Polish, Ruthenian, and Lithuanian cooperation.[132] The account's author made recourse to the November Uprising of 1830 and the joining together of Poles and Ruthenians through the union of the Churches. Texts of this type that were concerned with authentic events created an atmosphere of accord conducive to the upcoming jubilee celebrations of the Blessed John of Dukla.

An article that appeared in *Gazeta Narodowa* just prior to the celebrations showed how an inhabitant of Lviv had interpreted the Blessed John of Dukla:

> And so sometimes this abused capital of Red Rus' is honoured, if only during such sieges in which [John of Dukla] plays an eminent role, with such pages of history, ones that would be the envy of royal capitals far older and more famous. The man from Dukla returned schismatics to the Union, and his memory was holy particularly for Ruthenians, who together with Catholic Poles surrendered themselves to his care— and this at a time, as the chronicles relay, when they, held captive by Cossacks, would betray their co-religionists to the Tatars or Turks. What a beautiful testimony to the relations of Poles to Ruthenians, of Catholics to schismatics.[133]

Further on, the author of the article recalls how the figure of John of Dukla appeared in the heavens, forcing Hetman Bohdan Khmelnytsky to halt the attack on Lviv, accept the ransom, and forfeit his demand for the surrender of the city's Jewish residents. Having risen to iconic status in the Ruthenian historical consciousness, here the Cossack leader is etched into this particular story as a *de facto* raider of the half-brother Ruthenians living as one with Poles and Jews in the capital of Red Rus'. These two historical narratives clashed during the 400th anniversary commemorations of the death of John of Dukla; the Cossacks (and Khmelnytsky), increasingly mythicized by the Ruthenians, were placed in opposition to the idea of Polish-Ruthenian fraternity, personified by the heavenly defender of Lviv, John of Dukla. In this way John's blessedness and the legends attached to him were to become

---

[132] "Objaw prawdziwy zgody między Rusinami a Polakami. Z Borszczowskiego d. 6. lipca," *Gazeta Narodowa* no. 158 (10 Jul. 1884), p. 2.
[133] "Lwów d. 12 lipca," *Gazeta Narodowa* no. 161 (13 Jul. 1884), p. 1.

instruments in solving the problems between Poles and Ruthenians of modern Galicia.

The commemorations devoted to the "defender of Lviv" commenced on 13 July 1884 with a march from Lviv market square to the Bernardine Church, where the laying of a wreath at the grave of John of Dukla took place. The speaker of the national chamber, Mikołaj Zyblikiewicz, took part in the proceedings. At this time, the red banner of the Blessed John was also consecrated. It depicted the priest in a kneeling position with his arms raised, while the reverse side was embroidered with the following inscription:

> To the Blessed John of Dukla, Patron of Poland, Rus', and Lithuania, special Guardian of Lviv, on the 400th anniversary of his death, from his worshippers and the III order of St. Francis 1484–1884.[134]

A ceremonial dinner followed the commemorations, during which a toast was raised to the Ruthenians.

The jubilee finished with another procession, this time from the Bernardine Church to the cathedral and back. Members of all three denominations took part, with Father Iuliian Pelesh accompanied by a Ruthenian chapter house from the Uniate side, despite what the editor of *Gazeta Narodowa* called the "wanton aggression of *Dilo* and *Slovo*."[135] The homily was given by clergy from the three rites, with 30,000 faithful taking part in the commemorations,[136] including a sizeable percentage of Ruthenians. In 1886 one of the Lviv Bernardines involved in the event's organization, Father Norbert Golichowski, published a work devoted to the Blessed John of Dukla.[137] This book reveals that the Ruthenian press vehemently questioned the initiative to reconcile the Poles and Ruthenians who had inhabited Lviv for centuries. The author, defending himself from these periodicals that had accused him of incorrectly calling John the patron of Rus', listed examples to prove the long-standing practice of observing his cult on the part of the Uniate clergy:

> (…) Leon Szeptycki, Piotr Bielański etc. celebrated pontifical liturgies in our Lviv Bernardine Church at the commemorations of the Blessed

---

[134] "Obchód 400-letniego jubileuszu błog. Jana z Dukli," *Gazeta Narodowa* no. 162 (15 Jul. 1884), p. 2.

[135] "Uroczystości jubileuszowe," *Gazeta Narodowa* no. 167 (20 Jul. 1884), p. 2. In the quote there is mention of the article: "Prymyrenie tserkvei," *Slovo* no. 76 (12 [24] Jul. 1884), p. 1.

[136] "Kronika miejscowa i zamiejscowa dnia 21 lipca," *Gazeta Narodowa* no. 168 (22 Jul. 1884), p. 2.

[137] Norbert Golichowski, *Pamiątka uroczystości 400-letniej rocznicy śmierci Błogosł. Jana z Dukli zakonu OO. Bernardynów, odbytej we Lwowie i w innych klasztornych kościołach r. 1884* (Lviv, 1886).

Jan of Dukla, and Ruthenian parish priests such as Michał Kieszewski [Mykhailo Keshevsky] of Znesinnia and Michał Mogilnicki [Mykhailo Mohylnytsky] of Horodok gave sermons in Polish at the ceremony of this Saint.[138]

The best evidence of interdenominational cooperation over the cult of Saint John of Dukla was the translation of his relics to the Church of the Assumption of the Blessed Virgin Mary, colloquially known as the Wallachian Church. Although the Ruthenian periodicals *Slovo* and *Novyi Prolom* [*New Breakthrough*] reported on the religious event with an air of reservation, others expressed their enthusiasm regarding the commemorations;[139] an article in the ecclesiastical journal *Ruskii sion* [*Ruthenian Zion*] noted that "such a large religious turnout has not been seen in our town for ages."[140]

The jubilee spawned numerous poems, several of which were even censored.[141] The works contained in the compilation *Memory* [*Pamiątka*] by Father Norbert Golichowski were among those deemed problematic. The publisher did not include the fragments marked with a dot and questioned by the censor. A cursory reading of the poems reveals that many of them are not so much religious in character as they are social and political. The question of the relations between Poles and Ruthenians, as well as Poland's regaining of independence, appear in the majority of the poems. The collection opens with "A Prayer to Blessed John of Dukla" [Modlitwa do Bł. Jana z Dukli] by Maria Bartus. This work includes an invocation to Jan of Dukla first as the patron of Poland, then of Rus' — "(...) what arm in arm / She strode with us through the field of service" — and finally of Lithuania. Unfortunately we do not know how the poem ended, as the last two lines were censored.[142] The next work in the collection is entitled "Song for the 400th Anniversary Commemoration of the Death of St. John of Dukla (29 September 1484)" [Pieśń na 400-letnią rocznicę zgonu błog. Jana z Dukli (29. września 1484)]. Already in the first few lines the author asks Blessed John for help in protecting the fatherland, including the "Ruthenian lands," from enemies. John of Dukla appears in the work not so much as an evangelist as a preacher who gives homilies in Polish, Ruthenian, and German. Further on we read about an appeal that Lviv become the city

---

[138] "Braterskie słowo do pism ruskich," in Golichowski, *Pamiątka*, p. 86.

[139] "Prymyrenie tserkvei"; B. A. selianyn", "Iz" Zavyshnia," *Novyi prolom"* no. 156 (18 [30] Jul. 1884), p. 2; Cf.: "Braterskie słowo," p. 85.

[140] "Myssiia tserkovna v" Lvově," *Ruskii sion"* no. 14 (16 [28] Jul. 1884), p. 438.

[141] Aleksander Zyga, "Wkład ziemi krośnieńskiej w literaturę polską do 1903 roku," in *Inteligencja południowo-wschodnia ziem polskich*, eds. Halina Kurek and Franciszek Tereszkiewicz (Cracow, 1998), p. 88.

[142] Marys Bartus, "Modlitwa do Bł. Jana z Dukli," in Golichowski, *Pamiątka*, p. 36.

of Lev [Danylovych], Uniate but loyal to Poland and Catholicism. The subsequent lines are a plea:

> For there not to be differences
> In hearts between a Pole and a Ruthenian
> As a sign that each in this Fatherland
> Is a son and a servant of the Mother of God!

The poem asks that John of Dukla accept the hymn of praise as the patron of Poland, Lithuania, and Rus', while the lands of Halych, Podilia, Volhynia, Ukraine, Samogitia, Latvia, Żuławy and Podlachia give a goblet of their tears as an offering to the Lord. It closes by summoning the Blessed John:

> Let me return to the fatherland,
> To the immeasurable Imperium of stars![143]

One poem that addressed Ruthenian matters and was subsequently heavily censored was Maria Konopnicka's "On the Four Hundredth Anniversary of the Blessed John of Dukla Patron of Poland, Rus', and Lithuania" ["W czterechsetną rocznicę błogosławionego Jana z Dukli Patrona Polski, Rusi i Litwy"].[144] The first part of the work addresses the difficult situation in the fatherland, here understood as the fraternity of Poland, Lithuania, and Rus'. Lamenting their fate, the author calls upon them:

> Oh my Lithuania! Oh my Polish Crown!
> Oh Rus' which you no longer call "holy"
> Your freedom and voice have been taken from you
> While your faith – violated!
> Oh Vilnius of old! Oh Warsaw so bleak!
> Oh Kyiv drowning your tears in the Dnipro!
> Where are Your Eagles and Vytis of fame?
> Where is your mettle and health?
> The torn breast of my nation grows numb
> Without the Host of the spirit of fraternal sharing ...
> And the hearts grow numb from hunger and cold
> Without a tomorrow, without the ideal of old!

Konopnicka wrote with the purpose of inspiring awe in the lands of Lithuania, Rus', and the Crown, and to honour the fact that a brother

---

[143] X. Wł. Jul. J..., "Pieśń na 400-letnią rocznicę zgonu błog. Jana z Dukli (29. września 1484)," in Golichowski, *Pamiątka*, pp. 36–43.

[144] [Maria Konopnicka] Marja K., "W czterechsetną rocznicę błogosławionego Jana z Dukli Patrona Polski, Rusi i Litwy," in Golichowski, *Pamiątka*, pp. 45–47.

belonging to these lands—Blessed John of Dukla— was already an angel. The poem ends with an appeal for prayer for the fatherland:

> Oh my Lithuania! Oh my Polish Crown!
> Oh Rus' which you no longer call "holy!"
> Cast onto the old earth of yours your bosom
> And pray in tears – for your voice has been taken!

Special attention ought also to be paid to the poem by Platon Kostecki entitled "The Jubilee of St. John of Dukla" ["Jubileusz bł. Jana z Dukli"]. Here the poet does not fail to express the ideas he normally expounds, presenting Blessed John as patron of such ideas:

> Angel of authority, dispenser of miracles,
> Sincere son of the fatherland ,
> The Crown blesses you with tears and entreaties
> Rus' and Lithuania bless you,
> And across the whole world in a chorus erected
> The Church's prayer blesses –
> Teach us to love our fatherland,
> Like the angels do paradise
> For we from the grave as a fiery star
> Like you, would rush to help it.[145]

The author asks John of Dukla to intercede with God over the salvation of the fatherland, as he had "during the first centenary of the death" of the saint. He is not referring so much to the relatively inconsequential year of 1584, but rather to the period when Poland was a political power.

Many other works emphasized the important role played by John of Dukla in saving Lviv from Khmelnytsky's Cossacks, who were attacking not only Poles but the inhabitants of the city as a whole, Ruthenians included. The censored "Ballad on the Miraculous Saving of Lviv by Blessed John of Dukla" ["Ballada o cudownem uratowaniu Lwowa przez bł. Jana z Dukli"] by Anna Neumann "Kalina" clearly stresses that "Khmelnytsky wallows in fraternal blood."[146] Similarly, the poem "To the Honour of the Blessed John on the 400th Anniversary of his Blessed Demise" ["Ku czci błog. Jana w 400-letnią rocznicę Jego błog. Zgonu"] recalled "the rabid Khmelnytsky attacking Lviv with Tughay Bey."[147]

---

[145] Platon Kostecki, "Jubileusz Bł. Jana z Dukli," *Gazeta Narodowa* no. 153 (16 Jul. 1884), p. 2; Platon Kostecki, "Jubileusz Bł. Jana z Dukli," in Golichowski, *Pamiątka*, p. 54.
[146] [Anna Neumann] Kalina, "Ballada o cudownem uratowaniu Lwowa przez bł. Jana z Dukli," in Golichowski, *Pamiątka*, p. 48.
[147] Zyg. Kar., "Ku czci błog. Jana w 400-letnią rocznicę Jego błog. zgonu," in Golichowski, *Pamiątka*, pp. 55–57.

The commemorations of the anniversary of John of Dukla's death found favour within the Uniate Church, but were met with opposition on the part of Ruthenian activists. The greatest factor in the decision to organize such a grand commemoration had undoubtedly been the success enjoyed the previous year by the Viennese victory jubilee. However, the religious celebrations themselves had little effect on national relations. Nevertheless, they left a legacy of sorts, representing one more brick in the construction of the myth of the Commonwealth of Three Nations.

The Thousand-Year Anniversary Commemorations of the Death of Saint Methodius in Velehrad in 1885

The descriptions that appeared in the Polish press of the jubilees in 1883 and 1884 gave the impression that there was an indisputable sense of accord between Poles and Ruthenians. In some respects this was true: under the leadership of Sylvestr Sembratovych, the Greek Catholic Church had joined in the religious aspects of the historical commemorations. The situation was somewhat different, however, with the Ruthenian intelligentsia and Ruthenian politicians, who distanced themselves from these "Polish commemorations." This aside, the accounts given by the Polish media advanced the belief that the fraternal bonds between Poles and Ruthenians would be preserved in Galicia, grounded as they were in a common past. One figure who heartily subscribed to this mentality was Kostecki's Cracow acquaintance, Jan Matejko. In 1885, Matejko decided to engage himself in a work that would— in his opinion—lead to a realization of Polish-Ruthenian unity in Galicia. The pretext for Matejko's undertaking was the thousand-year anniversary of the death of St. Methodius, the apostle to the Slavs.

In 1880, Pope Leo XIII had issued the encyclical *Grande Munus*, in which he recalled how July 5 had been designated as the feast day of *Saints Cyril and Methodius* in the Catholic Church under his predecessor Pius IX. The Holy See sought to remind the Slavic nations of the Church's care for them by referencing the century-old tradition of the Slavic apostles' mission.[148] As a result of the papal designation of July 5 as a feast day, preparations for a great jubilee were organized in 1885 in Velehrad, Moravia. This celebration drew pilgrims from the whole of Slavdom. In various parts of the Austro-Hungarian monarchy pilgrim

---

[148] "Grande Munus" Encyclical of Pope Leo XIII on SS. Cyril and Methodius, 30 Sep. 1880, accessed 1 Sep. 2019, http://w2.vatican.va/content/leo-xiii/en/encyclicals/documents/hf_l-xiii_enc_30091880_grande-munus.html.

committees were set up, ordinarily with a religious profile. The co-creator of one such committee in Cracow was Jan Matejko. However, this committee was to take on not only a religious character but also a socio-political dimension as a result of Matejko's involvement.

In his article on Matejko's trip to Velehrad, Henryk Słoczyński wrote that the artist, who had been serving on the Cracow pilgrim committee founded under the direction of Bishop Albin Dunajewski, wanted

> (...) Poles to act together with the Ruthenians so that the overtone from the Velehrad celebrations would serve to strengthen the Greek Catholic faith, protecting it from the lure of Orthodoxy. Matejko's involvement in the matter was a result of his ambition to politically lead the enslaved nation. The conviction as to his own prophetic mission had developed under the influence of the Romantic literature read during the artist's early youth.[149]

Besides serving to propagate Polish-Ruthenian brotherhood, Matejko envisioned the pilgrimage as a response to the Pan-Slavist activities of tsarist Russia, which, following the banning of the Uniate rite in Ukraine as well as in the Kingdom of Poland (in the Chełm and Podlachia lands), aimed to win over Galician Ruthenians to the Great Russia idea. For this reason, the Polish elite embraced the commemoration of the thousand-year anniversary of the death of St. Methodius as an opportunity to display the Vatican's unity with the whole of Slavdom, including the Ruthenians, against the expansion of Orthodoxy and Moscow. This is suggested in the appeal of Father Władysław Chotkowski, a member of the pilgrim committee:

> God gave a huge hall but he did not give it the cement of unity and love. Now after a thousand years, however, the Slavs have started to think of unity, but two voices are calling them in different directions. On the one side are the calls of the Muscovites, who want all Slavic peoples to renounce unity with Rome and the Holy Father and to listen only to the tsar who rules in Petersburg. On the other side is the voice of Pope Leo XIII, who wants nothing but that the disunited family of Slavic nations be joined in the unity of the holy Roman Catholic faith.[150]

The organizers hoped that if Poles took the lead in planning the celebrations, the tone of the occasion would reflect Polish views on the question of Slavic unity. This was a move to combat the influences of

---

[149] Henryk Marek Słoczyński, "Dar dla Welehradu," *Przegląd Powszechny* no. 7–8 (791–92) (1987), p. 160.

[150] Władysław Chotkowski, *Żywot śś. Cyryla i Metodego Apostołów Słowiańskich napisany w tysiącletnią rocznicę chwalebnej śmierci św. Metodego z polecenia krakowskiego Komitetu Pielgrzymki przez ks. Chotkowskiego* (Cracow, 1885), p. 60.

Pan-Slavism with the counter-notion of Polish leadership over a unified Slavdom. As Marian Gorzkowski noted:

> Matejko himself presented the matter thus: It would be fitting if we Poles, as the best educated branch of Slavdom, were to take this commemoration into our own hands and to direct it, limiting our activity to purely religious practices, for all others can subsequently develop on their own. Therefore, to reach such an objective [Matejko tried to make sure], in particular, that the painting to be presented by him to Velehrad first be consecrated by the pope, and then sent from Rome to Velehrad as a gift from the Poles.[151]

The most important part in the undertaking was to be the presentation of Matejko's painting *Saints Cyril and Methodius* to the basilica in Velehrad. On the frame of the painting was the inscription "To the Slavs." The painting depicted both saints, with the background containing a cross with the image of the Częstochowa Madonna and the emblems of Poland (the Eagle), Rus' (the Archangel Michael), and Lithuania (the Vytis).[152] It should be noted that the coat-of-arms of Lithuania was in a subordinate position to that of Rus', positioned on the lower part of the cross where it was less visible. But this was not the only element underlining a Ruthenian motif in the picture. The depiction of the Black Madonna was an equally important element. Matejko often employed the image of the Częstochowa Virgin Mary in his work with the sole purpose of emphasizing the bond between Rus' and Poland: Prince Władysław Opolczyk's presentation of the icon to the monastery at Jasna Góra in the Middle Ages was considered by Matejko to be the most valuable gift that Rus' had had to offer Poland at that time. After all, the Black Madonna was to have been painted on a board from the Lord's Table by the Evangelist Luke himself, the legend of which the painter was clearly referring to in preparing the icons for the Greek Catholic church of St. Norbert in Cracow: in a parallel homage to the legend, St. Luke, whose face is that of Matejko, paints the Black Madonna.[153] The symbolism employed by Matejko in the painting *Saints Cyril and Methodius* revealed his vision of Polish-Ruthenian relations, of the religious and political community of Poles and Ruthenians, and finally of the role of historic Poland within the Slavic world, the multiethnic character of which was to act as proof of the possibility of combining various Slavic peoples into a political entity or federation. The Slavic unity envisioned by Matejko excluded Russia and its proclamation of Pan-Slavism, and represented a hegemony emanating from the care of the Vatican. Matejko recognized the reality of the growing rift

---

[151] Gorzkowski, *Jan Matejko. Epoka*, p. 294.
[152] Słoczyński, "Dar dla Welehradu," p. 163.
[153] Cf. Świątek, *'Lach serdeczny'*, pp. 79, 91, 125–30.

between Polish and Ruthenian politicians, but he sincerely believed in the ideas he expounded and had faith that his activities would result in a change in the current state of affairs, particularly as the pope had given his support to the commemorations. In the mind of the deeply religious artist, papal approval of the occasion could result in a miraculous union of Poles and Ruthenians as they undertook their pilgrimage to Moravia.

Matejko's lofty plans, however, were never realized. Initially the artist's attempts to gain support for his initiative from Adam Sapieha, Artur Potocki, Władysław Zamoyski and Stanisław Tarnowski ended in "everyone promising something and not doing anything."[154] Ultimately Zygmunt Cieszkowski travelled to Rome with a letter from the artist, in which was written:

> The Slavs are flocking to Velehrad, as we Poles are hurrying to get there in order to honour the Slavic apostles Saint Cyril and Saint Methodius at the tomb of Saint Methodius, and to unite ourselves through prayer as one and in permanence. On the 5th of July of this year, Polish pilgrims will present to Velehrad the gift of a painting of the Holy Apostles of Christendom. Desiring therefore, in the vein of historical tradition, sublimity and divine blessing as much for the Slavic peoples as for themselves, they turn to you, oh Vicar of Christ, with the beseeching request to bless their offerings and to celebrate a Holy Mass in front of this very image for our unhappy nation, which needs Divine Mercy the most. Solace arouses in us a still greater attachment to Your throne, and encourages the Ruthenians, undoubtedly more wretched than us , for they are tempted by schism. Your great heart, Holy Father, understands the significance of accord between nations based on love and commonality of faith, and therefore can best direct it.[155]

Despite a few difficulties, Cieszkowski was able to obtain the painting consecrated by the pope; however, its return to Cracow was met with the news that the Austrian authorities had banned Galicians from making pilgrimages to Velehrad under the pretext of an epidemic in Moravia. For this same reason the Velehrad celebration of July 5 took place at the Wawel in Cracow.[156] Nevertheless, the unbreakable Matejko decided to organize another pilgrimage to Velehrad for October 4 — the final day of the jubilee period designated by the Church. While the trip did materialize, Matejko was accompanied to Moravia by only a dozen or so pilgrims. In analyzing the Galician press, Henryk Słoczyński

---

[154] Gorzkowski, *Jan Matejko. Epoka*, p. 294.
[155] "Autograf Matejki. Brulion prośby zaniesionej do Ojca Świętego, ażeby odprawił mszę św. i pobłogosławił jego obraz śśww. Cyryl i Metody, który pielgrzymka polska ma zanieść do Welehradu," Cracow, 19 Jun. 1885, MNK, DJM, sygn. IX/2928.
[156] Słoczyński, "Dar dla Welehradu," pp. 163–64.

noted that up until the very last moment a desire to take part in the pilgrimage had been expressed by individuals such as Bishop Albin Dunajewski, Paweł Popiel, Artur Potocki, Stanisław Hushalevych and Franciszek Smolka, though ultimately none of them participated. Why, then, did they decide to abstain? Słoczyński explains:

> Can one point this time around to more discreet pressure on the part of Vienna? In examining the contemporary press, one cannot avoid the shocking impression that the papal consecration of the image was kept hidden. And yet, this was no small sensation and, at the same time, a serious argument as to why the artist's initiative should be supported. Similar disbelief is triggered by the absence of a priest on the pilgrimage to Velehrad (…) Was the total disregard of the pro-Uniate demonstration in Velehrad a reflection of the relations of the Latin clergy in Galicia towards the Greek Catholic faith?[157]

Given the circumstances, it is unsurprising that Matejko's plan to incorporate a large number of people, including Ruthenians, into the pilgrimage to Velehrad ended in a fiasco. The only Ruthenian to travel with Matejko to Moravia was Platon Kostecki. He later published an anonymous account of the pilgrimage in *Gazeta Narodowa*. From this article, entitled "The Submission of Matejko's Feretrum in Velehrad" ["Złożenie feretronu Matejki w Welehradzie"], we learn that a group numbering a dozen or so was received most cordially, and the painting was carried in the procession to the Gothic parish church in which the memorial service took place. The delegation submitted the documents presenting the image "to the honour and glory of God in the Trinity and the Slavic Apostles *Saints Cyril and Methodius* (…)." The document was signed by the participants: Jan Matejko, Zygmunt Cieszkowski, Ludwik Dębicki, Czesław Dołęga Lasocki, Władysław Markiewicz, Platon Kostecki, Władysław Miłkowski, Stanisław Nałęcz Cichocki, Leon Sapieha as well as by two priests, Józef Biba and Władysław Jaszkowski, both doctoral students in theology who had joined the pilgrimage in Vienna.[158]

The lack of Ruthenian response to this event can largely be attributed to the censor, but it is also doubtful that the Ruthenian elite in Lviv wished to involve themselves in an undertaking aimed—just like all the other anniversaries—at bringing about a Polish and Ruthenian accord. For this reason, as Henryk Słoczyński wrote, "Matejko's main goal—influencing the Ukrainian Uniates threatened by Orthodoxy— was not achieved."[159]

---

[157] Ibid., p. 167.

[158] [Platon Kostecki], "Złożenie feretronu Matejki w Welehradzie," *Gazeta Narodowa* no. 232 (11 Oct. 1885), pp. 2–3.

[159] Słoczyński, "Dar dla Welehradu," p. 167.

Anniversary Commemorations in the 1890s and the Beginning of the Twentieth Century

With time, anniversary celebrations were to become less widely upheld, although this custom remained reasonably widespread at the local level in the towns and smaller urban areas of Galicia. This was enhanced by the growth in the number of reading rooms, branches of the Sokół organization and the Association of People's Schools established in 1891. Schools also took it upon themselves to organize commemorations. School life, in which both Polish and Ruthenian youth participated, represented an opportunity to strengthen bonds; consequently, the notion of Polish-Ruthenian brotherhood was often promoted. In his work on the Przemyśl intelligentsia, Tomasz Pudłocki gives several interesting examples of schools bolstering the ideal of fraternity between nations. In 1887, during an Adam Mickiewicz evening held at a Przemyśl secondary school, the choir sang quite a few songs in Ruthenian; in turn, the graduate reunion masses at the cathedrals were jointly conducted for Roman Catholic and Greek Catholic pupils with a "toast to successful Polish-Ruthenian accord and unity" being raised during the subsequent banquets. A similar message was forwarded through events that took place at the 1st Secondary School in Przemyśl, where Roman Hamchykevych [Roman Hamczykiewicz] had formerly taught. In taking his leave of the graduates, this Ruthenian addressed the pupils by saying, "I love you, oh Polish youth," to which they responded by singing "Many Years!" ["Mnohaya lita"] in Ruthenian. At the same secondary school in 1892, Polish and Ruthenian youth lay flowers at the stone commemorating the Constitution of May 3, singing "God Thou Hast Poland" and "Ukraine Has Not Yet Perished" ["Shche ne vmerla Ukraina"].[160]

We learn about a similar act of cooperation between these two national communities from an account of a pupil, Wawrzyniec Dayczak, at the German secondary school in Brody. On the 100th anniversary of the Constitution of May 3, the Ruthenian secondary school catechist Grzegorz Jarema [Hryhorii Iarema] conducted a "solemn service" at the Uniate parish church.[161] The Ruthenian catechist for the town's youth, Father Jan Turkiewicz [Ivan Turkevych], annually prepared Polish and Ruthenian choirs to perform at the so-called Adam Mickiewicz and Taras Shevchenko morning concerts.[162]

---

[160] Tomasz Pudłocki, *Iskra światła czy kopcąca pochodnia? Inteligencja w Przemyślu w latach 1867–1939* (Cracow, 2009), pp. 414–15, 7.

[161] Wawrzyniec Dayczak, "Gimnazjum w Brodach na przełomie XIX i XX wieku we wspomnieniach byłego ucznia," introd. and ed. Maria Dayczak-Domanasiewicz, *Krakowskie Pismo Kresowe* 4: *Galicja jako pogranicze kultur* (2012), p. 28.

[162] Ibid., p. 55.

Despite the intentions of these events, their primary result was the spreading of patriotic feelings among Galician youth. These jubilee events stopped reflecting concrete political goals and exclusively became local manifestations of national or ideological views. They were considered a duty that had to be performed annually, usually with increasingly diminishing pomp. As Jadwiga Hoff wrote: "after a few years these anniversaries aroused less and less local interest and fostered a descent into patriotic lethargy."[163]

This did not mean, however, that there was a total rejection of jubilee events on the part of national organizations.[164] From the 1880s to the collapse of the monarchy, an array of interesting historical anniversaries took place that could be used to consolidate Polish-Ruthenian relations by referencing their common heritage. Yet with time, the Ruthenian angle became increasingly secondary, although it did not disappear entirely. The 100th anniversary of ratification of the Constitution of May 3, for example, was marked with national celebrations in which numerous Ruthenians were to have taken part. In Dobromyl a declaration propagating Slavic accord was issued, while in Sniatyn the slogan "We are brothers to you" was promulgated. As Adam Galos wrote, these sentiments might have resulted from the recently established Romanchuk–Badeni accord, which opened up a so-called "New Era."[165] Commemorations referencing Polish independence revolts, such as that marking thirty years since the January Uprising, no longer attracted Ruthenians other than the *gente Rutheni, natione Poloni*. The very idea of a federative uprising was still stressed during such jubilees, from the fiery speeches that opened the ceremonies to the small-scale leaflets printed for the occasion and distributed at their close. One such example is the *Jednodniówka* [One-day Newspaper] with its selection of poems and patriotic songs published in 1893.[166] Many of the works included forecasted another uprising, such as "It Was, Is and Will Be!" ["Była, jest i będzie!"]:

There was glory, there was fame
There was a battle but one bloody and of pain
There will be one fight more

---

[163] Jadwiga Hoff, "Inteligencja galicyjska – niepokorna czy lojalna?," *Rocznik Przemyski* 46, no. 4: *Historia* (2010), p. 57.

[164] Cf. Galos, "Obchody rocznicowe," pp. 89–112; Paweł Sierżęga, "Obchody rocznic narodowych w Galicji autonomicznej. Stan i perspektywy badań," in *Galicja 1772–1918. Problemy metodologiczne, stan i potrzeby badań*, vol. 2, eds. Agnieszka Kawalec, Wacław Wierzbieniec and Leonid Zaszkilniak, introd. Jerzy Maternicki (Rzeszów, 2011), pp. 420–33.

[165] Galos, "Obchody rocznicowe," p. 102.

[166] "*Jednodniówka* z festynu Uczestników powstania roku 1863," LNNBU, fond 5: Zbirka rukopysiv, avtohrafiv, hramot i dyplomiv biblioteky Natsional'noho zakladu im. Ossolins'kykh u m. Lvovi, op. 1: Rukopysy, spr. 6809/III: Varia 1791–1897, pp. 125–26.

And with our might will march Rus' and Lithuania
And when the bonds of enemies are cast aside
Holy Poland will again arise.

Also included were re-workings of well-known songs, often of dubious quality and worth, such as: "Hey, Kuba Drank to Jakób" ["Ej, pił Kuba do Jakóba"]:

Hey, Kuba drank to Jakób
Jakób to Michał:
Long live, Poland, Rus', and Lithuania,
Long live Poland whole!
And whoever doesn't drink
Then twice over shall they sink,
(...)

The final verse of this song considers Rus', though now from a critical viewpoint:

Poland – the mother, Lithuania – the daughter
And Rus' no stranger to us,
Though "in parts" vodka sips
And this from the tsarist pail
However the pail
Is drying up slowly
And so with a whack and a smack, and a smack and whack
Let's be of good will!

The three-part heraldic shield of the January Uprising of 1863 became an extremely popular symbol–the key to expressing the idea of federation of the three countries, and accompanied the next anniversary of the insurrection. All memorabilia from the times of the uprising enjoyed great reverence among later generations.

An interesting example is the banner from the church in Surazh near Vitsebsk, which a nobleman allegedly from the princely family Światopełk Mirski [Svyatopolk-Mirsky] brought to the celebration of the union in Horodło in 1861. Two years later he took the banner to the battlefield during the January Uprising. On the one side there was shown St. Kazimierz Jagiellończyk, on the other–the coat of arms of Poland, Lithuania, and Ruthenia. After the uprising the nobleman, under the assumed name Szymon Szydłowski, kept the banner during the celebrations organized by the veterans of January Uprising in Lviv until he died in 1906. After his death, the banner was still present during the anniversary of the uprising[167].

---

[167] In 1923 the banner was handed over to the Corps of Cadets No. 1 in Lviv in recognition of fighting during the Third Silesian Uprising. Today, the banner is an exhibit at

But cooperation with the Ruthenians was only truly possible during the organization of religious anniversaries. During the 300th anniversary of the Union of Brest in 1896, all three Catholic denominations were involved in the Lviv celebrations, as were Ruthenians such as Isidor Sharanevych.[168] By this time, those Ruthenians of Polish nationality who had been active in the past were already of an advanced age, and were simply unable to direct and coordinate such commemorations in the way they had in previous decades. Their absence is confirmed by the first point on the jubilee program, which stipulated that "this commemoration is to be as splendid as the greatest national church celebrations, but devoid of any political traits."[169]

A political-ideological tone and a degree of emotion did, however, accompany the erection of a monument to Adam Mickiewicz in Lviv. The design competition for the monument had attracted many entries, with the main prizes having been awarded to the Polish architect Antoni Popiel and his Ruthenian colleague Mykhailo Parashchuk in what was perhaps a symbolic move. In addition, during the official unveiling of the monument, which took place on 30 October 1904, the mayor of Lviv, Godzimir Małachowski, proudly announced that "swarms of admirers of this greatest Genius of our nation have been drawn from all parts of Poland, Lithuania, and Rus'."[170] In reality, the celebrations drew only a miniscule delegation from Navahrudak [Nowogródek], where the bard had been born. While there were certainly Jews in attendance, there was no mention of a single delegation from among the local Ruthenian population.

When the 500th anniversary of the Jagiellonian victory at Grunwald was celebrated in Cracow in 1910, there was simply no one left from among the Ruthenians of Polish nationality to attend. At that time, relations between Poles and Ruthenians were extremely antagonistic after a wave of Ukrainian peasants' strikes in Galicia from 1900 to 1904, conflict over Lviv University, and the assassination of the governor Andrzej Potocki in 1908. But even then, during the Grunwald celebrations, the Poles emphasized the idea of a federal Commonwealth.

---

the National Museum in Cracow. Józef Białynia Chołodecki, "Dzieje chorągwi Korpusu Kadetów we Lwowie," *Panteon Polski* no. 64 (1930), s. 2; Wacława Milewska, *Niepodległość. Wokół myśli historycznej Józefa Piłsudskiego* (Cracow, 2018), s. 190–191.

[168] See the celebration's program as well as the appeal to the "Brother Ruthenians": "Program uroczystego obchodu 300-letniej rocznicy Unii ruskiej Cerkwi z św. Stolicą Apostolską," LNNBU, fond 5, op. 1, spr. 6809/III, p. 505; Odezwa, LNNBU, fond 5, op. 1, spr. 6809/III: Varia 1791–1897, p. 508.

[169] LNNBU, fond 5, op. 1, spr. 6809/III, p. 505, point 1.

[170] "Kolumna Adama Mickiewicza we Lwowie," *Gazeta Lwowska* no. 250 (1 Nov. 1904), "Jednodniówka z festynu Uczestników powstania roku 1863", LNNBU, fond 5, op. 1, spr.6809/III: Varia 1791–1897, p. 3.

The Jubilee Celebrations of Private Individuals

The push to foster accord between Poles and Ruthenians continued through the organization of jubilees for public figures, these being representatives of Polish elites. The solemn atmosphere that permeated theatrical and literary elements of the commemorative programs inspired participants to express their views on this matter in an artistic form. Social meetings often created an opportunity for the voicing of visions, including those propagating the myth of the Commonwealth of Three Nations on the part of the elite. The press accounts of these jubilees as well as the occasional published recollections by known figures who attended these anniversaries have proven to be rich resources for understanding how the idea of Polish-Ruthenian brotherhood was vocalized. Platon Kostecki, a participant at many of the salons of the day, frequently wrote about these events. He grasped every opportunity to raise the issue of a common independence to be fought for not by a single nation, but by this fraternity of three peoples. His tendency to shoehorn this vision into any occasion was noted in *The Immortals* [*Nieśmiertelni*], an 1898 publication devoted to Lviv writers. Speaking of Kostecki, it reads:

> A traditional point of the program would be Kostecki's toast, and actually one of three toasts; for that number the venerable poet had in reserve. The use of one of these depends on the mood of the moment. In a normal mood Kostecki speaks in prose, and despite the severe stammer evident during a colloquial chat he turns out to be a most excellent public speaker. He talks at tremendous length, quite untiringly and with immense zeal. Sometimes the participants of the gathering try to interrupt this boisterous outpouring by applause, given after the first possible full stop. This does not work when the mood of the moment is exceptionally ceremonious and Kostecki draws on the second toast he has up his sleeve, ending with the litany in Poland's honour already known to all. Then his voice reverberates like the horn of an angel and even the orchestral fanfare from the gallery is unable to drown him out. The third type of toast is given in verse and will appear the following day in *Gazeta Narodowa*.[171]

One such jubilee in celebration of a renowned individual was that of the poet Seweryn Goszczyński. Celebrations in his honour took place on 7 March 1875 at the town hall reception room in Lviv. As was noted in the account published to mark the event, 160 people were in attendance, including a number of well-known literary figures.[172] Selected

---

[171] *Nieśmiertelni. Fotografie literatów lwowskich* (Lviv, 1898), pp. 15–16.
[172] [Agaton Giller] A.G. and [Józef Poliński] J.P., *Pamiątka uroczystości półwiekowego jubileuszu Seweryna Goszczyńskiego we Lwowie dnia 7. marca 1875. roku* (Lviv, 1875), p. 5.

guests gave speeches in honour of Goszczyński, and then addresses were read out from various individuals and institutions from all of the Polish lands and from abroad. The toasts that followed were peppered with noble ideas. Jan Grzegorzewski from Ukraine spoke in the spirit of Poland's brotherhood with Rus', stressing Goszczyński's own words on the subject of Rus' and recalling the various ways that the Ruthenian question could be viewed. Ultimately he raised "a toast to the brotherhood of Rus' and Ruthenian-Ukrainian national aspirations."[173] Platon Kostecki's toast, delivered in Ruthenian, took the subject broached by Grzegorzewski in a completely different direction. Kostecki emphasized how in his work, Goszczyński had captured the "historical triplet":

> For it is this triad that fashioned it: the Ruthenian-Mazurian [here meant a Pole]-Lithuanian. Whatever was immortal about what you forged, whatever was immortal in that which you penned in these very parts of the world, this was under the influence of this triad, or through or by this triad[174].

Kostecki's speech was greeted by extended applause, with Goszczyński responding that he himself was half-Ruthenian. Bolesław Limanowski supplemented the notion of brotherhood by raising a toast in Lithuanian. These toasts and speeches seemed to represent the continuity of the traditions of a multi-ethnic Poland.[175] Count Wojciech Dzieduszycki neatly drew the orations to a close, raising "a toast to Poland, Lithuania, and Ukraine!"[176]

Lviv had Platon Kostecki to thank for bringing the nationally appreciated Matejko to the city in 1888. This man of letters was already well acquainted with the artist, engaged in correspondence with him, had been on the pilgrimage to Velehrad, and wrote about him in *Gazeta Narodowa*. In June 1888 Platon Kostecki sent a letter to Cracow in which he wrote:

> I have a request to you, in my name and that of thousands of others, many, many thousands of others here in Red Rus', and in particular here in the capital. (...) these young people deserve to shake your hand, oh Master![177]

Several months later, Isidor Sharanevych, the senior member of the Lviv Stauropegion Institute, was to visit the painter with his own request, presumably connected with the exhibition of Ruthenian an-

---

[173] Ibid., p. 36.
[174] Ibid., p. 44.
[175] Ibid., p. 44; Limanowski, *Pamiętniki (1870–1907)*, pp. 120–21.
[176] [Giller] A.G. and [Poliński] J.P., *Pamiątka*, p. 45.
[177] "List od Platona Kosteckiego do Jana Matejki z zaproszeniem do Lwowa w imieniu młodzieży lwowskiej," Lviv, 30 Jun. 1888, MNK, DJM, sygn. IX/2845.

tiquities that was in development. Matejko arrived in Lviv in December of 1888 as the guest of the Greek Catholic metropolitan Sylvestr Sembratovych, where he visited the exhibition of Ruthenian antiquities, was serenaded with "Mnohaia lita", discussed Ruthenian matters,[178] and finally paid a visit to an artistic-literary circle of youth. To mark Matejko's visit to Lviv, Platon Kostecki wrote a special poem entitled "A Cordial Pole" ["Lach serdeczny"]. He addresses Matejko in verse:

> You are the first Pole whom a Ruthenian
> Invites to his cottage and to his heart.
> He prays for you to the Divine in the heavens…
> After all, Master, you are the cordial Pole
> And fraternal esteem shall follow you eternally![179]

This poem demonstrates how well both artists understood each other: what Matejko was able to put down on canvas, Kostecki was able to reflect in words.

Kostecki soon became the "jubilee poet," composing verses extolling eminent Poles and often making recourse while doing so to the theme of Polish-Ruthenian-Lithuanian unity. But he also wrote with the aim of commemorating important historical events. With his poem "January 22" ["22 stycznia"][180] he commemorated the nineteenth anniversary of the outbreak of the January Uprising, "The Third of May" ["Trzeci Maja"][181] praised the constitution of 1791, while John III Sobieski's victory was honoured in the work "On the Two Hundredth Anniversary of the Relief of Vienna" ["W dwusetną rocznicę odsieczy Wiednia"].[182] Kostecki not only recalled in his work the service rendered by well-known Poles to the fatherland, but also made reference to the idea of Polish-Ruthenian brotherhood and raised the issue of the need to build a Commonwealth of Three Nations.

After years of intensive work on national unity, the man who had raised so many toasts to Rus' and Poland was to instead have toasts raised in his honour by Lviv society. The spirit of *gente Rutheni, natione Poloni* could be felt in the way that Kostecki celebrated his jubilee of creative work in the press. The commemoration of his thirty years of editorial work and his position as an icon of sorts for the entire formation of Ruthenians of Polish nationality became an opportunity for an impressive manifestation of his views on Polish-Ruthenian-Lithuanian brotherhood. The celebration was so grand that it was covered by

---

[178] Gorzkowski, *Jan Matejko. Epoka*, pp. 361–63.
[179] Platon Kostecki, "Lach serdeczny", MNK, DJM, spr. IX/2795.
[180] Platon Kostecki, *22 stycznia* (Lviv, 1882).
[181] Platon Kostecki, *Trzeci Maja* (Lviv, 1871).
[182] Platon Kostecki, "W dwusetną rocznicę odsieczy."

almost all of the eminent journals in Galicia as well as in the other two areas of partition.

On Wednesday, 18 January 1888 the decorated room at the City Casino on Akademicka Street (today Taras Shevchenko Avenue) in Lviv was already full to the breaking point by 12:30. Among those assembled was the mayor, Edmund Mochnacki, the Galician Diet deputy and editor of the journal *Nowa Reforma* Tadeusz Romanowicz, the editor of *Gazeta Narodowa* Władysław Zajączkowski, the editor of *Dziennik Polski* Kazimierz Ostaszewski-Barański, and other eminent representatives of Galician social life. When the clocks struck 1:00, Platon Kostecki was led on stage by the mayor. Mochnacki welcomed him with a speech in which he stressed his service to journalism and the significance of the "struggle" in which he had engaged throughout his life by means of his pen. He praised his "eagle flight of thought and spirit," and concluded by noting that he constituted a model of civic virtues and patriotism. In the name of all those assembled, Mochnacki presented Kostecki with an expensive watch engraved with an Eagle, Vytis, and Archangel Michael along with the dedication: "To Platon Kostecki on the 30th anniversary of his work for national journalism, his compatriots 18 January 1888." The first line of "Our Prayer", emphasizing the unity of Poland, Lithuania, and Rus' was also engraved. A visibly moved Kostecki voiced his thanks, echoing his father's words: "there are three powers—God, one's fatherland, and one's family." He stated that he had tried to direct his life on the basis of these values, adding: "Nation and only nation, only for the good of the fatherland is my motto." He thanked his "compatriots" for the celebration, and prompted by the watch's inscription moved to explain "Our Prayer":

> And here on this watch is etched my *Mołytwa*. This song came to me like a Divine revelation – on hands and knees, with tears I merely copied it. This song fulfils all that is pure, free of hatred, that which faith heralds![183]

Praises were heaped upon Kostecki by the editor Tadeusz Romanowicz and November Uprising veteran Mieczysław Darowski. Following their speeches, three girls appeared in front of the stage dressed in Cracovian, Ruthenian, and Lithuanian folk costumes, who then earnestly recited the verses of "Our Prayer".[184] Kostecki kissed the girls and read out his new work, "The Three Hopes" ["Trzy nadzieje"], in which with feeling and affection he described the lands constituting his fatherland: the Crown, Lithuania, and Ukraine— the "three hopes" of the title.

---

[183] „Jubileusz Platona Kosteckiego," *Gazeta Narodowa* no. 15 (19 Jan. 1888).
[184] Dressed as a Ruthenian was Maryla Wolska, as a Cracovian Kazimiera Winnicka, and as a Lithuanian Jadwiga Zielonczanka. Maryla Wolska, "Quodlibet," in Maryla Wolska, Beata Obertyńska, *Wspomnienia* (Warsaw, 1974), p. 115.

After the recital, the guests continued to deliver speeches until 2:30. That evening a splendid banquet was given, attended by two hundred people—double the number anticipated—including the chief figures of Galicia's elite. Kostecki was accompanied by the likes of Leon Sapieha, Florian Ziemiałkowski, Euzebiusz Czerkawski and Wojciech Dzieduszycki. Referring to the idea broached by Kostecki which he himself revered, Dzieduszycki "spoke about the artificial split that has taken hold of the fraternal tribes, expressing at the same time the hope that the moment was nigh when a truth stronger than ill will and historical necessity would remove the barriers and join together that which evil people had divided."[185]

Not everyone congratulated Kostecki personally; he received many letters which were read out during the supper. These letters expressed not only admiration for Kostecki but also for the views he held. Leon Syroczyński raised a toast in a similar vein:

> You *Gente Ruthenus, natione Polonus...* though ethnographically Ruthenian, have been Polonized so superbly, and yet you have not forgotten your native tongue. And while we respect the historic traditions of Cracow and Warsaw, we do not have today a city more Polish than Lviv, yet no one sees anything strange in that a Ruthenian from the banks of the Dnister, a Ukrainian from the banks of the Dnipro, or a Mazurian from the banks of the Vistula should speak on its behalf. You, like our city, have resisted all violence whether Tatar or other—you have also resisted the frenzied Cossacks, and you resist all forms of Germanization, from Franz Joseph's *Sprechzeichen* and ankle-boots, to the latest, constitutionally loyal Viennese parliamentarianism.[186]

These sentiments were to return a dozen or so years later in 1907, albeit on a lesser scale, when the ailing 75-year-old Kostecki celebrated 45 years of journalism in *Gazeta Narodowa*. This celebration was organized by his doctors, and he was visited by his colleagues from the editorial board. Here also he received many well wishes and greetings by post, and again the newspapers wrote at length about the work of this "patriarch of Lviv journalism," as he was referred to by *Kurier Lwowski*. One of the editors of *Słowo Polskie* praised this famous bard of Polish-Ruthenian brotherhood:

> The respect that generally surrounded him overwhelmed me. Bent over his desk, he mystically adopted Wernyhora's profile, while his industriousness was impressive. (...) For this Ruthenian, who has never denied that he is a Ruthenian, was able to love Poland genuinely and deeply (...).[187]

---

[185] "Obchód jubileuszowy Platona Kosteckiego," *Dziennik Polski* no. 20 (20 Jan. 1888).

[186] "Bankiet na cześć Platona Kosteckiego," *Gazeta Narodowa* no. 16 (20 Jan. 1888).

[187] See for the words from various Polish newspapers "45-lecie Platona Kosteckiego," *Gazeta Narodowa* no. 253 (3 Nov. 1907), p. 2.

The Funerals of Ruthenians of Polish Nationality

Platon Kostecki died a year later, on 1 May 1908. His funeral mass took place with the participation of clergy from both Catholic denominations on 3 May 1908 at the Boim Chapel in Lviv.[188] And then the body was interred at the Lychakiv cemetery. The date of burial coincided with the 117th anniversary of the ratification of the Constitution of 3 May, and thus the funeral took on a somewhat patriotic character. Initially the clergy of the Greek Catholic Church wavered over taking part in the ceremony, but finally decided to accompany Kostecki's body along with representatives of the other two Catholic denominations. Despite this outward display of cooperation, speeches were removed from the program so as not to inflame with any possible political content the already tense situation that existed between Poles and Ruthenians in Lviv; only a few weeks earlier, a Ruthenian student named Myroslav Sichynsky had assassinated the Galician governor Andrzej Potocki. Despite these restrictions, crowds turned out, including many well-known figures, and—as it was reported—a "silent" national manifestation took place.[189] Obituaries appeared following Kostecki's death in all the Polish newspapers published in each of the three areas of partition.[190] He was remembered not only for being both a Ruthenian and a Pole and an advocate of reconciliation, but above all as a good and decent man who was devoted to his country. As the eulogy published in *Lechita* [Lechite] noted,

> He was famous for his cheerful disposition, tireless hard work and kindness. A superb speaker, often at a ceremonious moment he would utter words imbued with a love for the fatherland, placing before the gaze of the youth an image of national and political idealism in their most beautiful connotations. He was one of those, today so few in number, who proudly spoke about himself as *gente Ruthenus, natione Polonus*, and served Poland as his fatherland for the whole of his life.[191]

Kostecki's death, and the specific form the funeral took, symbolically brought to a close this epoch in the history of Ruthenians of Polish nationality. With his burial, the *gente Rutheni, natione Poloni* voice in the public domain suddenly fell silent. Kostecki had been predeceased by

---

[188] *Słowo Polskie* no. 205 (2 May 1908).

[189] A.B., "Ze Lwowa. Lwów 3 maja (Trzeci maja – Pogrzeb śp Platona Kosteckiego)," *Czas* no. 103 (4 May 1908), p. 3. Cf. also: Marian Tyrowicz, "Kostecki Platon," in *PSB*, vol. 14 (Wrocław–Warsaw–Cracow, 1968–1969), p. 340.

[190] See for example: "Ś. p. Platon Kostecki," *Czas* no. 102 (evening edition) (2 May 1908), pp. 3–4; *Słowo Polskie* no. 205 (2 May 1908); *Goniec Wileński* no. 3 (3 May 1908); *Przewodnik Gimnastyczny 'Sokół'* no. 6 (Jun. 1908); *Lechita* no. 20 (15 May 1908).

[191] *Lechita* no. 20 (15 May 1908).

other well-known Ruthenian figures who had advocated and promoted Polishness. Their funerals represented a final opportunity to demonstrate the duality of their identity; for this reason, *gente Rutheni, natione Poloni* funerals often developed a public dimension out of what was initially a private religious service of family mourning. Some even became overt manifestations of wider socio-political issues, assembling the local society who wanted to pay their respects to those who had been adherents of Polish-Ruthenian accord.

The funeral of Mikołaj Zyblikiewicz in 1887 was one such occasion. His burial at the Rakowicki cemetery in Cracow was accompanied by a long speech given by another *gente Ruthenus, natione Polonus*, the former Galician Diet deputy Zygmunt Sawczyński. Another speaker was Dr. Wawrzyniec Styczeń, president of the Cracow Bar (Izba Adwokatów w Krakowie), who asked the deceased to accept "from the Bar words of the highest respect and recognition," as was paid to him by "Rus' and the whole of Poland at the grave."[192] This type of rhetoric was extremely common at such funerals. Sometimes words were said by other *gente Rutheni*, praising the services of the deceased; such was the case at the funerals of Jan Dobrzański and Henryk Rewakowicz. At the funeral of the former in 1886 it was Platon Kostecki who spoke,[193] while Teofil Merunowicz gave an address for the latter in 1907.[194] When Anatol Lewicki passed away in 1899, words of condolence over his passing were expressed by Stanisław Smolka: "We had in him (...) a noble embodiment of a beautiful, ancient yet today disappearing breed: *gente Ruthenus, natione Polonus*. He loved his Rus' with a passion, but he adored her within the boundaries of Poland." He concluded his speech with an appeal for "eternal memory!"[195]

The speeches given at the funerals of well-known representatives of *gente Rutheni, natione Poloni* emphasized the two-tiered identity of the deceased, as well as the worldview they held. This is not only proof of the contribution made by these figures in the building of brotherly bonds between Poles and Ruthenians in Galicia, but it also bears witness to the fact that by the turn of the twentieth century, the escalating Polish-Ruthenian conflict in the Austrian realm of partition meant that attitudes typical of the *gente Rutheni, natione Poloni* had to be promoted and underscored. It appears that the passing of an era was clearly felt, along with the regret over the deaths of those who had created it. For in the last two decades of the nineteenth century and the first of the

---

[192] "Pogrzeb Zyblikiewicza," *Czas* no. 118 (25 May 1887), p. 2.
[193] "Pogrzeb Jana Dobrzańskiego," *Gazeta Narodowa* no. 127 (3 Jun. 1886), p. 2.
[194] "Pogrzeb zwłok ś. p. Henryka Rewakowicza," *Gazeta Lwowska* no. 228 (4 Oct. 1907), pp. 3–4.
[195] "Pogrzeb ś. p. prof. Dra Anatola Lewickiego," *Czas* no. 98 (29 Apr. 1899), p. 3.

twentieth the most notable Ruthenians of Polish origin passed away: Jan Dobrzański (d. 1886), Mikołaj Zyblikiewicz and Antoni Dąbczański (both d. 1887), Julian Szemelowski (d. 1891), Zygmunt Sawczyński (d. 1893), Euzebiusz Czerkawski (d. 1896), Anatol Lewicki (d. 1899), Julian Horoszkiewicz (d. 1900), Henryk Rewakowicz (d. 1907) and finally Platon Kostecki (d. 1908). Their departure came at a time when a completely different perspective on the nationality question was developing. Consequently, the impassioned speeches given at the graves of *gente Rutheni, natione Poloni* not only expressed heartfelt remorse over the passing of eminent figures, but also articulated a yearning for the fading epoch in which Ruthenians were able to feel Polish.

Teofil Merunowicz's *Ruthenian Question*: The Final Manifestation of the Ideas of *Gente Rutheni, Natione Poloni*

One more name must be added to the annals of the most eminent sociopolitical activists who shared the dual identity of *gente Rutheni, natione Poloni*: that of the long-serving Galician Diet and Imperial Council deputy, Teofil Merunowicz. In observing the discrepancy between his immediate surroundings and his ideals, he decided to write a book that would constitute the definitive political voice for the entire *gente Rutheni, natione Poloni* formation. In January 1919 the Gubrynowicz Publishing House in Lviv published Merunowicz's work, *The Ruthenian Question and the Peace Congress* [*Sprawa ruska i kongres pokojowy*].[196] Its release came at a time when the capital of the former Austrian area of partition was already under the control of the Polish army as part of the ongoing war with the Ukrainians over Eastern Galicia, with battles still raging for the remaining areas of what had been Red Rus'. At this time the Polish lands, which after 123 years of annexation once again constituted a single state entity, witnessed many diverse conceptions of the future shape of Poland's eastern borders, as well as varied proposals over resolving the complex relations with the inhabitants of these former Lithuanian-Ruthenian territories. Merunowicz also advanced his own proposal for the post-war order in this part of Europe. His main premise was the creation of a Commonwealth, one federal in character, composed of Poland, Lithuania, and Rus'.

Merunowicz, who had devoted his entire life to the integration of Poles and Ruthenians within the framework of a single state structure,

---

[196] Teofil Merunowicz, *Sprawa ruska i kongres pokojowy. Referat, opracowany dla polskiego biura prac kongresowych* (Lviv, 1919).

did not want to admit that Ukrainians had come into their own as a separate nation. In writing his treatise *The Ruthenian Question*, he undertook a thorough analysis of the broad spectrum of matters connected with the Ruthenian/Ukrainian question.

First, Merunowicz drew attention to the existence of a range of different definitions of Ruthenian nationality, none of which was universally accepted by the Ruthenians themselves. Furthermore, he demonstrated that each Ruthenian political party and faction understood the nationality it represented in a different way.[197] The Ukrainian party, following the example of Hrushevsky, used the term "Ukraine" for the entirety of Rus', while Merunowicz believed this name should have retained its former definition, restricted to the territories along the Dnipro River. Old Ruthenians used the designation "the Ruthenian nation"; Russians called them "Little Russians"; while others employed the adjective "Ruthenian" to differentiate them from Russians. Most ordinary Ruthenians, save for certain circles of the intelligentsia and Poles, used the term "the Ruthenian people."[198]

47. *The cover of Teofil Merunowicz's brochure* The Ruthenian Question and the Peace Congress... *(Lviv, 1919)*

Merunowicz opposed the slogan "Drive the Poles back over the San River!", recalling that a sizeable part of those ripe for expulsion had in the past been Ruthenians who had voluntarily undergone the process of Polonization. However, in stating this, he emphasized that he was speaking as someone torn between a Ruthenian ethnos and Polish nationality:

> There have existed for centuries and exist to this day such families which in maintaining the Eastern rite, considered by us to be the characteristic trait of a Ruthenian, act in civil life as if they belonged to the Polish nation. These are the so-called *Gente Rutheni natione Poloni*. For they consider that by the Union of Lublin of 1569, which "brought and forged into a single people" Poland, Lithuania, and Rus', joining these

---

[197] Ibid., p. 3.
[198] Ibid., p. 4.

nations "into a single inseparable and diverse body, into a single Commonwealth," the concept of historical Poland as the unification of three
nations through a voluntary union was definitively settled. Some say
that such Ruthenians are rare birds, and on their way to extinction.
Quite possibly. Yet, for as long as they live—and live they will—they
have loyally served, serve, and will serve the ideals of a common fatherland. To these ideals belongs the principle that in mutually respecting
one's individuality, Lithuania, Poland and Rus' are to consider themselves as joined historically by the bond of brotherhood in the state
union of Poland.'[199]

Thus, Teofil Merunowicz returned in this text to the subject of the
Union of Lublin after half a century had passed since the 300th anniversary celebrations in 1869. This time around, however, the national
consciousness of the Ruthenian population of Eastern Galicia had been
transformed in character. By recalling in *The Ruthenian Question* the
Lublin Diet of 350 years before, the author was no longer appealing
for a joint Polish-Ruthenian act but was addressing the Polish office
working at the Versailles Conference. He was very well aware that the
increasing numbers of *gente Rutheni, natione Poloni*, most of whom had
not played any political role whatsoever in years, had no chance of seeing the realization of this noble federative plan.

In writing about the need to instigate a federation, Merunowicz was
referring now not to a brotherhood offering mutual benefit in a situation of external threat, but to a historical act, one that would cement the
common existence of Poles, Ruthenians, and Lithuanians. The Ukrainian notion of statehood, not to mention the fact that a separate Ukrainian nation aspiring to independence already existed at that time, was
at loggerheads with such a vision. The author referenced history as
a means of questioning the very existence of the Ukrainian nation, to
which, according to widely held opinions concerning his own ethnic
roots, he also should belong, and yet did not want to belong.

Merunowicz argued that Rus' had Poland to thank for its level of development, for it had been Poland that had conducted a civilizing mission in the East—a mission guided by the spirit of fraternity and respect
for "individuality."[200] What is more, the influence exerted ended up being bilateral; while Rus' was Polonized, Poland was also Ruthenianized
to a degree, as seen in its language. Consequently, "Ruthenians and
Poles understand one another immediately, while the Russian tongue
is similarly foreign to both a Pole and a Ruthenian."[201]

---

[199] Ibid., pp. 6–7.
[200] Ibid., p. 7.
[201] Ibid., p. 9.

Merunowicz attributed the disagreements between Poles and Ruthenians to the differences in the rites of the same religion. He also questioned whether a singular Rus' had ever existed, for even after the unification of numerous lands by individual princes these states soon dissolved. It was only the union with Poland that ensured Rus' stability based on brotherhood, for Ruthenians were guaranteed freedoms, privileges, and religious tolerance within the Polish realm. This state of affairs was, according to the author, only to change in the nineteenth century, as threats to the Ruthenian people and the Uniate Church began to emanate from tsarist Russia.[202]

Merunowicz bolstered his arguments by analyzing various events from Ukrainian history, and in particular from the Cossack period. In accordance with the Polish point of view, he emphasized the importance of the conciliatory character of the Treaty of Hadiach, and with sorrow recalled its failure to transpire. He identified the main causes of the conflict as religious antagonism and the estate demands of the Cossacks, and not—according to him—the nationality question, which for Merunowicz did not play a role at the time. Merunowicz corroborated his views by quoting the words of Taras Shevchenko, claiming that it would have been better if Khmelnytsky had not been born or had died in the cradle.[203] He criticized not only the Ukrainian recognition of this Cossack hetman as being "a warrior of the first order for the freedom of the Ukrainian nation," but also the notion that the Koliivshchyna rebellion of 1768 had been an "act of national defence on the part of the Ruthenians against oppression by the Poles." Merunowicz argued that the "Massacre of Uman was an act of social revenge, and that it had nothing to do with Ruthenian national politics."[204] According to Merunowicz, the Ruthenians remained positively disposed towards the Poles, to whom they were connected by fraternal bonds. Merunowicz pointed to instances where Austrians had engaged in conflict with Poles in Galicia, such as their introduction of Ruthenian as a language of instruction at Lviv University and filling the department with Ruthenians, to prove that:

> (...) not only did the Ruthenian intelligentsia not display any hostility towards the Poles, but quickly was to almost totally Polonize itself. And never had Polonization in Galician Rus' made such inroads as it did at

---

[202] Ibid., pp. 10–17.

[203] Merunowicz here referred to the verse by Shevchenko entitled *Iakby to ty, Bogdane p'janyi...* from 1859, and more precisely the following lines: "(...) Iakby ty na svit ne rodyvs' \ Abo v kolystsi shche upyvs'... \ To ne kupav by ia v kaliuzhi \ Tebe preslavnoho. Amin". Taras Shevchenko, *Zibrannia tvoriv*, vol 1: *Poeziia 1837–1847* (Kyiv, 2003), pp. 252–53.

[204] Merunowicz, *Sprawa ruska*, pp. 17–22.

the turn of the nineteenth century as a result of the protection afforded to the Ruthenian language by the loathed German bureaucracy.[205]

A Ruthenian by provenance, he at least did not question the cultural achievements of compatriots like Ivan Kotliarevsky, Taras Shevchenko, Panteleimon Kulish and Mykola Kostomarov, as well as the members of the Ruthenian Triad in Galicia.[206]

Merunowicz believed the cause of the present day conflict to be the Revolution of 1848,, which was supposed to have taken care "of the estate (social) interests of the Ruthenian clergy, and supported all the directives of the German bureaucracy (...)."[207] He set about characterizing the contemporary Ruthenian/Ukrainian political options, emphasizing that they were only linked by "a hatred of Poles, and an envious implacable opposition towards them."[208] He considered this to be highly unjust, in the same way he viewed the Ruthenian accusations of Polish oppression.

According to Merunowicz, during the period of autonomy the Ruthenian language had been one of the languages of administration; half of the Galician judiciary were Ruthenian; Ruthenian education progressed thanks to the protection afforded it by the National School Board, of which the majority of trustees were Poles; Ruthenian newspapers prospered; the Shevchenko Scientific Society and the Prosvita organization received grants, as did smaller societies in the countryside; and Uniate parishes grew in size and importance. He posed the rhetorical question: "is this the oppression of the Ruthenian nationality?"[209]

The final part of *The Ruthenian Question* was dedicated to the political situation in the face of the war raging for Eastern Galicia, as well as the plans for a peace treaty that would decide the future of Rus'. Merunowicz recalled that "radical Ruthenian parties provoked and aroused by traditional vengeance and social and national envy" had undertaken aggressive acts. He listed as examples the killing of the governor Andrzej Potocki in 1908, the shootings at Lviv University in 1910, and finally the occupation of Lviv on 1 November 1918 by the Ukrainians, but added that the latter took place "under the command of Prussian officers and with the active aid of the German-Austrian military."[210] He contrasted these events with Polish desires for the Ruthenian lands:

---

[205] Ibid., p. 29.
[206] Ibid., pp. 23–27, 30–32.
[207] Ibid., p. 33.
[208] Ibid., p. 43.
[209] Ibid., pp. 45–47.
[210] Ibid., p. 48.

Poles want nothing more than for a return of the old Commonwealth, of course, not a nobiliary one, but a democratic one; this means that they want to bring back to life the fraternal union of Poland, Lithuania, and Rus' under the slogan "the free with the free – the equal with the equal." And with this intention alone they appeal to the coalition of Western powers, possibly to the peace congress, with the request to settle the Ruthenian question in the spirit of the brotherhood of nations and self-determination.[211]

Merunowicz stressed that the best way to end the Ukrainian-Polish war was a fair agreement that guaranteed benefits to both sides, and which would be approved by both Poles and Ukrainians in terms of the Versailles congress. His proposal covered six points that might constitute the basis for any future treaty.

The first point of the draft suggested granting Rus' (in the sense in which he understood this term, that is including parts of Rus' territories which had hitherto belonged respectively to the Russian and the Austro-Hungarian empires) political independence and governance with the guarantee of minority rights. The next point proposed the creation of a state within the borders of pre-1772 Poland that would be a federation of equal subjects: Poland, Lithuania, and Rus'. The lands of Eastern Galicia, Volhynia, Podilia, and the Right-Bank Ukraine were to fall within the boundaries of this Rus'. Another independent state based on the resolutions of the Treaty of Pereiaslav of 1654 and in a federal union with Russia was to be formed out of the remaining Ukrainian lands. The third demand proposed the "conciliatory resolution" of affairs that were mutual and common to the federation and others, to be resolved at the local diets of each of the states. The fourth and fifth points foresaw separate constitutions, administration, and judiciaries for each member of the federation. The final resolution called for an end to the fighting.[212]

Merunowicz's proposal, although not entirely realistic and perhaps naive by present day standards, can be regarded as the last example of the political thinking characteristic of the representatives of the vanishing socio-political formation that was *gente Rutheni, natione Poloni*. The war between the Poles and Ukrainians over Eastern Galicia brought an end to this period of accord and coexistence, with the representatives of both nationalities succumbing to the growing nationalisms that were to shape the attitudes of European societies during the first half of the twentieth century. This evolution of views, accelerated by the First World War and the collapse of the Austro-Hungarian

---

[211] Ibid., p. 49.
[212] Ibid., pp. 50–51.

monarchy, particularly in the context of national self-determination which had up to this point moved forward at a relatively slow pace, was to conclude a significant chapter in the history of the border zone that was nineteenth-century Eastern Galicia. Under these new circumstances, the two nations struggled with each other to determine the boundaries between them in the face of war over state existence.

Conclusion

Many books on Galicia begin by giving percentages: what percent of this crown land of the Habsburg Monarchy were Poles (usually determined by the declaration of Roman Catholicism as the religious denomination as given in the Austrian censuses as well as the declaration of Polish as the language of social intercourse), Ukrainians (those declaring Greek Catholic denomination or the Ruthenian language), Jews, and members of other nationalities. These categorizations are indicative of the common trend in scholarship of writing about the past from a modern instead of a historical perspective. The impression of distinct nationalities presented in these statistics is not without foundation; given that a bloody Polish-Ukrainian war over Eastern Galicia raged in 1918–19, while the twenty-year interwar period saw rising antagonism between the two nations before reaching its apogee during the course of World War II, there simply had to have existed two societies opposed to each other prior to these events, whose joint history was filled with escalating antagonism. However, these distinct identities recognized by contemporary Poles and Ukrainians do not reflect the entire picture of this period. Rather, there are stories of individuals, organizations, and ideas which did not have sufficiently strong support to win them a permanent place in this collective memory. One such story is that of the fate endured by *gente Rutheni, natione Poloni*—Ruthenians who felt a kinship with Polishness. The designation itself forces one to reconsider the aforementioned statistics presented in the subject literature, for it is unknown to which nationality these individuals have been assigned by those writing Galicia's history. The matter is made even more complicated when one takes into account the many Armenians and Jews who had a highly developed sense of belonging to the Polish nation, not to mention the German and Czech government officials who were Polonized during their time in Galicia. However, the opposite process also occurred: a part of the Roman Catholic peasantry underwent Ruthenization, while some Poles were Germanized. These nebulous identities reinforce the need for caution when writing about Galicia and its inhabitants. The nineteenth century was a period of rapid creation of national identities in general, with these identities often being fluid and heterogeneous. This was particularly visible in the case of the Ruthenian population, for in the mid-nineteenth century it was not yet decided which national option would ultimately win out among the Ruthenians: the Polish, Russian, Austrian, or the eventual victor, the Ukrainian. This option would not have been victorious if it had not been for the rivalry not only with the "others," but also with "one's own." Without the Ruthenians who felt an affinity to Polishness as well as the Russophile circles, with both of whom the Ruthenian national populists engaged in polemics, an intermediate identity would never have developed between Poland (although it did not actually exist on the map of Europe) and Russia.

This study has sought to recall one of those alternative scenarios in the shaping of national consciousness among Ruthenians during the duration of the partitions: the Polish scenario. The most significant problem here is undoubtedly the question as to how the notion of *gente Rutheni, natione Poloni* is currently comprehended, and how it was understood in the mid-nineteenth century when it became popular. This term has been used by various historians to describe the identity of the Ruthenian gentry in the Poland of the early modern epoch. At that time, the notion of identity and national affiliation was understood quite differently. In the nineteenth century, during the course of the partitions, however, this term had become something more than a mere attachment to a former state, representing instead a conscious choice. There is an ongoing attempt to define *gente Ruthenus, natione Polonus* as a world outlook, an idea, the self-designation of a group as well as also a two-tiered identity. It seems that the last of these is the most apt definition, though it must be emphasized that within this formulation there lurks a definite hierarchy—namely *gens*, understood as an ethnicity subordinated to the second component, nationality. This does not imply, however, the exclusion of the Ruthenian element in the case of Ruthenians of Polish nationality. This would indicate assimilation, whereas the nineteenth-century *gente Rutheni, natione Poloni* may be defined as a group of individuals situated at the phase between acculturation and assimilation. The *gente Rutheni, natione Poloni* were ethnic Ruthenians who considered Poland to be their ideological fatherland, although they would remain strongly attached to their own private homeland —Rus'. They lived among Poles as Ruthenians and did not deny their Ruthenian roots, so *de facto* they had not undergone full assimilation to Polishness. Such a state of affairs in a period when nationality was decided on by conscious discovery or choice could not be maintained for long. Hence the consciousness of being *gente Ruthenus, natione Polonus* could serve two, at most three, generations of a given family as an appropriate designation. At this point, either total Polonization or, more rarely, the adoption of a Ruthenian (Ukrainian) national identity occurred. The enigmatic nature of the *gente Ruthenus, natione Polonus* formation, its unspecified forms, and the oscillation and mutability of some of its representatives mean that the creation of a universal definition of the concept for research purposes is highly problematic.

It is worth asking whether the self-identification of some Ruthenians as Poles represented a manifestation among various layers of Galician society of an identity born from feudalism. In the case of the gentry, an attachment to historic Poland had been preserved in family memory. The nineteenth-century nobility, and in particular the landed gentry, recalled the participation of their forefathers in the governing of the former state: they recollected their attendance at diets, the royal distribution of lands, the levy en masse, and their holding of official state offices. This led to a natural sense of Polish patriotism, one justified by family history. The nineteenth century was, however, a period during which the social hierarchy would gradually dissolve, bringing to the fore a new estate that would take responsibility for social, cultural, and ultimately political matters. This new class was the intelligentsia, recruited from all social strata, including, in the last decades of the nineteenth century, also the peasantry. As it is often the source material (records of participation in uprisings, conspiracies, manifestations of Polishness in society, etc.) that allows us to determine whether representatives of the upper social spheres felt themselves to be Poles or not, in those social strata where the preserved source material is sparse at best, such an undertaking becomes more complicated. National consciousness and awareness only developed within the lower strata during the second half of the nineteenth century, particularly during its last decades. Furthermore, we are only able to determine whether they did indeed have a national consciousness when they left behind sources that answered the question as to who they felt they were.

In as far as we are able to conduct qualitative research into those whose identity is evidenced by extant sources relating to *gente Rutheni, natione Poloni*, it is much more difficult to carry out any research of a quantitative nature. Censuses in the Habsburg Monarchy were conducted every ten years for the duration of the second half of the nineteenth century, which forced its inhabitants to answer a series of questions including ones about denomination/rite and the language used for social interaction. There was no question on nationality, which was presumed to be that of state affiliation; that is, affiliation to the Austrian crown. We, however, are interested in how many Greek Catholics would have declared themselves to be of Polish nationality. The subject literature has attempted to establish the number of Ruthenians of Polish nationality on the basis of how many Greek Catholics gave Polish as their main language of social interaction, in doing so adopting the premise that the language declared was in fact the chief indication of national affiliation; and yet, it is unwise to consider this the sole criterion of the possession of a national orientation. These factors make it difficult to ascertain how many Ruthenians of Polish nationality actually inhabited Galicia in the subsequent decades of the nineteenth century and the beginning of the twentieth century, particularly given that the differences in the figures arrived at by various researchers are large (Józef Buzek in 1909 gave a figure of 107,000, Stanisław Pawłowski in 1910 saw 235,000, while Tadeusz Jagmin in the 1930s registered 430,000 Ruthenians of Polish nationality).

The problem also arises of establishing the geographical scope within which the identity phenomenon of *gente Rutheni, natione Poloni* occurred. It was most commonly seen in the larger urban centres of Eastern Galicia as well as on the actual cultural border area, in those locations where the Polish and the Ruthenian ethnoses were mixed: for example, in the Lemko region or the Sambir region. In addition, Polish culture was adopted by those Ruthenians who migrated to the large towns of Western Galicia, chiefly to Cracow. If multiculturalism—and by extension, inter-culturalism—had not pervaded various regions of Galicia, manifesting itself in public life (contacts made in the common public expanse) and in family life (mixed marriages), the extent of the phenomenon of *gente Rutheni, natione Poloni* would have been greatly reduced, if it had even arisen at all. Yet it should be mentioned that among those factors that led many Ruthenians to choose Polishness were other exceptionally important elements of daily life, situations of so-called ethnic conflict, or those events which forced one to choose sides. Such situations or factors included the use of Polish as the language of service in the Greek Catholic Church, which was to survive until the mid-nineteenth century; schooling, the Germanized character of which discouraged the youth from Polish patriotic self-organization; and fascination with the romantic-revolutionary literature of the day, which was written in Polish.

Polish literature, alongside historiography and historical painting, was to play an important role in the shaping of national identity under the partitions, even for Ruthenians. To explore the relationship between literature and identity, it is necessary to first establish how "fatherland"— a particularly popular term during this time—was understood in the nineteenth century. Numerous Polish poets and writers, particularly during the period of Romanticism, propagated among their readers their conceptualization of "fatherland" as well as their sense of affiliation to it. This fatherland was conceived as encompassing the entirety of the pre-partition Polish lands. There was no place within such conceptualizations for the exclusion of Ruthenian lands, as it was believed that these lands were inseparably linked to the history of Polish statehood and the notion of Polish nationality that went along with it. Romanticism would also introduce new social ideas directed towards the common people. In Galicia, folklorists gathered Ruthenian folk songs, on the one hand rousing interest among Ruthenians in their own folk culture, while on the other hand painting these songs as a composite element of a broadly understood Polish culture, viewing them as another cultural achievement of historic Poland. Poets, writers, historians, and painters considered Rus' to be an inseparable part of Poland. There is no absence in their ranks of the *gente Rutheni, natione Poloni*: individuals like Platon Kostecki, who in his numerous poems proclaimed the unity of Poland, Rus', and Lithuania, or Anatol Lewicki, the author of a school textbook entitled *An Outline of the History of Poland and the Rus' Lands Attached to It*. They helped to create the myth of the Commonwealth of Three Nations, cultivated as well by many Polish writers and artists. Jan Matejko's view of Ruthenian history reflected this myth; in his painting of numerous scenes depicting aspects of Polish history, he often emphasized the union of the Rus' lands and the Ruthenians themselves with Poland. Henryk Sienkiewicz, who was to have an immense influence on Polish society, continued to propagate the image of the Ruthenian Polish patriot, making a positive hero out of Prince Jeremi Wiśniowiecki in *With Fire and Sword*. The intent behind this type of nineteenth- -century Polish literature, historiography, and art was two-fold: to build a connection for Poles with the Rus' lands of pre-partition Poland, and to convince them, on the basis of historical arguments, that the Ruthenians should in the future reconstruct a joint state with the Poles. The presence in Galician social life of Ruthenians of Polish nationality merely confirmed that this was a realistic scenario.

The origin of the term *gente Ruthenus, natione Polonus* — constituting a component of the myth of the Commonwealth of Three Nations as well as the formulation itself can be found in the events and political thought of the turn of the nineteenth century. During the Enlightenment, the demand for state centralization came into vogue along with the accompanying eradication of any regional particularism. Hand in hand with this went the need to unify the whole of Polish society regardless of the different historical traditions of the various lands of the Polish-Lithuanian Commonwealth, as well as unifying the various ethnicities inhabiting the state. Although the southern lands of Poland had fallen beyond its political control already in 1772, resulting in Galicia's exclusion from the majority of the enlightened Warsaw reforms such as that seen in the area of education, ideas were nevertheless propagated in the Polish capital that reached compatriots in the Austrian zone of partition as a result of maintained contact between the nobility on both sides of the border. After the collapse of Poland in 1795, these ideas would also emanate from émigré groups through various types of publications. In the letters of Stanisław Staszic and Tadeusz Kościuszko, as well as in the writings of Hugo Kołłątaj, we can find

expressions of the need for a close union of the Ruthenians with Poland and the Polish nation (e.g., through the abandoning of the Julian
calendar in the Greek Catholic Church). But many Ruthenians did not
need to be convinced of their Polishness, for they continued to manifest their attachment to their former state after the partitions by serving
in the Polish Legions and fighting in the Napoleonic Wars or the November Uprising of 1830. If they had not up to this point taken part en
masse in the battles beyond the border, this was to change significantly
in a very short time. After the defeat in the uprising of 1830–31, the
Austrian area of partition began to be flooded with leaflets and brochures urging people to fight for a new and better Poland. During this
time, post-November Uprising emigrants played a significant role in
directing the discourse. After Adam Mickiewicz wrote that the Lithuanian and the Pole were brothers and members of a single nation, similar voices, particularly those of émigrés from the Rus' lands, began to
speak out on the subject of Ruthenians, whom they viewed as children
of the common fatherland of Poland. Although the majority of émigrés
interpreted the term Ruthenian more in terms of the inhabitants of the
Rus' lands than actual ethnic Ruthenians, certain political circles of the
Great Emigration started to reflect on the social causes and reasons behind the collapse of the uprising. A number of émigré factions attributed its failure to unresolved social problems. This perspective explained
the creation of propaganda focused on convincing the common people
to fight for Poland through a reconstruction of the feudal social order.
A similar objective was demonstrated in the activities of the numerous conspiratorial organizations that arose in Galicia. They had to take
into consideration not only the interests of the Polish people but also
of the Ruthenians, who needed to be addressed in their own language.
A specific political propaganda also developed at this time which addressed not only social questions but also the subject of Polish-Ruthenian brotherhood, in the spirit of which Kasper Cięglewicz and Julian
Horoszkiewicz wrote. Its result was the creation in the 1830s and 1840s
of numerous conspiratorial organizations which assembled both Polish and Ruthenian youth, including the students of the Greek Catholic
seminary in Lviv as well as members of the nascent intelligentsia. Even
though the conspirators' activities resulted in the disbanding of these
secret organizations and court sentences for their members, from their
midst arose legends about those fighting for Poland and looking out for
both Poles and Ruthenians. When those convicted were granted amnesty during the revolutions of 1848, not only were they welcomed with
recognition in Galicia, but they also claimed leadership positions in the
political organisms forming at the time and continued to proclaim the
ideals of Polish-Ruthenian fraternity.

The year 1848 was immensely significant in the development of the Ruthenian nationality in Galicia, for it was during this year that the Ruthenians first formulated their political demands. The Greek Catholic hierarchy represented at the time a conservative position loyal to the Austrian Empire. This was at odds with the demands for freedom coming from Lviv democrats, whose ranks contained both Poles and Ruthenians rallying for social changes. At the same time, these individuals emphasized their affiliation to Polishness. With the establishment of the first Ruthenian political organization of a national populist leaning, the Supreme Ruthenian Council, the Ruthenians aligned with the Lviv democratic circles created an analogous organization, the Ruthenian Sobor, in cooperation with the Polish Central National Council. There was a rivalry over who would lead the Ruthenian people and become the Ruthenian elite. This power struggle was won by the Greek Catholic clergy, for within the Ruthenian Sobor the circles were neither united nor unanimous on policy. The organization contained both Polish landowners and members of the intelligentsia who defined their Ruthenianness not ethnically but territorially, as well as actual Ruthenians of Polish nationality who were attached to their rite and language but for whom there could be no other imaginable route for political development than a joint one with Poles. The latter strongly accentuated their Ruthenianness, often using it in conjunction with the word "nationality," which caused controversy among the Poles who considered there to be but a single Polish nationality of which Ruthenianness was merely a component. Arguments of this nature revealed the fundamental problem that plagued those straddled between two cultures. Since a Ruthenian political program distinct from the Polish one had emerged, these individuals would have trouble reconciling two contradictory identities. From 1848, politically active figures had to choose whether they fell on the Ruthenian or the Polish side of the proverbial fence. Those who were to subsequently describe themselves as *gente Rutheni, natione Poloni*, made that choice, firmly subordinating the Ruthenian element of their identity to Polish nationality. The year 1848 and the activity of the Ruthenian Sobor were a point of reference for them. They saw in the activities of this organization the roots of their political thought, different from the ideas of Ruthenians of the national populist current or of those considered Russophiles.

The collapse of the revolutions of 1848 as a result of Franz Joseph's pacification of provincial democratic demands temporarily halted the development of the political aspirations of Polish society in Galicia, including those of Ruthenians of Polish nationality. However, the return of absolutist governance in the 1850s would not stop the process of separating the Ruthenian elites from the Poles. The period between the revolutions of 1848 and the beginning of the 1860s was characterized by conflicts over the language of instruction in folk primary schools, the struggle for equal representation for the Ruthenian language, and finally the discussion over which alphabet Ruthenians should employ. Agenor Gołuchowski, the former governor of Galicia and the Austrian minister of the interior, as well as the *gente Ruthenus, natione Polonus* Euzebiusz Czerkawski, were particularly vocal proponents of using the Latin script for Ruthenian. It never became the official alphabet despite the widespread use of Ruthenian in the Latin script, something especially cultivated by Ruthenians of Polish nationality. The fight put up by the Ruthenian elites to maintain the use of Cyrillic was to a large extent an element in the struggle with the Poles over Ruthenian identity. The irreversible Ruthenian rejection of Polishness was made clear with the outbreak of the January Uprising of 1863. Although earlier Polish conspiracies involving Ruthenian youth had occurred in Galicia, and although the January Uprising itself had attracted many Ruthenians, attempts by the National Government to incorporate the previously unarticulated addition of Rus' to the brotherhood of Poland and Lithuania came far too late. None of the efforts undertaken by representatives of the Polish government to win over Ruthenians in the fight for the independence of a joint state were to end in success. Finally, the vagueness of Polish views on the Ruthenian question became apparent: they offered nothing concrete apart from the merely symbolic designation of Rus' as an allegedly equal member of any future federation.

The January Uprising, and in particular its iconography, was to play a significant role in developing the myth of a Commonwealth of Three Nations. The Uprising advanced the notion of the union of Poland, Lithuania, and Rus' as the form for the future state, an idea that had been circulating since the commemorations of the 448th anniversary of the Union of Horodło in 1861. Hope for the swift achievement of independence was, however, gradually extinguished in subsequent years. Sovereignty was not brought about by the Uprising nor the struggles of Polish democrats towards the end of the 1860s; it became an even dimmer possibility with Napoleon III's loss of the war with Prussia in 1871, which killed any Polish hope for France's help in the rebuilding of Polish statehood. From the 1860s onwards Galician society had to satisfy itself with concessions made on the part of the Austrian monarchy in relation to provincial self-governance, such as the creation of autonomous organs of power like the Galician Diet in Lviv. Political activity would ultimately be conducted in the forum of the Imperial Council in Vienna, where influence could be exerted on legislation. Politicians from *gente Rutheni, natione Poloni* operated in these representative bodies. Their two-tiered identity meant that they were especially inclined to support those social developments which would maintain accord between Ruthenians and Poles in Galicia. One cause championed for this purpose was determining the language of instruction in schools and administration. Two Ruthenians of Polish nationality, Zygmunt Sawczyński and Euzebiusz Czerkawski, were responsible for reaching solutions that to a certain degree stopped the development of the Ruthenian language at the upper levels of education, at least until the time it had actually "formed." Instruction in Polish at the majority of secondary schools and in most subjects at higher institutions in Lviv could have resulted in the Polonization of Ruthenians who aspired to higher positions only accessible through Polish education.

The positions of the main political camps from the period of so-called Galician autonomy regarding Rus' and Ruthenians are also of interest. At a time when the Ruthenian national populist movement had become well developed, there was simply no room for the ideas forwarded by Ruthenians of Polish nationality. The Cracow Stańczyk group tried to compromise with the Ruthenians of the national populist orientation, the democrats acted in a similar fashion, while the socialists completely changed the perspective from one of national orientation to one of class interests. In turn the Polish populists and nationalists maintained a vision of the Polish nation built on the notion of a Polish ethnos, and not on the tradition of the former multi-ethnic Commonwealth of Poland and Lithuania. For this reason, the peasant activists were prepared to completely give up their vision of a future Poland comprising those territories that were not ethnically Polish. On the other hand, for the nationalists there was simply no room for "half-Poles," although this camp would eventually warm up to the idea of moving beyond ethnographic conceptions of territory to historically conditioned conceptions, which would encompass the Ruthenian lands.

Etched into other aspects of public life in Galicia were well-known Ruthenians of Polish nationality. Poles arriving in Galicia in the 1860s from the Ukrainian lands located in the Russian area of partition brought a certain revival to the idea of a Polish-Lithuanian-Ruthenian state, a notion that had been defeated during the January Uprising. Because of their provenance, they were especially interested in emphasizing the inclusion of Rus' in any future independent Polish state. Although they did not represent the *gente Rutheni, natione Poloni* formation, their writings, sometimes composed in Ruthenian, breathed life into the ideals of Polish-Ruthenian fraternity and unity. Their opinions differed only on the question of whether Ruthenians were one of the Polish tribes, or a separate nationality in its own right that in the future would create a common federative state with the Poles.

The idea of Polish-Lithuanian unity was also stressed in Galicia during the commemorations of important Polish historical anniversaries. The commemoration of the 300th year anniversary of the conclusion of the Union of Lublin in 1869, the 200th anniversary of the Relief of Vienna in 1883, the 400th anniversary of the death of St. John of Dukla, the miraculous defender of Lviv from the Cossacks in 1648, in 1884, or even the 1000th anniversary of the death of St. Methodius were aimed not only at celebrating historical figures and events but also at using historical examples to convince the population that Poles and Ruthenians had to strive together for a common future as they had once done. The Ruthenians of Polish nationality involved in the organization of these events helped set the specific tone. Although these events, particularly those of 1883 and 1884, actually saw the participation of the Ruthenian population and the Greek Catholic hierarchy, this in no way halted the development of the Ruthenian national movement. Meanwhile, Polish society wanted to believe that Ruthenians would take that specific route that had been actively marked out in Galicia by *gente Rutheni, natione Poloni* activists. It was only when the representatives of this formation had died off that there was reflection over the void left by their departure. The funerals of dignitaries like Mikołaj Zyblikiewicz, Zygmunt Sawczyński, Euzebiusz Czerkawski, and Platon Kostecki at the turn of the twentieth century often became the final opportunities for the manifestation of ideas the deceased had once borne. After their deaths, no one picked up the torch to continue their work.

The *gente Rutheni, natione Poloni* have left behind written relics preserving the ideas that defined them: poems, journalistic pieces, texts of a political content and nature. These texts help to establish the role that the *gente Rutheni, natione Poloni* played in the history of Galicia. In the Ukrainian political tradition, constructed on national values, Ruthenians of Polish nationality were simply Polonized Ruthenians. The views articulated by the *gente Rutheni, natione Poloni* concerning plans to construct a Poland encompassing Rus' only served to encourage Ruthenians of national populist leaning to formulate their own state visions, unrelated to the question of Poland's existence. Similarly, the desire on the part of Ruthenians of Polish nationality to be considered as the Ruthenian elite in Eastern Galicia provoked Ruthenian national populists to oppose them and to strengthen their own position in Ruthenian society. *Gente Rutheni, natione Poloni* did not have a fighting chance, for they lacked the support of the Greek Catholic clergy, which constituted the main authority among the Ruthenian population of Galicia.

For Polish society under partition, *gente Rutheni, natione Poloni* represented the ideal profile for Galician Ruthenians. Their presence in the political and cultural life of Galicia made it appear as though the Ruthenians did indeed wish to build a joint state with the Poles. These figments of the popular imagination were maintained thanks to literary and artistic works created not only by Ruthenians of Polish nationality but also by other Polish writers and artists. In practice, however, none of the Polish political camps in Galicia envisioned supporting these circles after the main activists recruited from the *gente Rutheni, natione Poloni* formation had disappeared from the political stage. The result was a certain dichotomy: on the one hand, the Polish conservative politicians in power started to support the Ruthenian national populists out of a fear of Russophilism; on the other, Polish society, fed propagandistic ideas in art and literature and assured by the attitude of well-known Ruthenians of Polish nationality and references to a common past, lived with the conviction that Rus' would most certainly be a joint founder of any future Poland. This deceptively coloured the Polish understanding of Polish-Ruthenian relations, resulting in a picture that did not reflect reality. The Poles were to experience immense disillusionment during the first decades of the twentieth century, for only in the face of the violent conflict that was the Polish-Ukrainian War would they understand that they were not dealing with "brother Ruthenians" or the "the children of a common mother Poland," but with the Ukrainian nation striving for independence through whatever methods were at its disposal.

Bibliography

Archives:

Cracow:

The National Archives in Cracow (*Archiwum Narodowe*)
- zesp. 29/1571: Archiwum Franciszka Piekosińskiego,
  - o   F 93: Archiwum galicyjskich organów Rządu Narodowego 1863.

The Jagiellonian Library (*Biblioteka Jagiellońska* [BJ])
- sygn. 10065 IV: Łoziński, Bronisław. "Materiały warsztatowe do książki *Agenor hrabia Gołuchowski w pierwszym okresie rządów swoich (1846–1859)*, Lwów 1901."

The Jagiellonian University Museum Collegium Maius (*Muzeum Uniwersytetu Jagiellońskiego Collegium Maius*)
- Archiwum Fotografii,
  - o   sygn. 638: Jaworski Walery.

The National Museum. The Jan Matejko House (*Muzeum Narodowe w Krakowie. Oddział Dom Jana Matejki* [MNK, DJM])
- sygn. IX/2928: "Autograf Matejki. Brulion prośby zaniesionej do Ojca Świętego, ażeby odprawił mszę św. i pobłogosławił jego obraz śwśw. Cyryl i Metody, który pielgrzymka polska ma zanieść do Welehradu." Cracow, 19 Jun. 1885.
- sygn. IX/2795: Kostecki Platon, "Lach serdeczny".
- sygn. IX/2845: "List od Platona Kosteckiego do Jana Matejki z zaproszeniem do Lwowa w imieniu młodzieży lwowskiej." Lviv, 30 Jun. 1888.
- sygn. IX/2921: "Pismo Towarzystwa Przyjaciół Sztuk Pięknych we Lwowie w sprawie dwóch stypendiów ufundowanych przez Matejkę." Lviv, 22 Nov. 1870.

Lviv:

Central State Historical Archives of Ukraine in Lviv (*Tsentral'nyi derzhavnyi istorychnyi arkhiv Ukrainy u Lvovi* [TsDIAU]):
- fond 93: Zemialkovs'kyi Florian 1817–1900 rr., op. 1,
  - o   od. zb. 5: Protokoly narad pol's'koï deputatsiï u Krakovi ta Vidni.
  - o   spr. 4: Shchodennyk (frakhmenty).
  - o   spr. 6: Shchodennyk Zemialkovs'koho F. – chlena i sekretaria deputatsiï vid pol's'ko-shliakhets'kykh kil Halychyny u Vidni.
- fond 102: Kolektsiia dokumentiv pro pol's'ke povstannia 1863–1864 rr., op. 1,
  - o   spr. 28: Spysky uchasnykiv povstannia, zasudzhenykh viis'kovym sudamy v mm. Zolochevi, Peremyshli, Riashevi, Ternopoli ta n.

- fond 146: Halytske namisnytsvo m. Lviv, op. 7, Vol. 2,
  o spr. 4005: Perepiska s ministrerstvam vnutrennikh del i greko-kato-
     licheskoi konsistoriei ob antigosudarstvennoi agitatsii v propov-
     Ediakh greko-katolicheskikh sviashchennikov.
- fond 146: Halytske namisnytsvo m. Lviv, op. 66, Vol. 2,
  o spr. 1708: Materialy pro borot'bu ukraïns'koho naselennia proty
     latynizatsii i polonizatsii ukraïns'koi shkil'noi molodi v m. Khyrovi
     (donesennia, lystuvannia i inshi).
- fond 358: Sheptytsky Andrei, op. 2,
  o spr. 5: Pastyrs'ki poslannia Sheptyts'koho do dukhovenstva i na-
     rodu.
- fond 474: Kolektsiia dokumentiv pro pol's'ki povstannia 1830–1831 ta
  1848 rr., op. 1,
  o spr. 15: Vidozvy, zvernennia i proklamatsiï pol's'kykh i ukraïns'kykh
     suspil'no-politychnykh, students'kykh ta relihiinykh tovarystv
     i orhanizatsiï u m. Lvovi periodu revoliutsiï 1848 roku.
  o spr. 18: Virshi pro pol's'kyi natsional'nyi rukh druhoï chverti XIX st.,
     napysani pid vplyvom revoliutsiï 1848 r. Vol. 1.
  o spr. 19: Virshi pro pols'kyi natsional'nyi rukh druhoï chverti XIX st.,
     napysani pid vplyvom revoliutsiï 1848 r. Vol. 2.

The Lviv National Vasyl Stefanyk Scientific Library of Ukraine (*Lvivs'ka
natsional'na naukova biblioteka Ukraïny imeni Vasylia Stefanyka* [LNNBU]):
- fond 4: Biblioteka Bavorovs'kykh u m. Lvovi, op. 1: Rukopysy,
  o spr. BAW. 1630/III: Zubrzycki Dyonizy, "Rys Historyi Narodu ru-
     skiego w Galicyi przez Dyonizego Zubrzyckiego. Zeszyt drugi od
     roku 1340 do roku 1596."
- fond 5: Zbirka rukopysiv, avtohrafiv, hramot i dyplomiv biblioteky Natsional'noho zakladu im. Ossolins'kykh u m. Lvovi,
  o op. 1: Rukopysy,
     – spr. 532/III: Czynności posiedzeń sekcji polskiej i ruskiej kongre-
       su słowiańskiego zwołanego do Pragi.
     – spr. 2972/I: Cięglewicz, Kasper. "Wskazówka dla nauczycieli
       ludu ruskiego." Lviv, 1840 [!] [Julian Horoszkiewicz. "Łysty do
       pryjateliw myru"].
     – spr. 3063/II: Kostecki, Platon. "W sprawie ruskiej." [Lviv, 1863].
     – spr. 3535/III: Bogdański, Henryk. "Notaty do pamiętnika Ryszar-
       da Hermana." Lviv, 1868.
     – spr. 4545/I: Fedkowicz, Józef Sielcz. "Historya Rzeczypospolitej
       litewsko-rusko-polskiej dla młodzieży." 1878.
     – spr. 5792/III: Rok 1848. Dokumenty, autografy, listy XIX w.
     – spr. 6807/III: Archiwum Darowskich. Miscellanea historyczno-
       -polityczne 1794–1877.
     – spr. 6809/III: Varia 1791–1897.

o   op. 2: Avtohrafy,
- spr. 5146/II: Kostecki, P[laton]. "Nasza molytwa." Lviv, 1891.
• fond. 9: Okremi nadkhodzhennia,
- spr. 2295: Zbirka vidozv, oholoshen', statutiv tovarystv, vypysky z hazet ta in.
• fond 45: Arkhiv Didushyc'kykh,
o   op. 1: Rukupysy biblioteky poturyts'koï Didushyts'kykh,
- spr. 201: *Protest Rusinów przeciw adresowi do tronu podanego przez deputację świętojurców.* [Lviv], 1861.
• fond 76: Kolektsiia Pavlikovs'kykh,
o   op. 1: Rukupysy biblioteky Pavlikovs'kykh,
- spr. 254: Materiały do dziejów 1848 r. w Galicji.
o   op. 2: Arkhiv Pavlikovs'kykh,
- spr. 214: Kostecki, Platon. "11 listów i wiersze, listy do Mieczy-sława Romanowskiego." Lviv–Shehyni, 1854–83.
o   op. 3: Arkhiv Pavlikovs'kykh,
- spr. 276: Zbiór materiałów dotyczących wydarzeń politycznych w Galicji 1848 r., 1847–1849.
- spr. 280: Zbiór różnych materiałów dotyczących wydarzeń społeczno-politycznych 1848 r.
• fond 215: Zbirka pol's'kykh aftohrafiv,
o   spr. ZA 427, folio 5: Kostets'kyi, Platon. "Virshi."

Warsaw:
The Museum of Independence (*Muzeum Niepodległości w Warszawie*)
• sygn. P-629: Pocztówka "Boże zbaw Polskę".

The National Library (*Biblioteka Narodowa*)
• sygn. 1.984.365 A Cim.: [Jabłoński, Henryk] Podolak z za Kordonu. *Piśń o Wyszniowśkim* (Lviv, 1848).
• sygn. F.2594/W: Stefan Laurysiewicz.
• sygn. Poczt. 1282: Konstanty Dzbański. Założenie kamienia węgielnego "Kopca Unji" przez Fr. Smolkę, we Lwowie na wysokim zamku dnia 11 sierpnia 1869.

Wrocław:
The Ossolineum (*Zakład Narodowy im. Ossolińskich we Wrocławiu* [ZNiO])
• sygn. 5923/II: Schmitt, Henryk. "Niezgodni bracia. Trajedja w 5 dzia-łaniach."
• sygn. 6725/I (MF 2490): Dzieduszycki, Maurycy. "Zapiski. Pamiętnik z r. 1846, chronologia domu Dzieduszyckich 1844–1857, statystyczne dane o Towarzystwie Jezusowem (1845), przepowiednie Wernyhory i o. Marka."
• sygn. 7527/II: Papiery Towarzystwa Przyjaciół Sztuk Pięknych we Lwo-wie. Akta Sekretariatu. Kopiariusz z lat 1886–1891.

- sygn. 7939/II (MF 2107): Archiwum Rozwadowskich. Korespondencja Wiktora Rozwadowskiego z lat 1848–1852. Listy od różnych osób.
- sygn. 12038/II: Autografy różnych osób z lat 1663–1910. Lit. M.
- sygn. 13129 I: Drohojowski, Marceli. „Pamiętnik."
- sygn. 13535/II (MF 3269): Opałek, Mieczysław. "Książka o Lwowie i mojej młodości. Kartki z pamiętnika 1881–1901." Frysztak, 1958.
- sygn. 17094/II: Papiery dotyczące obrazu Jana Matejki *Unia Lubelska* w Zakładzie Narodowym im. Ossolińskich we Lwowie.

Printed sources:
Lists, protocols and stenographic records:
Protokoły Koła Polskiego w wiedeńskiej Radzie Państwa (lata 1867–1868). Eds. and introd. Zbigniew Fras and Stanisław Pijaj. Cracow, 2001.

Protokoły posiedzeń Rady Narodowej Centralnej we Lwowie (14 Apr.–29 Oct. 1848). Eds. Stefan Kieniewicz and Franciszek Ramotowska. Prepared for printing by Adam Gałkowski et al. Warsaw, 1996.

Sprawozdania stenograficzne z posiedzeń Sejmu Krajowego galicyjskiego we Lwowie odbytych od dnia 15. do 26. kwietnia 1861 r.

Stenograficzne sprawozdania z trzeciej sesyi Sejmu Krajowego Królestwa Galicyi i Lodomeryi wraz z Wielkiem Księstwem Krakowskiem w roku 1865–1866. Vol. 1: *Posiedzenie 1–40.*

Stenograficzne sprawozdania z trzeciej sesyi Sejmu Krajowego Królestwa Galicyi i Lodomeryi wraz z Wielkiem Księstwem Krakowskiem w roku 1865–1866. Vol. 2: *Posiedzenie 41–80.*

Sprawozdanie stenograficzne z 4 sesyi Sejmu Krajowego Królestwa Galicyi i Lodomeryi, wraz z Wielkiem Księstwem Krakowskiem w roku 1866.

Stenograficzne sprawozdania z 1. sesyi 2. peryodu Sejmu Krajowego Królestwa Galicyi i Lodomeryi wraz z Wielkiem Księstwem Krakowskiem z roku 1867. Posiedzenie 1-10.

Stenograficzne sprawozdania z drugiego peryodu drugiey sesyi Sejmu Krajowego Królestwa Galicyi i Lodomeryi wraz z Wielkiem Księstwem Krakowskiem z roku 1868. Posiedzenie 1–34.

Stenograficzne sprawozdania z trzeciey sesyi drugiego peryodu Sejmu Krajowego Królestwa Galicyi i Lodomeryi wraz z Wielkiem Księstwem Krakowskiem w roku 1869.

Sprawozdanie stenograficzne z rozpraw galicyjskiego Sejmu Krajowego. 1. posiedzenie 2. sesyi 3. peryodu Sejmu galicyjskiego z dnia 14. września 1871.

Sprawozdanie stenograficzne z rozpraw galicyjskiego Sejmu Krajowego. 5. posiedzenie 2. sesyi 3. peryodu Sejmu galicyjskiego z dnia 19. września 1871.

Stenograficzne sprawozdania z trzeciey sesyi trzeciego peryodu Sejmu Krajowego Królestwa Galicyi i Lodomeryi wraz z Wielkiem Księstwem Krakowskiem w roku 1872.

Stenograficzne sprawozdania z czwartej sesyi trzeciego peryodu Sejmu Krajowego Królestwa Galicyi i Lodomeryi wraz z Wielkiem Księstwem Krakowskiem w roku 1873–1874.

Stenograficzne sprawozdania z pierwszej sesyi czwartego peryodu Sejmu Krajowego Królestwa Galicyi i Lodomeryi wraz z W. Ks. Krakowskiem w roku 1877. Posiedzenie 1–15.

Stenograficzne sprawozdania z czwartej sesyi czwartego peryodu Sejmu Krajowego Królestwa Galicyi i Lodomeryi wraz z Wielkiem Księstwem Krakowskiem w roku 1881. Posiedzenie 1–29.

Stenograficzne sprawozdania z drugiej sesyi piątego peryodu Sejmu Krajowego Królestwa Galicyi i Lodomeryi wraz z Wielkiem Księstwem Krakowskiem z roku 1884.

Stenograficzne sprawozdania z trzeciej sesyi piątego peryodu Sejmu Krajowego Królestwa Galicyi i Lodomeryi wraz z Wielkiem Księstwem Krakowskiem z roku 1885/6.

Stenograficzne sprawozdania z czwartej sesyi piątego peryodu Sejmu Krajowego Królestwa Galicyi i Lodomeryi wraz z Wielkiem Księstwem Krakowskiem z roku 1886/7 od 9. Grudnia 1886 do włącznie 25. stycznia 1887.

Stenograficzne sprawozdania z drugiej sesyi szóstego peryodu Sejmu Krajowego Królestwa Galicyi i Lodomeryi z Wielkiem Księstwem Krakowskiem z roku 1890. Posiedzenie 1–29.

Proclamations, brochures, writings and discourses:

Abramowski, Edward. "Ludność Polski." In Edward Abramowski. *Pisma publicystyczne w sprawach robotniczych i chłopskich.* Ed. Konstanty Krzeczkowski: 279–87. Warsaw.

Abramowski, Edward. "Pomniejszyciele ojczyzny." In Edward Abramowski. *Pisma publicystyczne w sprawach robotniczych i chłopskich.* Ed. Konstanty Krzeczkowski: 268–78. Warsaw, 1938.

Adama Mickiewicza wspomnienia i myśli z rozmów i przemówień. Collected and ed. Stanisław Pigoń. Warsaw, 1958.

Adress mieszkańców Galicyi. [Lviv, 1848].

Adres Rusinów. [Lviv, 1848].

Chotkowski, Władysław. *Żywot śś. Cyryla i Metodego Apostołów Słowiańskich napisany w tysiącletnią rocznicę chwalebnej śmierci św. Metodego z polecenia krakowskiego Komitetu Pielgrzymki przez ks. Chotkowskiego.* Cracow, 1885.

Cięglewicz, Kasper. *Die roth-reukischen Angelegenheiten im Jahre 1848.* Vienna, 1848.

[Cięglewicz, Kasper] Baltazar Szczucki. *Do moich bratej ludu Hałyckaho.* [Lviv] Buchach, 1848.

[Cięglewicz, Kasper]. "Instrukcya dla nauczycieli ludu ruskiego, [1837–1838]." In *Społeczeństwo polskie i próby wznowienia walki zbrojnej w 1833 roku.* Eds. Władimir Djakow, Stefan Kieniewicz, Wiktoria Śliwowska and Feodosij Steblij: 673–78. Wrocław–Warsaw–Cracow–Gdańsk–Łódź, 1984.

[Cięglewicz, Kasper] Baltazar Szczucki. *Rusin i Mazur. Dyalog przez Bałtazara Szczuckiego.* Lviv, 1848.

Cięglewicz, Kasper. *Rzecz czerwono-ruska 1848 roku.* Lviv, 1848.

[Cięglewicz, Kasper and Ignacy Kulczyński]. "Odezwa do ludu ruskiego, [1835]." In *Społeczeństwo polskie i próby wznowienia walki zbrojnej w 1833 roku.* Eds. Władimir Djakow, Stefan Kieniewicz, Wiktoria Śliwowska and Feodosij Steblij: 659–63. Wrocław–Warsaw–Cracow–Gdańsk–Łódź, 1984.

Czajkowski, Michał. "Kilka słów o Rusinach w roku 1831. Zapomniany artykuł Michała Czajkowskiego." Ed. Józef Weniger. *Ruch Literacki* 5, no. 10 (Dec. 1930): 314–17.

[Czartoryski, Adam]. *Mowy Xięcia Adama Czartoryskiego od roku 1838–1847.* Paris, 1847.

Czerkawski, Euzebiusz. "Łacińskie czcionki w języku ruskim." *Dodatek Tygodniowy przy Gazecie Lwowskiej* no. 24 (18 Jun. 1859): 99–102; no. 26 (2 Jul. 1859): 109–12.

Czerkawski, Euzebiusz. *Rozprawy i wnioski komisyi powołanej w roku 1879 przez galicyjską Radę Szkolną Krajową do zbadania sprawy gimnazyów.* Lviv, 1882.

Czerkawski, Euzebiusz. *Uwagi o nauce języka niemieckiego w gimnazyach i szkołach realnych z językiem wykładowym polskim i ruskim.* [Lviv, 1880].

[Czerwiński, Jan]. *O Rusinach i dla Rusinów.* Cracow, 1891.

[Daniluk Leon] Ukrainiec. *"Wiz i perewiz" czyli Ukraina galicyjska w prawdziwem oświetleniu.* Lviv, 1904.

Dąbczański, Antoni. *Wyjaśnienie sprawy ruskiej.* Lviv, 1848.

Dmowski, Roman. „Półpolacy," *Przegląd Wszechpolski* no. 11 (Nov. 1902): 801-5.

"Do Braci Rusinów." In *Dokumenty Komitetu Centralnego Narodowego i Rządu Narodowego 1862–1864.* Prepared for print by Dawid Fajnhauz, Stefan Kieniewicz, Franciszka Ramotowska [et al.]. Wrocław, 1968: 44–45.

Do bratej Rusyniw. [Lviv], 1848.

Dwa wyroki śmierci w c.k. sądzie karzącym lwowskim wydane przeciw Teofilowi Wiśniowskiemu i Józefowi Kapuścińskiemu. Paris, 1847.

Fedko znad Pełtwy. Rusin do Polaków. [Lviv, 1848].

Golichowski, Norbert. *Pamiątka uroczystości 400-letniej rocznicy śmierci Błogosł. Jana z Dukli zakonu OO. Bernardynów, odbytej we Lwowie i w innych klasztornych kościołach r. 1884.* Lviv, 1886.

Gorzkowski, Marian. *Przegląd kwestyj spornych o Rusi.* Cracow, 1875.

Gregorowicz, Kazimierz. *Z jakich powodów zmieniony został herb państwa polskiego. Odczyt miany podczas obchodu 23-letniej rocznicy horodelskiego zjazdu dnia 10 października 1884 r. w Paryżu.* Paris, 1884.

Heltman, Wiktor. *Demokracya Polska na emigracyi. Wyjątki z pism.* Lepnitz, 1866.

[Horoszkiewicz, Julian]. "Łysty do pryjateliw myru, 1837." In *Społeczeństwo polskie i próby wznowienia walki zbrojnej w 1833 roku*. Eds. Władimir Djakow, Stefan Kieniewicz, Wiktoria Śliwowska and Feodosij Steblij: 663–73. Wrocław–Warsaw–Cracow–Gdańsk–Łódź, 1984.

Horoszkiewicz, Julian. *Mowa Juliana Horoszkiewicza na pierwszem publicznem posiedzeniu zboru ruskiego we Lwowie dnia 15go Czerwca 1848*. [Lviv], 1848.

[Horoszkiewicz, Julian]. Gente Ruthenus natione Polonus. *Podstawa do zgody w narodzie*. Lviv, 1871.

Horoszkiewicz, Julian. *Rada familijna*. Paris, 1861.

Jireček, Joseph. *Über den Vorschlag das Ruthenische mit lateinischen Schriftzeichen zu schreiben. Im Auftrage des k. k. Ministeriums für Cultus und Unterrich*. Vienna, 1859.

[Kalicki, Bernard]. *Kwestya ruska*. Lviv, 1871.

Kalinka, [Waleryan]. *Internat ruski XX. Zmartwychwstańców we Lwowie*. Lviv, 1881.

Kalinka, Waleryan. "Konspiracya dzieci we Lwowie." In Waleryan Kalinka. *Pisma pomniejsze*. Part 2: 193–202. Dzieła ks. Waleryana Kalinki. Vol. 4. Cracow, 1894.

Kalinka, [Walerian]. *Schyzma i unia. Dwie konferencje powiedziane w kościele P. Maryi w Krakowie, 16 i 17 marca 1883 roku*. Lviv, 1883.

Kalinka, [Walerian]. *Stosunek Polaków i Rusinów do internatu ruskiego XX. Zmartwychwstańców we Lwowie (Sprawozdanie odczytane na Walnem Zgromadzeniu Stowarzyszenia Opieki nad tymże internatem, w marcu 1884)*. Lviv, 1884.

Kołłątaj, Hugo. *Listy Anonima i Prawo polityczne narodu polskiego*. Vol. 2. Eds. Bogusław Leśniodorski and Helena Wereszycka. Warsaw, 1954.

Kołłątaj, Hugo. *Uwagi nad teraznieyszem położeniem tey części ziemi polskiej, którą od pokoiu tylzyckiego zaczęto zwać Xsięstwem Warszawskim*. Leipzig, 1810.

[Koźmian, Stanisław, Józef Szujski and Stanisław Tarnowski]. *Teka Stańczyka. Osobne odbicie z 'Przeglądu Polskiego'*. Cracow, 1870.

Krasiński, Zygmunt. "O stanowisku Polski z Bożych i ludzkich względów." In Zygmunt Krasiński. *Pisma filozoficzne i polityczne*. Ed. and comments Paweł Hertz. Warsaw, 1999.

Kruszyński, Józef. *Odpowiedź na protest niby kleru ruskiego Dekanatu Kulikowskiego, rzeczywiście zaś podpisany przez Alexandra Kmicikiewicza, ogłoszony w Nrze 73 tak zwanego Dziennika Narodowego*. [1848].

Lelewel, Joachim. "Manifest Polaków znajdujących się w Belgii." In Joachim Lelewel. *Polska. Dzieje i rzeczy jej rozpatrywane*. Vol. 20: 221–29. Poznań, 1864.

Lelewel, Joachim. "Przewielebni i wielebni, nam w Bogu mili prawowiernej Cerkwi wschodniej Kapłani!." In Joachim Lelewel. *Polska. Dzieje i rzeczy i jej rozpatrywane*. Vol. 20: 482–86. Poznań, 1864.

[Leontowicz, Teodor] L. *Odpowiedź na artykuł o nieistnieniu Rusinów umieszczony w Numerze 2gim Dziennika Narodowego*. [1848].

[Łokietek, Józef] Jił. *Sprawa ruska. Wspomnienia, spostrzeżenia, uwagi, wnioski. Uwagi na czasie.* Vol. 1. Cracow, 1891.

Łozyńskyj, Josyf. *O zmianie narodowości pod względem na narodowość ruską.* 1848.

Merunowicz, Teofil. *Do wyborców kuryi IV okręgu wyborczego Lwów–Gródek– Jaworów słów parę od byłego ich posła do Rady państwa.* Lviv, 1900.

Merunowicz, Teofil. *Katechizm obywatelski dla Polaków i Rusinów w Galicyi i w Krakowskiem.* Lviv, 1884.

Merunowicz, Teofil. *Nad czem nasi posłowie w Sejmie radzili? (1886/7).* Lviv, 1887.

Merunowicz, Teofil. *O czem radzono w Sejmie krajowym w sesyi roku 1885 i 1886.* Lviv, 1886.

Merunowicz, Teofil. *O czem radzono w Sejmie w roku 1884.* Lviv, 1884.

Merunowicz, Teofil. *O wyborze posłów do wiedeńskiej Rady Państwa.* Lviv, 1885.

Merunowicz, Teofil. *Pamiatka 300-litnoj ricznyci unii Lublińskoj 1869 roku.* [Lviv, 1869].

Merunowicz, Teofil. *Pamiątka 300-letniej rocznicy unii Lubelskiej 1869 roku.* Lviv, 1869.

Merunowicz, Teofil. *Pismo do gmin wiejskich powiatu Lwowskiego.* Lviv, 1882.

Merunowicz, Teofil. *Sprawa ruska i kongres pokojowy. Referat, opracowany dla polskiego biura prac kongresowych.* Lviv, 1919.

Merunowicz, Teofil. *Stańczyki a konserwatyzm polski.* Lviv, 1879.

Merunowicz, Teofil. *Wewnętrzne sprawy Galicji. Spostrzeżenia i uwagi.* Lviv, 1876.

Merunowicz, Teofil. *Wolski czy Dobrzański? Głos wyborcy lwowskiego w sprawie kandydatur na krzesło poselskie w Radzie Państwa.* Lviv, 1877.

Merunowicz, Teofil. *Wyniki samorządu w Galicji.* Lviv, 1916.

Miłkowski, Zygmunt. *Sprawa ruska. Prowodyrowie Rusi spółcześni.* Poznań, 1879.

Miłkowski, Zygmunt. *Sprawa ruska w stosunku do sprawy polskiej.* Lviv, 1902.

Niemirowski, Jan. *Pojednanie braci duchownych i świeckich rzymsko- z grecko--katolickiemi w drodze zlania obódwóch obrządków w jedno ciało, czyli Wieniec Haliczanki Skromnej i Nadobnej ułożone i kobietom zacnym ofiarowane.* Lviv, 1848.

Orzechowski, Stanisław. *Wybór pism.* Wrocław, 1972.

Ostatni Słowa Teofyla Wyszniowskoho do Mury Hałyćkoho pysani dnia 28 Łypcia 1847 hoda po publykowanym dekreti. Trans. Jan Karol Cybulski. Lviv, [1848].

Podolinski, Bazyli. "Słowo przestrogi." In Ed. Feodosii Steblii. *Zapysky Naukovoho tovarystva imeni Shevchenka.* Vol. 228: *Pratsi Istorychno-filosofs'koï sektsiï:* 444–62, Lviv, 1994.

Pol, Wincenty. *Historyczny obszar Polski.* Cracow, 1869.

Popławski, Jan L. „Dwie cywilizacje," *Głos* 7 (1(13) Nov. 1886): 98–100.

Popławski, Jan L. „Środki obrony III," *Głos* 41 (3(15) Oct. 1887): 634.

"Protest" halytskykh rusynov" protyv" prazdnovan'ia rochnytsy 'Uniy Liublynskoi' na Rusy." *Slovo* no. 58 (23 Jun. [4 Aug.] 1869): 1–3.

Sawczyński, Zygmunt. *Języki wschodniej części kraju naszego.* Cracow, 1861.

Schmitt, Henryk. *Kilka słów bezstronnych w sprawie ruskiej.* Lviv, 1861.

Srokowski, Konstanty. "Polska racya stanu w sprawie ruskiej." *Krytyka* 9 (1907). Part. 1: 320–27, 446–54; Part 2: 62–74.

Staszic, Stanisław. *Pisma filozoficzne i społeczne.* Ed. and introd. Bogdan Suchodolski. Vol. 1. Warsaw, 1954.

Szeptycki, Andrzej. *Pisma wybrane.* Comp. Maria H. Szeptycka and Marek Skórka. Cracow, 2000.

W.K. "Sprawa rusko-ukraińska." *Sioło* no. 3 (1867): 135–58.

Wiśniowski, Teofil. "Panslawizm czyli Wszechsłowiańszczyzna." *Pismo Towarzystwa Demokratycznego Polskiego* 3 [1843]: 180–208.

[Wysłouch, Bolesław]. "Szkice programowe. II. (Narodowość)." *Przegląd Społeczny* 1, no. 4 (Apr. 1886): 251–58.

[Wysłouch, Bolesław]. "Szkice programowe. IV. (Polska Etnograficzna. Nasze zadania narodowe)." *Przegląd Społeczny* 1, no. 6 (Jun. 1886): 395–403.

[Zakrzewski, Stanisław] Z. "Niemcy, Rosja i kwestia polska. Z powodu książki Dmowskiego pod tymże tytułem." *Ateneum Polskie* 4 (1908): 65–76.

Zoria Halytskaia iako al'bum" na hod" 1860. Lviv, 1860.

Source editions:

Co mnie dzisiaj, jutro tobie. Polskie wiersze nagrobne. Comp. Jacek Kolbuszewski. Wrocław, 1996.

"Grande Munus" Encyclical of Pope Leo XIII on SS. Cyril and Methoius. 30 Sep. 1880. Accessed 1 Sep. 2019. http://w2.vatican.va/content/leo-xiii/en/encyclicals/documents/hf_l-xiii_enc_30091880_grande-munus.html.

Galicja w powstaniu styczniowym. Eds. of vol. Stefan Kieniewicz and Ilia Miller. Wrocław–Warsaw–Cracow–Gdańsk, 1980.

Pamiątka dla rodzin polskich. Krótkie wiadomości biograficzne o straconych na rusztowaniach, rozstrzelanych, poległych na placu boju, oraz zmarłych w więzieniach, na tułactwie i na wygnaniu Syberyjskiem, 1861–1866 r. ze źródeł urzędowych, dzienników polskich, jak niemniej z ustnych podań osób wiarygodnych i towarzyszy broni. Part 2. Collected and ed. Zygmunt Kolumna [Aleksander Nowolecki], introd. Bogdan Bolesławita [Józef Ignacy Kraszewski]. Cracow, 1868.

Społeczeństwo polskie i próby wznowienia walki zbrojnej w 1833 roku. Eds. Władimir Djakow, Stefan Kieniewicz, Wiktoria Śliwowska and Feodosij Steblij. Wrocław–Warsaw–Cracow–Gdańsk–Łódź, 1984.

Wydawnictwo materyałów do historyi powstania 1863–1864. Vol. 1: *Księga pamiątkowa 25-letniej rocznicy powstania styczniowego* [Lviv, 1888]; Vol. 2: *Pamiętnik Pułkownika Strusia, moje notatki, Bentkowski, z pamiętnika dla moich wnuków Deskura, wspomnienia z roku 1863 S. Duchińskiej;* Vol. 3:

Dokumenta do historyi powstania 1863/64. I. Galicya. Collected and ed. [Jan Stella Sawicki] Pułkownik Struś. Lviv, 1890.

"Złota Hramota." In Stefan Kieniewicz. *Powstanie Styczniowe*: 755–56. Warsaw, 2009.

Memoirs, diaries, journals, correspondence:

Baranowski, Bolesław Adam. "Kołomyjska *Kreis-Hauptschule* i gimnazjum w Stanisławowie." In *Galicyjskie wspomnienia szkolne*: 233–52. Ed. Antoni Knot. Cracow, 1955.

[Baranowski, Ignacy]. *Pamiętniki Ignacego Baranowskiego (1840–1862)*. Ed. Adam Wrzosek. Poznań, 1923.

Batowski, Aleksander. *Diariusz wypadków 1848 roku*. Ed. and introd. and footnotes Marian Tyrowicz. Wrocław–Warsaw–Cracow–Gdańsk, 1974.

Bogdański, Henryk. *Pamiętnik 1832–1848*. Ed. Antoni Knot. Cracow, 1879.

Chłędowski, Kazimierz. "Karta szkolna z pamiętnika literata i ministra 1853–1861." In *Galicyjskie wspomnienia szkolne*: 253–75. Ed. Antoni Knot. Cracow, 1955.

Chłędowski, Kazimierz. *Pamiętniki*. Vol. 1: *Galicja (1843–1880)*. Ed. Antoni Knot. Cracow, 1957.

Cichocki, Władysław. *Sambor przed pół wiekiem. Ku upamiętnieniu 40-tej rocznicy matury zdawanej w samborskim gimnazjum w czerwcu 1884 roku*. Cracow, 1925.

Czajkowski, Michał. *Kozaczyzna w Turcyi. Dzieło w trzech częściach*. Paris, 1857.

[Czaplicki, Ferdynand M. Władysław] Autor "Powieści o Horożanie." *Pamiętnik więźnia stanu*. Lviv, 1862.

[Czaplicki, Ferdynand M. Władysław] F. M. Władysław Cz. *Powieść o Horożanie*. Lviv, 1862.

Czaplicki, Ferdynand M. Władysław, *Rzeź w Horożanie i pamiętnik więźnia stanu*. Cracow, 1872.

Daszyński, Ignacy. *Pamiętniki*. Cracow, 1925.

Dayczak, Wawrzyniec. "Gimnazjum w Brodach na przełomie XIX i XX wieku we wspomnieniach byłego ucznia." Introd. and ed. Maria Dayczak-Domanasiewicz. *Krakowskie Pismo Kresowe* 4: *Galicja jako pogranicze kultur* (2012): 13–65.

Dayczak-Domanasiewicz, Maria. "Z dni wielkich przemian. Wspomnienia architekta Wawrzyńca Dayczaka (1882–1968)." *Rocznik Biblioteki Naukowej PAU i PAN w Krakowie* 53 (2008): 399–442.

Dąbczańska-Budzynowska, Helena. "Pamiętnik." Ed. Józef Fijałek. *Rocznik Biblioteki Polskiej Akademii Nauk w Krakowie* 9 (1963): 307–60.

[Dąbczański, Antoni]. *Antoni Dąbczański i jego pamiętnik (z portretem)*. Lviv, 1912.

Doboszyński, Józef. "Pamiętnik." In *Pamiętniki urzędników galicyjskich*. Eds. Irena Homola and Bolesław Łopuszański. Cracow, 1978.

[Giller, Agaton] A.G. and [Poliński Józef] J.P. *Pamiątka uroczystości półwie-kowego jubileuszu Seweryna Goszczyńskiego we Lwowie dnia 7. marca 1875. roku.* Lviv, 1875.

Gorzkowski, Marian. *Jan Matejko. Epoka od r. 1861 do końca życia artysty.* Eds. Kazimierz Nowacki and Ignacy Trybowski. Cracow, 1993.

Gregorowicz, Kazimierz. *Zarys główniejszych wypadków w województwie lu-belskim w r. 1861.* Ed. Wiesław Śladkowski. Lublin, 1984.

Horoszkiewicz, Julian. *Notatki z życia.* Ed. Henryk Wereszycki. Wrocław–Cracow, 1957.

Jabłonowski, Ludwik. *Złote czasy i wywczasy. Pamiętnik szlachcica z pierwszej połowy XIX stulecia.* Introd. Stanisław Wasylewski. Poznań, 1928.

Jackowski, Michał. "Pamiętniki podpułkownika, byłego dowódcy bry-gady jazdy Michała Jackowskiego 1807–1809." In *Pamiętniki polskie.* Vol. 1: 271–384. Selection Ksawery Bronikowski. Przemyśl, 1883.

Józefczyk, Andrzej. *Wspomnienie ubiegłych lat (Przyczynek do historyi spisków w Galicyi).* Cracow, 1881.

Kozarynowa, Zofia. *Sto lat. Gawęda o kulturze środowiska.* Wrocław–War-saw–Cracow, 1992.

Lasocki, Wacław. *Wspomnienia z mojego życia.* Vol. 1: *W kraju.* Prepared for print by Michał Janik and Feliks Kopera. Cracow, 1933.

Limanowski, Bolesław. *Pamiętniki (1835–1870).* Introd. Adam Próchnik. Warsaw, 1957.

Limanowski, Bolesław. *Pamiętniki (1870–1907).* Ed. Janusz Durko. Warsaw, 1958.

Longchamps de Bérier, Bogusław. *Ochrzczony na szablach powstańczych... Wspomnienia (1884–1918).* Eds. Włodzimierz Suleja and Wojciech Wrze-siński. Wrocław–Warsaw–Cracow–Gdańsk–Łódź, 1983.

[Matejko, Jan]. *Listy Matejki do żony Teodory 1863–188.* Ed. and preface Ma-ciej Szukiewicz. Cracow, 1927.

Matkowski, Józef. "Zbiór niektórych szczegółów życia mego." Preface by Ryszard Grabowski. In *Pamiętniki z lat 1792–1849*: 95–176. Ed. Ryszard Grabowski. Wrocław, 1961.

Mochnacki, Klemens. *Pamiętnik spiskowca i nauczyciela 1811–1848.* Ed. Anto-ni Knot. Cracow, 1950.

Morgenbesser, Aleksander. *Wspomnienia z lwowskiego więzienia.* Ed. Rafał Leszczyński. Warsaw, 1993.

[Mułkowski, Stefan]. *Kufstein. Więzienie stanu i dola Polaków w nim osadzo-nych.* Poznań, 1848.

"Nieznane listy Juliana Macieja Goslara z 1848 r." [Ed.] Jan Kozik. *Przegląd Historyczny* 66 (1975): 609–20.

Pisma Tadeusza Kościuszki. Selection, comments, and introd. Henryk Moś-cicki. Warsaw, 1947.

Rawita-Gawroński, Franciszek. *Ludzie i czasy mego wieku. Wspomnienia, wy-padki, zapiski (1892–1914).* Comp. Eugeniusz Koko. Gdańsk, 2012.

Reitzenheim, Józef. "Galicya. Wyjątek z pamiętników Józefa Reitzenheima." In *Pamiętniki polskie*. Vol. 2: 179–217. Selection Ksawery Bronikowski. Przemyśl, 1884.

Sapieha, Leon. *Wspomnienia (z lat od 1803 do 1863 r.)*. Introd. Stanisław Tarnowski. Ed., introd., and fragments of a correspondence Bronisław Pawłowski. Lviv–Warsaw–Poznań, [1914].

Sawczyński, Zygmunt. "Galicyjska szkoła elementarna przed 1848 r." In *Galicyjskie wspomnienia szkolne*: 153–57. Ed. Antoni Knot. Cracow, 1955.

Serafińska, Stanisława. *Matejko. Wspomnienia rodzinne*. Cracow, 1955.

Słotwiński, Adam. *Wspomnienia z niedawnej przeszłości*. Part 1: *1860–1871*. Cracow, 1892.

Smolka, Franciszek. *Dziennik Franciszka Smolki 1848–1849 w listach do żony*. Ed. and introd. Stanisław Smolka. Warsaw–Lublin–Łódź–Cracow, 1913.

[Stella-Sawicki, Jan] Pułkownik Struś. *Szkice z powstania 1863 roku*. Cracow, 1889.

[Stella-Sawicki, Jan] Pułkownik Struś. *Moje wspomnienia (1831–1910). (Rosja, Polska, Francja)*. Ed., introd., and footnotes Eugeniusz Barwiński. Lviv, [1921].

Swieżawski, Stefan. *Wielki przełom 1907–1945*. Ed. Mirosław Daniluk. Preface by Tadeusz Fedorowicz. Lublin, 1989.

Szeptycka, Zofia. *Młodość i powołanie ojca Romana Andrzeja Szeptyckiego zakonu św. Bazylego Wielkiego opowiedziane przez Matkę jego 1865–1892*. Ed. Bogdan Zakrzewski. Wrocław, 1993.

Szeptycka, Zofia. *Wspomnienia z lat ubiegłych*. Introd. Bogdan Zakrzewski. Wrocław–Warsaw–Cracow, 1967.

Tarnowski, Stanisław. "Dwa lata na ławie szkolnej z Józefem Szujskim." In *Galicyjskie wspomnienia szkolne*: 195–232. Ed. Antoni Knot. Cracow, 1955.

Tarnowski, Stanisław. *Matejko*. Cracow, 1896.

Tyrowicz, Marian. *Wspomnienia o życiu kulturalnym i obyczajowym Lwowa 1918–1939*. Preface by Julian Maślanka. Wrocław–Warsaw–Cracow–Gdańsk–Łódź, 1991.

W promieniu Lwowa, Żukowa i Medyki. Listy Mieczysława Romanowskiego 1853–1863. Eds. Bolesław Gawin and Zbigniew Sudolski. Warsaw, 1972.

Wolska, Maryla. "Quodlibet." In Maryla Wolska and Beata Obertyńska. *Wspomnienia*. Warsaw, 1974.

Zawadzki, Władysław. *Literatura w Galicji (1772–1848). Ustęp z pamiętników*. Lviv, 1878.

Ziemiałkowski, Florian. *Pamiętniki*. Part 1–2. Cracow, 1904.

Zubryts'kyi, Mykhailo. „Avtobiohrafia." In Mykhailo Zubryts'kyi. *Zibrani tvory i materialy u tr'okh tomakh*. Eds. Frank E. Sysyn et al. Vol. 2: *Materialy do biohrafii*: 53–101. Ed. Vasyl Sokil. Lviv, 2016.

[Zyblikiewicz, Mikołaj]. "Autobiografia Mikołaja Zyblikiewicza." *Czas* no. 116 (22 May 1887): 1.

Literature:

Prose and poems:

Album lwowskie. Ed. Henryk Nowakowski. Lviv, 1862.

A.Ł. *Piśń radosty.* [Lviv, 1848].

Bartus, Marys. "Modlitwa do Bł. Jana z Dukli." In Norbert Golichowski. *Pamiątka Pamiątka uroczystości 400-letniej rocznicy śmierci Błogosł. Jana z Dukli zakonu OO. Bernardynów, odbytej we Lwowie i w innych klasztornych kościołach r. 1884*: 35–36. Lviv, 1886.

[Boczkowski, Juwenal]. *Powiastka.* Lviv, 1848.

Czajkowski, Michał. "Trech-tymirow." In *Pisma Michała Czajkowskiego.* Vol. 7: *Koszowata i Ukrainki*: 215–33. Leipzig, 1865.

Czaykowski, Michał. *Wernyhora. Wieszcz ukraiński. Powieść historyczna z roku 1768.* Vol. 1–2. Paris, 1838.

Do selskoho ludu. [Lviv, 1848].

Duchińska, Seweryna. *Pieśń na cześć Jana Sobieskiego.* Lviv, 1883.

Dydacki, Franciszek. *[Lew, Orzeł, Anioł].* [Lviv, 1848].

Głoskowski, M. *Do bratej Rusyniw.* [Lviv, 1848].

Goszczyński, Seweryn. *Zamek kaniowski. Powieść.* Warsaw, 1828.

Groźba orlika białego świętojurskim maram. Przemyśl, [1848].

Hushalevych, Ivan. *Vospomynan'e posviashchenno Ioannu III Sob'eskomu koroliu pol'skomu, osvoboditeliu Vĕdnia ot' Turkov' dlia 12 verenia 1663 v den' dvokhsotlĕtneho iubileiu prasdnovannoho 11 i 12 veresnia 1883 vo Lvove.* [Lviv, 1883].

Jakubowski, Julian. *Zgoda. Poemat historyczny. Ruskiej braci poświęca Julian Jakubowski.* Lviv, 1874.

[Konopnicka, Maria] Marja K. "W czterechsetną rocznicę błogosławionego Jana z Dukli Patrona Polski, Rusi i Litwy." In Norbert Golichowski. *Pamiątka 400-letniej rocznicy śmierci Błogosł. Jana z Dukli zakonu OO. Bernardynów, odbytej we Lwowie i w innych klasztornych kościołach r. 1884*: 45–47. Lviv, 1886.

Kostecki, Platon. *22 stycznia.* Lviv, 1882.

Kostecki, Platon. *Braci naszej od Zachodu na powitanie.* Lviv, 1871.

Kostecki, Platon. "Jubileusz Bł. Jana z Dukli." In Norbert Golichowski. *Pamiątka uroczystości 400-letniej rocznicy śmierci Błogosł. Jana z Dukli zakonu OO. Bernardynów, odbytej we Lwowie i w innych klasztornych kościołach r. 1884*: 52–54. Lviv, 1886.

Kostecki, Platon. *Na uroczystość założenia kamienia węgielnego pod gmach Towarzystwa Gimnastycznego "Sokół" we Lwowie dnia 1. czerwca 1884.* Lviv, 1884.

Kostecki, Platon. *Poezyi.* Lviv, 1862.

Kostecki, Platon. *'Projekt pomnika'. Wiersz na cześć Jana Dobrzańskiego pracownika na polu obywatelskiem, literackiem i scenicznem, twórcy i głównego filaru 'Sokoła' i gmachu 'Sokoła'.* Lviv, 1886.

Kostecki, Platon. *Przy wręczaniu sztandaru od Polek na srebrne gody 'Sokoła' lwowskiego dnia 27 marca 1892 roku.* Lviv, 1892.

Kostecki, Platon. *Saturninowe gody*. Lviv, 1863.

Kostecki, Platon. *Trzeci Maja*. Lviv, 1871.

Kostecki, Platon. "Trzy nadzieje." *Gazeta Narodowa* no. 15 (19 Jan. 1888): 3.

Kostecki, Platon. *W dwusetną rocznicę odsieczy Wiednia*. Lviv, 1883.

Lam, Jan. *Wielki świat Capowic*. Cracow, 1869 (last ed. 2002).

[Laskownicki, Józef] A. Maryan. *Rusini*. Lviv, 1869 (2nd edit. 1878).

Lubowicz, Antim. *Jastrib i kury*. Lviv, 1848.

[Levytsky, Ostap] Ostap Kowbasiuk. Gente Ruthenus, natione także Ruthenus. *Uciekinierzy, poemat à la „Konrad Wallenrod."* Lviv, 1863.

Malczewski, Antoni. *Marja. Powieść ukraińska*. Warsaw, 1825.

Mickiewicz, Adam. *Księgi narodu polskiego i pielgrzymstwa polskiego*. Paris, 1832.

Mickiewicz, Adam. *The Books and the Pilgrimage of the Polish Nation*. London, 1833.

[Neumann, Anna] Kalina. "Ballada o cudownem uratowaniu Lwowa przez bł. Jana z Dukli." In Norbert Golichowski. *Pamiątka uroczystości 400-letniej rocznicy śmierci Błogosł. Jana z Dukli zakonu OO. Bernardynów, odbytej we Lwowie i w innych klasztornych kościołach r. 1884*: 48–50. Lviv, 1886.

Ostrowski, Krystyn. *Złote gody czyli unia lubelska. Hymn dziejowy (1569)*. Lviv, 1870.

Padurra, Tymko. *Ukrainky z nutoju*. Warsaw, 1844.

Pol, Wincenty. *Pieśni Janusza*. Vol. 1. Paris, 1833.

Rawita-Gawroński, Franciszek. "Śmierć Wernyhory. Baśń ukraińska." *Tygodnik Illustrowany* no. 25 (6[18] Jun. 1893): 489–510.

Shevchenko, Taras. *Zibrannia tvoriv*. Vol 1: *Poeziia 1837–1847*. Kyiv, 2003.

Siemieński, Lucjan. *Trzy wieszczby*. Paris, 1841.

Słowacki, Juliusz. *Beniowski. Poema. Pięć pierwszych pieśni*. Paris, 1841.

Słowacki, Juliusz. *Sen srebrny Salomei. Romans dramatyczny w pięciu aktach*. Paris, 1844.

Słowacki, Juliusz. *Wacław*. Lviv, 1879.

[Szaszkiewicz, Antoni]. *Pieśni Antoniego Szaszkiewicza wraz z jego życiorysem*. Published by Stefan Buszczyński. Cracow, 1890.

Wróblewski, Henryk Hugon. *Unja. Poemat*. Cracow, 1869.

"Wspomnienie poświęcone Janowi III Sobieskiemu królowi polskiemu, oswobodzicielowi Wiednia od Turków dnia 12. września 1683 r., w dzień dwusetletniego jubileuszu, święconego 11. i 12. września 1883 roku we Lwowie (Dosłowny przekład dumy ruskiej)." Trans. Jan Guszalewicz. *Gazeta Narodowa* no. 206 (1883): 1–2.

Wł. Jul. J. "Pieśń na 400-letnią rocznicę zgonu błog. Jana z Dukli (29. września 1484)." In Norbert Golichowski. *Pamiątka uroczystości 400-letniej rocznicy śmierci Błogosł. Jana z Dukli zakonu OO. Bernardynów, odbytej we Lwowie i w innych klasztornych kościołach r. 1884*: 36–43. Lviv, 1886.

Zacharyasiewicz, Jan. *Jarema. Studium z wewnętrznych dziejów Galicji*. Ed. Maria Janion. Warsaw, 1957.

Zachariasiewicz, Jan. *Św. Jur. Powieść w trzech częściach*. Lviv, 1862.

Zachariasiewicz, Jan. *Święty Jur. Jarema. Dwie powieści współczesne*. Vol. 1–2. Leipzig, 1873.

Zaleski, Józef Bohdan. *Poezija*. Paris, 1841.

Zaleski, Józef Bohdan. *Poezye*. Lviv, 1838.

Zoria Galitskaia iako al'bum" na god" 1860. Lviv, 1860.

Zyg. Kar. "Ku czci błog. Jana w 400-letnią rocznicę Jego błog. Zgonu." In Norbert Golichowski. *Pamiątka uroczystości 400-letniej rocznicy śmierci Błogosł. Jana z Dukli zakonu OO. Bernardynów, odbytej we Lwowie i w innych klasztornych kościołach r. 1884*: 55–57. Lviv, 1886.

Folkloristic, linguistic, ethnographic and geographic publications:

Horoszkiewicz, Julian. *Strój narodowy w Polsce*. Cracow, 1900.

Horoszkiewicz, Julian. *Świat popularnie opisany*. Lviv, 1853.

Horoszkiewicz, Julian. *Taniec polski według dawnego zwyczaju*. Lviv, 1897.

Łoziński, Józef. *Grammatyka języka ruskiego (mało-ruskiego)*. Przemyśl, 1846.

Łoziński, Józef. "O wprowadzeniu abecadła polskiego do piśmiennictwa ruskiego." *Rozmaitości* (Lviv) no. 29 (19 Jul. 1834): 228–30.

Łozynśkyj, J[osyf]. *Ruskoje wesile*. Peremyszeł, 1835.

Pauli, Żegota. *Pieśni ludu ruskiego w Galicyi*. Vol. 1–2. Lviv, 1839–40.

[Plater, Stanisław] S.H.P. *Jeografia wschodniey części Europy czyli opis krajów przez wielorakie narody słowiańskie zamieszkanych obejmujący Prusy, Xięztwo Poznańskie, Szląsk Pruski, Gallicyą, Rzeczpospolitę Krakowską, Królestwo Polskie i Litwę*. Wrocław, 1825.

Stupnicki, Hippolit. *Galicya pod względem geograficzno-topograficzno-historycznym*. Lviv, 1849.

Wagilewicz, Jan. *Grammatyka języka małoruskiego w Galicii*. Lviv, 1845.

Wagilewicz, Jan Dalibor. *Pisarze polscy Rusini wraz z dodatkiem Pisarze łacińscy Rusini*. Preparation for printing and introd. Rostysław Radyszewśkyj. Przemyśl, 1996.

[Węgliński, Leon Euzebiusz] L. Kost'. Prawdolubec z Jezupola. *Hôrkij śmich. Skazki i obrazki z żytia w Hałyczyni*. Cracow, 1885.

Węgliński, Leon Euzebiusz. *Nowyi poezyi małoruski t. j. piśny, dumy, dumki, chory, tańci, ballady etc. w czystom jazyci Czerwono-Rusyniw wedla żytia, zwyczaiw ich i obyczaiw narodnych*. Vol. 1–3. Lviv–Przemyśl, 1858.

[Węgliński, Leon Euzebiusz]. *Zwuki ôd našych seł i nyv. Pińja Lirnyka Nad--Nistrańskoho*. Vol. 1–2. Cracow, 1885.

[Zaleski, Wacław]. *Pieśni polskie i ruskie ludu galicyjskiego z muzyką instrumentowaną przez Karola Lipińskiego*. Coll. and publ. by Wacław z Oleska. Lviv, 1833.

Zawadzki, Władysław. *Obrazy Rusi Czerwonej*. Poznań, 1869.

Zawadzki, Władysław. "Obrazy Rusi Czerwonej." *Tygodnik Illustrowany* 9 (1864): 223–32.

Historiographical works:

Bandtkie, Jerzy Samuel. *Dzieje Królestwa Polskiego*. Vol. 1. Wrocław, 1820.

Bobrzyński, Michał. *Dzieje ojczyste ze szczególnem uwzględnieniem historyi Galicyi*. Cracow, 1879.

Gawroński, Francieszek Rawita. *Kozaczyzna Ukrainna w Rzeczypospolitej Polskiej do końca XVIII wieku. Zarys polityczno-historyczny*. Warsaw–Cracow–Lublin–Łódź–Poznań–Vilinus–Zakopane, 1922.

Gorzkowski, Marian. *O rusińskiej i rosyjskiej szlachcie*. Cracow, 1876.

Hrushevs'kii, Mykhailo. *Istoriia Ukraïny-Rusy*. Vol. 1–9. Lviv, 1898–1928.

Lelewel, Joachim. *Dzieje Litwy i Rusi aż do unji z Polską w Lublinie 1569 zawartej*. Poznań, 1844.

Lelewel, Joachim. *Dzieje Polski potocznym sposobem*. Warsaw, 1829.

Lewicki, Anatol. *Nieco o unii Litwy z Koroną*. Cracow, 1893.

Lewicki, Anatol. *Obrazki najdawniejszych dziejów Przemyśla*. Ed. Stanisław Stępień. Przemyśl, 1994.

Lewicki, Anatol. *Powstanie Świdrygiełły. Ustęp unii Litwy z Koroną*. Cracow, 1892.

Lewicki, Anatol. *Zarys historyi Polski i krajów ruskich z nią połączonych*. Cracow, 1884.

Lewicki, Anatol. *Zarys historyi Polski i krajów ruskich z nią połączonych. Podręcznik szkolny aprobowany przez wysoką C.K. Radę Szkolną Krajową. Wydanie skrócone*. Cracow, 1893.

Lewicki, Anatol and Friedberg, Jan. *Zarys historii Polski od zarania do roku 1922*. Warsaw–Komorów, 1999.

Naruszewicz, Adam. *Historya narodu polskiego od początku chrześcijaństwa. Panowanie Piastów*. Vol. 6. Warsaw, 1785.

Schmitt, Henryk. *Dzieje Narodu Polskiego od najdawniejszych do najnowszych czasów, krótko i zwięźle opowiedziane*. Vol. 1. Lviv, 1861.

Schmitt, Henryk. *Unja Litwy z Koroną dokonana na sejmie lubelskim 1568–1569. Szkic dziejowy*. Lviv, 1869.

Schmitt, Henryk. *Zdarzenia najważniejsze z przeszłości narodu polskiego zestawił w potocznym opowiadaniu*. Lviv, 1869.

Starczewski, Eugeniusz. *Sprawa polska*. Cracow, 1912.

Szajnocha, Karol. *Jadwiga i Jagiełło 1374–1413. Opowiadanie historyczne*. Vol. 4. Lviv, 1861.

Szajnocha, Karol. "Jak Ruś polszczała." In Karol Szajnocha. *Szkice historyczne*. Vol. 4: 173–90. Lviv, 1869.

Szujski, Józef. *Dzieje Polski podług ostatnich badań spisane*. Vol. 2: *Jagielloni*. Lviv, 1862.

Szujski, Józef. *Historyi polskiej treściwie opowiedzianej ksiąg dwanaście*. Warsaw, 1880.

Tarnowski, Stanisław. *O Rusi i Rusinach*. Cracow, 1891.

Waga, Teodor. *Historya Xiążąt i Królów Polskich krótko zebrana*. Vilnius, 1816.

Wagilewicz, Jan Dalibor. *Pisarze polscy Rusini wraz z dodatkiem Pisarze łacińscy Rusini*. Ed. Rostysław Radyszewśkyj. Przemyśl, 1996.

Zakrzewski, Stanisław. "Polacy i Rusini na Ziemi Czerwieńskiej w przeszłości." In Eugeniusz Romer, Stanisław Zakrzewski and Stanisław Pawłowski. *W obronie Galicyi Wschodniej*: 15–57. Lviv, 1919.

Zakrzewski, Stanisław. "Z powodu czwartego wydania 'Dziejów Polski w zarysie' Michała Bobrzyńskiego." In Stanisław Zakrzewski. *Zagadnienia historyczne*. Vol. 1: 237–41. Lviv, 1936.

Zakrzewski, Stanisław. "Zachód i Wschód w historji Polski." In Stanisław Zakrzewski. *Zagadnienia historyczne*. Vol. 2: 1–50. Lviv, 1936.

Zakrzewski, Stanisław. "Ze studiów nad dziejami unji polsko-litewskiej." In Stanisław Zakrzewski. *Zagadnienia historyczne*. Vol. 2: 177–229. [Lviv, 1936].

The press and periodicals:
Ateneum Polskie, 1908.
Czas, 1861, 1869, 1882–1883, 1887, 1892, 1899, 1908.
Czytelnia dla Młodzieży, 1861.
Djabeł, 1883.
Dnewnyk Ruskij / Dnevnyk' Ruskii, 1848.
Dodatek Tygodniowy przy Gazecie Lwowskiej, 1859.
Dziennik dla Wszystkich, 1879–1880.
Dziennik Literacki, 1861.
Dziennik Mód Paryskich, 1848.
Dziennik Narodowy, 1848.
Dziennik Polski (Lviv) 1876, 1883, 1888.
Dzwonek, 1850–1851.
Gazeta Lwowska, 1814, 1859, 1883, 1904, 1907.
Gazeta Narodowa, 1848, 1862–1863, 1867, 1874, 1882–1886, 1888, 1907, 1913.
Głos, 1861.
Głos Narodu, 1913.
Goniec Wileński, 1908.
Greko-Katolik, 1934–1935.
Greko-Polak, 1936.
Halychanyn, 1894.
Kłosy, 1881.
Kraj i Emigracja, 1839.
Krytyka, 1907.
Lechita, 1908.
Muzeum, 1896–1898.
Novyi prolom, 1884.
Nowa Reforma, 1883, 1913.
Pismo Towarzystwa Demokratycznego Polskiego, 1843.
Polak Greko-Katolik, 1838–1839.
Postęp, 1848.
Przegląd Lwowski, 1880.
Przegląd Polski, 1866, 1869, 1883–1884.

Przegląd Powszechny (later: *Dziennik Polski*) (Lviv), 1860–1861.
Przegląd Społeczny, 1886.
Przewodnik Gimnastyczny 'Sokół', 1908.
Przewodnik Naukowy i Literacki, 1875.
Rada Narodowa, 1848.
Rozmaitości (Lviv) 1834.
Ruskii sion, 1884.
Sioło, 1866–1867.
Slovo, 1869, 1884.
Słowo Polskie, 1908.
Sylwian, 1892.
Szkoła, 1893.
Światowid, 1935.
Tygodnik Illustrowany, 1864, 1883, 1885–1888, 1907.
Wędrowiec, 1896.
Zoria Halytska, 1854–1855.

Studies:

Adadurov, Vadim. "Halyts'ki rusyny u kontseptsiiakh pol's'koï polityky Frantsiï ta Avstriï 1805–1812 rokiv (do postanovky pytannia)." *Ukraïna v mynulomu* (1996): 38–60.

Adamczyk, Mieczysław. *Edukacja a awans społeczny plebejuszy 1764–1848.* Wrocław, 1990.

Adamczyk, Mieczysław. "Społeczno-gospodarcze położenie ludności unickiej diecezji przemyskiej w latach 1772–1848." *Przemyskie Zapiski Historyczne* 4–5 (1986–1987): 89–122.

Althoen, David. "Natione Polonus and the Naród szlachecki: Two myths of national identity and noble solidarity." *Zeitschrift für Ostmitteleuropa-Forschung* 52 (2003): 475–508.

Arkusha, Olena. "Krakivs'kyi konservatyzm ta problema ukraïns'ko-pol's'kykh vzaiemyn u Halychyni na pochatku XX stolittia." *Zapysky naukovoho tovarystva imeni Shevchenka* 256: *Iuvileinyi zbirnyk na poshanu Iaroslava Isaievycha* (2008): 282–316.

Arkusza, Ołena. "Polacy i Ukraińcy w Galicji wobec 'dużych i małych ojczyzn.' Ewolucja pojęcia ojczyzny jako wynik modernizacji świadomości narodowej na przełomie XIX i XX stulecia." In *Duża i mała ojczyzna w świadomości historycznej, źródłach i edukacji.* Eds. Bogumiła Burda and Małgorzata Szymczak: 43–58. Zielona Góra, 2010.

Arkusza, Ołena. "Ukraińskie przedstawicielstwo w sejmie galicyjskim." In *Ukraińskie tradycje parlamentarne. XIX–XXI wiek.* Ed. Jarosław Moklak: 13–57. Cracow, 2006.

Arkusza, Ołena and Marian Mudryj. "XIX-wieczna arystokracja polska w Galicji Wschodniej wobec ruskich (ukraińskich) aspiracji narodowych." *Krakowskie Pismo Kresowe* no. 4: *Galicja jako pogranicze kultur* (2012): 145–71.

Artymiak, Antoni. *Lwowianin Henryk Schmitt (spiskowiec, powstaniec, bibliotekarz, publicysta, historyk, organizator szkolnictwa)*. Jędrzejów, 1939.

AV. "Lwów oczami Ukraińców." *Kultura* (Paris) no. 9 (1956): 137–143.

Babiński, Grzegorz. *Pogranicze polsko-ukraińskie. Etniczność – tożsamość narodowa – zróżnicowanie religijne*. Cracow, 1997.

Baczkowski, Michał. "Galicjanie w armii austriackiej wobec wydarzeń lat 1848–1849." In *Galicja w 1848 roku. Demografia, działalność polityczna i społeczna, gospodarka i kultura*. Eds. Andrzej Bonusiak and Marian Stolarczyk: 89–97. Rzeszów, 1999.

Baczkowski, Michał. *W służbie Habsburgów. Polscy ochotnicy w austriackich siłach zbrojnych w latach 1772–1815*. Cracow, 1998.

Banach, Andrzej Kazimierz. *Młodzież chłopska na Uniwersytecie Jagiellońskim w latach 1860/61–1917/18*. Cracow, 1997.

Bańkowska, Anna. "Opowieść o Janie IV." *Rocznik Lwowski* (1995–1996): 139–149.

Barowicz, Antoni. *Marcin „Lelewel" Borelowski. Rękodzielnik – pułkownik*. Rzeszów, 1913.

Bartel, Wojciech M. "Michał Bobrzyński (1849–1935)." In *Spór o historyczną szkołę krakowską. W stulecie Katedry Historii Polski UJ 1869–1969*. Eds. Celina Bobińska and Jerzy Wyrozumski: 145–89. Cracow, 1972.

Bauman, Zygmunt, "Soil, Blood And Identity." *The Sociological Review* 40, no. 4 (1992): 675–701.

Bardach, Juliusz. "Od narodu politycznego do narodu etnicznego w Europie Środkowo-Wschodniej." *Kultura i Społeczeństwo* 37, no. 4 (1993): 3–16.

Bednarski, Adam. "Borysiekiewicz Michał." In *Polski słownik biograficzny*. Vol. 2: 357. Cracow, 1936.

Beiersdorf, Otton. "Galicja wobec powstania styczniowego." In *Powstanie styczniowe 1863–1864. Wrzenie, bój, Europa, wizje*. Ed. Sławomir Kalembka: 389–425. Warsaw, 1990.

Binder, Harald. "Ukraińskie przedstawicielstwo w austriackiej Izbie Posłów, 1879–1918." In *Ukraińskie tradycje parlamentarne. XIX–XXI wiek*. Ed. Jarosław Moklak: 127–62. Cracow, 2006.

Bobiatyński, Konrad. "Polska historiografia wobec unii hadziackiej." In *350-lecie unii hadziackiej (1658–2008)*. Eds. Teresa Chynczewska-Hennel, Piotr Kroll and Mirosław Nagielski: 661–83. Warsaw, 2008.

Bończa-Tomaszewski, Nikodem. *Źródła narodowości. Powstanie i rozwój polskiej świadomości narodowej w II połowie XIX i na początku XX wieku*. Wrocław, 2006.

Borys, Włodzimierz. "Do historii ruchu społeczno-politycznego studentów Uniwersytetu i młodzieży rzemieślniczej Lwowa w latach 1832–46." *Przegląd Historyczny* 54, no. 3 (1963): 418–31.

Borys, Włodzimierz. "Galicyjski okres w życiu Ignacego Kulczyńskiego (w świetle archiwaliów lwowskich)." *Przegląd Historyczny* 68, no. 1 (1977): 127–42.

Borys, Włodzimierz. "W kręgu rewolucyjnym Szymona Konarskiego, Piotra Kotkiewicza i Ignacego Kulczyńskiego." *Przegląd Historyczny* 66, no. 3 (1975): 461–72.

Borys, Włodzimierz. "Wyprawa J. Zaliwskiego i polskie organizacje spiskowe w Galicji w latach 1832–1835." In *Społeczeństwo polskie i próby wznowienia walki zbrojnej w 1833 roku*. Eds. Władimir Djakow, Stanisław Kieniewicz, Wiktoria Śliwowska and Feodosij Steblij: 83–105. Wrocław–Warsaw–Cracow–Gdańsk–Łódź, 1984.

Borys, Włodzimierz. "Z dziejów walk o wyzwolenie narodowe i społeczne w Galicji w pierwszej połowie XIX w." *Przemyskie Zapiski Historyczne* 4–5 (1987): 223–30.

Brock, Peter. "Ivan Vahylevych (1811–1866) and the Ukrainian National Identity." *Canadian Slavonic Papers* 14, no. 2 (1972): 153–90.

Brock, Peter. *Nationalism and Populism in Partitioned Poland: Selected Essays.* London, 1973.

Brock, Peter. "The Polish Identity." In *The Tradition of Polish Ideals: Essays In History and Literature*. Ed. Władysław Józef Stankiewicz: 23–51. London, 1981.

Brock, Peter. "Joseph Cowen and the Polish Exiles." *The Slavonic and East European Review* 32, no. 78 (1953): 52–69.

Brock, Peter. *Z dziejów wielkiej emigracji w Anglii.* Warsaw, 1958.

Broda, Józef. "Hołowkiewicz Emil." In *Polski słownik biograficzny*. Vol. 9: 599–600. Wrocław–Cracow–Warsaw, 1960-61.

Bruchnalski, Wilhelm. *Historya Rozmaitości. Pisma Dodatkowego do Gazety Lwowskiej 1817–1848 i 1854–1859.* Lviv, 1912.

Bryła, Stanisław. *Język ruski w szkolnictwie.* Lviv, 1913.

Budzyński, Zdzisław. *Kresy południowo-wschodnie w drugiej połowie XVIII wieku.* Vol. 3: *Studia z dziejów społecznych.* Przemyśl–Rzeszów, 2008.

Bujak, Franciszek. *Galicya.* Vol. 1: *Kraj, ludność, społeczeństwo, rolnictwo.* Lviv–Warsaw, 1908.

Bułhak, Henryk. "Sawczyński Adam Tymoteusz." In *Polski słownik biograficzny*. Vol. 35: 287–89. Warsaw–Cracow, 1994.

Buszczyński, Stefan. "Historyczne wspomnienie o Antonim Szaszkiewiczu. Przyczynek do dziejów naszej walki o wyzwolenie." In [Antoni Szaszkiewicz]. *Pieśni Antoniego Szaszkiewicza wraz z jego życiorysem*. Published by Stefan Buszczyński: 3–31. Cracow, 1890.

Buszko, Józef. "Historycy 'szkoły krakowskiej' w życiu politycznym Galicji." In *Spór o historyczną szkołę krakowską. W stulecie Katedry Historii Polski UJ 1869–1969*. Eds. Celina Bobińska and Jerzy Wyrozumski: 191–207. Cracow, 1972.

Buszko, Józef. *Polacy w parlamencie wiedeńskim 1848–1918.* Warsaw, 1996.

Buzek, Józef. *Rozsiedlenie ludności Galicyi według wyznania i języka.* Ed. Tadeusz Pilat. Lviv, 1909.

Charnets'kyi, Stepan. *Istoria ukraïnskoho teatru v Halychyni. Narysy, statti, materialy, svitlyny.* Lviv, 2014.

Chlebowczyk, Józef. *O prawie do bytu małych i młodych narodów. Kwestia narodowa i procesy narodotwórcze we wschodniej Europie Środkowej w dobie kapitalizmu (od schyłku XVIII do początków XX w.)*. Warsaw–Cracow, 1983.

Chlebowczyk, Józef. "Świadomość historyczna jako element procesów narodotwórczych we wschodniej Europie Środkowej." In *Polska, czeska i słowacka świadomość historyczna XIX wieku. Materiały sympozjum Polsko-Czechosłowackiej Komisji Historycznej 15–16 XI 1977*. Ed. Roman Heck: 9–24. Wrocław–Warsaw–Cracow–Gdańsk, 1979.

Chołodecki, Józef Białynia. *Do dziejów powstania styczniowego. Obrazki z przeszłości Galicyi*. Lviv, 1912.

Chołodecki, Józef Białynia. "Dzieje chorągwi Korpusu Kadetów we Lwowie." *Panteon Polski* no. 64 (1930): 2.

Chołodecki, Józef Białynia. *Lwów w czasie wojen Napoleona Wielkiego w latach 1809–1814*. Lviv, 1927.

Chornovol, Ihor. "Ieretyk. Ivan Vahylevych." *Lvivs'ka hazeta* no. 156 (2 Sep. 2005).

Chornovol, Ihor. "Ostannii gente Rutheni, natione Poloni. Platon Kostets'kyi." *Lvivs'ka hazeta* no. 119 (13 Jul. 2007).

Chwalba, Andrzej. *Historia Polski 1795–1918*. Cracow, 2005.

Chwalba, Andrzej. "Krajobrazy etniczne Galicji Wschodniej." In *Poprzez stulecia. Księga pamiątkowa ofiarowana Profesorowi Antoniemu Podrazie w 80. rocznicę Jego urodzin*: 173–82. Ed. Danuta Czerska. Cracow, 2000.

Chynczewska-Hennel, Teresa. "Gente Ruthenus—Natione Polonus." *Warszawskie Zeszyty Ukrainoznawcze 6–7: Spotkania polsko-ukraińskie. Studia Ucrainica*. Ed. Stefan Kozak (1998): 35–44.

Chynczewska-Hennel, Teresa. *Świadomość narodowa szlachty ukraińskiej i kozaczyzny od schyłku XVI do połowy XVII w.* Warsaw, 1985.

Chynczewska-Hennel, Teresa and Natalia Jakowenko. "Społeczeństwo, religia, kultura." In *Między sobą. Szkice historyczne polsko-ukraińskie*: 111–51. Eds. Teresa Chynczewska-Hennel and Natalia Jakowenko. Lublin, 2000.

Cichocki, Władysław. *Sambor przed pół wiekiem. Ku upamiętnieniu 40-ej rocznicy matury zdawanej w samborskiem gimnazjum w czerwcu 1884 roku*. Cracow, 1925.

Czołowski, Aleksander. "Dąbczański Antoni." In *Polski słownik biograficzny*. Vol. 4: 466–67. Cracow, 1938.

Czyż, Anna Sylwia and Bartłomiej Gutowski. *Cmentarz Miejski w Buczaczu*. Warsaw, 2009.

[Dąbrowski, Józef] J. Grabiec. *Rok 1863. W pięćdziesiątą rocznicę*. Poznań, 1913.

Demiańczuk, Jarosław. "Ukraińcy galicyjscy wobec powstania styczniowego." *Biuletyn Polsko-Ukraiński* 6, no. 3 (17 Jan. 1937): 29–32.

Deszczyńska, Martyna. "W sprawie świadomości historycznej polskich elit intelektualnych początku XIX w." In *Społeczeństwo w dobie przemian. Wiek XIX i XX. Księga jubileuszowa profesor Anny Żarnowskiej*: 419–24.

Eds. Maria Nietyksza, Andrzej Szwarc and Krystyna Sierakowska. War-saw, 2003.

Dmowski, Roman. „Półpolacy." *Przegląd Wszechopolski* no. 11 (Nov. 1902): 801–5.

Duchińska, Seweryna. *Bohdan Zaleski*. Poznań, 1892.

Duć-Fajfer, Helena. "Udział Łemków w życiu religijnym, umysłowym, kul-turalno-społecznym Galicji w 2. połowie XIX i na początku XX wieku." In *Poprzez stulecia. Księga pamiątkowa ofiarowana Profesorowi Antoniemu Podrazie w 80. rocznicę Jego urodzin*). Ed. Danuta Czerska: 199–212. Cra-cow, 2000.

Dudziński, Jarosław. "Działania Piotra Strzyżewskiego w Galicji Wschod-niej w czasie wojny polsko-austriackiej w 1809 roku." *Roczniki Humani-styczne. Historia* 55, no. 2 (2007): 143–73.

Dunin-Wąsowicz, Krzysztof. "Rewakowicz Henryk Karol." In *Polski słow-nik biograficzny*. Vol. 31: 169–72. Wrocław–Warsaw–Cracow–Gdańsk–Łódź, 1988–89.

Dunin-Wąsowicz, Krzysztof. "Próba analizy składu społeczno-zawodo-wego oddziału powstańczego z 1863 roku." *Kwartalnik Historyczny* 70, no. 4 (1963): 873–88.

Duszkiewicz, Wiesława. "Euzebiusz Czerkawski i jego poglądy na szkol-nictwo średnie." In *Biografie pedagogiczne. Szkice do portretu galicyjskiej pedagogii*. Eds. Czesław Majorek and Jerzy Potoczny: 25–40. Rzeszów, 1997.

Dutkowa, Renata. "Polityka szkolna w Galicji 1866–1890." In *Nauka i oświa-ta*. Eds. Andrzej Meissner and Jerzy Wyrozumski: 137–49. Rzeszów, 1995.

Dutkowa, Renata. *Polityka szkolna w Galicji. Między autonomią a centralizmem (1861–1875)*. Cracow, 1995.

Dzieduszycki, Maurycy. "Przeszłowieczny Dziennik Lwowski." *Przewod-nik Naukowy i Literacki* 3, no. 1 (1875): 33–51; no. 2 (1875): 130–144; no. 3 (1875): 238–245.

Eberhardt, Piotr. *Polska i jej granice. Z historii polskiej geografii politycznej*. Lu-blin, 2004.

Estreicher, Karol. "Czyrniański Emilian." In *Polski słownik biograficzny*. Vol. 4: 378–79. Cracow, 1938.

Filar, Tadeusz. "Miejsce społeczności ukraińskiej w XIX i XX-wiecznym Krakowie do 1918 roku." *Krakowskie Zeszyty Ukrainoznawcze* 1–2 (1992–93): 433–58.

Fiutowski, Teofil. *Szkolnictwo ludowe w Galicyi*. Lviv, 1913.

Forst de Battaglia, Otto. "Ze studjów genealogicznych nad epoką Jana III Sobieskiego." *Miesięcznik Heraldyczny* 12, no. 9 (1933): 132–41.

Franko, Ivan. "Stara Rus." In Ivan Franko. *Zibrannya tvoriv*. Vol. 37: *Litera-turno-krytychni pratsi (1906–1908)*. Ed. Ihor Dzeverin. Comment. Mykola Hryciuta: 79–110. Kyiv, 1982.

Fras, Zbigniew. *Demokraci w życiu politycznym Galicji w latach 1848–1873.* Wrocław, 1997.

Fras, Zbigniew. *Florian Ziemiałkowski (1817–1900). Biografia polityczna.* Wrocław–Warsaw–Cracow, 1991.

Fras, Zbigniew. *Galicja.* Wrocław, 2000.

Fras, Zbigniew. "Rola emigrantów w życiu politycznym Lwowa i Krakowa w 1848 roku." In *Galicja w 1848 roku. Demografia, działalność polityczna i społeczna, gospodarka i kultura.* Eds. Andrzej Bonusiak and Marian Stolarczyk: 27–47. Rzeszów, 1999.

Fras, Zbigniew. "Sawczak Damian." In *Polski słownik biograficzny.* Vol. 35: 284–85. Warsaw–Cracow, 1994.

Fras, Zbigniew. "Sawczyński Zygmunt." In *Polski słownik biograficzny.* Vol. 35: 290–94. Warsaw–Cracow, 1994.

Galos, Adam. "Obchody rocznicowe na prowincji zaboru austriackiego." In *Studia z dziejów prowincji galicyjskiej.* Ed. Adam Galos: 89–112. Wrocław, 1993.

Gancarz, Bogdan. *My, szlachta ukraińska. Zarys życia i działalności Wacława Lipińskiego 1882–1914.* Cracow, 2006.

Gąsowski, Tomasz. "Struktura narodowościowa ludności miejskiej w autonomicznej Galicji." *Prace Historyczne* 125. Ed. Krzysztof Baczkowski (1998): 89–108.

Gierowski, Józef A. "Józef Szujski jako historyk czasów nowożytnych." In *Spór o historyczną szkołę krakowską. W stulecie Katedry Historii Polski UJ 1869–1969.* Eds. Celina Bobińska and Jerzy Wyrozumski: 83–93. Cracow, 1972.

Giller, Agaton. *Bohdan Zaleski.* Poznań, 1882.

Głaz, Elżbieta. "Zygmunt Sawczyński – pedagog, polityk i działacz oświatowy." In *Biografie pedagogiczne. Szkice do portretu galicyjskiej pedagogii.* Eds. Czesław Majorek and Jerzy Potoczny: 41–58. Rzeszów, 1997.

Górski, Artur. *Podolacy. Obóz polityczny i jego liderzy.* Warsaw, 2013.

Grodziski, Stanisław. *Sejm Krajowy Galicyjski 1861–1914.* T. 1–2. Introd. Marian Małecki. Cracow, 2018.

Grodziski, Stanisław. *Wzdłuż Wisły, Dniestru i Zbrucza. Wędrówki po Galicji dyliżansem, koleją, samochodem.* Cracow, 2016.

Grott, Bogumił. "Nacjonalizm ukraiński w cerkwi greckokatolickiej i jego praktyka dyskryminacji Polaków i polskości w latach II Rzeczypospolitej." In *Różne oblicza nacjonalizmów. Polityka, religia, etos.* Ed. Bogumił Grott: 269–84. Cracow, 2010.

Gruchała, Irena. "Pasja bibliofilska Heleny Dąbczańskiej." In *Kraków – Lwów. Książki, czasopisma, biblioteki XIX i XX wieku.* Vol. 9. Eds. Halina Kosętka, Barbara Góra and Ewa Wójcik: 265–76. Cracow, 2009.

Gruchała, Janusz. *Rząd austriacki i polskie stronnictwa polityczne w Galicji wobec kwestii ukraińskiej (1890–1914).* Katowice, 1988.

Grünberg, Karol and Bolesław Sprengel. *Trudne sąsiedztwo. Stosunki polsko--ukraińskie w X–XX wieku.* Warsaw, 2005.

Grzędzielska, Maria. "Drogi Jana Zachariasiewicza." In *Z dziejów kultury i literatury ziemi przemyskiej. Zbiór szkiców, opracowań i utworów literackich*. Ed. Stefania Kostrzewska-Kratochwilowa: 107–24. Przemyśl, 1969.

Hampel, Józef. *Chłopów polskich drogi do demokracji. Studia i szkice*. Cracow, 2008.

Handelsman, Marceli. *Ukraińska polityka ks. Adama Czartoryskiego przed wojną krymską*. Warsaw, 1937.

Herbil's'kyi, Hryhorii. *Peredova suspil'na dumka v Halychyni (30-i – seredyna 40-kh rokiv XIX stolittia)*. Lviv, 1959.

Herbil's'kyi, Hryhorii. *Rozvytok prohresyvnykh idei v Halychyni u pershii polovyni XIX st. (do 1848 r.)*. Lviv, 1964.

Himka, John-Paul. "The Construction of Nationality in Galician Rus': Icarian Flights in almost All Directions." In *Intellectuals and the Articulation of the Nation*. Eds. Ronald Grigor Suny and Michael D. Kennedy: 109–64. Ann Arbor, 2001.

Himka, John-Paul. "The Greek Catholic Church and Nation-building in Galicia, 1772–1918." *Harvard Ukrainian Studies* 8, no. 3–4 (1984): 426–52.

Hlystiuk, Iaroslav. "Diial'nist' students'kykh tovarystv hreko-katolyts'koï dukhovnoï seminariï u L'vovi (1849–1914)." *Visnyk Lvivs'koho universytetu. Seriia Istorychna* special no.: *Lviv. Misto, suspil'stvo, kul'tura.* Vol. 6: *Lviv–Krakiv. Dialoh mist v istorychnii retrospektyvi*. Eds. Olena Arkusha and Marian Mudryi (2007): 246–94.

Hoff, Jadwiga. "Inteligencja galicyjska—niepokorna czy lojalna?." *Rocznik Przemyski* 46, no. 4: *Historia* (2010): 51–58.

Hoff, Jadwiga. *Mieszkańcy małych miast Galicji Wschodniej w okresie autonomicznym*. Rzeszów, 2005.

Hoff, Jadwiga. "Żydzi, Polacy i Rusini w małych miastach Galicji Wschodniej w drugiej połowie XIX w. Sąsiedzi, obcy, wrogowie?." In *Społeczeństwo w dobie przemian. Wiek XIX i XX. Księga jubileuszowa profesor Anny Żarnowskiej*. Eds. Maria Nietyksza, Andrzej Szwarc and Krystyna Sierakowska: 337–44. Warsaw, 2003.

Homola-Dzikowska, Irena. *Kraków za prezydentury Mikołaja Zyblikiewicza (1874–1881)*. Cracow, 1976.

Homola-Dzikowska, Irena. *Mikołaj Zyblikiewicz (1823–1887)*. Wrocław–Warsaw–Cracow, 1964.

Hroch, Mirosław. „National Self-Determination from a Historical Perspective." *Canadian Slavonic Papers* 37, no. 3–4 (1995): 283–99.

[Hrycak, Jarosław]. *Ukraina. Przewodnik krytyki politycznej. Z Jarosławem Hrycakiem rozmawia Iza Chruślińska*. Preface by Adam Michnik. Gdańsk–Warsaw, 2009.

Hryciuk, Grzegorz. *Przemiany narodowościowe i ludnościowe w Galicji Wschodniej i na Wołyniu w latach 1931–1948*. Toruń, 2005.

Hrytsak, Yaroslav. *Iwan Franko and His Community*. Trans. Marta Olynyk. Edmonton–Toronto, 2018.

Ianovs'kyi, Matsei. "Syroty Rechi Pospolytoï. Vid stanovoho suspil'stva do suchasnykh natsiï 1795–1918." In *Pol'shcha. Narys Istoriï*. Eds. Vlodzimiezh Mendzhets'ki and Iezhy Bratsysevich. Trans. Ivan Svarnyk: 209–10. Warsaw, 2015.

Inglot, Mieczysław. "Padurra Tomasz." In *Polski słownik biograficzny*. Vol. 25: 13–15. Wrocław–Warsaw–Cracow–Gdańsk, 1980.

Jagiełło, Michał. *Narody i narodowości. Przewodnik po lekturach*. Vol. 1. Warsaw, 2010.

Jagmin, Tadeusz. *Polacy grekokatolicy na ziemi czerwieńskiej*. Lviv, 1939.

Janion, Maria. "Pieśniarz czerwonoruski." *Życie Literackie* no. 37 (19 Sep. 1954): 4–5.

Janion, Maria. "Polski korowód." In *Mity i stereotypy w dziejach Polski*. Ed. Janusz Tazbir: 185–242. Warsaw, 1991.

Janion, Maria. "Powieść o chłopskim buntowniku." In Jan Zacharyasiewicz. *Jarema. Studium z wewnętrznych dziejów Galicji*. Ed. Maria Janion: 5–17. Warsaw, 1957.

Janowski, Maciej. *Inteligencja wobec wyzwań nowoczesności. Dylematy ideowe polskiej demokracji liberalnej w Galicji w latach 1889–1914*. Warsaw, 1996.

Janowski, Maciej. *Polska myśl liberalna do 1918 roku*. Cracow, 1988.

Jarosz, Jan Piotr. "Akcja repolonizacyjna na terytoriach południowo-
-wschodnich Rzeczypospolitej w latach 1935–1939." In *Polacy i Ukraińcy dawniej i dziś*. Ed. Bogumił Grott: 61–66. Cracow, 2002.

Jarowiecki, Jerzy. *Dzieje prasy polskiej we Lwowie do 1945 roku*. Cracow–Wrocław, 2008.

Kalembka, Sławomir. *Wiosna Ludów w Europie*. Warsaw, 1991.

Kamela, Małgorzata and Andrzej A. Zięba. "Stebelski Włodzimierz." In *Polski słownik biograficzny*. Vol. 43: 40–45. Warsaw–Cracow, 2004–5.

Kapralska, Łucja. *Pluralizm kulturowy i etniczny a odrębność regionalna Kresów południowo-wschodnich w latach 1918–1939*. Cracow, 2000.

Karolczak, Kazimierz. "Sprawy narodowościowe w Galicyjskim Sejmie Krajowym w latach 1861–1873." In *Galicyjskie dylematy. Zbiór rozpraw*: 31–49. Eds. Kazimierz Karolczak and Henryk Żaliński. Cracow, 1994.

Kasjan, Jan Mirosław. "Wernyhora." In *Życiorysy historyczne, literackie i legendarne*. Vol. 2. Eds. Zofia Stefanowska and Janusz Tazbir: 155–80. Warsaw, 1989.

Kasznica, Stanisław and Marcin Nadobnik. *Najważniejsze wyniki spisu ludności i spisu zwierząt domowych według stanu z d. 31 grudnia 1910 r*. Lviv, 1911.

Katsnel'son, Dora. "K istorii uchastiia Slavian k vengerskoi revoliutsii 1848–1849 gg. (Po materialam lvovskikh arkhivov)." In *Tsentral'naia i Iugo-vostochnaia Evropa v novoe vremia. Sbornik statei*. Selection, ed., and introd. Iurii Pisarev: 171–181. Moscow, 1974.

Kieniewicz, Stefan. *Adam Sapieha 1828–1903*. Warsaw, 1993.

Kieniewicz, Stefan. *Czyn Polski w dobie Wiosny Ludów*. Warsaw, 1948.

Kieniewicz, Stefan, "Fedorowicz Władysław Walenty." In *Polski słownik biograficzny*. Vol. 6: 390–91. Cracow, 1948.

Kieniewicz, Stefan. *Konspiracje galicyjskie (1831–1845)*. Warsaw, 1950.

Kieniewicz, Stefan. "Popiel Michał." In *Polski słownik biograficzny*. Vol. 27: 563–64. Wrocław–Warsaw–Cracow–Gdańsk–Łódź, 1983.

Kieniewicz, Stefan. "Powstanie listopadowe na tle ruchów rewolucyjnych w Europie." In *Powstanie listopadowe 1830–1831. Geneza, uwarunkowania, bilans, porównania*. Eds. Jerzy Skowronek and Maria Żmigrodzka: 279–86. Wrocław–Warsaw–Cracow–Gdańsk–Łódź, 1983.

Kieniewicz, Stefan. *Powstanie styczniowe*. Warsaw, 2009.

Kieniewicz, Stefan. "'Rusyn na praznyku' i dalsze jego losy." In *Problemy wiedzy o kulturze. Prace dedykowane Stefanowi Żółkiewskiemu*. Eds. Alina Brodzka, Maryla Hopfinger and Janusz Lalewicz: 327–41. Wrocław–Warsaw–Cracow–Gdańsk–Łódź, 1986.

Kieniewicz, Stefan. "Schmitt Henryk Leonard." In *Polski słownik biograficzny*. Vol. 35: 559–62. Warsaw–Cracow, 1994.

Kieniewicz, Stefan. *Sprawa włościańska w powstaniu styczniowym*. Wrocław, 1953.

Kieniewicz, Stefan. "Z problematyki badań nad społeczną historią 1863 roku." *Prace Historyczne* 78: *Struktury, ruchy, ideologie XVIII–XX wieku*. Ed. Halina Kozłowska-Sabatowska (1986): 61–7.

Kieniewicz, Stefan and Maria Domańska-Nogajczyk. "Stella-Sawicki Jan." In *Polski słownik biograficzny*. Vol. 43: 352–357. Warsaw–Cracow, 2004–5.

Kizwalter, Tomasz. *O nowoczesności narodu. Przypadek Polski*. Warsaw, 1999.

Kłak, Czesław. "Glosa do *Czerwonej czapki* Jana Zachariasiewicza." In Czesław Kłak. *Pisarze galicyjscy. Szkice literackie*: 57–76. Rzeszów, 1994.

Kłak, Czesław. "Literacka młodość Jana Zachariasiewicza." In *Z tradycji kulturalnych Rzeszowa i Rzeszowszczyzny. Księga pamiątkowa dla uczczenia X-lecia rzeszowskiego oddziału Towarzystwa Literackiego im. Adama Mickiewicza*. Eds. Stanisław Frycie and Stefan Reczek: 141–82. Rzeszów, 1966.

Kłak, Czesław. "Powieści biograficzne Jana Zachariasiewicza." In *Z dziejów kultury i literatury ziemi przemyskiej. Zbiór szkiców, opracowań i utworów literackich*. Ed. Stefania Kostrzewska-Kratochwilowa: 125–72. Przemyśl, 1969.

Kłak, Czesław. "Powieści historyczne Jana Zachariasiewicza zwierciadłem sporów politycznych między demokratami i konserwatystami galicyjskimi." *Prace Humanistyczne. Rzeszowskie Towarzystwo Przyjaciół Nauk. Wydział Nauk Humanistycznych. Komisja Historycznoliteracka* 1. Series 1. no. 1 (1970): 153–92.

Kłoskowska, Antonina. *National Cultures at the Grass-root Level*. Budapest, 2001.

Knot, Antoni. "Czerkawski Euzebiusz." In *Polski słownik biograficzny*. Vol. 4: 333–34. Cracow, 1938.

Knot, Antoni. *Dążenia oświatowe młodzieży galicyjskiej w latach 1815–1830.* Wrocław, 1959.

Knot, Antoni. "Dolnicki Julian." In *Polski słownik biograficzny.* Vol. 4: 288. Cracow, 1938.

Knot, Antoni. "Michalewicz Mikołaj." In *Polski słownik biograficzny.* Vol. 20: 571–72. Wrocław–Warsaw–Cracow–Gdańsk, 1975.

Knot, Antoni. "Wstęp." In *Galicyjskie wspomnienia szkolne.* Ed. Antoni Knot: i–lviii. Cracow, 1955.

Koko, Eugeniusz. *Franciszek Rawita-Gawroński (1846–1930) wobec Ukrainy i jej przeszłości. Studium archaizmu.* Gdańsk, 2006.

Koko, Eugeniusz. "Przedmowa." In Franciszek Rawita-Gawroński. *Ludzie i czasy mego wieku. Wspomnienia, wypadki, zapiski (1892–1914).* Ed. and footnotes Eugeniusz Koko: 7–20. Gdańsk, 2012.

Koko, Eugeniusz. "Rusini czy Ukraińcy? Kształtowanie się nowoczesnego narodu ukraińskiego w poglądach Franciszka Rawity-Gawrońskiego." In *Polacy i sąsiedzi – dystanse i przenikanie kultur. Zbiór studiów.* Part 1. Ed. Roman Wapiński: 31–35. Ostaszewo Gdańskie, 2000.

Komorowski, Jarosław. "Platona Kosteckiego Hołd Calderonowi." *Pamiętnik Teatralny* 48, no. 3–4 (1999): 96–108.

Koropeckyj, Roman. "Wizerunek narodowego ruchu ruskiego w powieści Jana Zachariasiewicza 'Święty Jur'." *Krakowskie Zeszyty Ukrainoznawcze* 3–4 (1994–1995): 305–23.

Kosiek, Zdzisław. "Kulczycki Włodzimierz Sas." In *Polski słownik biograficzny.* Vol. 16: 137. Wrocław–Warsaw–Cracow–Gdańsk, 1971.

Kot, Stanisław. *Historja wychowania. Zarys podręcznikowy.* Vol. 2: *Wychowanie nowoczesne (od połowy w. XVIII do współczesnej doby).* Lviv, 1934.

Kot, Stanisław. "Świadomość narodowa w Polsce w. XV–XVII." *Kwartalnik Historyczny* 52, no. 1 (1938): 15–33.

Kowalski, Tadeusz Antoni. *Mniejszości narodowe w siłach zbrojnych Drugiej Rzeczypospolitej Polskiej (1918–1939).* Toruń, 1997.

Koziebrodzki, Władysław. *Repertorjum czynności galicyjskiego Sejmu Krajowego od roku 1861 po rok 1883.* Vol. 1. Lviv, 1885.

Koziebrodzki, Władysław. *Repertorjum czynności galicyjskiego Sejmu Krajowego od roku 1883 po rok 1889 (sześć sesji piątego periodu).* Vol. 2. Lviv, 1889.

Kozik, Jan. *Między reakcją a rewolucją. Studia z dziejów ukraińskiego ruchu narodowego w Galicji w latach 1848–1849.* Warsaw–Cracow, 1975.

Kozik, Jan. "Stosunki ukraińsko-polskie w Galicji w okresie rewolucji 1848–1849. Próba charakterystyki." *Prace Historyczne* 54: *Z dziejów współpracy Polaków, Ukraińców i Rosjan* (1975): 29–53.

Kozik, Jan. *Ukraiński ruch narodowy w Galicji w latach 1830–1848.* Cracow, 1973.

Kozik, Jan. *The Ukrainian National Movement in Galicia 1815–1849.* Ed. and introd. Lawrence D. Orton. Trans. Andrew Gorski and Lawrence D. Orton. Edmonton, 1986.

Kozłowska-Sabatowska, Halina. *Ideologia pozytywizmu galicyjskiego 1864–1881.* Wrocław–Warsaw–Cracow–Gdańsk, 1978.

Kozłowska-Sabatowska, Halina. *Między konspiracją a pracą organiczną. Młodość Tadeusza Romanowicza.* Cracow, 1986.

Kozłowski, Eligiusz. *Legion polski na Węgrzech 1848–1849.* Warsaw, 1983.

Kozłowski, Maciej. *Między Sanem a Zbruczem. Walki o Lwów i Galicję Wschodnią 1918–1919.* Cracow, 1990.

Kozłowski, Maciej. *Zapomniana wojna. Walki o Lwów i Galicję Wschodnią 1918–1919.* Introd. Bohdan Skaradziński. Bydgoszcz, 1999.

Krajewski, Józef. *Tajne związki polityczne w Galicyi (od r. 1833 do r. 1841).* Lviv, 1903.

Kochmal, Anna. „Stosunki międzywyznaniowe i międzyobrządkowe w parafiach greckokatolickiej diecezji przemyskiej w latach 1918-1939." In *Polska–Ukraina. 1000 lat sąsiedztwa.* Vol. 3: *Studia z dziejów greckokatolickiej diecezji przemyskiej.* Ed. Stanisław Stępień: 219–29. Przemyśl, 1996.

Krotofil, Maciej. "Ukraińcy w Wojsku Polskim w okresie międzywojennym." In *Mniejszości narodowe i wyznaniowe w siłach zbrojnych Drugiej Rzeczypospolitej 1918–1939. Zbiór studiów.* Eds. Zbigniew Karpus and Waldemar Rezmer: 123–52. Toruń, 2001.

Książek, Tadeusz and Zygmunt Młynarski. *Udział Rosjan, Litwinów, Białorusinów, Ukraińców w powstaniu styczniowym (1863–1864).* Warsaw, 1962.

Księga pamiątkowa ku uczczeniu dwudziestej piątej rocznicy założenia Towarzystwa Gimnastycznego 'Sokół' we Lwowie. Lviv, 1892.

Kubiak, Hieronim. "Asymilacja." In *Encyklopedia socjologii. Suplement.* Comp. Zbigniew Bokszański et al. Eds. Hieronim Kubiak et al.: 29–36. Warsaw, 2005.

Kuczera, Aleksander. *Samborszczyzna. Ilustrowana monografja miasta Sambora i ekonomii Samborskiej.* Vol. 1–2. Sambor, 1935.

Kwaśniewski, Krzysztof. "Konflikt etniczny." *Sprawy Narodowościowe. Seria nowa* 3, no. 1 (4) (1994): 39–52.

Kwiecińska, Magdalena. "Drobna szlachta w Galicji — między polskim a ukraińskim ruchem narodowym." *Sprawy Narodowościowe. Seria Nowa* 34 (2009): 83–97.

Kwiecińska, Magdalena. "Poczucie tożsamości stanowej i narodowej rodu Kulczyckich z Kulczyc koło Sambora, na Ukrainie Zachodniej." *Literatura Ludowa* no. 4–5 (2004): 105–24.

Latos, Tomasz. "Stojałowski Stanisław." In *Polski słownik biograficzny.* Vol. 44: 11–17. Warsaw–Cracow, 2006–7.

Lechicki, Czesław. "Laskownicki Józef Albin." In *Polski słownik biograficzny.* Vol. 16: 525–26. Wrocław–Warsaw–Cracow–Gdańsk, 1971.

Lechicki, Czesław. "Łoziński Józef." In *Polski słownik biograficzny,* Vol 18: 455–56. Wrocław–Warsaw–Cracow–Gdańsk, 1973.

Levitskii, Ivan Em[eryk]. *Galitsko-russkaia bibliografiia XIX. stolětiia s" uvzgliadnen'em" russkikh izdanii, poiavivshikhsia v" Ugorshchině i Bukovině (1801–1886).* Vol. 1: *Khronologicheskii spisok" publikatsii (1801–1860).* Lviv, 1888.

Levyts'kyi, Kost'. *Istoriia politychnoï dumky halyts'kykh Ukraïntsiv 1848–1914 na pidstavi spomyniv*. Lviv, 1926.

Lewestam, Franciszek. "Jan Zacharyasiewicz. Szkic biograficzno-literacki." *Tygodnik Illustrowany* no. 230 (20 Feb. 1864): 65–66.

Lewicki, Jan. *Ruch Rusinów w Galicji w pierwszej połowie wieku panowania Austrji (1772–1820)*. Lviv, 1879.

Lewicki, Karol. "Czerlunczakiewicz Józef." In *Polski słownik biograficzny*. Vol. 4: 336. Cracow, 1938.

Lewicki, Karol. "Hordyński Mikołaj." In *Polski słownik biograficzny*. Vol. 9: 623. Wrocław–Warsaw–Cracow, 1961.

Lewicki, Karol. *Uniwersytet Lwowski a powstanie listopadowe*. Lviv, 1937.

Lisiewicz, Jerzy and Anna Pituch. "Merunowicz Józef." In *Polski słownik biograficzny*. Vol. 20: 454–55. Wrocław–Warsaw–Cracow–Gdańsk, 1975.

Litwin, Henryk. "Katolicyzacja szlachty ruskiej a procesy asymilacyjne na Ukrainie w latach 1569–1648." In *Tryumfy i porażki. Studia z dziejów kultury polskiej XVI–XVIII w.*. Ed. Maria Bogucka: 47–73. Warsaw, 1989.

Litwin, Henryk. "Narody pierwszej Rzeczypospolitej." In *Tradycje polityczne dawnej Polski*. Eds. Anna Sucheni-Grabowska and Alicja Dybowska: 168–218. Warsaw, 1993.

Łepkowski, Tadeusz. "Ojczyzna historyczna a etniczna w XIX i na początku XX w." In Tadeusz Łepkowski. *Rozważania o losach polskich*: 56–65. London, 1987.

Łopuszański, Bolesław. "Krzyżanowski Romuald." In *Polski słownik biograficzny*. Vol. 15: 615–16. Wrocław–Warsaw–Cracow, 1970.

Łopuszański, Bolesław. "Łapczyński Marcjan." In *Polski słownik biograficzny*. Vol. 18: 209. Wrocław–Warsaw–Cracow–Gdańsk, 1973.

Łopuszański, Bolesław. "Matkowski Józef." In *Polski słownik biograficzny*. Vol. 20: 203–04. Wrocław–Warsaw–Gdańsk–Cracow, 1975.

Łopuszański, Bolesław. *Stowarzyszenie Ludu Polskiego (1835–1841). Geneza i dzieje*. Cracow, 1975.

Łopuszański, Bolesław. "'Wskazówka dla nauczycieli ludu ruskiego' Kaspra Cięglewicza (z literatury chłopomańskiej pierwszej połowy XIX w.)." *Rocznik Muzeum Etnograficznego w Krakowie* 5 (1974): 239–56.

Łosowski, Janusz. *Anatol Lewicki*. Przemyśl, 1981.

Łosowski, Janusz. "Anatol Lewicki jako historyk." In Anatol Lewicki. *Obrazki najdawniejszych dziejów Przemyśla*: vii–xxxviii. Przemyśl, 1994.

Łossowski, Piotr and Zygmunt Młynarski. *Rosjanie, Białorusini i Ukraińcy w powstaniu styczniowym*. Wrocław, 1959.

Łoziński, Bronisław. *Agenor hrabia Gołuchowski w pierwszym okresie rządów swoich (1846–1859)*. Lviv, 1901.

Maciak, Dariusz. *Próba porozumienia polsko-ukraińskiego w Galicji w latach 1888–1895*. Warsaw, 2006.

Maciesza, Aleksander. "Dutkiewicz Melecjusz." In *Polski słownik biograficzny*. Vol. 6: 15–16. Cracow, 1948.

Madurowicz-Urbańska, Helena. "Karta z dziejów lwowskiej nauki. 'Ziemia Czerwieńska'—Rocznik Oddziału Polskiego Towarzystwa Historycznego we Lwowie (1935–1938)." In *Poprzez stulecia. Księga pamiątkowa ofiarowana Profesorowi Antoniemu Podrazie w 80. rocznicę Jego urodzin*. Ed. Danuta Czerska: 299–307. Cracow, 2000.

Magocsi, Paul Robert. *A History of Ukraine: The Land and its People*. Toronto–Buffalo–London, 2010.

Majorek, Czesław. *Historia utylitarna i erudycyjna. Szkolna Edukacja historyczna w Galicji (1772–1918)*. Warsaw, 1990.

Malczewska-Pawelec, Dorota. "Obraz Ukrainy i stosunków polsko-ukraińskich w podręczniku Anatola Lewickiego *Zarys historii Polski i krajów ruskich z nią połączonych*." In *Stosunki polsko-ukraińskie w szkolnej edukacji historycznej od XIX do XXI wieku. Materiały konferencji naukowej 21–22 października 2004 r., Cedzyna k. Kielc*. Ed. Hanna Wójcik-Łagan: 145–61. Kielce, 2005.

Marachow, Grigorij. "Polsko-ukraińskie związki rewolucyjne (50.–70. lata XIX wieku)." *Prace Historyczne* 54: *Z dziejów współpracy Polaków, Ukraińców i Rosjan* (1975): 55–70.

Maternicki, Jerzy. "Michał Bobrzyński wobec tzw. idei jagiellońskiej. Ewolucja poglądów i jej uwarunkowania." *Przegląd Humanistyczny* 21, no. 12 (1977): 131–42.

Maternicki, Jerzy. "Początki mitu jagiellońskiego w historiografii polskiej XIX wieku. Karol Szajnocha i Julian Klaczko." *Przegląd Humanistyczny* 32, no. 11–12 (1988): 33–48.

Micińska, Magdalena. *Galicjanie – zesłańcy po powstaniu styczniowym. Zesłanie w głąb Cesarstwa Rosyjskiego – Działalność księdza Ludwika Ruczki – Powroty*. Warsaw, 2004.

Mikietyński, Piotr. *Generał Stanisław hr. Szeptycki. Między Habsburgami a Rzecząpospolitą (okres 1867–1918)*. Cracow, 1999.

Milewska, Wacława. *Niepodległość. Wokół myśli historycznej Józefa Piłsudskiego*. Cracow, 2018.

Mitkowski, Józef. "Lewicki Anatol." In *Polski słownik biograficzny*. Vol. 17: 224–25. Wrocław–Warsaw–Cracow–Gdańsk, 1972.

Moklak, Jarosław. "Spór o Internat Ruski we Lwowie." In *Poprzez stulecia. Księga pamiątkowa ofiarowana Profesorowi Antoniemu Podrazie w 80. rocznicę Jego urodzin*. Ed. Danuta Czerska: 191–97. Cracow, 2000.

Moklak, Jarosław. "Spór polsko–ukraiński o język obrad sejmu galicyjskiego (1865–1866). Wnioski Antona Petruszewycza i Aleksandra Borkowskiego. Przyczynek do kształtowania się nacjonalizmów w Galicji Wschodniej." *Biuletyn Ukrainoznawczy* 9 (2003): 40–51.

Moklak, Jarosław. "Stanowisko posłów polskich gente Ruthenus i ruskich (ukraińskich) w Sejmie Krajowym galicyjskim wobec projektu ustawy o języku wykładowym w szkołach ludowych i średnich w 1866 r." *Biuletyn Ukrainoznawczy* 8 (2002): 28–41.

Moklak, Jarosław. *W walce o tożsamość Ukraińców. Zagadnienie języka wykładowego w szkołach ludowych i średnich w pracach galicyjskiego Sejmu Krajowego 1866–1892*. Cracow, 2004.

Monolatii, Ivan. *Razom, ale, maizhe okremo. Vzaiemodiia etnopolitychnykh aktoriv na zakhidnoukraïns'kykh zemliakh u 1867–1914 rr.* Ivano-Frankivs'k, 2010.

Morineau, Michel. "La douceur d'être inclu". In *Sociabilité, pouvoirs et société. Actes du Coloque de Rouen, 24/26 Novembre 1983*. Coll. by Françoise Thelamon: 19–32. Rouen, 1987.

Moszumański, Zbigniew. "Trening militarny żołnierza w aspekcie historycznym." In *Trening militarny żołnierzy*. Vol. 10. Eds. Andrzej Chodała, Jarosław Klimczak and Andrzej Rakowski: 8–33. Szczytno, 2006.

Możdżeń, Stefan Ignacy. *Historia wychowania 1795–1918*. Sandomierz, 2006.

Mudryj, Marian. "Adam Świątek, *Gente Rutheni, natione Poloni. Z dziejów Rusinów narodowości polskiej w Galicji*, Cracow 2014, Księgarnia Akademicka, ss. 512, il. Studia Galicyjskie, t. 3 [review]." *Kwartalnik Historyczny* 123, no. 4 (2016): 857–61.

Mudryi, Marian. "Aktyvizatsiia suspil'no-politychnoho zhyttia u 60-70-kh rokakh XIX st." In *Istoriia Lvova*. Vol. 2: *1772 – zhovten' 1918*. Ed. Iaroslav Isaevych: 233. Lviv, 2007.

Mudryj, Marjan. "Dylematy narodowościowe w Sejmie Krajowym galicyjskim (na przykładzie posłów formacji gente Rutheni natione Poloni)." In *Ukraińskie tradycje parlamentarne. XIX–XX wiek*. Ed. Jarosław Moklak: 59–94. Cracow, 2006.

Mudryj, Marian. "Formacja gente Rutheni, natione Poloni w XIX-wiecznej Galicji a pojęcie ojczyzny." In *Formuły patriotyzmu w Europie Wschodniej i Środkowej od nowożytności do współczesności*. Eds. Andrzej Nowak and Andrzej A. Zięba: 285–98. Cracow, 2009.

Mudryi, Marian. "*Gente Rutheni* v Pol's'kii Tsentral'nii Radi Narodovii 1848 roku." *Zapysky Naukovoho Tovarystva imeni Shevchenka* 256: *Pratsi filosofs'koï sektsiï*. Ed. O. Kupchyns'kyi (2008): 244–81.

Mudryi, Marian. "Ideolohiia chy svitohliad? Do pytannia pro teoretychni zasady Rus'koho Soboru 1848 roku." *Visnyk L'vivs'koho universytetu. Seriia istorychna* 44 (2009): 75–106.

Mudryi, Marian. "Ideia pol's'ko-ukraïns'koi uniï ta 'Rusyny pol's'koï natsiï' v etnopolitychnomu dyskursi Halychyny 1859–1869 rokiv." *Visnyk L'vivs'koho universytetu. Seriia istorychna* 39–40 (2005): 83–148.

Mudryi, Marian. "'Jesteśmy rozdwojonymi członkami jednego ciała'. Do pytannia pro vidnosyny mizh Holovnoiu Rus'koiu Radoiu i Rus'kym Soborom 1848 roku." *Zapysky Naukovoho tovarystva imeni Shevchenka* 265: *Pratsi Istorychno-filosofs'koï sektsiï* (2013): 54–80.

Mudryj, Marian. "Kwestia tożsamości wśród ruskich elit politycznych w Galicji." *Prace Historyczne* 144, no. 2: *Kształty galicyjskich tożsamości*. Ed. Adam Świątek (2017): 255–75.

Mudryj, Marian. "Nieznana rewolucja. Wydarzenia 1846 roku w Galicji w historiografii ukraińskiej." In *Rok 1846 w Krakowie i Galicji. Odniesienia, Interpretacje, pamięć*. Eds. Krzysztof K. Daszyk, Tomasz Kargol and Tomasz Szubert: 261–74. Cracow, 2016.

Mudryi, Marian. "Pol's'ki liberal-demokraty ta ukraïns'ke pytannia v Halychyni u 80-kh rr. XIX st." *Visnyk Lvivs'koho universytetu. Seriia istorychna* 32 (1997): 99–109.

Mudryj, Marian. "Poszukiwania tożsamości narodowej i pojęcie ojczyzny w dziewiętnastowiecznej Galicji (na przykładzie gente Rutheni, natione Poloni)." In *'Duża i mała ojczyzna' w świadomości historycznej, źródłach i edukacji*. Eds. Bogumiła Burda and Małgorzata Szymczak: 29–42. Zielona Góra, 2010.

Mudryj, Marian. "Powstanie styczniowe a środowisko gente Rutheni, natione Poloni w Galicji." In *Powstanie styczniowe. Odniesienia, Interpretacje, pamięć*. Ed. Tomasz Kargol: 67–78. Cracow, 2013.

Mudryi, Marian. "Rusyny pol's'koï natsiï (gente Rutheni, natione Poloni) v Halychyni XIX st. i poniattia vitchyzny." *Ukraïna. Kul'turna spadshchyna, natsional'na svidomist', derzhavnist'* 15: *Confraternitas. Iuvileinyi zbirnyk na poshanu Iaroslava Isaievycha* (2006–7): 461–74.

Mudryi, Marian. "Rus'kyi sobor 1848 roku. Istoriohrafichnyi ta dzhereloznavchnyi ohliad." *Visnyk Lvivs'koho universytetu. Seriia knyhoznavstvo, bibliotekoznastvo ta Informatsiini tekhnolohiï* 8 (2014): 193–206.

Mudryi, Marian. "Rus'kyi sobor 1848 roku. Orhanizatsiia ta chleny." *Ukraïna. Kul'turna spadshchyna, natsional'na svidomist', derzhavnist'* 16: *Iubileinyi zbirnyk na poshanu Ivana Patera* (2008): 107–26.

Mudryi, Marian. "Sichneve povstannia ta seredovyshche 'rusyniv pol's'koi natsiï' (gente Rutheni, natione Poloni) v Halychyni." In *Galicja a powstanie styczniowe*. Eds. Mariola Hoszowska, Agnieszka Kawalec and Leonid Zaszkilniak: 135–46. Warsaw–Rzeszów, 2013.

Mudryi, Marian. "Sproby ukraïns'ko-pol's'koho porozuminnia v Halychyni (60–70-i roky XIX st.)." *Ukraïna. Kul'turna spadshchyna, natsional'na svidomist', derzhavnist'* vol. 3–4: *Zbirnyk naukovykh prats'* (1997): 58–117.

Mudryi, Marian. *Ukraïns'ko-pol's'ki vidnosyny v Halychyni u 1867–1890 rr. Politychnyi aspekt. Dysertatsiia na zdobuttia naukovoho stupenia kandydata istorychnykh nauk*. Lviv, 1996 [unpublished work].

Nabywaniec, Stanisław. "Ksiądz Józef Łoziński – człowiek pogranicza." In *Dwa pogranicza. Galicja Wschodnia i Górny Śląsk. Historia – problemy – odniesienia*. Eds. Zdzisław Budzyński and Jolanta Kamińska-Kwak: 121–28. Rzeszów, 2003.

Najdus, Walentyna. *Polska Partia Socjalno-Demokratyczna Galicji i Śląska 1890–1919*. Warsaw, 1983.

Nakonechny, Ievhen. *Ukradene im'ia. Chomu rusyny staly ukraïntsiamy*. Introd. Iaroslav Dashkevych. Lviv, 2004.

Nance, Agnieszka B. *Literary and Cultural Images of a Nation without a State. The Case of Nineteenth-Century Poland*. New York, 2008.

Nazarko, Irynei. *Kyivski i halyts'ki mytropolyty: Biohrafichni narysy (1590–1960)*. Toronto, 1962.

Niebelski, Eugeniusz. *Duchowieństwo lubelskie i podlaskie w powstaniu 1863 roku i na zesłaniu w Rosji*. Lublin, 2002.

Niedźwiedź, Jakub. "Gente Ruthenus natione Polonus." In *Kultura pogranicza wschodniego. Zarys encyklopedyczny*. Eds. Tadeusz Budrewicz, Tadeusz Bujnicki and Jerzy Stefan Ossowski: 136. Warsaw, 2011.

Nieśmiertelni. Fotografie literatów lwowskich. Lviv, 1898.

Nikodem, Jarosław. „Anatol Lewicki i jego 'Powstanie Świdrygiełły'." In *Anatol Lewicki. Powstanie Świdrygiełły. Ustęp z dziejów unii Litwy z Koroną*: 9–19. Oświęcim, 2015.

Nowak, Joanna. "Gente Ruthenus, natione Polonus. Rusini w refleksji Wielkiej Emigracji." *Sprawy Narodowościowe. Seria Nowa* 23 (2003): 43–62.

Nowak, Magdalena. *Dwa światy. Zagadnienie identyfikacji narodowej Andrzeja Szeptyckiego w latach 1865–1914*. Gdańsk, 2018.

Olszański, Kazimierz. *Prasa galicyjska wobec powstania styczniowego*, Wrocław–Warsaw–Cracow–Gdańsk, 1975.

Orton, Lawrence D. "'The Stańczyk Portfolio' and the Politics of Galician Loyalism." *The Polish Review* 27, no. 1–2 (1982): 55–64.

Osadczy, Włodzimierz. "Dialog arcybiskupów. Andrzej Szeptycki i Józef Teodorowicz o stosunkach międzobrzędowych w Galicji Wschodniej na przełomie XIX i XX wieku." *Chrześcijanin w Świecie* no. 2 (1995): 95–103.

Osadczy, Włodzimierz. "Galicyjski mit unii polsko-litewsko-ruskiej." In *Unia lubelska. Unia Europejska*. Ed. Iwona Hofman: 169–75. Lublin, 2010.

Osadczy, Włodzimierz. "Kler katolicki obu obrządków wobec polsko-ruskiej rywalizacji w Galicji Wschodniej w XIX i XX wieku." In *Prace Komisji Środkowoeuropejskiej*. Vol. 7. Eds. Jan Machnik and Irena Stawowy-Kawka: 75–91. Cracow, 2000.

Osadczy, Włodzimierz. *Kościół i Cerkiew na wspólnej drodze. Concordia 1863. Z dziejów porozumienia między obrządkiem greckokatolickim a łacińskim w Galicji Wschodniej*. Lublin, 1999.

Osadczy, Włodzimierz. *Święta Ruś. Rozwój i oddziaływanie idei prawosławia w Galicji*. Lublin, 2007.

Ossowski, Stanisław. "Analiza socjologiczna pojęcia Ojczyzna." In *Stanisław Ossowski. O ojczyźnie i narodzie*: 15–46. Warsaw, 1984.

Ossowski, Stanisław. "Ziemia i naród." In *Stanisław Ossowski. O ojczyźnie i narodzie*: 47–57. Warsaw, 1984.

Osterkamp, Jana. "Imperial Diversity In the Village: Petitions for and against the Division of Galicia in 1848". *Nationalities Papers* 44, no. 5 (2015): 731–50.

Pachoński, Jan. *Oficerowie Legionów Polskich 1796–1807*. Vol. 1: *Korpus oficerski Legionów Polskich 1796–1807*. Cracow, 1999.

Pannenkowa, Irena. *Walka Galicji z centralizmem wiedeńskim. Dzieje rezolucji Sejmu galicyjskiego z 24. września 1868. W 50. rocznicę uchwały rewolucyjnej*. Lviv, 1918.

Papierzyńska-Turek, Mirosława. *Od tożsamości do niepodległości. Studia i szkice z dziejów kształtowania się ukraińskiej świadomości narodowej.* Toruń, 2012.

Partacz, Czesław. *Od Badeniego do Potockiego. Stosunki polsko-ukraińskie w Galicji w latach 1888–1908.* Toruń, 1997.

Partacz, Czesław. "Stosunki religijne w Galicji Wschodniej. Rusini łacinnicy i Polacy grekokatolicy." *Rocznik Przemyski* 28 (1991–1992): 123–46.

Pavlyshyn, Oleh. "Dylema identychnosty, abo istoriia pro te, iak 'latynnyky' (ne) staly ukraïntsiamy/poliakamy (Halychyna, seredyna XIX–XX st)." *Ukraina moderna* 21: *Natsionalizm na skhodi Evropy. Chyslo na poshanu Romana Shporliuka* (2014): 179–218.

Pawlikowska-Butterwick, Wiolleta. "A 'Foreign' Elite?: The Territorial Origins of the Canons and Prelates of the Cathedral Chapter of Vilna In the Second Half of the Sixteenth Century." *Slavonic and East European Review* 92, no. 1 (2014): 44–80.

Pawłowski, Bronisław. *Lwów w 1809 r. z 20 rycinami w tekście.* Lviv, 1909.

Pawłowski, Stanisław. *Ludność rzymsko-katolicka w polsko-ruskiej części Galicji z dwoma mapami.* Lviv, 1919.

Pawłowski, Stanisław. "Stosunki narodowościowe w Galicyi Wschodniej." In Eugeniusz Romer, Stanisław Zakrzewski, and Stanisław Pawłowski. *W obronie Galicyi Wschodniej*: 59–81. Lviv, 1919.

Pelczar, Roman. *Rzymskokatolickie szkoły trywialne w Galicji w latach 1774–1875.* Lublin, 2014.

Pelczar, Roman. *Szkoły parafialne na pograniczu polsko-ruskim (ukraińskim) w Galicji w latach 1772–1869.* Lublin, 2009.

Pijaj, Stanisław. "Lwowskie wybory parlamentarne w 1873 roku." *Visnyk Lvivs'koho universytetu. Seriia istorychna* spec. no.: *Lviv. Misto, suspil'stvo, kul'tura.* Vol. 8. Part 1: *Vlada i suspil'stvo.* Eds. Olena Arkusha, Marian Mudryi (2012): 96–114.

Pijaj, Stanisław. *Między polskim patriotyzmem a habsburskim lojalizmem. Polacy wobec przemian ustrojowych monarchii habsburskiej (1866–1871).* Cracow, 2003.

Pijaj, Stanisław. *Opozycja w wiedeńskiej Radzie Państwa w latach siedemdziesiątych XIX w. (skład, organizacja, funkcjonowanie).* Cracow, 2011.

Pijaj, Stanisław. "Posłowie ruscy w parlamencie wiedeńskim w latach 1848–1879." In *Ukraińskie tradycje parlamentarne. XIX–XXI wiek.* Ed. Jarosław Moklak: 95–126. Cracow, 2006.

Plokhii, Serhii. *The Origins of the Slavic Nations. Premodern Identities in Russia, Ukraine, and Belarus.* Cambridge, 2006.

Prokopovych, Markian. "Kopiec Unii Lubelskiej. Imperial Politics and National Celebration in Habsburg Lemberg." *Ece-urban* no. 3 (2008). Accessed 1 Sep. 2019. http://www.lvivcenter.org/en/publications/ece-urban.

Prus, Edward. *Hulajpole. Burzliwe dzieje Kresów Ukrainnych (od słowiańskiego świtu do Cudu nad Wisłą).* Wrocław, 2003.

Pucek, Zbigniew. "Galicyjskie doświadczenie wielokulturowości a problem więzi społecznej." In *Społeczeństwo i gospodarka*. Eds. Jerzy Chłopecki and Helena Madurowicz-Urbańska: 11–25. Rzeszów, 1995.

Pudłocki, Tomasz. *Iskra światła czy kopcąca pochodnia? Inteligencja w Przemyślu w latach 1867–1939*. Cracow, 2009.

Pulnarowicz, Władysław. *U źródeł Sanu, Stryja i Dniestru. Historia powiatu turczańskiego*. Turka, 1929.

Radyszewśkyj, Rotysław. "Przedmowa." In Jan Dalibor Wagilewicz. *Pisarze polscy Rusini wraz z dodatkiem Pisarze łacińscy Rusini*. Ed. Rotysław Radyszewśkyj: 5–22. Przemyśl, 1996.

Radzik, Ryszard. "Ewolucja narodowa społeczności Kresów Wschodnich." *Kultura i Społeczeństwo* 35, no. 2 (1991): 57–72.

Radzik, Ryszard. "Społeczne uwarunkowania formowania się ukraińskiej świadomości narodowej w Galicji wschodniej w latach 1830–1863." *Kultura i Społeczeństwo* 25, no. 1–2 (1981): 295–311.

Rawita-Gawroński, Franciszek. *Rok 1863 na Rusi*. Vol. 1: *Ruś Czerwona i Wschód*. Lviv, 1902.

Romaniuk, Myroslav and Mariia Halushko. *Ukraïns'ki chasopysy L'vova 1848–1939*. Vol. 1: *1848–1900*. Lviv, 2001.

Röskau-Rydel, Isabel. *Niemiecko-austriackie rodziny urzędnicze w Galicji 1772–1918. Kariery zawodowe, środowisko, akulturacja i asymilacja*. Cracow, 2011.

Ruda, Oksana. "Otsinka Liublins'koï uniï 1569 r. u pol's'kii istoriohrafiï kintsia XIX – pochatku XX st." In *Bahatokul'turne istorychne seredovyshche L'vova v XIX i XX stolittiakh / Wielokulturowe środowisko historyczne Lwowa w XIX i XX wieku*. Vol. 4. Eds. Leonid Zashkil'niak and Jerzy Maternicki: 316–31. Lviv–Rzeszów, 2006.

Rudnytsky, Ivan L. "Carpatho-Ukraine: A People in Search of Their Identity." In Ivan Rudnytsky. *Essays in Modern Ukrainian History*. Ed. Peter L. Rudnytsky: 353–73. Edmonton, 1987.

Rudnytsky, Ivan L. "Ukrainians in Galicia under Austrian Rule." In Ivan L. Rudnytsky. *Essays In Modern Ukrainian History*. Ed. Peter L. Rudnytsky: 315–52. Edmonton, 1987.

Rzemieniuk, Florentyna. *Unickie szkoły początkowe w Królestwie Polskim i w Galicji 1772–1914*. Lublin, 1991.

Schnür-Pepłowski, Stanisław. *Obrazy z przeszłości Galicyi i Krakowa (1772–1858)*. Part 1: *Lwów i lwowianie*. Lviv, 1896.

Schnür-Pepłowski, Stanisław. *Obrazy z przeszłości Galicyi i Krakowa (1772–1858)*. Part 2: *Dziatwa Apollina*. Lviv, 1896.

Schnür-Pepłowski, Stanisław. *Teatr polski we Lwowie (1780–1881)*. Lviv, 1889.

Schnür-Pepłowski, Stanisław. *Teatr ruski w Galicji*. Lviv, 1887.

Schnür-Pepłowski, Stanisław. *Z przeszłości Galicyi (1772–1862)*. Lviv, 1895.

Sedliar, Oleksandr. "'Dnevnyk Ruskii'." In *Entsyklopediia L'vova*. Vol. 2. Ed. Andrii Kozyts'kyi: 101. Lviv, 2008.

Semczyszyn, Magdalena. "Społeczno-polityczne postawy ziemiaństwa wschodniogalicyjskiego w świetle lwowskiej 'Gazety Narodowej'." In *Społeczeństwo, polityka, kultura. Studia nad dziejami prasy w II Rzeczypospolitej*. Ed. Tomasz Sikorski: 7–23. Szczecin, 2006.

Serczyk, Władysław A. *Historia Ukrainy*. Wrocław, 2001.

Serednicki, Antoni. "Polsko-ukraińskie pismo 'Sioło'." *Nad Odrą* no. 1–2 (2007): 12–13.

Sereda, Ostap. "Formuvannia natsional'noï tradytsiï. Ukraïns'ke kozakofil'stvo u Halychyni v 60-x rokakh XIX stolittia." In *Istoriia, mental'nist', identychnist'*. Vol. 4: *Istorychna pam'iat' ukraïntsiv i poliakiv u period formuvannia natsional'noï svidomosti v XIX–pershii polovyni XX stolittia*. Eds. Leonid Zashkil'niak, Joanna Pisulińska and Paweł Sierżęga: 395–403. Lviv, 2011.

Sereda, Ostap. "Pavlyn Svientsitsky u suspil'nomu zhytti Halychyny. Do istoriï pol's'koho ukraïnofil'stva." *Ukraïna. Kul'turna spadshchyna, natsional'na svidomist', derzhavnist'* 15: *Confraternitas. Iuvileinyi zbirnyk na poshanu Iaroslava Isaєvycha* (2006–7): 475–86.

Sereda, Ostap. "'Ruś będzie tańczyć!' 'Rus'ki baly' u L'vovi iak faktor pol's'ko-ukraïns'kykh vzaiemyn u Halychyni kintsia 40-kh – 60-kh rokiv XIX st." *Visnyk L'vivs'koho universytetu. Seriia Istorychna*, spec. no.: *L'viv. Misto, suspil'stvo, kul'tura*. Vol. 6: *L'viv–Krakiv. Dialoh mist v istorychnii retrospektyvi*. Eds. Olena Arkusha and Marian Mudryi (2007): 316–38.

Shchurat, Vasyl. "Zolota hramota z 1863 r. i nezolota z 1830 r." In Vasyl Shchurat. *Na dosvitku novoï doby. Statti i zamitky do istoriï vidrozhennia Hal. Ukraïny*: 68–73. Lviv, 1919.

Shtakel'berg, Iurii. "Nekotorye rezul'taty izucheniia sfragistiki Pol'skogo vosstaniia 1863–1864 gg." In *Tsentral'naia i Iugo-vostochnaia Evropa v novoe vremia. Sbornik statiei*. Eds. Vladilen Vinogradov, Dmitrii Markov and Il'ia Miller: 291–303. Moscow, 1974.

Sierżęga, Paweł. *Obchody 200. rocznicy odsieczy wiedeńskiej w Galicji (1883 r.)*. Rzeszów, 2002.

Sierżęga, Paweł. "Obchody rocznic narodowych w Galicji autonomicznej. Stan i perspektywy badań." In *Galicja 1772–1918. Problemy metodologiczne, stan i potrzeby badań*. Vol. 2. Eds. Agnieszka Kawalec, Wacław Wierzbieniec and Leonid Zaszkilniak. Introd. Jerzy Maternicki: 420–33. Rzeszów, 2011.

Sierżęga, Paweł. "Obchody rocznicy unii lubelskiej na terenie Galicji w 1869 roku." In *Działalność wyzwoleńcza*. Ed. Jadwiga Hoff: 146–192. Rzeszów, 2001.

Siwicki, Piotr. "Duszpasterstwo greckokatolickie w Wojsku Polskim 1918–2003." In *Historia duszpasterstwa wojskowego na ziemiach polskich*. Eds. Jan Ziółek et al.: 383–408. Lublin, 2004.

Siwicki, Piotr. "Miejsce nie-Ukraińców w Ukraińskim Kościele Greckokatolickim w świetle nauczania Metropolity Andrzeja Szeptyckiego

(Konferencja naukowa z okazji 10-lecia ustanowienia Diecezji Wrocław-sko-Gdańskiej, Wrocław, September 29, 2006)." *Kościół Unicki na Hrubie-szowszczyźnie.* https://unici.forumoteka.pl/temat,16,metr-a-szeptycki-o-grekokatolikach-nie-ukraincach-w-ukgk.html.

Skórski, Alexander. "Euzebiusz Czerkawski." *Muzeum* 12 (1896): 685–99, 751–61, 815–31; 13 (1897): 12–26, 87–93, 166–71, 238–44, 342–49, 503–19; 14 (1898): 99–131, 169–82, 225–37, 297–318, 583–95, 698–705.

Skruteń, Jozafat. "Demkowicz Leon." In *Polski słownik biograficzny.* Vol. 4: 105–6. Cracow 1938.

Skulimowski, Mieczysław. "Jaworski Walery." In *Polski słownik biograficz-ny.* Vol. 11: 113–15. Wrocław–Warsaw–Cracow, 1964–65.

Skwara, Jacek. "Konserwatyści wschodniogalicyjscy – podolacy wobec kwestii ukraińskiej w okresie namiestnictwa Michała Bobrzyńskiego 1908–1913." *Rocznik Historyczno-Archiwalny* 11 (1996): 13–38.

Slyvka, Liubov. *Halyts'ka dribna shliakhta v Avstro-Uhorshchyni (1772–1914 rr.).* Ivano-Frankivsk, 2009.

Słoczyński, Henryk Marek. "Dar dla Welehradu." *Przegląd Powszechny* no. 7–8 (1987): 158–69.

Słoczyński, Henryk Marek. *Światło w dziejarskiej ciemnicy. Koncepcja dziejów i interpretacja przeszłości Polski Joachima Lelewela.* Cracow, 2010.

Smith, Anthony D. *The Cultural Foundations of Nations: Hierarchy, Covenant, and Republic.* Malden, MA–Oxford–Carlton, 2008.

Sokulski, Justyn. "Dąbczański Leszek." In *Polski słownik biograficzny.* Vol. 4: 468–69. Cracow, 1938.

Sosnowska, Danuta. *Inna Galicja.* Warsaw, 2008.

Stabryła, Władysław. *Wernyhora w literaturze polskiej.* Cracow, 1996.

Starzyński, Stanisław. *Historya Uniwersytetu Lwowskiego.* Part 2: *1869–1894.* Lviv, 1894.

Stawecki, Piotr. "Kilka uwag o roli wojska w procesach integracyjnych i dezintegracyjnych II Rzeczpospolitej." In *Drogi Integracji społeczeństwa w Polsce XIX i XX w..* Ed. Henryk Zieliński: 193–215. Wrocław, 1976.

Stawecki, Piotr. "Polityka narodowościowa w wojsku Drugiej Rzeczypo-spolitej." In *Mniejszości narodowe i wyznaniowe w siłach zbrojnych Drugiej Rzeczypospolitej 1918–1939. Zbiór studiów.* Eds. Zbigniew Karpus and Waldemar Rezmer: 11–36. Toruń, 2001.

Stebelski, Piotr. "Lwów w 1848 roku. Na podstawie aktów śledczych." *Kwartalnik Historyczny* 23 (1909): 303–61, 507–64.

Steblii, Feodosii. "Ukraïntsi i poliaky Halychyny v 30–40-kh rr. XIX st. Po-shuky politychnoho partnerstva." In *Polska – Ukraina. Historia, polityka, kultura. Materiały międzynarodowej konferencji naukowej.* Ed. Stefan Zabro-warny: 44–61. Szczecin–Warsaw, 2003.

Steblij, Feodosij. "Polskie spiski lat trzydziestych XIX w. a społeczeństwo ukraińskie w Galicji." In *Społeczeństwo polskie i próby wznowienia walki zbrojnej w 1833 roku.* Eds. Władimir Djakow, Stefan Kieniewicz, Wiktoria Śliwowska and Feodosij Steblij: 106–18. Wrocław–Warsaw–Cracow–Gdańsk–Łódź, 1984.

Stępień, Stanisław. "Spory wokół języka i alfabetu Ukraińców galicyjskich. Druki ukraińskie wydane alfabetem łacińskim w Przemyślu w XIX i XX wiekach." In *Do dzherel. Zbirnyk naukovykh prats' na poshanu Oleha Kupchyns'koho z nahody ioho 70-richchia*. Vol. 1. Eds. Ihor Hyrych et al.: 190–212. Kyiv–Lviv, 2004.

Stępnik, Andrzej. *Ukraina i stosunki polsko-ukraińskie w syntezach i podręcznikach dziejów ojczystych okresu porozbiorowego 1795–1918*. Lublin, 1998.

Stokolos, Nadiia. *Konfesiino-etnichni transformatsii v Ukraïni (XIX – persha polovyna XX st.)*. Rivne, 2003.

Stolarczyk, Marian. *Działalność Lwowskiej Centralnej Rady Narodowej. W świetle źródeł polskich*. Rzeszów, 1994.

Studyns'kyi, Kyrylo. "Pol's'ki konspiratsiï sered rus'kykh pytomtsiv i dukhovenstva v Halychyni v rokakh 1831–1846." *Zapysky Naukovoho Tovarystva imeny Shevchenka* 80, vol. 6 (1907): 53–108; 82, vol. 2 (1908): 87–177.

Studyns'kyi, Kyrylo. *Lvivs'ka dukhovna seminariia v chasakh Markiiana Shashkevycha (1829–1843)*. Lviv, 1916.

Studyński, Cyryl. "Powstańcy polscy z r. 1863 w redakcji ukraińskiej 'Mety'." *Ziemia Czerwieńska* 3 (1937): 69–111.

Sviontek, Adam. "Mystetstvo na sluzhbi narodu. Rol' maliarstva u formuvanni uiavlen' poliakiv pro rus'ki zemli v period podiliv." *Istorychni ta kul'turolohichni studii* 6–7 (2014–15): 62–80.

S'v'yontek, Adam. "'Vid kolysky na vse zhyttia' – shchodennyk pol's'koho politychnoho diiacha ta pis'mennyka Zygmunta Milkovs'koho (Teodor Tomash Iezh) iak kraieznavche dzherelo do vyvchennia istoriï Podillia." In *Kraieznavstvo v systemi rozvytku dukhovnosti i kul'tury rehionu. Materialy Mizhnarodnoï naukovo-praktychnoï konferentsiï 21–23 zhovtnia 2008 r.*. Eds. M. Spytsia et al.: 23–26. Vinnytsia, 2008.

Szacka, Barbara. *Wprowadzenie do socjologii*. Warsaw, 2008.

Szacki, Jerzy. "Świadomość historyczna a wizja przyszłość." *Studia Filozoficzne* no. 8 (1975): 41–52.

Szeptycki, Jan Kazimierz. "Gdy w rodzinie ważyły się losy syna… (Rzecz o Romanie Marii Aleksandrze Szeptyckim – późniejszym metropolicie Andrzeju – w świetle dokumentów rodzinnych)." In *Polska–Ukraina. 1000 lat sąsiedztwa*. Vol. 1: *Studia z dziejów chrześcijaństwa na pograniczu etnicznym*. Ed. Stanisław Stępień: 183–98. Przemyśl, 1990.

Szklarska-Lohmannowa, Alina. "Sawczyński Jan Henryk." In *Polski słownik biograficzny*. Vol. 35: 289–90. Warsaw–Cracow, 1994.

Szubert, Tomasz. "Polscy więźniowie w twierdzy Kufstein w XIX wieku." *Śląski Kwartalnik Historyczny Sobótka* 60, no. 4 (2005): 439–76.

Ścigaj, Paweł. *Tożsamość narodowa. Zarys problematyki*. Cracow, 2012.

Śladkowski, Wiesław. "Idee federacyjne Kazimierza Gregorowicza." *Annales Universitatis Mariae Curie-Skłodowska. Sectio F. Historia* 51 (1996): 63–73.

Śladkowski, Wiesław. "Pod znakiem Orła, Pogoni i Michała Archanioła. Idee unijne i federacyjne w dobie powstania styczniowego." In *Unia lubelska. Unia Europejska*. Ed. Iwona Hofman: 132–49. Lublin, 2010.

Śliwa, Joachim. "Egipskie piramidy w polskim krajobrazie. Grobowiec rodziny Kulczyckich w Międzybrodziu koło Sanoka." *Rocznik Biblioteki Naukowej PAU i PAN w Krakowie* 52 (2007): 499–503.

Śliwa, Tadeusz. "Polański Tomasz." In *Polski słownik biograficzny*. Vol. 27: 281–282. Wrocław–Warsaw–Cracow–Gdańsk–Łódź, 1983.

Ślusarek, Krzysztof. "Zanim nadeszła rabacja. Uwagi na temat sytuacji społecznej na wsi galicyjskiej w latach czterdziestych XIX wieku." In *Rok 1846 w Krakowie i Galicji. Odniesienia, Interpretacje, pamięć*. Eds. Krzysztof K. Daszyk, Tomasz Kargol and Tomasz Szubert: 25–37. Cracow, 2016.

Śreniowska, Krystyna. *Stanisław Zakrzewski. Przyczynek do charakterystyki prądów ideologicznych w historiografii polskiej 1893–1936*. Łódź, 1956.

Świątek, Adam. "Grobowiec weteranów z 1831 i 1863 roku na cmentarzu Rakowickim w Krakowie. Materiały z projektu inwentaryzacyjnego." *Sowiniec* no. 43 (2013): 19–51.

Świątek, Adam. "Kostecki Platon." In *Przemyski słownik biograficzny*. Vol. 1: 39–44. Przemyśl, 2009.

Świątek, Adam. *'Lach serdeczny'. Jan Matejko a Rusini*. Cracow, 2013.

Świątek, Adam. "Platon Kostecki – swój czy obcy w polsko-ukraińskim społeczeństwie Galicji Wschodniej drugiej połowy XIX wieku." In *'Swój' i 'obcy'. Materiały z I Międzynarodowej Sesji Humanistycznej. Toruń 17–19 V 2009*. Eds. Anna Zglińska et al.: 175–84. Toruń–Warsaw, [2009].

Świątek, Adam. "Patron Polski, Litwy i … Rusi? Rzecz o lwowskich obchodach czterechsetnej rocznicy śmierci Jana z Dukli w 1884 roku." *Rocznik Przemyski. Historia* 51, no. 3 (2015): 79–104.

Świątek, Adam. "Platon Kostecki – zapomniany propagator unii polsko-rusko-litewskiej." In *Shevchenkivs'ka vesna. Materialy mizhnarodnoï naukovo-praktychnoï konferentsiï molodykh uchenykh*. Vol. 6. Part 2: *Pratsi aspirantiv ta studentiv*. Vol. 2. Ed. V. Kolesnyk: 241–244. Kyiv, 2008.

Świątek, Adam. "'Poległ wśród boju nauczycielskiego'. Wspomnienia pośmiertne na łamach czasopisma „Szkoła" jako źródło do historii nauczycielstwa galicyjskiego." In *Addenda do dziejów oświaty. Z badań nad prasą XIX i początków XX wieku*. Eds. Iwonna Michalska and Grzegorz Michalski: 119–30. Łódź, 2013.

Świątek, Adam. "Problem patriotycznego wychowania ludu na łamach lwowskiej 'Szkoły' w czasach autonomii galicyjskiej." In *Czasopiśmiennictwo XIX i początków XX wieku jako źródło do historii edukacji*. Eds. Iwonna Michalska and Grzegorz Michalski: 169–84. Łódź, 2010.

Świątek, Adam. "Przypadek gente Rutheni, natione Poloni w Galicji." *Prace Historyczne* 144, no. 2: *Kształty galicyjskich tożsamości*. Ed. Adam Świątek (2017): 303–22.

Świątek, Adam. "'Rusyn, Polak to dwa tiła, szczo jedneho serdcia syła.' Polska agitacja względem Rusinów galicyjskich w dobie Wiosny Ludów na przykładzie wybranych druków ulotnych." In *Druki ulotne w procesie komunikacji społecznej w XIX wieku (do 1918 roku)*. Ed. Małgorzata Karpińska: 49–71. Warsaw, 2018.

Świątek, Adam. "Rusini, Ukraińcy czy Polacy? Przyczynek do badań nad problematyką narodowości studentów obrządku greckokatolickiego studiujących na Uniwersytecie Jagiellońskim w latach 1850/1851–1917/1918." In *Amico, socio et viro docto. Księga ku czci profesora Andrzeja Kazimierza Banacha*. Eds. Tomasz Pudłocki and Krzysztof Stopka: 343–68. Cracow, 2015.

Świątek, Adam. "Ruś i Rusini w pismach społeczno-politycznych Teofila Merunowicza." In *Nowożytnicze Zeszyty Historyczne*. Vol. 3: *O kształt Europy Środkowo-Wschodniej*. Ed. Stanisław Witecki: 131–42. Cracow, 2011.

Świątek, Adam. "'Serdeczny Mistrzu, Tyś dziejów nie mierzył. Łokciem dziesiątków lat, Ty w Ruś uwierzył.' Platon Kostecki a Jan Matejko – historia niezwykłej znajomości." In *Per aspera ad astra. Materiały z XVI Ogólnopolskiego Zjazdu Historyków Studentów*. Ed. Adam Świątek: 169–77. Cracow, 2008.

Świątek, Adam. "*W sprawie ruskiej* Platona Kosteckiego." *Galicja. Studia i materiały* 3 (2017): 350–413.

Świątek, Adam. "Wizja Rzeczypospolitej w twórczości literackiej Platona Kosteckiego." In *Piłsudski i jego czasy*. Eds. Marek Hańderek and Adam Świątek: 203–10. Cracow, 2007.

Świątek, Adam. "Z rozważań nad problematyką tożsamości narodowo--etnicznej Gente Rutheni, natione Poloni w XIX-wiecznej Galicji." In *Odmiany tożsamości*. Eds. Robert Szwed, Leon Dyczewski and Justyna Szulich-Kałuża: 93–106. Lublin, 2010.

Tazbir, Janusz. "Procesy polonizacyjne w szlacheckiej Rzeczypospolitej." In *Tryumfy i porażki. Studia z dziejów kultury polskiej XVI–XVIII w.*. Ed. Maria Bogucka: 9–45. Warsaw, 1989.

Tazbir, Janusz. "Tradycje wieloetnicznej Rzeczypospolitej." In *Inni wśród swoich*. Ed. Wiesław Władyka: 12–23. Warsaw, 1994.

Temchin, Sergei. "Rech' Pospolitaia (Pol'sha, Rus' i Litva) kak Sviataia Troitsa. Srednevekovaia predystoriia poeticheskogo obraza Platona Kostetskogo (1861)." *Slavistica Vilnensis* 62 (2017): 265–75.

Tershakovets', Mykhailo. "Do zhyttiepysu Markiiana Shashkevycha." *Zapysky Naukovoho Tovarystva imeny Shevchenka* 105, vol. 5 (1911): 77–133.

Trevor-Roper, Hugh. "History and imagination." *Times Literary Supplement* no. 835 (25 Jul. 1980).

Trusevych, Stepan. *Suspil'no-politychnyi rukh u Skhidnii Halychyni v 50-70-kh rokakh XIX st.* Kyiv, 1978.

Turii, Oleh. "Ukraïns'ke dukhovenstvo i natsional'no-politychna borot'ba v Halychyni pid chas reVoliutsiï 1848–1849 rokiv." *Ukraïna. Kul'turna spadshchyna, natsional'na svidomist', derzhavnist'* 9: *Iubileinyi zbirnyk na poshanu Feodosiia Stebliia* (2001): 159–80.

Turii, Oleh. "Hreko-katolyts'ka Tserkva i revoliutsiia 1848–1849 rr. u Haly-chyni." In *Rok 1848. Wiosna Ludów w Galicji. Zbiór studiów.* Ed. Włady-sław Wic: 72–91. Cracow, 1999.

Tyrowicz, Marian. "Czubaty Dymitr." In *Polski słownik biograficzny.* Vol. 4: 371. Cracow, 1938.

Tyrowicz, Marian. "Daniluk Józef." In *Polski słownik biograficzny.* Vol. 4: 410–11. Cracow, 1938.

Tyrowicz, Marian. "Gudziak Jan." In *Polski słownik biograficzny.* Vol. 9: 137–38. Wrocław–Cracow–Warsaw, 1960–61.

Tyrowicz, Marian. "Kostecki Platon." In *Polski słownik biograficzny.* Vol. 14: 340–41. Wrocław–Warsaw–Cracow, 1968–1969.

Tyrowicz, Marian. "Krynicki Onufry." In *Polski słownik biograficzny.* Vol. 15: 463. Wrocław–Warsaw–Cracow, 1970.

Tyrowicz, Marian. *Prasa Galicji i Rzeczypospolitej Krakowskiej 1772–1850. Studia porównawcze.* Cracow, 1979.

Tyrowicz, Marian. "Próby wciągnięcia wsi wschodnio-galicyjskiej do kon-spiracji demokratyczno-rewolucyjnej (1833–1839)." *Rocznik Naukowo--Dydaktyczny* no. 35. *Prace Historyczne* 5 (1970): 133–44.

Tyszkowski, Kazimierz. "Czapelski Tadeusz." In *Polski słownik biograficzny.* Vol. 4: 164. Cracow, 1938.

Uhma, Stefan. "Hrabyk Piotr." In *Polski słownik biograficzny.* Vol. 10: 50. Wrocław–Warsaw–Cracow, 1962–64.

Věntskovskii, Dmitrii. *Grigorii Iakhimovich" i sovremennoe russkoe dvizhenie.* Lviv, 1892.

Vurlaka, Halyna et al. *Biblioteka Ivana Franka. Naukovyi opys u chotyr'okh tomakh.* Vol. 1. Foreword Mykola Zhulyns'kyi. Kyiv, 2010.

Walicki, Andrzej. *Idea narodu w polskiej myśli oświeceniowej.* Warsaw, 2000.

Walicki, Andrzej. "Koncepcje tożsamości narodowej i terytorium narodo-wego w myśli polskiej czasów porozbiorowych." *Archiwum Historii Fi-lozofii i Myśli Społecznej* 38 (1993): 215–31.

Walicki, Andrzej. "Naród i terytorium. Obszar narodowy w myśli politycz-nej Dmowskiego." *Dziś* no. 7 (Jul. 2002): 22–41.

Wasyl, Franciszek. *Ormianie w przedautonomicznej Galicji. Studium demogra-ficzno-historyczne.* Cracow, 2015.

Wasylewski, Stanisław. "Dobrzański Jan." In *Polski słownik biograficzny.* Vol. 5: 266–67. Cracow, 1939–1946.

Wasylewski, Stanisław. "Mikołaj Michalewicz. Redaktor Gazety Lwow-skiej 1827–1834." In *Stulecie Gazety Lwowskiej 1811–1911.* Vol. 1. Part. 2: *Życiorysy.* Ed. Wilhelm Bruchnalski: 1–13. Lviv, 1911.

Wereszycki, Henryk. "Horoszkiewicz Julian." In *Polski słownik biograficzny.* Vol. 10: 10–11. Wrocław–Warsaw–Cracow, 1962–1964.

Wereszycki, Henryk. *Pod berłem Habsburgów. Zagadnienia narodowościowe.* Cracow, 1986.

Wierzbicki, Andrzej. *Historiografia polska doby romantyzmu.* Wrocław, 1999.

Wilson, Andrew. *The Ukrainians. Unexpected Nation*. New Haven–London, 2015.

Wilczyński, Włodzimierz. "*Gente Ruthenus, natione Polonus.*" In Włodzimierz Wilczyński. *Ukraina. Leksykon. Historia, gospodarka, kultura*: 75. Warsaw, 2010.

Wisłocki, Władysław Tadeusz. *Kongres Słowiański w 1848 r. i sprawa polska*. Lviv, 1927.

Wisłocki, Władysław Tadeusz and Zofia Horoszkiewicz. "Cięglewicz Kasper Melchior Baltazar." In *Polski słownik biograficzny*. Vol. 6: 71. Cracow, 1938.

Wiśnicki, Janusz. "Konserwatyści polscy w Galicji wobec kwestii ukraińskiej (1864–1914)." *Przegląd Humanistyczny* 43, no. 5 (1999): 45–55.

Wojciechowski, Krzysztof. "Łopatyński Konstanty." In *Polski słownik biograficzny*. Vol. 18: 409. Wrocław–Warsaw–Cracow–Gdańsk, 1973.

Wójtowicz-Huber, Bernadetta. *'Ojcowie narodu'. Duchowieństwo greckokatolickie w ruchu narodowym Rusinów galicyjskich (1867–1918)*. Warsaw, 2008.

Wroński, Andrzej. "Powstanie styczniowe na Ukrainie." In *Powstanie styczniowe 1863–1864. Wrzenie, bój, Europa, wizje*. Ed. Sławomir Kalembka: 372–88. Warsaw, 1990.

Wróbel, Anna. "Od 'Galileuszy' do Polaków. Wejście do polskiej inteligencji przedstawicieli ludności napływowej i mniejszości w Galicji w XIX w." In *Inteligencja polska XIX i XX wieku. Studia 5*. Ed. Ryszarda Czepulis--Rastenis: 173–90. Warsaw, 1987.

Wróblewski, Kazimierz. *Kornel Ujejski (1823–1893). W dodatkach garść listów Ujejskiego, Szajnochy i Bohdana Zaleskiego*. Lviv, 1902.

Wysocka, Felicja. "List pasterski arcybiskupa Andrzeja Szeptyckiego do Polaków obrządku greckokatolickiego z roku 1904." In *Unia brzeska – geneza, dzieje i konsekwencje w kulturze narodów słowiańskich*. Eds. Ryszard Łużny, Franciszek Ziejka and Andrzej Kępiński: 139–50. Cracow, 1994.

Zajewski, Władysław. *Powstanie listopadowe 1830–1831*. Warsaw, 1998.

Zakrzewski, Stanisław. "'Ogniem i mieczem' Sienkiewicza w świetle krytyki historycznej." In Stanisław Zakrzewski. *Zagadnienia historyczne*. Vol. 1: 71–101. Lviv, 1936.

Zashkil'niak, Leonid. "Ivan Vahylevych na tli svoho chasu ta istoriohrafiï." In *Bahatokul'turne istorychne seredovyshche L'vova v XIX i XX stolittiakh Wielokulturowe środowisko historyczne Lwowa w XIX i XX wieku*. Vol. 4. Eds. Leonid Zashkil'niak and Iezhy Maternits'ki: 146–53. Lviv–Rzeszow, 2006.

Zaszkilniak, Leonid. "Iwan Wahyłewicz (1811–1866)." In *Złota księga historiografii lwowskiej XIX i XX wieku*. Eds. Jerzy Maternicki and Leonid Zaszkilniak: 63–80. Rzeszów, 2007.

Zaszkilniak, Leonid. "Polsko-ukraiński spór o Galicję na początku XX wieku. Między świadomością historyczną a realiami." In *Narody i historia*. Ed. Arkady Rzegocki: 156–69. Cracow, 2000.

Zathey, Hugo. *Młodość Bohdana Zaleskiego (1802–1830)*. Cracow, 1886.

Zayarnyuk, Andriy. *Framing the Ukrainian Peasantry In Habsburg Galicia, 1846–1914.* Edmonton–Toronto, 2013.

Zayarnyuk, Andriy. "The Greek Catholic Rustic Gentry and the Ukrainian National Movement In Habsburg-Ruled Galicia." *Journal of Ukrainian Studies* 35–36 (2010–11): 91–102.

Zborucki, Zygmunt. *Euzebjusz Czerkawski i galicyjska ustawa szkolna z 1867 r.* Lviv, 1927.

Zborucki, Zygmunt. *Lwów w dobie powstania listopadowego (Szkic historyczny w 100-letnią rocznicę powstania 1830/31).* Lviv, 1930.

Zborucki, Zygmunt. *Proces studentów samborskich (1837–1839).* Lviv, 1927.

Zdrada, Jerzy. "Rząd narodowy wobec udziału Galicji w powstaniu styczniowym 1863–1864." In *Galicja a powstanie styczniowe.* Eds. Mariola Hoszowska, Agnieszka Kawalec and Leonid Zaszkilniak: 13–42. Warsaw–Rzeszów, 2013.

Zdrada, Jerzy. "Lwowska 'Ojczyzna' z roku 1875." *Rocznik Biblioteki Polskiej Akademii Nauk w Krakowie* 15 (1969): 252–78.

Zdrada, Jerzy. "Ławrowski Julian." In *Polski słownik biograficzny.* Vol. 18: 282–83. Wrocław–Warsaw–Cracow–Gdańsk, 1973.

Zdrada, Jerzy, "Merunowicz Teofil." In *Polski słownik biograficzny.* Vol. 20: 455–57. Wrocław–Warsaw–Cracow–Gdańsk, 1975.

Zdrada, Jerzy. "Wybory do galicyjskiego Sejmu Krajowego w 1867 r." *Rocznik Biblioteki Polskiej Akademii Nauk w Krakowie* 9 (1963): 39–96.

Zgórniak, Marian. *Polska w czasach walk o niepodległość (1815–1864).* Cracow, 2001.

Zgórniak, Marian. *Za Waszą i naszą wolność.* Warsaw, 1987.

Zięba, Andrzej A. "Polacy galicyjscy, czy Polacy w Galicji – refleksje na temat przeobrażeń tożsamości polskiej w zaborze austriackim." *Zeszyty Naukowe Uniwersytetu Jagiellońskiego. Prace Historyczne* 144, no. 2: *Kształty galicyjskich tożsamości.* Ed. Adam Świątek (2017): 215–32.

Zięba, Andrzej A. "Gente Rutheni, natione Poloni." In *Prace Komisji Wschodnioeuropejskiej.* Vol. 2. Eds. Ryszard Łużny and Andrzej A. Zięba: 61–77. Cracow, 1995.

Zięba, Andrzej A. "Inne 'Tamte światy'." In *Rzecz o roku 1863. Uniwersytet Jagielloński wobec powstania styczniowego.* Ed. Andrzej A. Zięba: 79–100. Cracow, 2013.

Zięba, Andrzej A. "Profesor Emilian Czyrniański." In *Łemkowie i łemkoznawstwo w Polsce.* Ed. Andrzej A. Zięba: 15–27. Cracow, 1997.

Zięba, Andrzej A. "Srokowski Konstanty." In *Polski słownik biograficzny.* Vol. 41: 231–37. Warsaw–Cracow, 2002.

Zięba, Andrzej A. "Srokowski Stanisław Józef." In *Polski słownik biograficzny.* Vol. 41: 238–44. Warsaw–Cracow, 2002.

Zięba, Andrzej A. "Tożsamość etniczna jako obiekt manipulacji politycznej. Przypadek Rusinów łemkowskich XVIII–XX w. (część pierwsza)." *Rocznik Ruskiej Bursy* (2007): 59–94.

Zięba, Andrzej A. "Tożsamość etniczna jako obiekt manipulacji politycznej. Przypadek Rusinów łemkowskich XVIII–XX w. (część druga)." *Rocznik Ruskiej Bursy* (2008): 59–71.

Zięba, Andrzej A. "W sprawie genezy decyzji Romana Szeptyckiego o zmianie obrządku." In *Metropolita Andrzej Szeptycki. Studia i materiały.* Ed. Andrzej A. Zięba: 43–64. Cracow, 1991.

Zyblikiewicz, Lidia A. "Powszechne spisy ludności w monarchii Habsburgów." In *Celem nauki jest człowiek... Studia z historii społecznej i gospodarczej ofiarowane Helenie Madurowicz-Urbańskiej.* Ed. Piotr Franaszek: 387–400. Cracow, 2000.

Zyga, Aleksander. "Ludowa pieśń ukraińska w polskiej krytyce lat 1820–1845." *Rocznik Przemyski* 28 (1991–92): 43–58.

Zyga, Aleksander. "Wkład ziemi krośnieńskiej w literaturę polską do 1903 roku." In *Inteligencja południowo-wschodnia ziem polskich.* Eds. Halina Kurek and Franciszek Tereszkiewicz: 37–123. Cracow, 1998.

Żygulski, Zdzisław. "Barewicz Witold." In *Polski słownik biograficzny.* Vol. 1: 304. Cracow, 1935.

Encyclopedias and dictionaries:

Corpus studiosorum Universitatis Iagellonicae 1850–1918. [Vol. 1:] *A–D.* Ed. Jerzy Michalewicz. Cracow, 1999.

Encyklopedia socjologii. Editorial committee Zbigniew Bokszański et al. Eds. Andrzej Kojder et al. Vol. 1–2, 4, Suplement. Warsaw, 1998–2005.

Encyklopedyja powszechna. Vol. 7: *Den.–Eck.* Warsaw, 1861.

Kultura pogranicza wschodniego. Zarys encyklopedyczny. Eds. Tadeusz Budrewicz, Tadeusz Bujnicki and Jerzy Stefan Ossowski. Warsaw, 2011.

Polski słownik biograficzny. Vol. 2–44. Cracow, 1936–2007.

Wilczyński, Włodzimierz. *Ukraina. Leksykon. Historia, gospodarka, kultura.* Warsaw, 2010.

Entsyklopediia L'vova. Ed. Andrii Kozyts'kyi. Vol. 2. Lviv, 2008.

Webography:

http://www.cyrylimetody.marianie.pl
http://dziedzictwo.polska.pl
http://www.historycy.org
http://forum.fidelitas.pl
http://litopys.org.ua
http://www.lvivcenter.org

List of Illustrations

Chapter 3

Chapter 4

27. Antoni Dąbczański. Source: [Antoni Dąbczański], *Antoni Dąbczański i jego pamiętnik (z portretem)* (Lviv, 1912), p. 5.
28. An illustration from Boczkowski's leaflet *The Tale* (Lviv, 1848). Source: [Boczkowski], *Powiastka* (Lviv, 1848).
29. An illustration from Franciszek Dydacki's leaflet [*Lion, Eagle, Angel*] (Lviv, 1848). Source: Franciszek Dydacki, [*Lew, Orzeł, Anioł*] ([Lviv, 1848]).
30. Henryk Jabłoński's poem about Teofil Wiśniowski adressed to the Ruthenians (Lviv, 1848). Source: BN, sygn. 1.984.365 A Cim.: [Henryk Jabłoński] Podolak z za Kordonu, *Piśń o Wyszniowśkim* (Lviv, 1848).

Chapter 5

31. Euzebiusz Czerkawski. Source: *Wędrowiec*, no. 39 (14/26 Sep., 1896), p. 245.
32. The masthead of the newspaper *Zoria Halytska* under the editorship of Platon Kostecki. Source: *Zoria Halytska* no 27 (6 Jul., 1855).
33. The cover of Zygmunt Sawczyński's book *The Languages of our Country's Eastern Part* (Cracow, 1861). Source: Zygmunt Sawczyński, *Języki wschodniej części kraju naszego* (Cracow, 1861).

Chapter 6

34. The coats-of-arms of Poland, Lithuania, and Ruthenia at the building of the Polish Higher School founded by Prince Adam Jerzy Czartoryski in 1849 at 80 boulevard du Montparnasse in Paris. Source: Photography by Janusz Pezda.
35. Father Stefan Laurysiewicz during the holy mass on the occasion of the 448th anniversary of the Union of Horodło, 1861. Source: [Józef Dąbrowski] J. Grabiec, *Rok 1863. W pięćdziesiątą rocznicę* (Poznań, 1913), p. 144.
36. Father Stefan Laurysiewicz. Source: BN, sygn. F.2594/W.
37. The coat-of-arms used by the insurgents during the January Uprising of 1863. Postcard „Boże zbaw Polskę" from 1903. Source: Muzeum Niepodległości w Warszawie, sygn. P-629.

Chapter 7

38. Mikołaj Zyblikiewicz. Source: *Tygodnik Illustrowany*, no. 229 (21 May, 1887), p. 333.
39. Zygmunt Sawczyński. Source: *Dziennik dla Wszystkich*, no. 29 (1 Oct., 1880), p. 1.
40. Teofil Merunowicz. Source: [Dąbrowski] J. Grabiec, *Rok 1863*, a part of illustration 3 after p. 464.
41. The cover of the Teofil Merunowicz's book *The Civil Catechism for Poles and Ruthenians...* (Lviv, 1884). Source: Teofil Merunowicz, *Katechizm obywatelski dla Polaków i Rusinów w Galicyi i w Krakowskiem* (Lviv, 1884).

Index of Names

Index of Locations

Index of Institutions, Organizations, Political Camps, and Press Titles